Documents on

Communism, Nationalism, and

Soviet Advisers in China

1918-1927

Documents on
Communism, Nationalism, and
Soviet Advisers in China
1918-1927

PAPERS SEIZED IN THE 1927 PEKING RAID

Edited, with Introductory Essays, by
C. Martin Wilbur and Julie Lien-ying How

Columbia University Press New York 1956

Copyright © 1956 Columbia University Press, New York

Library of Congress Catalog Card Number: 56-6813

Published in Great Britain, Canada, India, and Pakistan
by Oxford University Press
London, Toronto, Bombay, and Karachi

Manufactured in the United States of America

PREFACE

The principal purpose of this book is to make available to scholars
a collection of documents which provide new information on a phase
of the revolutionary movement in China of which Communism has
been a part. The book is the result of a cooperative project, "Studies
in the History of Chinese Communism," which is part of the research
program of the East Asian Institute of Columbia University. The
project undertook to discover, translate, and publish important historical documents dealing with the Chinese Communist movement
in order to increase the basic information available to all persons
seeking to understand or interpret modern revolutionary China.

The project was made possible by a grant from the Rockefeller
Foundation to Columbia University for the East Asian Institute.
Several persons engaged in the work were recipients of grants under the Program of Emergency Aid to Scholars administered by the
United States Department of State. Much of the time which the undersigned devoted to the book was available because of a grant from
the Council on Research in the Social Sciences of Columbia University. The foregoing does not imply, however, that any of these organizations are responsible for the contents of this volume. On the
contrary, the authors take full responsibility for the selection of
the documents translated and for any comments or opinions expressed in other parts of the book.

In a research venture in which all the members assisted each
other in many ways, it is difficult to disentangle the several major
contributions. The general conception, over-all supervision, and a
considerable amount of the research, writing, and editing were provided by the undersigned who also saw the book through the press.
Miss Julie Lien-ying How deserves the major credit for the book.
She performed most of the bibliographic work and general research.
She checked all the translations, edited the documents, and wrote
the historical essays.

The authors are particularly indebted to Mr. Jennings Wong and
Dr. K. C. Wang, who made most of the preliminary translations,
checked one another's work, and performed some of the research.
Dr. Wang also inscribed the Chinese characters in the glossaries
and bibliography.

Many other people assisted in various phases of this study, which
drew upon the resources of several libraries. We express our ap-

preciation to Mr. Howard Linton and members of the staff of the
East Asiatic Library of Columbia University, especially Mr. Richard
Howard, for their resourceful and obliging help; and to Dr. Arthur
Hummel and members of the staff of the Division of Orientalia of
the Library of Congress for help in Miss How's search for rare
source material, much of it uncatalogued. The Hoover Institute and
Library on War, Revolution, and Peace and the Chinese-Japanese
Library, Harvard-Yenching Institute, Harvard University, kindly
made available many Chinese works not found elsewhere. Archival
material of the State Department dealing with China before 1929,
now in the National Archives, was made available through the
courtesy of Dr. E. Taylor Parks, and guidance in making use of
these files was given by Dr. Carl Lokke and members of his staff.
The library of the Department of State lent a copy of an English
translation of the "Brief History," which was helpful as a check on
our translation.

In our search for information about the circumstances of the raid
upon the office of the Soviet Military Attaché in Peking on April 6,
1927, which produced the documents in this volume, and in our unsuccessful quest for facts about the present whereabouts of the
originals, we were kindly assisted by General John Magruder, Dr.
T. F. Tsiang, and Dr. Hollington K. Tong, and by Mr. W. G. Graham
of the China Section, Research Department of the British Foreign
Office.

Mr. Ichiro Shirato gave invaluable assistance on Japanese sources
and helped with difficult problems of Japanese translation. He and
Mr. Paul Langer discovered the four collections of Japanese translations of the seized documents used in this study. Dr. Edwin Beal
and Mr. Peter Berton assisted in the search for other such Japanese collections. Mr. Andrew Kuroda made notes for us on one of
the Japanese collections housed in the United States National Archives. Mr. Tong Te-kong called our attention to several important
Chinese sources, including the invaluable published diaries of
Chiang Kai-shek. Professor Franklin Ho directed attention to
several important telegrams in these collections. Colonel Maynard
G. Moyer's gift of a copy of the basic Chinese publication, Su-lien
yin-mou wen-cheng hui-pien, greatly facilitated our work.

Miss Mary Kawai made preliminary translations of the three
documents in the present volume that were found in Japanese versions. Mr. Leo Gruliow and Mr. David Dallin gave expert advice
on problems of authenticity of some of the Russian texts and also
translated certain items from the Russian. Miss Gay Humphrey
checked a number of Russian documents. Mrs. Esther Corey and
Mr. Theodore Shabad helped us in reconstructing some of the Russian names based on Chinese and Japanese translations. Dr. Huang
Ling-shuang identified several persons mentioned in "A Brief History of the Chinese Communist Party." Mr. Ken'ichi Hatano, an

eminent Japanese authority on Chinese Communism, read a preliminary version of some of the documents and made useful comments. The authors are indebted to Mr. Chang Kuo-t'ao, who
provided them with important information on the early years of the
Chinese Communist Party. They wish also to thank Mr. Robert A.
Burton for his helpful suggestions.

Valuable aid on the manuscript was given by Miss Gwendolyn
Fillman, Mrs. Ruth Alexander Kaiden, Miss Frances Weinberg,
and Mr. and Mrs. Charles F. Steffens. The entire volume has
benefited by the skillful editing of Miss Helen Stroop.

This list of credits indicates the degree to which this was a cooperative project, demanding as it did skill at research in Chinese,
Japanese, and Russian sources. The authors offer their sincere
thanks to all who so generously helped with the work. We owe a special debt to Dr. Hugh Borton, Director of the East Asian Institute,
and to members of the Institute's Executive Committee, who warmly
encouraged the research program which made the volume possible.

                                    C. Martin Wilbur
March, 1956   Associate Professor of Chinese History

CONTENTS

Many summary headings not appearing
in the text are here included.

PREFACE (v)

ABBREVIATIONS (xix)

INTRODUCTION (3)

THE PROBLEM OF AUTHENTICITY (8)

External Evidence (8). The Raid on the Premises of the Soviet Embassy (8); The Position of the Peking Government, the USSR, and the Kuomintang (9); Selection and Translation of the Seized Documents (13); The First Documents Made Public (15); Arguments against Authenticity (18); Arguments for Authenticity (20); Conclusions regarding Contemporary Arguments (21).
Internal Evidence (22). Original Chinese Documents (23); Russian Documents (27); Errors of Translation (29); Two Doubtful Russian Documents (32).
Summary of Conclusions (36). Original Chinese Documents (37); Russian Documents (37).

PART I: INTRODUCTION TO "A BRIEF HISTORY OF THE
    CHINESE COMMUNIST PARTY" (38)

Document 1: A Brief History of the Chinese Communist Party (41)
Introduction (41); The Effects of World War I in China (43); Changes in the Labor Movement (44); The Peking-Hankow Railway Workers' Strike, February, 1923 (45); The National Liberation Movement (46); The May Fourth Movement, 1919 (47); Ch'en Tu-hsiu's Activities, 1918-1919 (47); Organization of the Shanghai Communist Group, 1920 (48); Organization of the Peking Communist Group, 1920 (49); Organization of the Canton Communist Group, 1920 (50); The First Congress, May, 1921 (52); Organization of Labor Unions, 1921 (55); The First Congress of the Toilers of the Far East, January, 1922 (57); The Second Congress, June, 1922 (58); Conflict between Sun Yat-sen and Ch'en Ch'iung-ming, 1922 (60); Communist Policy of Collaboration with the Kuomintang, 1922 (16); "Down with Imperialism!" and "Down with Militarism!" (62); The Strike Movement, 1922 to

February, 1923 (64); The Third Congress, June, 1923 (66); Feng Yü-hsiang's Coup d'État, October, 1924 (70); The Fourth Congress, January, 1925 (71); Development of the Revolutionary Movement, 1925 (72); Current Weaknesses of the Chinese Communist Party (74); Objectives of the Chinese Communist Party (76).

PART II: THE ORGANIZATIONAL POLICIES OF THE CHINESE CHINESE COMMUNIST PARTY, 1920 to July, 1926 (79)

Establishment of the Chinese Communist Party, 1920-1921 (79); Policy of Collaboration with the Kuomintang, 1922 (81); Organizational Policies Adopted by the Third Congress, Summer, 1923 (85); Organizational Policies from the Third Congress to the May Thirtieth Movement, Summer, 1923, to May, 1925 (88); The Effect of the May Thirtieth Movement on Organizational Policies, to July, 1926 (90); Party Structure (95); The Party's Training and Propaganda Policies, to July, 1926 (97).

Document 2: Resolutions on the Question of Organization (100)
Workers' Strikes and the National Revolutionary Movement (100); Absorb, Train, and Lead the Masses (100); Questions of Party Organization and Development (101); Organize Sectional Committees (101); Consolidate the Party's Influence among the Masses (102); Mistakes of the Kwangtung Regional Committee (102); Tendency of Party Members to Work as Individuals among the Masses (103); Expand the United Front and Cooperate with the Kuomintang Left Wing (103); Underground Activities in Certain Reactionary Areas (103); Assist the Communist Youth Corps (103).

Document 3: Plans on the Organization of Party Cells (104)
Significance of Cell Organization (104); Standards for Internal Party Education and Propaganda (105); Principles of External Agitation and Activities (105); Cell Meetings (106); Responsibilities of Cell Secretaries (107); Responsibilities of Educational Propagandists to Party Cells (107); Meetings of Cell Secretaries (108); Technical Work (109).

Document 4: Resolutions on the Question of Organization (110)
Experiences in Party Development and Weaknesses (110); The Significance of Organizational Work (111); The Significance and Methods of Work of Party Cells (112); The Work of Party Fractions (114); Party Organs (115).

Document 5: Circular Notice on Relations between the Chinese Communist Party and the Chinese Communist Youth Corps (117)
Functions of the Communist Youth Corps (117); Problems of Communist Party-Communist Youth Relations (118); Measures to Improve Relations (119).

Document 6: Resolutions on the Chinese Communist Youth Corps (120)
Accomplishments and Failure of the Communist Youth Corps (120);

Tasks of the Communist Youth Corps (120); Organizational Rela-
tionship between the Communist Party and the Communist Youth
Corps (121).
Document 7: Resolutions on the Question of Propaganda (122)
Need for and Principles of Mass Agitation and Propaganda (122);
Propaganda Mobilization (123); Workers' Clubs (123); Internal
Agitation in Party Cells (123); Party Schools (124); Collection of
Material and Party Publications (124).
Document 8: Resolutions on the Work of the Propaganda
Department (125)
The Problem of Publications (125); The Department's Duties (126);
The Problem of Editorial and Translation Work (127); The Problem
of Local Reports (127); Correspondence with Workers and Peas-
ants (128).
Document 9: An Outline of the Curriculum of the Chinese Commu-
nist Party's "A" and "B" Party Schools (130)
Outline of Curriculum for "A" Party Schools (130); Outline of
Curriculum for "B" Party Schools (132).
Document 10: A Concrete Guide to the Work of Training (135)
Systematize Thought and Study (135); Discipline Action (136); Col-
lectivize Individuality (136); On Service (137).

PART III: CONSOLIDATION OF THE REVOLUTIONARY BASE
    IN KWANGTUNG, 1921-1925 (138)

Sun Yat-sen's Early Contact with Soviet Russia, 1918-1920 (138);
Sun Yat-sen's Negotiations with Dalin and Joffe, 1922 to January,
1923 (140); Exchange of Missions, 1923 (143); Reorganization of
the Kuomintang, January, 1924 (144); Opposition to the Admission
of Communists, to January, 1924 (148); Organization of the Whampoa Academy, January to May, 1924 (150); The Chinese Communist
and Soviet Positions in Canton, 1924 (151); The Merchant Corps
Incident and the First Eastern Expedition, October, 1924, to April,
1925 (154); The Effect of Sun Yat-sen's Death on the Kuomintang's
Policies, March to June, 1925,(157); Anti-British Policies, Summer, 1925 (160); Reorganization of the Army and Government, Summer,
1925 (162); Ascendancy of the Kuomintang Left Wing, to September,
1925 (164); The Soviet Position in Canton, to September, 1925 (166);
Execution of Reorganization Policies and the Unification of
Kwangtung, to December, 1925 (168).
Document 11: Borodin's Report on the Revolutionary Committee (171)
Meeting of the Revolutionary Committee on October 14 (171); Politi-
cal Policies Adopted at a Conference on October 12 (172); Measures
Carried Out Prior to October 14 (172); Inside Plans for Action (173).
Document 12: Galen's Letter to Chiang Kai-shek (174)
Recommends Setting Up Special Class for Training Communications
Experts (174).

Document 13: Chiang Kai-shek's Letter to Galen (176)
Shameen Incident Points to Need for Anti-British Military Prepara-
tions (176); Political and Military Views (177); The Question of
Military Funds (177); Expansion of the Army (177); Army Organiza-
tion (177); Military Preparations (178); Expansion of the Military
Academy (178); Suggested Budget (179).
Document 14: Chiang Kai-shek's Speech to the Military
Council (181)
Britain and Other Imperialist Countries Instigate Militarist Dis-
orders (182); Divine Duty to Struggle against Imperialists (182).
Document 15: Minutes of the Military Council (183)
Organization of the Military Council (183); Important Problems
and Decisions of the Military Council (184).
Document 16: Kisanko's Report on Military Developments in
Kwangtung (186)
Situation at Canton in Late October, 1925 (186); Suppression of
Yunnan and Kwangsi Armies (186); Opposition to Centralization of
Finance (187); Support Rendered by British Hongkong to Anti-
Government Groups and Armies (187); Internal Consolidation (188);
Plans for Dealing with Enemy Armies (188); The Military Council
(189); The General Staff (190); The Political Training Department
(190); The Armies of the National Revolutionary Government (191);
Ammunition, Communications, Sanitation, Arsenals (192); Army
Schools (194); The Navy (196); Aviation (196); Obstacles to the
Work of Soviet Advisers (197); Objectives of the Canton Soviet
Group (197); Suggested Measures for Improving the Work of the
Canton Soviet Group (199).
Document 17: Regulations of Political Departments in the National
Revolutionary Army (200)
Commissars in the Armies (200); Political Commissars at Army
Headquarters and Various Organs (201); Appointment of Commis-
sars (202).
Document 18: Plans on the Establishment of the Central Military
and Political Academy (203)
Objectives in Organizing the Academy (203); Measures to Be
Taken (203); Organization of the Academy (204); Students of the
Academy (204); Period of Training at the Academy (204).
Document 19: Regulations on the Organs of the Kuomintang and
the National Government (205)
The Kuomintang Political Council (205); The Military Council (205).

PART IV: FRICTION AND RECONCILIATION IN THE
         REVOLUTIONARY CAMP, July, 1925, to July, 1926 (206)

The Emergence of Tai Chi-t'ao's Theories and Communist Policy,
July to October, 1925 (206); The Western Hills Conference, November 23 to December 5, 1925 (209); The Soviet Position in the

Military Establishment, to December, 1926 (212); The Second
Kuomintang Congress, January 4-19, 1926 (213); Chiang Kai-shek
and the Soviet Advisers, January to Early March, 1926 (215);
Communists in Kuomintang Organs, to May, 1926 (217); The
March Twentieth Coup d'État and the Immediate Communist Re-
action, March 20 to Early April, 1926 (218); Chiang Kai-shek's
Attitude and Assumption of Power, March 20 to April 1926 (221);
Comintern Policy and Opposition Currents in the Chinese Com-
munist Party, March to July, 1926 (224); Agreement for a Modus
Vivendi, May to June, 1926 (227); Policy of the Chinese Communist
Party, July, 1926 (230).
Document 20: Resolutions on Relations between the Chinese Com-
munist Party and the Kuomintang (234)
Class Differentiation within the Kuomintang (234); Formation of
the Kuomintang New Right Wing (235); Communist Policy toward
the Kuomintang (235); Means of Executing the Communist Party's
Policy (235); Definition of the Kuomintang Right and Left Wings
and the Reactionaries (237).
Document 21; Communist Attitude toward the Kuomintang in the
North (238)
Reactionary Atmosphere in the Kuomintang in the North (238);
Taichitaoism, a Reactionary Weapon (238); Failure of the Right in
Southern and Central China (239); Weakness of the Left Wing in
Peking (239); Need for a United Front between the Communists
and the Left Wing (239); Propaganda to Create an Anti-Right At-
mosphere (240); Principles of Propaganda—Taichitaoism Is Not
Sunyatsenism (240); Conspiracy of the Right and Reactionaries
to Destroy the Kuomintang (241); Need for Cooperation between
the Chinese Communist Party and the Kuomintang (242).
Document 22: Soviet Report from Canton (245)
The General Staff (245); Position of Soviet Advisers (245); Weak-
nesses in the Revolutionary Government (246); Policies to Be
Followed (247).
Document 23: Stepanov's Report on the March Twentieth Coup
d'État (248)
A Brief Account of the Incident (248); Recent Situation in Canton
(250); Errors of the Soviet Advisers (250); Errors of the Chinese
Communist Party (251); Estimate of Chiang Kai-shek and Tactics
for Dealing with Him (251); Plans for the National Revolutionary
Army (253);
Document 24: Stepanov's Report to a Meeting of the Soviet Group
at Canton (254)
Chiang Kai-shek's Moves following March Twentieth (254); Need
to Continue Cooperation with Chiang Kai-shek (255); Military
Developments (256); Plans for the Northern Expedition (256);
Soviet Military and Political Tasks (257); Questions and Criticisms

concerning Stepanov's Report (257); Errors of Chinese Communists (258); Need to Strengthen the Kuomintang Left (259); Activities of the Sunyatsenist Society and the Mechanics' Union (260); Varying Estimates of Chiang Kai-shek (262).

Document 25: Seifulin's Report on the Situation at Canton (266)
The Right Wing (266); The Situation in Canton (267); The Left Wing and the Left-Right Struggle (267); Conciliatory Measures (268); The Situation in the Army (269); The Military Situation (269).

Document 26; Political Report of the Central Committee of the Chinese Communist Party (271)
Changes in the Political Situation and the Party's Policies since October, 1925 (271); Imperialist Policy toward China (273); The Attitude of Various Social Forces toward the National Revolution (273); Dissensions within the Kuomintang (275); The Future of the National Revolutionary Movement (275); The Development and Work of theParty since October, 1925 (276).

Document 27: Resolutions on Relations between the Chinese Communist Party and the Kuomintang (278)
Anti-Communist Offensives (278); The Party's Errors (278); Policy toward the Kuomintang (279); The Party's Tactics in Dealing with the Kuomintang (280); The Anti-Right Struggle (281).

PART V: THE CHINESE COMMUNIST PARTY'S POLICIES IN
        THE MASS MOVEMENT, July, 1926 (282)

Document 28: Resolutions on the Labor Movement (288)
The Rise of Labor's Consciousness following May Thirtieth (288); Policies in Guiding the Labor Movement (289); Problems of the United Front (289); Party Publications for Workers (290); The All-China Federation of Labor (290); Methods of Organizing Labor Unions (291); Workers' Demands (292); The Labor Movement in Various Industries and Cities (292); The Central Committee's Committee on the Labor Movement (295).

Document 29: Resolutions on the Peasant Movement (296)
Tendencies in the Peasant Movement (296); Economic and Political Demands (297); The Problem of Organization (297); The Problem of Propaganda (298); Policy toward Landlords, the Min-t'uan, and Local Governments (298); The Problem of the Agrarian United Front (299); Attitude toward the Church (299); Policy toward Bandits (300); Armed Self-Defense (300); Relations between the Peasant Movement and the Kuomintang (300); The Party's Development in the Villages (301); Methods of Work (301).

Document 30: Resolutions on the Red Spears Movement (303)
Nature of the Red Spears (303); Methods of Assisting the Red Spears in Organization (304); Organize a United Front of Red Spears (305); Policy toward the Red Spears (305).

Document 31: Resolutions on the Merchant Movement (306)
Division of Chinese Merchants into Three Groups (306); Organiza-
tion of the Middle and Petty Merchants (306); Policy toward the
Kuomintang in the Merchant Movement (307).
Document 32: Resolutions on the Women's Movement (308)
Need to Penetrate the Masses (308); Problems of a United Front of
All Women's Groups (308); Female Labor, Students, and Peasants
(309); Problems of Publications, Organization, and Training (309).
Document 33: Resolutions on the Student Movement (311)
Position of Students in the National Revolutionary Movement (311);
Principles to Be Followed in the Student United Front (311).
Document 34: Resolutions on the Relief Movement (313)
The Relief Movement as a Tool to Promote the United Front (313);
The Party's Tasks in the Relief Movement (313).
Document 35: Resolutions on the Military Movement (316)
The Objective Situation (316); The Party's Accomplishments and
Failure (316); Immediate Tasks (317).

PART VI: KUOMINTANG AND SOVIET RELATIONS WITH
        FENG YÜ-HSIANG, October, 1924, to September, 1926 (318)

Feng Yü-hsiang's Coup d'État, October 23, 1924 (318); The Kuomintang, the Chinese Communist Party, Feng Yü-hsiang, and Tuan
Ch'i-jui, November, 1924, to March, 1925 (319); Soviet Negotiations with
Feng Yü-hsiang, April to June, 1925 (321); Feng Yü-hsiang and the
National Revolutionary Movement, to October, 1925 (323); Outbreak of
the Anti-Mukden War, October, 1925 (324); The November Twenty-
eighth Demonstration, 1925 (326); Feng Yü-hsiang's Retirement and Re-
lations with Soviet Advisers, December, 1925, to February, 1926
(327); The March Eighteenth Incident, 1926 (329); Feng Yü-hsiang's
Change of Attitude, April to Early May, 1926 (330); Feng Yü-hsiang
in Moscow, Summer, 1926 (333); Feng Yü-hsiang's Entry into the
Kuomintang, September 16, 1926 (334).
Document 36: Jen Te-chiang's Letter to Frunze on Alliance with
Feng Yü-hsiang (336)
Reasons for Contacting Feng Yü-hsiang (336); Negotiations with
Feng Yü-hsiang (337); Estimates of and Alternative Policies to-
ward Feng Yü-hsiang (338); Concrete Results Obtained by the Rus-
sians (339); Criticism of Karakhan (339); Suggested Policy toward
Feng Yü-hsiang (340).
Document 37: Letter to Karakhan on Feng Yü-hsiang (341)
Alternative Estimates of Feng Yü-hsiang's Political Attitude (341);
Feng Yü-hsiang as a Militarist (341); Test of Feng Yü-hsiang's
Sincerity (343); Alternative Measures if Feng Yü-hsiang Rejects
Soviet Demands (343).

Document 38: Record of a Meeting at the Soviet Embassy in
Peking (344)
Schools Established in the Kuominchün (344); The General Staff
(347); Arms and Troop Concentration (349); Communist Propagan-
da Work (350); Relations between the Russians and Feng Yü-hsiang
(351); Feng Yü-hsiang on the Anti-Mukden War and Japan (352);
Feng Yü-hsiang and the November Twenty-eighth Demonstration
(353); Feng Yü-hsiang's Negotiations with Other Provinces (354).
Document 39: Ya-en's Report on the Kalgan Soviet Group (355)
Evaluation of Soviet Work in Establishing Schools (355); Soviet
Failure to Gain influence (356); Rejection of Idea of Winding Up
Work (357); Suggestions to Create a Model Army (357); Need to
Establish Direct Influence over Feng Yü-hsiang (358); Recommen-
dations on Selection of Soviet Personnel (359).
Document 40: Draft Outline on the Organization of a Volunteer
Militia in Peking (360)
Objectives (360); Explanations to the Kuominchün (360); Explana-
tions to the Public (361); The Role of the Kuominchün and the
Kuomintang (361).
Document 41: Resolutions on the Question of Cooperation between
Party Members and the First Kuominchün (363)
Evidence of Kuominchün Responsibility for the March Eighteenth
Incident (363); Conditions for Continued Cooperation with the First
Kuominchün (364).
Document 42: Soviet Report on the Political Attitude of Feng
Yü-hsiang and First Kuominchün Officers (365)
Class Character of the Officers of the First Kuominchün (365);
Political Leadership by Dissatisfied Officers (366).

PART VII: KUOMINTANG-COMMUNIST RELATIONS DURING THE
     NORTHERN EXPEDITION, July, 1926, to April 6, 1927 (367)

Victory in Hunan and Hupeh and the Emergence of T'ang Sheng-
chih, July to October, 1926 (367); Communist Policy and the Kuomintang Joint Conference, July to October, 1926 (370); Victory in
Kiangsi and Fukien and Relations between Chiang Kai-shek and the
Communists, November to December, 1926 (372); Communist Policy, December, 1926 (375); Development of Wuhan-Nanchang Conflict, December, 1926, to January, 1927 (381); Communist Policy,
January, 1927 (384); The Wuhan-Nanchang Controversy, February
to March, 1927 (386); The Communist Propaganda Offensive, February to March, 1927 (388); Anti-Chiang Military Alliance, to
March, 1927 (393); Communist Alliance with the Wuhan Left Wing,
February to March, 1927 (396); The Chinese Communist Central
Committee and Moscow, January to April, 1927 (401); Communists
and the Left Wing at Peking, to April 6, 1927 (403).

Document 43: Pavlov's Report on the Eighth Army (410)
Political and Military Cliques (410); Estimate of T'ang Sheng-
chih (411).
Document 44: Teruni's Report to Borodin on the Situation at
Wuhan (413)
Lack of Communication and Coordination (413); The Capture of
Wuchang (414); The Kiangsi Campaign (414); Policy toward Sun
Ch'uan-fang (415); T'ang Sheng-chih's Attitude and Relations with
Chiang Kai-shek and the Communists (416); The Paoting Clique
(418); Criticism of Liu Tso-lung (418); Military Developments (419);
Suggestions on Military Strategy (419); Inadequate Political Work
and Weakness of the Left Wing in Wuhan (420).
Document 45: Resolutions on the Chinese Communist Youth
Corps (422)
Endorsement of the Resolutions on the Chinese Question of the Ex-
ecutive Committee of the Communist International (422); The
Nature and Actual Condition of the Corps (423); Political Tasks of
the Communist Youth Corps (423).
Document 46: Minutes of a Meeting of the Provisional Joint Council
of the Kuomintang's Central Executive Committee and the National
Government Council (425)
T'ang Sheng-chih's Report on Conditions in Western Hupeh (425);
Problem of Military Funds (426).
Document 47: Political Report of the Central Committee of the
Chinese Communist Party, January 8, 1927 (427)
Chang Tso-lin's Strategy (427); Weakness of the Kuominchün (427);
The Situation in Honan (427); Yen Hsi-shan's Position (428); Views
on the Shanghai Problem (428); Revolutionary Character of the Mass
Movement (428); Conflict among Leaders of the National Govern-
ment (429); Policies of Britain and Japan (429); The Central Com-
mittee's Military Policies and Political Slogans (429).
Document 48: Political Report of the Central Committee of the
Chinese Communist Party, January 26, 1927 (431)
Policy of the Foreign Powers (431); Policy of the Militarists (432);
Rise of the Right Wing (432); Alliance of Imperialism, the Right
Wing, and the Moderates (433); Need to Strengthen Mass Support
for the National Government (433); Propaganda Points—The Revolu-
tion Is Not Finished (433); Attack Bourgeois Ideology (433); Con-
centrate on the Anti-British Movement (434).
Document 49: Soviet Report on the Split between Chiang Kai-shek
and T'ang Sheng-chih (435)
Chiang Kai-shek's Loss of Political and Military Support (435);
Military Plans (436).
Document 50: Report on the Work of the Peking Local Committee in
the National Movement (437)
Analysis of the Circumstances of Work (437); Working Plans in the

National Movement—Movement against the New Right Wing (438);
The Left Unification Movement (440); Analysis of Left Organiza-
tions (442); Practical Society (443); New Army Society (445);
Szechuan Revolutionary Youth Society (446); New Yunnan Society
(447); The Reform Society (447); Soul of Hainan Society and the
Ch'iung-yai Association (448); Chung-shan Study Society and New
China Study Society (449); Recent Elections of the Municipal Party
Headquarters and Communist Policy (450); Organization of the
New Municipal Committee (453); The Left's Attitude toward the
Communist Party (454); Conclusions (455).

CONCLUSIONS (457)

NOTES (471)

GLOSSARY A: Special Terms and Names of Organizations and
    Party Organs (537)

GLOSSARY B: Names of Chinese Persons Mentioned in the Docu-
    ments and Essays (548)

GLOSSARY C: Names of Relatively Obscure Russians Mentioned
    in the Documents and Essays (562)

BIBLIOGRAPHY (565)

INDEX (595)

ILLUSTRATIONS

Instructions to the Soviet Military Attaché, Page 1   Facing page 16
Instructions to the Soviet Military Attaché, Page 2   Facing page 17

ABBREVIATIONS

KMT   Kuomintang, Nationalist Party

CEC   Central Executive Committee of the Kuomintang

CSC   Central Supervisory Committee of the Kuomintang

KCT   Kung-ch'an-tang, Chinese Communist Party

CC   Central Committee of the Chinese Communist Party

CY   Chinese Communist Youth Corps

CI   Communist International or Comintern

ECCI   Executive Committee of the Communist International

SY   Chinese Socialist Youth Corps

Documents on

Communism, Nationalism, and

Soviet Advisers in China

1918-1927

INTRODUCTION

The nineteen-twenties were important and turbulent years in China's modern revolutionary history. The Nationalist Party was revitalized and acquired military power with assistance from Soviet Russia. The Chinese Communist Party, working within the Kuomintang by direction from the Comintern, grew rapidly and its leaders gained revolutionary experience. A violent anti-imperialist movement swept the country. The Nationalists, with Communist help, launched the Northern Expedition, a great military campaign to put down warlord opponents and reunite the country. Then some of the leaders of the Kuomintang turned upon the Communists and drove them from the coalition in a purge in April, 1927. Other Kuomintang leaders continued to cooperate with the Communists until July, 1927. Then a second purge took place and the Russian advisers were driven from China. The purified Kuomintang went on to unify the country, at least nominally, and to establish a national government which won international recognition.

The documents in this collection pertain only to the events before the purge in April, 1927. They have a rather peculiar interest, for most of them are "action" documents written on the spot by participants in the revolution. Among them are instructions, reports, minutes, letters, and resolutions drawn up by men planning and carrying out the revolutionary program. The writers probably never expected the documents to be made public. It is through a quirk of history that they are available.

The fifty documents here printed in translation are from a much larger number seized in a raid on the office of the Soviet Military Attaché in Peking on April 6, 1927. The raid was conducted by Chinese police and gendarmes under orders from Chang Tso-lin. The Soviet Attaché's office was a directing point for Soviet agents working as advisers and instructors among Chinese revolutionary groups. Other raided buildings in the Soviet Embassy compound were serving as refúge for Chinese Communists and Kuomintang members; hence the intimate nature of many of the documents discovered. Subsequently, three hundred and twenty-four of the documents were published in Chinese, about fifty were published in English, and several compilations were prepared by the Japanese. The raid and its revelations created a considerable international storm in 1927.

This promising source of information about the early history of Chinese Communism, about the Kuomintang, and about the role of Soviet agents in the Chinese Revolution has not been adequately

utilized by Western historians. This may have been due partly to
the cloud of doubt regarding their authenticity which was raised almost immediately and partly to the difficulty of the languages into
which they were translated. The Chinese and Japanese versions
are in many cases most obscure.

The documents in the present collection, save for a few, have
not been available previously in English. In selecting this group
for translation we looked for documents which dealt with Chinese aspects of the Revolution. Previous collections have all laid stress
upon the activities of Soviet agents, whether these activities were
related to Chinese political developments or not.

There is a certain adventitiousness about the availability of the
documents. Of those which escaped burning only a small proportion
was published. Of those published not many dealt with the Chinese
Revolution directly. Therefore they do not provide a full and con-
secutive narrative. In chronology they are scattered irregularly
over several years, and they deal with events in various parts of
China. They are raw materials of history, rather heterogeneous in
nature. To provide coherence we have grouped together documents
which are interrelated and have provided each group with historical
essays which discuss in some detail the broader events to which
the several documents in the group pertain. We also point out ways
in which the several documents contribute to an understanding of
these events. The documents in each part follow a chronological
sequence. The parts overlap one another, but generally progress in
historical order.

The first document is a confidential history of the Chinese Communist movement from 1918 until September, 1926. It provides a
general framework for understanding many of the items which follow. The next group relates to the Chinese Communist Party's organizational policies. Beginning with Part III, attention is focused
on Kwangtung, where the Kuomintang revolutionary base was consolidated with the help of Russian advisers and Chinese Communist organizers. As the revolutionary movement gathered strength
in Kwangtung, friction and deep cleavages developed within the
Kuomintang over the radicalization of the movement, the influence
of Soviet advisers, and the increasingly important role played by
Chinese Communists. Similarly, contention grew within the Communist movement over the policy of cooperation with the Kuomintang. And both Communist and Kuomintang leaders found themselves
at odds with their Russian advisers. A number of documents in Part
IV illustrate this phenomenon. Part V deals with Communist policy
toward the mass movements which the Party dominated but which
its leaders dared not allow to become too militant for fear of disrupting the alliance with the Kuomintang just on the verge of the
Northern Expedition.

Highly successful in Kwangtung, Soviet agents attempted to play a similar guiding role in creating a revolutionary nucleus in the North with the armies of Feng Yü-hsiang. They also tried to link these armies with the Kuomintang in South China. Documents that illustrate this venture are brought together in Part VI.

In Part VII is a group of reports written during the course of the Northern Expedition. They reflect the growing tension within the Kuomintang and between the Nationalists and the Communists which culminated in the split of April, 1927.

The reader may be interested in a few examples of the types of historical data available in the documents in this volume. One type is the observations of Russian advisers who were attempting to direct the revolution in China. Needless to say, they had many frustrations. Their evaluations of events with which they were closely connected have a certain fascination in addition to their historical importance.

On March 20, 1926, General Chiang Kai-shek shattered the Russian-fostered coalition between the Kuomintang and the Chinese Communists in Canton by a direct display of his military power. He arrested the Communist deputy chief of the Navy Bureau and a number of Party representatives in the Army. His troops seized strategic points, surrounded the headquarters of various Communist-led organizations, and disarmed the guards who protected the residences of the Soviet advisers. Among our documents is a vivid contemporary description of this event in a report by General Stepanov, Russian adviser to Chiang's First Army. Stepanov analyzes Chiang's action, which "came as a lightning shock to our comrades," in the light of errors made by the Russian advisers and the Chinese Communists. Then he analyzes the character of "the chief culprit in the incident, Chiang Kai-shek." Chiang's most prominent characteristic, according to his Russian adviser, was his "lust for glory and power and craving to be the hero of China." Stepanov proposed that in order to continue to use Chiang to carry on the revolutionary struggle an effort be made by the Russians to satisfy his lust for power. He might be appointed commander-in-chief of the Army. "If we could inject into him a small dose of revolutionary ideology and surround him with the brave influence of the Left, we would ensure against repetition of the March 20 Incident."

But Chiang's coup d'état could not be easily wished away. In a second report early in April, 1926, Stepanov sees two possible conclusions regarding Chiang's subsequent actions: either that he sincerely intended to temper the incident and cooperate with the Left for the cause of the national revolution, or that his actions were meant only to deceive his opponents in preparation for another hostile move. If the second conclusion were adopted "we must be prepared to fight him." "Our basic policy," said Stepanov, "is to

cooperate with Chiang to the very end possible." He admitted that
the March Twentieth Incident "may dishearten us, but we must forget it and keep up our efforts." The report concludes with a record
of the discussion among the members of the Soviet advisory group.
The questions and answers reveal the grave misgivings of men involved in a situation they did not clearly comprehend.

Secret resolutions of the Chinese Communist Party's Central
Committee, meeting in plenary sessions, are another type of historical data in this collection. These are very important, as they
reveal the Party's official appraisal of the objective situation in
China at the time and the major strategy and tactics to be followed
to exploit the situation. Among the seized documents were three
resolutions from the Enlarged Plenum held in Peking in October,
1925, and what are apparently the complete resolutions of the
Second Enlarged plenum held in Shanghi in July, 1926. These decisions of meetings of the Central Committee at a crucial period
in the Party's history do not seem to be available in any other
source. They are analyzed in their historical context in the appropriate introductions.

These examples perhaps suffice to indicate that this collection is
intended to contribute to our knowledge of the Revolution from the
point of view of the participants themselves. One tendency in studies
of Communism in China is to emphasize the theoretical doctrines
that presumably guided the participants in revolution. Another is
to focus attention upon the Comintern leadership, which rested in
Russia. The documents in this collection and the essays offered to
illuminate them place the focus upon what actually happened in
China, the policies established on the scene, and the individuals
directly involved. They provide only a little information about the
formulation of policies in Moscow but considerable insight into the
execution of such policies. Furthermore, the documents provide information about the Kuomintang in action. Accordingly, published
sources on Kuomintang history, generally neglected in the West,
have been drawn upon to illuminate the account of the Nationalist-
Communist coalition.

The historical value of the documents in this collection depends
entirely upon their authenticity. The stigma of forgery was attached
to them by spokesmen for Soviet Russia even before the first
documents allegedly discovered in the Soviet Military Attaché's
office were published. Therefore it has been one of our major concerns to gather and weigh all available evidence on this question
and to draw conclusions.

Two lines of approach were followed. The first was to examine
all available external evidence, that is, information about the raid,
the circumstances of publication of the documents, and the testimony of persons who have expressed opinions as to their authentic-

ity. The second approach was to weigh internal evidence. How do
the documents stand up, individually, under historical scrutiny? Do
they reveal inaccuracies, inconsistencies, or anachronisms that
make them suspect? The first essay presents the evidence we have
accumulated on this issue, and our conclusions.

THE PROBLEM OF AUTHENTICITY

EXTERNAL EVIDENCE

The Raid on the Premises of the Soviet Embassy

At eleven o'clock on the morning of April 6, 1927, a party of three
hundred police and plain-clothes detectives from the Peking Metropolitan Police Headquarters and the Third and Fourth Regiments of
the Ankuochün Gendarmes approached the Legation Quarter of
Peking. Under the personal command of the Chief of Police, Ch'en
Hsin-ya, the men were admitted into the quarter by the sentries on
duty. They proceeded to the premises of the Soviet Embassy, surrounding it on three sides. Simultaneously, armed British soldiers
appeared on the wall of the British Legation, which adjoined the
Soviet Embassy on the north.

The raiding party began a systematic search of the residential
quarters of Embassy personnel in the western portion of the Embassy compound, and of the Peking offices of the Chinese Eastern
Railway and the Dalbank. As the searchers entered the office of the
Chinese Eastern Railway, a shot was fired from within. A short
while later, a Russian was seen being handcuffed and led away. Subsequently another group of prisoners, including Li Ta-chao, Chinese
Communist leader in North China, was taken into custody.

At two in the afternoon it was discovered that there was a fire
in the office of the Soviet Military Attaché, situated in the barracks
of the former Imperial Russian Legation Guard. A number of Russians had locked themselves into the office and were burning piles
of documents. Fire equipment was rushed to the scene. A hose was
laid over the roof of the building and water was pumped down the
chimney. The flames were thus brought under control.

By five o'clock, seven truckloads of documents salvaged from the
fire in the Military Attaché's office, some badly scorched, had been
carted away. In addition, an assortment of Kuomintang and Chinese
Communist banners and seals, two machine guns, fifteen rifles, and
quantities of small arms were seized.[1] A number of Chinese and
Russian prisoners were taken to police headquarters.[2] The raid
ended at seven o'clock. A portion of the raiding party withdrew; the
rest remained in the Embassy compound.

The incident attracted immediate and widespread interest. Amidst
speculation that there would be war between the Soviet Union
and the Peking Government,[3] two major issues emerged: the

degree of responsibility of the Diplomatic Corps, and the legality of the raid.

According to a later account given by William J. Oudendyk, the Minister of the Netherlands and <u>doyen</u> of the Diplomatic Corps, the following had taken place prior to the raid. Wu Chin, Vice-Minister of Foreign Affairs of the Peking Government and chief of the Foreign Department of the Ankuochün, called on Oudendyk. Wu said he believed that the Chinese Eastern Railway and Dalbank offices, protected by the Soviet Embassy's diplomatic status, were being used as Communist headquarters for staging an insurrection in Peking. He suggested putting an end to such activities, and, when informed that the Legation police could do nothing, requested permission for the Chinese police to enter the Legation Quarter and search these two buildings. When Oudendyk submitted Wu Chin's request to the other ministers, they agreed with him that it should be granted. On the morning of April 6, 1927, Oudendyk signed a warrant for the Metropolitan Police to search the offices of the Chinese Eastern Railway and the Dalbank in the Soviet Embassy compound.[4]

That same evening, Oudendyk lodged a formal protest with the Chinese Foreign Office, charging that the searching party had exceeded its authorization when it entered the office of the Military Attaché.[5] It was widely reported in the press, however, that the protest was merely technical and that no further action was expected from the Diplomatic Corps.[6] On April 7 and again the following day, the Protocol ministers extended the original permit in order that the search could be continued.[7]

Thus, the Diplomatic Corps showed that they at least approved of the raid by sanctioning it in the first place, by not taking positive action when the raiding party exceeded its warrant, and by twice extending the original permit for the search.

The Position of the Peking Government, the USSR, and the Kuomintang

The official statements of the Peking authorities clearly indicate that they assumed full responsibility for the raid. No mention was made of the Diplomatic Corps in the proclamation of the Peking Metropolitan Police Headquarters[8] or the note of the Chinese Foreign Minister, Wellington Koo, to the Soviet Chargé d'Affairs,[9] both dated April 6, 1927. The Peking Government's position was that the harboring of Li Ta-chao and other revolutionaries within the Soviet Embassy compound, where they conspired against the state and disseminated Communist propaganda, violated the Sino-Soviet Agreement of May, 1924, and the principles of international law.[10] This position was reiterated in the instructions of the Chinese Foreign Office to the Chinese Chargé d'Affairs in Moscow. The Foreign Office justified the raid as an act of self-protection by

the state and resorted to two additional arguments: (1) The raid
was not without precedent; and (2) The Soviet Embassy proper was
not searched.[11]

The Peking Government's stand was promptly challenged by the
USSR in a note from Litvinov, Acting People's Commissar for Foreign Affairs, to the Chinese Chargé d'Affaires in Moscow on April
9, 1927. Litvinov denounced the raid as an unprecedented breach of
international law and indirectly accused the Diplomatic Corps. He
declared that the cooperation between the Peking police and the
Diplomatic Corps suggested the real "springs" from which arose
the breach of international law.[12] Thus, the issues of legality and
responsibility of the Protocol ministers became intertwined.

Chang Tso-lin had ordered the raid at a time when the Kuomin-
tang was winning new and decisive victories in the campaign to
unify the country. The party's National Revolutionary Army had
occupied Shanghai on March 22, and Nanking two days later. The
Kuomintang was torn, however, between two factions: the Left
Wing, supported by the Communists, and elements headed by
Chiang Kai-shek, Commander-in-Chief of the National Revolutionary
Army.

The Third Plenum of the Kuomintang's Central Executive Committee, meeting at Wuhan between March 10 and 17, had entrenched
the Left Wing in control of the party and the government and had
ousted Chiang Kai-shek and his supporters from key positions.[13]
The latter were quick to retaliate. On March 28, two days after
Chiang entered Shanghai, members of the Kuomintang's Central
Supervisory Committee met and decided to convene an emergency
session on April 2. On that day they voted to invalidate all decisions made by the Hankow Joint Council and the Third CEC Plenum
on the ground that they were manipulated by Left Wing leaders
under Borodin's direction. The Shanghai meeting of the CSC is of
even greater historical significance, for it launched the Kuomintang's Party Purification Movement. The CSC adopted a resolution
to hand over to the Kuomintang CEC for decision and action a list
of names of Communists who were accused of engaging under foreign direction, in activities detrimental to the Kuomintang. The
emergency session of the CSC voted at the same time to notify the
military and police to place these Communists under surveillance
or detention, but stipulated that all measures were to be executed
in a peaceful manner, pending final decision at a plenary session of
the CEC.[14]

The emergency session of the CSC was followed by a series of
conferences of top Kuomintang leaders, including Wang Ching-wei,
leader of the Left Wing, who had arrived at Shanghai from Europe
on April 1. According to a Kuomintang document, Wang Ching-wei
agreed to carry out immediately a number of measures restricting

the activities of Communists and labor unions and invalidating the orders issued by the party and government at Wuhan. Other KMT leaders, on the other hand, accepted his proposal to solve outstanding problems peacefully at a joint session of the CEC and CSC to be convened at Nanking on April 15.[15] Several months later, Wang Ching-wei confirmed that he had agreed at the Shanghai conferences to convene a plenum of the CEC at Nanking to discuss the demand of Chiang and others for the immediate dismissal of Borodin and the ousting of Communists from the KMT. He then left for Wuhan on April 6, Wang declared, for the purpose of persuading Left-Wing leaders there to attend the plenum at Nanking.[16] Thus, according to his own testimony, Wang Ching-wei was ready to subject to reexamination the Party's policy of admitting Communists into its ranks and cooperating with Soviet Russia. Two days before he left Shanghai, however, Wang issued a joint declaration with Ch'en Tu-hsiu, head of the Chinese Communist Party, which reaffirmed the policy of cooperation between the Kuomintang and the Chinese Communist Party, and denied all rumours of an impending break.[17]

The raid thus occurred in the midst of uncertainty as to the Kuomintang's future course, but denunciation of Chang Tso-lin's action came promptly from both factions. Despite his insistent demand for dismissing Borodin and ousting the Communists, Chiang Kai-shek expressed sympathy with the Soviet Embassy. In a note to Chernykh, the Soviet chargé d'affaires in Peking, dated April 8, 1927, Chiang denounced the raid as an unprecedented outrage maneuvered by the imperialists with the aim of destroying the Chinese National Revolution and bringing about international conflict.[18] Eugene Chen, Foreign Minister of the National Government at Hankow, expressed profound regrets in a wire to Chicherin, the Soviet People's Commissar for Foreign Affairs. He declared that the National Government would take strong action against the "wanton violation" of the sovereignty and dignity of the Soviet Republic.[19] On April 22, the Kuomintang at Wuhan formally issued a manifesto denouncing the Diplomatic Corps for instigating or at least sanctioning the raid because of fear that the Legation Quarter would soon no longer serve as the base of imperialist operations.[20]

The charges against the Diplomatic Corps made by the USSR and the Kuomintang were seconded by a segment of the independent press. The highly respected periodical Hsien-tai p'ing-lun (The Contemporary Review) declared that the Peking Governments was used as a tool by the Diplomatic Corps.[21] The editor of the independent China Weekly Review, John B. Powell, roundly denounced the Diplomatic Corps and challenged the legality of the raid.[22]

The USSR raised the issue of authenticity of the seized documents before any of them had been made public (the first document was released on April 19, 1927) by linking it to the question of the Diplo-

matic Corps' responsibility. The gist of the Soviet contention was
that the Diplomatic Corps, in particular the representatives of
England, had pushed Chang Tso-lin into staging the raid in such a
manner that counterfeit documents could be smuggled in, thereby
providing "proof" of hostile Soviet activities and an excuse for war.

In the first Soviet note submitted to the Chinese Foreign Office
immediately after the raid, the Soviet Chargé d'Affaires protested
that no one from the other portions of the Embassy was allowed
near the scene of the search. He declared that the responsible
officials of the Embassy were roughly pushed back by the police.[23]
On the following day, Russian representatives in Peking suggested
further that, in the absence of official Soviet and foreign observers,
the police could produce any document they wished and falsely allege
that they were seized on the Soviet premises.[24]

England was singled out by the USSR for denunciation. On April
8 Moscow newspapers reported that the Foreign Affairs Commissariat was without authentic information on the Peking events and
was therefore unable to interpret the significance of the incident.
Nevertheless, a communiqué was issued the same day stating that,
notwithstanding the paucity of news, it was already clear that England
was the chief instigator of the provocation.[25] On the same day,
Pravda accused England of wanting to provoke the USSR in order to
have an excuse for intervention in China. It added that England might
have expected to find "proofs" of the interference of the USSR in the
domestic affairs of China.[26]

Litvinov's note of April 9 linked the allegedly provocative intentions of the foreign powers to the circumstances of the raid in a
way designed to cast doubt on everything reportedly seized from the
Soviet Embassy premises. In it Litvinov declared that, in view of the
circumstances of the raid, the hostile foreign influences which inspired and sanctioned it could use anything they wished against the
USSR under the pretense of their having been found on the Soviet
premises.[27]

On April 11, Alexis I. Rykov summed up the Soviet case in a
speech at the All-Russian Congress of Soviets. Denouncing the
Diplomatic Corps for instigating the raid and thereby provoking the
USSR to war, Rykov proceeded to the accusation that counterfeit documents could have been smuggled in during the raid. To illustrate
this point, he referred to a document from a Chinese source which
he claimed was absolutely reliable. This was allegedly a record of
a conference which took place at Harbin under orders from Chang
Tso-lin's headquarters, at which secret-service chiefs were told
they must absolutely find stores of Communist literature and arms
in Soviet premises. For this purpose they were to make use of the
stores of the police administration if necessary. Rykov introduced
another argument. He cited the use of Russian White Guards in con-

nection with the raid as proof of provocative intentions against the
USSR. He did not specify, however, in what capacity he believed the
White Russians were employed.[28]

While the USSR sought to cast suspicion on the seized documents,
it simultaneously demanded their return. Litvinov demanded in his
note of April 9 the return of all documents and other seized property
as well as the release of the prisoners. Until these demands had
been satisfied, he stated, the USSR was recalling its chargé
d'affaires and Embassy staff from Peking, leaving only personnel
for performing consular functions.[29] Accordingly, the Soviet Embassy staff prepared to leave Peking by April 15.[30] On April 16,
the Peking Government rejected the Soviet demands,[31] and the withdrawal of the Soviet Embassy took place on April 17,[32] two days
before the first seized document was made public.

During this period, the Soviet Union was alone in raising the
issue of the documents' authenticity, although the Russians' accusation that Chang Tso-lin was a tool of the Diplomatic Corps was
echoed in other quarters.

Selection and Translation of the Seized Documents

A study of contemporary sources and subsequent publications
which mention the seized documents indicates that the major lines
of argument on authenticity, pro and con, were drawn in the brief
period of one month following the release of the first document.
Hence, it is necessary to examine in some detail the nature and number of the first group of documents released and the manner of their
selection, translation, and publication.

Examination of the documents began immediately after the raid.
By midnight of April 6 it was reported that a staff of experts had
been assembled at the Metropolitan Police Headquarters.[33] Chang
Kuo-ch'en, Commissioner of Foreign Affairs for Chahar, was
appointed head of the Commission for Translation and Compilation
of Soviet Documents. On April 8 the Metropolitan Police Headquarters announced that they would shortly publish the seized documents
as a state paper.[34]

The military attachés of the American, British, and French legations played a substantial, if not leading, role in the initial work of
sorting and translating the documents into English. Two days after
the raid, it was reported that the foreign military attachés had already examined the seized documents.[35] In a telegram to Secretary
of State Kellogg dated April 27, 1927, the United States Minister,
MacMurray, reported that theoretically the Chinese authorities were
making the documents equally available to all Protocol legations.
However, benefit in fact accrued principally to the British, French,
and American legations, whose military attachés had pooled their
resources to work on the documents under the direction of Captain

John P. Ratay, U.S. Army. According to MacMurray, they had been
given facilities for sorting, photographing, and translating those
documents regarded as of possible value, and trustworthy Russians
had been employed for translation work under Ratay's supervision.[36]
According to General (then Major) John Magruder, who was American Military Attaché in Peking at the time, Captain Ratay took
charge of selecting as well as translating the documents into English and directly supervised their publication by the Chinese authorities.[37]

On April 12, Ankuochun headquarters issued the first public statement on the character of the documents.[38] A fuller account was
sent to Minister MacMurray; in this twenty general types of documents were listed, with emphasis on Russian documents dealing with
Soviet intelligence and espionage and aid to the KMT and Feng Yü-
hsiang.[39] The following day the Metropolitan Police Headquarters
announced that a full examination of the documents would require
some time, in view of the large quantity of documents seized and
the burned and damaged condition of some of them. Many, it was
stated, were barely legible.[40]

The Peking authorities were apparently aware of the magnitude
of the task and seemed willing to accept advice.[41] Minister Mac-
Murray reported that while the Government was most anxious to
obtain the widest possible publicity for the documents, it was handicapped by lack of system and understanding of publicity as well as
by a scarcity of translators from Russian.[42]

On April 27, the Protocol ministers were invited to an exhibit of
the seized documents.[43] An exhibit for newspaper correspondents
was held the following day. According to the London Times correspondent, a number of photographs were exhibited with certified
translations of some of the documents by foreign officials. Translations of those documents which more especially connected the
Soviet government with the Chinese revolutionary movement were,
according to The Times correspondent, checked by non-Russian
foreigners acquainted with the language.[44]

Among the papers exhibited were various documents which presumably had been stolen from the British Legation. These included
telegrams between British Minister Sir Miles Lampson and the
British Foreign Office concerning the Hankow Incident and instructions issued by the British Legation to British consuls, as well as
minute records of conversations and seating plans for British Legation functions.[45]

It was widely reported at the time that papers belonging to other
foreign legations had also been discovered in the mass of Soviet
documents. In a memorandum dated May 3, 1927, Major Magruder
reported the discovery of numerous documents from the British
and Japanese legations as well as papers from the Italian, Spanish,

and Belgian legations and the Chinese Foreign Office. No material
from the American Legation, according to Magruder, had yet been
found.46

A number of documents originating in other foreign legations were
apparently removed from the Metropolitan Police Headquarters.
Major General Shigeru Honjo, the Japanese Military Attaché, reported to the Vice-Minister of War in Tokyo that the seized documents had been disappearing and that some of them were known to
be embarrassing to certain foreign nations.47 The London Times
correspondent reported that some papers not submitted to the press
for inspection were known to include privileged statements which
in wrong hands would be diplomatic indiscretions. Hence, it was
deemed expedient to suppress them.48

Certain other documents were suppressed because the authorities feared that their publication would hamper the surveillance
and arrest of those Communists whose party affiliation was exposed
by the documents.49

The First Documents Made Public

On April 19, nearly two weeks after the raid, the first document
allegedly seized in the Soviet Military Attaché's office was made
public. It purported to be instructions to the Soviet Military Attaché
based on the resolutions of the Seventh Enlarged Plenum of the Executive Committee of the Communist International in Moscow. The
document was released in English and Chinese translations, accompanied by a facsimile of the original Russian. A Reuters dispatch
headlined the translation: "Startling Document Made Public as Outcome of Raid of Police and Military on the Soviet Embassy."50

The document made a great impact on the public mind, both because it was the first Soviet document to be released and because
of its sensational character. It is included in every publication we
have seen which contains translations of the seized documents.51

Since a great deal of controversy centers about this document,
we include here an independent English translation prepared by Mr.
Leo Gruliow from a photograph of the original Russian text. There
were many typing errors in the original text.52

C[ompletely] Secret

To the Military Attaché in China.

Enclosing herewith the resolution on the Chinese question adopted
at the [recent?] augmented plenary session of the E.C.C.I., we are
sending you instructions to be carried out, worked out on the basis
of this resolution.

1. All attention should be concentrated at present on giving the
revolutionary movement in China an exclusively national character.
For this purpose agitation is necessary in favor of the Kuomintang

as the party of China's national independence. Make broad use of the
Hankow events and Britain's position in them as proof, first, of the success of the Kuomintang in national work, and, second, of the European
states' undoubted weakness in combating the Chinese revolution.

2. It is necessary to organize anti-European53 riots on the territory held by Chang Tso-lin's troops.

3. It is necessary to discredit Chang Tso-lin's activity, presenting him as a hireling of international, capitalist and imperialist...
[burned] who is hindering the Kuomintang in its work for the liberation of China from [economic?] dependence.

[4. It is necess?] ary to organize agitation against European use
of force...[at this point only a few disconnected words are legible
at the bottom of the burned page]

[5. It is necess?] ary to take all measures to arouse the masses
of the people against...[burned, and a word cut off]...[burned] for
these purposes necessary to see to it that the foreign pow...[burned]
use...[burned] in fighting the crowds of people. To bring on interference by the foreign...[burned] do not hesitate to use any measures,
including even robbery and beatings. In case of clashes with European troop detachments make broad use of these incidents for agitation.

6. Be careful not to carry through the Communist program at
this time. This could strengthen Chang Tso-lin's position and intensify the split in the Kuom...ng. [A line at this point is indecipher-
able—washed out of the photo or blinded out by a highlight] ...
[burned] too sharp pressure on capitalist [ungrammatical case end-
ing] elements, making it one's task until Chang Tso-Lin falls to
keep all strata of the population, including the bourgeoisie, in the
Kuomintang.

7. In directing this movement against Europeans it is extremely
important to preserve the existing antagonism between the individual foreign powers. It is particularly important to isolate Japan, as
a country that might land large military forces in China very
swiftly. For these purposes during any demonstrations it is necessary to be careful to see to it that none of the victims are Japanese
residents. However, in conducting agitation against foreigners, to
set Japan apart might create an unfavorable impression. Therefore
it is necessary to conduct agitation against foreigners in the form
of an anti-British movement.

...[burned] essary immediately to send to all department chiefs
and leadersh...[burned]

The selection of this document, with its emphasis on antiforeign
and anti-British activities, as the first document to be released
reflects the widespread apprehension over the outbreak of antiforeign riots in territories occupied by the Kuomintang. The Nanking

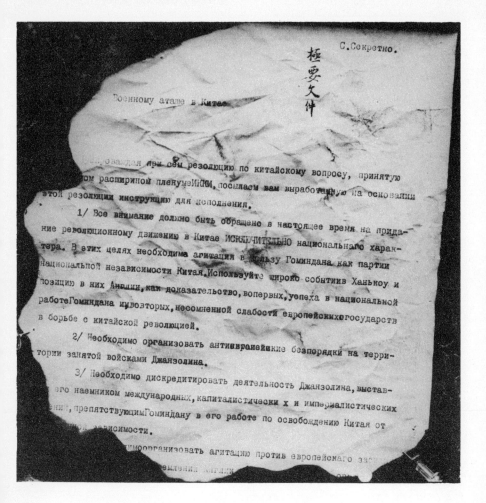

Instructions to the Soviet Military Attaché, Page 1

The first document published by the Peking Commission investigating the documents allegedly seized in the raid of April 6, 1927. The authenticity of this document has been

...но принять все меры к побуждению народных масс против и... этих целях необходимо добиться применения иностранными дер... борьбе с народной толпой. Чтобы вызвать вмешательствоиностранн... ...не останавливайтесь ни перед какими мерами вплоть до граб ей и ... ...биений. В случае столкновения с европейскими воинскими частями широко ...льзуйте эти случаи для агитации.

...6/ Остерегайтесь проводить в жизнь в настоящее время коммунистичес... ...програму. Это может укрепить положение Джанзолина и усилить раскол в Гом... не. Наши отдачо ...тю ...онических ... ...слишком резкаго напора на капиталистическия элементы ставя своей задач ...до падения Джанзолина, сохраня. Б в Гоминдане все слои населения включая ...уржуазию.

7/При проведении настоящаго движения против европейцев чрезвычайно важно сохранить существующий антагонизм между отдельными державами. Особо но важно изолировать Японию, как страну могущую кротчайший срок доставит... в Китай большие воинские силы. В этих целях при всякаго рода выступлениях ...еобходимо строго наблюдать, чтобы не было пострадавших среди японских рез... ...тов. Однако при ведении агитации против иностранцев выделениеЯпонии мо... ...произвести неблагоприятное впечатление. Поэтому необходимо проводить ...нию против иностранцев под видом антибританскаго движения.

...ую немедленно разослать всем заводтделам и руководст...

Instructions to the Soviet Military Attaché, Page 2

challenged (for a discussion of this question, see pages 34–36). Photograph from the Archives of the United States Department of State

Incident, in which a number of foreigners were killed at the time
of the occupation of Nanking by the National Revolutionary Army
had preceded the raid by two weeks. An attack by a mob on the
Japanese Concession in Hankow had taken place only three days
before the raid.

On April 22, MacMurray forwarded a translation of the first
document to the Secretary of State with the remark that the Chinese authorities had already found among the documents important
evidence of Soviet activity, especially of antiforeign agitation in
China. The translation, he added, had been verified by Senior Minister Oudendyk.[54]

Emphasis on antiforeign Soviet documents is again evident in the
selection of documents which followed the first one to be released.
On April 22, four additional documents were made public. The subject of two of these is Soviet espionage in foreign legations; one is
an agreement signed by a Chinese to hire spies in foreign legations,
and the other contains instructions on methods of hiring spies in
foreign legations.[55]

On April 28, additional documents in English and Chinese translations were made available at the exhibit for newspaper correspondents. The North China Star published a total of twelve English
translations of documents the following morning.[56] The first publication of English translations in pamphlet or book form appeared
on May 11, when fourteen translations of the seized documents
were put out by the North China Daily News and Herald of Shanghai.[57] Comparison of this pamphlet with other pamphlets issued
about the same time,[58] with documents published in the press, and
those dispatched by Minister MacMurray to the Secretary of State,
reveals that only about fifteen documents had been released by
May 11, 1927, and approximately thirty had been made public by
the end of June.[59]

There was a fair amount of criticism of the handling of the documents. As early as April 22, the London Times correspondent had
reported that the documents were not being used to the best advantage and that the translations were given out indiscriminately
and without the necessary information as to dates, places of origin,
and signers of the documents.[60] Similar criticism was voiced in a
Reuters dispatch which reported that criticism was increasing in
foreign official and journalistic circles.[61] Randall Gould, a United
Press staff correspondent, complained on April 25 that few persons had had access to the seized documents and that the translations as published were unsatisfactory because of incompleteness
and lack of proof of authenticity. He emphasized the scarcity of
impartial experts.[62]

Impatience was expressed in certain quarters. The London Times
editorial of May 6, 1927, for instance, expressed the hope that the

Peking Government would not wait until all the captured documents had been examined before publishing a White Book. It pointed out that any long delay in publication would encourage charges that the documents had been forged or tampered with.[63]

Documents released during this period were mainly Russian documents on Soviet espionage, supplies to the Kuomintang and Feng Yü-hsiang, and the work of Soviet advisers at Canton and Kalgan. Not one paper from the 514 files of original Chinese documents which were listed as having been seized,[64] was included.

The disproportionate emphasis on Russian documents and on Soviet activities is evidenced also by the Peking Metropolitan Police Headquarters in the foreword to the Chinese Government White Book which was dated April, 1927. The foreword states that the following had been proved conclusively by the seized documents: (1) The Soviet Embassy had an extensive political and military secret-service apparatus in China, which conducted espionage everywhere, even in the foreign legations; (2) Soviet advisers and instructors in China were members of Kuomintang and Chinese Communist councils and were paid through the Soviet Military Attaché; and (3) The Soviet government, through its Peking Embassy, furnished arms, munitions, and other war supplies to the enemies of the Peking Government.[65]

The tendency was to accept or reject the entire collection of documents in accordance with one's attitude toward the Soviets. Contemporary discussions of their authenticity reveal little effort at objective analysis of their substance. Judging by the accounts in the contemporary press, there was no noticeable effort to check data in the documents against independent sources or to search for internal historical inconsistencies. There were, however, a number of specific arguments used to attack or defend the validity of the documents.

Arguments against Authenticity

While the overwhelming majority of newspapermen in Peking accepted the documents as genuine, there were at least two notable exceptions; they were Randall Gould, a staff correspondent for the United Press, and the correspondent of the Berliner Tageblatt.

Gould's dispatch of April 25, 1927, is especially interesting because it foreshadowed the arguments of the Soviet government and the Communist International. Gould cited the Soviet officials in Peking as his source, but apparently did not question their arguments. His article introduced the following contentions: (1) The use of the "old style" spelling in the first facsimile of a Russian document released proves that the documents are forgeries; (2) "Curious" mistakes and misspellings in this same facsimile prove that the documents are forgeries; (3) The most damaging papers have nothing to do with the

Soviet government proper, but are open and previously published accounts of CI proceedings; and (4) Data which seems to indicate warlike Soviet intentions could be found in the office of every other foreign military attaché in Peking.

One argument presented in Gould's dispatch but not subsequently mentioned in Soviet denials is that the burned edges of this first document are too carefully scalloped and shaped around to have been the result of ordinary burning. The White Russians, according to Gould's dispatch, had manufactured the documents, even to the point of carefully burning their edges with matches. Gould repeated previous Soviet charges that the circumstances of the raid provided every opportunity for the fabrication of documents.[66]

The Peking correspondent of the Berliner Tageblatt, in a dispatch dated April 29, 1927, also asserted that the use in some instances of the old Russian orthography cast doubt on the documents. What he considered to be the really compromising documents, he said, were published three weeks after the raid because of the laughter allegedly aroused by the first documents which were published.[67]

Moscow's first formal denial of authenticity was made on April 29, 1927, in a declaration issued by the Secretariat of the Executive Committee of the Communist International. The ECCI repeated previous charges that the raid was staged to conceal the British system of forgery and questioned the first document released, "Instructions to the Soviet Military Attaché," on grounds of policy. It pointed out that the CI would not stir the masses against foreigners in China, as that would only cause foreign intervention, and that it would not encourage pillage and murder of foreigners regardless of class origin.[68]

On May 5 Litvinov officially raised for the first time the issue of orthography and incorrect Russian. He declared that a photographic copy of a document published in a Peking English-language newspaper proved the document was forged because of use of the old Russian orthography and incorrect Russian.[69] Although he did not identify the document, Litvinov was apparently referring to the "Instructions to the Soviet Military Attaché," for in an interview the following day he repeated the charge and identified the document as the only one "hitherto published." He also introduced officially the argument that most of the seized material consisted of the usual informatory reports which could be found in the offices of every military attaché in Peking, adding, however, that this in no way proved they were authentic.[70]

On the same day, an article in Pravda, entitled "The Peking Provocateurs Unmasked: False Documents in the Service of Chang Tsolin and Chamberlain: Falsification with the Object of Provocation," recapitulated the Soviet arguments. In addition, the article pointed out that the resolutions of the Seventh Enlarged Plenum of the ECCI,

the sixth document released, had been published in Moscow and in
all newspapers and had been issued as a separate booklet. The implication was that this document could have been copied. Pravda
also refuted the contention of foreign correspondents who had seen
the documents that it would be impossible to forge such a mass of
documents in a short time, by asserting that this said nothing in
favor of their validity. The dispatch of the Berliner Tageblatt
correspondent was quoted by Pravda to support the charge that the
use of the old orthography and linguistic errors in the first document proved the documents to be forgeries. Pravda pointed out that
the new orthography had been introduced in the USSR ten years before, and attributed the crudeness of the forging to the Ankuochün's
haste in forging a document of a compromising nature.[71]

Soviet denials of authenticity were accompanied by continued denunciation of the foreign powers, especially England, and of Chang
Tso-lin, and protest against the circumstances of the raid. In a
statement on May 5, Litvinov linked the Peking documents with
papers seized from Soviet couriers aboard the S.S. "Pamiat Lenina"
on the previous February 28. He suggested that interested persons
had placed counterfeit documents in the couriers' luggage and that
a similar maneuver had been carried out in Peking. Finally, Litvinov
warned that the publication of further documents revealing Soviet
propaganda, intervention, and antiforeign agitation in China was to
be expected, but that all these documents would be false also, concocted to besmirch the Soviet government and injure Soviet-Japanese
relations.[72]

Arguments for Authenticity

The documents were regarded as genuine by foreign diplomatic
officers and the majority of the newspapermen in Peking who had
an opportunity to view them.

According to a Japanese Foreign Office report, all the ministers
believed in the authenticity of all of the documents. The report adds
that the ministers were shocked by the evidence of "wicked conspiracy" at the exhibit.[73] The Japanese Military Attaché, Shigeru
Honjo, apparently entertained no doubt of the documents' authenticity, judging by his letters to the Japanese Vice-Minister of War.[74]
Total acceptance of the documents' authenticity is indicated in the
telegrams and dispatches of United States Legation personnel.[75]
The tendency to accept the documents was so strong, in fact, that
few reasons were given to support this acceptance.

Among the arguments advanced in favor of authenticity was the
contention that the voluminousness of the seized material precluded
the possibility of forgery, since it was impossible to fake such a
mass of documents.[76] Another argument was that the handwriting
and signatures of leading Soviet officials in Moscow and China had

been identified and offered incontrovertible evidence of authenticity.[77]

Certain Soviet arguments were directly contradicted in the contemporary press. In answer to the charge that the circumstances of the raid cast doubt on the documents, it was pointed out that the papers were exactly as they were taken away from the Embassy premises and that many were still wet with paraffin and partly burned.[78] Furthermore, it was contended that the circumstances of the raid in fact guaranteed authenticity, since many police cars which had arrived empty at the Soviet Embassy departed with a huge mass of documentary material.[79]

The North China Daily News reported on the reactions of a group of former Russian officers at an exhibit of fourteen documents in Shanghai. The Russians, according to the article, found that the documents were written in "a style peculiar to old-time military men, staff officers and the like, which none but the cleverest would dare to imitate. Others found in the long dissertations upon Red policy a variety of Yiddish phraseology which it would be equally impossible for any but a bred-in-the-bone Bolshevist to reduplicate, especially since these great masses of persiflage are in the new Russian phonetic spelling."[80]

Conclusions regarding Contemporary Arguments

Contemporary arguments on authenticity, pro and con, tend to fall into two types: arguments based on circumstantial evidence, and those based on internal evidence.

Circumstantial evidence is used in the following arguments against authenticity: (1) The raid was staged so that counterfeit documents could be smuggled in; (2) Papers similar to the seized documents could be found in any foreign legation in Peking; and (3) Most of the papers had previously been published (the implication being that they could have been copied). On the other hand, the following arguments for authenticity are circumstantial in character: (1) Empty police cars were filled with documents following the search of the Soviet Military Attache's office; and (2) The quantitiy of the seized documents guarantees authenticity.

Evidence internal to the documents is cited in the following arguments against authenticity: (1) Use of the old orthography; (2) Linguistic errors; and (3) Erroneous policy statements. One document, "Instructions to the Soviet Military Attaché," was cited to support all three contentions. The first two contentions were directly contradicted by persons defending the papers as genuine. In addition, it was asserted that the signatures and handwriting of leading Soviet officials had been positively identified in the documents.

The general tendency was to accept the documents as authentic. The issue was not even raised in most discussions. Positive arguments for authenticity, it appears, were advanced only after Soviet charges of forgery had been publicized. The few contentions, pro and con, which were advanced were based on an extremely limited number of documents. Although stacks of papers were open for inspection at the exhibits of April 27 and 28, the actual number available for study by the press and public in facsimile reproduction and in English and Chinese translations did not exceed fifteen at the end of five weeks. The entire mass, on the other hand, consisted of 1,285 files of documents.[81] Furthermore, the papers released during this period were far from representative because of the exclusion of original Chinese documents. There was no attempt at correlating the scattered documents or objective analysis.

Hence, we believe that the arguments formulated within five weeks of the raid are inconclusive.

INTERNAL EVIDENCE

Important as are the tests of orthography, linguistic style, and identification of signatures and handwriting as means of ascertaining authenticity, they are applicable only to original Russian documents. Unfortunately, photographs of only twenty-nine Russian documents are presently available;[82] this is an inadequate basis for forming any but the most fragmentary conclusions.

The present location of the original documents, if they still exist, remains a mystery. We have received conflicting information on their disposition following the publication of Su-lien yin-mou wen-cheng hui-pien, but lack any evidence as to their present whereabouts. There would seem to be several possibilities. They may be in Japan, taken there either from Manchuria (if Chang Tso-lin took them on his retreat from Peking in the summer of 1928), or from China during World War II; (2) They may be in Taiwan, if taken there during the Communist conquest of the mainland of China in 1949; or (3) They may be in Communist China.[83]

In the absence of the original documents, we attempted an evaluation, on the basis of their content, of the authenticity of a portion of those published. By checking these documents against contemporary sources and searching for internal proof of authenticity on historical grounds as well as for evidence suggesting forgery, it may be possible to form at least tentative conclusions.

Each published document must be evaluated individually. The discovery of evidences of forgery in a few documents does not condemn the whole collection, nor does obvious authenticity of some documents validate the rest. However, the cumulative weight of many bits of evidence may lead toward either a generally hostile or generally favorable view of the whole.

From the 337 documents presently available in Chinese,[84] two

groups were selected for investigation: (1) Original Chinese documents, constituting about 15 percent of the 337;[85] and (2) Translations of documents in Russian which are reports from China pertaining to Chinese situations and to Chinese revolutionary groups,
the Kuomintang, the Chinese Communist Party, and the Kuominchün.
These represent approximately 30 percent of the total and include
some fifteen Russian translations of original KMT and KCT documents.[86]

Excluded from this examination are all documents on Soviet organizations in China per se, such as elaborate regulations, statutes,
and budgets, and documents on Soviet espionage in China and other
countries. These constitute roughly 45 percent of the documents
translated into Chinese. Especially voluminous are the detailed espionage instructions and reports.[87] There are two principal reasons
for excluding these documents: (1) Unlike reports on the Chinese
scene, which can be checked against contemporary sources, these
documents on Soviet organization and espionage seem difficult either
to confirm or refute; and (2) Although Soviet espionage doubtless was
an important facet of Soviet activity in China in the mid-1920's, it is
beyond the scope of this study. Another group of documents dealing
with the Chinese Eastern Railway, Manchuria, and Mongolia, which
represents roughtly 10 percent of the total,[88] is also excluded as
outside the limits of this study.

Each document in the two groups selected for analysis was examined on its own merits. The following are our conclusions.

Original Chinese Documents

With the exception of several Kuomintang papers which the Peking
Commission classified by mistake as Communist texts,[89] the original
Chinese documents are papers of the Chinese Communist Party. They
are for the most part documents of the Central Committee, the Northern Regional Committee, and the Peking Local Committee.

In our opinion, the original Chinese documents are wholly genuine.

The chief reason for this conclusion is their extraordinary accuracy,
when checked against independent contemporary sources. There are
innumerable instances of striking corroboration, but it is possible
here only to cite a few examples.

One instance of corroboration concerns the interpretation of the
defection of the KMT's Old Right Wing following Sun Yat-sen's death
in March, 1925 and the rise of the New Right Wing following the May
Thirtieth Movement of 1925. The first two resolutions outlining this
interpretation in Document 20, resolutions on KMT-KCT relations
adopted by the Central Committee of the Chinese Communist Party in
October, 1925 [Doc. 20, pp. 1-2], correspond closely with the opening
section of an article published two months later by Ch'en Tu-hsiu, Chairman of the Central Committee and General Secretary of the Party.[90]

It is of course conceivable that a forger might have used Ch'en's article as a basis upon which to reconstruct these two resolutions. This possibility is unlikely, however, in view of a major difference between Document 20 and Ch'en's article. The resolutions drafted in October, 1925, state that the KMT New Right Wing was opposed to the KMT Left and the KCT. On the other hand, Ch'en asserted in late December, 1925, that the New Right Wing was opposed to Soviet Russia as well as to the KMT Left and the KCT. This difference is of course due to the fact that on December 4, 1925, the new Right Wing declared the termination of Borodin's contract as adviser to the KMT.[91]

Another instance of corroboration applies to Communist arguments against the KMT New Right Wing. We found that a large number of the propaganda arguments outlined in Document 21, a document of the KCT's Peking Local Committee dated November 25, 1925, were utilized one month later by Chang Kuo-t'ao in an open letter to KMT members.[92] It was stated in both Document 21 and Chang's letter, for instance, that the Western Hills conference of the New Right Wing was illegal and that class struggle does not harm but, on the contrary, helps the National Revolution.

Again it is conceivable but unlikely that a forger might have manufactured Document 21 on the basis of Chang's letter. Although the two documents use similar arguments, they implementate them differently. Document 21, which is an "internal" document outlining policy for Communist members, instructs them to deny that they joined the KMT for ulterior motives by posing a series of questions calculated to emphasize the KMT's impotence before the Communist entry [Doc. 21, pp. 153-54].

Chang Kuo-t'ao, who as a reserve member of the KMT Central Executive Committee was expelled by the Western Hills Faction, employed different tactics in arguing the same point. Repudiating the accusation that Communists sought to monopolize KMT organs, he asserted that they in fact lacked sufficient strength and were therefore unable fully to serve the KMT, for which they were most apologetic, Chang emphasized their dedication to the cause of the National Revolution and declared that there was in fact no basic difference between Sun Yat-sen's Three People's Principles and communism.

Yet another instance of corroboration pertains to Communist policy in the period between October, 1925, and July, 1926, as stated in Document 26, the Political report of the Central Committee, Chinese Communist Party, at the Second Enlarged Plenum held at Shanghai between July 12 and July 18, 1926 [Doc. 26, pp. 62-63].

For the period between October and December, 1925, according to the report, the Party's policy was to advance the slogan, "Extend the nature of the Anti-Mukden War!" with the objective of publicizing the war as a struggle for the people's freedom. This is confirmed by a document, "Manifesto on the Anti-Mukden War," signed by the Central Committees of the Chinese Communist Party and the Chinese Communist Youth Corps on October 20, 1925, which called on the masses to support the war against Mukden.[93] For the period between December, 1925 and April, 1926, according to Document 26, the KCT proposed that the National Government dispatch troops against Wu P'ei-fu, who was attacking the Kuominchün in Honan. Again, this is confirmed by a contemporary document, "Statement to the People of the Country on the Alliance Between Wu P'ei-fu and Mukden against the Kuominchün," signed by the Central Committees of the KCT and the CY on February 7, 1926, which called for troops to aid the Kuominchün in Honan.[94] Again, for the period between April and June, 1926, according to the report, the Party advocated assistance to T'ang Sheng-chih in Hunan against Wu P'ei-fu. This too is confirmed by an article in the May 15, 1926 issue of Hsiang-tao chou-pao, in which Ch'en Tu-hsiu urged that troops be sent to aid T'ang immediately.[95]

Finally, the current situation and the Party's policies outlined in the CC's Political Report are mirrored in the "Manifesto of the Chinese Communist Party on the Current Situation," issued by the Second Enlarged Plenum of the CC on July 12, 1926.[96] The Manifesto presented a twenty-three-point minimum platform for struggle jointly with the KMT, the continuance of which was called for by the CC's political report, Document 26.

Again, while it is not impossible that a forger could have reconstructed the CC's political report on the basis of several documents previously published at various dates, the possibility is slight because of marked differences between the report and the Party's manifestos. For instance, the Party's manifesto of July 12, 1926, denounces the Right Wing of the bourgeoisie and urges the continuation of the united front in general terms. The CC's political report, on the other hand, spells out in detail the Party's tactics of united front: Build up the force of workers and peasants, get hold of the petty bourgeoisie, and force the bourgeoisie to the Left. Translated into strategy regarding the Kuomintang, these tactics called for close collaboration between the Communists with the KMT Left Wing (petty bourgeoisie) in the struggle for revolutionary leadership against the New Right Wing (bourgeoisie) [Doc. 26, pp. 66-67].

There is great consistency within and between the original Chinese documents. Thus, for example, the CC's resolutions on Kuomintang - Communist relations adopted in October, 1925 [Doc. 20] are restated correctly in Document 27, the CC's resolutions on Kuomintang-Communist relations adopted in July, 1926 [Doc. 27, p. 70].

Likewise, the Party's current policies and views as revealed in Document 1, "A Brief History of the Chinese Communist Party,"

written in September, 1926, are corroborated by the resolutions of
the Second Enlarged Plenum of July, 1926. For example, the "Brief
History" considers as a chief weakness of the Party its shortage of
trained personnel. It warns that no good results would be achieved,
despite the rapid growth of Party membership, unless such growth
was accompanied by a corresponding increase of Communist directing personnel [Doc. 1, p. 43]. The CC expressed the same concern
in more specific terms in the resolutions on organization. It revealed
that the available force of qualified directing personnel met only one
third of the total requirements [Doc. 4, p. 80].

Another factor which strongly argues for the authenticity of the
original Chinese documents is the complete absence of anachronisms.
Apart from the question of accuracy, in their general style the
Chinese papers bear all the earmarks of authenticity. Particularly
telling is the occurrence of certain abbreviations and codes characteristic of Chinese Communist documents of this period. Examples
are the insertion of the English letters "CP" and "CY" in Chinese
texts and the use of the codes "Our School" and "People's School" to
designate the KCT and the KMT respectively.[97]

A skillful forger would presumably imitate Communist style and
use Communist codes. However, the hypothesis of forgery, which
cannot be categorically excluded, requires that the forger must have
been very skillful and well informed about the inner workings of the
Party. Against this hypothesis is the obvious fact that the translators
in Peking who put the Russian documents into Chinese were very
poorly informed about details of the Chinese Communist movement.
They did not even know the names of many leading Chinese Communists, including that of Chang Kuo-t'ao, judging by the frequent
errors in proper names in Chinese translations of Russian documents.[98] Such errors could very easily have been straightened out
by the hypothetical expert who forged the Chinese documents. Thus,
the great accuracy of the original Chinese documents on the one
hand, and the numerous inaccuracies of translation from Russian
into Chinese in matters pertaining to Chinese Communism and
events in South China on the other hand, argue against forgery.

The absence of any mention of Soviet connections with the
Chinese Communist Party also suggests authenticity. According to
the Preface of Su-lien yin-mou wen-cheng hui-pien, original Chinese
documents were included in that collection for the purpose of "making clear who was the guilty party." While the papers did not emanate
directly from the Soviet Union, it states, they were nevertheless
products of the Soviet conspiracy against China, for their ultimate
purpose was to further Soviet agitation and propaganda.[99] As
"making clear who was the guilty party" was thus the avowed purpose of the Peking Commission, it would appear that if these documents were forged, Soviet manipulations would have been given

prominence. The documents mention neither the Comintern nor the USSR.

Finally, the available historical record reveals no evidence that the Chinese Communist Party ever raised the issue of authenticity.

The original Chinese documents published in Su-lien yin-mou wen-cheng hui-pien were spared from damage by burning; in this group there are no fragmentary documents or evidently missing passages. This suggests the possibility, for which we know of no evidence, that the Chinese documents did not come from the Military Attaché's office, where the burning was done, but from some other part of the Soviet quarters. They might have been the working file of the Peking Local Committee of the Chinese Communist Party and might have been seized in the part of the compound where Li Ta-chao and other revolutionaries were in refuge.[100] This seems quite as likely as the assumption that they were stored in the office of the Soviet Military Attaché.

Russian Documents

Russian translations of KMT and KCT documents.—As in the case of the original Chinese documents, we believe that the Russian translations of KMT and KCT documents are genuine, despite inaccuracies resulting from triple translation (Chinese-Russian-Chinese). The documents have a high degree of historical accuracy when checked against contemporary KMT and KCT sources.

For example, Document 17, "Regulations of Political Departments in the National Revolutionary Army," drafted around the end of 1925, corresponds closely to the KMT's instructions on the position of Party representatives issued in July, 1925.[101] The regulations are actually a detailed elaboration of the functions and prerogatives of political commissars outlined in the instructions.

We found in independent sources the original Chinese texts on which the Russian translations of two documents in this group were presumably based. Document 13, a letter from Chiang Kai-shek to Galen, dated June 26, 1925, and enclosing military plans, is included in Chiang Kai-shek's diary, which was not published until 1936.[102] Thus, in effect Chiang validates Document 13. In the diary, however, the letter is addressed not to Galen but to the Military Council and is dated July 1, 1925. It is possible that Chiang Kai-shek first sent the letter and plans to Galen for advice before submitting them to the Military Council. It is interesting to note the only discrepancy between the two texts, aside from errors of translation. In the letter to Galen, Chiang recommended having more Russian advisers on a national defense committee to be orgainzed within the Military Council. There is no mention of Russian advisers, on the other hand, in the letter to the Military Council published in 1936.

Another document for which we were able to locate the original

Chinese text is Document 14, which gives excerpts from a speech
delivered by Chiang Kai-shek to the Military Council on July 26,
1925. The text of the complete speech is printed in a pamphlet published by the Political Department of the First Army, apparently,
issued shortly after August 26, 1925, when the First Army was organized.[103] Thus, a forger could have used this published version
to make a digest in Russian of a speech delivered nearly two years
before in Chinese. Then it is assumed that the Peking Commission
translated the Russian digest back into Chinese, with mistakes.
Such deviousness, however, rather stretches credulity. Excerpts
from the same speech are recorded also in Chiang's diary entry for
July 26, 1925.[104]

The types of errors—wrong characters for proper names, incorrect figures, and meaningless terms—which are found in the
Russian translations suggest that it is unlikely that the documents
were forged in Russian, based on original Chinese texts. (See discussion of this point below.)

Soviet reports from China.—In our opinion, the weight of evidence
suggests that the Russian reports from China are for the most part
authentic despite inaccuracies.

The most compelling argument for authenticity is the confirmation by independent sources of minute details discussed in the Soviet
reports. Our acceptance of these documents was gradual. The more
thoroughly that irrelevant and unimportant details were checked,
the stronger the impression of authenticity became.

One instance of such confirmation pertains to the movements of
Chiang Kai-shek immediately after the coup d'état of March 20, 1926.
Document 23, a contemporary account by General Stepanov, Soviet
adviser with the First Army,[105] is almost completely corroborated
by Chiang Kai-shek's diary.[106]

According to Stepanov, Ao-li-chin (his Russian name is not known),
the acting chief adviser at the Central Military and Political Academy,[107] and another Russian, Ivanovskii,[108] called on Chiang in
the afternoon of March 20; Chiang's diary entry for that day records
a visit from Ivanovskii and another Soviet adviser. On March 22,
according to Stepanov, Solovyev, councilor of the Soviet Embassy,[109]
went to see Chiang; Chiang's diary mentions the visit of a councilor
of the Soviet Embassy. On March 23, according to Stepanov, Wang
Ching-wei suddenly disappeared and could not be found anywhere,
although he was reportedly in a hospital; Chiang's diary states that
Wang had gone away for medical treatment. On March 24, Stepanov
asserts, Chiang and Ivanovskii had a talk at a farewell party given
in honor of some Russians who were leaving Canton; Chiang's diary
records the conversation he had with Ivanovskii that same day when
he said goodbye to him. Finally, according to Stepanov, Chiang left
Whampoa for Canton on March 26 to look in vain for Wang Ching-wei,

and then headed for Hu-men; Chiang's diary recounts that he went to Canton to find Wang on the 25th and, failing in his attempt, left for Hu-men on the 26th.

Feng Yü-hsiang's diary similarly confirms details reported by Soviet advisers. One example concerns the withdrawal of the Kuominchün armies from Peking to Nankow on November 11, 1925,[110] during the Anti-Mukden War. On December 2, Henry A. Lin, who was chief Soviet adviser to Feng Yü-hsiang,[111] reported to Ambassador Karakhan that the withdrawal to Nankow was made on the advice of the Russians. Lin said this indicated the extent of Soviet influence with the Kuominchün. Yet he admitted that the final selection of the site for troop concentration was made independently by the Kuominchün in disregard of Soviet plans [Doc. 38, pp. 5-6]. Feng Yü-hsiang's diary corroborates and sheds further light on this incident. It reveals that on November 11, the day of the withdrawal, "Adviser Lin" and Feng disagreed on the position of the Nankow defence line and that the final orders were based on Feng's own plans.[112]

The dates of a number of the Soviet reports are themselves suggestive of authenticity. One such example is Document 11, Borodin's report on the Kuomintang Revolutionary Committee and its plans to attack the Canton Merchant Corps, known as the "Paper Tigers." Borodin described the measures which had been carried out by Kuomintang leaders prior to October 14 and revealed doubt as to the loyalty of certain troops affiliated with the KMT. The fact that the report was written on the morning of October 14 is significant because the troops suspected of disloyalty did join in the raid on the Merchant Corps on the morning of October 15. The doubt could only have existed before the event, and could scarcely have been known to a forger two and a half years later. Furthermore, it appears the Peking Commission which published the documents did not understand who the Paper Tigers were, for it referred to them as bandits.[113]

Errors of Translation

Although the translations into Chinese of the Russian documents reveal a generally high degree of historical accuracy, errors of various types are scattered throughout them. By cross-checking Chinese translations against the Russian originals, when available, and against presumably independent English and Japanese translations, some of the inaccuracies can be identified as errors made by the translators. The following types of errors of translation are the most common.

Errors in proper names.—According to the preface of Su-lien yin-mou wen-cheng hui-pien, Russian transliterations of Chinese proper names presented great difficulties to the Peking translators. Hence, warning is provided by inserting the word "transliteration" following any proper name which could not be identified, to indicate that characters were selected for their phonetic value to reproduce the sound in Russian.[114] Many such transliterations are found in the Chinese translations, at times without proper warning. The Peking Commission failed to identify, for instance, most of the Chinese proper names in Document 43, a report on the Eighth Army written by a Russian agent, Pavlov,[115] on August 9, 1926. The Chinese translation of the document sometimes refers to T'ang Sheng-chih, commander of the Eighth Army, as "T'an Yen-k'ai." This is obviously incorrect, because Pavlov's report concerns T'ang Sheng-chih and the Eighth Army in Changsha exclusively, while T'an Yen-k'ai, commander of the Second Army, was at that time in Canton.

There are also numerous errors in the names of places, organizations, and groups.

The fact that many of the Russian transliterations of Chinese proper names were based on the Cantonese pronunciation contributes to the confusion, for the translators in Peking retransliterated the proper names into Chinese according to the Northern pronunciation. Thus it has not always been easy to identify the original Cantonese name.

Absurdities.—Failure to identify proper names occasionally leads to ludicrous results. For instance, "Tai Chi-t'ao chu-i," meaning the principles of Tai Chi-t'ao, or Taichitaoism, is translated in at least two documents as "Ta Ch'i-tao chu-i," or "principle of great prayer."[116] "Hsi-shan p'ai," meaning "the Western Hills Faction," is translated as "Hsin-shih p'ai," or "modern faction."[117] Sometimes ordinary words are mistakenly translated as proper names. In one document the words "T'ung-ling," meaning "command," are translated as a proper name, "Tung Ling." Thus, the system of command discussed in the document becomes distorted as "Tung Ling's system."[118]

Meaningless terms.—Occasionally terms occur in the Chinese translations which are impossible to understand. One such example is the term "Tan-ko ti she-hui-tang," meaning literally "single socialist party."[119] Other examples are the terms "Ta Ti-san kuo-chi" and "Hsiao ti-san kuo-chi," meaning literally "big Third International" and "small Third International."[120]

Omissions.—According to the Peking Commision, passages considered unimportant or redundant were omitted, with indication of such omission at the proper place. The Commission also explains that the translation process was divided into two stages. In the first stage, a Russian document was translated literally; in the second, "free translation" was employed to polish rough spots and elucidate obscure passages.[121] The Commission occasionally condensed whole paragraphs or sections without proper warning. This at times results in the loss of important segments of the text.

In a few instances, such omission by condensation was apparently intentional. For example, in one passage the Chinese translation omitted a sentence referring to the elimination of Chang Tso-lin and Wu P'ei-fu.[122] In another passage the Chinese translation refers to a "well-known reactionary party," whereas the English translation states specifically: "confounded reactionary and militarist to the core.... Marshal Chang Tso-lin."[123]

On the whole, however, omission and condensation appear to have resulted from ignorance or carelessness rather than intentional suppression.

Distortion.—The translators' evident unfamiliarity with the situation in South China sometimes resulted in serious distortion of meaning. One example is the passage in the "Brief History" concerning deliberations at the Third Congress of the Chinese Communist Party in the summer of 1923. According to the Chinese translation, the Congress engaged in long debates with the KMT and finally decided that the KMT should have influence among the workers and peasants because the KMT needed the KCT for the latter's help in organizing the masses.[124] The English version of the same document, which is historically correct, states that the KMT problem aroused long debates at the Congress and that it was finally resolved that the KMT should have influence among the masses. The reason was that the KCT could not expect to win over the entire masses in the near future and it therefore needed the KMT as a means to organize them.[125]

The Commission's confusion about the respective natures and functions of the KMT and KCT is particularly pronounced. As previously mentioned, it classified a number of Kuomintang texts as communist documents. It was frequently unable to distinguish between the various organs of the KCT, the KMT, the National Government, and the National Revolutionary Army. Thus, for instance, the name of the KMT Political Council is frequently translated as that of the Political Department of the National Revolutionary Army, and vice versa. The translations occasionally betray confusion even between the Kuominchün (People's Army) and the Kuo-min ko-ming chün (National Revolutionary Army).

Such errors suggest considerable ignorance on the part of the translators. They also argue for the authenticity of the Russian documents, since it is highly improbable that absurd terms and proper names which do not represent actual persons should have been forged intentionally.

While it is impossible to determine the source of inaccuracies in those Chinese translations of Russian documents which cannot be cross-checked against other versions, it may be assumed that at least some of such inaccuracies derive from mistranslation.

But the strong preponderance of accuracy over inaccuracy suggests that the Russian documents relating to events in China are generally authentic.

Furthermore, the substance of many of the Soviet reports indicates the improbability of forgery. The bewilderment of the Soviet advisers following Chiang Kai-shek's coup of March 20, 1926, and Soviet uncertainty as to Feng Yü-hsiang's attitude[126] would hardly be prominently discussed in forged documents. Such information, in fact, detracts from the picture of Russian advisers masterminding the Chinese Revolution which the seized documents allegedly prove.

Finally, the manifest ignorance of the translators concerning the situation in South China suggests the unlikelihood of their being able to forge either the original Chinese or the Russian documents. It appears improbable that persons who could not even identify Tai Chi-t'ao, the ideologist of the KMT New Right Wing, could have forged the detailed and accurate information on the New Right Wing, much less the Chinese Communist Party's tactics in dealing with it.

To summarize the discussion, the internal evidence points strongly to the following conclusions:

1. The documents in the Chinese language, mostly papers of the Chinese Communist Party, are wholly authentic.

2. The documents in Russian which are translations of original Chinese documents and those dealing with Chinese affairs and Russian participation in these affairs appear to be authentic as to historical fact.

3. The documents in Russian which were translated into Chinese suffer from numerous errors, principally due to the ignorance of the translators.

Two Doubtful Russian Documents

There are many documents, originally in Russian but published in Chinese translation in Su-lien yin-mou wen-cheng hui-pien which we were unable to subject to detailed historical criticism for reasons previously mentioned. They are documents on Soviet organizations in China per se and documents on Soviet espionage activities in China and elsewhere. When photographs of the originals exist or when translations had been made into English, however, we were able to secure useful advisory opinion from experts on these matters. But there still remains for some other student the interesting problem of studying Soviet organization and espionage in the mid-1920's and the authenticity of documents purporting to reveal information on these matters.

In contrast to the voluminous instructions on Soviet espionage, there are surprisingly few documents allegedly emanating from Moscow which deal with general policies in the Chinese revolutionary movement. Two important documents of this type are the "Theses on the Chinese Question" adopted at the Seventh Enlarged Plenum of the Executive Committee of the Comintern, and the "Instructions to the Soviet Military Attaché" based on the "Theses." Both documents were widely publicized a few weeks after the raid.

"Theses on the Chinese Question."—A copy of the "Theses" written in Russian, which was allegedly seized in the Soviet Military Attaché's office contains at the end two theses and one paragraph[127] which are totally absent from official Comintern publications.[128] Although there is no other discrepancy, the extra theses raise a challenging question: Are they authentic portions of an ECCI document, or are they material grafted on to an otherwise genuine text by interested parties in Peking?

In defense of the first interpretation it may be argued that the extra theses were indeed adopted at the ECCI Plenum but were kept secret when the rest of the theses were published. It must be remembered, however, that the Seventh Enlarged Plenum was attended by a large number of delegates and reports of the deliberations were widely published. It would seem difficult to maintain secrecy under such circumstances.

An analysis of the content of the extra theses fails to provide definite clues. The extra theses are consistent with the preceding ones. They seem, in fact, to reiterate in a general fashion the policies discussed in detail earlier in the document.[129] One particular portion bears a strong resemblance to a speech delivered by Stalin before the Chinese Commission of the Plenum on November 30, 1926.[130] Thus there would seem to be little ground for veiling the extra theses in secrecy. It may on the other hand, be argued, that the very consistency of the extra theses argues for authenticity.

A second possible way to account for the extra theses is that they were included in a preliminary draft of the document, but were eliminated from the final one adopted at the Seventh Enlarged Plenum.[131]

It may be significant that neither the Soviet government nor the Comintern, to our knowledge, repudiated this document. No mention was made of the extra theses. Rather the Soviets pointed out, when the document was first released, that it had already been widely published, implying that all the seized papers were merely copied from published sources. This may, in fact, be interpreted as tacit acceptance of the document's authenticity. Soviet representatives in Peking took a similar position.[132]

The evidence is, in short, inconclusive. The extra theses may have been genuine portions of a Comintern document at one time, or they may have been forged and tacked on to an otherwise authentic document.

Mr. David J. Dallin, an authority on Soviet policy in the Far East,

very kindly examined the photographs we were able to assemble
of original Russian documents. He also studied the documents
previously published in English translation. He had the following to
say with respect to the "Theses on the Chinese Question," on the
basis of a photograph of the original Russian document and an English translation:

"As far as the last two theses of this document are concerned
(embracing points 23 through 28) it is hard to reach a definite conclusion. On the one hand, they contain no revelations which could be
expected to be found in a forged document. On the other hand, they
do not contain any information or note any decisions which were not
known otherwise and which the Comintern had reason to conceal.
Weighing the pros and cons, I tend to doubt the authenticity of these
chapters. My reasons are the following:

"a. Whereas resolutions of the Comintern, prepared and discussed
    in commissions, were usually conceived in grammatically
    correct Russian, the main sentence of Point 23 ("Dlya etogo
    neobkhodimo") is written in poor, unclear language.

"b. A term is used with regard to Communist political work in
    the Army ("neobrabotannyi korpus") which does not fit into a
    resolution of the Comintern.

"c. In general it would have been a strange procedure to make
    secret a part of the Plenum's resolution. The 'Plenum' in 1926
    was actually a crowded congress. After the session its mem-
    bers returned to their respective countries. Some among them
    were known to be heretical or on their way out. If a secret
    decision was to be taken, the small 'Presidium' rather than
    the 'Plenum' would be the more suitable place.

"If the two chapters are not authentic, the only motive for forgery
could have been an attempt to discredit the Kuomintang army, ex-
posing it as an organism directly subordinated to the Comintern, and
Thesis 10, which appears to be genuine, was attached to conceal the
operation of Thesis 9."[133]

"Instructions to the Soviet Military Attaché."—This document
(see above, pp. 15-16) was repeatedly cited by the Soviets as
proof of the spuriousness of the entire collection of seized documents. It was the only document specifically attacked. In our opinion, it is open to question because of its partial use of old Russian
orthography and evidence of historical contradiction.

Out of twenty-nine original Russian documents of which we have seen
photographs, this is the only one which employs old Russian orthography. All adjectives in the document have the old endings (-ago instead of -ogo).[134] While there is some division of opinion as to how
swiftly and completely the new orthography came into use, it appears extremely doubtful that an allegedly official document emanating from
Moscow in early 1927[135] should have employed the old orthography.

Although it is specifically stated that the "Instructions" were
drafted in accordance with the "Theses" of the Seventh Enlarged
ECCI Plenum, there are serious inconsistencies between the "Instructions" and the "Theses" on policy toward imperialism. The
third instruction (to discredit Chang Tso-lin as a hireling of the
imperialists) and the seventh instruction (to preserve existing an-
tagonisms between the foreign powers) are fully in line with Comintern policy and are corroborated by the "Theses."[136] There is
direct contradiction, however, on the means to be used in struggling
against imperialism.

The second instruction to the Soviet Military Attaché calls for the
organization of anti-European riots in the territories of Chang Tso-
lin. The fifth instruction calls for bringing on interference by foreign
powers through all possible means, including robbery and beating.
(It is not stated whether this policy was to be carried out in territories occupied by the Kuomintang or in militarist areas, or both.)
This policy of direct violent struggle against foreign powers is at
variance with the tactics outlined in the "Theses."

The anti-imperialist program in areas under Kuomintang control
was carefully defined in the "Theses." The Kuomintang government,
that document states, was revolutionary, first of all because of
its anti-imperialist character. Such being the case, the Chinese
Revolution and the revolutionary government must strike at the
roots of imperialist power in China. The abolition of the unequal
treaties and the return of territorial concessions were not sufficient
for this purpose; it was necessary to strike at the economic foundation of imperialist power. Hence, the Kuomintang government must
gradually nationalize railway concessions, mills, mines, banks, and
enterprises financed by foreign capital. Communists were instructed
to join the Kuomintang governmental apparatus in order to exert a
direct influence over the formulation and execution of policy.[137] In
short, in areas under KMT control, the anti-imperialist program
was to be primarily economic, to be gradually executed by the
National Government.

In territories under militarist control, according to the "Theses," Communists should concentrate on revolutionary work among the peasantry for
the purpose of breaking up reactionary militarist armies.[138] Thus,
for the time being, imperialism was to be hit indirectly through the
defeat of Chinese militarists.

Such evidence of historical contradiction and the use of old
Russian orthography suggest the possibility of forgery. It appears
that the "Instructions" may be completely spurious, or a genuine
document was "doctored" by alteration of its contents or by addition of new material.

Considerable leeway was exercised in preparing the English and
Chinese translations of the allegedly seized Russian original. The

sensational character of the "Instructions" was heightened by insertion and reconstruction of phrases and words. For example, in
the English and Chinese translations, the word "massacre" was reconstructed from the Russian word "beating" as a method to be used
to provoke foreign interference.[139]

Mr. Dallin believes, on the bases both of the English translation
and a photograph of the Russian "original," that this document was
forged. He states: "One document, namely, 'Instructions to the Military Attaché,' was clearly forged. Moreover, it is obvious that the
person who forged it was a Japanese agent or was seeking contacts
with Japanese Intelligence. The naive instruction to 'organize anti-
European disorders,' 'discredit the activities of Chang Tso-lin,'
'isolate Japan,' and a number of other similar ones, together with
the old-style spelling, leave no doubt in my mind that this document
is a forgery."[140]

SUMMARY OF CONCLUSIONS

The Soviet government attempted to cast suspicion upon the documents from the first. Before any of them were published representatives of the USSR charged that counterfeits would be produced. As
soon as the first documents were published they denounced them as
forgeries. On the other hand, most of the Western-language press in
China defended the authenticity of the documents, and the foreign
diplomatic corps in Peking apparently accepted them as genuine.

In so far as arguments regarding authenticity were based upon
the documents themselves, they were based upon only a few examples. Soviet representatives tried to prove their case by contend-
ing that use of old-style orthography, linguistic errors, and erroneous policy statements proved the documents were forged. One
document, "Instructions to the Soviet Military Attaché," was cited
to support all three charges. The main lines of argument, pro and
con, had been drawn by the time fifteen documents were published.

In our opinion, previous arguments based upon external evidence
or upon only a few of the documents are inconclusive. Our own conclusions are based upon an intensive study of two groups of the
documents which make up about 45 percent of those now available
in published form. They are (1) the original Chinese documents,
and (2) translations of Russian documents pertaining to Chinese
situations or Chinese revolutionary organization. Our conclusions
are restricted to these two groups of documents, the contents of
which can be checked against contemporary Chinese sources. We
offer no opinion upon the authenticity of documents pertaining to
Soviet organizations in China, to Soviet espionage activity, and to
the Chinese Eastern Railway, Manchuria, and Mongolia.

Original Chinese Documents

These are, in our opinion, wholly genuine. They proved extraordinarily accurate when checked against independent contemporary sources. There is great consistency within and among these documents. We could find no evidence of anachronisms. The general style of the Communist documents conforms to the style characteristic of Communist writing of the period, even to the use of certain abbreviations and codes.

Russian Documents

1. Among the translations of Russian documents a number were originally Chinese Communist and Kuomintang documents. These show a high degree of historical accuracy though containing many errors due to double translation (from Chinese to Russian, then back into Chinese). We believe them to be authentic.

2. The second group of Russian documents we have studied, Soviet reports from China, appears to be authentic despite inaccuracies. The most compelling argument for their authenticity is confirmation by independent sources of minute details discussed in the reports.

The documents in Russian which were translated into Chinese (1 and 2 above) suffer from many errors which appear to be due principally to the ignorance of the translators about the persons and events mentioned.

Two doubtful documents among the groups we did not attempt to authenticate are the "Theses on the Chinese Question" adapted by the Seventh Enlarged ECCI Plenum and "Instructions to the Soviet Military Attache," purportedly based upon the "Theses." The first may have been altered by the addition of two theses and one paragraph. The second may have been wholly or partially forged.

In sum, the documents we present in this collection appear to us to be authentic and valuable sources of historical information.

PART I

INTRODUCTION TO
"A BRIEF HISTORY OF THE CHINESE COMMUNIST PARTY"

"A Brief History of the Chinese Communist Party," written in Russian, discusses the Party's development from its inception around 1918 up to September, 1926. This translation is based on the Chinese translation, prepared by the Peking Commission, of the original Russian document, augmented and corrected by cross-checking an independent English translation.[1]

The author is not identified. The reader is informed merely that he is ignorant of the Chinese language, but that he based the "Brief History" entirely on Chinese sources [Doc. 1, p. 1]. According to Reizo Otsuka, a Japanese expert on Chinese Communism, Li Tachao has been credited with drafting the preliminary text as a report from the Chinese Communist Party to Comintern.[2] Whoever supplied the documentary data, the final version of the "Brief History" is an interesting structure of blocks of narrative laced together by the author's interpretative comments. Thus, it has a double nature: it offers a generally accurate account of the Party's history[3] plus the revealing observations of the author.

The "Brief History" is valuable first of all because of its early date; it was apparently written shortly after September 3, 1926.[4] Certainly it is one of the earliest Party histories known to have been compiled. It is unorthodox Party history, since it predates the standardization of the official Communist interpretation of the Party's early history and the Great Revolution of 1925-27. Furthermore, it is of value for its "inside" approach, which is particularly pronounced when the author passes judgment on the party's record.

The author discusses the growth of the Chinese Communist Party as a purely indigenous development without reference either to the Comintern or the Soviet Union. While he does on one occasion link the Chinese Revolution with the World Revolution and the Chinese Communist Party (KCT) with the Comintern (CI) [Doc. 1, pp. 2-3], he offers no information on KCT-CI relations, either in terms of policy direction from Moscow or on-the-spot activities of Soviet advisers and Comintern representatives. Thus, strict limitations are set upon the scope of the "Brief History."

In contrast to the orthodox Communist denunciation of the Chinese

Communist leadership for opportunism during the early and middle 1920s, the author completely supports the Party leaders. He tends particularly to glorify Ch'en Tu-hsiu, secretary of the Party and chairman of the Central Committee. While orthodox Communist histories accuse Ch'en of being chiefly responsible for the debacle suffered by the Chinese Communist Party in 1927, the author of the "Brief History" is loud in his praise. There is in fact such emphasis on Ch'en Tu-hsiu's personal role that other leading Chinese Communists are almost completely ignored. Thus, Ch'en Tu-hsiu is represented as having been the only person who undertook Communist work in 1918 [Doc. 1, p. 10], although Li Ta-chao was equally responsible for organizing the Marxist Study Group in Peking in that year.[5]

Parallel to this emphasis on Ch'en Tu-hsiu is the prominence attached to Shanghai, headquarters of the Central Committee. It must be emphasized, the author states, that Ch'en Tu-hsiu and his group laid the real foundation of the Party for all China and that Shanghai was the real center of the Party [Doc. 1, p. 13].

This double emphasis on Ch'en and Shanghai coincides with repeated expressions of support for and justification of the policies of the Central Committee. To cite one example, the author regards as dangerous the tendency of certain Communists to advocate breaking all relations with the Kuomintang. Such currents of thought, he said, must be counteracted at once by the Central Committee [Doc. 1, p. 45]. In July, 1926, the CC had convened the Second Enlarged Plenum in Shanghai and had decided to continue cooperating with the Kuomintang through membership in that Party. This decision was adopted against opposition from various groups within the Party, the most formidable being the Kwangtung Regional Committee. The Kwangtung Communists, who had their headquarters in Canton, demanded immediate, direct struggle for seizure of leadership of the Kuomintang. Guided by Borodin, they played the key role in executing Communist policy in territory controlled by the KMT. They thus commanded a strategic position, acting with considerable independence from the authority of the Shanghai Central Committee, with which they disagreed.[6]

Save for a passing tribute to the Kwangtung Regional Committee for its leadership of the Hongkong-Canton Strike [Doc. 1, p. 41], the author of the "Brief History" is silent on the Committee's accomplishments. In commending the Party for its success in the villages of Kwangtung [Doc. 1, p. 46], for instance, he neglects to mention that the pioneering work was done by the Kwangtung Regional Committee. This silence on matters concerning the Kwangtung Regional Committee contrasts sharply with his staunch support of Ch'en Tu-hsiu and the Central Committee and suggests the possibility that he was deliberately seeking to bolster the Central

Committee against internal opposition. Since the Central Committee's decisions were adopted under Comintern direction,[7] the author was in effect upholding the Comintern's policies in China.[8]

Although the "Brief History" has been utilized as important source material in Japanese histories of the Communist movement in China,[9] there is little mention of the document or, for that matter, the entire collection of seized documents, in Chinese Communist literature. In 1951, however, an article appeared in the Chin-pu jih-pao in Tientsin, signed by Professor Chin Yü-fu, which accepts the "Brief History" as an accurate and valuable source on the early history of the Chinese Communist Party.[10] Since Professor Chin does not to our knowledge hold a responsible office in the Chinese Communist Party or the Central People's Government, we cannot assume his opinion to be representative of the Party's. It appears significant, nevertheless, that an article accepting the "Brief History" as genuine was allowed to be printed in one of the more important newspapers in Communist China.

In the translation which follows, the bracketed headings have been supplied. Numbers in brackets in the left-hand margin refer to the corresponding page in the four-volume edition of Su-lien yin-mou wen-cheng hui-pien. (See Bibliography.)

DOCUMENT 1

A BRIEF HISTORY OF
THE CHINESE COMMUNIST PARTY

[Introduction]

[1] It is not an easy task to present the entire history of the Chinese Communist Party in the context of general Chinese history and the history of the Chinese Revolution. In this concise narrative I hope to point out a direction of study to those who are interested in the problem. This brief history, however, is based entirely on Chinese data and the writer has encountered many difficulties due to his ignorance of the Chinese language. Suggestions from readers for correction of unsatisfactory points will therefore be appreciated.

The Chinese national revolutionary movement has advanced considerably in the last two or three years. It has absorbed a great portion of the masses and it is characterized by solid organization and the following explicit objectives:

1. National independence. To attain this objective, it is first necessary to eliminate imperialism.

2. National unification. To attain this objective, it is necessary to fight the internal enemy, militarism.

Three years ago, not only the majority of Chinese society in general but the higher levels of society were unable to understand the significance of these two objectives. Now, however, they have become crucial problems of the Chinese people.

This situation was brought about by the determination of a small group, the Chinese Communist Party. We call it a small group because, in the four years between 1920 and 1923, KCT membership was not quite one thousand. Adding the membership of the Youth Corps, the total membership was barely three thousand. In the

[2] two years of 1925 and 1926, however, membership increased tenfold to approximately thirty thousand. Of course, the KCT's position is not determined by the quantity but by the quality of its members, by their moral influence and weight. An agricultural country, China is culturally very backward. These thirty thousand organized, disciplined, and conscious members of one tight organization are capable of playing a most decisive role. Though representing an insignificant portion of the population, they have a well-defined program of immediate struggle which promises good prospects for the future.

Revolutionary work has been temporarily suspended in Europe, all the more so in the United States. It is a fact that capitalism has managed to delay the day of its collapse, even though it has not achieved complete stabilization. History has taught us that social revolution can be successfully carried out even in agricultural countries, as in Soviet Russia, and we believe that present conditions in China are similar to those in Russia in 1905. In a few more years, China will become the second Soviet Union and the peasants and workers will exercise power throughout the country. In order to reach this goal, the peasants and workers should devote all their efforts to work and struggle.

The KCT will undoubtedly assume direction of this struggle of the masses because it is superior to all other parties in absorbing the ideas of internationalism and in its capacity to realize them. The slavery to which China has been subjugated by the bourgeoisie of European capitalist countries and the United States has compelled the world proletariat and the Communist parties of several countries to study the Chinese problem and to assist the Chinese Communist Party and the Chinese national liberation movement.

Aid must first come, and it has already come, from the Russian proletariat and its vanguard, the Communist Party of the Soviet Union. The majority of the Russian masses, the peasants and workers, should be well informed about the struggle of the Chinese masses and should know who are the leaders of this struggle. In other words, they should be informed about the Chinese Communist Party.

It is a well-known fact, already noted at the last [Sixth] plenary session of the Comintern [March, 1926], that the greatest attention and aid must be rendered the Communist parties of Britain and [3] China in order to further the World Revolution. We will try to prove, in terms of history and concrete facts, that their achievements are indeed great. If the KCT follows this course of advance, we can truly say that the Chinese proletariat has found a loyal guide and the CI an excellent member in the KCT.

Ten years ago in China it was impossible to find anything that could have served as the foundation of a Communist Party. Even an embryonic organization was lacking, since there was no organized group of comrades for the study of Marxism who could at some future time serve as the nucleus of a new mass organization. China did not even have an organized social democratic party, from which men most devoted to the revolutionary cause could be detached (as was the case in several European countries and the United States).

Of course there were revolutionaries in China, but they were ideologically far from Marxist. Most of them were either followers of Dr. Sun or anarchists. There were also socialists, however.

A few prominent revolutionaries, most of them old but some young, were interested in Marxism and devoted themselves to the study of Marxist doctrines. While they individually professed interest in ideology, however, none of them (individually or organized in groups) possessed a concrete program of action or slogans to attract and organize the masses.

[The Effects of World War I in China]

China's participation in the European War produced far-reaching consequences, as follows:

1. The imperialist countries, particularly European countries, forced their bourgeoisie to leave China alone and concentrate instead on domestic affairs. Hence, the Chinese national bourgeoisie was able to develop. At the same time, there was continuous development of the position in China of such countries as the United States and Japan, which formerly were of secondary importance.

2. Due to the above, there was great expansion of Chinese national capital and industry as well as Japanese and American capital in China.

3. What we regard as important is the extensive development of [4] Chinese national industry, the final result of the simultaneous expansion of Chinese national capital and Japanese and American capital. In view of the failure of Britain, France, and Germany adequately to supply the Chinese market with necessary commodities, these are now produced for consumption in China by Chinese factories.

4. Following the development of Chinese industry, not specifically industry founded with Chinese capital but industry in China generally, the Chinese proletariat developed to a certain extent.

At the end of the World War we paid much attention to the great increase of all types of Chinese workers who were already exposed to the "training" offered by British and Japanese factory foremen. Chinese men and women laborers thus directly encountered their enemy, the enemy which has enslaved China for many decades.

At the Versailles Peace Conference following the imperialist war, the victorious nations robbed the defeated. China, one of the victors, appealed for justice on the basis of her rights as a victorious nation. Her delegates demanded the return of Shantung, Tsingtao, Weihaiwei [Weihai], and other territories formerly occupied by Germany. The result of the imperialist war, however, was the transfer of these territories to the hands of the allies, Britain and Japan.

The imperialist nations at the Peace Conference had very little sympathy or concern for enslaved China; their major concern was the protection of their own respective interests. It was a great humiliation for China! Although this was not China's first taste of humiliation its impact was singularly profound, and it will never be forgotten by the progressive masses of the Chinese people, especially the urban masses. The development of the working class and the moral and spiritual humiliation of Versailles were special phenomena of China in 1919.

[5]   These two forces were of unusual significance and they were properly utilized by the true revolutionaries who joined the Communist movement as individuals for the purpose of organizing an embryo for the future Communist Party.

[Changes in the Labor Movement]

Many Chinese revolutionaries had previously studied anarchism, socialism, and communism. Their activities, however, were confined to study and they did not attend to propaganda work. Although the pre-1911 revolutionary movement continued to exist, the number participating from the masses was small and the movement was largely confined to the lowest [lumpen] proletariat (with the exception of the intelligentsia). The factory workers stood on the sidelines and watched without participating.

In the two years of 1912 and 1913, there were signs of the beginnings of a labor movement. The organizations, however, were not composed of pure labor elements but included members of the petty bourgeoisie, artisans and politicians. Politicians are basically managers of the Chinese bourgeoisie and the propertied class in general. The urban and rural bourgeoisie took a keen interest in the movement for the sole purpose of using such organizations to get votes to the Parliament. They falsely proclaimed to the masses of the unions that since China is a republic, each citizen has the right to elect and to be elected to office. First of all, however, it was necessary to organize and elect good members to Parliament before such blessings could materialize.

Each politician organized a trade union and lent it his assistance with the idea of absorbing people who thereafter had to vote for their master. Members of trade unions (among them craftsmen, small shopkeepers, and the lowest elements of the proletariat) were given the assurance that they would have no more employment worries once their masters were elected to Parliament. Such was the character of the labor unions when first organized.

[6]   Due to the imperialist war and its consequences for China, a change was brought about in the labor movement. The old type of labor movement gradually disappeared and there appeared genuine labor organizations among workers (the industrial proletariat).

The railway workers are the most experienced among the industrial proletariat because the existence of railways and foreign capitalist interest in Chinese railways date back to the prewar period. The railways were essential to the foreign capitalists in absorbing the resources of the Chinese people (China's raw materials) and importing into China manufactured goods at exorbitant prices.

When Wu P'ei-fu had ambitions of becoming a national hero and unifying the country by force, he took an interest in, and wanted to make use of, the railway workers. He at first sanctioned and supported to a certain extent the organization of a labor union by workers on the Peking-Hankow Railway, hoping thereby to win them as allies. He was aware of the inevitability of economic conflict between workers and employers and categorically forbade political activities among the workers. However, he thought that encourage-

ment of union organization before the workers started an active
struggle for it would be to his own benefit. Thus he readily gave his approval when the workers requested permission to organize a union.

A new situation was created following the war, in which Chinese
labor found itself in a disadvantageous economic position with rising
living costs and low wages. Hence, the first strike of the Peking-
Hankow Railway workers occurred in 1923. The strike, which was at
first purely economic, later became political. Details will be presented as follows.

[The Peking-Hankow Railway Workers' Strike, February, 1923]

In February, 1923, Peking-Hankow Railway workers presented various economic demands to the railway administration at the same time
that the first congress of representatives of the Peking-Hankow Railway Union was to take place. When the administration rejected their
[7] demands, clashes broke out between workers and the railway authorities. Wu P'ei-fu, convinced that capitalist interests must be protected, forbade the convocation of the congress which he had previously approved. His action was clearly a direct provocation by him
and the capitalists supporting him. They were well aware that the
workers would regard such action as provocative and that the strike
would thus assume a political nature, at which time drastic action
could be taken in accordance with martial law. Subsequent developments justified their expectations.

The prohibition of the holding of the congress and rejection of
the workers' economic demands by the capitalists aroused such tension that the workers actually made several demands of a political
nature. Consequently, Wu P'ei-fu not only suppressed the strike but
closed all labor organizations along the railway, arresting all leaders. The important ones were shot; many are still imprisoned.

This was a hard blow to those working for the labor movement,
especially because the Peking-Hankow Railway workers had the most
powerful and the largest labor union. The strike was not well organized and plans were not fully prepared in advance so that the
workers were disbanded almost without resistance.

It may seem wasteful to relate this event in such detail. A careful
explanation of this most important historical motivating force is
essential, however, and this subject will again be discussed in the
following chapter.

The incident was not entirely without benefit, for it drew greater
attention to the labor movement and convinced the laboring masses
that they themselves were responsible for the weakness of their
organization.

When unions [labor unions organized by Communists] were first
organized there was opposition even among the workers. It was due
largely to labor's lack of thorough understanding of their own ob-

jectives and to the fact that the older unions were organized principally to get votes for Parliament. The workers were therefore
extremely suspicious of any plans imported from other quarters
and considered Communists as outsiders because they had nothing
[8] at all to do with the manufacturing industry.

The above difficulties did not prevent the Chinese Communist
Party from advancing, however. It continued to agitate among the
laboring masses, explaining to them the necessity of organizing
labor unions. It disseminated propaganda so that the workers could
gradually understand the meaning of labor unions. Such work was
done exclusively by the KCT, which achieved extensive results
despite its numerical weakness.

[The National Liberation Movement]

Following the close of the European war, there was great development of the national liberation movement of oppressed peoples,
such as the Koreans, Filipinos, and Indians. With even greater success, the movement has spread over wide areas of China, which has
become the center of the movement.

The other peoples are under one hundred percent de facto and
de jure enslavement, and their countries have become colonies.
China's case is different. Though no less oppressed than other
nations, she nevertheless maintains national sovereignty and may
be considered a semicolony. Her national liberation movement can
therefore develop with far greater ease. Foreign troops are
stationed in Korea, the Philippines, and India, where foreigners
control administrative power. Although garrisons of foreign nations
are stationed in Peking, Tientsin, Shanghai, and a few other places
in China, it can hardly be said that they occupy the whole of China.
Chinese administrative organs do not everywhere oppose the national
liberation movement, nor are they always able to oppose it to the
fullest extent. This has been proved by recent events. For instance,
in 1925, the confounded reactionary and militarist, Marshal Chang
Tso-lin, was forced to give this movement material as well as
a moral support.

The national liberation movement first assumed broad dimensions at the end of the imperialist war in 1919 and it has been
characterized thereafter by opposition to Japan and the pro-Japanese Anfu regime.

At that time the most effective antigovernment movement prevailed throughout the country. Newspapers everywhere carried
[9] such loud protests as that the government was selling the country to
the Japanese. The masses then realized it was futile to resist the
government and the Japanese merely through protests and peaceful
demonstration movements. Since 1912, all movements had been of
a purely peaceful nature, and it was not until 1919 that the masses

began to believe that peaceful struggle must be abandoned to give way to active, even armed, struggle. Thus, a turning point was reached in terms of the people's psychology and their methods of struggle.

[The May Fourth Movement, 1919]
If we wish to fix a date marking the birth of the KCT, May, 1919, is that date because, on May 4th of that year, the tide of the Anti-Japanese movement swept the country.

The movement was caused by the open and fearless treachery of the Anfu Clique heading the central government. Japan utilized the opportunity to negotiate with this government a treaty amounting to surrender, under which China would hand over to the Japanese all national railway trunk lines. This event coincided with the drafting of the Versailles Treaty and China's humiliation at the Peace Conference. Hence, Chinese youths, especially university students, who had hoped China would gain her freedom after the European war, were greatly agitated and resorted to drastic action. Unfortunately, the movement lacked proper organization and developed into an alarming situation. The Chinese minister to Japan was beaten up. In Peking, government offices were mobbed and assassination attempts were made on cabinet ministers. In Paris, an attempt was made on the life of the Chinese minister and the leader of the Communications Clique.

This was the beginning of the active revolutionary movement of the masses which at first was composed of only university students, and later included the laboring masses of Peking, Shanghai, and other cities.

At that time labor was already aware of the difference between its interests and those of the people in general.

Conscious of this difference, workers in Peking and Tientsin in North China hoped to have some political organization of their own. [10] It was at this juncture that the Group of Ten made its appearance. (The Group of Ten was a labor organization. Each group was composed of ten persons.) This indicates the workers' desire for political organization, even though they were not sufficiently developed to organize a party.

Veteran Chinese revolutionaries at that time were studying various theories with the hope of pushing forward the Revolution. However, nothing concrete was accomplished and it was all in vain. It is not men who create history; history creates men. This is well understood by those who study Marxism. From the historical standpoint, men who are created by history occupy the most important positions in the development of any social movement.

[Ch'en Tu-hsiu's Activities, 1918-1919]
In discussing the beginnings of the KCT, reference must be made

to the important position occupied by Ch'en Tu-hsiu. Ch'en is now
Secretary-General and leader of the Party. In 1918, Ch'en was the
only person who engaged in Communist work. He began by grouping
around himself the best revolutionaries. (At that time, he was professor of literature at Peking University. We cannot go into detail
here on his personal life.) History repeats itself. Prominent individuals step forward, organize themselves into groups, and attract
the best elements of society, especially workers.

Ch'en began publication of a weekly, Mei-chou p'ing-lun [weekly
review] [in December, 1918], in which he cautiously promoted the
cause of labor and discussed such questions as political organization of labor. He was chief editor and concurrently business manager, but later on found two or three comrades to assist him. He
also regularly published pamphlets under the title "To the Peking
People." His activities were soon cut short by imprisonment, however.

As the country was greatly agitated just then over the problem of
national liberation, the authorities felt it unwise to take drastic
measures with Ch'en Tu-hsiu and he was released after several
months. Since it was no longer possible for him to continue his work
in Peking, he proceeded to Shanghai, where Tai Chi-t'ao was then
living. Tai was also engaged then in publishing an organ for the discussion of Marxist doctrines.

As Shanghai is the most industrialized area and has greater
numbers of laborers than anywhere else in China, Ch'en Tu-hsiu
used it as the base of the labor movement and the center of his
work. It is clear that Ch'en Tu-hsiu devoted the greater part of his
attention to the labor movement. He fully realized the close con-
[11] nections between party and labor organization. Since China had
neither labor unions nor a [Communist] party, Ch'en decided to
promote both organizations simultaneously. He hoped, after one
year's painstaking effort (1919), to gather together a forceful group
in preparation for the organization of the KCT.

[Organization of the Shanghai Communist Group, 1920]
At the beginning of 1920 (the ninth year of the Chinese Republic),
seven persons, Ch'en and his associates, organized a group in
Shanghai. They were: (1) Ch'en Tu-hsiu; (2) Tai Chi-t'ao; (3) Shen
Hsüan-lu; (4) Ch'en Wang-tao (who soon left the Party); (5) Li Han-
chün (who also left the Party); (6) Shih Ts'un-t'ung (still in the
Party); and (7) Yüan Hsiao-hsien (still in the Party). Of the seven,
four have left the Party (the group, actually) and only three remain.

As for Tai Chi-t'ao, who subsequently left the Party, a brief remark is necessary in order to understand him. Tai was a founder
and active member of the organization but he split with the KCT and
is now a member of the KMT Right Wing. Tai is an extremely ca-

pable man and is very well versed in Marxism, but he is now constantly waging an ideological struggle against the KCT. Tai Chi-t'ao is among those ideologists of the KMT who claim that China does not suit Communism and Communism does not suit the KMT.

At the beginning, the group published a [weekly] for workers [Lao-tung-che] and a periodical especially for Shanghai clerical workers [Huo-yu]. Since a violent reaction was in force at the time, it was compelled to devise various measures in order to enlist young revolutionaries. Its organization was named the Foreign Language School, composed of the best revolutionaries, who were trained for: (1) work in China; (2) study at the Communist University for the Toilers of the East in the Soviet Union. In 1920 there were altogether 60 people at the Foreign Language School, mostly members of the Youth Corps. (In China and a few other places, the Youth Corps was organized before the KCT. Elsewhere, both organizations appeared at the same time.)

It was planned to have a group of the students of the school work in China and, under the direction of Ch'en Tu-hsiu, plant the seeds [12] of a Communist party in Shanghai. The most important task of the group was the organization of labor unions in Shanghai. (There was then no organization at all in Shanghai.)

The first trade union to be successfully organized in Shanghai was the mechanics' union, followed by the printers' union and the textile workers' union. Organization of trade unions was successful first of all among skilled workers. Ch'en directed the work single-handed, handicapped by lack of funds and many other difficulties. It is significant that the only source of income was profit on the magazine, Hsin ch'ing-nien (La Jeunesse), Ch'en was aware that contemporary youths were engulfed by extreme revolutionary agitation and were therefore most interested in whoever could offer solutions to their difficult problems.

In sum, by the beginning of 1920, an embryo of the KCT existed in Shanghai.

By the middle of 1920 this organization numbered about seventy persons wielding influence over labor and able to direct the labor movement.

It is obvious that such a movement could not be confined to the area of Shanghai. If it were, it would soon be extinguished. However, with the establishment of an organization of Communist comrades in Shanghai, its influence did not fail to reach other areas in China.

[Organization of the Peking Communist Group, 1920]
Similar developments took place in Peking in September, 1920. An organized group appeared there also. Of the eight comrades in the group, six were anarchists and two Communists. The anarchists were led by Huang Ling-shuang and the two Communists were

Li Ta-chao and Chang Kuo-t'ao, now members of the Central Committee of the Chinese Communist Party. The Shanghai group was
also heterogeneous including anarchists as well as Communists.
This "alliance" did not last long. Three of the anarchists soon withdrew from the Peking organization, which was, however, strengthened by the addition of four new members: (1) Teng Chung-hsia;
(2) Lo Chang-lung; (3) Liu Jen-ching; and (4) name unknown. It
[13] published leaflets, pamphlets, and a daily [weekly], Lao-tung yin.

In view of the extremely reactionary situation in Peking, it was
impossible to carry on concrete work. After a few months, however,
an evening class for workers was established at Ch'ang-hsin-tien,
a Peking-Hankow Railway station not far from Peking. The workers there were even more backward than the Shanghai proletariat.
The work was therefore even more difficult.

In considering the measures taken by the Peking group, such as
publication of various types of provocative literature and establishment of the school, one must conclude that it was working under
the advice, if not direct supervision, of the Shanghai organization.
The fact must be emphasized that Ch'en Tu-hsiu and his group laid
the real foundation of the Chinese Communist Party for all China
and that Shanghai is the real center of the Party.

At any rate, there were two organizations of the Communist
Party by the beginning of the second half of 1920, one at Shanghai
and the other at Peking.

[Organization of the Canton Communist Group, 1920]
In the autumn of the same year, Mo Jung-hsin, governor of
Kwangtung, was driven out by Ch'en Ch'iung-ming, who took over
the governorship. Ch'en Ch'iung-ming was then a self-styled national
revolutionary. Following the capture of Kwangtung, he invited Dr.
Sun from Shanghai to assume political leadership in Kwangtung. He
also invited Ch'en Tu-hsiu to take charge of education in the province (it is not clear whether he did so directly or through Dr. Sun).
Ch'en, having enjoyed a certain degree of success in organizing the
Communist force in Shanghai, hurried to Canton with the hope of
utilizing the opportunity to plant the seeds of a Communist organization there. He had not the slightest intention of pursuing the
work of education but did not want to miss this excellent opportunity.

On arriving in Kwangtung, Ch'en moved immediately to organize
the Communist force and enlisted the following comrades: (1) T'an
P'ing-shan; (2) Ch'en Kung-po; (3) T'an Chih-t'ang. Several anarchists also joined him. He was able to work with relative freedom
in Kwangtung and, with the experience gained in previous work in
Shanghai and Peking, Ch'en was able to draft a program for the
Party and to present it to the Kwangtung organization. However, the

anarchist members regarded the Party program as irreconcilable
with their basic ideas and did not wish to remain in the organization.

Fortunately, their withdrawal did not adversely affect the organization. As at Shanghai and Peking, it was of no consequence. The
[14] Chinese anarchists are basically not different from anarchists in
general. In China, they were little known, or even unknown, to the
masses, for they made no effort to work among them. Their withdrawal from the organization therefore produced no reaction at all
among the masses, if one may use the term "masses" when speaking of that period. The basic organization in Kwangtung finally accepted Ch'en Tu-hsiu's draft party program (unanimous approval
was of course impossible) and organized a school of propaganda and
agitation in Canton to train personnel for future work not only in
Canton but in other areas as well. The organization also published
a daily [weekly], Lao-tung sheng, which exerted a great influence.

With the successful establishment of the Kwangtung organization,
the first chapter of the history of the KCT may be considered
closed.

The three cities of Shanghai, Peking, and Canton dominate almost
the whole of China. They are the centers of the social and revolutionary movement. The development of the KCT proceeds from these
places, and Ch'en Tu-hsiu should be recognized as the founder of
organizations in all other areas.

Shanghai is the center of the nation's industry and commerce,
Peking is the political and university center, and Canton is the
center of the national revolutionary movement. With the foundation
laid in these three important places, the Communist movement continued to develop. Within less than six months, Communist nuclei had
been established in Hupeh, Hunan, and Honan. Furthermore, the
Communist movement spread to Chinese students studying abroad,
who organized small organizations in Tokyo, Paris, and other places.

Although our work was developing, we felt many inadequacies in
the work of direction and encountered numerous difficulties. The
scope of our activities was one such problem. Since it was impossible to undertake all social movements with our available strength,
we decided to proceed with the most urgent task of the day, the organization of labor.

While the number of the laboring class was daily increasing, the
progress of the labor movement was slow and reactionary elements
[15] were also found mixed in with the laboring class. One may state
and prove now from the historical point of view that the decision to
emphasize labor organization has already been justified by subsequent developments.

The work of the three years from 1918 to 1920 was concentrated
on grouping together individual revolutionaries and organizing them
into small units capable of serving as nuclei at different places.

Efforts were also made to examine in Party publications the basic problems of the masses. Thus the initial work of collecting material for laying the Party's foundation may be said to have been accomplished in three years. The KCT had by the beginning of 1921 an outline for the future.

After three years of perserverance and hard work by the small group of comrades working under the direction of Comrade Ch'en Tu-hsiu, the following results were achieved:

The Shanghai organization was composed of approximately seventy persons. Since the Party had not then been established, these persons cannot be called Party members but only comrades. There were about ten comrades in Peking and ten in Canton. There were three newspapers, one each in Peking, Shanghai, and Canton. In addition, there was the Chinese Socialist Youth Corps, with a membership twice as large as that of the organizations. A small number among our comrades had had some experience and this served as the foundation of their future work.

What did our comrades undertake in 1921 in proceeding with their work?

Since small groups of comrades were already in existence, we had to group our forces together and organize them, particularly in view of the confused political situation. Otherwise we would not have been able to proceed with our work.

[The First Congress, May, 1921]

In May, 1921, the First Congress of the Party was held in Shanghai. At that time persons connected organizationally with the Party and those taking part in actual Party work totaled not more than sixty or seventy. The rest were mainly "sympathizers." Eleven delegates attended the Congress, which took place in the Shanghai French Concession, beyond the reach of Chinese law. Fortunately, no untoward incident occurred despite a search by police and gendarmes.

The organizers, including Ch'en Tu-hsiu, had hoped to solve at the Congress all outstanding problems relating to the Communist movement. Ch'en Tu-hsiu was busy in Canton and did not attend the Congress, but he sent his draft of the Party platform to be discussed at the meeting.

[16]   The Congress reflected the real condition of the Party at that time. Men of divergent ideas, political outlooks, and frames of mind assembled. The situation of heterogeneity previously characterizing the local groups in Peking, Shanghai, and Canton repeated itself once more at the Congress. Among the eleven delegates there were: (1) students of socialism; (2) democratic socialists; (3) anarchists; and (4) Communists. It was not easy, therefore, to find thorough solutions to any of the problems under discussion.

The program outlined and sent by Ch'en Tu-hsiu was brought for-

ward for discussion. Ch'en was very cautious in drafting the program and emphasized the following points: (1) education and training
of Party members; (2) guidance [of the Party] in accordance with
democratic principles; (3) discipline; and (4) need of caution in approaching the masses with a view to bringing them into the Party
fold. Seizure of political power, it was stated, was a problem for
the future, since the Party was not yet established and efforts
should first be devoted to work of a preparatory character. The nature of the draft program was already extremely mild and yet, when
presented at the Congress, certain delegates considered it too radical and others too impractical. Still others believed it unnecesary
to adopt a concrete program.

One of the delegates, Li Han-chün (now out of the Party), argued that
despite similarities the Russian and German revolutions had many
differences. In Russia the Communist Party was dictatorial while
the democratic system existed in Germany. The right and wrong of
these systems, Li said, had yet to be determined. Li argued that the
problems of a Party platform and political policy raised by Ch'en
Tu-hsiu should be deferred, pending the despatch of comrades to
Russia and Germany for study and inspection.

It is obvious that with such opportunistic currents of thought at
the Congress, it was impossible to discuss or even raise the question of the Chinese Communist Party joining the Comintern.

Li Han-chün rejected all forms of active revolutionary work,
interference of the Party in the labor movement, and publication of
Communist literature, and even opposed taking part in the politics
in general. He and his group favored only the study of communism.
This attitude is a reflection of Chinese conditions. It is also connected to some extent with the belief of Dr. Sun that it is not difficult
to act but difficult to know. Li believes that action is easy if preceded by thorough study and understanding. He therefore advocated
studying the conditions of the Russian, German, and Western Euro-
[17] pean revolutions before selecting our own course. His position
thus coincides with Dr. Sun's repudiation of the old proverb, "To
know is not difficult; to act is."

The disputed points on knowledge and action had nothing at all to do
with Marxist doctrines or the original aims set forth at the First
KCT Congress. Had the wavering opinion of Li Han-chün and Ch'en
Kung-po not been repudiated at once our Party would have been extinguished and become a miscarriage. Although the laboring masses
in the revolutionary movement were not in a position to exert pressure on their leaders (the Congress was to a certain extent playing
the role of leader), and the general environment precluded the possibility of such pressure, the majority of the delegates felt it imperative to resist firmly the current of thought of the "sitting on the
fence" group and decisively rejected the position of Li Han-chün.

Almost all of Ch'en Tu-hsiu's proposals on Party centralization, discipline, and the Party's ultimate objective (seizure of power) were approved. These policies were to form the basis of the future program of the Party. It was also decided that the Party was to be called the Communist Party and that the principles of Communism should guide the Party in its work.

The decision on the ultimate objective of the Party—seizure of political power by proletarian organizations under the leadership of the KCT—was the most objectionable point to the "sitting-on-the-fence" clique of Li Han-chün and others. Finally, in accordance with the decision of the Congress on the withdrawal of all those who have non-Communist tendencies, Li and the others were ordered to leave the Party. This made it possible for the first election of the Central Committee to be carried out smoothly. Ch'en Tu'hsiu was elected Secretary-General, a decision which was of great benefit to the KCT.

Upon his election as Secretary-General, Ch'en left Kwangtung for Shanghai to direct the CC in performing the work of the labor movement in accordance with his principles. Ch'en, however, was arrested soon after his arrival in Shanghai. It was only after his release that he could, with considerable difficulty, again begin his work.

Once more Ch'en Tu-hsiu followed his old principles and devoted himself first of all to developing the labor movement, particularly since the situation at the time was favorable. A special bureau, [18] headed by Chang Kuo-t'ao, was organized to direct the labor movement.

A publishing office was also established to handle such communist books as Program of the Communist Party, Wage-Labor and Capital, Manifesto of the Communist Party, The Soviet System of Power, and Program of the Communists (Bolshevists). Most works were translated from English; only a few were directly translated from Russian. The publishing office failed shortly after it was set up because the directors of the office thought that books of that kind would command very few buyers and therefore sent them out free. The office was consequently forced to close down. The fault, however, was not only with the directors, but even more with the Central Committee, which directed the office.

This incident is characteristic and reveals that even such stalwart Communists as Ch'en Tu-hsiu and others were not quite confident of their own strength. They doubted whether their literature could be readily sold on the book market, even though it was not being published in millions of copies but in much smaller quantity! Thus underestimation of their own forces led to an erroneous decision. The slow progress in the work of agitation and propaganda was paralleled by slow advance in the distribution of literature. This, however, was not due to lack of interest among the Communists or

the masses, who were full of revolutionary spirit, but to incompetence in handling publishing work and selecting materials for printing and publication.

While the work of agitation and propaganda was not very successfully carried out (particularly among workers), the labor movement
advanced with rapid strides.

[Organization of Labor Unions, 1921]
The labor movement progressed rapidly throughout China (wherever there were industrial enterprises and workers). The KCT
was able to organize big labor unions instead of the small organs
it had previously established among the laboring masses. Organization of big unions first took place in Shanghai among the mechanics,
printers, and textile workers. Membership in such unions was not
confined to laborers, however. Employees in general could also
join.

The mass labor movement coincided with the rise and development of industry. In contrast to the prosperous growth of industry,
the workers were left in a deplorable state. Hence, a so-called
"active labor movement" was initiated. It was of an exclusively
economic character and expressed itself in economic strikes.

The first strike occurred in the Shanghai British-American
[19] Tobacco Company [on October 24, 1921]. Members of the Chinese
Communist Party took an active part in this movement, mixing
themselves in with the laboring masses to agitate for economic
struggle and to stir the workers to the realization of the need for
big labor unions.

The Party was confronted with numerous difficulties in this work
because the laboring masses, though greatly agitated, regarded the
Party's actions as dangerous and radical. They believed that the
labor movement should stay within legal limits and the most conservative among them even suspected the purity of our motives,
thinking that our action were propaganda devices. This was due to
the older unions of 1912-1913, which were well known to the workers. The unions did not recognize the KCT, which was unable to
show its real face in view of its illegal status. On witnessing the
fiery actions of the Communists, the laborers suspected them of
being spies for the capitalists or propagandists for Sun Yat-sen. In
short, the workers feared being utilized by others as instruments
of violent struggle.

A very amusing episode may be related here. At a meeting, some
Communists proposed to date all documents with the year 1921 instead of the 11th year of the Republic of China and the workers
suspected them of being emissaries of the Manchus, sent to stir up
revolt against the Republic! The KCT was actually forced to put up
a fight on this very elementary question, which should not have

caused doubts even among the least conscious. It was only after all
kinds of explanations that the laborers were brought to understand
and to recognize the Communists. Such were the difficulties in the
work of the Party.

Party development proceeded in a strict and orderly manner.
From the big proletarian center of Shanghai it gradually expanded
to Peking, Canton, Hankow, etc. The same order applies to the
trade union movement.

The big trade-union movement developed at approximately the
same time in Peking and Tientsin in North China. As mentioned
[20] above, an evening class was organized for laborers (mostly railway
workers) near Peking. The Foreign Language School in Shanghai
was a center of Communist propaganda and training of Party workers. The evening class at Ch'ang-hsin-tien was a center of agitation
among workers, Communist propaganda, and enlistment of Party
members. It is different from the Shanghai Foreign Language
School, which does not enlist Party members but gives them systematic training.

Aside from the evening class, KCT members frequently met
workers at places where they relaxed, such as tea-houses, cafes,
etc. This was done not without difficulty because Chinese workers
(with the exception of the majority of railway workers) were in
most cases completely dependent on their contractors, so that Party
members had first to develop contacts with contractors, labor
bosses, and all the other classes above the workers. Actually, of
course, the Communists had nothing in common with the contractors, nor did they have any message intended for the contractors,
but the only way was to try to alienate the workers from their
bosses.

After half a year, in May, 1921, some results were apparent when
more than a thousand workers of Ch'ang-hsin-tien Railway Station
assembled at a meeting at which the problem of contract labor was
raised. This meeting was part and parcel of the campaign conducted
cautiously and constantly by the Communists among individual workers and small groups. The Party stated at this meeting that the time
for liberation from contract labor had arrived and that workers
should take into their own hands the right to take any action they
chose. The slogan for organizing big labor unions was also issued
and it met with the complete approval of the masses of workers.
Thus in May, 1921, the beginnings of a mass trade-union movement
were evident in North China.

The year 1921 may be called the year in which the foundation of
the mass trade-union movement was laid in all industrial centers
cf China. Various labor unions were organized among Shanghai
workers and railway workers' organizations were set up.

The labor movement (including the miners of Honan, Chihli,

Hunan, etc.) was well organized and it manifested proper characteristics. By "proper," we mean that the movement was actually in
the hands of the workers and the workers' Party and was entirely
different from the labor movement of 1912 and 1913, which was
[21] sponsored and organized by politicians and various "sitting-on-the-
fence" cliques. Now the movement is promoted and directed exclusively by the KCT. Although a foundation has been laid, however,
further efforts are required to strengthen it and to prevent the in-
flux of profit-seekers as in the old days.

[The First Congress of the Toilers of the Far East, January, 1922]
    The same year witnessed another important event for the KCT.
As a result of the KCT's efforts, China was able to participate in
the First Congress of the Toilers of the Far East which took place
in Moscow [January 21 to February 2, 1922]. Its objective, roughly,
was to organize the peoples of the Far East to oppose the Washington Conference and its decisions.(Details on the Washington Conference cannot be related here.) The KCT tried by various ways
and means to organize a Chinese delegation to the Congress. At
meetings in open-air speeches, and in its newspapers, the Party
insisted on the necessity of sending a Chinese delegation. Although
this was strongly opposed in many quarters, the KCT finally
succeeded in organizing a delegation of thirty persons, representing students, workers, the KMT, and the KCT. It was a delegation
representing four organizations and three classes of Chinese society, namely, labor, the intelligentsia, and the urban middle and
petty bourgeoisie. (The last refers to the KMT, which was then in
close contact with the petty bourgeoisie).
    With few exceptions, members of the delegation had no organiza-
tional affiliation. At the Congress, they had no definite political
program, unified opinion, or clear comprehension of their own position. The Communists were in a difficult spot and could not help the
situation.
    The above-mentioned inadequacies did not lessen the importance
of the Congress, which was of international significance. Its importance was partly due to the fact that the Washington Conference devoted nine tenths of its time and work to the so-called Pacific Ques-
[22] tion, the greater part of which is the China Question. We may
venture the opinion that had the Chinese delegation not attended the
Moscow Conference, the latter would have lost all its significance.
The KCT did its very best in this matter.
    One more episode. Among the Chinese delegates was a woman
named Huang Pi-hun. On arriving in Moscow she went to call on
[Alexandra] Kollontai, representing herself as the leader of the
Chinese women's movement. She behaved badly. One of the first
things she asked for was an appropriation of funds allegedly for use

in the women's movement. After her return to China she was revealed as a propagandist for Ch'en Ch'iung-ming, on whose instruction she made an attempt to assassinate Sun Yat-sen. Sun Yat-sen later ordered her to be shot.

Though optimism is not warranted by the women's movement, certain results have been achieved, also as a consequence of promotion by the KCT.

Good as well as harm (the word "unpleasantness" would be more correct) was done by the Chinese delegation in Moscow. At that time the famine in Russia was well known to all. Food provisions for the delegation, though not too substantial, were far better than those enjoyed by the Russian workers and people in general. This should not have been a question of principles or politics and should not have been an issue at all to the politically conscious. However, it did produce a very great effect. The devastation in Russia resulting from famine and war created a very bad impression on the delegates, particularly KMT members. Communist members of the delegation were extremely young and politically inexperienced. They did not bother to explain to the other delegates the causes of disorder, famine, and other defects in Russia, but simply started quarrels. Without resorting to reason, they demanded that their fellow delegates admit the correctness of their Communist point of view. They merely relied on the following line of argument, "All is well, but to you all seems to be bad," which was usually accompanied by insults.

Many members of the delegation, especially KMT members, returned to China and declared that on the basis of the actual conditions observed, the treatment they received in Russia, and the experience of traveling with the Communists, it was doubtful whether the KCT could be of benefit to the country. Some of the delegates, such as Chang Ch'iu-pai and other KMT members, declared that the Chinese Communists were their enemies and precautions must be taken against them.

The foregoing relates the general experience and work of the KCT [23] from the First Congress·to the beginning of 1922.

[The Second Congress, June, 1922]
Following the Moscow Conference, the KCT held its Second Congress in June and July, 1922. Its position at that time was much stronger than at the first Congress. Not only had Party membership increased; its quality had also improved. The Party was also a great deal more experienced.

The difference between the two congresses was that the people who gathered at the Second Congress were united in Marxist doctrines, platform, and objectives, and they were all capable of dialectical reasoning. The Party Platform was completely passed at the Second Congress, the most important provision being the decision to join the Comintern. The Congress also passed a manifesto stating the Party's views on domestic and international problems.

One of the most important questions brought up for discussion at the Congress was the necessity of carrying on an active struggle for a democratic united front. The Party had become conscious of itself, of its strength and role, and the masses had also come to know the Party. The KCT thus had to present its political policies and clarify its stand. The political program adopted by the Congress comprised the following seven points:

1. Struggle against militarism to secure internal peace.

2. Struggle against imperialism until it is completely eliminated from the country; in other words, fight for the independence of the Chinese nation and people.

3. Create a united and democratic country (republic).

4. Grant the right of self-determination to the frontier peoples of Mongolia, Tibet, and Sinkiang.

[24] 5. Organize the Republic of China on the federal principle.

6. Establish universal, direct, equal, and secret election; freedom of speech, press and assembly; and the right to strike.

7. Enact labor legislation and land laws.

a) <u>Labor legislation</u>: Labor legislation should provide for the study of means to improve the worker's living and working conditions; abolish the system of contract labor; enact regulations for the eight-hour day in all factories, mills, mines, and railways; establish free medical care and dispensaries for workers in all factories and mills; enforce the principles of hygiene; provide workers with life insurance; enact a special law to protect child labor and old workers; and establish organs to render assistance to the unemployed.

b) <u>Legislation on the peasant problem</u>: Abolish the <u>likin</u> and other abnormal taxes and levies, substituting for them a consolidated income tax; enforce fixed land rents.

c) <u>Other legislation</u>: Abolish all laws restricting the freedom of women; grant women equal political and economic rights; improve the education of the people.

The resolution of the Second Congress covered all fundamental problems of the Chinese national revolutionary movement. The [25] Congress could not end its duty with mere resolutions, however; their execution required the unification of all democratic revolutionary forces in China. Hence, the Congress decided further that the newly elected CC should call all genuine democratic revolutionary forces to a unification conference. In other words, it strove to create a united front of the revolutionary elements in the Chinese social structure.

The importance of the Second Congress in the history of the KCT is due to the following:

1. The Party Platform was passed to define the Party's objectives with reference to current and future problems.

2. With the passage of the Party Platform and the adoption of the name "Kung-ch'ang-tang," the Party clearly revealed its true countenance, standing squarely on the path of Marxism.

3. The KCT established its connections with the World Revolution. By joining the CI, it has become an integral part of the world Communist movement.

4. The decision of the Congress on the absolute necessity of building a united front testifies to the fact that the KCT, though small in membership, was quite experienced and capable of finding solutions to the problems of the Chinese people.

5. The Congress declared that while the KCT was confronted with numerous problems, the basic task was development of the labor movement, that is, absorption of the working class by the Party. This was correct.

At the time of the Second Congress, there was a change in the frame of mind of the masses who had begun to take an active interest in the Party. This is proved by the zeal with which they immediately bought up the Party's literature. The masses wanted to know what the KCT was saying, what proposals it was making, and how it was thinking. More than twenty delegates attended the Second Congress.

[26]   The revolutionary movement advanced with great speed in 1922, not in terms of numerical increase but in improvement of the quality of personnel. The moral weight of the real revolutionary forces was gaining strength. The revolutionaries revealed undaunted courage in struggling for their objectives and solving the problems before them. This produced alarm among those who were in name democratic but who secretly harbored undemocratic principles. The true revolutionary movement was given a blow by these people. Although the blow was not aimed directly at the Chinese Communist Party, the Party had to face considerable unpleasantness.

[Conflict between Sun Yat-sen and Ch'en Ch'iung-ming, 1922]

On July 12, 1922 [June 16, 1922], at the close of the Second Congress, Ch'en Ch'iung-ming staged a political coup in Canton and drove out Sun Yat-sen. The incident was precipitated by Sun's demand that Ch'en organize a northern expeditionary force. Sun was concerned solely with revolution without taking into consideration his actual and potential strength. The only force he could rely on was the revolutionary spirit of the Chinese people and the comrades of his own Party, and he made his plans accordingly.

Even without Sun's demand for the northern expedition, Ch'en would certainly have been jealous of Sun as an elder revolutionary. Ch'en pretended to play the part of a revolutionary, but he differed from Sun in that he had no great ambition to unify China. Ch'en had already become a typical Chinese militarist, bent on robbery and oppression. He was also a wealthy merchant with close connections with the propertied classes of Kwangtung. As a pretext for rejecting Sun's demand, Ch'en proposed that efforts should first be concentrated on the building up of Kwangtung before the northern expedition could even be discussed.

Ch'en's proposal doubtless represented the opinion of the compradors and other capitalists of Canton and Hongkong, who realized that the enormous expense involved in the northern expedition would eventually fall on them. They believed it cheaper to feed Ch'en and his army, no matter how corrupt, than to shoulder the great burden of the northern expedition.

When we estimate the actual strength and influence of Sun Yat-sen, it becomes evident that the northern expedition would have been doomed to failure. The KCT was not sympathetic to Sun, but it did not openly support Ch'en Ch'iung-ming. The KCT had not then acquired an important position and therefore could not express any 27] definite opinion of its own. Furthermore, it did not have confidence in the success of the northern expedition.

The opinion of other political, social, and revolutionary elements was also unfavorable to Sun Yat-sen. The best-educated and the most democratic elements were on Ch'en Ch'iung-ming's side and were dissatisfied with Sun Yat-sen's program. Take, for instance, the noted Chinese scholar, Dr. Hu Shih. In his speeches and writings, Hu Shih considered Ch'en Ch'iung-ming as a genuine revolutionary and regarded Sun Yat-sen as in the wrong. Many of Sun's friends and followers advised him to give up political life completely in view of his demonstrated inefficiency. Sun Yat-sen then proceeded to Shanghai.

[Communist Policy of Collaboration with the Kuomintang, 1922]

The Chinese Communist Party believed that the time had come when it should play its first act in the political arena, that is, carry out the basic resolution of the Second Congress to build a fighting front in the Revolution. Despite the fact that Sun was an insignificant figure, having just lost his base in Kwangtung, the KCT believed that he and his comrades were the only democratic elements who, given an opportunity, could be expected to succeed. The KCT therefore sent representatives to call on Sun and presented him with a proposal for KMT-KCT cooperation, while promising all kinds of assistance. Sun did not disappoint the confidence of the KCT and accepted its proposal at once. In this decision he was supported firmly by the most prominent KMT members in Shanghai, such as Wang Ching-wei, Liao Chung-k'ai, Hu Han-min, and others.

At the time there was already a [KMT] Right Wing which opposed

this decision and regarded the KCT's proposal as an act of deception for the purpose of expanding the KCT by means of KMT
strength. Even now, people of the Right Wing still maintain that the
KCT developed on the strength of the KMT. Honest KMT members
admit that this statement is contrary to the facts and is sheer
nonsense from beginning to end. The KMT's expansion is actually
due to the help rendered by the KCT through its work.

[28]   The talks between the representatives of the CC of the KCT and
Dr. Sun led to definite results. In August, 1922, the entire question was raised again in a broader sense at the plenary meeting
called by the CC of the KCT at Hangchow, capital of Chekiang province. The meeting adopted a resolution to try to bring about an
amalgamation of the KMT and the KCT in terms of internal organization. The resolution was adopted unanimously, although some individual comrades were opposed to it.

The adoption of this resolution was necessitated by the situation
at the time, for the working class and its Party were unable, with
only their own forces, to handle their colossal problems. It was
particularly difficult to work among the vast masses of the whole
social structure whose interest in politics was growing constantly.

On the other hand, the KMT was inactive; in fact, it did not even
exist. When the KCT conveyed the resolution to Dr. Sun, he expressed complete approval and was very pleased. The KMT was so
weak at that time that all leading members, even those who never
professed Leftist principles, such as Hu Han-min, endorsed Sun's
decision.

The KCT foresaw the difficulties engendered by the decision to
ally with the KMT, which was actually not a party at all but a collection of groups and individuals espousing Sun Yat-sen's principles.
Having no contact with each other, KMT members did not have any
Party program or regulations. They had many prejudices. It is sufficient to cite here only one example to show how backward the KMT was.

The Party practiced several ceremonies of an ordinary bourgeois
character, completely devoid of revolutionary spirit, in initiating
new members into the Party. Each candidate took an oath of allegiance to Sun Yat-sen and in place of the seal made an impression
with his finger. These were the most characteristic rituals, but
there were countless others which testify to the fact that the KMT
was a religious sect rather than a political party. The KCT was willing
to cooperate with such a "party" and concluded an alliance with Sun
because this provided the only legal access to the mass movement.

["Down with Imperialism!" and "Down with Militarism!"]
The KCT decided to take up the most pressing problems with the
KMT and build them up as slogans of the day. The two slogans were

"Down with imperialism!" and "Down with militarism!", which
covered all the urgent internal and external issues of that time.

The slogans were for the vast masses almost what the discovery
of America was for the people of the Middle Ages. However, their
significance had scarcely been comprehended previously by the
lower classes or even by the intelligentsia who are supposed to be
the leaders of society. The KCT was forced to carry on agitation
among the middle and lower social classes and to struggle for the
recognition of these slogans. Strange though it may seem, the Com-
29] munists had to fight against the leaders of society, professors, etc.

Of the two, the slogan "Down with militarism!" was understood
and adopted with greater speed because it strikes at an oppressive
burden borne directly by the masses then and in the past. Militarism, in short, does not allow the people to live in peace. It was a
great deal more difficult, however, for the masses to understand,
let alone accept, the slogan "Down with imperialism!" The cause
lay in the existence of opposition even within the circle of revolutionaries. Dr. Hu Shih, for instance, published a series of articles
in the Nu-li chou-pao (The Endeavor) to the effect that the Chinese
had not been oppressed by the imperialists, that the imperialists
had given China many benefits and treated the Chinese very well,
and that it was groundless to accuse them of insulting the Chinese.

Hu Shih's position did not merely represent that of the foremost
Chinese intellectuals, but larger circles of Chinese society as well.
This is because the imperialists never directly carried out their
policies but did so indirectly, in most cases through the comprador-
bourgeoisie and the militarists. They were able to cover up their
mischief so well that sometimes they were peace-makers in the
eyes of the masses.

Although there was in the Chinese mind no opposition to imperialism, Japan was the exception. The Chinese masses despised Japan
and were anxious to take revenge against her, but they regarded
the anti-Japanese movement and the anti-imperialist struggle as
two different matters. Not only was this the psychology of the
masses, but it was true also of the leaders of society, the KMT,
and other revolutionary organizations, which singled out Japan as
the enemy but remained silent about the other imperialist countries.
Furthermore, the anti-Japanese movement was not of an entirely
independent nature, as it was closely connected with the antigovernment movement of the time (opposition to the Anfu Clique). This
coincidence militated against a clear comprehension of the real
situation, for the hatred of the Japanese was in fact obscured to an
extent by the hatred of the government.

The "good-neighbor" relations with foreigners and the hospitable
attitude towards them stem from the artful policy of the imperialists. Parallel to the robberies and violence they were committing

in China, the foreigners founded schools, newspapers, and peasant societies, which formed an all-embracing apparatus for imperialist agitation and propaganda. They were thus able to deceive and cheat the Chinese people. There was a monopolistic character to their agitation, for there was nothing at all to oppose it for many years. In such a backward country as China, the results of this agitation are great. The people did not even react at first to this most urgent question of struggle against their bitter foe, imperialism.

[30]   The KCT devoted two years of active propaganda to popularizing these slogans and to arousing the people's interest in them. As a result, they are now popular and known everywhere in China. With the exception of the reactionaries, the tools of imperialism, and those nationalists who are mentally childish and so anxious for the return of China's past glory that they have become fanatics, every Chinese understands the meaning of the slogans and is permeated with hatred for militarism and imperialism.

[The Strike Movement, 1922 to February, 1923]

Following the Second KCT Congress, the entire country began to be covered by a network of labor unions (where a proletarian population and appropriate conditions existed). This time the labor movement differed from the previous movement because it was backed by strikes. In many places the strike movement developed faster than the labor movement, which meant that the unions were not able to cope with the rapid growth of labor activity.

Almost all the railways in the country were confronted with the strike movement. However, since the strike movement did not correspond with the strength of the leading organs of labor organizations, it terminated as easily as it had developed rapidly. Of the eighteen railways in China, nine were under the control of strong labor organizations (all in central China), while control over the other nine was very weak.

Although the KCT itself was numerically weak and was thus unable to supervise the entire movement, guidance of the unions' work was almost everywhere in its hands. While party membership, including CY members, did not total more than two to three hundred, the number of labor unions was considerable. Unions in the vicinity of Shanghai alone numbered thirty. There were over ten each in Changsha, Hankow, Tientsin, and Canton. Altogether, 125,000 to 150,000 workers were under Communist guidance.

Many strikes of that period ended in victories for the workers, testifying to the organized character of the labor movement in many places and the ability of labor unions to champion the workers' interests. This was not true of the labor movement everywhere, however. Furthermore, this period of rapid growth of the labor

1] movement came to an abrupt end on February 7, 1923, when the reactionaries struck with a deadly blow.

When things first began to develop on the Peking-Hankow Railway, the masses were in a revolutionary frame of mind. The authorities were inclined to be tolerant and even sanctioned the convocation of a congress. Later, alarmed at the continuous advance of the labor movement which threatened their own position, they determined to destroy it. February 7, 1923, is therefore one of the anniversaries in the history of the KCT and the Chinese labor movement.

The above results were derived from the fact that the KCT was too weak to exert control over the entire labor movement. Furthermore, the incredibly sudden and rapid development of events allowed Communist leaders no time for thorough investigation of all the issues which were arising daily. For instance, had some demands of the workers, even those of a purely economic nature, been adequately studied, they would not have been brought up at all, because the labor unions were then in no position to back them up. Emotion triumphed over reason when such demands were raised.

The KCT did advise the workers and their representatives that the time was not ripe for an aggressive policy and that they should reduce their demands to the minimum and proceed carefully. But such advice was given when developments were pressing. The KCT's responsibility is not lessened, however, and it should not be exonerated from blame. Neither should we minimize the gravity of the mistakes it committed. Most Party workers were members of the educated class, but they led a poor and hard life, sometimes even harder than that of workers. Their spirit of self-sacrifice is rarely equaled but they understood little of the workers' interests and living conditions, since most of them confined themselves to central labor organs and failed to penetrate the lower levels of the laboring masses. Had they exerted control over, or even penetrated low-level labor organizations, they would have understood how the laboring masses lived and breathed.

The incident of February 7, 1923, was a blow to the entire KCT as well as the labor movement. It amounted to big rocks being thrown at KCT organs in order to smash them. One of the consequences was the rise of conflict among young Party members, who began to feel nervous. This conflict grew in intensity when many comrades gathered at Shanghai. Some believed that the leaders of the Central Committee were responsible for all failures because of their incorrect policy. The CC, on the other hand, blamed the local
32] committees for poor execution of work. This situation did not last long, however, and order was soon restored.

This phase of development of the Chinese Revolution and the Chinese Communist Party corresponds to the post-1905 period of the Russian Revolution and the Russian Communist Party. The KCT followed in the footsteps of the late Comrade Lenin, who said in 1905, "One must hurry up with the revolution." Members of the Communist Party must be courageous in admitting and correcting their own mistakes, for improvement comes only through correction of mistakes. The KCT, after experiencing these setbacks, adhered to the words of Lenin and realized the futility of despair and downheartedness. Only by hard work and experience can the Party examine its own strength and the capacity of its members to hold to their original purpose.

In the one year following the Second Congress, the KCT encountered difficulties in many ways and suffered a serious defeat, but it was able to escape total destruction.

[The Third Congress, June, 1923]

In June, 1923, the Third KCT Congress was held in Canton under conditions a great deal more difficult than those which characterized the two previous congresses. The First and Second Congresses merely laid the foundation of the Party, while the Third Congress was charged with finding solutions to problems of broader dimensions. The KCT was almost connected with the KMT and this situation alone charged it with great responsibilities. The Party had gained the recognition of the masses and the labor movement was under its direction. Its forces, however, were weak. Such, then, was the situation in which the Third Congress had to carry out its work.

The most important resolutions of the Third Congress were as follows:

1. The Congress decided that the KCT's activities should be centered on the development of the national revolutionary movement.

2. The KCT should recognize the KMT as the nucleus around which the national revolutionary movement should be organized and the leader of this movement because of its historical connections.

[33]   3. KCT members, by virtue of the above, should join the KMT.

4. The KCT should positively help in the creation and formal organization of the KMT as the political party of the great masses.

5. The KCT should help strengthen the KMT's influence among workers and especially peasants.

6. The KCT should take the initiative in the reorganization of the KMT in order to transform it into a genuine political party.

The Third Congress confirmed the resolutions of the Plenary Session of the Central Committee, which took place between the Second and Third Congresses [August, 1922], on the amalgamation of the KCT with, or its entry into, the KMT. The Third Congress believed that labor was incapable of independent struggle and that the progress of its struggle depended on the development of the great national revolutionary movement. Hence, emphasis was laid in the resolutions of the Congress on the necessity of creating a political party capable of controlling and directing the national revolutionary movement.

The KMT problem aroused long debate. It was finally resolved that the KMT should have influence among the working masses, especially the peasantry, since the KCT could not expect to win over the entire masses in the near future. Had the KCT resolved otherwise, that is, that the KMT should not have access to the workers and peasants, the negotiations on the amalgamation with the KMT would have lost their significance. The KCT, in fact, needed the KMT as a means of organizing and influencing the vast masses and of directing the national revolutionary movement.

Although the KCT decided definitely at the Third Congress the question of cooperation and mutual relations of the KMT and the KCT, its decision was not final, because the last word in this matter rested with the KMT. The KMT decided on this problem in a positive sense only in 1924.

The significance of the Third Congress is further increased because of passage of the following points in its basic political platform:

1. Abolish all unequal treaties concluded between China and the imperialist powers. Restrict the privileges enjoyed by foreigners in expanding their economic and political influence (that is, special privileges in developing industry, such as the construction of factories and other enterprises, obtaining concessions, establishing schools and peasant societies). A new law should be promulgated to revise tariff policies. (The foreigners have already expressed approval of this.)

34] 2. Eliminate the militarists and confiscate their property for the development of national industry.

3. Large-scaled industries and businesses (railways, banks, and mines) should be controlled by the government—that is, nationalized.

4. Institute universal and direct election by secret ballot. Elections should be held on holidays or festivals.

5. Grant the people freedom of speech, press, and assembly; repeal the Special Police Act which restricts political freedom (promulgated during Yuan Shih-k'ai's time and still in effect), and the special strike laws.

6. Grant women complete equality.

7. Grant the people freedom of political expression; the right to influence removal of incompetent officials and appointment of high government officials, diplomats, and delegates to international conferences; and the right to elect all responsible officials of the local and central governments.

8. Grant the peoples of Tibet, Mongolia, and Sinkiang the right of self-determination. They may unite with China if they so wish.

9. Organize local self-government throughout the country to administer local affairs.

10. Centralize the financial policy. Prohibit the uncontrolled issue of an unlimited amount of coins and the circulation of foreign paper [35] money on the market. Publicity should be given the financial policy of the country to make it clear to the masses.

11. Abolish the <u>Likin</u> (transit duties between provinces or even counties). Introduce an income tax on movable and immovable property. Taxes should be fixed annually and then enforced by law.

12. Public instruction should be free and universal. Religion should not be taught in the schools. There should be separation of the church and school (or separation of the church and state, which is practically the same). Prohibit misuse of funds provided by the budget for education. Grant teachers one month's annual leave with double pay and provide pensions, in case of old age and sickness, to persons working in the field of public instruction.

13. The work of judicial organs should be revised and placed on a more proper footing. Repeal the death penalty and abolish corporal punishment. Law courts should not charge any fees.

14. Prohibit [establish] voluntary enlistment in the army and abolish compulsory military service. Enact special laws to regulate pay for military men.

15. Build new houses for the poor and repair and improve old dwellings. Regulate house rents by special laws.

16. Fix by law the ceiling price of daily necessities.

17. Protect by law the interests of the peasantry in the following ways:

a) Establish by law a unified land tax throughout the country which should not be a burden on the peasantry. The illegal and corrupt practices of tax collectors should be abolished. (The collectors usually draw no salary but take a certain percentage of the tax as compensation. His functions are reminiscent of those of the public officers charged with executing the decisions of law courts.)

b) Promulgate laws improving land leases to permit peasant associations to lease land collectively.

c) Solve by special legislation the problem of distribution of water sources, that is, the order of their utilization. Improve the method of cultivation of grain and tilling of the soil. (Agricultural schools).

[36]   d) The state should assist the poor peasants with grain and agricultural implements.

e) Regulate by law minimum prices of agricultural products.

18. Labor legislation:

a) Abolish by law the system of contract labor. Labor unions should be recognized as legal organizations empowered to conclude contracts.

b. Prescribe by law the eight-hour working day and prohibit shifting workers from day working hours to night working hours.

c) Allow all workers thirty-six hours of rest weekly.

d) Fix the wages of equally qualified men and women workers on an equal basis. Women workers should be given maternity leave of three weeks with pay both during and following confinement.

e) Prohibit the employment of children under fourteen years of age. Persons between fourteen and eighteen should not work more than six hours during the day or night.

f) Compel industrialists by law to provide for and pay the cost of appropriate sanitation in their factories under state supervision. Unions should have the right to participate in such arrangements and the right of inspection.

g) Promulgate laws on workers' life and health insurance and [7] protection in case of sickness and death. Labor unions representing the workers should take part in such insurance organs.

h) Lend assistance to the unemployed as provided by labor legislation.

Although Party membership was still very small at the time of the Third Congress compared with its present strength, the KCT was conscious of its moral force and the consequent responsibility to the masses. Hence, the Party had the right as well as the duty to reveal its "political face" in a more or less complete form. Judging by the program, or rather the draft program, passed at the Third Congress, we see that the Party had high hopes of assuming a position of responsibility in the national movement as well as organizing the laboring masses. The program included provisions for the peasantry, the intelligentsia, and the petty bourgeoisie. In all these points and in the whole program generally, the KCT took a proper position which in a very short time enabled it to reach a leading position in the national revolutionary movement. Credit for this must be given the Chinese Communist Party and its leaders because of their thorough understanding of Chinese conditions and foresight with regard to the development of the national movement. This and the absence of extraneous influences can be proved by the fact that the resolutions were formulated prior to the reorganization of the KMT and the KMT's final decision on the problem of Communist entry into the KMT. It can be said definitely that the extremely important resolutions and comprehensive program passed by the Third Congress contributed significantly to the unification of the KMT and the KCT, for the KMT leaders perceived that the KCT expressed in its program the desire to cooperate in directing the national movement.

In August, 1924, the KMT finally called a plenary session [Second Plenum of the CEC], at which the problem of the KCT's entry into the KMT was completely solved.

[38]   At this meeting members of the KMT CEC accepted all the proposals of the KCT concerning its entry into the KMT. This raised the morale of those KCT members who had been rather downhearted. The question of a united front was most important from the very beginning. It was raised in its entirety as early as the Second KCT Congress. However, the KMT's [final] decision on this question was long delayed, thus causing dissatisfaction among certain KCT members, particularly in view of the development of the national revolutionary movement and the consequent need of direction. The KMT procrastinated and delayed organizing a party capable of gathering and organizing the national revolutionary forces, especially the active elements. The resolutions of this plenary session of the KMT, however, heartened and inspired the KCT.

Through 1924 and the beginning of 1925, the KCT made great efforts and progress towards the consolidation of the organization of the KMT.

Increase of KCT membership failed to keep pace with the growth of Communist influence over the masses. It is necessary here to summarize the work of the KCT since the Third Congress, that is, 1923. During this period, the Party experienced several difficult moments. It suffered defeat but also gained several victories. The Peking-Hankow Railway Incident of February 7, 1923, was a great defeat because it resulted in some confusion among Party members which, fortunately, did not last long. The incident was not a total defeat, however, because it stimulated the rise of the national revolutionary movement which continues to grow daily in depth and breadth.

The February Seventh Incident and the ensuing rise of national revolutionary consciousness contributed greatly to the final solution of the cardinal question of a bloc between the KMT and KCT. The positive settlement of this question must be considered a victory. The problem was all the more crucial because of the rapid growth of the national revolutionary movement and its lack of direction.

[Feng Yü-hsiang's Coup d'État, October, 1924]

The above-mentioned points necessitated the holding of the Fourth KCT Congress in January, 1925, which coincided with the occurrence of a great event in China. This so-called great event was the recurrence of conflict between two strong militarist groups, Mukden and Chihli, around the end of 1924. The conflict precipitated great

[39] changes within the Chihli Clique and resulted in the coup d'état of the Christian General, Feng Yü-hsiang.

It is still difficult to form definitive conclusions on the causes of the coup. Doubtless, disagreements of a typically Chinese character, that is, lack of complete accord between Feng Yü-hsiang and Wu P'ei-fu, were responsible. The affront Feng received at the hands of Wu might also have been a contributing factor. However, it seems clear that Feng would not have attempted what he did had the national revolutionary consciousness of the masses not been highly developed. At the most, Feng would probably have started a simple armed conflict with Wu, to which end he could easily have joined some other militarist group.

It is highly significant that Feng, having staged the coup d'état apparently in alliance with Chang Tso-lin, remained independent and preferred to ally himself with the national revolutionary movement. Thus, for the first time in the history of Chinese militarism in the last twelve or thirteen years, military men appeared who oriented themselves towards the people and called themselves the Kuominchün [the People's Army]. The three Kuominchün armies which were established in North China in 1924 and 1925 would have been an impossibility without the proper objective revolutionary conditions.

[The Fourth Congress, January, 1925]

The rise of the national revolutionary movement, the appearance of the revolutionary forces in the North, and the rapid rise of the labor and peasant movements stimulated KCT expansion. By this time, Party membership had increased to between 900 and 1,000 and CY membership to 2,000. With these forces at its disposal, the Party convened its Fourth Congress, which devoted the greater part of its attention to the work that had been carried out in accordance with resolutions of the previous congresses. The Congress formulated concrete plans of direction and noted points of weakness in the Party's work for correction. It did not pass any new resolutions which altered in any way the resolutions of the previous congresses.

One of the most important problems confronting the Congress was policy in coping with the situation in the North. The question of the convocation of a national assembly was raised. At the time, Dr. Sun had just arrived in North China and the KCT had to withstand all the attacks which were aimed at the movement for a national
40] assembly. At the same time, the KCT had to struggle against the attempts of Tuan Ch'i-jui to convene a conference with limited representation, that is, a conference of representatives of the bourgeoisie only. The question of these two conferences was the crucial one at the time.

The imperialists were aware that a national assembly, if convened, would give a legal form to the demands and wishes of the vast masses under the influence of the national revolutionary movement. They therefore wished to see it crushed at any cost. At their

instigation, the Anfu Clique, led by Tuan Ch'i-jui, proposed a reconstruction conference with the purpose of obstructing Sun's plans
for a national assembly. The imperialists hoped that by delaying
the convocation of a national assembly they could strike an organized blow at the national revolutionary movement and thus
eliminate the dangers it threatened for them.

[Development of the Revolutionary Movement, 1925]

The labor movement, accompanied by the strike movement, developed parallel to the national revolutionary movement. All the
important centers of the country fell under their influence. Twenty
Japanese factories were involved in strikes affecting 40,000 workers in Shanghai alone at the beginning of 1925. Similar conditions
existed in Tsingtao, Hankow, and other cities.

The labor movement was making swift progress and was to be incorporated later into the revolutionary movement on a national
scale.

On May 1, 1925, the First [Second] National Labor Congress was
convened. This bore testimony to the fact that the Chinese labor
movement had left the embryonic phase and was becoming a definite force with an important role to play in the future. Thus, the
legalization of the movement was quite naturally the first problem
discussed, since the labor movement had heretofore existed only
as an underground movement.

Although the imperialists were aware of the development and
steady consolidation of the labor movement, they did not expect a
revolutionary movement of such broad dimensions within this
short period of time. While they were skeptical that the workers
would resort to positive action at that time, they realized that the
growth of the labor movement would eventually lead to more
drastic activities and decided therefore to provoke the labor movement and drown it in a "sea of blood."

[41]   The May Thirtieth Incident of 1925 is an illustration of the degree of imperialist provocation. It would, however, be a mistake
to assume that the imperialists were acting completely alone, for
behind them stood the Chinese comprador-bourgeoisie.

Following the incident, an unprecedented revolutionary movement occurred in Shanghai, Tientsin, Peking, and Canton, and
rapidly spread throughout the country. Labor was the most active
element in this movement. In Shanghai alone 500,000 workers
were on strike and a major strike broke out in Kwangtung against
the most powerful imperialist nation, Great Britain.

This movement of world significance was directed by the KCT.
Otherwise, it would not have gained such vast dimensions. Without
the guidance of the Kwangtung Communist Party [Kwangtung Regional Committee], the Hongkong strike would not have become a

political factor on a national scale or assumed international significance because it dealt severe blows at Great Britain. Let us assume that the strike would have broken out anyway without Communist guidance, as a result of mass indignation over the shootings
at Shanghai, Tsingtao, Shameen, etc. In that case, the strike would
not in the first place have enjoyed such an organized character; in
the second place it would not have lasted for such a long time; and
in the third place, it would have not brought about the boycott of
British goods. Furthermore, the strike was and still is of tremendous political significance and has contributed greatly to the
unification of Kwangtung. (Kwangtung, the base of the Chinese
national revolutionary movement, was for a long time molested by
provincial militarists who fought among themselves. It was only at
the beginning of 1926 that the revolutionary forces of the KMT
succeeded in unifying the province.)

The May Thirtieth Incident aroused an unprecedented wave of
indignation among the great masses. It would have been extremely
easy at the time to provoke them to fight imperialism and militarism, and it was only the KCT's expert guidance which restrained
the national revolutionary movement from attempting some premature course of action. The only possible result of such action,
had it taken place, would have been the liquidation of the national
revolutionary movement. The KCT followed the development of
events with extreme care, studied every minute detail, and acted
very opportunely in adopting tactics suited to the requirements of
the situation.

At the initial stage of the movement following May Thirtieth,
the active revolutionary forces, the workers and students, were
isolated from each other and they acted independently. The Chinese
Communist Party immediately moved to correct this by organizing
central organs to direct the students and workers and centralizing
in the CC the power to supervise these active elements. Under KCT
guidance, a central organ of the labor movement was established to
guide the workers and an organ of the student movement was organized to guide the students. The petty bourgeoisie and the intelligentsia also participated in the national revolutionary movement,
however. Thus, it was necessary to centralize the entire movement. The KCT created under its direction an organ [the Joint
2] Committee] consisting of representatives of labor unions, students,
small shopkeepers and merchants (the petty bourgeoisie). Since
the KCT held the power of direction of the labor and student movements and since labor and students were the most active elements
and formed the majority in this organ, the KCT succeeded in centralizing in itself the power of directing the revolutionary movement.

Judging by the Party's work during this period, its resolutions,

and the confidence it enjoyed among the masses, it is clear that the
KCT was developing rapidly and that it was capable of directing the
national revolutionary movement. Yet practical difficulties were
not reduced but were even increased in some instances. Take the
Hongkong strike, for instance. While the KCT took upon itself the
organization of the strike and all the consequent difficulties, the
KMT Right Wing not only opposed the strike but took active measures to suppress it at its start. The KMT Left Wing was irre-
sponsible and brought up many unrealistic suggestions, such as
declaration of war against Britain, demand for the return of Hongkong, etc. In terms of the relative balance of forces at the time, it
was utterly impossible to have declared war against Britain. Only
silly idealists could have suggested such an absurd idea!

The KCT therefore had to struggle against the KMT Right on the
one hand (the Right had always objected to fighting the imperialists
in any way) and against the KMT Left on the other (the Left took
the extreme opposite position, which was equally impractical).
Even then, the KCT demonstrated its ability to carry out a wise
and sound policy. It advocated prudence and cautioned against
forcing events or being provoked by the British.

Recently, on September [3d], 1926, the British attempted to provoke the National Government at Canton with a view to causing disturbances in the rear and thus undermining the success of the
Northern Expedition. Two British gunboats approached Canton and
seized landing positions on the river. This provocative action
failed to produce the expected results, however, and credit for this
must again be attributed to the Communists, who restrained the
Strike Committee from taking rash measures. In short, the KCT's
activities during this period prove that it is the only political
party in China capable of handling all problems with sobriety and
determination and pursuing a national policy.

[43]   It must be remembered that at that time—May, 1925—KCT membership was still 1,000, plus a CY membership of 2,000, although
the Party's influence was such that it could guide the entire revolutionary movement. The masses understood the significance and
purpose of the KCT, which attracted wide attention and was very
popular among the masses. The Party began to grow rapidly from
that time on. Within half a year, Party and CY membership jumped
to 10,000 each. Thus the Party grew tenfold, a phenomenal advance
exceeding all expectations!

[Current Weaknesses of the Chinese Communist Party]

This tremendous growth is not unaccompanied by serious difficulties. The KCT is confronted with a great shortage of workers to
carry out Party policies among the masses in local areas. Most of

the Party workers sent to the various localities are inexperienced and incapable of directing work among the masses. It is clear that no good would result if the Party continues growing at the same rapid speed, since the work of direction definitely will not be able to keep pace with such growth. If we can find a large number of able directing personnel, however, the future of the Party will be brilliant. The principal weakness of this period is inability of many Party members to direct the work among the masses.

The second weakness is that many Party members are too interested in big politics and neglect the daily, pressing problems of the masses.

The third weakness, though affecting only a limited number of Party members, is most dangerous. It is the tendency not to distinguish between the national revolutionary movement and the Communist and labor movements. Once a certain newspaper article discussed the future of the national revolutionary movement and advocated communizing the movement. It also claimed all credit for the KCT. The result was the withdrawal of representatives of the petty bourgeoisie from the Shanghai Joint Committee.

One further weakness, and that is, the tendency of our comrades to classify the masses into the Left, Right, and Center. This is both wrong and dangerous. There is no absolute criterion by which we may classify the workers as the Left, the students as the Center, and the petty bourgeoisie as the Right. (Even if this is usually the case, we must not approach this question with such a conventional point of view, particularly since there are exceptions to the rule.)

The KCT's position in 1926 is markedly different from its
[44] previous situation. It was formerly a study organization devoted to theoretical discussion and devoid of practical work. Now the Party concentrates its efforts on concrete, practical work. It has not abandoned theoretical study, however.

Two or three years ago the KCT was merely taking an interest in politics, whereas it is now "making politics" itself and exerting a great influence. A minor mistake of an individual Party member, let alone mistakes committed by the Party generally, adversely affects the entire Party. In this respect, a study of the events which transpired at Canton on March 20, 1926, and May 15, 1926, would be particularly instructive and would prove that mistakes were made by the Party. (The incidents are discussed in separate reports and will not be related here.) The above incidents resulted largely from the KCT's erroneous policy in working among the masses. This problem necessitates careful study in order to avoid repetition.

[Objectives of the Chinese Communist Party]

The immediate objective of the KCT is to gain influence among the entire working masses and to approach the peasantry. The Party's ability to accomplish good work among the peasantry is proved by its record in Kwangtung. Although KMT influence is stronger there than anywhere else, the KCT has been able to direct the peasant movement in Kwangtung with such success that it has almost completely monopolized the entire work.

The KCT should also assume direction over the student movement. Mistakes in the past were due to the fact that CY members held the power of directing the students. The situation will definitely improve as soon as the CC takes over control of this work.

With reference to the bourgeoisie, the important question is that of the petty bourgeoisie. Also important is the problem of neutralizing the middle bourgeoisie. The big bourgeoisie should be considered a dangerous enemy because it will always be on the imperialist side and has never been connected with the national revolutionary movement. The imperialists are well aware of this and are now trying every means to establish closer relations with the big bourgeoisie and, through it, the middle and petty bourgeoisie. For instance, the Chinese bourgeoisie living in the foreign concessions of Shanghai are allowed to feel very much "at home." Relations between the Chinese bourgeoisie and imperialism will always be close because the Revolution ultimately threatens both to an equal extent.

The KCT fully understands this situation. It recently toned down slogans on "big" issues and is concentrating instead on daily problems, particularly those of a local character and those which involve the interests of the masses. This is the only means of winning the confidence of the petty bourgeoisie and alienating it from the big bourgeoisie.

In accordance with what has already been pointed out at the Fourth Congress, Party work should be so organized as to afford both central and local organs responsibility for carrying out Party work. Past relations between central and local organs have not been smooth. We must correct this weakness in every possible way.

The KCT currently is confronted with one great problem: the Northern Expedition. There was at first no unanimous opinion on this among Party members. Certain organs and comrades opposed the Expedition. This situation will of course be detrimental to the Party if allowed to be prolonged. These comrades forget that a successful Northern Expedition would conclude the initial stage of liquidation of the militarists and, consequently, the imperialists. Even if we assume that the defeat of Wu P'ei-fu and Chang Tso-lin does not mean the complete extermination of militarism, a successful Northern Expedition would still be an asset to the national revolutionary movement, since the new militarists are better disposed towards the national movement than the old militarists. (The word "new" is not absolute but relative. Some militarists have connections and struggle together with the KMT while other militarists oppose the KMT and the national revolutionary movement. Hence, they are classified as "new" and "old.")

The KCT has issued explicit directives for the organization of a campaign to support the Northern Expedition. It has declared that unity is essential and that the peasants should be aroused to the support of the Northern Expedition.

Although certain members advocate breaking off all relations with the KMT and entering the political arena independently, the KCT continues to exert all its efforts toward realizing the policy of the unification of all revolutionary forces. The tendency towards independence from the KMT may appear to be of a revolutionary character but it actually contains the danger of alienation from the masses. In breaking off all relations with the KMT, the Party would lose the means of carrying on work among the masses legally, which is a factor of great importance. The CC must counteract at once this dangerous phenomenon.

[46] The real cause of the unceasing development of the Communist movement and the fact that it will continue to advance in the future is not Russian rubles or Russian agitators, as is claimed by the imperialist and anti-Communist Chinese press. It is rather the poverty and hunger of the Chinese people and the policy of the imperialists and militarists, which pushes the people into the arms of the only force which shows them the first and only solution to their dilemma. This force is the Chinese Communist Party, and the only political party able and willing to carry on an active struggle and to lead the fight for the liberation of the Chinese people.

The history of the KCT for the past seven or eight years shows that the Party has been treading an extremely difficult path and that it has written many glorious pages into its history. Nevertheless, there are numerous difficulties lying ahead.

The time has now come when the KCT must become a true political party of the masses. It faces many serious problems, among them the question whether it will advance by pursuing a correct policy or decline by pursuing a wrong policy. The Party's influence is now so great that a minor mistake can seriously affect the Party itself and its mass following.

We can prove that the progress of the urban laboring masses has been great. The Party should have two objectives in the nearest future: (1) to strengthen and advance our position in the cities; and (2) to gain influence in the villages.

Many difficulties confront the KCT with reference to the agrarian problem because the villages are extremely backward and conservative and cannot be compared with the cities. The problem is not a hopeless one, however. The KCT has gained both experience and good results in its work in the villages of Kwangtung. The Party has widespread and solid roots there and a considerable percentage of Party members there are peasants. This proves that the KCT is in a position to organize its own nuclei among the peasantry. Before doing so, however, it is first necessary to organize all the active elements in the villages, with primary attention to the poor peasants who constitute the majority of the population.

The KCT has paid and is now paying great attention to work in [47] the army. Some concrete results have already been obtained. The events of March 20, 1926, notwithstanding, the work done by the KCT in the National Revolutionary Army previous to that date has not been obliterated and will not be obliterated in the future. Political departments and political work still exist in the Army. Despite the temporary withdrawal, Party work in the National Revolutionary Army will be resumed at an opportune time with even greater vigor than before March 20th. There are already signs to this effect.

PART II

THE ORGANIZATIONAL POLICIES OF
THE CHINESE COMMUNIST PARTY, 1920 to July, 1926

Establishment of the Chinese Communist Party, 1920-1921

The author of the "Brief History" discusses a number of historical
factors which were conducive to the birth of the Communist movement in China, such as the growth of industry and the parallel development of labor during World War I, the widespread disappointment over the Versailles Treaty, and the May Fourth Movement.
[Doc. 1, pp. 3-5, 8-9]. He neglects to mention, however, the impact
of the Russian Revolution and the 1919-1920 Soviet declarations of
policy toward China. The USSR renounced all treaties concluded
between the Czarist government with and concerning China, re-
linquished privileges and concessions in China, and promised
support to the Chinese people in the struggle to obtain complete
freedom.[1] The Soviet declarations evoked an enthusiastic response,
particularly among the Chinese intelligentsia, many of whom were
disillusioned.with the democratic West and already impressed by
the success of the Russian Revolution.[2]

   While there were Chinese intellectuals who were favorably
inclined toward communism, the organization of the Communist
party was carried out under Comintern guidance. In the spring of
1920, Gregory Voitinskii, secretary of the Comintern's Far
Eastern Bureau, arrived at Peking with his wife and a Chinese
Communist named Yang Ming-chai. The Comintern had entrusted to
Voitinskii the task of making contact with intellectuals for the purpose
of establishing a Communist party. Voitinskii went first to see Li
Ta-chao, Professor of History at Peking University. Li referred
him to Ch'en Tu-hsiu, formerly head of the Department of Literature at Peking University, who was then residing in Shanghai.
After conferences with Voitinskii, Ch'en Tu-hsiu rounded up a
mixed group of revolutionaries which included socialists, anarchists, and communists. In September, 1920, Ch'en called a conference to formulate concrete plans for the group,[3] the main task
of which was to plant the seeds of a Communist party in Shanghai.
The majority of the members of the group belonged to the Chinese

Socialist Youth Corps, which had been organized the previous
month under Voitinskii's guidance.4

The Chinese Communist Party was formally inaugurated in the
summer of 1921 at the First Party Congress held in Shanghai.
Maring, a Dutch Communist whose real name was Sneevliet,
attended the Congress as a delegate of the Comintern.5 Ch'en T'an-
ch'iu later recalled that the delegates voted to make use of Bolshevik experience in organization and in setting conditions for
Party membership. Party statutes were adopted which set the
Party irrevocably on the Bolshevik path.6 It was decided to expel
all those who had non-Communist tendencies [Doc. 1, pp. 16-17].
Furthermore, according to Tung Pi-wu, a resolution was passed
for a "closed-door policy," designed to keep membership secret
and "pure." Party members were forbidden to join any other political party.7

A bona fide Chinese Communist Party thus emerged from the
heterogeneous groups of revolutionaries which had been recruited
in Shanghai, Peking, and Canton. However, Party membership
was infinitesimal; persons who were organizationally connected
with the Party totalled no more than sixty or seventy [Doc. 1, p. 15].
It was therefore decided not to organize a formal central committee but to establish a provisional central bureau to maintain contact with the various local Communist nuclei. According to Ch'en
T'an-ch'iu, Ch'en Tu-hsiu, Chang Kuo-t'ao, and Li Ta were elected
to the central bureau. Chou Fu-hai, Li Han-chün, and Liu Jen-
ching were elected as reserve members.8 Only two departments
were organized: the Organization Department, headed by Chang
Kuo-t'ao, and the Propaganda Department, headed by Li Ta.9

The Congress endorsed Ch'en Tu-hsiu's view that while seizure
of power was the Party's ultimate goal, it was a problem for the
future. For the time being, it was decided, the Party was to devote
itself to work of a preparatory character. In the Party platform he
drafted,10 Ch'en stressed the need for caution in approaching the
masses in order to bring them into the Party fold [Doc. 1, pp. 16-
17].

Party leaders had from the beginning conceived of the tasks of
organizing the Party and the masses as interrelated. Mass organization at that time was practically synonymous with labor organization. Communists had in fact turned to labor organization even before the Party was officially established [Doc. 1, pp. 11-13]. The
First Party Congress strengthened the emphasis on labor organization. It established the Chinese Labor Union Secretariat, headed
by Chang Kuo-t'ao and composed of twenty-six members,11 nearly
half the total Party membership.

Some sources assert that the First Congress discussed the question of policy toward Sun Yat-sen, who was then collaborating with

Ch'en Ch'iung-ming at Canton. According to Ch'en T'an-ch'iu, the Congress decided to adopt a critical attitude toward Sun's doctrines but to support his practical and progressive activities on a basis of "non-party collaboration," that is, outside the Party.12

Policy of Collaboration with the Kuomintang, 1922

The Chinese Communist Party's "closed-door" policy gave way within a year to a series of decisions which culminated in the entry of Communists into the Kuomintang for the purpose of joint struggle in the Chinese national revolutionary movement.

The theoretical basis for the reversal was provided by the "Theses on the National and Colonial Question," adopted by the Second Congress of the Comintern in the summer of 1920. Comintern policy, according to the "Theses," was chiefly to bring about "a union of the proletarian and working masses of all nations and countries for a joint revolutionary struggle leading to the overthrow of capitalism." Communist parties in backward areas were ordered to give "active support" to revolutionary movements for national liberation. At the same time, however, they were to support and revolutionize the peasant movement against landowners and "all feudal survivals," and were to organize the peasantry and all the exploited into Soviets. The "Theses" state: "It is the duty of the Communist International to support the revolutionary movement in the colonies and in the backward countries, for the exclusive purpose of uniting the various units of the future proletarian parties—such as are Communist not only in name—in all backward countries and educate them to the consciousness of their specific tasks, i.e., to the tasks of the struggle against the bourgeois democratic tendencies within their respective nationalities. The Communist International must establish temporary relations and even unions with the revolutionary movements in the colonies and backward countries, without, however, amalgamating with them, but preserving the independent character of the proletarian movement, even though it be still in its embryonic state."13

Thus, the Comintern called for temporary cooperation with other revolutionary groups in the liberation movements of colonial and backward countries, to be combined with the development of an independent proletarian movement and the preparation of forces for future struggle against bourgeois tendencies.14 The "Theses" had no immediate effect on Communist policy in China, since a Chinese Communist party had yet to be organized. It was not until January, 1922, at the First Congress of the Toilers of the Far East held in Moscow and Petrograd, that the strategy outlined in the "Theses" was defined in concrete terms for execution by the Chinese Communist Party.

The First Congress of the Toilers of the Far East, which was

attended by a Chinese delegation which included Communists and
Kuomintang members, resolved that: "The struggle for national
emancipation of the masses of China, Korea, and Mongolia is at the
same time a struggle for the international proletariat, headed by
the workers and peasants of Soviet Russia, against the world imperialists, it is at the same time a struggle for the freedom and
independence of all oppressed nations."[15] The specific tasks of
the Chinese working class and Communists were mapped out in a
report by Safarov entitled "The National and Colonial Question and
the Communist attitude." This report stated: "The chief task with
which they are confronted is to achieve their emancipation from
the foreign yoke. It is the duty not only of Communists, but of all
honest Chinese democrats, to criticize most unsparingly the various Chinese politicians who are entering into any kind of understanding with any of the imperialist gangs...It is imperative to conduct an energetic struggle for the overthrow of that regime which
is supporting the feudal anarchy...All Chinese democrats must fight
for the federative Chinese republic." In short, the principal duty of
Chinese Communists and other democratic revolutionaries was to
struggle against imperialists and Chinese militarists. In line with
the warning of the Second Comintern Congress against Communist
amalgamation with national revolutionary groups, Safarov declared:
"The Chinese workers must tread their own path, must not connect
themselves with any democratic party or any bourgeois elements."
And he continued, "We support any national revolutionary movement, but we support it only in so far as it is not directed
against the proletarian movement."[16]

The Second Congress of the Chinese Communist Party was convened in May, 1922. The Party voted to join the Communist International[17] and issued a manifesto in accordance with the policy
outlined by the First Congress of the Toilers of the Far East.[18]
The Party called for a democratic united front of the proletariat,
poor peasantry, and petty bourgeoisie against imperialism and
militarism. The proletariat should support the democratic revolution in view of Chinese political and economic conditions, the Party
declared, but this did not mean that the proletariat were surrendering to the petty bourgeoisie. Upon the successful conclusion of the
democratic revolution, the proletariat were to struggle against the
bourgeoisie and establish the dictatorship of the proletariat in alliance with the poor peasantry. This second phase of the struggle
could be successful immediately upon the victory of the democratic
revolution, provided that the proletariat's organization and fighting
capacity had been adequately strengthened. The Party stressed the
need for workers to fight for their own class interests, and to organize themselves in the Party and in labor unions. They must develop their strength in preparation for the establishment of Soviets

in alliance with the poor peasantry. The Chinese Communist Party was a section of the Comintern, the Manifesto declared, and it called on all Chinese workers and peasants to rally to its banner. It called on all the oppressed masses of China to struggle together with the workers and poor peasants under the Party's banner.[19]

On June 17, 1922, the Party's Central Committee published another declaration, known as the "First Manifesto of the Chinese Communist Party on the Current Situation." The CC reiterated the need for the proletariat temporarily to join a democratic united front and confirmed that its ultimate goal was proletarian revolution. But there were significant differences between the two declarations. In the "Manifesto of the Second Congress" issued in May, 1922, the Party had called on the oppressed masses, the workers, and peasants to rally under the Party's own banner in the struggle for the democratic revolution. It had called for a democratic united front of workers, peasants, and the petty bourgeoisie. The June manifesto, on the other hand, made no distinction between the petty bourgeoisie and the bourgeoisie and shifted the emphasis to cooperation with democratic political parties. Furthermore, the Central Committee singled out the Kuomintang as a potential ally. While the CC criticized it for various defects, the CC declared that of all the political parties in China only the KMT could be considered a revolutionary party. The CC called for a joint conference with revolutionary elements of the KMT and revolutionary socialists to build a united front on the basis of an eleven-point program.[20]

These differences suggest that the decision to seek an alliance with the Kuomintang was a product of the Second Congress. Its timing may also have been influenced by the difficulties which were besetting Sun Yat-sen in Canton. On June 16, 1922, the day before the "First Manifesto" was published, a coup d'état was staged by Ch'en Ch'iung-ming against Sun Yat-sen, who escaped to Shanghai.[21]

Shortly after Sun's arrival in Shanghai, Dalin, a delegate of the Young Communist International, called on him with a proposal for an alliance between the Chinese Communist Party and the Kuomintang. Sun rejected the offer but told Dalin he would be willing to allow members of the Chinese Communist Party and the Youth Corps to enter the Kuomintang as individuals.[22]

Maring, who had just returned from a trip to Moscow, then convened a special plenum of the KCT's Central Committee at West Lake, Hangchow. Sun Yat-sen's condition for cooperation was accepted by the Central Committee, but sources conflict on how this was brought about. According to Ch'en Tu-hsiu's testimony in 1929, Maring took the position that the Kuomintang was not a party of the bourgeoisie, but a party representing the alliance of various classes. Communists should therefore join the Kuomintang to improve it and push forward the Revolution. Maring's suggestion, Ch'en asserts, was unanimously opposed by the five members of the Central Committee who attended the Plenum: Ch'en himself, Li Ta-chao, Chang Kuo-t'ao, Ts'ai Ho-shen, and Kao Chün-yü. According to Ch'en, the CC members contended that entry into the KMT would confuse class organization and curb the KCT's independent policy. Maring then asked if the Chinese Party would obey the decision of the Comintern. Thus, for the sake of respecting international discipline, Ch'en asserts, the CC decided to adopt Maring's proposal.23

According to Maring, on the other hand, the majority of the CC, including Ch'en Tu-hsiu, favored his proposal. Those who were opposed, particularly Chang Kuo-t'ao, based their position on the belief that the Kuomintang was weak and not worth supporting.24

Chang Kuo-t'ao's account of the Special Plenum tends to substantiate Ch'en Tu-hsiu's testimony. Maring based his position on the decisions of the Second Congress of the Comintern, Chang recalls. It was Maring's view that the Chinese Communist Party was too small to form a united front with the large Kuomintang, and he therefore pressed for the entry of Communists into the Kuomintang as individuals.25

The "Brief History" supports the impression that the Communists' numerical weakness contributed to the decision to enter the Kuomintang. The decision of the Hangchow Plenum, the "Brief History" states, was necessitated by the objective situation. The working class and its party were incapable of handling their colossal problems on their own, and it was difficult to work among the vast masses. Hence, the Chinese Communist Party was willing to cooperate with the Kuomintang because it provided an access to the mass movement. Labor was distrustful of the Communist intellectuals, the "Brief History" relates, and regarded their actions as radical and dangerous [Doc. 1, pp. 18-19, 28]. At that time, it must be remembered, the combined membership of the Chinese Communist Party and the Youth Corps did not total more than two or three hundred [Doc. 1, p. 30]. The Kuomintang, on the other hand, had a membership of about 150,000.26

Following the Hangchow Plenum, individual Communists began to enter the Kuomintang. According to Wang Ching-wei, Li Ta-chao was the first Communist to join the Party. Li told Sun Yat-sen, Wang asserts, that he could not relinquish membership in the Comintern, and Sun agreed to this condition.27 Li Ta-chao's case set the precedent for dual membership in the Kuomintang and the Chinese Communist Party.

The Chinese Communist decision to collaborate with the Kuomintang was fully endorsed by Moscow. In a letter to Chiang Kai-shek dated November 21, 1922, Sun Yat-sen informed his subordinate that the Russians in Moscow had been advising the Chinese Communists to join the Kuomintang.28 On January 12, 1923, a formal resolution was passed by the Executive Committee of the Comintern to the effect that the Kuomintang was the political party dedicated to the National Revolution, that it represented many classes, and that the Chinese Communists should cooperate with it.[29]

Organizational Policies Adopted by the Third Congress, Summer, 1923

The Chinese Communist Party officially adopted the policy of entering the Kuomintang at the Third Party Congress in the summer of 1923. In the "Resolutions on the National Movement and the Kuomintang Problem" adopted at the Congress, the Party defined its reasons: "The working class has not yet become great and powerful. Hence it is impossible to create a powerful Communist Party—a Party of the great masses to meet the immediate needs of the Revolution. The Executive Committee of the Comintern and the Central Committee of the Chinese Communist Party have therefore resolved that the Chinese Communist Party should cooperate with the Kuomintang and that Communist members should enter the Kuomintang...We enter the Kuomintang, but preserve still our own organization. Furthermore, we should exert every effort toward absorbing from among workers' organizations and the Kuomintang Left Wing revolutionary elements who possess class consciousness, gradually expanding our organization and tightening our discipline in order to build the foundation for a strong Communist Party of the masses...We should strive to expand the Kuomintang's organization throughout China in order to centralize all Chinese revolutionary elements in the Kuomintang for the purpose of meeting the immediate needs of the Chinese Revolution...the immediate political struggle naturally means only the national movement, the movement to overthrow foreign power and militarism. Hence, there is need for large-scale propaganda in favor of the National Revolution among the laboring masses in order to expand the Kuomintang which stands for the National Revolution. At the same time, all revolutionary elements who comprehend the necessity for the National Revolution and who, furthermore, have class consciousness should as far as possible join our organization. We should also disseminate propaganda among the masses on the necessity of supporting the interests of the laboring class in the national movement."[30]

The Congress issued a manifesto recognizing the Kuomintang as the central force of the National Revolution. The Party expressed hope that all revolutionary elements would rally around the Kuomintang. It stated, however, that the Communist Party would always support the interests of workers and peasants, and that its special task was to undertake organizational and propaganda work among the masses and lead them to join the National Revolution.[31]

The policy of collaboration was adopted amidst intense controversy.

According to orthodox Communist histories, two extremist views
were advanced at the Third Congress. The Right deviationist tendencies were represented by Ch'en Tu-hsiu, who advocated centralizing all work in the KMT. Such a policy, these orthodox sources
assert, meant the complete amalgamation of the Communist Party
with the Kuomintang and the liquidation of the Communist Party.
Ch'en's erroneous views, they state, are betrayed in the "Manifesto
of the Third Congress." On the other hand, orthodox histories
assert that Chang Kuo-t'ao favored Left-deviationist, "closed-door"
policies. Chang allegedly opposed expanding the KMT's organization
among the masses and insisted that the proletariat should participate in the National Revolution under the banner of its own party.[32]

The orthodox Communist argument that Ch'en Tu-hsiu wished to
liquidate the Chinese Communist Party hinges on the phrase, "centralization of work in the Kuomintang." The "Resolutions on the
National Movement and the Kuomintang Problem" prove, however,
that the Chinese Communist leadership had no intention of sacrificing the Communist Party's own organization while helping the
Kuomintang to expand. They show, on the contrary, that Communists were instructed to make every effort to develop their own
organization and to absorb revolutionary elements into the Party
for the purpose of laying a foundation for a strong Communist party
of the future. This concept of simultaneously developing the Kuomintang and the national movement on the one hand, and preparing
the Communists' independent forces on the other, is basic to the
strategy outlined in the Comintern's "Theses on the National and
Colonial Question." Hu Hua, author of a recent orthodox Communist
history, in fact accepts the resolutions of the Third KCT Congress
as correct and attributes their formulation to Mao Tse-tung and
Ch'ü Ch'iu-pai.[33]

The real issue then was not whether the Party leadership intended
to expand the Kuomintang at the expense of the Chinese Communist
Party, but what attitude Communists should adopt with regard to the
Kuomintang in the labor movement—whether Communists should
expand the KMT's organization among labor and encourage the
entry of workers into the Kuomintang.

Chang Kuo-t'ao recalls that he proposed at the Third Congress
the following resolutions on the labor movement: (1) The KCT
should strengthen its leadership in the labor movement during the
National Revolution and develop Party organization among workers;
(2) The KCT should cooperate in the labor movement with KMT-led
trade unions and KMT members in the unions. But, except for a
few, workers who were Communist Party members should not join
the KMT; and (3) The KCT should take a neutral position on the
question of bringing non-Communist workers into the KMT. Chang's
resolutions were defeated.[34] According to the author of the "Brief

History," who consistently backs the official policies of the Central Committee, the Congress finally resolved that the KMT should have influence among the working masses, particularly the peasantry. This was because the KCT could not expect to win over the entire working masses in the forseeable future. Had it been resolved otherwise, that is, to the effect that the Kuomintang should not have influence among the working masses, he continues, the entire policy of amalgamation with the KMT would have lost its usefulness, because the KCT needed the KMT as a means to organize and influence the vast masses and to direct the national revolutionary movement [Doc. 1, p. 33].

Earlier in the year, on February 7, Wu P'ei-fu's suppression of the Peking-Hankow Railway workers' strike had brought to an end a period of impressive gains for the Communists in their work of fomenting strikes and organizing labor unions. The February Seventh Incident encouraged the growth of the idea that the KCT was too weak—membership was still barely 300 in the summer of 1923[35]—to control the labor movement. Therefore, it should help develop Kuomintang influence among the workers and peasants as a means of indirectly strengthening the Communist position. The author of the "Brief History" states flatly that the February Seventh Incident, which resulted in serious intra-Party disputes and loss of confidence in the CC, occurred because the KCT was too weak to exert full control of the labor movement [Doc. 1, pp. 6-7, 31]. Orthodox Communist historians accuse Ch'en Tu-hsiu of losing faith in the proletariat because of "February Seventh" and trace his Menshevism to the time of the incident.[36] In November, 1923, a group of KMT members accused Ch'en Tu-hsiu and the Communists of utilizing the KMT with added vigor following the February Seventh Incident.[37]

The record thus suggests that the Chinese Communist leadership did place new emphasis at the Third Congress on developing the Kuomintang as a means to expand the Communists' own organization and influence. Ch'en Tu-hsiu made no defense of his position at the Third KCT Congress in his letter to members of the Chinese Communist Party in 1929.[38] Chang Kuo-t'ao, however, recalls that Maring was the main driving force behind the policy of having all Communists join the Kuomintang and work actively for that party. Ch'en Tu-hsiu cast the deciding vote against his resolutions on the labor movement at the Third Congress, Chang asserts, but he did so principally to avoid opposing a Comintern resolution which Maring cited as the basis for his position. Although Ch'en drafted the "Manifesto of the Third Congress," according to Chang, it actually expressed the ideas of Maring with the Comintern's blessings.[39] At any rate, Ch'en Tu-hsiu at least acquiesced in the decisions of the Third Congress, although he personally may not have agreed with Maring.

At its Second Congress in August, 1923, the Chinese Socialist
Youth Corps endorsed the Party's policy and adopted the following
resolutions: "In joining the Kuomintang, members of the Youth
Corps should be directed by the executive committees of various
levels of the Corps, which should in turn follow the directions of
the Central Committee and the executive committees of various
levels of the Chinese Communist Party regarding the entry of Corps
members into the Kuomintang. Members of the Corps in the Kuomintang should: (1) Support the policies of Communist Party members
and maintain with them complete unanimity of speech and action;
and (2) Preserve the strict and independent organization of the
corps."[40]

Members of the Chinese Communist Party and the Socialist Youth
Corps had entered the Kuomintang as individuals prior to the summer of 1923. Communists were active in carrying out the Kuomintang's "First Reorganization" designed to revitalize the Party.[41]
They helped in the secret organization of KMT branches in important centers of the country—Li Ta-chao in the North, Tung Pi-wu
in Hupeh, Wu Yü-chang in Szechuan, and Mao Tse-tung, Lin Tsu-han,
and Hsia Hsi in Hunan.[42]

Organizational Policies from the Third Congress to the
May Thirtieth Movement, Summer, 1923, to May, 1925

Although Sun Yat-sen was firm in holding down KMT elements
opposed to his decision to admit Communists into the Kuomintang,
he was equally insistent that Communists who joined the KMT should
abide by its discipline and render it full allegiance. In his comments
on a petition to impeach the Communists in late 1923, Sun stated
that the Communists, whom he referred to as "youngsters," wished
to monopolize Russian aid. The Russians, however, were not fooled
by them and ordered them to join the Kuomintang. If Russia wished
to cooperate with China, Sun declared, she must cooperate with the
KMT. Should Ch'en Tu-hsiu disobey the Party, he would be expelled.[43] According to Ch'en Tu-hsiu, Sun Yat-sen told Maring on
many occasions that since the Chinese Communists had joined the
Kuomintang, they must obey its discipline and not openly criticize
it. If they did not obey the Kuomintang, Sun said, he would expel
them. Sun told Maring, furthermore, that if Soviet Russia should
support the Chinese Communist Party, he would oppose Soviet Russia at once.[44]

Although Communists were elected to the Kuomintang Central
Executive Committee at the First KMT Congress in January, 1924,
their status in the Kuomintang was still insecure. There were repeated protests against their entry into the Kuomintang. The polarization of the Kuomintang into the Left, which supported Sun Yat-
sen's decision to admit Communists, and the Right, which stood

opposed, steadily increased. It was not until August, 1924, that the Kuomintang's CEC adopted formal resolutions to permit admission of Communists into the party.45

To strengthen their position in the KMT, Communists formulated two principal tactics: alliance with the KMT Left Wing and organization of Communist Party fractions in the KMT.

According to Chang Kuo-t'ao, when Gregory Voitinskii came to China in late 1923 to replace Maring as Comintern delegate, he sought to correct the emphasis on developing the Party within the KMT. Voitinskii, Chang recalls, stressed the independent development of the Chinese Communist Party as a political party while Communists remained within the KMT. At the same time, Voitinskii proposed a new line which distinguished three groups within the KMT: the Right, Left, and Center. Communists were to ally with the Left to attack the Right with help from the Center. This concept of differentiation of the Kuomintang, however, was not adopted until May, 1924, when a plenum of the Central Committee resolved to put the tactic into effect.46   Chang's account is substantially corroborated by a booklet, "What Party Members Should Know," published by the KCT in 1925.47

In June, 1924, Borodin said that the Chinese Communists organized Party fractions in the Kuomintang three months after they entered it.48 According to the CC, the function of Party fractions is "to represent collectively the opinion of the Party" in order to realize Party policies. "Independent opinion on the part of any individual is not allowed. All decisions of the Party organ [to which a given fraction is subordinated] must be executed." Each and every member of the Party fraction must be mobilized to carry out such decisions. Communist Party fractions were not independent units of the Party structure, nor did they compose a separate system. They were established under Party organs of all levels and were under their supervision, from the Central Committee down to executive committees of Party cells. Party fractions were provisional and changeable. Their existence was determined by Party headquarters of various levels [Doc. 4, pp. 78-79].

In short, Communist Party fractions were established, sometimes temporarily, in organizations other than the Chinese Communist Party, such as labor unions, peasant associations, and merchant associations, to carry out the Party's decisions. Although theoretically Communists joined the KMT as individuals, as members of Communist fractions in the KMT they were bound to act collectively to carry out policies assigned to them by regular Communist Party organs. This contradiction became a source of friction between "pure" Kuomintang members and Communist-Kuomintang members. As early as June 18, 1924, Chang Chi, Hsieh Ch'ih, and Teng Tse-ju, members of the KMT Central Supervisory Committee, accused

members of the KCT and CY of disloyalty to the KMT and violation
of KMT discipline. Communists joined the KMT not as individuals,
they charged, but as a body by organizing Communist Party fractions. Acting as members of Communist fractions, they sought to
force their own policies on the KMT, resulting in the formation of
a party within a party. Thus, they declared, Communists had no
semblance of KMT spirit and were loyal only to the Comintern and
the Chinese Communist Party.[49]

To strengthen the Communist position outside the Kuomintang,
the Party reversed its attitude toward the Kuomintang in the labor
movement which had been adopted at the Third Congress. According to Chang Kuo-t'ao, Voitinskii stressed Communist leadership
of an independent labor movement in late 1923.[50] In other words,
Communists were to keep the labor movement free of Kuomintang
influence.

At the same time, the Communist Party turned systematically
to organization of the peasantry in areas of Kwangtung which fell
within the Kuomintang's jurisdiction. P'eng P'ai had started
organizing peasant associations in Hoifung as early as 1921,[51]
but it was not until after the Third Congress that the Party as
a whole devoted serious efforts to organization and training of the
peasantry.[52]

In discussing the Communist program it is important to bear in
mind the Party's numerical weakness. By the Fourth Congress in
January, 1925, Party membership had reached 994, a threefold increase since the summer of 1923; Youth Corps membership had
jumped to 2,365.[53] However, the combined Party and Corps membership still lagged far behind the growth of Communist influence
in the labor and peasant movements—by May, 1925, the Party had
under its leadership 540,000 organized workers[54] and 400,000 organized peasants in Kwangtung.[55]

Dual membership imposed a further strain on the available Communist personnel. Borodin told KMT leaders in June, 1924 that all
members of the KCT and the Youth Corps were supposed to join
the Kuomintang.[56] The majority of Communist members had joined
the KMT by the following year.[57] As Kuomintang members they had
additional opportunities for strengthening Communist influence
among the masses, but they had also to devote themselves to work
for the Kuomintang.

The Effect of the May Thirtieth Movement
on Organizational Policies, to July, 1926
As a direct result of the May Thirtieth Movement, Communist
Party membership increased tenfold, from 1,000 in May, 1925, to
10,000 six months later [Doc. 1, p. 43]. The membership of the
Chinese Communist Youth Corps had jumped to 9,000 by September,

1925.58 Impressive as they are, these figures fall short of indicating the full impact of the May Thirtieth Movement on the organization of the Chinese Communist Party.

The May Thirtieth Movement revealed to the Communists the strength of the labor movement and, by virtue of its control of the labor movement, the potential power of the Communist Party itself.

The Shanghai General Strike was led by the General Labor Union, itself a product of the May Thirtieth Incident. The General Labor Union became the driving force behind the Joint Committee, composed of delegates of labor unions, student federations, and street unions of the petty bourgeoisie, which was formed under Communist auspices to promote an anti-imperialist united front. Since Communists controlled the General Labor Union and were able also to win control of the student federations, they in fact dominated the Joint Committee. Thus, in the words of the "Brief History," the Communist Party succeeded in centralizing in itself the power of directing the revolutionary movement [Doc. 1, pp. 40-42].59

Strikes in British and Japanese-owned factories, accompanied by national revolutionary slogans, reached a peak in July and the early part of August. They then began to decline. Negotiated settlements were arranged, beginning with agreements ending strikes in Japanese-owned textile mills. Meanwhile, militarists of the Mukden Clique began actively to suppress the labor movement. The General Labor Union was closed down in mid-September. Labor leaders were arrested. Communist sources assert that the decline of the May Thirtieth strike wave was facilitated by bourgeois compromise. They point out that the Chinese chambers of commerce, which they regard as organs of the big bourgeoisie, refused in the first place to participate in the Joint Committee, and later acted as intermediaries between foreign owners and striking workers. As early as July 10, 1925, when the strike wave was at its height, the Chinese Communist Party issued a declaration accusing the big bourgeoisie of compromise. It drew a line of demarcation between the national revolutionary forces—workers, students, and the petty bourgeoisie —and the big bourgeoisie.60 The Communists later also accused the petty bourgeoisie of vacillation and held it partly responsible for the decline of the strikes.61

Thus, to the Communists, the May Thirtieth Movement demonstrated the hostility of the big bourgeoisie and the vacillation of the petty bourgeoisie, at the same time revealing the potentiality of their own party.

As the strike wave began to decline in August, the Central Committee of the Chinese Communist Party ordered a policy of retreat. Anti-imperialist national revolutionary slogans were replaced by minimum economic demands for workers and political demands of a local nature. The Party justified this as necessary, in order first to preserve whatever gains that had been made, secondly, to prevent complete smashing of the labor movement, and, thirdly, to maintain the good will of the petty bourgeoisie.62 The CC rejected the course of armed insurrection designed to establish proletarian dictatorship which was advocated by certain Party members and workers. Such a Left-deviationist course was born of moods of despair, the CC said, and signified not the will to victory but the seeking of a "noble" way out of a difficult situation.63

At the beginning of October, 1925, an enlarged plenum of the CC was convened in Peking. The CC took stock of the objective situation which had changed so radically as a result of the May Thirtieth Movement and re-evaluated its policies. A major organizational question was what effect, if any the May Thirtieth Movement had had on the relations between the Kuomintang and the Chinese Communist Party. The need to re-examine Kuomintang-Communist relations was accentuated by the growing influence of Tai Chi-t'ao's views, which centered on the argument that Communists were utilizing the Kuomintang to develop their own organization and influence.64

Ch'en Tu-hsiu later asserted that he had submitted a proposal to the Political Resolution Committee at the Plenum which stated that Tai's pamphlets were not random expressions but were indicative of the bourgeoisie's attempt to strengthen their own power for the purpose of checking the proletariat and going over to the counter-revolution. He had proposed then, Ch'en asserted, the immediate withdrawal of Communists from the KMT in order to maintain the Chinese Communist Party's own political independence and in order to lead the masses without being checked by the KMT's policies. This proposal, according to Ch'en, was opposed by the Comintern delegate and responsible members of the CC on the ground that it would be equivalent to opposing the KMT. Ch'en said that he was thus unable to maintain his proposal and accepted the majority opinion of the CC and international discipline.65

The Enlarged Plenum resolved that Communists should remain within the Kuomintang. To cope with the challenge of Taichitaoism, the CC re-emphasized the policy, first introduced by Voitinskii in late 1923, of allying with the Left Wing against the Right. The CC ordered Communists to distinguish clearly between the Right and Left wings and above all to avoid confusing themselves with the Kuomintang Left. (See Part IV, pp. 208-9)

The caution against confusing Communists with the Left Wing was part of the policy of strengthening the independent character of the Chinese Communist Party which was emphasized at the Plenum. This too was a concept Voitinskii had previously suggested in order to counteract Maring's tendency to stress developing the Communist position within the Kuomintang. However, some Communists found it difficult to strike a correct balance between executing the tasks of the Kuomintang and of the Chinese Communist Party. This was particularly the case with Communists who joined the Communist Party and the Kuomintang almost simultaneously after 1922. In 1925, according to "What Party Members Should Know," Right-deviationist tendencies were even more dangerous and prevalent among Party members than Left-deviationist tendencies. While Left-inclined members insisted on conducting an independent proletarian revolutionary movement to establish proletarian dictatorship, Right-inclined Communists neglected the Communists' own organizations.66 Such Rightist tendencies were severely criticized in Document 2, the resolutions on organization adopted by the CC at the Enlarged Plenum. Party members were apt to work as individuals in labor unions, in the Kuomintang, and among the masses, the CC said. Such persons appeared to be representatives of the various mass movements in the Chinese Communist Party, the CC declared, rather than executors of the KCT's policies among the masses [Doc. 2, p. 5].

Communists in Canton were particularly exposed to the pitfalls of dual membership, since many leaders of the Kwangtung Regional Committee held important posts in the Kuomintang. T'an P'ing-shan, for instance, was a member of the KMT Central Executive Committee and headed the all-important KMT Organization Department.67 They tended to stress achieving Communist objectives by infiltrating Kuomintang organs, particularly after Sun Yat-sen's death in March, 1925.

The Kwangtung Communists were singled out for criticism by the CC. They had failed to utilize the revolutionary tide to consolidate and develop the Party, said the CC. Although they were able to influence the workers and peasants ideologically, they had failed to consolidate this influence organizationally. The Kwangtung comrades, the CC continued, worked individually in the KMT, the labor unions, and the peasant associations, and ignored the interests of the Party as a whole. They had failed to make use of the Hongkong-Canton strike to absorb workers and peasants into the Communist Party [Doc. 2, p. 4].

In order to build up an independent Communist working force, the CC resolved that unless absolutely necessary Communists should not join the Kuomintang or engage in its work. The CC at least considered ordering Communists not to help develop KMT organization wherever Communists had not already established an influence among the masses, particularly in South and Central China [Doc. 20, p. 3].

The CC stressed the need for expansion along with Party independence. It declared that the Chinese Communist Party's propaganda and organization must be independent and expanded, particularly in

Kwangtung. Communists must expand the Chinese Communist Party everywhere, particularly where the Kuomintang had influence [Doc. 20, p. 4]. The CC declared that the Party was in a period of transition from a small organization to a mass party and that the transitional phase should end as soon as possible [Doc. 2, p. 5].

The building of a mass party required not only increase of Party membership but improvement of the Party's social composition, which had been predominantly intellectual.68 In line with this objective, the CC denounced as erroneous the idea of many local Communists that every Party member must understand Marxism and possess a high degree of working capacity. The idea that quantitative growth was contingent upon development of the Party's capacity for internal education, the CC declared, was a unique obstacle to becoming a mass party. The CC ordered the elimination of "cumbersome formalities" in enlisting workers, peasants, and students. While it set the probation period for intellectuals at three months, it set the probation period of workers and peasants at only one month [Doc. 2, p. 4].

The CC laid new stress on the need to win over the masses of workers and peasants. It declared: "It is absolutely true that the future destiny of the Chinese revolutionary movement depends entirely upon whether or not the Chinese Communist Party will be able to organize and lead the masses."[Doc. 2, p. 2]. The Enlarged Plenum paid special attention to organization of the peasantry on a national scale. In a letter to the peasantry dated October 10, 1925, the Enlarged Plenum outlined demands for the peasantry and the method of organizing peasant associations. Although some people might say that the peasantry in Kwangtung were able to organize because of the assistance of the National Government, the letter states, such a statement was only half true. The National Government in Kwangtung had unquestionably helped the peasants. At the same time, however, there had been instances of collaboration between the Kuomintang Right Wing, the landlords, the Merchant Corps, and the Army with the aim of destroying peasant associations and oppressing the peasantry; about these the National Government could do nothing. Thus, it was up to the peasants themselves to struggle for their own organization. The Enlarged Plenum pledged Communist support to the peasantry of the entire country.69

By July, 1926, Party membership had expanded threefold, from 10,000 to 30,000 [Doc. 4, p. 73; Doc. 1, p. 2]. The CC nevertheless continued to stress the need for further expansion. An Enlarged Plenum emphasized the slogans, 'Expand the Party!' and 'Enlist more revolutionary workers, peasants, and intellectuals!'"[Doc. 4, p. 76].

A comparison of the Central Committee's resolutions on organization of July, 1926, with the resolutions of October, 1925, reveals that the CC was increasingly concerned over the quality of the

Party membership. It was particularly anxious over the shortage
of directing personnel. Although a minimum force of 355 responsible Party workers was needed, the CC said, only 120 persons at
most were available [Doc. 4, p. 80]. Leading Party workers were
criticized. They tended to be mere employees, and had a tendency
toward corruption. The CC concluded that Party headquarters of
all levels, from the CC down to Party cells, lacked sufficient
strength of leadership and training [Doc. 26, p. 68]. The Party was
short of personnel for work among the masses, particularly in the
labor and women's movements [Doc. 28, p. 96; Doc. 32, p. 111].

Party Structure
The Party's structure was based on the Bolshevik principle of
democratic centralism. The CC defined the system as follows:
"The organic system of the Party extends from the Central Committee to the regional or local committees, from the regional or
local committees to sectional committees, and from the sectional
committees to the executive committees of Party cells and conferences of unit chiefs. The interrelationship of this system must be extremely close" [Doc. 4, p. 78].
The Party cell was the basic unit in the organizational structure.
Party cells were not divisions, the CC explained, but were the
nuclei of the Party, joined together according to the Bolshevik pattern. There were two types of Party cells: (1) cells in factories,
villages, and schools; and (2) cells of districts and streets. The
cells were responsible for the Party's development and activities.
The Party slogan, "All work to Party cells!" typifies the importance attributed to cell organization [Doc. 4, pp. 76-77].
Party cells were particularly important as the Party's organ of
contact with the masses. This is illustrated in Document 3, "Plans
on the Organization and Development of Party Cells," issued by the
Party's Northern Regional Committee on December 10, 1925. Here
it is stated: "The cell is the kernel of the Party among the masses
...the Party's ears, eyes, arms and legs among the masses." [Doc.
3, pp. 31-32]. Members of Party cells were indoctrinated with
Bolshevik principles of centralization and discipline. They were
instructed to "collectivize life; oppose individualism; have absolute
confidence in the Party; oppose all subjective points of view" [Doc.
3, p. 33].
In big cells, small units were established to carry out such tasks
as collection of dues. In big industrial centers and villages, sections
were formed by grouping together a number of neighboring cells.
As the CC emphasized, the small units and sections were not regular
divisions of the Party, but were merely organs set up in accordance
with the need to facilitate the work of Party cells [Doc. 4, pp. 77-78].
It is indicative of the Party's growth after the May Thirtieth Move-

ment that sections were not ordered established until October, 1925 [Doc. 2, p. 3]. Small units were ordered set up only in July, 1926 [Doc. 4, p. 77].

The organization of regional committees suggests flexibility in the Party's approach to organization. There was apparently no strict regulation on the jurisdiction and authority of the regional committees. When first organized, the Hunan Regional Committee had jurisdiction over the local committees of Pingsiang and Anyuan in Kiangsi in addition to the province of Hunan.70 The Northern Regional Committee supervised Party work in Hopeh, Shansi, and Manchuria, but the Peking Local Committee was subordinated directly to the CC. [Doc. 2, p. 30].

The Kwangtung Regional Committee, with authority over Party work in Kwangtung and Kwangsi, was by far the largest of the regional committees. With headquarters at Canton, this committee exerted direct influence on Communists working in KMT organs and the Army. By 1925, the Kwangtung Regional Committee had a fully developed organization headed by Ch'en Yen-nien, the eldest son of Ch'en Tu-hsiu. There were six departments concerned respectively with organization, propaganda, and the military, labor, peasants, and women's movements. The Committee ran its own training classes for Party cadres, its own newspaper, the Jen-min chou-k'an, and its own Party School.71

The Central Committee in Shanghai, on the other hand, apparently had only four departments: the organization and propaganda departments set up in 1921, and the women's and publications departments in addition. It was only in October, 1925 that the CC ordered the establishment of committees on the peasant movement, the labor movement, and the military movement [Doc. 2, p. 2]. By July, 1926, however, only the committee on the labor movement had been established.72 Although the Central Committee was the highest Party organ,73 considerable autonomy was exercised by the regional committees, particularly the Kwangtung Regional Committee.

Beginning in the fall of 1925, the Central Committee launched a number of moves to centralize authority in its own hands. It placed new emphasis, for instance, on the role of special commissioners appointed by the CC. In october, 1925, the CC declared it had done very little directing work in many localities. It ordered an increase in the number of special commissioners authorized to direct the regional and local committies in the execution of their tasks [Doc. 2, p. 2].74 The tendency toward centralization is evident also in the CC's decision to transfer from the Youth Corps to itself the authority to direct the student movement.

Prior to the May Thirtieth Movement, the Youth Corps had served the Party in a unique capacity. Since the membership of the Corps was consistently two or three times as great as the Party's, the

Youth Corps constituted a much-needed auxiliary. However, Party membership caught up with Corps membership during the May Thirtieth Movement. By November, 1925, memberships in Party and Corps each stood at 10,000 [Doc. 1, p. 43]. The Corps continued through 1926 to lag behind the Party. By April, 1927, there were 35,000 Youth Corps members, compared with 57,963 in the Party.[75]

As Party membership began to outdistance that of the Corps, Party-Corps relations became increasingly strained. Document 5, a circular notice on relations between the Party and Youth Corps issued by the Northern Regional Committee on March 26 [1926], states in part: "The CP's policy is carried out among the masses of youths by the CY, which receives its political policies directly from the CP. No one has ever doubted this ...In recent months, relations between the Party and the Youth Corps under the jurisdiction of the Northern Regional Committee have not been very satisfactory" [Doc. 5, p. 54].

At the Second Enlarged Plenum held in July, 1926, the Central Committee criticized the CY's failure to become "genuinely popular" and announced the decision to transfer leadership of the student movement from the CY to the Party [Doc. 6, pp. 115-16]. The "Brief History" asserts that mistakes had been made in the student movement because the CY had held leadership. The situation would definitely improve, it states, as soon as the Central Committee took over control of the student movement [Doc. 1, p. 44].

The Party's Training and Propaganda Policies, to July, 1926

The Party's expansion following the May Thirtieth Movement brought the question of internal education to the forefront. In Document 7, resolutions on propaganda adopted in October, 1925, the CC stated: "Special attention should also be paid to agitation within the Party. Such agitation should encourage the entire membership from bottom up to participate in positive political life" [Doc. 7, p. 57].

The Party subjected every member of every cell to a continuous program of training and education. Such indoctrination was the special responsibility of the "educational propagandists," who were regarded as the central elements of Party cells. Their duty was to carry out the Party's political and ideological propaganda, help cell members to analyze current problems from the theoretical point of view, help them to understand the Party's policies, and improve their political interest and working capacity. Document 3 emphasizes the importance of the discussion method in stimulating interest and participation of cell members, and cautions educational propagandists against employing "injection-type" lectures [Doc. 3, pp. 36-38].

By 1925-1926, the KCT had developed two types of Party schools to supplement the training provided members through participation in cell activities. General schools were established under local committees to train workers as mass agitators. The training period was fixed at two weeks, or at most one month. Directing personnel for the Party were trained in advanced Party schools set up under regional committees. The training period in such schools was three months. The CC emphasized that Party members attending such schools must not become separated from the masses. They were required simultaneously to work among the masses in order to acquire true proletarian ideas [Doc. 7, p. 59].

Document 9 is an outline of the curriculum of the two major types of Party schools, giving detailed instructions on lecture topics and reference material. It reveals a strong emphasis on theory and reliance on standard Western works. The curriculum of the advanced schools included a heavy dose of the history of the socialist movement and the Russian revolutionary movement. The attention given to theory, even in the curriculum of schools for workers, reflects the Party's concern over its lack of theoretical capacity. In July, 1926, the CC stated that in view of the Party's lack of members with a command of theory, all the strength it did possess in this connection was to be concentrated in the periodical Hsin ch'ing-nien. Theoretical articles in other Party periodicals were therefore to be published in the Hsin ch'ing-nien [Doc. 8, p. 81].

Aside from regular Party schools, the KCT set up training classes to prepare personnel for specialized work among the masses. In July, 1926, training classes for low-level cadres working in the labor movement were ordered established in the big cities. Party headquarters of all levels were instructed to set up training classes to prepare women members working among peasant women and female laborers [Doc. 28, p. 96; Doc. 32, p. 112].

The most promising Party members were sent to the Soviet Union for training. According to the "Brief History," the Shanghai Communist group began in 1920 to dispatch members to study at the Communist University for the Toilers of the East [Doc. 1, p. 11]. The Sun Yat-sen University for Chinese Toilers was established in Moscow in January, 1926 under the presidency of Karl Radek.76 The student body included Kuomintang members as well as Communists.

A detailed guide to the principles and objectives of Communists being trained in Moscow is given in Document 10, which gives detailed instructions on the means of systematizing thought and study, disciplining action, collectivizing individuality, and training members to become professional revolutionaries. Drawn up by members of the Chinese Socialist Youth Corps and the Chinese Communist Party Branch in Moscow, the document offers an insight into the Party's conception of the ideal Chinese Communist.

The KCT's program of internal training and propaganda was

carried out simultaneously with an expanding program of disseminating propaganda outside the Party. The great importance attached to propaganda activities is evident in the fact that, besides the Organization Department, the Propaganda Department was the only department established at the First Party Congress.

Party cells, particularly the small units of Party cells, were charged with the special responsibility of propaganda work among the masses. The duty of small units, said the CC, was to enable labor comrades to know and understand every detail of the daily struggle [Doc. 7, p. 58]. The CC outlined two principal methods of mass agitation: propaganda mobilization and the establishment of worker's clubs. The function of propaganda mobilization, said the CC, was to focus the attention of all classes on certain specific events or problems, and should be well planned in advance. The CC stated that workers' clubs had served an important purpose before the Party was established. The Party should further develop them by making use of their good points and introducing certain changes to suit the Party's needs. Especially important were the "self-study groups" of the clubs, which were charged with the duty of absorbing non-Party members. Communists were instructed to carry on such activities as discussion of newspaper articles and interpretation of current events in the self-study groups [Doc. 7, pp. 57-59].

The CC's resolutions of July, 1926, on the work of the Propaganda Department suggests that the Communist propaganda program was by that time fairly well developed. The resolutions reveal a keen awareness of the importance of public opinion. The CC ordered the establishment of a publicity section to furnish Party organs with weekly and monthly summaries of the editorials and news reports of Chinese and foreign newspapers and magazines. The CC also ordered the Propaganda Department to conduct a general survey of intellectual and press opinion, to be followed by monthly surveys of the reaction of the general public and various groups to Communist "propaganda mobilization" campaigns. A program of workers' and peasants' correspondence was initiated to encourage workers and peasants to write to the Party freely about their living conditions, attitudes, and problems. [Doc. 8, pp. 82, 83, 86].

Communists in all phases of propaganda work were told to adjust the language and content of propaganda to the level of those to whom the propaganda was directed. "To be effective in our work of agitation," the CC declared, "we must enable the masses, even the most backward workers and ricksha coolies, to understand our propaganda ...it is best to point out the Party's accomplishments and the fact that the Party has already fought for and obtained concrete benefits for the working class and the peasantry. Such accomplishments are our point of departure in getting hold of the masses." [Doc. 7, pp. 56-57].

This document is translated from the original Chinese text of the resolutions on organization adopted at an enlarged plenum of the Central Committee of the Chinese Communist Party. The document is not dated, but the resolutions appear to have been adopted at the Enlarged Plenum of the CC held in Peking in October, 1925. This deduction is confirmed by Document 4, which summarizes the October, 1925 resolutions [Doc. 4, p. 80]. Our translation is based on a copy of the original Chinese text made by the Japanese in Peking and sent with a letter of transmittal by Major General Shigeru Honjo, Japanese Military Attaché in Peking, to the Japanese Vice-Minister of War on May 26, 1927. The copy was filed in <u>Mitsu dai nikki,</u> 1927, V, and is available on microfilm at the East Asiatic Library, Columbia University.

RESOLUTIONS ON THE QUESTION
OF ORGANIZATION

[1]   1. Several hundred thousand workers of Shanghai, Hongkong, and Canton participated in the latest national revolutionary movement by instituting strikes. The most backward portion of the proletariat in northern and central China also took up arms for the same cause. Thus, several million workers have become conscious of political and economic struggle. This is a period unprecedented in Chinese history! The Chinese Communist Party should give special attention to the struggle of the proletariat and guide its participation in the national liberation movement.

2. As a result of the high tide of the national revolutionary movement and the enthusiastic participation of the immature proletariat, the function of the Chinese Communist Party has naturally been enhanced many times. We must on the one hand assemble and organize [2] the proletariat; on the other hand, we must provide it with political training and education. Through study we have come to understand the means of unifying the peasantry and allying it with other democratic elements. Before we can perform this historically significant duty, however, we must first of all expand our Party by absorbing into the Party the proletariat and the most revolutionary elements of the advanced intelligentsia. The present phase of the Chinese Communist movement and the national revolutionary movement is marked by the daily rising of the revolutionary tide among the masses. It is absolutely true that the future destiny of the Chinese revolutionary movement depends entirely upon whether or not the

Chinese Communist Party will be able to organize and lead the masses.

3. The KCT should be able to direct and organize the revolutionary workers, handicraftsmen, and intellectuals, admit them into the Party, and provide them with proper organization. Within the Party, it is necessary to have a centralized organization of active elements, from the lower levels to the higher levels, from the cells to the CC. There must also be clearly defined and close relations between the low and high levels.

In view of the increase of Party membership, we plan to enlarge the CC considerably at the next congress. There should be definite organization of and clear relationships between the various departments of the CC, such as the Organization, Propaganda, Women's, Publications, and Distribution departments. If possible, the secretaries of the CC and the regional committees should not hold concurrent posts in the departments. Committees on the labor, peasant, and military movements should be established under the CC, to be responsible for the execution of regular tasks connected with such movements. The number of special commissioners appointed by the CC should be increased so that they may be able actually to direct the regional and local committee in the execution of their tasks.

Our experience of the past few months indicates that the CC has done very little directing work at many places, particularly in the [3] North, and that there has been uneven distribution of directing personnel. The Party's development is of the utmost importance in a period following a high revolutionary tide. We should pay particular attention to the North, because the majority of workers there have not yet taken part in the present movement. The failure at both Tientsin and Tangshan necessitates an acceleration in the development of our Party's work in that area. We should therefore strengthen the organization of the Northern Regional Committee to enable it to supervise Party work in Chihli, Shansi, and the Three Eastern Provinces. The Peking Local Committee is independently organized and is not subordinated to the Northern Regional Committee.

4. The regional and local committees should on the one hand carry out all the CC's instructions and, with reference to questions of political strategy, ask the CC. . . [missing. Burned?] and send men to various places (departments, party fractions, workers' clubs, and research societies) under their jurisdiction to supervise the routine work of our Party.

At certain places such as Shanghai, our Party has already expanded considerably. We must organize sectional committees with the sections defined by area, under [local and regional] committees. This new method of organization is absolutely essential because: (a) it is convenient in terms of direction; and (b) it provides an even easier means to expand Party organization.

The duties of Party cells, particularly those in factories, are to consolidate our influence organizationally and continuously, and regularly to absorb revolutionary workers into the Party.

5. At present the most important organizational problem is the consolidation of our Party's influence among the masses. With the revolutionary tide running high, the mere fact that the masses are willing to accept our proposals is insufficient to prove that we really have influence among them and can actually direct them. We [4] must utilize the revolutionary high tide as follows:

a) Eliminate cumbersome formalities in enlisting revolutionary workers, students, and peasants into the Party. The probation period of workers and peasants is one month; the probation period for intellectuals is three months.

b) Organize cells and party fractions in labor organizations, peasant associations, and organizations of revolutionary intellectuals.

It is only by joining our Party that the revolutionary elements of society may receive Party training and really comprehend Party theories. We must not indulge the vain hope that many ready-made Party members can be acquired from Chinese society or that workers in big industries are natural members of the KCT and may join the Party as long as they are class-conscious and loyal to the Revolution, without fulfilling other conditions.

During this revolutionary period, many of our responsible comrades in various localities entertain the erroneous idea that every Communist member should understand Marxism and possess a high capacity for work. They think that if Party membership develops merely in quantity instead of quality, this would not only be without benefit to the Party but would further intensify the looseness of Party organization. Hence, many of them believe that the quantitative development of our Party should be contingent upon the development of the Party's capacity for internal education. This erroneous conception is a unique obstacle to making our Party a Party of the masses.

During the period of high tide in the revolutionary movement and active struggle of the Hongkong workers, the Kwangtung Regional Committee failed to utilize the opportunity to consolidate and develop our Party. The Kwangtung Regional Committee is able to influence the ideas of the masses of workers and peasants but it has failed to consolidate such influence organizationally by absorbing worker and peasant elements into the Party and establishing Party fractions in various organizations. This is erroneous.

[5]   Our Kwangtung comrades work individually in the KMT, labor unions, peasant associations, and the Army. They do not stand on the ground of Party interests as a powerful Party, organized and properly supervised, to lead the proletariat to struggle for position in the national revolutionary movement.

6. Our comrades and committee members of various levels (the CC and local committees) generally work as individuals in labor unions and the KMT, and among the student masses, or they limit their direction to certain specific tasks. Hence, they appear to be representatives of the various movements in the KCT rather than executors of the Party's policies and tasks while participating in such movements.

Such phenomena occur during the period of transition of the Party from a small organization to a party of the masses. This transitional phase should come to an end in the shortest possible time. We should enable the entire Party to come into contact with the proletariat, the peasantry, and the intelligentsia.

7. At this time, the question of the united front of the proletariat, peasantry, petty bourgeoisie, and all democratic elements is largely the question of relations between the KCT and the KMT. Hence, in our organizational policies, we should pay particular attention to our Party's organization wherever the KMT has influence, for instance Kwangtung, so that we may expand the united front and strengthen our cooperation with the KMT Left Wing.

8. The recent reactionary and oppressive policy of the militarists and capitalists is first of all the inevitable result of the development of economic struggle and, secondly, the result of the failure of the majority of the laboring masses to participate fully in the revolutionary movement.

In view of the existence of reaction, we should resort to secret [6] underground work at certain places. This does not mean, however, that we should revert to the previous condition of our Party, under which we merely carried on underground work among the laboring class and the intelligentsia. We should simultaneously build up a clandestine organization and exert every effort to engage openly in the political movement. At all times, we must firmly fix in mind the fact that our Party cannot become a party of the masses through secret work alone.

9. Aside from the development of our Party's organization and work, the development and expansion of the CY to penetrate the masses of labor and peasant youths and the students is of great significance and assistance to the work of making our Party a Party of the masses and to the national revolutionary movement. Hence the Enlarged Plenum considers the rendering of assistance toward the expansion and consolidation of the CY organization and the educational training of CY members as tasks of great importance at the present time.

Document 3 is translated from an original Chinese document, which was issued as Correspondence Circular No. 1 by the Organization Department of the Northern Regional Committee of the KCT on December 10, 1925. Our translation is based on a copy made by the Japanese in Peking and sent with a letter of transmittal by the Japanese Military Attaché in Peking to the Vice-Minister of War in Tokyo on June 14, 1927. The copy is avialable in <u>Mitsu dai nikki,</u> 1927, V, and is also on microfilm at the East Asiatic Library, Columbia University.

PLANS ON THE ORGANIZATION
OF PARTY CELLS

[30] <u>Significance of Cell Organization</u>

1. The cell is the basic organ and organizational unit of the Party. Without cell organization, the Party would lack foundation; if the cells are not strong, the Party would become loose. Hence, solidity of Party organization is completely dependent on the strength of cell organization.

2. The cell is the Party's school for education and propaganda. If [31] we desire to learn proletarian revolutionary theories and policies, the only way is to go through the cell. If we want our ideas and actions to be proletarian, the cell again is the only place where we can attain this goal. Hence, if we desire to understand proletarian revolutionary theories and policies and to make our ideas and actions proletarian, we cannot do all this in what we call universities or research institutes, but in cells.

3. The cell is the kernel of the Party among the masses. All policies and plans of the Party must go through Party cells before they can materialize. Otherwise, even if the Party had very sound policies and plans, they would be mere empty words. We depend entirely on Party cells to explain the Party's policies and plans and to carry [32] out propaganda and agitation among the masses.

4. The cell is the Party's instrument for development. If the Party is in need of development, it is entirely dependent on Party cells to bring this about. The cell is the organization of the Party among the masses. Since the life of the cell is the life of the masses, if there is no life among the masses, there is no life in the cell. The cell comes in contact with the masses daily, and the Party develops with the masses as its objective. Hence the Party depends upon the cell for its development.

5. The cell is the Party's ears, eyes, arms, and legs among the masses. The Party must have cell organization before it can understand the demands of the masses and the masses can recognize the guidance of the Party. Only thus can the Party function among and lead the masses.

6. The cell is the center of life of the Party and of every Party member. The life of every Party member should be a part of the life of the Party and the life of the Party is concentrated in Party cells. Therefore the life of every Party member cannot be separated from the cell. If a Party member separates his or her life from the cell, then he or she cannot understand the whole life of the Party. The separation of a Party member from the life of the cell is equivalent to separation from the life of the Party; and separation from the life of the Party is equivalent to separation from the Party.

7. The cell is the Party's weapon of struggle. In order to acquire fighting strength, it is necessary for the Party to absorb the vast organized masses. The cell represents a part of the organized masses of the Party. It is the synthesis of the Party's crack army.

8. In short, the significance of cell organization is as follows:

   a) It is the basic organ and organizational unit of the Party.
   b) It is the school of the Party for education and propaganda.
   c) It is the kernel of the Party among the masses.
   d) It is the instrument for development of the Party.
   e) It is the center of life of the Party.
   f) It is the Party's weapon of struggle.

Standards for Internal Party Education and Propaganda

9. Politicalize ideas; oppose the hatred of politics in the minds of intellectuals and scholars.

10. Discipline action; oppose anarchist tendencies.

11. Systematize studies; oppose romantic and academic tendencies.

12. Collectivize life; oppose individualism.

13. Have absolute confidence in the Party; oppose all subjective points of view.

14. Cultivate the proletarian revolutionary philosophy of life and become professional proletarian revolutionaries; oppose petty bourgeois romantic revolutionary ideas and actions.

Principles of External Agitation and Activities

15. See clearly the objective environment and the objectives of the masses.

16. Study the psychology and demands of the masses.

17. Make use of various types of slogans to summon, assemble, and organize the masses.

18. Make sure that all our slogans are adapted to the demands of the masses; the simpler and the clearer the slogans, the more practical they will be.

19. In our practical work we must always get hold of the progressive elements among the masses. Only by so doing can we avoid isolating ourselves.

20. When we lead the masses to engage in daily struggle, we always absorb the progressive elements into our Party in order to [34] strengthen the Party's directing capacity and to expand our organization.

21. Make use of every means and opportunity to raise the demands and courage of the masses, particularly when they are in despair.

22. When the masses are assembled, we should plan to organize and lead them to realize our policy.

23. Every opportunity should be utilized to engage in agitation among the masses so that our flag will march at the head of every movement.

24. When the Party's masses achieve victory, we should hold out new demands or augment old ones in order to strengthen mass organizations. We should explain to them that not all our victories are presented to us by the objective situation, but that they are the results of our own struggle.

25. When our Party achieves victory we must not be arrogant. We should be judicious in further consolidating the foundation of our mass organizations in order to strengthen our fighting force. Only by so doing can we resist new oppression.

26. When we fail we need not be disappointed. We must study with great care the causes of our failure from the subjective and objective points of view. In particular, we must study our errors. Only thus can we enrich our experience in struggle so that we may prepare for new struggles to come.

Cell Meetings

27. Content of cell meetings:
   a) Political report
   b) Discussion of concrete methods to realize the Party's policies
   c) Discussion of means to develop the Party
   d) Discussion of· the distribution of work among our comrades
[35]   e) Comment on the work of our comrades
   f) Report and discussion of life within and outside the Party
   g) Proposals

28. Cell meetings should be held weekly, and there should be a definite time and place for such meetings.

29. It is unnecessary for the cell secretary to be chairman at every cell meeting, but it is his duty to designate comrades to serve as the chairman by rotation so that they may practice the techniques of chairmanship.

30. If a comrade is unable to attend a cell meeting due to reasons

of business, he should ask the cell secretary for leave of absence
and present the reasons for such request prior to the meeting. Those
who fail to ask for leave of absence are considered absentees without
cause.

31. When a cell meeting is in session, any comrade who wishes to
leave halfway through the meeting or earlier must explain to the
chairman his reasons for doing so. He may leave only with the consent of the chairman.

32. Cell secretaries should talk to those comrades who fail to
attend cell meetings without cause. They should employ all means
to make every Party member attend meetings and take an active
interest in them.

Responsibilities of Cell Secretaries

33. Cell secretaries are not merely technical experts but Party
organizers. Hence they are vested with the responsibility of carrying
out the policies and plans entrusted to them by the local committees.

34. Cell secretaries bear the responsibility of educating our comrades. In order to achieve this aim, they must be active among their
cell comrades. They must get to know them and study their inclina-
tions and demands, their good points as well as shortcomings. Only
36] thus can they lead their comrades to work.

35. Since cell secretaries direct all members of the respective
cells, they must pay attention to their own behavior, ideas, and
speech. When they commit an error, it is not merely a personal
error. It affects all other cell members as well.

36. Cell secretaries should take cognizance of the external situation and the capacity of their cell comrades, motivate them to engage
in activities among the masses, agitate and organize the masses,
and be responsible for the Party's current proposals and policies.

37. Cell secretaries should formulate concrete plans of work for
the cells so that all work may be carried out methodically. They
should also enable every comrade to work. Only thus can Party cells
become alive and able to function among the masses.

38. Cell secretaries should pay special attention to the progressive
elements among the masses, motivate themselves and other comrades to engage in activities among the masses, and absorb to the
fullest extent the progressive elements into the Party.

39. Cell secretaries should do their best to attend cell meetings of
the CY in order to present political reports and to carry out the
Party's supervision of the CY. They are responsible for the execution of all the Party's duties with reference to the CY.

Responsibilities of Educational Propagandists to Party Cells

40. The most important tasks of educational propagandists of Party
cells consist of the work of political education and ideological

propaganda. More important still, political propagandists should enable comrades in general to analyze various current problems from the theoretical point of view. Such are the duties of educational propagandists.

[37]   41. Since the responsibility of educational propagandists is so great, they should not have to recite the propaganda outline word for word or pronounce stereotyped theories at cell meetings. It is their duty, however, to enable our comrades to acquire a clear and precise understanding of reports after they are presented and to comprehend the significance of Party policies. It is their duty also to increase our comrades' interest in politics, capacity for work, and tools for carrying out Party directives.

42. In order to realize the above tasks, educational propagandists should avoid "injection-type" reports to the best of their ability and rather employ the method of stimulating our comrades at cell meetings, drawing questions from them and encouraging discussion. At the end of meetings, they should formulate conclusions to resolve the difficult questions raised by our comrades and criticize our comrades' point of view. This is the means to enable our comrades to understand certain kinds of problems with greater clarity.

43. Especially when attending cell meetings of worker comrades, educational propagandists should pay even greater attention to their objective capacity to understand. Before making reports or discussing questions, they should take note of their degree of understanding of and interest in such questions. Great care must be exercised even in selecting the language to be used so that it may properly convey our message. If this is not done, it would not be easy to make our worker comrades really understand and take interest in these problems.

44. Educational propagandists not only take charge of the work of political education and ideological propaganda in Party cells but render assistance to cell secretaries in the entire work of direction. Hence there should be close relations between educational [38] propagandists and cell secretaries. We may say that educational propagandists are the central elements in Party cells.

Meetings of Cell Secretaries

45. Since Party cells are the foundation of our Party, and since cell secretaries are organizers of the Party and directors of the cells, cell secretaries should frequently hold meetings to review and criticize the work of the various cells and to discuss concrete methods of execution of work.

46. Meetings of cell secretaries are called by the organization departments of local committees. In addition to the above-mentioned tasks, representatives of local committees appointed to attend meetings of cell secretaries should present reports on important current problems.

Technical Work

47. One day before cell meetings, cell secretaries must send out notices to all cell members and to educational propagandists who attend such meetings.

48. At each meeting cell secretaries should fill out the attendance record of each Party member. (This type of record is issued by local committees.)

49. Cell secretaries should distribute and sell all publications and propaganda material not only to Party members, but to non-Party members.

50. Cell secretaries should shoulder the responsibility of collecting Party membership dues. However, they should pay attention to the following:

a) Party members who are concurrently members of the CY do not pay Party membership dues.

b) The rules governing collection of Party membership dues are based on the section on collection of dues in the regulations revised at the Fourth Congress of our Party.

Upon the collection of membership dues each month, cell secretaries immediately turn them over to the local committees.

51. Cell secretaries should make reports on the work of the cells. (Forms on which such reports are made are issued by the Organization Department.)

52. Cell secretaries should order every comrade to submit weekly reports. (Report blanks are issued by the Organization Department.)

The following translation is based on the original Chinese text of
the resolutions on organization adopted at the Second Enlarged
Plenum of the Central Committee of the Chinese Communist Party
held in Shanghai, between July 12 and July 18, 1926. The resolutions
are part of a document which contains the CC's political report and
twelve resolutions adopted at the Plenum, introduced by the following
note prepared by the Secretariat of the Conference: "The Second Enlarged Conference of the Central Committee convened on July 12,
1926 and closed on July 18, 1926. The agenda consisted of fifteen
items. Twelve important resolutions were adopted. A number of
them, such as the resolutions on the peasant movement and the resolutions on the labor movement, require further supplementation.
(Note that this does not mean changing the meaning of the resolutions
but giving fuller explanations.) It was therefore decided to send the resolutions to the Secretariat for revision and printing. However, local
demand for the resolutions was so urgent following the conference that we
cannot wait until the process of revision is completed. Hence, the Secretariat has mimeographed the resolutions in their original form for
preliminary distribution. The resolutions will later be revised and
printed. The Enlarged Conference instructs all local Party headquarters to convene meetings of our comrades upon receipt of this
document. They should make detailed reports and enable every comrade to understand the important points of these resolutions and to
apply them in actual work. It is also hoped that our comrades will
be encouraged to discuss the resolutions. Results should be reported
to the Central Committee." This document is available in Su-lien
yin-mou..., III, "KCT," 60-121; see pages 73-81 for our Document 4.

RESOLUTIONS ON THE QUESTION OF
ORGANIZATION

[73] Experiences in Party Development and Weaknesses
    1. Since the last Enlarged Conference (October, 1925), our Party
organization has expanded threefold. In the past eight months, despite
the gradual ebbing of the tide of the May Thirtieth Movement, our
Party at all levels has been able to lead the mass movement under
various conditions. From the standpoint of the national revolutionary
movement, our Party has actually become a political nucleus. From
[74] the standpoint of the local mass movements, our Party has been assuming in many respects the position of leadership.
    2. We have gained the following experiences from organizational work:

a) Through movements of various kinds, we have been able to get close contacts with the great masses, to develop mass organizations, and to expand the Party itself.

b) Due to the emphasis on expanding our work, our Party has been able, where the revolutionary tide is relatively high and the mass movement is relatively developed, to absorb the masses, among whom we are building our basic organizations.

c) Due to the attention which we have begun to pay to the work of Party cells, the Party has improved its social composition, absorbed progressive elements, and penetrated the proletarian masses. Thus, we have secretly built a preliminary foundation.

3. While the experiences gained from actual work are fruitful, our Party is still extremely young organizationally and it has many major defects. Chief of these are:

a) Our Party at all levels still does not realize the real meaning of organizational work. Not grasping the political significance of organizational work, many regard it as merely technical.

b) The work of Party cells has not been truly established. The Party cells already in existence have merely acquired outward form. The Party at all levels fails to understand the significance of Party cells or their methods of work.

c) The work of Party fractions is extremely bad.

d) Party organs are unhealthy.

The Significance of Organizational Work

4. The significance of organizational work is not only technical but political. In other words, organizational work is the axis from [5] which the Party directs the mass movement. Without good organization the Party cannot direct an extensive mass movement or implement its policies. Good policy cannot be realized without good organization. A major characteristic of a Bolshevik Party is its organizational work. A young party depends on good organizational work in order to become Bolshevik, to grow from a small organization into a party of the masses, from an organization [for the study] of theories into a party of action, and to organize mass action through the basic work of Party cells.

5. Our Party is developing organizationally. There is, however, a great danger which may occur any time. This is the danger of weakness of the leadership and the failure of subjective capacity to meet objective requirements, resulting in the loss of many opportunities for action. Weakness of the leadership would incur especially great losses in times of mass political action. This is the most serious organizational problem.

The objective course of the revolutionary movement is daily developing. Our Party's chief organizational duty is to push forward the revolutionary movement, hold the center of the movement, and

guide it in every possible way. This is the duty not only of the Organization department of Party headquarters of all levels. The present
Enlarged Conference has decided that hereafter the Central Committee should frequently dispatch special commissioners to the regional
committees, which should in turn send special commissioners to the
local committees, to inspect and execute these tasks. In times of
crisis at any particular place, the commissioners would be all the
more necessary.

6. What is the greatest obstacle to organizational work? It is the
skeptical psychology towards developing organizational work. Under
the present temporary militarist reaction, the development of the
revolutionary movement depends not only on the reactionary situation
but on the revolutionary masses of workers, peasants, and intellectuals. The problem at this time is: If the masses are not brought to
close contact with the proletarian Party's forces, they may easily
[76] walk into the camp of the comprador-bourgeoisie. From May Thirtieth to the present, the problem of the mass movement is: To
which force is the majority of the masses in the united front to belong? If our Party fails to expand and lead the masses, the forces of
the bourgeoisie and counterrevolution will be daily strengthened.
Consequently, the Enlarged Conference has directed its serious
attention to this problem and restates the Party's slogans, "Expand
the Party!" and "Enlist more revolutionary workers, peasants, and
intellectuals!"

7. One of the Party's chief organizational tasks is work among the
nonpartisan and unorganized masses. Our current important work is
to develop under many different forms and organizations masses
sympathetic to our Party. We have accomplished a great deal through
our work in the relief association, for instance, although local Party
organs do not pay sufficient attention to it. We should hereafter further direct our attention to and activate such organizations as relief
associations and athletic, educational, and cultural organizations.

The Significance and Methods of Work of Party Cells

8. A Party cell is not a division but the nucleus of our Party in
various factories, mines, schools, or areas. These many social
nuclei are joined together into one Party according to Bolshevik
principles. The organization of cells is precisely determined by
social and living conditions. However, the majority of our present
cells have lost this significance. They are merely divisions of our
Party organized on the basis of revolutionary elements gathered
from various social organizations or areas, and to whom Party
training is given. Party cells fail to make themselves the nuclei of
these social organizations or areas. Unless they perform this function, Party cells will never be capable of contacting and leading the
masses. This most serious defect must be remedied at once.

7]   9. There are five ways by which the above defects may be remedied in order to establish true Party cells.

a) At present, our Party is still founded on the local committees rather than Party cells, on the active workers of the local committees rather than those of Party cells. Hereafter, we must build the foundation of our Party on cells. We must hold the cells responsible for the establishment of the basic activities of the Party. Each cell should see that its activities are well distributed among its members so that each member should know and execute the slogan, "All work to Party cells!" Each cell should carry on the activities of the entire Party (such as the labor and peasant movements, cooperatives, relief associations, the women's movement, the youth movement, distribution of books and magazines, introduction of members, intelligence reports, communication of messages, etc., in accordance with the condition, membership, and the needs of each cell). During the period of secrecy, big Party cells may find it inconvenient to hold regular conferences of Party cell members because of the large membership. They may therefore be divided into small units to execute such tasks as the collection of Party dues, communication of orders, etc. We must remember, however, that the existence of small units is predicated on the above-mentioned situation and that they are not the basic organizations of the Party but merely subdivisions [of cells] in the factories, mines, and schools.

b) Powerful executive committees should be set up in **Party** cells to guide their work. In large cells where small units are established, the executive committee should be enlarged and should convene periodic meetings of the chiefs of the small units. The executive committee should have a planned, systematic, and progressive working program to carry out the resolutions and orders of the Party.

c) The nature of Party cells should be redefined in such a way that only Party cells of the following two types may be permitted to exist: (1) Party cells in factories, villages, or schools; (2) Party cells of streets or districts (determined on the basis of residential address). It is necessary to define the nature of Party cells in order to establish the work of Party cells and to avoid confusing their functions with those of Party fractions.

d) In big industrial areas (such as Shanghai, Hongkong, Wuhan, and Tientsin) and big villages, where organization is developed and the number of cells has increased, sectional committees, with the sections defined by area, should be set up under regional or local com-
78] mittees. When several neighboring cells are joined together, a sectional committee is organized to administer the work of all Party cells within the given area.

e) The organic system of the Party extends from the CC to the regional or local committees, from the regional or local committees to sectional committees, and from the sectional committees to the executive committees of Party cells and conferences of unit chiefs. The interrelationship of this system must be extremely close. The following organizational work should be strictly carried out among the masses, starting from the small units of Party cells: (1) Political action; (2) Development of work; (3) Distribution and circulation of books and newspapers; and (4) Collection of membership dues, etc.

10. In the process of development, any slackening and deficiency of organizational work may prevent the Party from taking action. All kinds of meetings must be held under any circumstances. A meeting of ten or twenty minutes may prove fruitful and effective if each member is well prepared prior to the meeting. Meetings of Party cells or small units are even more important. Every comrade has the duty of preparing his own reports and opinions. The duties of every unit chief, Party cell secretary, or administrative committee member are to convene meetings, to gather reports for formulating conclusions, and to execute Party resolutions and instructions. Under regional, local, or sectional committees, conferences of active elements or conferences of responsible working comrades should be held as often as possible.

The Work of Party Fractions

11. The function of Party fractions is to realize the Party's policy and to increase the Party's influence in nonpartisan organizations, such as labor unions, peasant associations, student federations, and various other organizations. Party fractions are different from Party cells in both function and organization. Party fractions are not themselves independent units, nor do they form a separate system. Party fractions are established in accordance with the organization of the Party, under Party organs of all levels and under their supervision. Party fractions of different levels and nature exist from the CC down to the executive committees of Party cells. Party fractions are often provisional and changeable. Their existence is determined by Party [79] headquarters of various levels, which also appoint executive committees for those Party fractions which have a large membership.

12. The work of Party fractions is to represent collectively the opinion of the Party in carrying through the Party's policies. Independent opinion on the part of an individual is not allowed. The decisions of Party organs must be executed, and to do this each and every member of the Party fractions should be mobilized. Majority decisions of the Party fractions, save those which have to be communicated to subordinate Party organs, must be executed by the mobilization of each and every fraction member. Within certain limits [members of] a Party fraction may discuss their work. In case of conflict of opinion between Party fractions and Party organs (such as between a Party fraction in a labor union at a certain factory and the executive committee of the Party cell of the same factory), it

should be immediately referred to a higher Party organ for settlement.

13. Many defects have been revealed in the work of the Party fractions. There is even lack of understanding regarding the meaning of
Party fractions. The fractions also tend to become a second organization of the Party. These defects should be immediately corrected.
Party organs of all levels must not overlook the fact that our comrades in Party fractions cannot be separated from the Party's basic
organization.

Party Organs

14. Political parties cannot be without organs. The Communist
Party, naturally, must have its organs also. Our Party organs are
what Lenin called the organs of "professional revolutionaries." The
function of Party organs is to develop the Party's organization and
to execute the Party's political and technical work. Particularly
when the Party is expanding, it cannot be without good organs and
proletarian, scientific organization.

15. Party organs require two essential conditions to be efficient
and healthy: (a) perfect organization, suited to the requirements;
[80] (b) sufficient and responsible working personnel. In the past Party
organs have been organized only in form, sometimes even to the
point of having only a name but no actual work. This defect has been
found in the organs of various departments and committees. It is
partly caused by the insufficiency of the working force, but also by
the failure of Party organs to meet the necessary requirements.
We must examine all defects from the organizational standpoint in
order to seek reform. At the same time we must reinforce and more
suitably distribute manpower so that responsible workers will be
increased and strengthened. According to the statistical report of
the CC's Organization Department based on present needs alone, the
minimum requirements for nation-wide directing personnel is 35
persons for regional work; 160 persons for local and sectional committee work; 160 persons for special or Party cell work, totaling
355 persons. At present, however, there are barely 120 persons responsible for the Party's work, an indication of the wide margin between actual needs and the available working force. We must train
more personnel in order to save the situation.

16. It was decided at the last Enlarged Conference that the departments of the Central Committee should have definite organization,
that the secretaries of the CC and regional committees should not
hold concurrent posts in the departments, and that committees on
the labor and peasant movements and a department of military
affairs should be organized under the CC to carry out regular duties.

Only a part of these decisions has been executed; the greater part
has not been realized. For instance, to this day there is no responsible

comrade in the CC's Organization Department. Responsible comrades on the Committee on the Labor Movement are often dispatched on special missions to various places for temporary work. The Committee on the Peasant Movement is still not organized.

Following this Enlarged Conference, we must endeavor to execute the above decisions and to correct our past errors. A central secretariat should be established to centralize the CC's technical work. Party organs at all levels likewise stand in need of reform. Unless the Party's organization is sound, we cannot push forward the revolutionary movement of the masses.

Relations between the CC, Party organs of all levels, and Party [81] cells should be close. Regular reports should be made by higher Party organs to lower Party organs and vice versa.

DOCUMENT 5

Document 5 is translated from an original Chinese document, signed by Lo Keng-ti and Li Jui-hsiang. Since "Li Jui-hsiang" is the code name for the Chinese Communist Party's Northern Regional Committee (see Su-lien yin-mou..., III, "KCT," p. 200), this document was apparently issued by the Northern Regional Committee of the Chinese Communist Party. "Lo Keng-ti" may have been the code name for the Northern Regional Committee of the Youth Corps. If this supposition is correct, the document was issued jointly by the Party and the Youth Corps. It is dated March 26 without indication as to the year, but its content suggests that this notice was written in 1926, after Party membership had caught up with and exceeded the membership of the Youth Corps. Document 5 is published under the title, "A Circular Notice of the Chinese Communist Party Explaining the Mutual Relations of the CY and the CP" in Su-lien yin-mou..., III, "KCT," pp. 53-56. The Peking Commission explained that the document was originally marked "Circular Notice No. 23."

[CIRCULAR NOTICE ON RELATIONS BETWEEN
THE CHINESE COMMUNIST PARTY AND
THE CHINESE COMMUNIST YOUTH CORPS]

53] The CY is a "hand" of the Party among the masses of youths. It is a youth organization directed by the Party. Aside from working in the political and labor movements under the Party's direction, it is entrusted with many kinds of work concerning proletarian youths and the oppressed masses of youths in general. Thus, it may be said that the CY's work is part of the CP's work. The proletariat is a complete entity. It has only one Leninist party. The masses of proletarian youths led by the CY should also stand under the CP's banner in order to unify action and struggle.

54] The economic position of proletarian youths is much more oppressed than that of adults. Their sentiment is therefore more radical and their interest more intense than that of adults. It is therefore necessary to have a special independent organization to guide and develop youths. However, the CY is not a youth political party, completely independent of the CP. It is a subsidiary organ of the CP, as are labor unions and peasant associations. In order to secure the vast masses of youths, the directing team of the Party cannot alienate itself from the Youth Corps merely because the latter has its own organizational independence.

The CY is the CP's instrument for development among the masses

of youths. The CP's policy is carried out among the masses of
youths by the CY, which receives its political policies directly from
the CP. No one has ever doubted this since the organization of the
Party and the Youth Corps.

How close should the relations be between local organs of the
Party and the Youth Corps in order to be of benefit to our work? In
recent months, relations between the Party and the Youth Corps under the jurisdiction of the Northern Regional Committee have not
been very satisfactory. Strictly speaking, it is due to lack of clear
understanding of the Party as a whole. The following are the major
errors and the problems which arise most frequently with respect
to relations between local Party and Corps organs.

1. The Corps does not send representatives to participate at meetings of Party organs of all levels, and vice versa.

2. Party organs of all levels neglect the work of the Corps.

3. Corps organs do not carry out decisions of the Party.

4. The Party freely transfers comrades of the Youth Corps without
notifying the Corps or paying any attention to its opinion.

5. The Party does not respect the organization of the Corps and
neglects the opinion of high-level organs of the Corps.

[55]   6. The Party does not assist in the development of the Corps. It
even compels Corps comrades to join the Party with a view to increasing Party membership in order to meet the requirements on
Party development prescribed by high-level organs.

7. The Corps is prohibited from expanding or establishing cells
in certain organizations or schools where there are masses of
youths.

8. The Central Committee's decision on determining Party or
Corps membership on the basis of age is not carried out.

9. Problems of relations between the Party and the Youth Corps
are not properly settled on the spot. Trivial matters are referred
to high-level organs.

The above mistakes are due to the tendency of local [organs],
which are hard pressed with work, to concentrate on finding means
to execute the directives of high-level organs. At the same time, it
cannot be denied that they forget that the Youth Corps' work is part
of Party work. They forget that the Corps is the Party's instrument
for development among the masses of youths and that, directed by
the Party, it is the leading organ of the masses of youths.

The Youth Corps is the reserve army of the Party. It is the
school of Leninism. It should be greatly developed among the masses
of youths and its membership should be greater than the Party's.
But what is the situation now? The work and numerical strength of
the Corps not only fail to keep pace with the development of the objective situation, they fail to keep pace with the Party. It should be
emphasized that the Corps' weakness or lack of development not only

imperils the Corps itself but is a loss to the Party. Lack of understanding of the Party and of communism is betrayed in the failure of
local party organs to pay attention to the organization and development of the Youth Corps and to provide for and promote its work. It
is likewise betrayed in the failure of Youth Corps organs to accept
the Party's direction and to act in unison with the Party.

Hereafter, local Party and Corps organs of all levels should hasten to reform relations between the Party and the Corps and to bring
them closer together. Not only should the Party and Corps mutually
supervise each other to correct past mistakes; Party organs should
plan how to help develop the Corps and to direct its work. Youth
Corps organs should strive to realize the Party's decisions and to
56] lead the masses of youths to stand under the Party's direction for
united action and struggle. Reports on the Party's work should
include the work of the CY.

Local Party headquarters are directed to pay the greatest attention to and execute the above.

DOCUMENT 6

The following is translated from the original Chinese text of the resolutions on the Chinese Communist Youth Corps adopted at the Second Enlarged Plenum of the KCT's Central Committee held between July 12 and July 18, 1926. The original document is published in Su-lien yin-mou..., III, "KCT," pp. 114-16.

RESOLUTIONS ON
THE CHINESE COMMUNIST YOUTH CORPS

[114] The organization of the Chinese Communist Youth Corps has developed greatly during the struggles of the past year. It is gradually getting close to the masses of young workers and has absorbed a
[115] portion of young revolutionary workers. By its actions, the CY has proved its ability to lead students, workers, and the masses of youths in general to participate in the political movement led by the KCT. The Enlarged Conference acknowledges its satisfaction in this respect.

The CY is a revolutionary youth organization which leads youths to struggle for their own interests and to participate in general cultural movements. Under the Party's direction, it also leads them in political struggles. The Youth Corps has failed to fulfill its mission, however. It has failed to become genuinely popular by adapting itself to the characteristics and demands of the masses of youths. Attention must be given to correct this.

Following the May Thirtieth Movement of last year, the Chinese labor and peasant movements and the general national revolutionary movement developed greatly. On the other hand, reactionary ideas and organizations resulting from class differentiation are daily expanding and exerting a strong influence on the masses of youths. Under such conditions, it is the responsibility of the Youth Corps to secure, ideologically and organizationally, on the basis of the self-interests of youths, a greater number of young workers, peasants, and students and, under the Party's direction, lead them to participate in the current revolutionary struggle.

The CY should devote its efforts not only to expanding its ranks and absorbing more revolutionary workers, peasants, students, and other oppressed youths in order to penetrate the lower levels of the masses of youths, but should adapt its work to the demands and characteristics of youths. Lacking work which is truly concerned with the actual needs of youths, the CY can never penetrate the masses of youths. Necessary political activities, however, must not be neglected.

The function of Chinese students in the national revolutionary movement will continue to expand. If the student movement can be developed under our direction, it would be of great benefit to the Party in the peasant and urban petty bourgeoisie movements. The Party should hereafter direct the Youth Corps in earnest, but the latter must not reduce its positive activities, thus adversely affecting the development of the student movement, because of the trans-

16] fer of political leadership of the student movement to the Party.

Although it has been decided that membership in the Party or the Youth Corps should be determined according to age, Party organization is still lacking at many places. Furthermore, it is more convenient and suitable at certain places to organize the Youth Corps first. Where Party organization is lacking, it is the duty of the Youth Corps to help the Party to organize and to execute the Party's resolutions. On the other hand, the Party should help the Youth Corps to organize where there is Party organization but no Youth Corps organization.

The Party should render greater aid to and direct the Youth Corps in its efforts to organize and to adapt its work to the interests of the masses of youths. In the labor movement, the Party should pay attention to and support the special economic interests of young and child workers. In guiding and assisting the Youth Corps, the Party must strive to preserve the independent spirit of the Corps and not interfere excessively in its activities, thus obstructing the development of its work. The local committees should pay attention to reforming the organizational relationships between the Party at the lower levels and the Youth Corps. [The Party] must not arbitrarily assign work to the responsible comrades of the Youth Corps. Those who are members both of the Party and the Youth Corps should positively participate in the work of the Corps to fulfill their duty of leading members of the Corps to positive action. The Youth Corps should stress the training of positive active elements through actual work in order to strengthen the capacity of its low-level leadership.

In short, the work of the Chinese Communist Youth Corps should be in greater conformity with the interests of the masses of youths. The Party should regard the work of the CY as part of the work under its direction and lend the Youth Corps its earnest guidance and assistance.

DOCUMENT 7

Document 7 is translated from the original Chinese text of the Central Committee's resolutions on propaganda, apparently adopted at the Enlarged Plenum in October, 1925. A comparison with Document 8, which gives the CC's resolutions on propaganda adopted in July, 1926, confirms this deduction. The Peking Commission published the original text of Document 7 in Su-lien yin-mou..., III, "KCT," pp. 56-60.

RESOLUTIONS ON THE QUESTION OF
PROPAGANDA

[56] 1. In view of the current high revolutionary tide, the duty of our Party is to absorb the masses of workers and the revolutionary intellectuals in order to strengthen and expand the Party's influence among the working class of the entire country. We should begin work among the peasantry in the villages and build the foundation of our Party among the peasant masses. Unless our Party becomes a real political party of the masses, we will not be able to strengthen our position of leadership of the struggle of the working class and of the National Revolution.

In order to fulfill these important tasks, our Party should undertake agitation and propaganda work among the masses. Wherever he may be, each and every Party member should endeavor to promote propaganda on our Party's principles and slogans.

2. To be effective in our work of agitation, we must enable the masses, even the most backward workers and ricksha coolies, to understand our propaganda. Hence, only the most popular language and writing should be used.

However, not only the language and writing but the content of agitation should also be close to the masses. The most important principle of mass agitation is that it must be concretely based on facts immediately confronting the peasant and working masses.

[57] Therefore, a Communist should not only direct and train the masses but be able to observe and analyze what they say and to understand their needs in order that our Party's oral and written propaganda may reflect their psychology.

In disseminating Party propaganda among the masses, it is best to point out the Party's accomplishments and the fact that the Party has already fought for and obtained concrete benefits for the working class and the peasantry. Such accomplishments are our point of departure in getting hold of the masses.

3. The first formula of mass agitation is "propaganda mobilization," which focuses the attention of all classes in the country (in the beginning, of course, only Party members and the working class) on a certain event or problem. "Propaganda mobilization" calls for the enlistment of the Party's total strength and influence. Hence, it must be planned well in advance. This does not mean, however, that Party organs of all levels should reduce their capacity to meet emergencies or to cope with important movements and upheavals.

4. The second formula of mass agitation is the workers' club. Before our Party was organized, the workers' club had served a great purpose. We should continue to develop the workers' clubs by making use of their good points and introducing certain changes so that they will become more suited to the functions of our Party. Some very good results may be obtained from such work.

5. Special attention should also be paid to agitation within the Party. Such agitation should encourage the entire membership from bottom up to participate in positive political life. This is one of our current basic tasks. The Party cell is the foundation in carrying out such work.

8]   The Party cell is the organ for realizing party tasks, just as the entire Party is the organ for realizing the workers' class struggle. The work of each cell must not deviate at any time from the actual circumstances of the particular cell. The agitation work of each cell should be based on the daily struggle of the Party and of the working class.

6. The Communist Party is an inseparable part of the working class. The only difference between the Communist Party and the entire working class is that the Party represents the portion which has the highest degree of class consciousness. In fact as well as words, the Party stands as vanguard in the workers' class struggle. Party members should see that their own class consciousness increases continuously, which is the sole guarantee of the Party's triumph. Each member should not only be able to fight for Party principles himself but lead others to fight and expand the Party's influence among the masses.

Mass propaganda to carry out the two above-mentioned functions provides the most intensive training for the entire Party.

The Party carries out mass propaganda through the small units of cells and the self-study programs of the clubs. Party cells, particularly those with large memberships, should be divided into many units for carrying out their work. The duty of small units of Party cells is to enable labor comrades to know and to understand every detail of the daily struggles in which they themselves participate, and which are reflections of the entire class struggle.

Hence, propaganda work of these small units should be coordinated with the entire work of the cells. We should exert every effort to improve the organization of small units to make them organs with well-defined plans. Particular attention should be directed to past experience in order to eliminate many defects and drawbacks.

The self-study groups of the clubs must absorb non-Party members. Propaganda in such groups should be particularly interesting [59] and realistic. Propaganda work should take the form of discussions of newspaper articles, interpretations of the current situation, and brief discussions of the history of the class struggle. Of course propaganda should be based on the degree of political knowledge of the workers. Propaganda, like agitation, should be easily understood or its goals will not be attained.

7. For mass agitation and propaganda work there must be competent personnel. Therefore the establishment of Party schools at various places is an important task.

In view of its present strength, the Party is in a position to open only two kinds of Party schools:

a) General Party schools under local committees for training agitators among the masses. Such schools should be provided only for workers and the length of time required for graduation should not exceed one month or half a month;

b) Advanced Party schools under regional committees to train our comrades of more advanced political knowledge and experience to become directing personnel. The time required for graduation should not exceed three months.

Training in the Party schools should be based on experience in the national revolutionary movement. The function of the Communist Party in the many revolutionary movements should be explained. Our comrades attending Party schools should not be separated from the masses. They should simultaneously work outside, among our comrades and non-comrades. Only thus can they acquire true proletarian ideas. Our experience with Party schools in Shanghai and other places has been highly satisfactory and we should review such experience for further improvement.

8. Fundamental tasks in written propaganda and agitation are the development and popularization of our Party papers, popular pamphlets, and songs, and the translation of books on Marxism. Material [60] of all kinds should be collected to facilitate the editing of Chinese Marxist writings to serve as the theoretical basis for forming solutions to the numerous problems of the National Revolution and the class struggle. It is necessary to establish an appropriate organ in the Central Committee to direct and plan the work of collecting material.

Only through such efforts in carrying out the Party's work can we guarantee the fulfillment of our duties.

DOCUMENT 8

Document 8 has been translated from the original Chinese text of the resolutions on the work of the Propaganda Department which were adopted at the Second Enlarged Plenum of the Central Committee of the KCT which met from July 12 to July 18, 1926. The resolutions are published in <u>Su-lien yin-mou...</u>, III, "KCT," p. 81-87.

RESOLUTIONS ON THE WORK OF
THE PROPAGANDA DEPARTMENT

[81] Having examined the Propaganda Department's report, the Enlarged Conference has decided that immediate reforms are necessary and that the following concrete measures should be adopted in our propaganda work.

The Problem of Publications

1. <u>Hsiang-tao</u>, the publication of the central political organ, should be made more stirring in order to reflect and guide the daily struggle of the Chinese revolutionary masses. Theoretical analysis should not be unduly emphasized and efforts should be made to: (a) Increase propaganda on the significance of local labor and peasant movements; (b) improve the communication of local political news so that important local events will not be neglected.

2. <u>Hsin ch'ing-nien</u>, the theoretical publication of the CC, should be published regularly every month to meet the needs of the revolutionary ideological struggle. In view of our Party's lack of theoretical ability, all the strength we do have should be concentrated for the time being in <u>Hsin ch'ing-nien</u>. (For instance, articles in <u>Hsiang-tao</u> emphasizing theoretical analysis and articles on historical theories in <u>Pei-ching cheng-chih sheng-huo</u> should be published in <u>Hsin ch'ing-nien</u>.) Studies on the Chinese economy and the history and theory of the labor and peasant movements should also be included in <u>Hsin ch'ing-nien</u>. Furthermore, the magazine should contain studies and discussions of CY problems, in order to make the <u>Hsin ch'ing-nien</u> a joint publication of the central committees of the CP and CY.

3. Popular publication of the CC. A periodical, <u>Lao Nung</u> or <u>Kung Nung</u> should be published, first as a monthly and later as a weekly. Such a publication should be able to furnish workers and peasants with political guidance, collect data on the conditions of workers and peasants and news concerning their political and economic struggle, and publish letters from workers and peasants from various places.

[82] The objective is to enable the masses of workers and peasants to understand the situation and significance of the national revolutionary struggle and to reflect the actual life and struggle of the workers and peasants.

4. Party newspapers. Further improvements are necessary in gathering data on the work and life of the Party in all departments of the CC and Party organs of all levels as material for training and guiding our comrades.

5. An editorial committee should be set up to review and censor periodically all publications of the CC and bring into closer relationship with the Party the official publications of our labor unions, peasants' associations, and women's and youth organizations. It should enable the CC to exercise proper supervision of and guidance over all local publications. The committee should be composed of the chief editors of Hsiang-tao, Hsin ch'ing-nien, Lao nung tang-pao, Chung-kuo ch'ing-nien (CY), Chung-kuo kung-jen (official publication of the All-China Federation of labor), and Chung-kuo fu-nu (official publication of the Federation of Women). The committee should meet at least monthly to report and review the condition of the official publications of the CC, local Party organs, and labor unions.

The Department's Duties

Up to the end of April of this year, the CC's Propaganda Department failed to carry out the duties of the Department. All forces must be positively reformed in order to carry out the following minimum activities:

1. Establishment of a publicity section to furnish the editorial staff of the official publications of all departments of the CC with weekly and monthly compilations of the editorials and news dispatches of Chinese and foreign newspapers and magazines.

[83] 2. Establishment of a library to index all important Chinese and foreign books by categories and date of publication and to collect all local and central publications (publications of the Party's labor unions, peasants' associations, students' and women's associations, and other official publications, books and publications of importance in Peking, Canton, Hankow, and Shanghai). When this work has been undertaken for a certain period, the indices should be distributed among organs of all levels. Regulations for loaning books should be fixed.

3. Daily routine: (a) draft outlines of propaganda on the political situation according to the Central Bureau's resolutions on propaganda, mobilization and interpretation of the current situation; (b) issue regularly circular notices on the duties of local propaganda departments; (c) correspond with local propaganda departments in answer to their letters and reports; (d) review and criticize monthly all local publications according to the decisions of the Editorial Committee (of course, it is still necessary to guide local publications through

regular correspondence); (e) make a general survey of intellectual and press opinion in the very near future. Such surveys should be conducted once a month thereafter to ascertain the reaction of the general public and various groups to our national and local "propaganda mobilization"; (f) make a preliminary survey in the nearest future on the condition and method of the regular educational work at different places (the work of Party cells in training our comrades in theory and Party duties) and the condition of specialized educational work (such as training classes). Thereafter, monthly reviews should be made on the results of such work.

The Central Propaganda Department should furnish the Central Bureau with written reports containing such items as the results of nation-wide investigation of the work of national propaganda and agitation, the number of issues of the Party's central and local publications, their editorials on important events, and their editorial and translation record.

[84] The Problem of Editorial and Translation Work
The Central Propaganda Department must immediately commence editorial and translation work.

1. Decide on a minimum plan for the translation of theoretical material to add to the collection of books on the ABC's of communism.

2. Textbooks for Party schools and educational outlines for Party members:

a). Ko-ming ch'ang-shih, a simple and popular interpretation of the most important problems of the Chinese Revolution.

b) Tang-wu ch'ang-shih, an interpretation and explanation of theory, methods of propaganda, and organization of the activities of the Party, labor unions, students and women (such as the significance of Party cells and the functions of Party fractions).

c) The teaching methods of lower Party schools (training classes) (practical curriculum and reference lists).

3. Stirring pamphlets: Very simple and popular pamphlets to explain the Fifth Manifesto of the Party on the current political situation [Manifesto of the Second Enlarged Plenum].

4. Collection of propaganda outlines on memorial occasions (such as the anniversaries of Lenin, February Seventh, March Eighth, March Eighteenth, May First, May Fourth, May Fifth, May Seventh, May Thirtieth, Relief Day, Youth Day, the Paris Commune, the October Revolution, Double Ten, Anti-Christianity Week, Anti-Imperialism Week, Workers' Memorial Week, anniversaries of Sun Yat-sen, Liao Chung-k'ai, etc.), with reference material attached.

The Problem of Local Reports
Regional and local committees must submit regular monthly reports and prepare the following items (in case work is lacking in

a certain category, an explanation is necessary so that plans for the initiation of such work may be prepared).

[85]   1. Monthly records of agitation. Leaflets and results of the work of propaganda mobilization of the central and local committees of our Party and other cliques should be included in general and centralized monthly reports with conclusions. In addition, urgent and separate reports should be submitted at various times.

2. Monthly records of propaganda. The work of theoretical propaganda in the clubs and research societies—Canton has enjoyed access to, and other places should at least make use of, the Central Committee's theoretical publications so that our comrades may attract the attention of noncomrades to our theories and carry on discussion with them through correspondence; local publications should pay more attention to our debates and discussions with other local groups. The results of such work must be embodied in monthly reports.

3. Monthly synthesized reports on the number of issues and the current slogans of local publications. Local publications should primarily stress local political agitation and problems. Publications of the Party's local labor unions, students' and women's associations should be sent regularly by express post to the CC's Propaganda Department. They should also be sent to the Committee on the Labor Movement, the Women's Department, and the CY. The Propaganda Department must not be overlooked merely because separate issues have been sent.

4. Monthly reports on the survey of popular opinion.

5. Monthly educational records. Party cells should hold monthly discussions of theory to test our comrades' understanding of doctrines, monthly discussions on the current situation to broaden the political understanding of our comrades and the masses, monthly discussions on discipline to correct the views of our comrades or certain tendencies which manifest themselves in problems of organization.

6. Monthly records of Party schools (the results, methods, and material of all training classes).

7. Monthly synthesized reports on the local effect of the CC's publications. Criticisms of the CC's publications by local comrades and noncomrades or the local need of ideological guidance.

[86]   8. Monthly synthesized reports on the size and content of correspondence of local comrades with the CC's publications on politics, theories, labor, and peasantry (Hsiang-tao, Hsin ch'ing-nien, Lao nung). Regardless who the writers are, all local propaganda departments should make reports on their correspondence.

Correspondence with Workers and Peasants

In our propaganda work, we must immediately execute the resolution on worker and peasant correspondence in order that our Party may know and examine the opinion of the masses, which is necessary in guiding them. Worker and peasant correspondence may be organized roughly in four ways.

1. The Propaganda Department selects among workers those who can write ordinary letters and asks them to write freely about their own living and home conditions, revealing their own reactions and knowledge of political problems.

2. The Propaganda Department selects and sends student comrades to workers' districts and peasant villages to record conversations and interviews with workers and peasants.

3. The Propaganda Department entrusts the responsible personnel of the Labor and Peasant Committees who work in worker and peasant districts, with the task of establishing such correspondence through various means.

4. In case of outbreaks of strikes or resistance to taxation, the Propaganda Department sends its own personnel to worker and peasant districts or delegates representatives of the Labor and Peasant Committees to gather the correspondence of the masses expressing their views and reaction towards such occurrence. Local propaganda departments should frequently prepare questionnaires for workers and peasants so that worker and peasant correspondents may fill in their answers.

Central and local propanganda departments must themselves be reformed in order to execute these tasks. The Central Committee and committees of all levels should maintain an exceptionally cautious and strict relationship with [their] propaganda departments in regard to distribution of personnel and administrative procedures.

The Enlarged Conference believes that not even 1 or 2 percent of the resolutions on propaganda adopted at the last Enlarged Conference (last October) has been carried out. It does not, however, hold the central and local propaganda departments responsible. Nevertheless, the resolutions on propaganda are still appropriate. The present Enlarged Conference believes that it is only necessary to outline very concrete methods of execution. Hence, the above concrete measures have been adopted which should be executed by central and local propaganda departments.

Document 9 is translated from an original Chinese document which is undated and unsigned. It is published in Su-lien yin mou..., III, "KCT," pp. 138-46.

AN OUTLINE OF THE CURRICULUM OF THE CHINESE
COMMUNIST PARTY'S "A" AND "B" PARTY SCHOOLS

[138] Outline of Curriculum for "A" Party Schools

"A" party schools are established for workers. The curriculum may be divided into six lecture topics, each followed by "problems." The number of lectures for each topic and the distribution of teachers are fixed by local propaganda committees. In view of the present shortage of theoretical works in Chinese, reference material is outlined only in general terms.

A. Capitalism

1. What is commodity? What is commodity economy? What is hired labor? (Marx, Wage-Labor and Capital, published by the People's Bookstore, Canton)

2. How do capitalists exploit labor?

[139]   3. What is capital? What is surplus value? (Kautsky, The Economi Doctrines of Karl Marx, published by the Commercial Press).

4. Why is capitalist society divided into many classes? Explain the special characteristics of the following classes: (a) the bourgeoisie— big capitalists who own the instruments and capital of production (materials of production); (b) the petty bourgeoisie—the handicraftsmen and farmers who own the tools of production; (c) the proletariat (workers)—who are unable to own the materials of production but can only sell their labor.

5. What is the significance of class struggle? (Manifesto of the Communist Party)

6. What is industrial and commercial competition? Will small handicraft production or big production triumph in this competition? Why are the small farmer and small handicraftsman bankrupt? What is the meaning of concentration of capital?

7. Why do capitalists want to employ more female and child laborers? This is a capitalist tactic of competition and exploitation of the working class.

8. What is the function of the state or government in the class struggle? (Note: The foregoing is a general outline of "The Nature of Capitalist Society." Aside from using the above-mentioned mate-

rial and such publications as <u>Hsin ch'ing-nien</u> and <u>Hsien-feng</u>, teachers should pay special attention to facts which are easily observed and understood by local workers and explain the following: (a) class struggle is unavoidable in capitalist society; in order to achieve liberation, the proletariat must take an active part in the class struggle and in the struggle to seize political power; (b) competition between the petty bourgeoisie and small capitalists is also unavoidable in

40] capitalist society; the poor peasants become daily more bankrupt and capital daily becomes more concentrated. The proletariat and the peasantry should therefore unite to oppose the capitalists. These are the two most important ideas contained in the above eight questions.)

9. What is the phenomenon of "anarchy in production" in capitalist society?

10. What is economic crisis?

11. Why is it that as capitalism develops, economic crisis deepens and class conflict in society becomes more violent?

12. What is the result of concentration of capital? What is the meaning of corporations and trusts?

13. What are the merits of concentration of capital and mechanized production as compared with small handicraft and small business?

14. In what way does capitalist development prepare the social and economic foundations for communism? (Marx, <u>Wage-Labor and Capital</u>; Bukharin, <u>Program of The Communists (Bolshevists)</u>; Kautsky, <u>The Class Struggle</u>).

(<u>Note</u>: The main purpose of the above six questions is to explain two important ideas: (a) capitalism must collapse through self-contradiction; (b) in the course of capitalist development, improvements in production methods and concentration of productive material have already laid the foundation for communism.)

B. Imperialism

1. What is the organizational method of industrial production during the period of financial capitalism?

2. What is the function of banks during the period of financial capitalism?

41]   3. What is the goal of capitalists when they unite in trusts and syndicates?

4. What is the tendency of concentration of capital during the period of financial capitalism? (must give illustrations).

5. What is imperialism?

6. Is it possible to avoid war between capitalist countries?

7. Why does the bourgeoisie of all countries fight for markets and colonies?

8. Give concrete examples of the partitioning of the world and seizure of colonies by the Powers during the second half of the nineteenth centry (illustrated on simple maps of the world). (Lenin, <u>Imperialism, the Highest Stage of Capitalism; A Popular Outline</u>,

translated by Li Ch'un-fan, published by the Shanghai Book Co.)

(Note: The central idea of these eight questions is to explain:
(a) capitalism has developed to become the world's economic system;
(b) in the period of financial capitalism, war and struggle for colonies among capitalist countries is unavoidable.)

9. What is the condition of imperialist aggression in China?
(Illustrate with the unequal treaties, rights of customs administration, consular jurisdiction, right to engage in railway, mining, and industrial enterprises, foreign loans, securities, etc.)

10. What is the connection between militarists and imperialists?

11. What is the power of imperialists in Chinese industry?

12. Give concrete examples of direct exploitation and oppression of Chinese workers and the common people by the imperialists and [142] foreign capitalists (including Christian mission schools).

13. Is China an independent nation or a semicolony?

14. During the imperialist period, why does conflict between the Powers and China and other oppressed peoples become daily more acute? (For material on the above questions use histories of Chinese foreign relations, current events and articles on the movements of oppressed peoples in various magazines (Hsin ch'ing-nien, etc.).

(Note: The central idea of these six questions is to explain: (a) The development of imperialism has caused the division of the world into two big camps. In one camp are the proletariat and poor peasantry of all countries and the oppressed peoples; in the other, the bourgeoisie of all capitalist countries and their imperialist governments;
(b) China is one of the oppressed peoples and the imperialists have oppressed her politically, economically, and culturally.)

C. Proletarian Dictatorship and Communism

1. Why does capitalist development inevitably lead to social revolution?

2. What is the system of proletarian dictatorship? What is a proletarian state?

3. Why is proletarian dictatorship transitional in nature? How will it be transformed from a proletarian state into a proletarian society?

4. Do classes still exist in a Communist society?

[143] 5. Does the system of private ownership of productive material still exist in a Communist society?

(Note: The meaning of communism is often misinterpreted by the Chinese as calling for the confiscation of all "private" daily consumers goods. Hence, among our workers comrades and especially the working masses, we should...[following missing; burned?]

Outline of Curriculum for "B" Party Schools

"B" party schools are established for comrades of more advanced standards. Two lecture topics may be added to the curriculum and lecture material may include more details. This would, however, accentuate the shortage of Chinese material. Hence, if the local committees have suitable propaganda workers, they should consult the following foreign books. If such personnel is not available, follow the outline for "A" schools.

A. The Development of Capitalism
  1. Period of natural economy
    a) Economy is the foundation of social development
    b) Primitive communism
    c) Patriarchal society
    d) Feudalism
    e) The rise of private ownership and international trade during the period of national economy
  2. Rise of capitalism and commercial capitalism
    a) Urban handicraft economy.
    b) Commercial capitalism
  3. Basic contradictions between industrial capitalism and capitalist society
    a) Peculiar characteristics of capitalism
    b) Process of development of industrial capitalism
    c) Basic contradictions in the capitalist society
    d) Capitalist country
  4. Financial capitalism, imperialism and the World War
    a) Alliance of capitalists
    b) Bank capital
    c) The struggle of the Powers for markets and export-capital imperialism
    d) The World War
  5. Leninism
B. Imperialism and China
  (Same as the outline for "A" schools—items nine to fourteen—but teaching material may be doubled for detailed treatment)
C. History of the Socialist Movement
  1. Evolution of socialism
    a) History is the history of class struggle
    b) Early communist theories—Christian communist movement
    c) "Heretical" communism
    d) The English and French bourgeois revolutions and the theory of communism (Babeuf)
    e) The Utopian [Socialists] Fourier, St. Simon, Owen
    f) The revolutions of 1830 and 1840 and scientific socialism
  2. The three Internationals
    a) The First International
    b) The Paris Commune
    c) The Second International
    d) The Third International
  3. Communist society.

D. History of the Russian social revolution (during lectures attention should be given to the history of the development of the Russian Bolsheviks and internal conflict within the Russian Socialist Party)

[146]

   1. History of the Russian revolutionary movement and the Bolsheviks
     a) The earliest revolutionary organization in Russia
     b) The rise of the Russian working class and its movement
     c) Before and after the 1905 Revolution
     d) From 1905 to 1914
     e) The European war and the Bolsheviks
   2. From the February, 1917 Revolution to the October Revolution
   3. The October Revolution and the period of military communism
     a) Meaning of the October Revolution
     b) National construction by the working class
     c) The October Revolution and the Russian Communist Party (The Seventh, Eighth, and Ninth Congresses of the Communist Party)

DOCUMENT 10

The following is a translation of an original Chinese document which was drawn up by the Moscow Branch of the Chinese Communist Party and the Chinese Communist Youth Corps. It is undated, but appears to have been drafted in the early 1920s, sometime before February, 1925, when the Chinese Socialist Youth Corps changed its name to the "Chinese Communist Youth Corps." The Chinese document is published in Su-lien yin-mou..., III, "KCT," pp. 49-53.

A CONCRETE GUIDE TO THE WORK OF
TRAINING

[49] A. Systematize thought and study—oppose romanticism. Romanticism is a condition which destroys organization.

1. Do not forget we come from a Chinese petty bourgeois background. We have various old concepts and ideas inherited from an economically backward, patriarchal society which are not suited to proletarian revolutionaries.

2. We want to cultivate a pure revolutionary philosophy of life and self-conscious training—we cannot be depended on if we lack a definite philosophy of life and rush into the revolutionary path on a moment's impulse.

3. We should stand firmly on class grounds. We must not observe all things in accordance with old concepts.

4. We should destroy family, local, and national concepts—the proletariat has no family, no local or national limitations.

5. Destroy unity based on sentiment—sentimental unity is petty bourgeois unity—we build our unity on Party interests.

[50] 6. There is within the organization no class distinction or division between workers and students—such psychology is completely divorced from class and Party consciousness. If such phenomena occur within an organization, the spirit of unanimity would be destroyed.

7. We must at all times strive to learn—we must not indulge even slightly in self-satisfaction, self-exaltation, or boastfulness. If we suffer from these weaknesses, we will not be able to progress.

8. We must employ in our work for the Party the same kind of interest we have in love and literature—love and literature are the foundation of romanticism.

9. We must define the class point of view before we study ideology. We must proceed from fundamental understanding of [basic principles]. We must not aim too high and achieve nothing in the end.

10. We should exert our efforts in accordance with the plans and methods of study prescribed by the organization.

11. We must studiously avoid academic-type study—academic-type study denies that theory is born of practice.

12. We must at all times prepare ourselves to return to our country to participate in actual revolutionary work—we must not feel our studies are inadequate and thus be unwilling to return to our country for service.

13. We must pay attention to the Russian language aside from our studies—we absolutely must not maintain the erroneous idea that we should first study Russian before we study ideology.

B. Discipline action—absolutely oppose anarchist tendencies. If we oppose iron discipline, we would be negatively helping the bourgeoisie to destroy the proletariat's revolutionary organization.

14. We must train political agitators and mass organizers—every Communist member is required to have the capacity [to serve as a political agitator and mass organizer].

[51]   15. We must at all times maintain the organization's unity of action.

16. We must strive to eliminate the [bad habits of the] intelligentsia —the bad habits of university students and the entire petty bourgeoisie. If we maintain these bad habits, we would not be truly surrendering to the proletariat. We would not be thorough proletarian revolutionaries.

17. We must at all times and everywhere mutually correct each other's errors of thought and action.

18. When we have opinions, we must express them—if we hide our opinions and do not express them, we would be standing outside the organization and encouraging counterrevolutionary [tendencies].

19. We must cultivate the habit of perseverance—Communists are always willing to "lie on faggots and taste gall" in order to struggle for the interest of the proletariat.

20. We must not forget to [disseminate] propaganda every time we write a letter—propaganda is the minimum duty of every Communist member.

21. Our attitude and action outside the organization should be extremely cautious—divulging the organization's secrets is [equivalent] to the conduct of enemy spies.

22. Every comrade must develop close relations with at least two other comrades (exclusive of comrades belonging to the same small unit) in order to achieve solidarity among our comrades.

C. Collectivize individuality—oppose individualism and the concept of private property. Proletarian action is adapted to the masses. [The proletariat] has no private property.

23. The organization's interest is the individual's interest. We must not obstruct the organization's advance because of individual interest—if we hamper the organization's progress because of individual interest, we would be negatively or positively betraying disloyalty to the proletariat's revolutionary organization.

24. We must not have excessive self-confidence. We must have the psychology of thoroughly trusting the organization—it is counter-revolutionary conduct not to trust the organization.

25. Our lives and our will must not be based on individual beliefs or the individual will—in accordance with the organization's life and will, we should absolutely collectivize and adapt to the masses our own lives and will. There is absolutely no such thing as individual life or individual free will.

26. We must strictly criticize our comrades' errors and humbly accept our comrades' criticism—it is not the attitude of a Communist to fear criticism, to reject criticism or not to criticize his comrades. Wherever he may be, every Communist must at all times criticize and supervise his comrades in accordance with the relations of mutual super-vision (the mutual relations of Communists mean mutual supervision)—criticism is a tool to train us to become iron-like Communist members.

27. Proletarian revolutionaries absolutely must not slight, deceive, or be mean to their comrades. They must not hold any other kind of attitude or indulge in any conduct which are incompatible with [their position] as Communists. They should always be closer and more intimate with their comrades than with their own brothers.

28. We must correct craftiness and other weaknesses derived from dishonesty—Communists cannot be anything but stark naked with their own organization and comrades.

29. We must absolutely and humbly correct pride, love of glory, and other weaknesses derived from not being solid.

30. If our nature is too temperate, we would reveal weakness and we would then be unable to accomplish anything. However, if our nature is too cruel, we would be inviting conflict and misunderstanding—in short, we must be calm and composed and observe facts with a cool head. We must have firm and positive spirit and skillful tactics in carrying out our work.

D. On service—experience is founded on our work and our own errors. We must also express through work our loyalty to the organization. Neglect of work is counterrevolutionary conduct.

31. Aside from revolution, Communist members have no other profession—we are professional revolutionaries.

32. The organization's work is our only work. Aside from the organization's work there is no so-called individual work—Communist members always positively participate in the work of the organization.

33. We must be responsible in our work. We must at the same time understand that we are a part of this machinery which is the Communist Party. We absolutely must not maintain the attitude of being compelled [by the Party] or hamper the work of this machinery.

34. The quantity and quality of a Communist member is determined in accordance with his capacity—true Communists never show off their accomplishments, fear hardship, or long for ease.

PART III

CONSOLIDATION OF THE REVOLUTIONARY
BASE IN KWANGTUNG, 1921-1925

Sun Yat-sen's Early Contact with Soviet Russia, 1918-1920

The reopening of the Peking Parliament in August, 1916, following the death of Yüan Shih-k'ai, appeared to lend new hope to the cause of republicanism in China. That hope was soon dashed, however, by bitter factionalism between leading political parties and by the rise of militarist power. In August, 1917, Parliament was dissolved by President Li Yüan-hung. In protest, Sun Yat-sen led a group of Parliament members to Canton, where they set up an opposition military government. Sun Yat-sen was elected Generalissimo, although it soon became evident that actual power was vested in the hands of the militarists in control of the southwestern provinces. In May, 1918, Sun's opponents pushed through a reorganization of the government which deprived him of what little authority he possessed. He then left Canton for voluntary retirement in Shanghai.[1]

It was shortly after this setback, severe even for Sun Yat-sen's strangely checkered career, that the first contact reportedly took place between the Chinese revolutionary leader and the new Soviet regime. In 1927, Wang Ching-wei traced the origin of the Kuomintang's policy of alliance with Soviet Russia to a telegram which Sun Yat-sen sent Lenin at this time, congratulating him on the triumph of the Russian Revolution.[2]

According to Gregory Voitinskii, Sun Yat-sen met with him in Shanghai in the autumn of 1920. Voitinskii was then engaged in organizing a Communist party in Shanghai. Sun Yat-sen asked him many questions about Soviet Russia and the Bolshevik Revolution, Voitinskii asserts, and expressed regret that the geographical location of Canton did not permit contact with Russia. Sun also asked him, according to Voitinskii, whether it was possible for the Russians to set up a powerful radio station at Vladivostok or Manchuria to establish communications with Canton, and informed him that he hoped to make use of a military victory in South China to develop the revolutionary movement in the central and northern provinces.[3] Voitinskii's account lacks confirmation by Kuomintang sources. If it is accurate, it would suggest that Sun Yat-sen's initial interest in

Soviet Russia was practical rather than ideological and that he was thinking primarily of the possibility of Soviet aid for a military campaign. Around the time of the reported interview, forces loyal to Sun Yat-sen were engaged in an attempt to recapture Canton. In October, 1920, the Kwangtung Army, commanded by Ch'en Ch'iung-ming, brought the campaign to a successful close. Sun Yat-sen returned in triumph to Canton, assuming the presidency of the new government the following spring.[4]

Having regained Canton as a base of operations, Sun Yat-sen was determined to launch an expedition against the northern militarists. In the fall of 1921, he established headquarters at Kweilin in preparation for a drive through Hunan on what became known as the "First Northern Expedition."[5] It was while he was at Kweilin in August or September, 1921, that Sun Yat-sen met Maring, Voitinskii's successor as Comintern delegate to the Chinese Communist Party.

The meeting between Maring and Sun Yat-sen is confirmed by both Kuomintang and Communist sources. Hu Hua, an orthodox Communist historian, asserts that Sun Yat-sen accepted two suggestions advanced by Maring. Maring pointed out that it was necessary to establish a good political party capable of uniting all classes, especially the masses of workers and peasants, in order to push forward the Chinese Revolution. The other suggestion according to Hu, was that it was necessary to develop an armed nucleus for the Revolution, that is, to establish a military academy. Hu Hua does not state, however, that any agreement was actually arrived at.[6] Other sources also indicate that the meeting failed to produce definite results. According to Li Chien-nung, Maring told Liao Chung-k'ai following the meeting that he was disappointed by the outcome.[7] According to Chiang Kai-shek's diary, another meeting took place between Sun and Maring on December 25, 1921. Chiang dates the origin of the idea of cooperation with Soviet Russia from this meeting,[8] although evidence that any concrete agreement was reached is lacking.

The meetings with Maring took place while Sun Yat-sen was in power at Canton. Thus Sun was probably not as receptive to Soviet aid, if any was offered, as he might have been had his own circumstances been less favorable. On the other hand, it appears that Maring's mission to see Sun Yat-sen was exploratory in character, part of an over-all Soviet program designed to sound out and establish contact with various Chinese leaders.

The record in fact suggests that the Russians were at first interested in Wu P'ei-fu as an ally. After Wu seized control of the Peking Government in alliance with Chang Tso-lin in July, 1920, an article appeared in Izvestia predicting that he would be oriented toward Soviet Russia.[9] According to Wang Ching-wei, while Maring was talking with Sun in 1921, Soviet representatives were

simultaneously negotiating with Wu P'ei-fu in North China.[10]
Katsuji Fuse, a Japanese journalist asserts that Soviet interest in
Wu was manifested shortly after Ignatius Yurin's mission to Peking
from late 1920 to the middle of 1921.[11] However Wu P'ei-fu was
not interested in the Soviet overtures.

Ignatius Yurin was the first of a number of Soviet representatives
sent to China to work toward the establishment of diplomatic relations between the USSR and the Peking Government. His official position was that of head of the Economic Mission of the Far Eastern
Republic. In a note to the Foreign Minister of the Peking Government,
Yurin announced his government's intention to establish friendly relations with China and to revise all treaties previously concluded
under the Czarist regime. Yurin failed in his mission but apparently
played an instrumental role in the Peking Government's withdrawal
of recognition of the Russian representative formerly appointed by
the Czarist government.[12] Following Yurin, A. K. Paikes was sent
to Peking. He also failed to establish treaty relations, although both
he and Yurin reportedly made fruitful contacts with elements of the
Peking intelligentsia.[13] In the summer of 1922, the Soviet government sent to Peking one of its top diplomats, Adolf Joffe, to continue
to press for treaty relations with the USSR. Joffe arrived on August
12, 1922.[14]

Sun Yat-sen's Negotiations with Dalin and Joffe, 1922 to January, 1923
    Two days after Joffe's arrival at Peking, Sun Yat-sen landed at
Shanghai following a harrowing experience. In the pre-dawn hours of
June 16, 1922, Ch'en Ch'iung-ming's troops suddenly surrounded
Sun Yat-sen's residence in Canton. Together with his principal
followers, Sun barely escaped falling into rebel hands. They found
refuge on a gunboat, where they remained for fifty-six days, finally
reaching Shanghai on August 14, 1922. The coup d'état of Ch'en
Ch'iung-ming, who had consistently obstructed the First Northern
Expedition, came shortly after Wu P'ei-fu had defeated Chang Tso-
lin at the end of the First Mukden-Chihli War. Chang Tso-lin's defeat had spelled disaster for the KMT's First Northern Expedition,
finally launched in February, 1922, since Sun Yat-sen had combined
with Chang against Wu.[15]

These events were to have fateful consequences. Within two weeks
of his arrival at Shanghai, Sun Yat-sen was to guide the Kuomintang
into collaboration with the Chinese Communists.

On June 17, the day after Ch'en Ch'iung-ming's coup, the Central
Committee of the Chinese Communist Party published a manifesto
singling out the Kuomintang as a potential ally in a democratic united
front. Shortly after Sun arrived at Shanghai, the Communist offer of
an alliance was conveyed to Sun by Dalin, a representative of the
Young Communist International. Sun rejected the proposal for a

two-party alliance, but said he was agreeable to admitting Communists into the Kuomintang as individuals. This condition was accepted by the Chinese Communist Central Committee, apparently under pressure from Maring, and Communists began to join the KMT. (See Part II, pp. 82-84)

Sun's decision to admit Communists was immediately followed by the decision to reorganize the Kuomintang, which had become ineffectual. The Party was organizationally weak; its members were tied together primarily by the personality of Sun Yat-sen. On September 4, 1922, Sun convened a meeting of fifty-three Kuomintang members, including Communists, and announced his decision to reorganize the Party. Two days later, he appointed a committee of nine members to draft reorganization plans. According to certain pro-KMT and Communist sources, the committee included Ch'en Tu-hsiu, leader of the Chinese Communist Party. On January 1, 1923, a new Kuomintang political platform was announced. Provisions were made in the Party constitution for the holding of annual Party congresses and monthly meetings of the heads of Party committees and departments.[16] Efforts were pushed to establish Kuomintang branches in all important centers of the country. Designed to pump new life into the party, these measures, which became known as the "First Reorganization," paved the way for the Reorganization of 1924 which brought about a fundamental transformation of the Kuomintang.

Important as were the decisions to admit Communists and revitalize the Party, the evidence suggests that at that time, and to Sun Yat-sen himself, their significance was eclipsed by the Kuomintang's gravitation toward Soviet Russia. The Chinese Communist Party had been founded only the previous year and its membership was infinitesimal. This consideration, as well as Sun Yat-sen's subsequent remarks on the nature of Kuomintang-Communist collaboration, suggest it is unlikely that he regarded the Communist entry as a major solution to the Party's problems. It appears almost certain that while negotiating with Dalin on cooperation with the Chinese Communists, Sun was taking preliminary steps in the direction of cooperation with Soviet Russia.

A letter from Sun Yat-sen to Chiang Kai-shek, dated August 30, 1922, suggests that correspondence between Sun and Adolf Joffe began simultaneously with the Sun-Dalin negotiations. "Their representative," said Sun, had sent him a special messenger with a letter inquiring about Far Eastern problems. He had answered the letter point by point, and it was expected that mutual consultations would be carried on more conveniently now that letters had been exchanged. Sun informed Chiang that "this representative" had a military aide with him on his mission and that Sun had asked him to send this aide down to Shanghai first for consultation on the military situation.[17]

Whether or not Sun was referring to Adolf Joffe, arrangements for a conference with Joffe were completed at the latest by November, 1922. On its part, the USSR had by then decided to throw full support behind the Kuomintang.[18]

A clue to Sun Yat-sen's immediate objective for which he sought a Soviet alliance, is provided by a letter he wrote to Chiang Kai-shek on November 21, 1922, four days before he began negotiations with Joffe in Shanghai.[19] Sun informed Chiang that he had made important connections in Shanghai. He confided that the matter was extremely complicated and difficult to handle, but said he was fortunate in having linked up with the right and important source and that it would be possible to develop closer relations in the future. Much depended on securing a base of operations, said Sun. To secure a base, it was necessary to recapture Kwangtung. After that, the southwestern provinces of China could be unified. With the southwestern provinces as a base, said Sun, the Kuomintang would be in a powerful position. Sun added that it was precisely because of the importance of securing a base that Moscow had advised the Chinese Communists to join the Kuomintang.[20]

Thus, Sun Yat-sen's immediate goal was the recapture and consolidation of Kwangtung province as a base for national unification. Apparently, the failure of the First Northern Expedition had only strengthened his attachment to the goal of unification by military means. On the other hand, Ch'en Ch'iung-ming's rebellion had forcefully demonstrated the dangers of reliance on militarist support. Clearly, some other means of support was necessary.

The decision to cooperate with Soviet Russia was by no means made on a moment's impulse, however. If Voitinskii's account is correct, Sun had toyed with the possibility of receiving material support from Soviet Russia as early as 1920. Furthermore, his attitude toward the Russian Revolution had been friendly; this is indicated, for instance, by his congratulatory telegram to Lenin. Sun's attitude was shared by considerable numbers of Chinese who were impressed by the 1919-1920 Soviet declarations of equality toward China and disillusioned with the West following the Versailles Conference. Sun himself appeared to have become increasingly alienated from the Western Powers, who had continued to deal with the Peking Government and had turned a deaf ear to his pleas for support.[21] Finally, although Sun's meetings with Maring failed to produce results, Kuomintang members attended the First Congress of the Toilers of the Far East which was convened in Moscow in January, 1922.[22]

On January 26, 1923, following a series of talks, Sun Yat-sen and Joffe issued a joint manifesto stating the general conditions of cooperation between the Kuomintang and Soviet Russia. They agreed that in view of Chinese conditions it was not possible to establish communism or even the Soviet system in China. Furthermore, the manifesto states, it was Joffe's belief that China's most pressing problems were the completion of national unification and attainment of national independence. Joffe had assured Dr. Sun of the Russian people's warmest sympathy and willingness to lend support toward these ends.[23]

The joint manifesto came on the heels of the recovery of Canton accomplished principally by the Kwangtung Army of Hsü Ch'ung-chih, the Kwangsi Army of Liu Chen-huan, and the Yunnan Army of Yang Hsi-min. On February 21, 1923, Sun Yat-sen again returned to power in Canton. He proceeded to organize a military government and assumed the position of Generalissimo on March 2, 1923.[24] Sun's victorious return ushered in the first phase of the National Revolution. Supported by Chinese Communists and Russians, the Kuomintang began the task of consolidating the revolutionary base in Kwangtung.

Exchange of Missions, 1923

The Sun-Joffe manifesto announced in broad terms Soviet willing-ness to aid China's struggle for national unification and independ-ence. Detailed plans remained to be worked out. Hence, Sun Yat-sen ordered Liao Chung-k'ai to accompany Joffe when the latter left Shanghai. For a month Joffe and Liao stayed at Atami, a hot-springs resort in Japan.[25] According to Katsuji Fuse, who interviewed Joffe at that time, Joffe and Liao drafted plans for a military acad-emy for training Party officers modeled upon the system developed by Trotsky.[26] Actually, their discussions covered the entire question of Kuomintang reorganization. Later (in late 1926), the Chinese Communist Party tended to play up Liao Chung-k'ai as equally responsible with Sun Yat-sen for the KMT's adoption of the so-called Three Great Policies.[27] Kuomintang sources likewise credit Liao with a major role in laying the foundation for the Party's reorganization in 1924.

To carry the Liao-Joffe talks one step further, the Kuomintang appointed a delegation headed by Chiang Kai-shek which was to study conditions in Soviet Russia. The group left Shanghai on August 16, 1923, accompanied by Chang T'ai-lei, an important member of the Communist Kwangtung Regional Committee. Chiang Kai-shek studied the Soviet system in Russia, paying special attention to military matters. He met many important leaders, including Chich-erin, Kalinin, Maring, Wu Ting-k'ang (Voitinskii), Lozovskii, Joffe, Zinoviev, Trotsky, and Kamenev.[28]

Chiang's diary reveals that he formed unfavorable impressions of the Soviet Union during his inspection trip. Hollington K. Tong asserts that Chiang submitted a report to Sun Yat-sen, the tenor of which was "Don't trust Russia," upon his return to Canton late in

December, 1923, but the report was ignored by Sun.[29] By that time, Michael Borodin (whose real name was Grusenberg) had been in Canton for more than two months and the Kuomintang had become fully committed to the policy of alliance with Soviet Russia.

The first Soviet adviser to serve with the Kuomintang in Canton was a general named Pavlov. However, little is known of his activities. He was killed at Sheklung in November, 1923, while participating in a battle against the forces of Ch'en Ch'iung-ming, who had launched a counterattack against Canton.[30]

Borodin's arrival marked the real beginning of Soviet-Kuomintang collaboration. According to Borodin's first report to Moscow, he arrived at Canton on October 6, 1923. During his first meeting with Sun Yat-sen, he conveyed to Sun the greetings of Moscow and of the Soviet Political Representative, Leo Karakhan, who had arrived in Peking the month before to continue Joffe's unsuccessful efforts to establish treaty relations with the Peking Government. During their conversation, Borodin reported, Sun expressed hope of controlling Central China and Mongolia and told Borodin that everything depended on the northward movement of his troops. Sun also expressed the belief that, with Soviet Russia at its rear, Mongolia offered great possibilities as a base. Nevertheless, Borodin said, Sun told him that his immediate objective was to hold Kwangtung, to which end it was necessary to increase and strengthen his army. Sun said he needed help for this purpose and suggested setting up a direct route by steamer from Vladivostok to Canton to transport much-needed military supplies from the Soviet Union.[31]

Borodin's report strengthens the impression that a military campaign for national unification was paramount in Sun's mind and that the decision to cooperate with Soviet Russia was largely prompted by desire for Soviet material aid.

Reorganization of the Kuomintang, January, 1924

The first task to which Borodin addressed himself was not military, however, but political—the reorganization of the Kuomintang into a centralized and disciplined party patterned upon the Communist system. He moved with impressive speed. On October 11, 1923, five days after his arrival at Canton, Borodin outlined his plans on reorganization of the KMT to members of the Chinese Communist Party's Kwangtung Regional Committee. Two days later he was able to report to the Kwangtung Communists that Sun Yat-sen and other prominent KMT leaders would probably proceed to reorganize the KMT in accordance with his suggestions.[32]

Borodin advocated as a preliminary step the organization of a committee of nine Kuomintang members. Accordingly, on October 25 Sun Yat-sen appointed nine members, including the Communist T'an P'ing-shan, to the Provisional Central Executive Committee

charged with drafting plans on Party reorganization.[33] After three
months, the Provisional CEC submitted for approval at the First
Kuomintang Congress a constitution and a political program which
were actually drafted by Borodin. According to Sun Yat-sen, Borodin
had at his request drafted the constitution and the Party program
in English. They were approved by Sun and then translated into
Chinese by Liao Chung-k'ai.[34]

Sun Yat-sen delivered the opening address at the First Congress
which convened at Canton on January 20. He called attention to two
important points: organization of the Kuomintang as a strong and
effective Party, and utilization of the Party's strength to rebuild
the nation. As he himself pointed out, the latter idea was not new.
He had for years advocated Party government in view of the chaos
in China. Now, however, he realized it was too early to speak of
Party government. The first duty of a revolutionary party, Sun declared, was to build the nation. The Chinese Revolution had thus far
failed, he said, because the Kuomintang's strength had been scattered.
Then he came to the central idea of the Reorganization. The most important thing about a political party, he said, was the need for every
member to be inbued with a cooperative spirit. Party members must
sacrifice their individual freedom and contribute to the Party their
total capabilities.[35]

The Soviet imprint on the new constitution of the Kuomintang is
unmistakable. It established a pyramidal Party structure starting
from sub-district headquarters and extending upwards through
district, hsien, and provincial headquarters. The National Party
Congress, which was to meet at least every two years, was the highest Party organ. During interim periods between meetings of the
National Congress, the Central Executive Committee was invested
with supreme authority. In line with the Communist principle of
democratic centralism, Party organs at each level were required
to render absolute obedience to higher Party organs. Although Party
members were given the right of discussion before a decision on
any question had been reached, once a decision had been made they
owed the Party unquestioning obedience in order to realize Party
policy. The constitution also provided for the organization of Party
fractions as in Communist Parties. What distinguished the Kuomintang constitution from its Communist prototype was the extraordinary powers granted Sun Yat-sen, who was designated chairman of
the National Congress and the Central Executive Committee. He was
given the power of final decision on all resolutions of the CEC.[36]

Although Sun Yat-sen was primarily interested in Soviet supplies
and techniques to help him achieve national unification, his new orientation effected significant changes in the Party's professed ideology.
This is particularly evident in the reinterpretation of the Three People's Principles expounded in the "Manifesto of the First Congress."

The most striking innovation was the new emphasis on anti-imperialism in the Principle of Nationalism. The Party had two principal objectives: (1) freedom and independence of the Chinese people; and (2) equality of all peoples or races within the Chinese Republic. Primary importance was attached to the former, however, as is evident in the following passage: "To whatever class, the meaning of nationalism is none other than the elimination of imperialist aggression....to the majority of the people, the objective in the struggle for national liberation is none other than anti-imperialism." The Party denounced imperialism as the source of all of China's afflictions. Chinese militarists, the chief target of attack in earlier Party pronouncements, now occupied only the second spot as conspirators allied with imperialists.[37]

In short, anti-imperialism was equated for all practical purposes with the Principle of Nationalism, which had hitherto tended to focus on relations between the five principal races constituting the Chinese Republic. Until the Revolution of 1911, in fact, its meaning was largely confined to opposition to the Manchus. While the new stress on anti-imperialism stemmed partly from Sun Yat-sen's disillusionment with the West, Communist influence is clearly discernible in the KMT's formulation of anti-imperialism as a conscious policy and in its program to build up anti-imperialist sentiment as the motive power of the National Revolution.

In accordance with Comintern policy, the Chinese Communist Party had raised the slogans of anti-imperialism and antimilitarism in a manifesto issued in May, 1922. The Party denounced imperialists as the principal enemies of the Chinese people and accused Chinese militarists of being their tools. Specifically, the Chinese Communist Party accused Britain of supporting Ch'en Ch'iung-ming against Sun Yat-sen in Kwangtung.[38] In contrast, in a manifesto issued on August 15, 1922, before his new orientation, Sun Yat-sen had made no adverse mention of imperialism in describing Ch'en Ch'iung-ming's coup of June 16, 1922.[39]

The Kuomintang's anti-imperialist policy was foreshadowed in the manifesto on the "First Reorganization" issued on January 1, 1923. The Kuomintang chastised the Manchus for sacrificing national rights and signing unequal treaties with the Powers, thus reducing China to the status of a colony. It advocated revision of the unequal treaties to recover China's position of equality and independence in international relations.[40] In the Party program of January, 1924, the Kuomintang went one step further and pledged itself to abolish the unequal treaties.[41]

Anti-imperialism was linked also with the Principle of Democracy. The Kuomintang advocated direct exercise by the people of the rights of election, initiative, referendum, and recall, and advocated division of the government into five functions or branches. The Party declared: "Only truly anti-imperialist individuals and organizations may enjoy all rights and liberty. All those, whether individuals or organizations, who betray the country and the people and who owe allegiance to imperialists and militarists are barred from the enjoyment of such rights and liberty." The democratic representative system was criticized. The so-called democratic system in various countries in modern times was often monopolized by the bourgeoisie and transformed into an instrument of oppression against the common people, the Party declared. The democracy championed by the Kuomintang, on the other hand, was the joint possession of the common people and not the private property of a minority.[42] Criticism of the representative system had also been voiced in the manifesto of January, 1923.[43]

Distrust of the representative system of government further bolstered the theory of political tutelage, envisaged early by Sun Yat-sen as a transitional stage between the military period of struggle to establish a republic and the final stage of constitutional government. During the period of political tutelage, power was to be wielded by the Party while it prepared the people for constitutional government. In January, 1924, the theory of political tutelage was fortified by the new stress on Party centralization. The Party declared that all means should be employed to educate and train Party members as revolutionary elements. It was necessary to disseminate nationwide propaganda so that the people would join the revolution to seize political power and to suppress the people's enemies. Upon seizure of power and establishment of a government, political power was to be exercised by the Party in order to forestall counterrevolutionary movements within the country, to deal with imperialist conspiracies against the Chinese people, and to eliminate all obstacles to the execution of the Kuomintang's principles. Only an organized and powerful Party, the KMT declared, was capable of carrying out such tasks for the benefit of the entire people.[44]

The most important provisions of the Principle of the People's Livelihood, according to the "Manifesto of the First Congress," were equalization of land tenure and regulation of capital. These ingredients were not new. What distinguished the 1924 manifesto from previous Party documents, including the January, 1923, manifesto, was the concept of the function of the masses in the National Revolution. Anti-imperialist sentiment of the poor peasants and workers was particularly strong because of their hard living conditions, the KMT declared. Victory in the national revolutionary movement therefore depended on the participation of the peasantry and labor throughout the country. On the one hand, the Kuomintang should lend its total strength to help develop the peasant and labor movements in order to strengthen the forces of the national revolutionary movement. The Party must, on the other hand, demand that peasants and workers join the Kuomintang and struggle ceaselessly together with the Kuomintang to promote the progress of the national revolutionary movement. The Kuomintang's struggle for national liberation, the "Manifesto" declared, was supported by intellectuals, workers, peasants, and merchants,45 reflecting the Communist analysis of the Kuomintang as a political party representing various classes.

The new stress on the political potentialities of mass action as a revolutionary force was a product of Sun Yat-sen's new orientation. Whereas he previously had tended to rely on militarist support in carrying out the Party's program, the Chinese Communist Party had from the beginning laid stress on the Party's position among the masses as its major source of power. By January, 1924, it already held a considerable edge over the Kuomintang in mass organization, particularly among workers. The Kuomintang established a labor department under Liao Chung-k'ai and a peasant department under the Communist Lin Tsu-han.46 In the Party's political program, it pledged itself to reform agrarian organization and improve the living conditions of the peasantry. It promised to enact a labor law, improve the living conditions of workers, and protect and help the development of labor organizations. Among other provisions in its fourteen-point domestic program, the Kuomintang advocated "complete" freedom of speech, press, assembly, and religion.47

The swiftness with which Borodin was able to push through reorganization plans and his authorship of the KMT constitution and program suggest that he won Sun Yat-sen's confidence within a relatively short time. On October 26, 1923, about three weeks after Borodin's arrival, Sun Yat-sen wired thanks to the "friendly Moscow Government and Party" for sending Borodin to aid the Kuomintang in Kwangtung. Simultaneously, he wired Chiang Kai-shek, then in Moscow, that it was very clear "who was a friend and who was not."48 On December 13, 1923, Sun officially appointed Borodin adviser to the Kuomintang.49

Opposition to the Admission of Communists, to January, 1924

Borodin's success is attributed by Ch'en Tu-hsiu to the promise of substantial material aid which came in "his briefcase."50 Sun's decision to make an alliance with Soviet Russia was virtually unopposed, at least not publicly, by Kuomintang members. In contrast, his decision to admit Communists into the Party was challenged from the beginning. A Kuomintang Right Wing which opposed this policy, according to the "Brief History," had already developed at the time of Sun's negotiations with Communist representatives in the summer of 1922 [Doc. 1, p. 27].

Even the Provisional Central Executive Committee which was organized in October, 1923, to draft plans for the KMT's reorganization was not free of doubts concerning the Communist's motives. Sun

Yat-sen had to deliver a stern warning against the "anti-Communists" on the committee, Chiang Kai-shek later reported, in order to bring them into line.[51]

Despite Sun's firmness, official protest against the admission of Communists came one month later. On November 29, 1923, eleven members of the Kwangtung Branch of the KMT presented a petition to Sun. They charged that Ch'en Tu-hsiu was the actual author of the KMT's political program and accused the Communists of utilizing the KMT for their own purposes. In his marginal notes on the petition, Sun assured them that Ch'en had no part in drafting the program and that he would be expelled if he should disobey the Party. The Russian Revolution had succeeded and the Chinese Revolution had not, said Sun, because KMT members still did not understand the Three People's Principles. There was actually no difference between the Principle of the People's Livelihood and Communism. Sun declared that the foreign powers had often helped the enemies of the Kuomintang to destroy the Party and that sympathy could only be expected from Russia, the oppressed nations, and the oppressed peoples.[52]

The oppositionist elements rallied under the leadership of Feng Tzu-yu at the First Kuomintang Congress.[53] Wang Ching-wei later recalled that they unsuccessfully sponsored a resolution prohibiting Kuomintang members from entering any other political party. If passed, this would have called upon the Communists either to give up Communist membership or withdraw from the Kuomintang.[54]

To allay suspicions, Li Ta-chao presented a statement of the purpose of KCT and CY members in joining the KMT. They did not do so to utilize the KMT for the Communist movement, Li said, and they joined the Party not collectively but as individuals. Hence, one might say that they "straddled" two parties, but not that there was a party within a party. Li said that the Communists had dual responsibility in the KMT: the ordinary responsibility of KMT members, and the responsibility arising from the alliance of the KMT with the world revolutionary movement.[55]

In the elections to the first Central Executive Committee of the Kuomintang, Communists won three of the twenty-four seats. They were T'an P'ing-shan, Yü Shu-te, and Li Ta-chao. Six Communists— Mao Tse-tung, Ch'ü Ch'iu-pai, Chang Kuo-t'ao, Lin Tsu-han, Han Lin-fu, and Yü Fang-chou—were elected to the seventeen-man Reserve CEC.[56] Although their representation on the Kuomintang CEC was not significant, Communists gained a strategic foothold in the Party when T'an P'ing-shan became head of the Kuomintang Organization Department,[57] by far the most important Party organ. Among its many powers, the Organization Department had authority to appoint personnel to positions at all levels of the Party hierarchy, select new members, and keep check on the Party membership in general.

Organization of the Whampoa Academy, January to May, 1924

The reorganized Kuomintang turned first to the organization of a military academy, as planned by Joffe and Liao Chung-k'ai. On January 24, 1924, Sun Yat-sen appointed Chiang Kai-shek as chairman of a preparatory committee charged with organizing the Party academy. The Whampoa Military Academy began functioning in the following May. Chiang was appointed president and Liao Chung-k'ai the Kuomintang's party representative to the Academy.[58] Liao's appointment was the KMT's first use of the Soviet Commissar system, which accords equal power to the commanding officer and the Party representative in each military unit and thus ensures Party supervision of the military. Wang Ching-wei, Hu Han-min, and other Kuomintang leaders were appointed as political instructors at the Academy to lecture on such topics as the Three People's Principles and the history of the Kuomintang.[59]

In a speech to the first class, which consisted of 460 students,[60] Chiang Kai-shek explained the Party's objectives. The Kuomintang's past weaknesses, he said, stemmed from Party members' lack of training. Chiang stressed the utter necessity of adherence to Party discipline. "Aside from 'obedience to order,'" he said, "no other phrase is allowed within the Academy."[61]

Chiang's diary mentions altogether thirty-two meetings of the preparatory committee, which was composed of seven Kuomintang members.[62] The diary makes no reference to Soviet direction in organizing the academy. The record suggests, however, that the dominant role was played by Borodin and General Vassili Blücher, who was known in China as Galen. He headed the group of about forty Soviet advisers who arrived at Canton with Borodin.[63] Many of the advisers were engaged as military instructors at the Whampoa Academy.[64] According to Hollington K. Tong, Chiang had met Galen on his trip to Russia and had personally selected him as his chief of staff at the academy. Tong also asserts that Borodin played an important role in establishing the school.[65]

The Russians were in fact able to exert such influence that as a gesture of protest Chiang Kai-shek resigned as chairman of the preparatory committee on February 21, 1924.[66] On the following March 14th, Chiang explained his move in a letter to Liao Chung-k'ai. He was dissatisfied, Chiang said, with the Kuomintang's current situation and policies. Sun Yat-sen's Soviet orientation was the principal cause of his misgivings. It was his belief, Chiang told Liao, that Kuomintang members should not encourage Sun Yat-sen to insist on his own views. The Russian Communist Party was dishonest; only thirty percent of what it said could be trusted. The Chinese in Moscow scorned Sun Yat-sen and had completely become slaves of the Russians. The Russian Communist Party's only policy toward China, Chiang declared, was to build up the Chinese Communist

Party and bring about its rise to power. He could not believe that the Kuomintang could actually cooperate permanently with the Chinese Communist Party. Furthermore, Chiang told Liao that the Russians considered the Manchus, Mongolians, Mohammedans, and Tibetans to be within the Soviet orbit, and that they were probably not wholly devoid of designs on China proper. Concluding with the view that the Russians' so-called internationalism and World Revolution were merely different terms for imperialism, Chiang expressed dismay that his report on Soviet Russia should have been ignored.[67]

Chiang later resumed his post upon the persuasion of Sun Yat-sen and other KMT leaders, principally Liao Chung-k'ai. In a letter to Sun, Chiang declared that he dared not disobey his leader and was therefore returning to Whampoa. He again voiced misgivings about the KMT's course and, in carefully worded phrases, complained that Sun did not have full confidence in him. He implored Sun to trust him completely and to believe that his actions had never been influenced by the slightest thought of personal gain.[68]

The Chinese Communist and Soviet Positions in Canton, 1924

Despite Sun Yat-sen's vast powers which were formalized by the new constitution, his decision to admit Communists into the Party continued to be challenged by dissident elements. While there was no open schism, the Party was increasingly split between two factions: the Left Wing, which supported Sun on the Communist issue, and the Right Wing, which stood opposed. On March 16, 1924, in a circular notice to Party members, Sun Yat-sen reminded them that they had no individual freedom and must unconditionally observe Party principles and execute Party policies.[69]

On June 18, 1924, another petition to impeach the Communists was submitted by three of the five members of the Kuomintang Central Supervisory Committee—Chang Chi, Hsieh Ch'ih, and Teng Tse-ju. They charged that the majority of KMT organizers sent out to the localities were Communists who were more interested in advancing their own Party. They accused Communist members of the Kuomintang of forcing their policies on the KMT and seeking to destroy it by criticism, propaganda, and the organization of Communist Party fractions. The authors of the petition cast suspicion also on Communist efforts in organizing peasant associations in Kwangtung. They concluded that while they were not opposed to the Communists' entry into the Kuomintang as individuals, the existence of a party within a party, the actual result of the Communist entry, threatened the very survival of the Kuomintang.[70]

The Second Plenum of the Kuomintang CEC, which convened on August 15 to discuss the CSC petition, ended in a decisive victory for the policy of admission of Communists. For the first time, the KMT adopted resolutions stating the reasons for and the conditions of this policy. The resolutions made three principal points. The

first point echoed the "Resolutions on the National Movement and the
Kuomintang Problem" adopted by the Chinese Communist Party in the
the summer of 1923 in calling for the centralization of all revolutionary elements in the KMT. The CEC explained that since China was
in a semicolonial status, all classes shared a common determination to struggle for independence and liberation from imperialist
oppression. The Kuomintang was the political party which represented all classes in the national revolutionary struggle. Hence, all
truly revolutionary elements should be centralized in the Kuomintang
regardless of class distinctions. In the second point, the CEC cited
the Kuomintang constitution to the effect that all those who were
willing to accept the Party's platform and to meet the obligations
of Party membership could become members. Hence, the CEC
stated, the Party had no right to interfere with members who did
not violate Party regulations. On the other hand, all members who
were unwilling to engage positively in the revolutionary movement in
accordance with the Three People's Principles, and who not only
failed to oppose imperialists and militarists but failed to support
the laboring masses, would be dealt with according to Party discipline without question as to their ideological commitments. In the
third point, the CEC referred specifically to the Chinese Communist Party. The Communist Party, it said, was not a product of individual speculation nor was it arbitrarily created and transplanted
to China. It was a political organization arising out of the natural
class struggle of the Chinese industrial proletariat and, as such,
was necessarily a part of the political organization of the international proletariat. Even if the Chinese Communist Party were to be
dissolved, the Chinese proletariat could not be destroyed and would
organize again. Thus, the KMT could only ask Communists who had
joined the Party whether their actions were in harmony with its
principles and platform and nothing more. The Party must govern
all Party members in accordance with its platform and constitution;
Communists who had accepted the Party's platform and had joined
the Party must be regarded as members of the Party and governed
as such.[71]

The CEC's positive settlement of the Communist issue was preceded by the organization on July 11, 1924, of the Kuomintang Political Council. No provision had been made for such an organ in the
KMT constitution; it was organized by Sun Yat-sen personally; he
assumed the position of chairman and appointed twelve members to
the Council. The Political Council adopted two resolutions on its
functions: (1) to be responsible to the CEC for Party affairs. It
could either report to the CEC before taking action or request rati-
fication by the CEC after taking action; and (2) to execute all diplomatic and political policies decided on by Sun Yat-sen.[72]

The authority which the Political Council granted to itself thus

superseded that of the twenty-four-man CEC, representing a step
in the direction of concentration of power within the KMT. However,
the authority of the Political Council was clearly dependent on Sun
Yat-sen, who held the power of deciding all diplomatic and political
matters. Thus, it appears, the Political Council was designed to
facilitate execution of Sun Yat-sen's policies and to hold down dissident elements of the Right Wing.

The passage of the resolutions on the admission of Communists
into the Kuomintang represented further defeat for the Right. The
resolutions were greeted enthusiastically by the Chinese Communists, who had been disheartened by the Kuomintang's failure to
formalize the policy of admitting them [Doc. 1, pp. 37-38]. Despite
this significant gain and Borodin's success in winning Sun Yat-sen's
confidence, however, some of the Soviet advisers were disappointed
with the initial results of their work in Canton. According to a later
Soviet report, they felt that it was futile to continue working in Canton and demanded a move to North China or the Yangtze valley
[Doc. 39, p. 79].

Their discouragement may have been influenced by the following
factors.

First, Soviet influence in Canton was represented to a great extent by Borodin's personal influence with Sun Yat-sen. Although the
Kuomintang had been reorganized, the government remained virtually
unchanged, with Sun Yat-sen as Generalissimo. The Kuomintang was
still dependent on the support of provincial "guest armies," over
which it had no real control. In the military sphere, Soviet influence
was almost exclusively confined to the Whampoa Military Academy.

Secondly, there seems to have been some impatience on the part
of Soviet advisers with Kuomintang policies. Although an ambitious
domestic program had been spelled out in the KMT platform, the
Party was largely preoccupied with military affairs. This was
necessitated by the precarious circumstances of Kuomintang rule
in Canton. The Party's foothold in Canton and surrounding areas
was continually threatened by internal dissident elements and enemy
armies in neighboring districts of Kwangtung. Under such conditions,
much of the social legislation adopted at the First Congress remained to be carried out. It was not until November, 1924, for instance, that the Labor Union Law containing among other provisions
recognition of the right to strike, was promulgated.[73]

Thirdly, the organization of the Soviet group had yet to be clearly
defined.[74] There were also problems of coordination with Moscow.
Karakhan had finally succeeded in negotiating a treaty with the Peking Government which was signed on May 31, 1924. However, the
Russian Embassy compound, in the custody of the Dutch Legation
following the Peking Government's withdrawal of recognition of the
old Russian representative, was not returned to the USSR until

September, 1924.[75] Thus, it was only toward the end of 1924 that an
intricate system of coordination began to evolve, with the Soviet
Embassy serving as the focal point for the transmission of instructions and funds to various groups working in China. The first shipment of Russian supplies did not arrive at Canton until October 7,
1924,[76] almost exactly one year after Borodin's arrival.

The Merchant Corps Incident and the First Eastern Expedition, October, 1924, to April, 1925

The supplies arrived at a propitious moment. The Kuomintang's
authority was threatened by the Merchant Corps, a militia maintained
by Cantonese merchants. Commanded by Ch'en Lien-po, comprador
of the Hongkong-Shanghai Banking Corporation, the Merchant Corps
was reportedly allied with Ch'en Ch'iung-ming, who had a powerful
army in the East River districts of Kwangtung. The crisis had been
precipitated by the government's seizure on August 10 of a con-
signment of rifles ordered by Ch'en Lien-po from a British concern.
Tension mounted as the Merchant Corps mobilized its forces throughout Kwangtung province; the strength of the Corps was estimated by
one source at 50,000.[77]

In a manifesto to foreign countries on the Merchant Corps crisis,
issued on September 1, Sun Yat-sen declared that the Merchant
Corps had risen in open rebellion with British support. The British
consul at Canton, Sun asserted, had conveyed to him the protest of
the Shameen Consular Corps and had intimated that British naval
forces stood ready to intervene should the government take drastic
measures. Sun expressed dismay that the British labor government
would threaten thus to overthrow the Canton Government, although
imperialist powers had consistently aided counterrevolutionary
forces diplomatically. A new era had just begun, he said, in which the
Chinese must devote themselves to the elimination of imperialist
intervention in China, the greatest obstacle to the completion of
the Revolution.[78] Ten days later, in a wire to the MacDonald
government, Sun accused the British consul of planning to destroy
the Canton Government.[79]

This was the first major crisis involving a foreign power to occur
since the Kuomintang had proclaimed anti-imperialism as its foremost policy. Despite Sun Yat-sen's declarations, however, he
appeared anxious to avoid direct conflict with the British; his attention was focused on the national scene. On September 18, 1924, two
days after the outbreak of the Second Mukden-Chihli War, Sun declared his support of the Mukden Army and launched the Kuomintang's Second Northern Expedition. In line with the Party's anti-
imperialist emphasis, Sun stated that the Northern Expedition was
anti-imperialist as well as antimilitarist. Since the Revolution of
1911, he asserted, the scourge of war had been caused directly by

Chinese militarists and indirectly by imperialists. From Yüan
Shih-k'ai to Wu P'ei-fu, he declared, Chinese counterrevolutionaries
had been supported by imperialists. Thus, the objective of the
Northern expedition was not merely the overthrow of Wu P'ei-fu
and Ts'ao K'un, but the prevention of future counter revolutionary
regimes. "In other words, the objective of this war is not only the
overthrow of militarists but also, and more particularly, the overthrow of imperialism upon which the existence of militarists depends.
This must be done so that the root of counterrevolution may be
forever eliminated and China may rid herself of her semi-colonial
status and become a free and independent nation."[80]

Sun ordered most of the Canton Governments' forces to proceed to
Shaokuan in preparation for the drive north against Wu P'ei-fu;
he himself went there to supervise preparations. A series of letters
exchanged between Sun and Chiang Kai-shek at this time suggests
that Sun was so preoccupied with the Second Northern Expedition
that he tended to ignore the dangers posed by the Canton Merchant
Corps. He instructed Chiang on October 7, the day the first Soviet
weapons arrived, to transfer them immediately to Shaokuan.[81] Two
days later, he ordered Chiang to organize a Revolutionary Committee to cope with the Merchant Corps.[82] On the same day, however, he sent Chiang a secret telegram with orders to abandon
Whampoa and to send all weapons and students to Shaokuan to concentrate on the Northern Expedition.[83] On October 11, Sun ordered
Chiang to move immediately to Shaokuan. The Northern Expedition
was bound to be successful, he said, and it was going to be started
even if there were no funds for the purpose. He told Chiang that
he definitely would not return to deal with the situation in Canton.[84]

According to his diary, Chiang Kai-shek defied Sun's orders. On
October 9 he wrote Sun warning him of the danger in Canton and
urging him to return.[85] On October 11, he told Sun that he would
hold Whampoa to the death. He urged Sun to send the troops back
to Canton to take prompt action. Sun must not, he said, waver and
delay in the belief that the Northern Expedition could be successful.[86] Sun Yat-sen apparently came around to Chiang's views and
finally decided to take firm measures against the Merchant Corps.
On October 14, he ordered the following units placed under Chiang's
command: the gendarmes, the workers' and peasants' self-defense
corps, the aviation unit, the armored car battalion, the arsenal, the
guard battalion, the Whampoa Military Academy and the Yunnan
Army School. That night Chiang, according to his diary, led an attack
on the stronghold of the Merchant Corps which ended in complete
victory for the KMT.[87]

Chiang's account is disputed by other sources. Chou Lu, who
later became a leading member of the KMT Right Wing, asserts
that during the crisis Chiang Kai-shek proposed retreating from

Canton. According to Chou, Hsü Ch'ung-chih and Liao Chung-k'ai
took the lead in organizing action against the Merchant Corps. It
was Hsü Ch'ung-chih's Kwangtung Army which assumed full responsibility for the move, Chou asserts.[88] Fan Shih-sheng, whose own
role is the subject of controversy,[89] asserts that the decision to
suppress the Corps was made at a meeting attended by Fan, Hu
Han-min, Liao Chung-k'ai, and others. According to Fan, it was
agreed that Hsü Ch'ung-chih, Wu T'ieh-ch'eng, and Li Fu-lin would
lead the action against the Corps.[90] Neither Chou Lu nor Fan Shih-
sheng mentions the Revolutionary Committee.

Document 11, Borodin's report on the Revolutionary Committee,
is an important addition to the available sources on this subject,
particularly since it is dated the morning of October 14, 1924, the
very day the suppression of the Merchant Corps took place.

Borodin's report offers striking corroboration of Chiang's own
record of the incident. It gives, for instance, an almost identical
list of the units placed under Chiang's command. While Borodin reported that Hsü Ch'ung-chih, Fan Shih-sheng, and other commanders were also scheduled to participate in the attack, he added that
in case their armies "declare unwillingness to move," the units
under the Revolutionary Committee's direct control would take
action [Doc. 11, pp. 10, 13]. Borodin thus showed confidence in
Chiang, who commanded these units, and doubt as to the loyalty of
the other troops.

This indirect expression of confidence in Chiang Kai-shek is
significant in the light of the evidence in Chiang's diary that Borodin
had sought to influence the appointment of members of the Revolutionary Committee. On October 9, 1924, Chiang wrote Sun Yat-sen
that Borodin had just paid him a visit at the Whampoa Academy.
During their talk, Chiang said, Borodin expressed himself strongly
against the inclusion of Wang Ching-wei and Hu Han-min on the
Revolutionary Committee. Chiang himself disagreed with Borodin
and requested Sun Yat-sen to include both Wang and Hu.[91] Sun Yat-
sen's reply is suggestive of Borodin's influence. It was unnecessary
to include Hu Han-min and Wang Ching-wei on the Revolutionary
Committee, Sun told Chiang, because the Revolution must follow the
Russian pattern and Hu Han-min had lost faith in this regard. Wang
Ching-wei, he said, was basically not a Russian-type revolutionary.
While both men were best fitted by nature for maintaining the status
quo, neither was suited for taking drastic action.[92]

Despite this letter, however, Sun Yat-sen appointed Wang Ching-
wei to the Revolutionary Committee on the following day, October
10. The other members were Chiang Kai-shek, Liao Chung-k'ai,
Hsü Ch'ung-chih, Eugene Chen, and the Communist T'an P'ing-shan.
Hu Han-min was excluded[93] although he was, as Deputy Generalissimo, theoretically the most important KMT leader at Canton.

Despite Borodin's apprehension, the troops not directly controlled by the Revolutionary Committee cooperated in the successful
attack. A direct result of the incident was the organization of the
Whampoa Training Regiment with arms seized from the Merchant
Corps.[94] Whampoa cadets had played their first active role during
the Merchant Corps Incident and were to become an increasingly
important political and military force in Canton.

Early in 1925, Kuomintang rule was again challenged when Ch'en
Ch'iung-ming led a counterattack against Canton. To meet the new
crisis, the Party launched the First Eastern Expedition on January
20, 1925 with Chiang Kai-shek as commander-in-chief. Swatow and
Chaoan were captured by the Expedition's forces in March and the
East River districts of Kwangtung, the stronghold of Ch'en Ch'iung-
ming, were soon after pacified.[95]

The Effect of Sun Yat-sen's Death on the Kuomintang's
Policies, March to June, 1925

The suppression of the Merchant Corps and the First Eastern
Expedition consolidated the Kuomintang's hold on Canton. At the
same time, the Party began again to play a national role. On October
23, 1924, Feng Yü-hsiang, a principal lieutenant of Wu P'ei-fu,
abruptly changed sides and seized Peking; this resulted in the collapse of the Chihli Clique in North China. The new Northern coalition centered around Feng invited Sun Yat-sen to Peking to cooperate
with the provisional government set up under its auspices. Sun left
Canton for Peking in November, elated at the chance to realize his
plans for convening a national assembly which he outlined in a manifesto issued on November 10, 1924. His negotiations with the provisional Peking government soon ended in deadlock, however. In
February, 1925, the provisional government exploded any remaining hopes of an agreement when it convened a reconstruction conference against Sun's opposition.[96] On March 12, 1925, Sun Yat-sen
died in Peking in an atmosphere of defeat.

In a document known as "Tsung-li's Will," Sun Yat-sen told his
followers that he had struggled for the National Revolution for forty
years, with freedom and equality for China as his objectives. Forty
years of experience had taught him, he said, that to realize these
objectives it was necessary to awaken the masses and to join in
common struggle with peoples of the world who treated the Chinese
as equals. The Revolution had not yet been accomplished, he said.
He charged his disciples with the duty of continuing to struggle for
the final success of the Revolution in accordance with his writings—
"General Principles of Reconstruction," "The Outline of Reconstruction," the "Three People's Principles," and the "Manifesto of
the First Congress." He had recently advocated the convening of a
national assembly and the abolition of the unequal treaties. These

objectives, he stated, should be realized within the shortest possible time.[97]

The Third Plenum of the CEC convened on May 18, 1925 at Peking,[98] whither many of Sun's followers had accompanied him. The CEC unanimously adopted resolutions completely to accept Sun Yatsen's will as the Kuomintang's bible. A manifesto announcing the CEC's decision declared that all who accepted Sun Yat-sen's will would be recognized as comrades. All who continued counterrevolutionary actions and received support and orders from imperialist powers to obstruct the progress of the National Revolution would be considered as enemies.[99]

The Third CEC Plenum reaffirmed and strengthened the policy of alliance with Soviet Russia. In a "Manifesto on the Current Situation," the CEC declared that Soviet Russia had abolished the unequal treaties between Russia and China on the one hand and, on the other hand, had supported the struggle of the Chinese people in the movement for abolition of the unequal treaties. Soviet Russia had destroyed imperialist Russia by the use of revolutionary force, the CEC declared, and was allied with the oppressed peoples of the world to destroy imperialism everywhere.[100]

In his will Sun Yat-sen stated the general policy of allying with peoples of the world who treated the Chinese as equals. This was in line with the political program adopted at the First KMT Congress, which stated that China would recognize as "most-favored nations" all countries willing to relinquish special rights in China and to abolish treaties compromising Chinese sovereignty.[101] The will makes no specific mention of an alliance with Soviet Russia. Hence, the CEC also cited a letter Sun Yat-sen wrote to the Soviet Government shortly before his death as the basis for the "Manifesto on the Current Situation.[102]

In his letter, addressed to the Central Executive Committee of the Soviet Government, Sun said that on his deathbed his thoughts turned to it as well as to the future destiny of the Kuomintang and China. The Soviet leaders were at the head of the union of free republics, a heritage left by the immortal Lenin to all suppressed peoples of the world. By means of this heritage, Sun said, the victims of imperialism would inevitably win their emancipation. He then stated: "I leave behind me a party which, as I always hoped, will be allied with you in its historical task of liberating China and other suppressed peoples from the yoke of imperialism. My charge to the Kuomintang party before all is that it shall continue to promote the cause of the national revolutionary movement for the emancipation of China, which has been degraded by imperialism into a semi-colonial country. I therefore charge my party to maintain permanent contact with you. I cherish the firm belief that your support of my country will remain unaltered. In taking my last leave of you, dear comrades, I express the hope that the day is approaching when the Soviet Union will greet in a free and strong China its friend and ally, and that the two states will proceed hand in hand as allies in the great fight for the emancipation of the oppressed of the whole world."[103]

The Kuomintang's Soviet orientation was solidified by a series of messages exchanged between the Kuomintang, the Russian Communist Party, and the Comintern. The Central Committee of the Russian Communist Party sent a telegram, signed by Stalin, extending condolences to the Central Executive Committee of the Kuomintang and expressing the conviction that the party would continue to fight for liberation from imperialism under Sun Yat-sen's banner. In a wire addressed to Stalin and Zinoviev, the KMT Central Executive Committee vowed to continue the work of Sun Yat-sen. The CEC was convinced, it said, that as true disciples of Lenin, the Russian Communists would fight along with the heirs of Sun Yat-sen. In reply, Zinoviev wired the Kuomintang CEC in the name of the Comintern. The Comintern, he said, was following the struggle of the Chinese people with great attention and, true to Lenin's charge, was teaching the workers of all countries to support the national revolutionary movements of the Eastern peoples, especially the people of China. The ECCI, said Zinoviev, would do all in its power to make clear to all workers of all countries the significance of Sun Yat-sen's work. The Comintern was convinced that all its sections would render support to the Kuomintang, which would lead Sun Yat-sen's cause to victory. Zinoviev added that the ECCI did not doubt that the Chinese Communist Party, which was cooperating with the Kuomintang, would also prove equal to the great historical tasks confronting it.[104]

Meanwhile, in a letter to the Central Executive Committee of the Kuomintang, the Chinese Communist Central Committee pledged full support to the KMT on behalf of the Chinese Communist Party, the Chinese workers and peasants, the proletariat of the world, and all friendly parties associated with the Comintern.[105]

The Third CEC Plenum reaffirmed the policy of admission of Communists into the Kuomintang. In the "Instructions of the Kuomintang of China on the Admission of Communists into Our Party," the CEC defended on a general level the concept of centralizing all revolutionary elements in the Kuomintang. It specifically confirmed the resolutions admitting Communists which were adopted at the Second Plenum in August, 1924. The CEC charged the imperialists and militarists with responsibility for the doubts which had arisen among the people in general and among certain KMT elements because of Communist membership in the KMT. Party members must understand, it said, that Communists joined the KMT because they accepted the principles and program of the KMT and shared its duty of carrying forward the National Revolution. The CEC added that revolution in any country was part of the World Revolution.

Since Sun Yat-sen's will makes no mention of either the concept of centralizing all Chinese revolutionary elements in the KMT or the policy of admission of Communists, the CEC based the "Instructions" on statements made by Sun during his lifetime. Sun had repeatedly made clear to all Party members, the CEC said, the reasons for the admission of Communists. Although the Kuomintang's organization was based on the system of democratic centralism, one supreme principle had always been in force. The Kuomintang was founded by the Tsung-li, and his Three People's Principles were the Party's eternal principles. When Sun Yat-sen was alive, he had the power of deciding the actions of Party members. Now that he had passed away, the CEC said, the actions of Party members must be completely determined by the teachings he had bequeathed to the Party.[106]

Kuomintang leaders took decisive action against Right Wing elements. Feng Tzu-yu, leader of the opposition against the admission of Communists at the First KMT Congress, had bolted Party discipline and had organized a separate organization, the Peking KMT Comrades' Club. The CEC immediately expelled Feng and others associated with him.[107]

The Kuomintang pledged itself to the realization of the immediate policies of convening a national assembly and abolition of the unequal treaties. In a series of declarations, the Third CEC Plenum called on all members to devote unceasing efforts toward the realization of the two objectives specifically mentioned by Sun Yat-sen in his will.[108]

Anti-British Policies, Summer, 1925

The later sessions of the Third CEC Plenum were held in Canton,[109] coincidentally with the outbreak of anti-imperialist demonstrations and strikes resulting from the May Thirtieth Incident in Shanghai. On May 30, 1925, Chinese students and workers held a parade protesting the shooting of a number of striking workers at Japanese-owned plants. When some of the demonstrators were arrested, the crowd headed for a police station where a British officer shouted orders to open fire. Twelve students were killed. In protest, Chinese merchants closed down shops. A general strike, led by the Communist-controlled General Labor Union, crippled Japanese- and British-owned enterprises. Patriotic riots and strikes broke out in Peking, Kiukiang, Hankow, Kaifeng, Amoy, Tientsin, and other major cities.

A general strike was declared in Canton on June 19. Four days later, on June 23, a demonstration parade of Whampoa cadets, workers, and students was fired upon by British forces, resulting in the death of a great number of demonstrators. The incident, known as the "Shameen Massacre," stirred anti-British sentiment to fever pitch.

What was the policy of the Kuomintang, which had pledged itself to eliminate imperialist influence from China and within the shortest possible time to abolish the unequal treaties? In a declaration issued at half past seven in the evening of June 23, the CEC made known its desire for peaceful settlement of the incident and announced the organization of an investigation committee. The CEC declared that it had decided not to rely on military force or on vengeful methods, and that it would adopt peaceful means to pursue its objective, the abolition of the unequal treaties.[110] In effect, the Kuomintang announced that it would not go to war against Britain.

Nevertheless, Party leaders repeatedly called for preparations for war. Document 13, a letter from Chiang Kai-shek to Galen, dated June 26, 1925, three days after the Shameen Massacre, illustrates this phenomenon. Chiang declared that in addition to employing a boycott of British goods and other such passive means of struggle, the Kuomintang should start military preparations, to be completed within half a year, for an extended period of armed struggle against the British. This struggle, Chiang added, might last for from three to five years. Enclosed with the letter were detailed plans for reorganizing the Party's military establishment. Although he had drafted plans on fighting the British before the Shameen Incident, he said, the current situation required the immediate execution of some of these plans [Doc. 13, p. 15].

In another set of plans presented on July 7, 1925, Chiang again declared that British imperialism must be recognized as the greatest and most immediate enemy. The British government, he said, had conspired with and rendered support to the Kuomintang's enemies in every crisis that had ever occurred in Kwangtung. The Hongkong Government was responsible for and guided Ch'en Ch'iung-ming's coup d'état of June 16, the Merchant Corps rebellion, Ch'en Ch'iung-ming's disturbances in the East River districts, and the rebellion of Liu Chen-huan and Yang Hsi-min. Chiang asserted that there could be no more room for compromise after the Shameen Incident. The Canton Government must clarify its attitude and call upon the masses to cooperate with it in a war to the death against Britain. However, Chiang pointed out that since Britain was sure to help Ch'en Ch'iung-ming and other enemies of the KMT in Kwangtung, the Party must first of all clear Kwangtung province of enemy troops. The Party should then launch a Northern Expedition. Finally, to strengthen its position, the Party must reorganize the Army and centralize finances.[111]

Both sets of plans were designed to realize the resolutions on reorganization of the Army which had been adopted earlier by the Third CEC Plenum with the warning that all who opposed military reorganization would be severely dealt with.[112] However, it is significant that both of Chiang Kai-shek's reorganization plans were linked to anti-British policies. Thus, it appears that military organization was being pushed through by Kuomintang leaders on the ground that they must prepare to fight British imperialism.

Conspiracy with the British was cited also to justify the ousting of two powerful generals, Liu Chen-huan, commander of the Kwangsi Army, and Yang Hsi-min, commander of the Yunnan Army. They had helped to recover Canton for the Kuomintang in January, 1923, but were provincial militarists of the old school and had no close ties with the Party.

Liu and Yang had been charged with the defense of Canton and its environs during the Eastern Expedition. In May, 1925, Chiang Kai-shek, Liao Chung-k'ai, Wang Ching-wei, and T'an Yen-k'ai conferred at the headquarters of the Eastern Expeditionary Forces at Swatow. It was decided to dispatch some of the troops back to Canton to deal with Liu Chen-huan and Yang Hsi-min. On June 12, 1925, Chiang Kai-shek was appointed garrison commander of Canton. The next day, on the outskirts of Canton, the troops of the Kwangsi and Yunnan armies were defeated and disbanded. Liu and Yang were ousted from the city.113

The Kuomintang explained their expulsion as necessary action against counterrevolutionaries who had obstructed the execution of the Party's revolutionary policies. Liu Chen-huan and Yang Hsi-min were accused of planning to overthrow the Canton Government with the connivance of Ch'en Ch'iung-ming and the Hongkong Government. Proof of such a conspiracy, according to Chiang Kai-shek's report to the Second KMT Congress, was discovered during the Eastern Expedition.114

Reorganization of the Army and Government, Summer, 1925

The ousting of Liu and Yang was the prelude to the launching of military reorganization, which had two principal objectives: centralization, and subordination of the military to Party control.

A move toward these two objectives was made in the establishment of the Military Council of the National Government on July 6, 1925. According to Document 19, the Military Council was the highest military organ of the National Revolutionary Army. However, it was subordinated to the Kuomintang Political Council, which had power to appoint the personnel and supervise the work of the Military Council, as well as to approve its important decisions.

That the Party controlled the Military Council is further confirmed by Document 15, minutes of a meeting of the Military Council held shortly after its establishment. Three of the eight original members of the Military Council—Wang Ching-wei, Liao Chung-k'ai, and Wu Ch'ao-shu—were what may be called purely civilian Party members, all with seats on the Political Council. Wang Ching-wei, who was concurrently chairman of the Political Council and the National

Government Council, served also as chairman of the Military Council. As chairman of the Military Council, Wang held the power of final decision on all questions [Doc. 15, p. 4]. In a letter to all officers and men, the Military Council summed up the principle of Party control of the military. The Kuomintang, it said, should direct and supervise all political and military organs of the Government.115

On August 26, 1925, the Military Council announced the incorporation of all military units into the National Revolutionary Army. There were to be five main armies: the Party Army commanded by Chiang Kai-shek was reorganized as the First Army; the Hunan Army, commanded by T'an Yen-k'ai, became the Second Army; the Yunnan Army, commanded by Chu P'ei-te, the Third Army; the Kwangtung Army, commanded by Li Chi-shen, the Fourth Army; and the Fukien Army, commanded by Li Fu-lin, the Fifth Army.116

A major feature of the reorganization was the application of the Party representative system to all military organs and units. Up to the summer of 1925, Liao Chung-k'ai was the only person to be appointed as a Party representative to the military; he served both the Whampoa Academy and the Party Army. In late June, 1925, Chiang Kai-shek proposed the establishment of political departments in all army groups, division, regiments, and brigades [Doc. 13, p. 19]. The following month, the Kuomintang Central Executive Committee ordered that all orders and regulations in the Party Academy and the Army were to be considered valid only when countersigned by the appropriate Party representatives.117

On June 14, 1925, the Political Council resolved to organize a national government based on the committee system. Party control of the new government was provided by two resolutions adopted by the Political Council: (1) The Political Council was organized within the Central Executive Committee for the purpose of directing the advance of the National Revolution; and (2) The Political Council was given power to decide on political policies and to execute them in the name of the National Government.118

Formally inaugurated on July 1, 1925, the National Government faithfully echoed Party policy. In a series of declarations, it announced that its foremost task was to abolish the unequal treaties. It pledged itself to work toward the convening of a national assembly.119

Individual Party leaders continued to denounce imperialism and vowed to eliminate its influence in China. In a speech to the Military Council on July 26, 1925 (Document 14), Chiang Kai-shek accused imperialist countries, particularly Britain, of backing Chinese militarists and other enemies of the Kuomintang. "How can we tolerate this?" he asked; "We must resolutely attack them until they are all eliminated!" Chiang declared that the military man's divine duty was to subdue imperialist countries.

Ascendancy of the Kuomintang Left Wing, to September, 1925

In short, the months following Sun Yat-sen's death witnessed intensification of his revolutionary policies: alliance with Soviet Russia, admission of Communists to the KMT, and promotion of the
anti-imperialist campaign. The army and government were transformed into instruments of the Party in accordance with the Soviet
pattern. These developments reflect the dominance of the Left
Wing, which carried out the program revolutionizing the Party's
organization and platform against the opposition of the Right.

The triumph of the Left Wing is demonstrated in the relative positions secured by Left and Right Wing members in the National
Government. A dramatic illustration is Hu Han-min's fall from
power. Reportedly sympathetic with the Right, Hu was Deputy Generalissimo in Canton following Sun Yat-sen's departure for North
China. Nominally he was the most important Kuomintang leader.
When the government was reorganized, however, he was named
Minister of Foreign Affairs.[120] This was an insignificant post, as
the KMT controlled only parts of Kwangtung province and the Government lacked diplomatic recognition.

Liao Chung-k'ai, the Left leader who most firmly supported Sun
Yat-sen's revolutionary policies, was named Minister of Finance.
This was a key position because the Kuomintang was determined to
centralize in its own hands the financial resources controlled by
army generals. In addition, Liao Chung-k'ai maintained the posts
of Party Representative to the Whampoa Academy and the Party
Army and remained chief of the Kuomintang Labor Department,
governor of Kwangtung, and minister of finance in the Kwangtung
Provincial Government.[121] Wang Ching-wei was elected chairman
of the National Government, the Standing Committee of the National
Government Council, the all-powerful KMT Political Council, and
the Military Council.[122]

On June 30, 1925, the day before the formal inauguration of the
National Government, a last-minute attempt was made by Teng
Tse-ju to forestall control of the government by the Left Wing.
Teng, a member of the Central Supervisory Committee, demanded
impeachment of the Political Council in a letter to the CEC. He
charged that the Political Council was controlled by a minority and
that it had arbitrarily announced the reorganization of the government in the name of the CEC, although the CEC had passed no resolution on the question.[123] Teng's protest was, in effect, ignored when
his official letter was answered the following day with a private
letter signed by four individuals: Hsü Ch'ung-chih, Wang Ching-wei,
T'an Yen-k'ai, and Liao Chung-k'ai. The four retorted that Sun Yat-
sen had given members of the Political Council special powers to
execute decisions before notifying Central Party Headquarters.[124]

The tense political situation in Canton erupted into violence on

August 20 1925, when Liao Chung-k'ai was assassinated while on his way to a meeting of the CEC. Later on the same day, a Special Committee was organized by the Central Executive Committee, the National Government Council, and the Military Council, acting jointly. Wang Ching-wei, Hsü Ch'ung-chih, and Chiang Kai-shek were appointed as its members. The Special Committee was empowered to take into its own hands all political, military, and police control.[125]

On August 25, the Special Committee arrested three suspects, including Lin Shih-mien. Other suspects, including Hu I-sheng, younger brother of Hu Han-min, escaped. Still others, one of whom was Liang Hung-k'ai, were detained at the Kwangtung Army's headquarters. It was there, according to Chiang Kai-shek's diary, that the authorities discovered proof of a conspiracy headed by British Hongkong to overthrow the National Government and to support Liang Hung-k'ai as commander-in-chief of the Army and Wei Pangp'ing as governor of Kwangtung.[126]

Thus, the assassination of Liao Chung-k'ai was attributed by the Special Committee to British bribery of Right Wing elements, and a series of anti-Right measures was put into effect. The most important of these was the decision of the Special Committee that Hu Han-min should go abroad because of his suspected implication, through the activities of his brother, in Liao Chung-k'ai's assassination. Hu Han-min was virtually exiled. In view of his prominent position, however, he was appointed representative of the Kuomintang to Soviet Russia on September 23, and left the same day on a Russian ship.[127]

The anti-Right coup d'état assumed even more serious proportions when Hsü Ch'ung-chih, a member of the ruling triumvirate, was himself forced to take a leave of absence in Shanghai on September 20. On the day before, the First Army, Whampoa cadets, and other units, acting under orders from Chiang Kai-shek, had disarmed the greater part of Hsü's Kwangtung Army as counterrevolutionary.[128] According to Chiang's diary, Hsü Ch'ung-chih had reached an agreement with Ch'en Ch'iung-ming as early as June, 1925.[129]

The action against Hu Han-min and Hsü Ch'ung-chih was followed by a migration of members of the Right Wing from Canton to Shanghai and elsewhere. The Canton of September, 1925, had become a stronghold of the Left Wing. The victory of the Left was accompanied by rapid concentration of power within the Left leadership. The three-man Special Committee superseded the twelve-man Political Council on August 20.[130] By the end of September, power was vested in the hands of two men, Wang Ching-wei and Chiang Kai-shek.

The appointment of Chiang Kai-shek to the Special Committee was

a turning point in his career. He had previously held no important
political post in party or government; he was not a member of the
CEC, the Political Council, or the National Government Council.
Chiang's military power was also considerably strengthened when
portions of Hsü Ch'ung-chih's Kwangtung Army were incorporated
into his First Army.[131]

The position of the Left Wing was defined by Wang Ching-wei in a
speech eulogizing Liao Chung-k'ai two days after the assination.
Those who wanted to oppose imperialism should turn to the Left,
Wang declared. Those who wanted to continue to live under imperialist oppression should turn to the Right. There was no need to
create the issue of communism vs. anticommunism; the only issue
was imperialism vs. anti-imperialism.[132] On August 31, Chiang
Kai-shek, speaking at a meeting held to commemorate Liao Chung-
k'ai, said that Liao was a victim in the struggle between revolution
and counterrevolution. Liao was definitely not a victim of the so-
called struggle between communism and anti-communism, Chiang
declared.[133] In short, the Left Wing defined itself as anti-imperialist and revolutionary, and defined the Right Wing as counterrevolutionary and subservient to imperialist interests.

The Soviet Position in Canton, to September, 1925

A similar interpretation of Liao Chung-k'ai's assassination was
advanced by Kisanko, the Russian who took over leadership of the
Canton Soviet group early in November, 1925.[134] In a report to
A. I. Egorov, Soviet Military Attaché,[135] drafted toward the end of
1925 (Document 16), Kisanko asserted that Liao's assassination was
a result of support rendered by British Hongkong to organizations
opposed to the National Government. Due to an alliance between dis-
gruntled generals, the KMT Right Wing, and the Hongkong Government, said Kisanko, all kinds of violence against the National Government and the Left Wing had been taking place [Doc. 16, pp. 32-33].

Kisanko's report suggests not only that the Russians approved of
the Left Wing's actions but that they actively supported Left Wing
leaders. In fact, Kisanko claimed chief credit for the Russians
for the ousting of Liu Chen-huan and Yang Hsi-min from Canton.
Although the Government's troops were generally credited with suppressing the rebellious armies of Liu and Yang, Kisanko stated,
achieving victory was actually beyond their ability and was due to
the assistance of the Russian advisers [Doc. 16, p. 32]. Such an admission of Soviet involvement in the internal struggle for power
lends credibility to the assertions of Kuomintang and other anti-
Communist sources that the Soviet advisers, Borodin in particular,
supported the Left Wing against the Right. One of the specific
charges is that Borodin engineered the anti-Right coup d'etat of
August-September, 1925.[136] It is certain, at any rate, that the Left

Wing's program of military reorganization was supported by the Russians, if not completely carried out under their direction, as Kisanko claimed [Doc. 16, p. 32].

The fundamental objective of military reorganization—a centralized and politically indoctrinated army, loyal to and controlled by the Party—was in the first place an ideal introduced by the Russians. The successive establishment of the Whampoa Academy, the Whampoa Training Regiment, and the Party Army was accomplished with Soviet support.

The close interest which Galen took in organizing the Party Army is suggested in Document 12, a letter he wrote to Chiang Kai-shek on April 16, 1925, three days after the Kuomintang CEC resolved to establish the Party Army.[137] Galen stressed the importance of communications organs and suggested setting up a special class at Whampoa to train communications specialists. He offered the services of a Russian colonel referred to by the name of Te-la-t'e-wen,[138] as chief instructor for the special course.

It is certain also that military reorganization paved the way for Soviet penetration of the Kuomintang's military apparatus. Soviet influence had previously been largely restricted to the Whampoa Academy. Although a contingent of high-ranking Soviet advisers had participated in the First Eastern Expedition,[139] they had not been given permanent appointments.

Soviet infiltration is most evident in the organization of the General Staff of the National Revolutionary Army. According to Document 15, minutes of the National Government's Military Council, the position of chief of the General Staff was assumed by General Victor P. Rogachev, who was also put in charge of naval and aviation affairs. Rogachev was the assistant chief of the Soviet group in South China and concurrently head of the South China Soviet Intelligence Branch.[140] The Military Council voted to distribute Russian personnel among all departments of the General Staff and resolved that the General Staff had power to determine, under Russian direction, the Army's size and finances [Doc. 15, p. 5].

Soviet advisers were appointed for the first time to most army units, the commissariat, arsenal, and other military branches. On July 1, 1925, a meeting of the Soviet group was held at which the Russians received assignments as advisers to various military units and organizations.[141]

The foothold which the Russians were able to obtain in the Kuomintang's military establishment represented a substantial gain. They had now the means of direct penetration, in addition to the powers of persuasion which Borodin had applied so successfully with Sun Yat-sen.

Execution of Reorganization Policies and the
Unification of Kwangtung, to December, 1925

Kisanko's report provides illuminating information on the execution of military reorganization up to the end of 1925. It offers an insight into the difficulties confronted by the Kuomintang, its accomplishments, and failures.

Kisanko noted among the generals a strong undercurrent of resentment against the system of Party representatives. He attributed part of the difficulty to the lack of precise regulations on the functions of Party commissars and consequent disagreement between army officers and Party commissars on the latter's functions. However, he reported that such regulations had just been drafted and were awaiting the Military Council's approval [Doc. 16, pp. 32, 50].

Document 17, the regulations referred to by Kisanko, confirmed the CEC's instructions, which were that all orders not countersigned by the appropriate Party representative were void. The regulations, applicable from the platoon level to the General Staff, stated in detail the functions and prerogatives of Party commissars. The Party commissar had power to impose penalties to be carried out by the military commander. Article Ten instructed the Party commissar to report to his superior any of the commander's orders which in his opinion endangered the National Revolution. In the event of possible rebellion, the Party commissar had authority to act on his own discretion without observing proclaimed orders.

Kisanko stressed the importance of a unified Party commissar system and suggested that it be carried out first by the First Army and then gradually by the other armies [Doc. 16, p. 50]. Thus it appears that by the end of 1925 the Party representative system had not yet been firmly established in the First Army and had yet to make any appreciable headway in the other armies.

The new chief of the Soviet group voiced harsh criticism of the quality of political training. He seemed particularly critical of the Whampoa cadets. He said they were "indifferent" to political problems. As a partial remedy, Kisanko recommended a complete change of Whampoa instructors and greater emphasis on political training. Kisanko also suggested centralizing all existing schools in one military academy [Doc. 16, pp. 56, 60].

On January 12, 1926, the Military Council voted unanimously to establish the Central Military and Political Academy, combining the schools of the various armies.[142] According to Document 18, which outlines the objectives and method of organization of the Central Academy, the Academy was to be subordinated directly to the Military Council. The goal was a centralized system of training closely supervised by the Party and emphasizing political as well as military training [Doc. 18].

The decision to centralize the academies was apparently made also in the interest of economy. The Kuomintang had been in financial straits much of the time since its return to Canton early in 1923. The minutes of a joint meeting of the Military Council and the Political Council on September 22, 1925, for instance, reveal that the Party suffered from serious financial shortages. According to Wang Ching-wei, the number of troops had increased while the available funds had decreased. T'an Yen-k'ai showed alarm because his troops were indignant at not having been paid for many months. Ch'eng Ch'ien reported that he had been forced to sell rifles in order to feed his troops.[143]

The National Government encountered determined opposition in executing the policy of financial centralization. According to Kisanko, individual generals were still appointing their own tax collectors and refusing to turn in revenue to the National Government. In short, Kisanko concluded at the end of 1925 that the task of financial unification had only just begun [Doc. 16, p. 54].

The National Government had difficulty too in centralizing supplies. The Military Council had appointed a supervisor at the main Canton arsenal as the first step in army reorganization. Later, a central commissariat was organized to control the distribution of supplies. However, the generals did not respect the Military Council's instructions, Kisanko reported, and some of them even hired their own people to manufacture ammunition. The Party's failure effectively to control distribution aggravated the already serious shortage of supplies. Furthermore, a large percentage of the weapons available to the National Government was obsolete, according to Kisanko [Doc. 16, pp. 53-54].

The Soviet Union had continued to transport supplies to Canton from Vladivostok following the first shipment in October, 1924. According to the draft of a telegram to Galen from the Soviet Military Attaché in Peking, dated June 4, 1926, the total cost of supplies shipped on credit to Canton up to December 1 [1925] amounted to 2,000,000 roubles.[144] These shipments contributed substantially to the store of supplies at Canton, although they fell far short of meeting the needs of an expanding military establishment.

The difficulties which beset the Kuomintang in its attempt to centralize military organization is vividly illustrated by Kisanko's discussion of Li Fu-lin's attitude. Li was commander of the Fifth National Revolutionary Army. However, according to Kisanko, neither the Military Council nor the Chief of the General Staff had received any report at all from Li. Kisanko predicted that conflict between Li and the National Revolutionary Army was inevitable and that Li would sooner or later display violent opposition to the reorganization [Doc. 16, p. 52].

The Kuomintang also had to cope with enemy armies threatening

Canton from the north, south, and east. The enemy in the North
was dealt with first. On September 28, 1925, the Second Eastern Expedition was launched, again with Chiang Kai-shek as commander-
in-chief.[145] The campaign brought quick results. By early November, 1925, the East River districts were recovered from Ch'en
Ch'iung-ming. By December 20, southern Kwangtung, with the
exception of Hainan Island, was pacified.[146] The Party had finally
completed the task of consolidation of Kwangtung, envisaged by
Sun Yat-sen as the first phase of the unification of China.

DOCUMENT 11

Document 11 was translated from Russian into Chinese by the Peking Commission and published under the title, "A Certain Gentleman's Report on the Proceedings of a Meeting of the Revolutionary Committee on October 14, 1924," in <u>Su-lien yin-mou...</u>, III, "Canton," pp. 10-13. The text gives no date or author. However, according to the "Catalogue of Russian Documents of Secondary Importance," <u>Su-lien yin-mou...</u>, I, p. 6, the report was written by Borodin on the morning of October 14, 1924.

[BORODIN'S REPORT ON THE REVOLUTIONARY COMMITTEE]

] [Meeting of the Revolutionary Committee on October 14]
The responsible Labor Party [Kuomintang] in South China elected members of the Revolutionary Committee at a meeting on October 14. Dr. Sun was elected chairman and Dr. Sun's deputy [Hu Han-min] was given only the right to speak.* It was decided that all orders issued by the Committee are to be signed by Dr. Sun and certified by the secretary. Liao Chung-k'ai was elected secretary.

General Chiang Kai-shek was elected chairman of the Military Committee with the following units placed under his control: (1) the Whampao Academy; (2) the aviation squadron; (3) armor car [battalion]; (4) General Wu T'ieh-ch'eng's school [for gendarmes]; (5) General Wu T'ieh-ch'eng's troops [gendarmes]; (6) the Yunnan [Army's] school; (7) General Ch'en Ch'i-mei's Hunan School;† (8) workers' police [pickets]; (9) peasant [self-defence] corps; and (10) the arsenal. Liao Chung-k'ai was appointed Political Commissar to the above units and T'an P'ing-shan his deputy.

The Political Department.—Wang Ching-wei was appointed

---

* According to Chiang Kai-shek's diary, which appears correct, Hu Han-min was not appointed to the Revolutionary Committee by Sun Yat-sen. Hence, he apparently had no voting power. See Chiang Kai-shek, <u>Chiang Chieh-shih hsien-sheng</u>, VIII, 15.
† On October 14, 1924, Sun Yat-sen ordered a number of military units to be subordinated directly to Chiang Kai-shek. The list given in Document 11 corresponds exactly with that given in Chiang's diary, except that the latter does not mention "General Ch'en Ch'i-mei's Hunan School." See Chiang Kai-shek, <u>Chiang Chieh-shih hsien-sheng</u>, VIII, 23.

Political Commissar for the whole province of Kwangtung‡ and Chou Wen-lai [Chou En-lai], Liao Chung-k'ai, and T'an P'ing-shan were named his deputies. They determine the actions of the Revolutionary Committee and the armed forces.

Political Policies Adopted at a Conference on October 12

At this time, when we are continuing to unite with the masses, we should unite with the Center and the Left to fight against the Tiger Party [Canton Merchant Corps]. With this objective in mind, we should settle accounts with the Tigers by force either at 10:00 o'clock in the evening of October 14, or at dawn, October 15. The Revolutionary Committee is not opposed to the people but wishes to unite with them to oppose those bandits who disturb peace and order, oppress the people, and hamper reforms.

1. The Revolutionary Committee should attempt to sever connections between the Tiger Party and the people and should adopt certain slogans for this purpose. A demonstration should be held in Central Park on October 15 to explain the relationship between the Revolutionary Committee and the people. Afterwards, we stage an armed movement.

2. The Revolutionary Committee should proclaim to the people in advance the objectives and meaning of the present Kuomintang struggle. We should use airplanes and armored cars to distribute leaflets today (October 14).

3. Concede to the demands of the printers at once so that the Kuo-min jih-pao, organ of the Revolutionary Committee [Kuomintang], may resume publication today.

Other political policies should also be adopted.

[12]   The demonstration should be so organized that it would not appear to have any connection whatsoever with our armed action.

In the event that armed action fails to take place, the question of independent action by the troops directly subordinated to Chiang Kai-shek will be decided on after the demonstration on October 15. Action should take place on the night of October 15.

Appendix

The following measures have been carried out by a group of Revolutionary Committee members prior to October 14.

1. Transferred Wu T'ieh-ch'eng's army from Shaoyang [Shaokuan] to Canton.

2. Reappointed Wu T'ieh-ch'eng chief of gendarmes.

---

‡ Hu Han-min was governor of Kwangtung province. Because Hu was not a member of the Revolutionary Committee, it appears possible that Wang Ching-wei was appointed to take charge for the emergency period.

3. Placed General Wu T'ieh-ch'eng and his troops under the direct control of the Revolutionary Committee.

4. Chiang Kai-shek entered the city as Commander-in-Chief, his position at Whampao filled by General Ho [Ying-ch'in] as his deputy.

5. The headquarters of the Revolutionary Committee was set up in the home of Liao Chung-k'ai (it will move later to its permanent home at Central Kuomintang Headquarters).

6. The headquarters of Communist Party members was established at the home of a certain comrade.

The armies were ordered to be absolutely obedient during this critical period. The question of control of the above armies will be discussed and decided on after the crisis is over.

Inside plans for action.—The Tigers' hideout in the western section of the city, Hsi-hua [Hsi-kuan], is to be raided and destroyed. The Tigers have been hiding there since martial law was proclaimed in this city. It has been decided to make a sneak attack on October 14, at 10:00 P.M.

Troops not under the control of the Revolutionary Committee but which are to take part in the action are:

[3]　　1. The Kwangtung First Division under the command of General Li Chi-shen.

2. The Kwangtung Second Division under the command of General Chang Ming-ta [Chang Min-ta].

3. The Yunnan troops under the command of General Fan Shih-sheng.

4. The Yunnan troops under the command of General Liao Chung-chou [Liao Hsing-ch'ao].

5. Other Kwangtung troops under the command of General Hsü Shun-ch'i [Hsü Ch'ung-chih].

The above troops obey Dr. Sun's orders. Liao Chung-k'ai and Wang Ching-wei also have connections with them.

In case they declare unwillingness to move, the troops under the control of the Revolutionary Committee will take action.

As Dr. Sun's deputy, Hu Han-min is to issue the order for action.

DOCUMENT 12

Document 12, a letter from Galen to Chiang Kai-shek, was
translated into Chinese from the Russian by the Peking Commission and published under the title, "A Letter from Galen to
Chiang Kai-shek, Dated April 16, 1925, on the Establishment of a
Special Course to Train Personnel for the Organization of Communications Organs in the Army," in Su-lien yin-mou..., III, "Canton," pp. 27-28. The Chinese text does not indicate whether the
letter was originally written in Russian or Chinese.

[GALEN'S LETTER TO
CHIANG KAI-SHEK]

[27]   It is clear from past battle experience that the communications
organs already established in the armies of the southern government cannot render proper assistance to army commanders. Communications organs should enable army commanders to contact
and direct their troops under all circumstances. At present, however, army commanders sometimes do not receive news of their
troops for several days. The local populace is relied on for help
in relaying information between officers of different units. The
small number of army telephones is almost completely unutilized
due to the shortage of specialists who understand the work of military communications. Special attention should be paid to this matter in organizing the new army at this time.

One of my subordinate officers, Te-la-t'e-wen, who is an expert on military communications, is now training a small unit of 22
soldiers at your Academy. I must point out however, that the problem of military communications cannot be solved by these soldiers
because: (1) Their training is limited to knowledge of telephones,
the most elementary phase of military intelligence; and (2) Due to
[28] the urgent need for specialists at the front, the training course is
limited to two or three weeks. It is therefore impossible within
such a short period to transform these soldiers, who are half-
educated and with only slight knowledge of the written language,
into specialists.

Other practical measures must be taken in order to establish
military communications organs. My opinion is that you should
set up a special class for 25 to 30 persons at the Whampoa Military Academy. They will be specially trained and organized into
a communications unit upon graduation.

Graduates of the engineering course should be selected for this
special course in order to achieve speedy results, since engineer-

ing students have a general background in technical matters.

As for instructors for the class, I can send Te-la-t'e-wen to your Academy for general direction. As he is not well versed in the Chinese language, please select the direct instructors from among those officers who have knowledge of telegraph, telephone, and military communications work.

According to this plan, a sufficient number of officers trained for military communications work should definitely be available within two or three months. They are indispensable in organizing a new army and in modern military operations.

This special course will not entail heavy expenses. A certain sum will be required for the purchase of tools for experimentation, such as telephones, telegraph, and other accessories. The amount involved, however, will not be too great. I shall appreciate hearing from you as to your opinion on this matter.

DOCUMENT 13

Document 13, a letter from Chiang Kai-shek to Galen dated June 26, 1925, was translated by the Peking Commission from Russian into Chinese under the title, "A Letter on Military questions from Chiang Kai-shek to Galen," and published in Su-lien yin-mou..., III, "Canton," pp. 14-21. The Russian text itself was presumably translated from Chinese. The following version is based on the Peking Commission's translation, checked and corrected against the original Chinese text published in Chiang Kai-shek's diary, Chiang Chieh-shih hsien-sheng, XI, 1-8. See above, "The Problem of Authenticity," p. 27.

[CHIANG KAI-SHEK'S LETTER
TO GALEN]

[14] Dear General Galen:

[15]   I had drafted plans prior to the Shameen Incident for fighting the British. In view of the present situation, it is necessary to carry out immediately the proposals on military construction suggested in my plans (e.g., repair of fortifications, establishment of mine factories and shipyards, etc.). The Government should complete within three to six months military preparations for an armed struggle against the British.

British influence in the Far East has indeed reached a climax! I believe that, besides employing peaceful means of struggle (such as boycott of British goods), our Party should start military preparations to be completed within half a year for a long period of struggle against the British (which may last for three to five years). It is therefore necessary to establish within the Military Council a special affairs department or a national defense committee, to which a large number of Russian advisers should be appointed. The Committee should be held responsible for distribution of work and the study and investigation of plans in order to centralize responsibility. What is your reaction to this suggestion?

I am enclosing for your reference a copy of my plans. It will be appreciated if you would treat them as confidential for the time being and add to them whatever suggestions you may have, so that they may be used to facilitate a decision at the meeting on military construction.

Chiang Kai-shek

Enclosure: The plans

POLITICAL AND MILITARY VIEWS
[THE PLANS]

The remnants of our enemy in southern Kwangtung and such places as Chaoan and Meihsien should be cleared up within three months. After this, we should carry out our plans for future development. Important points, however, can be started at once.

The Question of Military Funds

The sum of $35,000,000 can be collected in Kwangtung province. Upon the completion of financial reforms, this sum can be increased to $40,000,000 (including Chaoan, Meihsien, and southern Kwangtung).

16]   From the above funds, it is proposed to appropriate $18,000,000 to $20,000,000 for military planning; $15,000,000 to $16,000,000 for the navy and infantry; $2,000,000 to $4,000,000 for improving forts and arsenals, rehabilitating mine factories and shipyards, improving aviation, and expanding the Military Academy, etc.

The Army Should Be Expanded Temporarily to 65,000 Men

The first military group (Kwangtung Army) should be composed of three armies, totaling 30,000 men.

The Party Army should be expanded to two divisions, totaling 10,000 men. Lin's army (former Kwangsi Fifth Division) and Wu T'ing-shen's [Wu T'ieh-ch'eng's] army should be placed under the command of General Hsü.

The second military group (Hunan Army) should be reduced to three divisions totaling 12,000 men.

The third military group (Yunnan Army) should be fixed at two divisions, totaling 10,000 men.

The fourth military group (small units of the Northern Expeditionary Forces) should be fixed at one division, totaling 3,000 men.

The above reorganization is based on the military forces now available to us. By the end of 1926 or early in 1927, the government force is expected to expand to 80,000 to 100,000 men.

If the Government plans a northern expedition, the defense of Kwangtung province should be strengthened to resist possible attack from Hongkong and Fukien. At the same time, substantial forces should be prepared to launch offensives in the direction of Kiangsi and Hunan, or Hunan and Hupeh. To cope with the estimated enemy forces in these two directions, the northern expeditionary army would require a minimum of 70,000 men, a number barely sufficient for effective deployment.

17] ### The Army Organization Should Be Divided into Four Categories

1. Three companies to one battalion; three battalions to one regiment; three regiments to one division.

2. Four companies to one battalion; three battalions to one regiment; two regiments to one brigade; two brigades to one division.

3. Three companies to one battalion; three battalions to one regiment; three regiments to one brigade; three brigades to one division.

4. The gendarmes should be organized according to the former system of command.

The Problem of Military Preparation

1. The Hu-men and Ch'ang-chou forts should be repaired and commanded according to the former system, with one commander for each fort and a commanding general responsible for over-all direction.

2. The Whampoa shipyards and mine factory should be restored immediately. The training gunboats, S.S. "Fei-ying," S.S. "Wu-feng," and S.S. "Hu-ang" ["Fu-an"], should be repaired at once. A commander of the training fleet should be appointed.

3. Reorganize the river defense fleet, the salt gabelle fleet, and the training fleet. The S.S. "Chung-shan" should be placed under the direct control of the Navy Department. In three years, we must have six submarines.

4. Expansion of the arsenal.
   a) Establish a steel mill.
   b) Increase the number of factories manufacturing cartridges.

[18]
   c) Increase machinery for manufacturing rifles in order to increase output to at least 150 daily.
   d) Establish a cannon factory to produce at least four cannons per month. (In case of lack of funds this can be deferred.)

5. Establish a sewing factory to make uniforms for all the armies.

6. Establish an airplane factory and organize a relatively large-scale aviation school.

7. All cartridge factories should be controlled by the central arsenal.

The Question of Expansion of the Military Academy

1. Establish an officer training school. Cadets are to be limited to from 1,500 to 2,000 men. Special classes should be set up for training in aviation, infantry, cavalry, artillery, engineering, army service corps, and gas [chemical warfare].

2. Promote the second and the third classes of Whampoa Academy cadets to an advanced military school where separate classes for training in artillery, staff work, bombardment, airplane manufacturing, and gas [chemical warfare] will be set up. (If a naval academy is not to be established, then the advanced military school should include in its program courses on mines, navigation, shipbuilding, and submarines.)

3. Establish a naval academy for training naval personnel.

4. Establish a medical school and a military commissariat school.

5. Reorganize the surveying school.

Other Necessary Educational Institutions

[19]   1. Organize a central supervisory organ on military training.

2. Organize military training committees in all armies.

3. Organize an inspection and examination committee.

4. Establish political departments in all armies, divisions, regiments, and brigades to instruct officers and soldiers in common political knowledge.

Organs in Charge of Military Expenditures

1. Organize an army commissariat committee.

2. Organize an army commissariat supervisory committee.

3. Organize a committee to examine the military expenditures of all armies.

All organs connected with military training and expenditures and the army commissariat should be directly subordinated to the Military Council.

Improvement of the Economic Condition of Soldiers

Every soldier should receive a minimum monthly pay of ten dollars.

The Organization and Training of Peasant and Student Armies

[Peasant and student armies] of 100,000 men to be completed by the end of 1926.

The Budget

A. Monthly expenditures:

1. The standing army of approximately 65,000 men, organized

[20] into ten divisions and ten brigades, requires approximately $1,200,000 to $1,300,000.

2. The Navy (river defense fleet, the salt gabelle fleet, and the training fleet) requires approximately $40,000.

3. The forts require $15,000.

4. General expenditures of the military schools, the officers' schools, the medical school, army commissariat school, gas [chemical warfare] school, surveying school, and the advanced officers' school require approximately $250,000 to $300,000.

B. Special expenditures:

1. Repair of forts: $300,000.

2. Repair of the training fleet: $200,000.

3. Restoration of the Whampoa mine factory and shipyard: $1,000,000.

4. Establishment of an airplane factory: $1,000,000.

5. Establishment of a steel mill: $500,000.

6. Expansion of cartridge factories: $300,000.

7. Replacement of machinery for the manufacture of rifles: $500,000.

8. Establishment of a cannon factory: $1,000,000. This may be deferred in case of insufficient funds.

9. Establishment of a sewing factory: $500,000.

[20]   The total amount of monthly expenditures: $1,655,000. Annual expenditures: $19,860,000.

The total amount of special expenditures: $5,300,000.

The expenses covering purchase of submarines is not included.

If this great amount of funds cannot be provided this year, then the various items of special expenditures should be shifted to the budget for 1926. If, even in 1926, the special expenditures cannot be met with, we may establish first the aircraft factory, then the mine factory, and then the shipyard. It should not be too difficult to meet the cost of the above, which will not exceed two million dollars.

DOCUMENT 14

Document 14, excerpts from a speech delivered by Chiang Kai-shek on July 26, 1925, was translated by the Peking Commission from Russian into Chinese under the title, "Minutes of a Military Conference in Kwangtung Attended by Rogachev, Military Attaché at the Soviet Embassy in Peking, Borodin, Military Adviser in Kwangtung, and Others," in Su-lien yin-mou..., III, "Canton," pp. 2-4. The Chinese text does not indicate whether the excerpts, apparently an incomplete verbatim record of Chiang's speech, originally appeared in Russian or Chinese. Our translation is based on the above source, checked and corrected against the original Chinese text of the complete speech in Chiang Chieh-shih hsiao-chang tsai Kuo-min Cheng-fu Chün-shih wai-yüan-hui chiang-yen tz'u. Excerpts from the same speech are given also in Chiang's diary. See Chiang Kai-shek, Chiang Chieh-shih hsien-sheng, XI, 46-49. See above, "The Problem of Authenticity," p. 28.

CHIANG KAI-SHEK'S SPEECH TO
THE MILITARY COUNCIL

[2] It is my belief that the detailed reports thus far presented on military strategy, finances, and personnel are inadequate. Our army must have unified objectives and spirit. I propose that it be called the "Revolutionary Army" or "National Revolutionary Army" and that, in order to avoid confusion, the names "Hunan Army" or "Kwangtung Army" should no longer be used. Our mission is determined by principles and not by mere names.

Our army should be called the "Revolutionary Army" because Dr. Sun devoted nearly forty years to the Revolution. Following the overthrow of the Manchus, Yüan Shih-k'ai, Ts'ao K'un, and, currently, Tuan Ch'i-jui and Wu P'ei-fu, became the most stubborn counterrevolutionaries. If we allow them to imperil the nation without a declaration of war by a revolutionary army, what hope is there for the future of the nation? We are fully aware that other counterrevolutionaries would rise to power even if Tuan should step down and that all counterrevolutionaries are equally destructive.

[3] To this day, the people still do not realize the cause of our struggle against the counterrevolutionaries or that imperialism and militarism are one. The root must first be removed! Gentlemen, you must know that the imperialists, recognizing the inconvenience of starting a direct war against us, secretly control the

militarists and instigate disorders throughout our country. The imperialists aim at making profits and China is their field of plunder. I presume this is known to you all! We are sure to achieve success if we can fight the imperialists with unified objectives. Just think who is behind Yang Hsi-min and Lai Shih-huang? And why do people like T'ang Chih-yao, the slaves of imperialism and world capitalism, want to destroy the Kwangtung Government? Who actually dictates their actions? Clearly, the British and other imperialists utilize them against us. How can we tolerate this? We must resolutely attack them until they are all eliminated!

Our country has become extremely impoverished because the militarists absorb the fat of the land. The Northern militarists have never succeeded in unifying China because they are lined up with the imperialists. We, on the other hand, build our force on the mass movement as well as the army. Though our army is small, the imperialists consider it very strong because it is backed by the force of the masses, while the Northerners have only the army. The psychology of the imperialists have changed recently and they greatly fear our army. Although they have specialists and technicians, we have spirit—the spirit of struggling for justice— which is sufficient to fight them. The British realize it is impossible to wage open war with China since it would result in the loss of all their interests. Modern warfare, moreover, is different from that of the old days. Military strength alone is not enough. There must be due regard for justice and principles.

On examining the world today, we find workers everywhere who are the real force of the Revolution, for every worker is opposed to military force. Even though our revolution may not be victorious at the moment, this is only a temporary phenomenon. It is only right that our revolution should succeed. Like the venomous snake which is endowed with a beautiful lady's feet to tempt the weak and secure their obedience, the imperialists are employing clever and [4] tricky tactics in China to cause our countrymen to kill one another for their profit. Are you gentelmen not aware of this? I hope you will not fear the British but will have confidence in victory. Victory will then be assured. Though long oppressed, the people are still unconscious and it is difficult to make them understand. But you, gentlemen, surely comprehend and realize that the divine duty of every military man is to subdue the imperialist countries. The imperialists assist the Chinese militarists, exclaiming, "Come, we give you food, but we will get it back from you someday!" (Applause)

DOCUMENT 15

Document 15 was translated by the Peking Commission from Russian into Chinese under the title, "Minutes of a Military Conference in Kwangtung Attended by Rogachev, Military Attaché at the Soviet Embassy in Peking, Borodin, Military Adviser in Kwangtung, and Others," in Su-lien yin-mou..., III, "Canton," pp. 4-8. No date is given nor is there any indication as to whether the minutes were originally written in Russian or Chinese. The contents suggest, however, that the minutes were compiled shortly after July 18, 1925. We have omitted from our translation detailed information on minor issues given in the last section of the document.

[MINUTES OF
THE MILITARY COUNCIL]

[Organization of] the Military Council

[4] The Military Council is officially convened. All problems awaiting the Council's decision should first be referred to the Political Council for investigation. The agenda of the Military Council should also be referred to the Political Council for approval.

Note: Members of the Military Council are members of the Political Council.* They all hold responsible positions in the Government and the Army.

Wang Ching-wei, Chairman of the Political Council, serves concurrently as Chairman of the Military Council. Other members of the Military Council are:

Hsü Ch'ung-chih, Minister of War who supervises the affairs of the General Staff, a member of the Political Council.

T'an Yen-k'ai, superintendent of the arsenal.

Hu Han-min, member of the Political Council and Minister of Foreign Affairs of the National Government.

Chu P'ei-te, Commander of the Yunnan Army. (He is the only person not holding any governmental position.)

Liao Chung-k'ai, Secretary of the Kuomintang Central Executive Committee, member of the Political Council, Minister of Finance, supervisor of sanitation in the Army.

---

* Not all members of the Military Council belonged to the Kuomintang Political Council. The Military Council was organized on July 6, 1925, with eight members. See "Letter from the Military Council of the National Government to all Officers and Men," p. 50. Of the eight names, that of Chiang Kai-shek is the only one missing in Document 15.

Wu Ch'ao-shu, member of the Political Council, concurrently holding other positions.

The chairman of the Military Council has the power of decision.

[5]   Rogachev, Chief of the General Staff, concurrently supervisor of naval and aviation affairs.

The Military Council meets weekly...[Burned]

Important Problems [and Decisions] of the Military Council

Note: At the opening of each meeting, Tsung-li's Will should be recited. All members should rise and pay homage.

Appointment of heads of departments of the General Staff; distribution of Russian personnel among the departments; determination of the interrelationships between the General Staff and the Military Council.

Decision on the need for the General Staff to determine under Russian direction the Army's size and finances.

Decision on the plan of organization of the General Staff, which should not be amended.

Attention to sanitation in the armies and appointment of Liao Chung-k'ai as supervisor.

Liao Chung-k'ai, a member of the Military Council and Minister of Finance, reported on the unsatisfactory financial situation due to the failure of army commanders to turn in tax collections. Decision: Appointment of officials to investigate the actual condition and the quantity of arms of and the funds to be appropriated to each army.

On the 18th of July, the question of press opinion was discussed. In view of deteriorating Anglo-Russian relations, we should follow the Political Council's decision to continue the strike, to clear up eastern Kwangtung in the near future, and then, beginning with restoration of order in Kwangsi, carry on the Northern Expedition. The matter of clearing up eastern Kwangtung should be completed within three months. There is reason to believe that Feng Yü-hsiang and Chang Tso-lin of Mukden will clash early this winter. Chang is a tool of the imperialists.

Plans on the Northern Expedition should be executed. The expedition should proceed along two routes; one starting from Hunan
[6] and Kweichow to unite with mass organizations in the North, and the other by sea. Certain members of the Council do not believe that the Northern armies lack support, but this is immaterial. We must, however, seek to delay military action by Wu P'ei-fu because the military governors of Hunan, Hupeh, Anhwei, Kiangsi, Kiangsu, Chekiang, and Fukien are all members of Wu's clique. Wu would be an important figure once he takes action. In addition, we should try

to encourage Wu to proceed north and encounter Hu Ching-yi.†
Concerning this matter we must... [Burned]

Reports on the expansion of the Navy and Aviation have been made
to the Military Council and the General Staff. Wang Ching-wei is
appointed chief of the aviation squadron because he is a man of high
prestige and will live up to the people's expectations. A Navy Department is to be established to centralize and organize the Navy.
A part of the garrison force should be organized as the military
gendarmes.

Suspend the publication of war news in newspapers to avoid furnishing information to the enemy.

Decision on the dispatch of two Whampoa battalions to suppress
banditry in Shen county. The plans are to be formulated by General
Headquarters.

Decision on the summoning of military officers to explain the reorganization of the army, its objectives and tasks.

Prohibition of the shooting of the people at will by military officers. Abolition of the Military Department of the Kowloon railway
because of the killing of a railway employee. This matter should
be dealt with by the General Staff.

Decision on the regulations for checking arms. In the name of the
National Government, the Military Council should check on and
approve the size of each army.

Decision on the blockade of Hongkong and the stopping of all shipments of goods there. The General Staff is to formulate plans to
carry out this decision. It should dispatch the armored car battalion,
but instruct it absolutely to avoid precipitating any conflict with
British forces.

Appointment of responsible personnel (the Navy Department).

Decision on the withdrawal of troops from the city. The General
Staff is to be instructed on this.

[7]   Confirmation of the suspension of military reports in newspapers.
All military funds should be met by government revenues.

Four fifths of the revenues should be appropriated for military
expenditures. Estimates should be made of the expenditures of the
armies of the National Government and the provincial armies.
Priority will be given the former. [Remainder omitted.]

---

† Hu Ching-yi died on April 10, 1925. This evidence of historical
anachronism may have resulted from mistranslation from Russian
into Chinese. For instance, the Russian text may have referred to
Hu Ching-yi's army, which was then commanded by Yüeh Wei-
chün.

DOCUMENT 16

Document 16 was translated by the Peking Commission from Russian into Chinese under the title, "A Letter from the Chief of the Soviet Branch in South China to Egorov, Military Attaché at the Soviet Embassy in Peking, Reporting on the Entire Situation in Kwangtung, Military Developments, and the Condition of Various Kinds of Work," in <u>Su-lien yin-mou...</u>, III, "Canton," pp. 31-62. In our translation, we have omitted the middle section of the report giving detailed information on troop movements and battles during the Second Eastern Expedition and the war in Southern Kwangtung. The report, marked "Most Secret," was evidently written by Kisanko, head of the South China Group from November 1, 1925, to the end of March, 1926. According to the Chinese text, the document was dated May 3, but this appears erroneous. The National Revolutionary Army had gained control of all of Kwangtung Province except Hainan Island by mid-December, 1925, and the Fourth Army was ordered to attack the island on December 21. (See Chiang Kai-shek, <u>Chiang Chieh-shih hsien-sheng</u>, XIII, 40.) Since Kisanko's report was written shortly after the beginning of the offensive against Hainan Island, it is probably dated around the end of December. 1925.

[KISANKO'S REPORT ON MILITARY
DEVELOPMENTS IN KWANGTUNG]

[31] I arrived at Canton on October 29 and assumed my duties as Chief of the Group on November 1. At the time of my arrival, the fighting in the East against Ch'en Ch'iung-ming had ended, while the fighting in the South against Teng P'ei-ying [Teng Pen-yin] was still in progress. The greater part of the National Revolutionary Army, together with many of the Russian advisers was, therefore at the front, including Rogachev, former acting chief of the group, [32] and Chiang Kai-shek, Commander-in-Chief of the Eastern Expedition. Consequently, my survey of conditions in Canton and of our work here was greatly handicapped. As the reports available at Group headquarters are insufficient, a relatively longer period of time has been necessary in conducting the survey.

To understand the present situation and the plans and tactics resulting therefrom, it is necessary to draw our attention to past events.

In May of this year, the Government was faced with a critical situation: the armies of Yunnan [commanded by Yang Hsi-min] and

Kwangsi [commanded by Liu Cheng-huan] were on the verge of rebellion, and rendered help to the enemy. Although the final success
of the Government troops in suppressing the rebellious armies was
attributed to the former's determined efforts, victory was actually
beyond the ability of the Government forces and was due to the assistance of the Russian advisers. Since then the Government has
been in a stronger position politically and has begun to reorganize
the Army according to our directions. The following are basic problems in army reorganization:

Organization of a unified national revolutionary army; centralization of the military and financial system of the Government; regulation of the number of standing army units and the military budget;
centralization of all administrative and political organs; appointment of Party representatives to all Army units and administrative
organs; regulation of medical facilities for the Army. A part of the
above has already been put into effect. Furthermore, the National
Government has organized the Military Council [as] the central
directing organ and has established under it the General Staff and
the Political Training Departments. The Military Council is responsible for all problems.

Plans on the number of army units and organization of a model
army have been drawn up and are ready for execution. A further
step is now being taken to unify finances. On the surface, the
generals are unanimously in favor of this move. Actually, however,
they are completely opposed, because they consider as their own
private property territories where their troops are stationed. Thus,
they naturally oppose proposals which deprive them of revenues
and appoint Party supervisors to their armies. In view of all this,
generals are dissatisfied with the Government's new plans and
have united themselves into a strong organization with the support
of both the Kuomintang Right Wing and Hongkong.

At first, the National Revolutionary Government helped the striking workers of Hongkong by creating various public welfare projects
for their employment at Canton (such as the construction and repair
of streets, avenues, and roads to Whampoa, and work in the Army,
etc.). Hongkong was in serious economic difficulties and therefore
[33] gave substantial support to organizations opposed to the National
Revolutionary Government. The first incident resulting from such
support was the assassination of Liao Chung-k'ai. Subsequently,
there arose all kinds of violence against the Government and the
Kuomintang Left Wing and agitation in the Army for a military
coup in Kwangtung.

The anti-Government actions of Kwangtung University were instigated by the University's president, Chou Lu, with the motive of
overthrowing the Canton Government from within and without.
Ch'en Ch'iung-ming, with help from Hongkong, attacked Canton

from the east, Hsiung K'o-wu of the Szechuan Army from the north, Wei Pang-p'ing and Teng P'ei-ying [Teng Pen-yin] from the south. At the same time, Ch'en Ch'iung-ming got three battleships from Wu P'ei-fu to blockade Canton while his troops proceeded along the river from Hongkong toward Canton. The Government was subjected to serious pressure and faced the danger of total destruction. It was able, however, by swift and determined measures to resist internally the anti-Government organizations and, externally, the enemy armies, thereby acquiring a strong and firm position by November, 1925.

The Government's first step toward internal consolidation was the thorough disarming of unreliable troops. A number of them, however, had already joined Teng P'ei-ying [Teng Pen-yin].

The assassinated Liao Chung-k'ai was commander of the Second Kwangtung Army. Hu Han-min was exiled abroad because of his ideological connections with the secretary of the Political Council of the KMT Central Executive Committee* and revelations of the involvement of his brother [Hu I-sheng] in Liao's assassination.

In view of the serious situation at Canton, General Hsü Ch'ung-chih, whose revolutionary determination appeared wavering, was given leave of absence to go to Shanghai.

The following measures against our external enemies were considered necessary:

1. Extermination of Ch'en Ch'iung-ming's army because of its most violent hostility toward the Government and its close connections with the Hongkong Government. The disarming of Hsiung K'o-wu's troops in the North.

[34]   2. Extermination of the enemy in the southern route.

The Military Council adopted the following plans to distribute the Army for the battlefronts. For the eastern front, the First and Third divisions of the First Army, numbering 6,000 men, and the Fourth Army (excepting the Tenth Division) under Liao Fu-lin [Li Fu-lin],† about 6,000 men. For Tan-shui, about 3,000 men from the Fourth and Ninth brigades and 3,000 men from the two independent

---

* Either the Peking Commission made errors of translation or Kisanko was misinformed. Liao Chung-k'ai was not commander of the Second Kwangtung Army. According to the Chinese text, Hu Han-min had ideological connections with the secretary of the Political Council of the KMT Central Executive Committee. This may be a reference to Lin Shih-mien, secretary to Sun Yat-sen when the latter was Generalissimo, who was allegedly associated with Hu Han-min and who was a suspect in Liao's assassination.
† The Fourth Army was commanded not by Li Fu-lin, but by Li Chi-shen.

regiments of the former Kwangtung Army, seven battalions of the Independent Division under Wu Chi-hsin [Wu Chung-hsin], four regiments of 1,500 men under General Ch'eng Ch'ien, and 2,500 to 3,000 men from the provincial armies of Kiangsi, Hunan, and Hupeh, totaling about 20,000 to 21,000 men. For the northern route against the forces of Hsiung K'o-wu, part of the Second and Third armies and the Kwangsi troops, which offered to attack Hsiung's forces from the rear by way of Kiangsi [Kwangsi]. For the southern route in defense of the Southwest, the remaining portion of the Fourth Army (that is, the Tenth Division) of Li Fu-lin. ‡

The responsibility for preserving peace and order in the provincial capital was assigned to the Second Division of the First Army, the schools of the First, Second, and Third armies, and the Navy.

The attitude of the Fifth Army toward the Government has not been clear since the fighting started. Hainan Island, which it is attempting to occupy, is opposite Kwangtung, and in case of unfavorable fighting conditions on the Government's side, there is danger of revolt.**

Some advisers are at the southern front, others at the eastern front. Reorganization of the Army has therefore been delayed. All battle records will be forwarded by the next mail.

[Omitted: detailed battle record, pp. 34-48.]

48] The Military Council

The Military Council is actually the mastermind of the National Revolutionary Army. In spite of the independent power of the various generals and their habitual unwillingness to be subordinated to others, the Council has been able in a short space of time to win prestige in the National Revolutionary Army. The generals refer various problems, even minute ones which can be solved either by 49] themselves or by their headquarters, to the Military Council for instructions. Military plans, including [plans for] army reorganization, supplies, and distribution of ammunition, and plans on the principles of political work, and many minor problems are executed upon the Council's approval. We are endeavoring to guide the work of the Council in the right direction.

The standing members of the Military Council consist of myself, as chief adviser to the National Revolutionary Government, Rogachev, as Chief of the General Staff, and Ao-li-chin, as chief adviser

---

‡ See preceding note.
** The Fourth Army, not the Fifth Army, was engaged in the offensive against Hainan Island. There is no doubt, however, that Kisanko was expressing doubt as to the loyalty of the Fifth Army.

to the Political Council of the National Revolutionary Government.††

The Military Council recently solved the following important problems:

1. Approved battle plans for the eastern, southern, and northern routes.
2. Approved plans for suppressing banditry.
3. Approved the budgets of all armies and organs.
4. Established the censor's bureau.
5. Fixed the oath of military men.
6. Solved all problems relating to the supply of military uniforms.
7. Decided on plans for army reorganization and issued orders for reorganizing the Army and the [Political] Department. (Refer to Appendix No. 10.)

The General Staff

The General Staff should not be as inactive as before, since its position has been elevated. It must be noted that the Military Council, the actual directing organ of the Army, is not charged with minor and purely technical problems. The General Staff is the Council's assisting technical organ. The armies at first slighted the General Staff. The commanders referred directly to the Council matters which should have fallen within the jurisdiction of the [50] General Staff. This situation stemmed from the failure of high-ranking officers to realize the need for the General Staff and from the difficulty of selecting suitable personnel to head the departments of the General Staff.

At present, the General Staff has set up the following departments: (1) intelligence; (2) administration; (3) infantry; (4) artillery; (5) communications, (army communications, etc.); (6) engineering; and (7) sanitation. All the above departments are headed by a Chinese who is assisted by a [Russian] adviser, except the Communications Department, for which no suitable Chinese could be found. Therefore a Russian was employed to head the department. The problem which needs immediate solution is establishment of the General Staff in a firm position so that it will not be merely the secretariat of the Council as before.

The Political Training Department

This organ was established only recently. It has not been set up

---

†† Ao-li-chin was acting chief adviser at the Whampoa Academy in late 1925 and early 1926, according to lists of Soviet personnel seized in the raid. There is no available record that he was chief adviser to the Political Council, although that may have been the case.

in all armies. Political work in the Army is poor in many respects and is still in the initial stage. The following fundamental
tasks should be executed:

1. Carry out the unified commissar system. This system should
be carried out first by the First Army and gradually by other
armies. However, because regulations on the Political Department
had not been promulgated, the commissars themselves and the
army officers have varying interpretations of their function. Now
such regulations have been drafted and await the Council's approval
(see Appendix No. 11) [Document 17].

2. Establish a Military Court to impose penalties on the Army
for such crimes as the forceful occupation of territories, acceptance
of bribes, and embezzlement of public funds.

3. Give advanced political training to the Army, with particular
emphasis on the officers and cadets of the Military Academy.

4. Establish clubs in army schools.

[51]   5. Set up a unified curriculum of political courses at all army
schools.

The Armies of the National Revolutionary Government

The reorganization of the National Revolutionary Army is not
yet complete. The present organization is as follows.

First Army. Commander, Chiang Kai-shek. Consists of three
divisions, each division consisting of three regiments. The number
of men is as follows: The First Division, approximately 4,000; the
Second Division, approximately 3,500; the Third Division, approximately 3,100. The First and Third divisions are stationed in the
East bordering Fukien, and the Second Division is stationed in
Canton and environs.

Second Army. No organization into divisions. Consists of nine
regiments, two independent battalions, and the former Kwangtung
Nineteenth Independent Battalion, which fled at the time the
Kwangtung First Army was disarmed [September, 1925], but has
now returned to the Government's forces and is combined with the
Second Army (the former Hunan Army) because the majority of
the soldiers are Hunanese. The number of men in the Second Army
totals approximately 15,000, but cannot be definitely determined
because reorganization has just been launched. A part of the
Second Army has been dispatched to the new territories to the north
of Shaokuan.

The Third Army. Its organization is as follows: First Division
consisting of three regiments, one artillery company, and one
machine-gun company. Second Division, consisting of two regiments,
one artillery company, and one machine-gun company. Two independent brigades. One independent regiment and the Kiangsi Army.
[52] The total number of men is approximately 14,000 to 15,000 with

approximately 7,000 magazine guns, 14 machine guns, and 3 cannons. At present, a part of its forces is moving along the southern route.

Fourth Army. This group consists of three divisions and two independent regiments. It is difficult to determine the number of men because it is now on the southern route. Furthermore, enemy troops have often been incorporated into the Fourth Army.

Fifth Army. Although its commander, Li Fu-lin, is a member of the Military Council and has participated in its meetings and work, the Office of the Chief of Staff and the Military Council have received no report concerning the Fifth Army. The commander, Li Fu-lin, is close to the Canton Merchant Corps. Should the Fifth Army be disarmed, it would surely arouse the resentment of the Corps. Therefore, when some of the unreliable armies were disarmed, no such attempt was made with the Fifth Army. The Fifth Army is the largest of the National Revolutionary Armies but yet has no Russian advisers. However, for the sake of the final victory of the National Revolutionary Army, Li Fu-lin has consented to organize a political department in the [Fifth] Army and it will be possible from now on to infuse Kuomintang elements into it. Attention should be directed to the fact that Li Fu-lin will sooner or later display violent opposition to army reorganization and the National Revolutionary Army will encounter conflicts with his army.

The First Independent Division amounting to 3,000 men under General Wu Chi-hsin [Wu Chung-hsin], is stationed in the east of the province, as are also the Second Independent Division and the Third Independent Division under General Ch'eng Ch'ien.

In addition, there is a small army unit in the South which has no particular form of organization.

The above explains the organization of the armies. It is difficult at present to ascertain the total number of men in the National Revolutionary Army because most of the smaller units are in contact with the Operations Department only when they request funds [53] from the Military Council. When our troops were moving to the South, these small units actively declared their loyalty to the Government. At the beginning of the fighting on the southern front a rough estimate of the forces of the National Revolutionary Army was made. It is not possible to form an estimate now, however. Reorganizing or disarming these small units has been contemplated, but that would be a tremendous task.

Ammunition. Ammunition supply in the Army is very poor. Some of the armies still use obsolete guns. Each company possesses only seven to nine magazine guns. Machine guns are insufficient and there was a shortage of cartridges in the recent fighting.

In all units of the National Revolutionary Army, there are altogether 137 cannons, mostly 8 mm., 7.5 mm., 6.5 mm., 5.7 mm.,

4.7 mm., 4.5 mm., or 3.5 mm mountain guns manufactured by the British, Japanese, and Krupp factories. Most of the cannons are obsolete 1880 or 1890 models, lacking rapid firing power and pressure gauge. There is insufficient ammunition in store in all the armies. An army with seven cannons has only twenty shells. However, replenishment of ammunition at this time is impossible because the supply has to come from abroad or from other provinces. The arsenals in Kwangtung are not yet in a position to manufacture shells.

Communications. Army communications are not regulated. Technical communication is completely lacking; manpower communication is not organized. The local populace is relied on for transmitting telegrams. This is most inconvenient.

Sanitation. Sanitation is very essential in the Army. In previous fighting, the wounded frequently died en route to the rear. Recently, the General Staff has enlisted the support of the Sanitation Administration Department in sending the wounded to military 4] hospitals for treatment. But sanitary equipment in the various armies is still insufficient, owing to lack of funds, medicine, beds, and other supplies.

The arsenal. The replenishment of military supplies at this time is still difficult because of (1) financial shortage, and (2) collection of taxes and levies by the various generals. The Government must establish financial organs to replace the collectors appointed by the generals. The work has just begun and the revenues are still insufficient. The Commissariat Administration is now being organized to see that the manufacture of military supplies, cartridges and guns is handled by the arsenals. There are still a few generals, however, who hire people to manufacture such needed ammunition for themselves. The big arsenal's regulations on requisition of military supplies provide that any general may order unlimited quantities of necessary supplies, but he himself must pay for them. The Government does not subsidize the arsenal, which depends solely upon proceeds from the sale of arms to meet material and labor costs.

The first step taken by the Military Council in reorganizing the Army was the appointment of a supervisor at the arsenal. Without the Military Council's approval, no ammunition or supplies may be issued. However, the generals at present do not respect the Council's instruction and freely place their orders with the arsenal, not infrequently causing conflict with the Government. The arsenal's production is 125,000 cartridges per week.

Aside from this arsenal, there is a small arsenal of the former Yunnan Army which can produce from 15,000 to 20,000 cartridges per day or 20,000 to 25,000 per day and night. They are of 7.9, 6.8 or 6.5 caliber, used for Japanese-type guns.

The reason for operating the small arsenal is to increase the
quantity of cartridges on the one hand and, on the other, to combat
the monopoly of the big arsenal. There are some unstable elements
even at present among the workers at the small arsenal, partly because of economic reasons and partly [because these elements are]
under the influence of the anti-Government movement.

In order to explain [investigate] the causes of the workers' dissatisfaction with the Government, a special committee has been
[55] set up with one of our representatives participating (see Appendix
No. 12). Attached is the report of Ao-li-chin, who is working on
this committee.

Army Schools

There are officers' schools in the First, Second, Third, and
Fourth armies. We have had no reports from the Fifth Army. The
objective of the schools is to train low-ranking officers for the
armies. Lately the work of the schools has been unsatisfactory
because most of the Russian advisers have left for the front with
the troops and the schools lack proper direction. After fighting in
the East had ended, only one person was sent to join the schools of
the First, Third, and Fourth armies. Up to now there is no adviser
in the school of the Second Army. Since army officers must be
given solid political knowledge, the two Russian political workers
will be installed as political advisers at the schools as soon as they
arrive. (Now only two schools have one adviser each.)

The School of the First Army (Whampoa). The organization of the
school: (1) regular school; (2) preparatory school. High school and
college graduates who have had no military education enter the
preparatory school first and then, after a general military education, they enter the regular school. Each school has one thousand
students.

The regular school is located on Whampoa Island close to Canton
and the preparatory school is at the Hui-chou Fort. During the
recent fighting a number of students remained aboard the gunboats,
as the officers of some of the ships were suspected of being unreliable and the students, on the other hand, are trustworthy. Six months
are required for graduation from the regular school. Graduation
takes place in the first part of January.

As a result of the war, courses have not been given as scheduled
and the records of students due for graduation are below passing.
The reason is that the students were assigned to guard duties in
suburban areas during the fighting.

[56]   Instructors are engaged by invitation. Nine tenths of them have
no political background. The permanent instructors are politically
organized, but further efforts are necessary in this respect.

Tactics instructors, sufficient.

Ballistics [instructors], only 20 percent sufficient.

Survey instructors, only 70 percent sufficient.

Engineering [instructors], about 70 percent sufficient.

Artillery [instructors], about 50 percent sufficient.

The distribution of students is satisfactory, but classrooms are 70 percent short.

Clubs, none. It had been planned before the war to organize a club. The outbreak of war, however, obstructed its progress.

As yet there is no Sunyatsenist lecture group. Political courses and general political lectures are also lacking. There are only occasional lectures during classes.

All the students are revolutionary elements. Due to the weak political curriculum and the instructors' lack of political organization, however, the students have an indifferent attitude towards political problems.

With the war over, plans have already been formulated to institute reforms:

a) Change instructors. Elevate the political standards of the instructors who remain.

$7]   b) Appoint regular political instructors and fix a systematic political curriculum.

c) Organize clubs and define their activities.

d) Organize a Sunyatsenist lecture group.

e) Expand experimental work and increase the number of classrooms.

Schools of the Second Army. There are two schools in the Second Army: (1) officers' school; (2) enlisted men's school. Two hundred and eighty students graduated from the officers' school at the beginning of this month. The remainder, 470 students, will graduate in the first part of March.

Three hundred new students should be selected, with 150 to come from high schools and the rest from among enlisted men in the Army.

The enlisted men's school has 550 students recruited from five companies. The students of the Second and Third companies, totaling 280 persons, will complete their course in January. The rest will finish by February. The quality of the instructors and of the training is below average.

Schools of the Third Army. There are two schools in the Third Army: (1) the officers' school; (2) the supplementary school for low-ranking officers.

The officers' school was established in early September. It now has 800 students and 300 magazine guns. The position of president is filled by the Commander of the Third Army, General Chu P'ei-te.

The acting president is the Dean, General Kuo Ching-wei, who is a native of Kiangsi. He is a graduate of a Japanese military academy and possesses profound military knowledge.

The instructors are poorly organized. Tactical training is weak. The number of instructors is insufficient. Students are admitted without taking entrance examinations and their general and technical knowledge varies greatly.

[58] The supplementary school for low-ranking officers has about 600 students and 200 magazine guns.

Many of the students formerly were enlisted men and they lack military knowledge. Their age ranges from twenty-five to thirty. The school has actually ceased to function because of shortage of instructors. Dissolution of the school is now considered, with the older men to be repatriated to their native places and the strong ones (that is, useful elements) transferred to the officers' school.

The School of the Fourth Army. The school is still in the stage of organization. It is recruiting students and building a campus.

The Navy

During the recent fighting the Navy was charged with the following responsibilities: (1) protection of harbors and river mouths against attack by enemy ships and prevention of the transportation of armed personnel by ships sailing under foreign flags; (2) defense of Kwangtung and Fukien;‡‡ (3) suppression of banditry along the river front. The ships, though old, were capable of carrying out the first two duties but not the third. Although eight armed ships were captured from the rebels, the present strength of the Navy is still inadequate to destroy the bandits. More ships are needed in order to suppress the great number of bandits who are supported by Hongkong.

To repair the ships, a torpedo and mine factory was established. The factory has completed repairs on one torpedo boat, special repairs on one gunboat, and general repairs on six gunboats. It has prepared a dockyard for the gunboat "Chung-shan."

All unstable officers of the gunboats have been discharged since a Russian [Smirnov] became Chief of the Navy Department. New appointments of officers and [political] commissars of the ships have now been completed.

Aviation

There were six airplanes and one naval plane in the Aviation Bureau before the war. They were all old models and were regarded [59] by the Russian advisers and specialists as entirely unfit for use.

---

‡‡ The National Government succeeded in establishing control over Kwangtung province only in late 1925. Fukien province was under allegiance to Sun Ch'uan-fang. It is possible, however, that Kisanko may have meant that the navy of the National Government was charged with defending the approaches to neighboring Fukien.

However, at the Eastern and Southern fronts, the air force was able to achieve 50 percent of the duties assigned to it.

In mid-November, the Aviation Bureau established one air squadron and an aviation training school. Many Whampoa graduates came for training. A number of very fine miltiary air squadrons and instructors, absolutely indispensable in the development of aviation, can be turned out within a short time. Most of the present air force personnel have no military knowledge. Being sons of wealthy merchants, they have studied abroad. They have very little contact with the National Revolutionary Government and it is difficult for them to serve in the Army.

For geographical reasons, aviation in Kwangtung should be particularly stressed, as it would render great service to communications organization and army administration.

Our Work

We have already secured good positions in the various departments of the National Revolutionary Army. It is not possible, however, to penetrate further to obtain complete control because of the following major reasons:

1. Shortage of advisers. The presently available advisers are insufficient for distribution among the armies and the schools. There have been cases of one adviser handling the work of two persons. Much important work has been suspended because of such shortages.

2. Complete lack of interpreters. Most of the advisers do not understand foreign languages. Each adviser has to have one English-Russian and one English-Chinese interpreter. At present, we have only one English-Russian interpreter and one barely capable Russian-Chinese interpreter, and they are at the Eastern Front with the Army. The rest of the interpreters do not understand Russian speech, not to say writing. Consequently a good deal of time has been wasted and much of the real meaning has been lost through roundabout translation.

The regulations of our group, a report on its work, and the budget will be forwarded to you by the next mail.

[60] Our Present Duties. In view of the favorable situation in Canton's foreign relations, we should now direct our attention entirely to political training and the training of powerful combat troops loyal to the National Revolutionary Government. Those troops should be given considerable supplies. The tasks of the group in the immediate future are:

1. Suspend purely military work and engage in political-military work. As war activities have not yet ceased, our advisers are tied up with military activities and are unable to pay adequate attention to political work. Most of the armies are ignorant of political work. In the first stage, all the advisers should benefit army political

organs by their experience and knowledge and draw the officer's attention to political work so that a suitable groundwork can be laid.

2. Establish a centralized military academy, as previously mentioned. The schools of the armies are at present very much handicapped by lack of personnel and finances and have failed to provide adequate military-political training for officers. The establishment of a single military academy would bring economy in personnel and finances. The good elements of the four schools should be sent to the Army and given suitable appointments as officers (for details see Appendix No. 13). [See Doc. 18.]

3. The General Staff should be the actual administrative organ of the National Revolutionary Army. Abolish the generals' independent power. Only thus can a regular army controlled by the National Revolutionary Government be created.

4. Establish a central commissariat organ and promulgate laws regulating necessary supplies to the regular Army.

5. Reorganize the armed forces into five armies and two independent divisions. The present numberous small army units impose extra cost, waste actual strength, and considerably affect combat ability. (See Appendix No. 10 for instructions on army reorganization.)

[61]   6. The regular troops stationed at various places should expedite their movements through short-cut routes, setting up defense where the enemy could be attacked [could attack?] and establishing safe camps for training.

7. Establish supplementary classes for training reserve army officers, and establish a military study society among officer-instructors in the Army.

8. Fix the training curriculum. A uniform curriculum has not yet been fixed. The advisers independently formulate their own curriculum in the armies, resulting in great divergencies.

9. Establish a political and military publishing office. Chinese military science is completely lacking in the Army, and consequently Chinese officers are entirely ignorant of military science. All new publications on political and military matters should be translated into Chinese and distributed to the officers and political personnel of the National Revolutionary Army.

10. Revise Army Regulations. Most of the laws presently in force in the Army are translated from old Japanese and German laws. They are obsolete and unsuited to present needs.

11. Organize a strong Navy in view of the many water routes in Kwangtung.

12. Strengthen and expand aviation.

13. Organize and regulate sanitation in the Army.

The following should be done immediately in order to realize the above plans:

1. Increase the personnel of the Group. This question was put to Voronin [Egorov's predecessor], who consented to our request. The additional expenses should be borne by Moscow.

[62]   2. Send fifteen Russian-Chinese translators. The idea in Peking that interpreters working in Kwangtung need only understand the Kwangtung dialect is fundamentally erroneous. The officers and [Party] members here speak the Peking Mandarin in dealing with our advisers. Therefore, it is necessary to have translators who understand the Peking Mandarin.

3. Send ammunition and telephone and telegraph materials according to the amount requested.

In addition, it is necessary to establish liaison with your office for transmission of information. (a) Send two regular couriers to travel from Peking to Canton and back to Peking at least once a month; (b) Send us the military code, without which communication with your office is handicapped because (1) at present, there is only one secret code at Borodin's place. Those of us who are scattered at various places have to wait for our chance to send telegrams through Borodin, thus causing great delays; (2) the present procedure does not ensure secrecy, as the secret code is known to many people; (3) Borodin's decoding clerk often piles up telegrams without transmitting them; (4) if I had the secret code for direct communication with you, it would prove extremely beneficial.

This report will conclude here. Further reports will be sent by the next Soviet ship going to Shanghai.

DOCUMENT 17

Document 17 was translated by the Peking Commission from Russian into Chinese and published in <u>Su-lien yin-mou...</u>, III, "Canton," pp. 21-24. Presumably the regulations were originally written in Chinese. The document is undated. Kisanko reported in late December, 1925, however, that the regulations of political departments had just been drafted. See Doc. 16, p. 50.

REGULATIONS OF POLITICAL DEPARTMENTS IN
THE NATIONAL REVOLUTIONARY ARMY

[21] **Chapter I. Commissars in the Armies**

1. Political departments are organized to promote political education, instill a national revolutionary spirit, raise fighting capacity, solidify discipline, and realize Sunyatsenism in the Army.

2. The Political Commissar is the representative of the Kuomintang, responsible to Party headquarters for the political training of the troops. He helps carry out directives of Party headquarters and high-ranking officers, and assists army commanders in raising and solidifying the disciplinary foundation of the National Revolutionary Army.

3. The commissar is the director of Party organizations in the Army. He is responsible for the work of political education and [22] supervises such organs as army clubs, the League of Military Youth, and the Sunyatsenist Society. He directs Party members in these organs as well as his subordinates in the political department.

4. The commissar should know all the officers of the Army and inquire at all times into conditions of army life and the psychology of the officers and men.

5. The commissar should see that all deficiencies and obstacles in carrying out our work are removed. He should report to his superior in case such is not possible.

6. The commissar should carry out Party and political training in the Army and direct such work in accordance with orders of his superior. This work should be in harmony with the curriculum of instruction fixed by the army commander.

7. The commissar is the superior of the military personnel in the Army. His orders, like those of the commander, should be obeyed.

8. The commissar should have executive power to impose penalties which should be carried out by the commander.

9. The commissar should not interfere with the commander's administrative orders.

10. The commissar should report to his superior any of the commander's orders which in his opinion endanger the National Revolution. In the event of an apparent rebellion, he may act on his own discretion without observing proclaimed orders. Such action should be reported simultaneously to his superior, the Political Council, and the president of the Military Court.

11. In times of war, the commissar should set a good example to the officers and men by demonstrating personal bravery in fighting at the front.

12. The commissar should give attention to general affairs and army life; check whether the men get their food on time and on the quality of the food; train the men to protect national property; check that all newspapers and magazines are received on time and equality distributed in the Army.

13. The commissar should see to it that the troops do not disturb the people during wartime. He should explain to the soldiers their duty of liberating the people from foreign imperialism.

14. The commissar should maintain contact with the people where the army is stationed. He should exert special efforts to bring peasant and labor organizations close to the Army.

15. The commissar's work should be planned in accordance with Kuomintang organs in the Army. He should direct the work of Party organs and carry out through Party organs all important measures designed to strengthen the Army.

16. The commissar should have power to suspend resolutions of Party organs in case of conflict of opinion with Party organs. He should report such action to higher Party headquarters and to the appropriate Political Department.

17. The commissar should familiarize himself with all existing regulations of the National Revolutionary Army and such orders and circular instructions as concern his particular army.

18. The commissar should report monthly to his superior on his work. Reports on work and conditions in the Army should also be made at meetings of army officers and political workers.

19. All provisions in the first chapter of the regulations concern only commissars in regiments, battalions, companies, platoons, and the Navy. The duties and powers of commissars at army headquarters, commanders' offices, the various organs of the National Revolutionary Army, army groups, divisions, naval headquarters, the General staff, the sanitation bureau, the commissariat, and the arsenal, etc., will be enumerated in the second chapter.

Chapter II. [Political] Commissars at Army Headquarters and Various Organs

1. The commissar at army headquarters, commander's offices,

and various military organs should have powers and duties identical with those of respective commanding officers.

2. The commissar should have the power of military, political, and financial supervision.

3. The commissar receives and approves reports of subordinate officers together with the commander. He, together with the commanding officer, signs all orders and outgoing documents. Documents without the commissar's signature will be considered null and void.

4. The commissar should sign orders on which he conflicts with the commanding officer, but he sould report this to his superior. He may act in accordance with provisions of Article 10 [Chapter I] when he considers that any action of the commander betrays treacherous intentions.

Chapter III. Appointment of Commissars

1. The position of commissar should be filled by KMT members who are loyal to the National Revolution, politically experienced, and strictly disciplined.

2. Commissars in army units lower than regiments and equivalents should be appointed by the Political Departments.

3. Commissars in divisions and armies should be nominated by the Political Department with the consent of the Kuomintang Central Executive Committee, and appointed upon the approval of the Military Council.

utilized the Kuomintang to expand their own organization and influence. Why did the Communists not bring the name of their own
party out into the open? he asked. Was it because they realized that
communism could not possibly meet the needs of the nation and
people and had in fact no chance of success?

Tai Chi-t'ao made a number of specific complaints against the
Communists—they sought to oust non-Communist elements from
Kuomintang posts; they absorbed Kuomintang members into the
Communist Party and Youth Corps; they criticized the Kuomintang
with a view to destroying the people's confidence in the KMT. Tai
particularly denounced the Communists for stirring up trouble
between Kuomintang leaders in order to advance their own interests.
As examples, Tai complained that Communists were promoting
conflict between Chiang Kai-shek and Hsü Ch'ung-chih, and that they
were spreading rumors to the effect that Hu Han-min wished to
attack Wang Ching-wei and Hsü Ch'ung-chih.

Although Tai declared that it was necessary for China to ally
herself closely with Soviet Russia in order to achieve national independence and freedom and to participate in the World Revolution,
he warned that China must not abandon her independence and rely
completely on Soviet Russia. China must not forget her own needs,
he said, and blindly follow Russia.[3]

The publication of Tai's book took place just as the Kuomintang
Left Wing was reorganizing the government and army in Canton
with the support of Soviet advisers. Left leaders further consolidated
their position and instituted an anti-Right coup in August and September which was highlighted by the departure of Hu Han-min and
Hsü Ch'ung-chih from Canton. (See Part III, pp. 162-166). Although
the Left Wing was indisputably in control, Chinese Communist
leaders were worried over the appearance of Tai Chi-t'ao's
theories. In an open letter to Tai Chi-t'ao, dated August 30, Ch'en
Tu-hsiu defended Communist motives in joining the KMT. Ch'en
pointed out that very few KMT members had joined the KCT, compared with Communists who had joined the KMT. He warned Tai that
his book was being utilized as propaganda by the reactionaries.[4]

At the beginning of October, an enlarged plenum of the KCT's
Central Committee was convened in Peking. Ch'en Tu-hsiu later
asserted that he had served warning at the Plenum that Tai Chi-
t'ao's writings betrayed the bourgeoisie's intention of checking the
proletariat and going over to the counterrevolution, and that he
therefore proposed withdrawing from the Kuomintang. The CC, however, rejected his proposal and resolved to remain within the
Kuomintang. To strengthen the Communist position, the CC emphasized the need for strengthening the Communist Party's
independent character, expanding the Party, and stepping up efforts
to absorb the masses. (See Part II, pp. 92-94).

In recognition of the threat of Tai Chi-t'ao's theories, the CC
resolved that Tai and others like him should be regarded as the
principal enemies of the Communists. Tai's attitude resulted
from the intensified differentiation of Chinese society following
the May Thirtieth Movement,[5] the CC stated, and indicated the
efforts of the bourgeoisie to define their ideology and to consolidate themselves organizationally. People like Tai Chi-t'ao, the
CC said, were utilizing the signboard "The Real Three People's
Principles" to oppose the class struggle, the KMT Left Wing, and
the Communists. The CC concluded: "It becomes increasingly clear
every day that this faction has formed itself into the KMT Right
Wing" [Doc. 20, pp. 1-2]. To bolster the Communist position within
the Kuomintang, the CC re-emphasized the policy of alliance with
the Left against the Right. The CC stated: "Our Party members
should know our present policy toward the KMT: We oppose its
Right Wing and unite with its Left Wing by contracting a close alliance with it and helping it in every way possible to fight against the
Right" [Doc. 20, p. 3].

The Communist policy of alliance with the Left had been introduced by Voitinskii in late 1923 and had been formally adopted by
the CC in May, 1924.[6] However, this policy did not assume major
significance until after Sun Yat-sen's death in March, 1925. During Sun's lifetime, he held supreme authority over the Party and
government and it was mainly through Borodin's direct influence
on him that Communists sought to mould the KMT's organization
and policies.

Two major incidents are cited in KMT and other anti-Communist
sources to document the charge that, following Sun's death, Communists helped Left Wing leaders to consolidate their power against
the Right. These sources assert that Borodin and the Central Committee of the KCT were primarily responsible for Wang Ching-wei's
election as the first chairman of the National Government in July,
1925. They point out that previously Wang had been relatively unimportant, compared with Hu Han-min and Liao Chung-k'ai. The
Communists opposed Hu Han-min as a Rightist these sources say,
and maneuvered his demotion to the post of Foreign Minister. Communists preferred Wang Ching-wei to Liao Chung-k'ai as chairman
because Wang could be manipulated and Liao could not.[7] Secondly,
these sources assert that the anti-Right coup following Liao Chung-
k'ai's assassination was instigated by Borodin. According to Liu
Lu-yin, immediately after the assassination Borodin insisted to
Hsü Ch'ung-chih that five prominent Right Wing leaders—Hu Han-min,
Chou Lu, Ku Ying-fen, Teng Tse-ju, and Hsieh Ch'ih—be arrested.
Hsü's refusal, Liu asserts, led to his own expulsion from Canton.[8]

While it is difficult to ascertain the accuracy of specific details,
the charge that the Russians and Chinese Communists supported

the Left against the Right appears valid. The Kuomintang's revolutionary policies and the reorganization of the government and army in the summer of 1925 undoubtedly were carried out by Left leaders with Communist support, particularly since the CC had resolved to execute the tactic of allying with the Left against the Right as early as May, 1924.

Communist support of the Left Wing was confined to Left leaders. Apparently, neither Borodin nor the Chinese Communists encouraged the development of the Left Wing organizationally. The few Left organizations which did exist were either weak, like the Progressive Society, a secret organization at the KMT's Central Party Headquarters, or infiltrated by Communists, as was the New Student Society.[9] The Left therefore had no organized following, nor did it have a platform independent of the Party and Government.

In the resolutions adopted at the Enlarged Plenum in October, 1925, the CC revealed concern over the instability of an alliance with the Left Wing which hinged entirely on cooperation with Left leaders. The Left was "mere talk," the CC declared; it was not enough to be Left-inclined [Doc. 20, p. 4]. According to the two top Left leaders themselves, Wang Ching-wei and Chiang Kai-shek, the Left was anti-imperialist and revolutionary, and the Right was subservient to imperialists and counterrevolutionary.[10] The CC sought to establish a more precise definition of the Left Wing in accordance with political policies. The Right and Left, it declared, should be classified according to their attitude toward: (1) imperialism; (2) the labor and peasant movements; (3) militarism; (4) Soviet Russia and the Chinese Communist Party; and (5) reactionary policies. The Left Wing not only should oppose all reactionaries, imperialists, and militarists, the CC stated, it should assist the labor and peasant movements and cooperate with Soviet Russia and the Chinese Communist Party [Doc. 20, p. 5].

The CC warned against the danger of confusing Communists with the Left Wing. This erroneous tendency, said the CC, had led to neglect of their own position by the Communists as well as misunderstanding of the respective positions of the Communists and the Left Wing. The CC declared that it was incorrect to classify the Kuomintang into Right, Left, and Center. There were in fact only the Right and Left Wings in the KMT, the CC said. Members of the Center had either joined the Right or Left, while former Right Wing members, such as Feng Tzu-yu, had become openly reactionary [Doc. 20, pp. 4-5].

The Western Hills Conference, November 23 to December 5, 1925

Communist fears of the emergence of a new Right Wing of the Kuomintang were confirmed on November 23, 1925, when fifteen mem-

bers of the CEC and CSC convened what they called the "Fourth CEC
Plenum" before Sun Yat-sen's tomb in the Western Hills of Peking.
Signers of the telegram announcing the opening of the "plenum" included Tai Chi-t'ao, Chou Lu, Chang Chi, Lin Shen, Shao Yüan-
ch'ung, Yeh Ch'u-cheng, Shen Hsüan-lu, Hsieh Ch'ih, and Wu Chih-
hui. A manifesto was issued on the first day of the conference, denouncing the Communists for utilizing the KMT only in order to
expand the influence of their own Party and to support Soviet Russia. The "Fourth CEC Plenum" had therefore decided, the manifesto
stated, to annul the KMT membership of all Communist members
of the Kuomintang. However, it declared that the KMT and the KCT
could still cooperate as political parties in the interests of the
National Revolution. The Kuomintang was dedicated to the overthrow of imperialism of all kinds in order to obtain national independence. Although the Communist Party and the Kuomintang shared
a common determination to work for the National Revolution, said
the Western Hills Group, China and Russia had different historical
backgrounds and social conditions. The National Revolution and
class revolution could go hand in hand. It added, however, that the
Kuomintang should cooperate with anti-imperialist Russia whenever necessary in the course of revolutionary work.[11]

The immediate reaction of the Chinese Communists is revealed
in Document 21, drafted by the Peking Local Committee and dated
November 25.

The Peking Local Committee identified Tai Chi-t'ao as the leader
of the "New Right Wing" and labeled his theories "Taichitaoism."
Despite its assertion that the Right Wing was gathering in Peking
only because that was the only place it could "maintain its dying
life," the Peking Local Committee betrayed extreme nervousness.
The Right Wing had allied itself with the reactionaries, it said,
and Communists were seeking an alliance with the Left in order to
counteract the reactionary conduct of the Right. However, there
were hardly any Kuomintang Leftists in Peking, the Committee said,
and Party members were all inclined toward Taichitaoism. Under
such circumstances, the Peking Local Committee stated, "It is
extremely dangerous for the Communists to fight singlehandedly
against the Right within the Kuomintang." An isolated struggle by
the Communists not only could overthrow the Right but could enchance
its strength for, in such an event, "many shortsighted and wavering
elements who cannot see clearly that this is a struggle between
revolution and counterrevolution would mistake it for a struggle
between communism and anti-communism" [Doc. 21, p. 149].

The Peking Local Committee declared that the Northern Communists must attempt to form a Left Wing of the masses and, under
the united front of the Left and the Communists, from the bottom
level of the masses up to high-level organs, oppose the Right and

the reactionaries. It outlined point-by-point rebuttals of the arguments of the Right Wing (or New Right Wing) under three propaganda
headings: (1) Taichitaoism was not Sunyatsenism; (2) The Right
Wing and the reactionaries were conspiring to destroy the organization of the KMT and to violate Party discipline; and (3) It was
necessary to continue the cooperation between the Chinese Communist Party and the Kuomintang [Doc. 21, p. 150].

In an article, "What are the Right and Left Wings of the Kuomintang?" published in the December 3, 1925 issue of Hsiang-tao chou-
pao, Ch'en Tu-hsiu came out openly in support of the Left against
the Right. Tai Chi-t'ao's clique was the final development of the
KMT Right Wing, he said. What was the difference between the Right
and Left? Around the time of the First KMT Congress, he answered, the Left favored, and the Right opposed, anti-imperialist
and antimilitarist policies; the Left believed in, and the Right
denied, the Three People's Principles. Now, however, it was not
enough merely to believe in principles. Those who believed only in
principles were only ideologists, not revolutionaries, Ch'en said.
The Left Wing knew that it was useless merely to disseminate
propaganda on the Three People's Principles without defining concrete policies for their realization. In order to realize the Principles, the Left could not but support the policies calling for the Russian alliance, cooperation with the Communists, and nonopposition
to the class struggle, which were policies demanded by the actual
situation. Ch'en concluded: "In the Chinese national revolutionary
movement, we must support the Kuomintang Left Wing and oppose
its Right Wing!"[12]

Ch'en Tu-hsiu's definition of the Left's platform was echoed in
a circular notice to Party members issued by the Kuomintang
Central Executive Committee the following day, December 4. If
the Party did not ally with Soviet Russia, base itself on the peasantry and labor which constitute the majority of the people,
and admit Communist elements who stood for the interests of
peasants and workers, then the revolutionary force would fall into
isolation and the Revolution would never be accomplished. Under
the circumstances, the CEC declared, not to be revolutionary was
to be counterrevolutionary. There was absolutely no room for
neutrality. The CEC announced that it had already protested against
the Western Hills Conference.[13]

Meantime, on December 2, the Western Hills Group adopted
resolutions for the expulsion of Communist CEC members—T'an
P'ing-shan, Yü Shu-te, Li Ta-chao, and Lin Tsu-han—and Communist members of the reserve CEC—Mao Tse-tung, Ch'ü Ch'iu-
pai, Han Lin-fu, Yü Fang-chou, and Chang Kuo-t'ao. On December
4, it took the following measures: (1) Borodin's contract as adviser to the KMT was terminated; and (2) the Political Council was

dissolved. The next day, the Group decided to expel Wang Ching-wei from Party membership for a period of six months.[14]

On December 12, the CEC denounced Chou Lu and Hsieh Ch'ih, whom it identified as the principal leaders of the Western Hill Group, and issued a call for the opening of the Second Congress of the Kuomintang.[15] Formal action in dealing with the Western Hills Group was thus delayed until the Congress was convened on January 4, 1926, in Canton.

The Soviet Position in the Military Establishment to December, 1926

The Western Hills Conference took place just as the Second Eastern Expedition was drawing to a close. Soviet advisers participated in the campaign, which brought all of Kwangtung under KMT rule. On December 11, 1925, at a banquet at the Swatow headquarters of the Eastern Expeditionary Forces, Commander-in-Chief Chiang Kai-shek made generous acknowledgment of the Russians' services. He asked rhetorically why the National Revolutionary Army had not earlier been organized or the East River districts pacified. He then answered that these accomplishments were all due to execution of Sun Yat-sen's policy of alliance with Soviet Russia. Chiang said that the KMT should accept Russian direction of the Chinese Revolution, and compared this to the Allied command under Marshal Foch in World War I. He quoted Sun Yat-sen to the effect that Borodin's views represented Sun's own views. He referred to Sun's will calling on the KMT to unite with all peoples in the world who treated the Chinese as equals.[16]

The influence of Russian advisers in the Kuomintang's military apparatus reached its zenith with the conclusion of the Second Eastern Expedition. By the end of December, 1925, the newly organized Navy and Aviation bureaus were officially headed by Russians [Doc. 15, p. 5]. The Navy Bureau was taken over by Admiral Smirnov,[17] who promptly discharged all "unstable" officers on the gunboats and made new appointments of officers and political commissars [Doc. 16, p. 58]. The Aviation Bureau was headed by a Russian named Remi.[18] The Communications Department of the General Staff was also headed by a Russian. In view of the strong Russian position on the General Staff—Rogachev was Chief of Staff—the Chief of the Soviet Group in Canton sought to strengthen the General Staff's authority. The General Staff should not be merely the secretariat of the Military Council, Kisanko said, but the actual administrative organ of the National Revolutionary Army [Doc. 16, pp. 50, 60].

Whereas Borodin tended to rely on exerting influence indirectly through Left leaders, Kisanko apparently favored more aggressive methods aiming at Russian control of the Kuomintang's military

system. He complained, for instance, that despite the good positions
the Russians had been able to secure in various departments of the
National Revolutionary Army, it was as yet not possible for them
to penetrate further to obtain complete control because of the shortage of advisers and interpreters. He held an extremely low opinion
of Chinese officers, whom he considered entirely ignorant of military science [Doc. 16, pp. 59-61].

By this time, detailed regulations on the organization of the Soviet
Group in South China had been drawn up. The chief of the Group.
Kisanko, received instructions from the Soviet Military Attaché in
Peking and coordinated political policies with Borodin.[19]

The Second Kuomintang Congress, January 4-19, 1926

On December 26, 1925, the Presidium of the Fourteenth Party
Conference of the Russian Communist Party wired greetings to the
Presidium of the Second Kuomintang Congress which was scheduled
shortly to convene. The telegram expressed the Russians' conviction that the Kuomintang would follow the Russian Communist
Party's example by destroying the foundation of imperialist rule in
Asia. This task could be accomplished, it stated, if the Kuomintang
would strengthen the alliance of the Chinese working class and
peasantry, allow itself to be guided by their interests, and support
every movement which was directed against world capitalism.[20]

The Second KMT Congress responded with a telegram to the
Soviet Government which called upon it to cooperate still more
closely with the KMT in the fight against imperialism.[21] The Congress also issued a manifesto declaring that the Chinese Revolution was part of the World Revolution and that its objective was the
overthrow of imperialism and its tools—the militarists, bureaucrats, compradors, and local bullies.[22] The Second Congress addressed a message to the oppressed peoples of the world. It assured them that the Party's mission was to follow Sun Yat-sen's
directions to advance together with all the oppressed peoples and
classes to bring to fruition the National Revolution, help hasten the
World Revolution, and realize true peace for mankind.[23]

Such pronouncements reflect the dominance of the Left Wing
at the Second Congress. The Communists again vowed that their
only objective was the unification of the Kuomintang's revolutionary forces in order to further the National Revolution.[24]

Anti-Communist sources assert that Communists were in actual
control of the Second Congress. According to one source, behind-
the-scenes power was wielded by the Communist Party fraction of
90 members (out of a total of 256 Congress delegates), which was
headed by T'an P'ing-shan and later by Chang Kuo-t'ao.[25] Tung
Pi-wu later recalled that KMT Left leaders expressed the hope
that many Communists would be elected to the CEC. However, the

Communist Party did not wish to come out so openly in control and permitted only a few Communists to be elected.[26]

Seven Communists—Li Ta-chao, Lin Tsu-han, T'an P'ing-shan, Wu Yü-chang, Yang P'ao-an, Yü Shu-te, and Yün Tai-ying—were elected to the CEC, the membership of which was increased from twenty-four to thirty-six.[27] At the First Plenum of the CEC on January 22, 1926, three Communists—T'an P'ing-shan, Lin Tsu-han, and Yang P'ao-an—were elected to the nine-man Standing Committee of the CEC.[28] Wang Ching-wei and Chiang Kai-shek remained the top leaders. Wang maintained his positions at the head of the Party and Government. Chiang was elected for the first time to the CEC and also the Standing Committee of the CEC.[29]

Since the Western Hills Conference had expelled Wang Ching-wei from Party membership, his re-election to the highest political posts indicated repudiation of the "Fourth CEC Plenum." Earlier, on December 4 and 12, the CEC had disavowed the Western Hills Conference. However, the Second Congress did not resolve to expel all members of the Western Hills Group, as it had previously expelled members of the Peking Kuomintang Comrades' Club.[30] The "Resolutions Impeaching the Western Hills Conference" adopted at the Second Congress classified members of the Western Hills Group into three categories. Chou Lu and Hsieh Ch'ih were identified as the central elements of the Group and were expelled permanently from the Party. Warning was given twelve other members, including Chang Chi, Shen Hsüan-lu, Lin Shen, and Shao Yüan-ch'ung; they were threatened with expulsion if they continued to violate Party discipline. Tai Chi-t'ao, who signed the telegram convening the Western Hills Conference but later withdrew from the Conference, was merely reprimanded for publicizing his private opinions and thus promoting intra-Party conflicts.[31]

Furthermore, Tai was re-elected to the Central Executive Committee at the Second Congress.[32] The re-election of Tai, whom the Communist Central Committee had identified as the leader of the New Right Wing, suggests that the Communist position at the Second KMT Congress was not as strong as might be supposed from the revolutionary tone of the manifesto and the telegram to the oppressed peoples of the world which the Congress had issued.

According to anti-Communist sources, Tai Chi-t'ao's re-election was principally due to Chiang Kai-shek's support.[33] Prior to the Second Congress, on December 25, 1925, Chiang Kai-shek had denounced the Western Hills Group in a circular letter to Party members. He upheld the policy of admitting Communists into the KMT, defended Wang Ching-wei's actions, and defended Borodin against the accusation that he was despotic and dictatorial. The Russian advisers, Chiang declared, sincerely loved the Kuomintang and had not tried to dictate policy to the Party.[34]

By January 11, 1926, however, Chiang's attitude had undergone considerable revision. On that day he met with Sun Fo, who had just arrived from Shanghai, where many of the Western Hills Group had gathered. During their conversation, Chiang expressed his personal opinion that the resolution expelling members of the Western Hills Conference should be postponed until the Third Party Congress.[35]

Chiang Kai-shek and the Soviet Advisers, January to Early March, 1926

Around this time, critical references to the Russian advisers begin to appear in Chiang's diary. The entry for January 19, 1926, the last day of the Second Congress, states that Chiang had been unhappy of late about the policies of Rogachev, the Russian Chief of Staff, and Kisanko, Chief of the Soviet Group in Canton. Chiang said: "I treat them with sincerity but they reciprocate with deceit. It is impossible to work with them!"[36] On February 7, according to Chiang's diary, Kisanko ridiculed him.[37] On February 11, Chiang recorded the following: "My Russian associates are suspicious and envious of me. They deceive me. It may be, however, that they do so unintentionally. In view of the circumstances, the only course for me is to be guided by sincerity."[38]

Chiang Kai-shek made the first move to restrict Russian influence on February 16 when he proposed reorganizing the General Staff and removing Russians from administrative posts.[39] This suggestion was advanced in the absence of Borodin, who had left Canton for North China in the early part of February.[40]

Disagreement between Chiang and the Russians at this time centered on the question of launching the third Northern Expedition. On January 27, 1926, Wang Ching-wei had proposed to the Political Council that the Northern Expedition be launched. The resolution was adopted,[41] but no specific date was set. On February 24, the National Government established a unification committee for the two provinces of Kwangtung and Kwangsi, thus completing negotiations to bring Kwangsi under KMT jurisdiction. That same day, Chiang proposed an early decision to launch the Northern Expedition in order to rescue Feng Yü-hsiang's Kuominchün armies, which had been defeated in North China.[42] Chiang's proposal was made despite Russian opposition. Two days before, on February 22, most of the Russian advisers had counseled him to "go slow" on plans for the Northern Expedition.[43]

On February 26, Chiang proposed dealing with Kisanko specifically. According to the diary, he told Wang Ching-wei that Kisanko's dictatorial and contradictory behavior was a danger to the Party and country and that it would adversely affect Sino-Russian relations. However, Chiang made it plain that he regarded Kisanko as

an individual rather than as a representative of the Soviet authorities.[44] The following day, on February 27, Chiang dismissed
Wang Mou-kung, commander of the Second Division of the First
Army. According to Chiang, Kisanko and the other Russians had
been utilizing Wang Mou-kung in conspiracies against the KMT.[45]

Chiang's hostility toward Kisanko was apparently more than personal, however. In the absence of Borodin, Kisanko was the chief
Soviet representative at Canton. It is probably more than mere
coincidence that Chiang complained also of Rogachev, the second
most important Russian adviser then in Canton.

Document 22 is an extremely interesting report written at this
time by a Soviet adviser, possibly Kisanko. The Russians had played
an exceptionally important role at Canton, he said. The Kuomintang
as it existed in early 1926 was actually established by the Russians,
since its program, regulations, and work were planned under Russian leadership, according to the standards of the Russian Communist Party but conforming to actual conditions in China. The direction of the Party and Government had been carried on until recently
with the closest participation of the Russian political director
(Borodin), and there had not been a case in which the Russians' proposals were not accepted and put into effect by the Government. He
reported that the majority of KMT leaders (called by him the Center) was for the time allied with the Communists (whom he called
the Left), under the Russians' political leadership. He warned, however, that support of the Right Wing would grow if the Russian
advisers and the Communists tried to push the revolution too fast.
He stressed the need of continued Russian guidance, but pointed out
that the Communists should proceed with great caution. To counterbalance the Right and the vacillating Center, he emphasized the
organization of workers and peasants under the revolutionary slogans of the Left Wing of the KMT [Doc. 22, pp. 4-6].

Thus, the author of Document 22 appeared to be apprehensive
about the possibility of a split among Kuomintang leaders and
increase of the Right Wing's influence. He revealed also that Admiral Smirnov and Remi had been obliged to relinquish their official titles and resume the position of advisers. Rogachev had had
to give up the position of chief of staff and had become adviser to the chief
of staff.[46] He maintained, nevertheless, that the change did not
materially reduce Soviet influence. Russian advisers were in fact
at the head of all departments of the General Staff, he said, although
officially they were called advisers. The reason the Russians
reverted to the position of advisers, he explained, was that "it is
politically inconvenient for our advisers to hold official posts and
our influence does not suffer in the least by their becoming advisers again" [Doc. 22, pp. 2-3].

Despite his confident assertions, it is clear that by the end of

February, 1926, decisive steps had been taken to restrict Russian
control of the Kuomintang's military apparatus. Chiang's diary
indicates that additional measures were forthcoming. On March 8,
Chiang told Wang Ching-wei that revolutionary power must not fall
into the hands of foreigners and that certain limits must be set in
order to safeguard the Party's independence in its alliance with
Soviet Russia. According to Chiang's diary, Wang Ching-wei
agreed with him.[47] Four days later, however Chiang recorded in
his diary that Wang Ching-wei had implied that he should leave
Canton.[48]

Chiang's complaints against the Russian advisers beginning in
January had been accompanied by expressions of regret at the lack
of Party unity.[49] Beginning on March 7, entries in the diary refer
to the circulation of anti-Chiang propaganda in Canton.[50] Two days
later, it is definitely stated that Chiang was particularly perturbed
by the activities of Communists within the KMT.[51]

Communists in Kuomintang Organs, to May, 1926

Communists occupied approximately one fifth of the CEC seats
and one third of the Standing Committee seats. However, these
percentages do not give an accurate picture of Communist influence
in Kuomintang organs. By controlling the Organization Department—
T'an P'ing-shan had been department head since the reorganization—they commanded a strategic position within the Kuomintang
setup. According to Ch'en Kuo-fu, the majority of members of
provincial and municipal Party headquarters were Communists.
Twenty-six out of the twenty-nine persons on the staff of the
Organization Department in Canton were Communists.[52]

The Propaganda Department, often considered to be second in
importance only to the Organization Department, was headed by
Wang Ching-wei. Since Wang was busy with his other posts, control
of the Department fell to his deputy, Mao Tse-tung. The Peasant
Department was headed by the Communist Lin Tsu-han. Feng Chü-
p'o a Communist, served as secretary of the Labor Department.
Communists likewise held posts as secretaries in the remaining
divisions—the Youth, Overseas, Merchant, and Woman's departments. In addition, the Communist Liu Fen was chief secretary at
Central Party Headquarters.

Communists won responsible posts in the various training classes
set up by the CEC. Three out of five men in charge of the KMT's
Political Training Class were Communists. They were Mao Tse-
tung, Lin Tsu-han, and Li Fu-ch'un. Mao Tse-tung served also as
director of the KMT's Peasant Movement Training Institute, and
Teng Ying-ch'ao (Mrs. Chou En-lai), a Communist, served directly
under Ho Hsiang-ning (Mrs. Liao Chung-k'ai) in the Women's Movement Training Institute.[53]

Communists attempted to infiltrate military organs principally by obtaining posts as Party representatives. In December, 1925, Kisanko had stressed the need to push the appointment of Party commissars to the First Army [Doc. 16, p. 50]. With Chou En-lai heading the Political Department of the First Army, a high proportion of Party commissar posts in the First Army were subsequently taken by Communists. According to a Russian adviser, Communist Party representatives headed political work in four out of the five divisions of the First Army [Doc. 24, p. 81].[54]

The vice-chairman of the Political Department of the Central Military and Political Academy was Lu I, a Communist. The Communist Nieh Jung-chen was secretary. The Communist cell at the Academy was directly supervised by the Military Committee of the Chinese Communist Kwangtung Regional Committee, headed by Chou En-lai. In addition, Chou served also as deputy chairman of the political training classes sponsored by the Military Council.

Li Chih-lung, a Communist graduate of the first Whampoa class, headed the Political Department of the Navy Bureau and concurrently was deputy chief of the Bureau.[55]

The March Twentieth Coup d'État and the Immediate Communist Reaction, March 20 to Early April, 1926

During the night of March 18, Li Chih-lung ordered the gunboat S.S. "Chung-shan" to proceed to Whampoa. It anchored near Chiang Kai-shek's office and later returned to Canton. On the morning of March 19, Chiang went to see Wang Ching-wei. According to his diary, Chiang felt the urgent need to curb the Communist agitation immediately in order to save the Party and the country. That evening he held a secret conference with certain "trusted subordinates" (not further identified) which lasted until 4:00 o'clock in the morning.[56]

The morning of March 20, 1926, martial law was declared in Canton. Li Chih-lung and a number of Communist Party representatives were arrested. Guards at the residences of the Russian advisers and at the headquarters of the Strike Committee were disarmed. The coup d'état had a shattering effect upon the political situation at Canton.

A vivid description of the event and the reaction of the Russian advisers is given in Document 23, a report prepared by General Stepanov, adviser with the First Army, shortly after the incident.

According to Stepanov, the March Twentieth coup came as a great shock to the Russian advisers. Although they were aware of the significance of the movements of the S.S. "Chung-shan" on March 19, they had been clearly unprepared for the drastic measures taken by Chiang. Bewildered, they sought to find out Chiang's motives and future plans through other Chinese leaders, especially the generals, and from Chiang himself [Doc. 23, pp. 67-69].

Stepanov analyzed the causes of the incident in terms of the errors of the Russian advisers and the Chinese Communists and the personal characteristics of Chiang Kai-shek.

The Russian advisers, said Stepanov, pursued erroneous tactics by pushing the centralization of military organs too rapidly and by grabbing too much direct control over various organizations. This, combined with their excessive supervision of the Chinese generals and neglect of Chinese etiquette, aroused resentment among the Chinese military officers. Furthermore, the Russians failed to disseminate suitable propaganda in the Army. He criticized the Chinese Communists for similar errors. In his opinion, they failed to understand the tactic of organizing and then secretly transforming the Kuomintang, but concentrated instead on openly seizing control of Kuomintang organs. Thus, he said, they aroused envy among Kuomintang members [Doc. 23, pp. 70-71].

According to Stepanov, Chiang Kai-shek was an unusually egoistic and ambitious man. His entire personality was dominated by a lust for glory and power, to attain which he would utilize the Russians, the Chinese Communists, and the masses. These characteristics, in Stepanov's view, represented opportunity for the Russians to regain his friendship. He said, "We are trying to make Chiang cooperate with us again by satisfying his desire for glory and enabling him to achieve greater power and strength than he now enjoys....It is permissible to make a few concessions to Chiang's political demands as the price we pay." Stepanov thus hoped to win Chiang over by conciliatory measures and by helping him achieve greater power. In his opinion, Chiang was wavering between the Right Wing and the Communists. Hence, the Russians should surround him with Left influences and inject into him a strong dose of revolutionary ideology [Doc. 23, 71-73].

Stepanov's conciliatory policy was put into stronger terms in Document 24, a report he presented at a meeting of the Russian advisers in early April. It was necessary, he said, to continue to utilize Chiang for the National Revolution and cooperate with him as far as possible to the very end (emphasis ours), although he was not certain whether Chiang sincerely desired to cooperate with the Left or merely wished to deceive his enemies in preparation for a second coup [Doc. 24, p. 76].

In addition, he advocated the following policies: (1) strengthen the Kuomintang's unity; (2) strengthen in particular the KMT Left Wing; (3) eliminate the counterrevolutionary Right; and (4) strengthen the alliance of the Communists with the KMT and the Government [Doc. 24, p. 78].

In short, Stepanov's policy was two-pronged. Communists were to placate Chiang and draw him to the Left. At the same time, they were to strengthen the KMT Left and eliminate the Counterrevolutionary Right.

The second part of Document 24 records the Russian advisers' discussion of Stepanov's report at the meeting. It reveals that considerable disagreement existed among the Russians. One Soviet adviser believed that Chiang would definitely be persuaded to lean to the Left. Another was disturbed by Chiang's assumption of power and pessimistic about the possibility of genuine cooperation with him. While Stepanov himself was apparently optimistic about Chiang's future political orientation, he emphasized that it was impossible to guarantee that Chiang would always be allied with the Russians [Doc. 24, pp. 84, 86-87].

Despite misgivings on the part of certain of the Russians, the actual policy which they pursued as a group was conciliatory almost from the first day of the coup.

Solovyev, Councillor of the Soviet Embassy, called on Chiang two days after the incident. He asked Chiang whether the issue at stake was personal or one pertaining to relations with Soviet Russia. When Chiang answered that the issue was only personal, Solovyev said he was greatly relieved. He assured Chiang that Kisanko and Rogachev would be ordered to leave Canton.[57] That same evening, the Political Council resolved to relieve Kisanko and other Russians of their posts;[58] these advisers apparently left Canton immediately, on March 24.[59] On that same day, Smirnov was dismissed by the Kuomintang CEC.[60]

The departure of the Russians symbolized the Soviet policy of conciliation. The remaining Russian advisers retreated still further by revising their attitude toward the Northern Expedition.

On April 3, Chiang presented to the CEC a set of proposals on the Northern Expedition.[61] As late as March 12, Chiang and Kisanko had had a serious argument over the advisability of launching the Northern Expedition.[62] After the coup, however, the Russians more or less accepted Chiang's opinions. In his second report, Stepanov declared that the situation in North China was favorable to the launching of the Northern Expedition. He stressed the need for all Russians to study data pertaining to the Expedition and added that the Army might be moving north in two or three months [Doc. 24, pp. 77, 79].

The official Chinese Communist policy of this period following the coup was likewise conciliatory. According to Stepanov, Ch'en Tu-hsiu agreed with his analysis of Chiang's character. Stepanov further asserted that the CC, as well as the Kwangtung Communists, shared his belief that Chiang should be conciliated by satisfying his personal ambition [Doc. 23, pp. 71, 73]. In his political report to the Fifth Congress in April-May, 1927, Ch'en Tu-hsiu confirmed that the CC had adopted a policy of retreat following the coup d'état in the belief that the combined strength of the Communists and the KMT Left was insufficient to suppress Chiang.

The CC, said Ch'en, took into consideration the fact that Chiang had not yet openly betrayed his counterrevolutionary leanings.63

The Communist Party's actions in the period after the March Twentieth Incident were clearly conciliatory. According to Stepanov, the Kwangtung Regional Committee voluntarily withdrew Communist Party representatives from the First Army. The Communist-controlled League of Military Youth was disbanded. Both moves were of course designed to placate Chiang and to ease Kuomintang-Communist tension [Doc. 24, pp. 75, 82]. In an article published in Hsiang-tao chou-pao on April 23, 1926, Ch'en Tu-hsiu denied charges that the Communists had been involved in a conspiracy to overthrow Chiang on March Twentieth. He emphasized the Chinese Communist Party's desire to continue cooperating with the Kuomintang.64

The international Communist press even denied that a coup had taken place. An article published in the International Press Correspondence on April 8 asserted that a "lying report" had been circulated by Reuter's to the effect that Chiang Kai-shek had carried out a coup d'état. The Kuomintang, it states, was not a tiny group of people, but a mass party in the true sense of the word. It was of course impossible to carry out a coup overnight.65 One month later, Voitinskii, chief Comintern delegate in China, again declared that news of a coup was merely "an invention of the imperialists."66

Chiang Kai-shek's Attitude and Assumption of Power, March 20 to April, 1926

Soviet hopes of appeasing Chiang were increased by the public attitude of Chiang himself following the coup.

In the first place, Chiang's attitude toward the Chinese Communists appeared to be equivocal. While he implied that they had instigated the S.S. "Chung-shan" incident to overthrow him, he did not directly accuse them of conspiracy.

On March 22, in a speech to the cadets of the Central Military and Political Academy, Chiang declared that the question of guilt was not yet clear. He added that even if Li Chih-lung were guilty, it was an individual matter and not one involving the entire organization (that is, the KCT, since Li was a Communist).67

Furthermore, on the following day, March 23, Chiang officially took responsibility for the incident when he petitioned the Military Council for punishment for his arbitrary actions. However, he stated that the emergency measures he ordered were in the interests of the Party and Government.68 Chiang also gave the impression of minimizing the incident. He expressed the view that it was merely the result of enmity between the Suñyatsenist Society and the League of Military Youth.69

On April 3, Chiang Kai-shek's views on KMT-KCT relations

were considerably clarified when he proposed to the CEC the following: (1) a plenum of the Kuomintang Central Executive Committee was to be convened to regulate discipline and investigate certain elements in the Party and Army; (2) Communists must not
criticize Sun Yat-sen's character; they must be devoted to the
Three People's Principles in their work, abolish all secret organizations and activities within the KMT, notify KMT authorities
about all policies and instructions of the Communist Party, and
register all Communist members of the KMT with the proper KMT
authorities. Furthermore, they must not occupy more than one third
of the membership of the CEC; and (3) a joint KMT-KCT conference was to be called to settle all difficulties.[70]

Chiang's proposals were largely embodied in the resolutions
adopted by the Second CEC Plenum in the following month. While
they were designed to, and subsequently did, restrict Communist
activities within the KMT, they cannot be considered as totally
disadvantageous to the Communists. The proposal for a joint conference may in fact be interpreted as a concession to the Communists, for it implied tacit recognition of the idea of two-party alliance, which had been rejected by Sun Yat-sen. Furthermore, this
suggestion must have pleased the Russian advisers, who considered
the calling of just such a conference one of their immediate objectives [Doc. 24, p. 81].

On the specific issue of Communist Party representatives in the
Army, Chiang's attitude was hazy. On April 3, 1926, he proposed
the temporary withdrawal of all Party representatives for further
training on the ground that conflict between Communists and non-
Communists in the First Army had assumed dangerous proportions.
He also said that Communist and anarchist elements should be
withdrawn because the National Revolutionary Army was predicated
on the Three People's Principles. Yet, he declared that the system
of Party representatives should not be abolished.[71] After Communist Party representatives had voluntarily withdrawn from the
First Army on April 10,[72] Chiang praised the Communists for
their spirit. Their withdrawal, he said, was made because of their
great love for the Army and the Central Academy.[73]

Another cause of the Russians' apparent confusion is that
Chiang's attitude towards them was as equivocal as his attitude
towards the Chinese Communists. According to Stepanov, Chiang
made no definite demands or indications as to the work of the
Russian advisers. When he asked Chiang how the Russians should
work, Stepanov said, Chiang replied that they should continue as
before [Doc. 24, p. 79].

When Chiang presented his proposals on KMT-KCT relations on
April 3, 1926, he suggested that the Russians should not hold administrative posts of any type, but should serve strictly as advisers.

They should not, said Chiang, exceed the limits of their position without obtaining permission from their respective superior officers. However, he reaffirmed the policy of cooperation with the Russians as well as the Chinese Communists.[74]

Chiang made even stronger protestations of friendship with the Russians in an interview with a reporter of the Min-kuo jih-pao, a KMT organ. He expressed profound regret that the Russians had been inconvenienced on March Twentieth due to a misunderstanding of his orders by subordinates. Chiang denounced reports of his hostility towards the Russians and Communists as fabrications of "the running dogs of imperialists" who wished to take the opportunity to overthrow the Government. He emphasized that there was definitely no change in the policy of alliance with Soviet Russia.[75]

Nevertheless, on April 20, 1926, at a gathering of the Party representatives who had withdrawn from the First Army, Chiang obliquely accused the Communists of conspiratorial intent. This impression was further strengthened when he added that the whole story could not yet be told, but that he felt sure the conspiracy involved only a minority. He then referred to the belief, which he said was held by some people, that Kisanko had conspired to force him to go to Vladivostok on the S.S. "Chung-shan." Chiang said that he did not completely (emphasis ours) believe this story, and added that if Li Chih-lung were indeed involved, he was merely carrying out other people's orders.[76]

Yet another reason for the relative optimism felt by some of the Russians at this time was Chiang's series of attacks on the Right Wing of the KMT.

On April 4, Chiang issued a circular telegram denouncing the Second Congress held by the Western Hills Group in Shanghai [Doc. 24, p. 75]. According to his diary, he was distressed at the thought of the Right Wing's alliance with imperialists aiming to destroy the Kuomintang and the Government. He continued in subsequent speeches to denounce the Right Wing in no uncertain terms.[77]

Chiang also took steps to curb the Right Wing's activities in Canton. On April 5, when informed of the Right Wing's plans to hold a demonstration, he ordered Wu T'ieh-ch'eng, commander of the Gendarmes, to prevent the demonstration.[78] Toward the end of April, Chiang's anti-Right moves assumed the proportions of a second coup d'état. He ordered the dismissal of a number of Right Wing members of the KMT, including Ou-yang Chü, a close subordinate of Wu T'ieh-ch'eng. On April 24, Wu T'ieh-ch'eng himself was dismissed [Doc. 24, p. 75; Doc. 25, p. 2].[79]

Chiang had in the meantime assumed virtual control of the Kuomintang and the Government with the retirement of Wang Ching-wei.

Wang Ching-wei had fallen ill a few days before the coup. On

March 20, when he learned of Chiang's actions, he denounced
Chiang as counterrevolutionary. On March 23, Wang suddenly
disappeared and could not be found anywhere in Canton [Doc. 23,
pp. 68-69].[80] He wrote to Chang Ching-chiang, however, that he
was retiring from politics because he felt he was doubted and dis-
liked.

On March 26, Chiang Kai-shek wrote to Wang to ask for leave.
He also wrote T'an Yen-k'ai, Chu P'ei-te, Li Chi-shen, and other
generals, as well as T. V. Soong, the Minister of Finance. Chiang
told them that he planned to retire and urged the return of Wang
Ching-wei. That evening, according to Chiang's diary, T. V. Soong
went to see Chiang to convey the wish of the Party leaders that he
should remain in Canton. Chiang agreed.[81]

As Wang's whereabouts continued to be unknown, arrangements
were made for the distribution of his multiple positions. On April
16 a joint conference of the Central Executive Committee of the
KMT and the National Government Council was held. T'an Yen-k'ai
was elected chairman of the Political Council and Chiang was made
chairman of the Military Council; these were two of the important
posts vacated by Wang Ching-wei. Following this, Wang officially
declared his retirement and left Canton for Hongkong on May 9.
From Hongkong, he headed for Paris.[82]

Comintern Policy and Opposition Currents in the
Chinese Communist Party, March to July, 1926

Did Chiang Kai-shek meet with no opposition at all?

According to Stepanov, a number of KMT leaders[83] visited the
Russians' residence on March 20 and expressed disapproval of
Chiang's actions. T'an Yen-k'ai and Chu P'ei-te, Stepanov said,
called on Kisanko. They branded Chiang as a counterrevolutionary
and suggested taking serious measures against him. "In short,"
Stepanov asserted, "everyone expressed opposition to Chiang"
[Doc. 23, p. 68]. The existence of a potential anti-Chiang combination is confirmed by Document 25, a summary report prepared
by Seifulin, the Soviet Military Attaché,[84] on the bases of Borodin's
reports from Canton. It is dated June 3, 1926. Around March 20,
Seifulin said, Wang Ching-wei had attempted to form an anti-Chiang
alliance and, by the pressure of this alliance, to force Chiang not
to yield to the demands of the anti-Communist faction in the Kuomintang. The Russians, however, then considered such measures inappropriate [Doc. 25, p. 5]. The reports of Stepanov and Seifulin thus
suggest that Wang Ching-wei's retirement resulted partly from the
failure of an anti-Chiang alliance to materialize. They suggest further that the Russian advisers' disapproval of strong measures
against Chiang contributed materially to his assumption of power.

The conciliatory attitude of the Russian advisers was based on the premise that it was necessary to maintain the Kuomintang-Communist entente. This was the policy underlying the "Resolutions on the China Question," which were adopted at the Sixth Plenum of the ECCI on March 13, 1926, one week before the coup.

The ECCI defined the Kuomintang as "a revolutionary bloc of workers, peasants, intellectuals, and urban democracy on the basis of a community of the class interests of these strata in the struggle against the imperialists and the whole militarist-feudal order for the independence of the country and for a single revolutionary-democratic Government." It praised the Canton Government as a model for the future revolutionary-democratic order and called upon the Chinese Communists to work together with the Kuomintang to "democratize" the country. The ECCI reaffirmed the necessity for a single national revolutionary front of workers, peasants, and the bourgeoisie. It warned the Chinese Communist Party against the harmful tendency of Right Wing liquidationism, which ignored the independent class tasks of the Chinese proletariat and led to a "formless merging with the general democratic national movement." At the same time, it warned against "Left moods which try to skip over the revolutionary-democratic stage of the movement straight to the tasks of proletarian dictatorship and Soviet power, forgetting all about the peasantry, which is the most important and decisive factor of the Chinese national-liberation movement."[85]

In April, 1926, the ECCI sent instructions to the Chinese Communist Party ordering it to exert every effort to compel the KMT Right Wing to withdraw, or to expel it from the Party.[86] Communists were instructed to organize and strengthen the Left Wing as their central task [Doc. 24, p. 81]. These tactics were duly outlined by Stepanov at the meeting of Soviet advisers which followed the March coup [Doc. 24, p. 78].

Although in October, 1925, the Chinese Communist Central Committee had warned of the Left's weakness and had pointed out the need to strengthen it against the Right, Communists still did little to develop the Left Wing organizationally. The Communist policy of alliance with the Left still hinged on cooperation with individual Left leaders. Thus, the March Twentieth coup resulted in the almost total destruction of the Left Wing, since Chiang and Wang had been the two principal Left leaders. To paraphrase Nilov,[87] the Left Wing was absolutely empty; it had neither leaders nor masses [Doc. 24, p. 81].

It was precisely this view—that the Left did not even exist—which prompted members of the Communist Kwangtung Regional Committee to oppose the official Communist policy of conciliation of Chiang and alliance with the Left Wing. They advocated an independent Communist offensive against Chiang. According to one source, certain members of the Committee wanted Borodin to force Wang

Ching-wei to dismiss Chiang. They advocated calling on workers
to strike and planned a counteroffensive to be conducted by Com-
munists in the Army.[88] They had no notion of withdrawing from the
Kuomintang, however. In his report to the Sixth Party Congress,
Ch'ü Ch'iu-pai declared that most members of the Kwangtung
Regional Committee believed that the Left was nonexistent and that
Communists should seize leadership of the Kuomintang. They be-
lieved that Communists should eliminate the Right Wing and fill
the Kuomintang with the masses, thus converting it into a pure
Left organization.[89]

In short, certain members of the Kwangtung Regional Committee
demanded Communist seizure of the Kuomintang. The official
Communist policy was opposed from the opposite direction by members of the Chinese Communist Party who favored withdrawing
from the Kuomintang altogether.

According to Ch'en Tu-hsiu, after the coup he again proposed
immediate withdrawal from the KMT. He sent a report to the
Comintern expressing his personal opinion that cooperation with
the KMT by means of joint work should be replaced by a two-
party alliance outside the KMT, so that Communists could pursue
an independent policy and win the confidence of the masses. This
opinion, Ch'en asserts, was critiziced by Bukharin in an article
in Pravda, and Voitinskii was sent back to China to correct the
tendency toward withdrawal from the KMT.

The Central Committee in Shanghai, Ch'en asserts, resolved to
prepare independent military forces to oppose Chiang at the same
time it accepted the fact of his coup d'état. The CC sent P'eng Shu-
chih to Canton to consult the Comintern delegate, Voitinskii, on
this plan. Voitinskii opposed the CC's opinion, however, and insisted that the Communists continue to support Chiang, strengthen
the National Government, and carry on the Northern Expedition. He
would not even agree to the CC's request for 5,000 rifles with which
to arm the peasants of Kwangtung, Ch'en asserts, on the ground that
armed peasants could not fight against Ch'en Ch'iung-ming's forces
and could only arouse the suspicion of the KMT.[90]

Ch'en's account of P'eng Shu-chih's mission is partially confirmed by Stepanov, who reported that the representative of the
Central Committee had said that Chiang Kai-shek could easily be
isolated if he were opposed by the Communists and the KMT Left
Wing. Stepanov added, however, that he himself believed Chiang
would definitely not be isolated, since various groups throughout the
country attached great importance to him [Doc. 24, p. 86].

Orthodox Communist histories contradict Ch'en's assertions.
They hold him responsible for the Right-opportunist policy of capit-
ulation to the Kuomintang and Chiang Kai-shek following the March
Twentieth coup, thus sabotaging the interests of the Party.[91] In his

political report to the Fifth Congress held in April-May, 1927, Ch'en Tu-hsiu did indeed confirm and defend the CC's policy of retreat. It must be remembered, however, that Ch'en Tu-hsiu was speaking in his capacity as secretary of the Party, and the Party's policy then was still committed to remaining within the Kuomintang. It is interesting, therefore, that in the same political report he chastised himself for having proposed withdrawal from the Kuomintang. "I myself," he said, "have been guilty of this error."[92] Furthermore, Victor A. Yakhontoff, who cites Borodin as his source, asserts that Ch'en Tu-hsiu was opposed to the Communists remaining within the Kuomintang and advocated their withdrawal long before they were expelled. This view, Yakhontoff asserts, was condemned by the Comintern, which accused Ch'en of "following, and on certain points even going ahead of, Trotsky."[93]

Although it is difficult to draw conclusions on the position of individual Communists, there is ample evidence of the existence of two strong opposition currents within the Chinese Communist Party. Both opposition groups—those favoring immediate withdrawal from the Kuomintang and those advocating independent direct struggle to seize KMT leadership—were denounced at the CC's Second Enlarged Plenum in July, 1926. The opinion that the KCT should completely divorce itself from organizational relationship with the KMT, the CC declared, was erroneous, for it betrayed a misunderstanding of the long-range view of the Chinese National Revolution. It was in fact no different from that held by the KMT Right and the New Right in demanding that Communists withdraw from the Kuomintang. On the other hand, the view that Communists should monopolize KMT organs was equally incorrect, because it was not suited to the social foundation and organization of the KMT. Communist monopoly of the KMT, said the CC, would reduce that Party to a narrow organization because of excessive concentration of power, thus resulting in dispersion and loss of the petty bourgeoisie. Furthermore, said the CC, Communist experience in Kwangtung had already proved this policy to be thoroughly erroneous [Doc. 27, p. 71].

Agreement for a Modus Vivendi, May to June, 1926

Apparently Borodin was also dubious about the official Comintern policy when he first returned to Canton on April 29, 1926.[94] He immediately went into a series of conferences with Chiang Kai-shek,[95] which took place with increasing frequency just before the Second CEC Plenum convened on May 15.[96] However, the available sources conflict on the measures proposed by Borodin to replace the Russians' conciliatory policy. According to a letter written by three Comintern delegates on March 17, 1927, Borodin agreed with the Kwangtung Communists that the Left Wing did not

even exist. He therefore favored Communist withdrawal from the
Kuomintang.[97] At the Fifth Congress, Ch'en Tu-hsiu confirmed
that Borodin agreed with the Kwangtung Communists. According to
Ch'en, however, Borodin did not favor withdrawal but sided with
the Kwangtung Communists in demanding a direct offensive against
Chiang.[98]

It is certain at any rate that some of the Russians in Canton,
as opposed to the Comintern leaders in Moscow, questioned the
policy of conciliation and considered other measures of dealing
with Chiang. Seifulin reported on June 3, 1926, that Chiang Kai-
shek's demands confronted the Russians with two alternatives.
One was to accept his demands, in order to avoid a catastrophe
which would otherwise be inevitable. The other was to adopt
measures similar to those taken by Wang Ching-wei at the time of
the coup—to form an anti-Chiang alliance and force Chiang not to
yield to the anti-Communists in the Kuomintang. It was finally decided to continue the policy of conciliation, Seifulin reported. As
he put it, "The problem was solved by adopting a policy to satisfy
Chiang and to yield to his demands" [Doc. 25, p. 5].

This decision led to an agreement between Chiang and Borodin
on a modus vivendi between the Russians and Chinese Communists
on the one hand and Chiang on the other. Three principal points are
discernible within the framework of this "gentleman's agreement":
(1) Communists accepted Chiang's proposals for restricting their
activities within the Kuomintang; these proposals also indirectly
strengthened Chiang's control of the Party; (2) Chiang yielded to
Borodin's insistence that action be taken against the Right Wing;
and (3) Borodin agreed definitely to support the Northern Expedition.

On May 15, 1926, at the opening of the Second CEC Plenum,
Chiang Kai-shek proposed a set of resolutions on the "Adjustment
of Party Affairs." The first section, which dealt with Kuomintang-
Communist relations, was an elaboration of his proposals of April
3. They consisted of the following important points: (1) The KCT
should instruct its members to reform their speech about and attitude toward the KMT; they must not doubt or criticize Sun Yat-sen
and the Three People's Principles; (2) The KCT should hand over to
the chairman of the CEC a complete list of its members in the
KMT; (3) Only members who do not belong to any other party are
eligible to serve as department heads in the KMT's Central Party
headquarters; (4) KMT members should not convene Party conferences without the Party's permission; (5) KMT members should not
belong to any other organization or participate in any activity without the permission of KMT Party headquarters; (6) All instructions
and policies of the KCT and the CI must be passed by a joint KMT-
KCT conference; (7) KMT members should not join other Parties;

they may not rejoin the Party if they once have joined the KCT; and (8) Violators of the above rules are subject to expulsion.[99]

Chiang Kai-shek's proposals, slightly amended, were adopted by the CEC on May 17. The CEC decided further that Communists should not hold more than one third of the seats on the executive committees of the KMT's central, municipal, and district Party headquarters.[100]

In the second section of the "Resolutions," Chiang proposed the election of a chairman of the CEC to serve until the convening of the Third Kuomintang Congress. If the practice of electing the CEC chairman at each plenum were continued, the "Resolutions" stated, the proper execution of the decisions on Kuomintang-Communist relations might be hampered. This proposal was also adopted.[101]

The establishment of the CEC chairmanship was thus proposed and adopted as an instrument to execute the KMT's decisions regarding the Communists. It represented still another step in the Kuomintang's developing tendency toward concentration of power. The chairman of the CEC was invested with the highest authority, since the Political Council, which had hitherto been the controlling body, was subordinate to the CEC. Chang Ching-chiang, who was closely associated with Chiang Kai-shek, was elected as chairman of the CEC on May 19, 1926.[102] A great change of personnel took place at the Kuomintang's Central Party Headquarters in accordance with the decision that Communists could not head any of the departments. Chiang Kai-shek, with Ch'en Kuo-fu as his deputy, was elected to replace T'an P'ing-shan in the powerful Organization Department. Ku Meng-yü took over the Propaganda Department from the deputy chief, Mao Tse-tung. At the Peasant Department, Lin Tsu-han gave way to Kan Nai-kuang. At the Secretariat, Liu Fen was replaced by Yeh Ch'u-cheng.[103]

Communist acceptance of the decisions of the Second CEC Plenum was formally announced in a letter to the Kuomintang CEC from the Central Committee on June 4. The CC explained the "Resolutions" as a product of the Kuomintang's desire to eliminate envy and suspicion in order to consolidate the revolutionary forces. Since the "Resolutions" were an internal KMT problem, the CC stated, it had no right to express either approval or disapproval. The CC ended with the hope that the Kuomintang would purge the reactionaries more energetically in order to strengthen the internal situation.[104]

According to Seifulin, it was part of the general agreement that, upon the satisfaction of his own demands, "Chiang Kai-shek would take action to arrest, purge, and otherwise bring pressure against the Right" [Doc. 25, p. 6]. This is partially confirmed by the entry in Chiang's diary for May 27, ten days after the CEC's adoption of

Chiang's proposals. On that day, according to the diary, Chiang and Borodin conferred on the subject of liquidating the reactionaries.105

To be sure, Chiang had already taken active measures against the Right Wing prior to Borodin's return. However, Borodin apparently succeeded in extracting a commitment from Chiang that he would continue his anti-Right moves.

According to Document 25, Hu Han-min tried to persuade Chiang Kai-shek to arrest Borodin. Hu's attempt failed, however, and he decided to leave Canton. The document also mentions that Wu Ch'ao-shu, another prominent member of the Right Wing, was forced to go to Shanghai [Doc. 25, pp. 3, 7].106

Finally the available historical record points to the conclusion that Borodin agreed definitely to support the Northern Expedition.

When Borodin first returned to Canton, he was apparently still unwilling to accept Chiang's proposal to launch the Northern Expedition. On May 1, according to Chiang's diary, Borodin and Chiang disagreed on the subject of the Northern Expedition.107 Their differences were apparently ironed out during subsequent conferences. According to Hollington K. Tong, Borodin had to yield on the question of the Northern Expedition in exchange for nothing less than continued cooperation between the Communists and the Kuomintang.108

At the end of May, the National Government decided to send a unit of the Seventh Army to Hunan to rescue T'ang Sheng-chih, with whom it had been negotiating an alliance. T'ang himself was appointed commander of the Eighth Army on June 2, 1926.109 The Hunan campaign in effect became the first operation of the Northern Expedition.

On June 4, an emergency plenum of the CEC resolved to launch the Northern Expedition. Chiang was appointed commander-in-chief,110 and the Military Council was abolished in order to give him a freer hand.111 On June 29 Chiang was appointed a member of the National Government Council. On July 5 he was appointed chief of the KMT's Military Personnel Department, which had power to appoint and dismiss all Party representatives in the National Revolutionary Army and other military organs. Finally, on the following day, July 6, Chiang was formally elected chairman of the CEC Standing Committee. For the period of the Northern Expedition, however, Chang Ching-chiang was to serve as his deputy.112

Chiang Kai-shek thus obtained complete control of the Party's political and military organs partly as a result of the launching of the Northern Expedition.

Policy of the Chinese Communist Party, July, 1926

The launching of the Northern Expedition met with considerable opposition from the Chinese Communists.

The July 7, 1926, issue of Hsiang-tao chou-pao carried an article by Ch'en Tu-hsiu in which he declared: "The Northern Expedition signifying revolutionary military action has not become an issue because, judging by political conditions within the National Government, the strength of the National Government, and the fighting capacity and revolutionary understanding of the National Government's armies, the time has not arrived for a revolutionary Northern Expedition. The present problem is not how to carry on the Northern Expedition, but how to defend ourselves against Wu P'ei-fu's southern expedition, the invasion of Kwangtung by anti-Red armies, and the anti-Red activities of the compradors, local bullies, bureaucrats, and the Right Wing within Kwangtung."[113]

Ch'en Tu-hsiu's attitude is reflected in Document 26, the political report of the Central Committee at the Second Enlarged Plenum which convened in Shanghai on July 12, 1926. The Northern Expedition did not represent a real revolutionary force, the CC stated, but was only a defensive movement against the penetration of anti-Red armies into Hunan and Kwangtung [Doc. 26, p. 63]. Opposition to the Northern Expedition by Ch'en Tu-hsiu and other Communists apparently was serious. The "Brief History," written around September, 1926, states that the situation of divided opinion in the Party on the Expedition would become dangerous if allowed to be prolonged and that, in recognition of this, the CC had issued directives to correct the situation and to organize a campaign in support of the Northern Expedition [Doc. 1, p. 45].[114]

The documents of the CC's Second Enlarged Plenum suggest that a principal reason for the Chinese Communists' reluctance to support the Northern Expedition was fear of the increasing power of Chiang Kai-shek and the Kuomintang New Right Wing. Hence, the Communists were reluctant to embark on a campaign which might further expand the New Right Wing's power.

The Plenum repudiated deviationist tendencies of those who favored withdrawal from the KMT and those who demanded a direct anti-Chiang offensive and seizure of the KMT. It reaffirmed the policy of remaining within the Kuomintang. In line with the resolutions of the Sixth ECCI Plenum, the CC asserted that the Kuomintang embraced four classes: the workers and peasants, represented by the Communists; the petty bourgeoisie, represented by the KMT Left; and the bourgeoisie, represented by the KMT New Right Wing [Doc. 26, p. 66].

The CC reaffirmed the policy of alliance with the Left against the Right. Communists were to ally with the Left to struggle against the Center (or New Right)[115] for the power of directing the national movement, thus guaranteeing seizure of leadership of the National Revolution by the proletariat's party [Doc. 27, p. 71].

A comparison of the composition of and policy toward the KMT

New Right, as outlined in July, 1926, with the CC's resolutions of
the previous October (Document 20), reveals a number of significant differences.

In July, 1926, Chiang Kai-shek was classified as a leader of the
New Right, despite his anti-Right measures in April-May, 1926.
Thus he was grouped with Tai Chi-t'ao as a representative of the
bourgeoisie.116 The reactionary Right Wing was expanded to include members both of the Old Right Wing, such as Feng Tzu-yu,
and men sympathetic to and affiliated with the New Right Wing,
such as Sun Fo. Tai Chi-t'ao, however, was retained as a leader
of the New Right.

In October, 1925, the CC had identified the New Right Wing as
the real enemy of the Communists and had called for positive attack
against it in alliance with the Left Wing. The reactionary Right
Wing, according to the CC, was in fact no longer in the KMT, since
it had become openly reactionary. In July, 1926, on the other hand,
the CC's strategy was to ally with the Left to force the New Right
Wing to attack the reactionary Right. Thus, the reactionary Right,
rather than the New Right, was made the target of direct attack.
The shift was, in effect, a retreat.

The difference is more than theoretical. It reflects Chiang Kai-
shek's power after March Twentieth, as well as the CC's awareness of the Left Wing's weakness. The bourgeoisie (Chiang Kai-
shek) had acquired considerable force, the CC stated, and the
backward workers, filled with patriarchal ideas, could easily be
drawn into the ranks of the bourgeoisie. The petty bourgeoisie, said
the CC, were even more inclined towards the bourgeoisie [Doc. 26,
p. 66]. In the resolutions on KMT-KCT relations, the CC declared
flatly that the armed Center had seized power at Canton [Doc. 27,
p. 69]. The CC showed that it had few illusions about the New Right.
The bourgeoisie, declared the CC, were seeking concessions from
imperialism and, as soon as these had been secured, they would become nonrevolutionary [Doc. 26, p. 65]. Despite the nonrevolutionary tendencies of the bourgeoisie, the CC declared that it was still
necessary to cooperate with them for the Revolution, and to utilize
them for the time being. The reason was that if the Communists
attacked the bourgeoisie too severely, they would be drawn completely into the ranks of the imperialists, thus enhancing the enemy's
strength [Doc. 26, p. 66].

In view of the New Right Wing's dominance, the CC re-examined
the policy of alliance with the Left Wing. According to Nilov, the
Chinese Communists had engaged in critical re-evaluation of their
policies following the coup. They had come to realize their errors,
chief of which was the habit of openly expanding their influence and
position within the KMT and ignoring the Kuomintang Left. Nilov
said that they also realized the error of monopolizing the labor and

peasant movements, thus causing resentment among the majority of KMT members and a split between the Right Wing and the Communists [Doc. 24, pp. 80, 81].

Thus the CC declared at the Second Enlarged Plenum that the Communists' chief error was employing the wrong formula in working within the Kuomintang; under this plan the KMT Left Wing was tied down and unable fully to participate in Party work and the anti-Right struggle. The Communists themselves, said the CC, were responsible for creating a situation in which the KCT-KMT struggle was allowed to overshadow the struggle between the Left and Right [Doc. 27, pp. 69, 73].

To correct these errors, the CC formulated concrete measures to strengthen the KMT Left Wing.

The CC identified Wang Ching-wei and Kan Nai-kuang as the leaders of the Left Wing.

It instructed Communists to help form mass organizations of the Left Wing outside the Party, especially among the petty bourgeoisie. To add substance to the Left Wing within the Party, the CC said it was necessary that the KMT organizational system be more flexible in order to absorb new petty-bourgeois elements. To this end, KMT organs at lower levels should resemble political clubs. Social organizations with revolutionary tendencies should be allowed to join the Kuomintang as units [Doc. 26, p. 66, Doc. 27, pp. 72, 73].

This policy ran counter to the attempts of Chang Ching-chiang and Ch'en Kuo-fu to tighten the Kuomintang setup. Ch'en Kuo-fu later recalled that they amended Party regulations in order to reduce the number of Communists and to increase the number of "pure" KMT members in the Organization Department. They trained "pure" KMT members specifically to save the Party from the Communist conspiracy and later dispatched them to the provinces and cities. They organized a political training institute to develop cadres for the Kuomintang.[117]

Thus, Communist attempts to strengthen the KMT Left organizationally, which distinguished from the preceding phase the Communists' post-March Twentieth policy of alliance with the Left, coincided with the strengthening of the New Right under the leadership of Chang Ching-chiang and Ch'en Kuo-fu. The ensuing intra-Party struggle, climaxed by the split between the Left Wing under Wang Ching-wei at Wuhan and the New Right under Chiang Kai-shek at Nanking in April, 1927, had its origin in the spring and summer of 1926.

DOCUMENT 20

The following translation is based on a copy of an original Chinese document sent by the Japanese Military Attaché in Peking to Tokyo on May 26, 1927 and filed in Mitsu dai nikki, 1927, V. The resolutions are not dated or otherwise identified. Judging by their content, they were adopted at the Enlarged Plenum of the KCT Central Committee in Peking in October, 1925. This deduction is confirmed by Document 27, which summarizes the resolutions of October, 1925 (p. 70). The document is signed "Chün," probably a pseudonym.

RESOLUTIONS ON RELATIONS BETWEEN THE
CHINESE COMMUNIST PARTY AND THE KUOMINTANG

[1]   1. Since the Reorganization, class differentiation within the KMT, following class differentiation in Chinese society, has become daily more apparent.

Following the death of Sun Yat-sen, bureaucratic and comprador elements formally established separate organizations, such as the Peking KMT Comrades Club and the Shanghai Hsin-hai Comrades Club. The Peking KMT Comrades Club, headed by Feng Tzu-yu and P'eng Yang-ch'ung [P'eng Yang-kuang] was organized for the purpose of seeking compromise with the militarist government and expanding its influence in the North. The Shanghai Hsin-hai Comrades Club, headed by Chang T'ai-yen and T'ang Shao-i, was organized for the purpose of uniting with the influence of the militarists T'ang Chi-jao, Chao Heng-ti, and Ch'en Ch'iung-ming, and expanding their influence in the Southwest.

Although they differ in their attitude towards the Northern militarists, the two organizations take uniform action in opposing the Communists (the CP and CY) and the Left KMT, and even conspire with imperialist Great Britain to destroy the Canton Government.

They plan not only to expand the military influence of their own cliques in order to overthrow the Canton Government, but also to develop their own Party headquarters to oppose the KMT CEC at
[2] Canton. The Shanghai Club in particular has become the center of counterrevolutionary influence in the South.

2. In the last few months the high tide of the revolutionary movement has shown that the proletariat is an independent social force, and a very great and dynamic political force, capable of accelerating the progress of political development of the bourgeoisie. Such

a phenomenon is directly reflected in the KMT and the petty
bourgeoisie, who are making every effort to define their ideology
and to consolidate themselves organizationally.

In the KMT, a small portion of bourgeois elements (such
as Tai Chi-t'ao, etc.) has utilized the "signboard," "The Real
Three Principles of the People," and promoted slogans for compromise between classes, in order to oppose the class struggle,
the KMT Left, and the KCT. It becomes increasingly clear every
day that this faction has formed itself into the KMT Right Wing.
They do their best to distinguish themselves from such elements
as the Peking KMT Comrades Club and the Shanghai Hsin-Hai
Comrades Club of the militarists and compradors. However,
since they oppose the KMT Left and the KCT, their acts are objectively
equivalent to giving aid to counterrevolutionaries and imperialists.

3. The latest developments in the revolutionary movement have
[3] intensified the internal differentiation of the KMT. On the other
hand, they have also enabled the KMT to expand, especially in
the South, and to become the real political party of the masses and
of the National Revolution. Tens of thousands of peasants, workers,
and the urban petty bourgeoisie have joined the Party as new members.

4. At present it is more than ever the responsibility of the KCT
to cooperate with the KMT Government, to come into close contact
with the majority of the masses, and to do its utmost to assist the
KMT Left to enable it to develop the work of the revolutionary
movement. At the same time, our Party should make every effort
to oppose the slogans and strategy of the KMT Right.

Our Party members should know our present policy toward the
KMT: We oppose its Right Wing and unite with its Left Wing by
contracting a close alliance with it and helping it in every way possible to fight against the Right.

5. An important method of executing such strategy is to expand
and strengthen our Party everywhere, especially where the KMT's
influence exists. Our Party should actively enter the political
arena and carry out our ideological strategy and struggle everywhere. This is the second method by which we may attain our objectives. In concrete terms the method is as follows:

a) The KCT's political propaganda and organization should be independent and expanded, especially in Kwangtung.

b) We should win over the masses of workers and peasants.

c) Unless absolutely necessary, our new comrades should not
join the KMT or engage in its work, particularly the work of high-
level Party headquarters (with the exception of Party headquarters
which are absolutely under our influence).

d) Where we do not have any masses, we should not help the KMT to establish or develop its organization, particularly in Central and South China.*

e) Where the influence of the KMT Left and the KCT exists
[4] (especially in Kwangtung), we should cooperate earnestly with the KMT and impel it to take an active part in the national movement to the best of its ability. We must not shun the KMT intentionally or let it stand by in a negative and passive state. At the same time, we must not yield one inch of ground to the KMT in terms of the theory and practice of class struggle in all movements.

f) In the presence of KMT members, some of our comrades used to classify the KMT into the Left, Center, and Right, grouping KMT leaders with the Center. This is not only incorrect but strategically inappropriate. The first defect is that our comrades unconsciously neglect our own position and completely become members of the KMT Left Wing. The second defect is that Left-inclined elements of the KMT mistakingly think that the Left Wing is identical with the Communist faction. Hence, those who do not join the KCT or CY consider themselves to be members of the KMT Center and regard all policies of the KMT which are somewhat Left-inclined as the KCT's policies and refuse to approve them. The third defect is that the real KMT Right (such as Tai Chi-t'ao, Chou Lu, and Chao Yüan-ch'ung, etc.) regard the reactionaries as the Right and themselves as the Center. All those who formerly belonged to the so-called Right Wing have actually already left the KMT, and those who formerly belonged to the so-called Center have now either joined the Left or the New Right. Hence, at present, the KMT consists only of the Left and Right. At the moment, however, the so-called Left is mere talk. It is not enough to be Left-inclined! The Left should not violate the Manifesto of the First KMT Congress in its actions. In terms of concrete political policy, it should not merely be different from the reactionaries, but really closely united with the Communists. These [should be] the special characteristics of the KMT Left in this period. In our propaganda, we should classify the Left and Right Wings of the KMT and the reactionaries according
[5] to political policies as in the following chart.

---

* This point is crossed out in pencil. There is no indication whether this was so in the original document seized in the raid, or the marking was made by the Japanese who copied (or edited) the document.

[Policy]	Left Wing	Right Wing	Reactionaries
1. [Toward imperialism]	Oppose all imperialists from beginning to end	Oppose one imperialist and compromise with other imperialists because of the vigorous advance of the workers and peasants	Compromise with imperialists
2. [Toward the labor and peasant movements]	Assist the labor and peasant movements for the sake of the Revolution	Advocate compromise between capital and labor	Destroy the labor and peasant movements
3. [Toward militarism]	Oppose militarists for the sake of democracy	Oppose militarists for the sake of maintaining its own political influence	Compromise with militarists
4. [Toward Soviet Russia and the KCT]	Make connections with Soviet Russia and the KCT	Make connections with Soviet Russia in order to oppose the KCT	Oppose Soviet Russia and the KCT
5. [Toward reactionaries]	Eliminate all reactionary influence for the sake of political reform	Procrastinate in instituting reforms in order to preserve the reactionary influence for the sake of opposing the Left	They are themselves reactionary elements

DOCUMENT 21

Document 21 is translated from an original Chinese document, dated November 25, 1925. It is signed "Pai Wei" and appears to be a document of the Peking Local Committee of the Chinese Communist Party. This deduction is confirmed by Chang Kuo-t'ao, who asserts that Pai Wei was the code name of the Peking Local Committee at the time (Chang Kuo-t'ao, in an interview with C. Martin Wilbur, Hongkong, November 24, 1954). The Peking Commission published the document under the title, "The Attitude of the Communist Party," in <u>Su-lien yin-mou...</u>, III, "KCT," pp. 146-56.

OUR IMMEDIATE ATTITUDE TOWARD THE
KUOMINTANG IN THE NORTH

[146] 1. A very thick reactionary atmosphere has prevailed in the Kuomintang in the North in the last few months. Furthermore, such reactionary influence tends towards gradual concentration. The following facts will prove these phenomena.

[147] a) Widespread anti-Communist and anti-Soviet Russian propaganda.

b) The arrival of Chou Lu and Lin Shen in the North and their antagonistic attitude towards the Kwangtung Revolutionary Government.

c) The actions of Hsieh Ch'ih and others in seizing the Peking Executive Headquarters.

d) The arrival in the North of Tai Chi-t'ao, leader of the New Right, and the recently convened meeting of the Kuomintang Central Executive Committee at the Western Hills.

2. The above-mentioned phenomena prove that the Right Wing in the National Revolution is daily leaning farther to the Right and that its influence is concentrating in Peking. Such concentration does not mean expansion of the Right's influence, however, but on the contrary, its retrenchment.

3. The result of Taichitaoism is merely the formulation of the Right Wing's working principle in the Kuomintang: "Raise the left hand to drive out the Communists! Raise the right hand to overthrow the reactionaries." This principle not only cannot cause the Right Wing to be Left-inclined, it causes the Right to incline further to the Right. The value of Tai Chi-t'ao's theories lies solely in furnishing the reactionaries with a weapon to attack the Left and the Communists and to subdue the Right. It is otherwise not worth a cent! Consequently, since the appearance of Taichitaosim, the

Right has leaned further to the Right, to the extent that it has allied itself with the reactionaries to destroy the alliance of the Left and the Communists.

8]   4. The concentration in the North of the Right Wing's influence is not a result of expansion of the Right's influence but the fact that it is surrounded by the revolutionary force. The reactionary conduct of the Right is not tolerated in Kwangtung under the southern revolutionary regime. It has failed to secure a foothold in Central China, [such as] Shanghai, where the proletariat's organization is very strong. Consequently, the Right can only come to Peking, the center of political reaction in the North, to maintain its dying life.

5. The North, particularly Peking, is the nation's center of political reaction. Furthermore, there is lacking strong and organized proletarian masses [in the North]. Hence, the urban petty bourgeoisie in general are completely surrounded by the reactionary atmosphere. Their political outlook is extremely confused, and they are therefore easily influenced by Taichitaoism. Except for a very few old members, there is no real Left Wing in the Peking KMT. Party members are all inclined towards Taichitaoism. Under such conditions, the reactionaries regard Taichitaoism as a treasure, and avail themselves of the opportunity to utilize it. First, they use Taichitaoism to destroy the alliance of the Left and the Communists and then use the same weapon to threaten the manufacturer of the weapon. This may be seen in the reactionaries' recent attacks on Tai Chi-t'ao and the Right Wing. However, the Right does not realize the error and danger of its theory. It will eventually be subdued by the reactionaries and incline ever further to the Right.

6. Although there are a few old Party members in the North who may be considered Leftists, they have always paid scant attention to work among the masses and are unable to form a Left Wing within the Party on strong foundations. Due to the fact that they have not gotten hold of the vast masses and for other reasons, they do not employ
19] drastic means in dealing with the reactionaries, but maintain a watchful, wavering attitude. This is the situation of intra-Party struggle in the Northern Kuomintang: The Right has allied itself with the reactionaries to destroy the revolutionary organization of the Kuomintang, and the Communists are seeking an alliance with a vast and strong Left in the Northern Kuomintang to counteract the reactionary conduct of the Right.

7. Under such conditions, it is extremely dangerous for the Communists to fight singlehandedly against the Right within the Kuomintang. An isolated Communist struggle not only cannot overthrow the Right, but can enhance its strength. The reason is that in such an event many shortsighted and wavering elements who cannot see clearly that this is a struggle between revolution and counterrevolution would mistake it for a struggle between communism and

anti-communism. Henceforth, the highest principle of our work in
the Kuomintang is to build within the KMT a Left Wing with a vast
mass [following], and, under the united front of the Left and the
Communists, from the lowest level of the masses up to high-level
organs, oppose the Right and the reactionaries who are conspiring
to destroy the foundation of the Kuomintang.

8. In accordance with the above principles, we should endeavor
to carry out the following important propaganda work among the
masses and in our daily practical work. We must first create an
anti-Right atmosphere among the masses before we can attain our
objective, the formation of a Left Wing with a vast mass [following]
and a united front between the Left and the Communists.

a) We must make the wavering masses in general understand
[150] that Taichitaoism is not true Sunyatsenism. Attack the Right's
counterrevolutionary slogan, "Overthrow the Communists with
the left hand and the reactionaries with the right."

b) Expose the most recent conspiracy of the Right and the reactionaries to destroy the organization of the Kuomintang and to
violate discipline.

c) Explain to the masses the Kuomintang members' misunderstanding of the Communist Party and the Communist attitude toward the Kuomintang. We should make the masses understand the
mutual relations and necessity of cooperation between the KCT
and the KMT in the national revolutionary movement.

9. Regarding the first point, opposition to Taichitaoism, the
content of our propaganda should be:

a) Taichitaoism is not Sunyatsenism. The basic premise of
Sunyatsenism is the concept of a Chinese revolutionary movement
for national liberation, and not continuation of Confucian morality
or development of China's traditional civilization. In short, Sunyatsenism is Sun Yat-sen's revolutionary conception; not Confucius's
moral conception. Sunyatsenism is a theory of revolutionary struggle, not a doctrine of pacifist morality.

b) Class struggle does not harm the National Revolution.
Chinese workers have assumed leadership of the Chinese National
Revolution. This is a fact which no one can deny. Therefore, the
stronger the organization of Chinese labor, the stronger the national
revolutionary force. Hence, a strong organization of Chinese
labor not only does not harm but benefits the Chinese National
Revolution. Under the present semicolonial conditions of China,
class struggle for liberation is not harmful but necessary to the
National Revolution, just as, under the capitalistic conditions of
Russia, the struggle for national liberation was not harmful but
necessary to the proletarian revolution.

c) There is absolutely no possibility of the KCT destroying the
KMT in the national revolutionary movement. Revolution is a

51] form of social force. Each political party represents a certain
type of revolutionary organization. The Communist Party represents the interests of the proletariat. The Kuomintang is the political Party of the oppressed classes for the National Revolution.
These two organizations have different class natures and different
historical missions, and represent different social forces. While
these two social forces are both in an oppressed position and are
struggling together, it is impossible for one oppressed social force
to destroy the other. Thus, the KCT cannot now destroy the KMT,
just as the KMT cannot deny the existence of the KCT.

   d) Taichitaoism is a weapon of reactionary theory. Viewed from
all angles, Taichitaoism not only is not Sunyatsenism and cannot
train genuine Sunyatsenist revolutionary members for the Kuomintang, but can only furnish the reactionaries with a sharp weapon
to attack the revolutionary actions of the KCT, shake the ideological faith of the Left Wing, and intimidate the Right Wing with its
weak psychology.

   10. Regarding the second point, exposure of the conspiracy
of the Right and the reactionaries in destroying the organization
and discipline of the Kuomintang, the following should be pointed
out.

   a) The Kwangtung Revolutionary Government is publicly recognized by the revolutionary masses of the entire country as the only
existing Chinese revolutionary government. No one can deny that
this government is supported by the revolutionary masses of the entire country. The Kwangtung Revolutionary Government is daily
becoming stronger, while the people under its jurisdiction live in
relative freedom and peace. Yet Chou Lu and Lin Shen, as members
52] of the Central Executive Committee and representatives of the
Kwangtung Government, actually attack and insult the Kwangtung
Revolutionary Government at mass meetings and in declarations.

   b) The Peking Executive Headquarters is a legal Kuomintang
organization. Even if it were guilty of unlawful acts in violation
of Party principles, it should be dissolved in accordance with the
Party Constitution and not forcefully seized by any one clique. Chou
Lu, Lin Shen, and Hsieh Ch'ih actually led their own people to occupy
the Executive Headquarters and, in the name of the Headquarters,
convened the CEC in violation of Party principles. Can such action
have been taken by members who protect and cherish the Kuomintang?

   c) China has adopted the policy of the Russian alliance in international diplomacy. This is the course our people must take. Yet the
Right Wing follows the reactionaries in fabricating rumors to attack
Soviet Russia and the Kwangtung Revolutionary Government, thus
serving the interests of imperialism.

   d) Tai Chi-t'ao's publication of his personal definition and inter-

pretation of Sunyatsenism, freely attacking, without going through
Party censorship, the statements of the KCT, a friendly party, already has violated Party principles and discipline. Moreover, his
theory is actually used as a weapon by the reactionaries to destroy
the Party. Nevertheless, he still does not realize all this and is
in fact forming cliques within the Party. Without the consent of the
Party and in total disregard of Party decisions, he privately convened in the Western Hills of Peking an illegal CEC. Is this
intended to protect or destroy the Party organization?

e) The Kuomintang Political Council is an important organization
for directing the actual work of the Party. Party members and
organizations, even the CEC, cannot dissolve such an organization
[153] at will. Yet the Right Wing dared to propose to dissolve it at the
illegal CEC meeting. Who is actually trying to destroy the Kuomintang?

f) Communists participating in KMT work undertake the same
duties as pure KMT members. Similarly, KMT members who simultaneously belong to the KCT should enjoy the same privileges and
rights as pure KMT members. This is beyond doubt! Of course, KCT
members cannot necessarily be members of the KMT CEC, but
KMT members should not bar KCT members from the CEC. Yet
the Right Wing insisted that high-ranking Committee members
should not be permitted to join two parties. Who is actually attempting to dictate everything and bar all save its own clique?

g) The laws governing election to the Second National Congress
were determined by the Third CEC Plenum [May-June, 1925], and
therefore cannot possibly be changed at any illegal meeting. Yet
the Right Wing dared propose changing the election laws at the
illegal CEC meeting. Who is actually rebelling against the KMT?

11. On the third point, the KCT's attitude toward and relations
with the KMT, we should explain the necessity of cooperation between
these two basically different political parties in the national revolutionary movement and clarify the following misunderstandings.

a) A general misconception of the masses is that KCT members
joined the KMT either to utilize or destroy the KMT. On this point,
we should warn the people against being too shortsighted. They
need only refresh their memory of the condition of the KMT a few
short years ago and they will know whether KCT members joined the
KMT for utilizing or destroying it. We should pose the following
questions to be answered by the masses.

[154]   (1) What were the revolutionary objectives of the KMT before
              Communists raised such slogans as "Down with imperialism
              and militarism" and "National Revolution"?
          (2) What was the position of the KMT before Communists pro-
              claimed it the national revolutionary party of China.
          (3) What was the people's impression of Sun Yat-sen before

Communists declared to the broad masses that he should be
venerated as the leader of the Chinese National Revolution?

(4) What was the relationship between the KMT and the masses
before Communists pointed out that a revolutionary party
without a broad mass foundation is doomed to failure?

(5) What was the nature of the KMT organization before Communists joined the work of the KMT?

We need only request the people to think over the above questions.
Any faithful and loyal revolutionary may judge for himself whether Communist participation in the KMT is intended to destroy
and utilize the KMT or to develop its work and strengthen its
organization. We need not defend ourselves subjectively.

b) The Right Wing's attack on the Communists is centered on
the charge that the KMT has split into several cliques since the
Communist infiltration, Communists in the KMT having concentrated
on fomenting trouble for their own benefit. Actually, we need only
ask a few questions in order to stump the Right Wing.

(1) Did such phenomena as intra-KMT splits and conflicts occur
only after the Communist entry?

155]   (2) Can Communists be accused of fomenting trouble when Communists within the KMT lead the masses towards revolution
and Communists outside the KMT awaken it and criticize its
work?

(3) Can Communists in the KMT be accused of intentionally
attacking and expelling all cliques save their own when Communists in the KMT give warning to those who are nonrevolutionary, who look for political promotion and personal gain
under the shields of the KMT and Sun Yat-sen and to those
who align themselves with the enemy?

Only reactionaries can answer "yes." Any awakened person would
understand that these charges are not true.

c) Many people mistake the Left-Right struggle for a struggle
between communism and anti-communism. This is an erroneous
conception! Everyone knows that Communists have never advocated
communism in the KMT or attempted to carry out communism under the Kwangtung Revolutionary Government. This is entirely the
fabrication of the running dogs of imperialists and militarists,
who wish to destroy the people's organizations. The real nature of
the struggle between the Left and Right Wings of the KMT is a fight
between revolution and counterrevolution, not between communism
and anti-communism. The masses follow the reactionaries to mis-
interpret the struggle as one between communism and anti-communism because of ignorance of the real situation and of the meaning of the struggle and failure to see clearly their own revolutionary
responsibility. This is no slight deception!

12. At a time when the situation is so tense, when the Right Wing

has become so reactionary, when the masses in general are so unstable, and when a few leaders of the Left are taking a watchful
attitude, the duty of Communists, viewed from all angles, is to engage in positive propaganda and agitation among the masses of the
[156] lowest levels. Our comrades should raise this problem for discussion at KMT meetings and explain to the masses the dangers of the
Right Wing's mistake as well as their own heavy responsibilities.
They should be organized to form a strong Left Wing of the vast
masses which will be allied with the Communists to sweep away
the last reactionary influence remaining in the Party, thus strengthening the foundation of the National Revolution. This is the immediate objective of our work in the KMT for which all comrades
should be mobilized at once.

DOCUMENT 22

The following excerpts are translated from a Japanese translation of sections of a 58-page Russian report which was badly burned during the raid on the Soviet Embassy premises. We have checked the Japanese extracts against portions of the same document translated into English in Chinese Government White Book, pp. 259-65, and Soviet Plot in China, pp. 62-66. The Japanese translation is published in Pekin Rōnō Taishikan yori ōshū shitaru himitsu bunsho, XI, 1-6, under the title "Soviet Advisers in South China." The report is unsigned and undated, but appears to have been written after Borodin left Canton for North China at the beginning of February, 1926. It may have been written by Kisanko. In our translation, we have omitted passages of the Japanese excerpts which are incomprehensible as a result of burning. Underlining is in the original Russian document.

[SOVIET REPORT FROM CANTON]

2]   [Passages omitted.]
The General Staff
The General Staff is a technical organ of the [Military] Council. [Rogachev], our military director (assistant to the Chief of the Group) actually acts as chief of the General Staff, but his official position is that of adviser to the Chief of the General Staff. Up to December 8, 1925, there were no strict regulations governing the General Staff. Regulations had been prepared during the organization of the General Staff in June, 1925, but they were subject to continuous alterations in connection with the daily work. At that time, there were the following departments in the General Staff: the operations and intelligence departments (including communications
[3] service) and the departments of administration, inspection of supplies, and the Navy. The last two departments were considered independent and were subordinated directly to the Military Council. The Aviation Bureau claimed to be subordinated directly to the Political Council. Our advisers were, in fact, at the head of all these departments, but officially they were called advisers to the chiefs of departments. At the end of December, our advisers even held official posts as chief of the Navy [Smirnov] and chief of the Aviation Bureau [Remi]. Within a short time, however, they had to become advisers again, since it is politically inconvenient for our advisers to hold official posts and our influence does not suffer in the least by their becoming advisers again.
    [Passages omitted.]

The following are weak points in the Revolutionary Government. Insufficient unity and insufficient stability of the Kuomintang Center, which consists of quite diverse elements of the population and [4] is subject to constant vacillation. For the time being, the majority of the Center is influenced by and allied with the Left Wing, that is, the Communist Party and the CY, under our political leadership. In case we make mistakes in our direction and the Left Wing becomes too enthusiastic about plans (which are too radical for the present time), however, the possibility is that the Center will split and a considerable portion will go over to the Right Wing. Despite a series of defeats, the Right has not ceased struggling against the radical policies of the Kuomintang and the Revolutionary Government at Canton.

At one time, the big bourgeoisie succeeded in drawing to their side the middle and petty bourgeoisie, especially the merchant associations. They organized their own military force in Canton, the people's Corps* or the "Paper Tigers." These forces struggled against the Revolutionary Government but were suppressed and destroyed by the Government. These classes of the population, except the big bourgeoisie, now support the Government. In case of excessively radical policies or mistakes in our political leadership, however, they might again turn against the Revolutionary Government.

The Army lacks thorough political organization. Individual generals still enjoy considerable influence. Under favorable circumstances, some of them may rebel against the Government and unite with malcontent elements of the population under the political slogans of the KMT Right Wing. On the other hand, it is difficult to say whether they [the National Revolutionary Army] will successfully hold out against the technical superiority of the Northern armies. Of course, the defeat of the Revolutionary Army will give the counterrevolutionaries a favorable opportunity inside Canton itself.

[5]   In order that these weak points should not become fatal ones, our most skillful guidance is necessary. Our leadership plays an important role in Canton. Even the slightest mistakes will painfully affect the Left Wing and still more painfully the Center and the Revolutionary Government. If our leaders become eager for measures too radical for China's actual conditions, the Government will provoke the discontent of a portion of the population. The antigovernment faction among the Right Wing of the Kuomintang will immediately take advantage of the discontent and draw over to its side the majority of the petty bourgeoisie under the slogan, "Struggle against Bolshevism!"

---

* A mistranslation by the Japanese; should be "Merchant Corps."

To prove that our leadership plays an exceptionally important role, we need only remember that the Kuomintang as it now exists was established by us. Its program, regulations, and work were worked out under our political leadership according to the standards of the Russian Communist Party but conforming to conditions in China. The direction of the Party and Government has been carried on until recently with the closest participation of our political director. There has not been a case yet when a measure proposed by us was not accepted and put into effect by the Government.

The Party in its reorganized form has been in existence only for a short time (two years). Thus, a stable and skillful nucleus to guide the Party and Government has not yet developed. In our work of political direction, we have to take into consideration the element of social change in order to formulate correct policies.

The Left Wing of the Kuomintang will have to proceed with great care in the future with respect to radical Communist work. On the other hand, it must concentrate on the work of organizing the peasants and workers under the revolutionary slogans of the Left Wing of the Kuomintang.

Under the guidance of the Left Wing, these organizations will counterbalance to a considerable extent the Right Wing and the vacillating Center. Furthermore, they will contribute to the continuation of our influence and the influence of the Left over the [6] Government, composed of elements of the Center.

It is necessary to carry on extensive political work in the Army and to attempt to place as many workers from the Left Wing as possible in the political organs of the Army. (This has already been done.) The Army must be trained in new methods of warfare. Tactical preparedness must be improved. It is necessary to take measures to improve the Army's supplies and technical equipment. In this respect our material aid is necessary.

The Government already has a concrete financial foundation and it is working out plans for the economic development of Kwangtung province, such as improvement of the Whampoa [harbor], construction of roads, and so on. The Government still lacks proper organs of direction and administration, however. No such organs of course exist in any part of China! Embryos of these organs have been sprouting, but their development is slow. Thus, through our guidance, it is necessary to intensify work in this direction. Our attention is required to see that the Revolutionary Government does not undertake tasks which are beyond its capacity and thus waste its small resources. What resources it does possess should be used to carry out enterprises which can be easily accomplished and are more urgently needed.

DOCUMENT 23

This is a report prepared by Stepanov, adviser with Chiang Kai-
shek's First Army, shortly after the coup d'état of March 20, 1926.
A Chinese translation from the Russian was prepared by the Peking Commission under the title, "Stepanov's Report at a Meeting of
the Communist Party Branch of the Soviet Commissioners Group
in Kwangtung on the Split between Chiang Kai-shek and the Russian
Communist Party and Plans for Utilizing Chiang Kai-shek," in
Su-lien yin-mou..., III, "Canton," pp. 67-74. The report is undated
but was apparently drafted toward the end of March, before Chiang's
speech of April 3, in which he outlined demands against the Communists. This supposition seems likely although Stepanov mentioned Chiang as chairman of the Military Council (p. 72), and
Chiang was not elected to that post until April 16, 1926. Stepanov
might have meant that Chiang was in control of the Military Council, though not acting officially as chairman. The chairman, Wang
Ching-wei, had disappeared at the time of the report. Brief excerpts in English are available in Mitarevsky's World-wide Soviet
Plots, pp. 22-23.

[STEPANOV'S REPORT ON THE MARCH

TWENTIETH COUP D'ÉTAT]

[67]   Chiang Kai-shek's action against the Russian advisers and the
Chinese Communist Party on March 20th came as a lightning shock
to our comrades as well as the military and civilian population.
As a consequence, [our] work in the National Revolutionary Army
will have to suffer a long period of suspension. A thorough study of
this matter requires a review of the entire incident, the gathering
of all data, and an analysis of the various conditions. Only thus can
we form a substantiated judgment.

The purpose of this report is to provide some information on the
incident by a discussion of the causes of the incident, the policies
of our political advisers and the Chinese Communist Party, as well
as the consequences of the incident.

According to Chiang himself and others, the immediate cause of
the incident was the movement of the gunboat, S.S. "Chung-shan,"
from Canton to Whampoa.

Our group was originally scheduled to inspect the "Chung-shan"
on March 19. During the night between the 18th and the 19th, the
Navy Bureau received a telephone call for the gunboat to move to
Whampoa. The deputy chief of the Navy Bureau, Li Ch'eng-lung

[Li Chih-lung], took this as an order from Chiang. Without trying
[68] to get confirmation, he ordered the gunboat to head for Whampoa.
Our advisers seemed to have been aware of the inside story and
ordered the gunboat to return and it returned to the city around
midnight. The next morning, Li and other Communists were arrested by order of Chiang.

Several days before the incident, Chiang had received a series
of threatening letters. When, on the 18th [19th], Chiang learned that
the gunboat had first moved to Whampoa and had later returned to
Canton, anchoring in front of the Military Officers' Academy under
full steam and ready for action, he thought that someone was
planning an attempt on his life. The culprit, he thought, could be
none other than the Communist, Li, who had connections with the
Russians. He therefore decided to arrest the Communists on the
gunboat first and, around 9:00 o'clock on the morning of the 20th,
ordered troops to surround our residence at Tung-shan and to
disarm the guards. Meanwhile, in the city, the labor organizations,
railway stations, and the Central Bank were also surrounded and
Ta-sa-tao [Ta-sha-t'ou] was put under watch by an air squadron.

At 2:00 o'clock in the afternoon, the commander of the Fifth
Regiment came and Kisanko requested him to withdraw the besieging troops. After returning to the city, the commander came once
more to withdraw the troops and to return arms. The siege of the
labor organizations was also lifted, but the siege of other places
was not lifted until the 22d.

About one hour after the withdrawal of troops from our residence,
Mr. Sung [T. V. Soong?] came and said that Chiang's action was
imprudent. He was followed by Li Chi-shen and General Teng
[Yen-ta?], who also criticized Chiang.

When Kisanko sent Ao-li-chin to see Chiang, Chiang apologized
profusely. Ao-li-chin gently rebuked him and mentioned the death
of Pavlov. Ivanovskii and Ao-li-chin went to see Chiang again to
discuss problems of the future and Chiang promised to call on
Ivanovskii the following day to discuss everything.

Meanwhile, T'an Yen-k'ai and Chu P'ei-te called on Kisanko.
They said that Chiang was counterrevolutionary and suggested taking
serious measures against him. Wang Ching-wei, then sick in bed,
heard of Chiang's move and also branded it as counterrevolutionary.
In short, everyone expressed opposition to Chiang.

Chiang failed to call on Ivanovskii on the 21st. Various generals
who came from Chiang's place reported that he still insisted on
ousting the Russians and the Communists.

[69]   The situation was therefore still tense. Our group outlined means
of resolving the situation and decided to change our leader. We decided to delegate Solovyev to discuss the matter and all other problems with Chiang.

On the 22d, Solovyev and Chiang held discussions at the Political Department in the presence of Wang Ching-wei. Chiang left for Whampoa after the meeting. The generals considered this significant. They believed that even if Chiang did not immediately oust the Russians, he would make preparations for a second attempt against them. According to them, Chiang had been preparing for this incident for over a month.

On the 23d, Wang Ching-wei suddenly disappeared. He was reported to be in a hospital but could not be found anywhere. On the 24th, the Government gave those of our comrades who were leaving a farewell party, at which I was able to bring Chiang and Ivanovskii together. After this meeting, Chiang again left for Whampoa. On the 26th, Chiang came back from Whampoa to look for Wang Ching-wei, but in vain. Then Chiang again left for Whampoa on his way to Hu-men. Yesterday he came to Canton from Whampoa.

On the 24th, our comrades began to leave Canton.

The foregoing is a brief account of the incident. We now go into conditions and causes of the incident.

The recent situation is characterized by the following trends:

1. Since the military victories in Kwangtung, the National Government has been greatly strengthened.

2. The people have confidence in the Government's strength.

3. The people have confidence in the policies of Party headquarters.

[70]   4. All those individuals and organizations which had opposed and attacked the policies of the KMT Political Council have been defeated.

5. The Army has been brought under the control of the National Government.

6. The Military Council has succeeded in obtaining control over the military organization.

7. All organs have been working actively toward strengthening and centralizing military power.

8. Plans for construction, education, and training have been formulated.

In short, the National Revolutionary Army is preparing to become a strong force, able not only to destroy the militarists but to unify the whole of China under the National Government. We must pay attention to the political situation in the Army. If it is good, I daresay the above observations are definitely not overly optimistic. As for our errors, our working procedure has not been suitable. Furthermore, the situation created by the characteristics of certain Chinese individuals invite attack. Our errors may be elaborated as follows:

1. Too rapid centralization of military power. (For instance, the

establishment of the General Staff, the police, the commissariat, and other organs.)

2. Excessive supervision of the generals and various organs. (Russian advisers often assume leading positions, directly handling all matters.)

3. Inappropriate radical propaganda in the Army on the problems of imperialism, the peasantry, and communism.

The above points naturally and unavoidably caused unpleasant feelings among high-ranking military officers who, not entirely free from old militarist habits, managed at first to endure and be patient but finally resorted to open opposition. We normally pay no attention to Chinese habits, customs, and etiquette. This may be a minor blunder but is sufficient to cause unpleasant feelings against the Russian advisers among the Chinese.

The Chinese Communist Party has also committed many mistakes in Party work and propaganda in the Army. Its members fail to understand the process of organizing the Kuomintang and then secretly transforming it. They only try, as their primary policy, openly to expand the Chinese Communist Party and to grab complete control over everything everywhere. Thus, they have alienated the KMT and have aroused jealousy on the part of KMT members.

The KCT's mistakes, however, are in fact due to the insufficiency of our directive capacity and lack of liaison which make unified action impossible. Therefore, we too, and not the Chinese Communist Party alone, should take the blame.

In short, there are significant connections between the March Twentieth Incident and the individual characteristics of our comrades as well as those of the chief culprit in the incident, Chiang Kai-shek.

My observations of the character of Chiang Kai-shek are shared by the Chinese Communists, including the chairman of the Central Committee [Ch'en Tu-hsiu]. We consider Chiang Kai-shek a peculiar person with peculiar characteristics, most prominent of these being his lust for glory and power and craving to be the hero of China. He claims that he stands not only for the Chinese National Revolution but for the World Revolution. Needless to say, the degree of his actual understanding of revolution is quite another matter.

To achieve his goal, power and money are required. He does not, however, use money to enrich his own pocket. He never hesitates to spend huge sums of money for grants and rewards. He is extremely fond of subsidizing newspapers in order to enlist support for his programs. His analysis of Chinese and world problems is extremely good.

[72]   He acts entirely according to his individuality without depending on the masses. However, in order to obtain glory, which is his

goal, he sometimes wants to utilize the masses, the Chinese Communist Party, and ourselves.

With his ambition to be the hero of China and his desire to utilize the national revolutionary movement, Chiang finds himself constantly wavering between the Right and the Communists. He speaks of the "Red Disaster," attempting to accord with Chinese public sentiment because the term "Red Disaster" is at present drawing much attention in China.

Chiang possesses much determination and endurance. Compared with the average Chinese, he is unusually forthright. He often accepts suggestions and plans from trusted subordinates. Yet he is not free from suspicion and jealousy. No one is allowed to argue with him over any matter or to act for him. Such is my judgment of Chiang as a person, though it may not be entirely sound.

When we review our mistakes in the light of Chiang's desire to be a hero, we know that attacks on us are inevitable sooner or later. The main problem in our future work is whether we can avoid the above mistakes.

Some of these mistakes have already been rectified. Others we will attempt to avoid in our future work. Members of the Chinese Communist Party are also engaged in correcting errors in basic policy. Nilov will report on this in detail.

The important subjective cause [of the incident] is the individuality of Chiang Kai-shek. Should Chiang actually have the above-mentioned unusual characteristics, there is no doubt but that we should, in the light of the over-all program, utilize him by all means to carry on the revolutionary struggle.

The possible future appointment of Chiang to the post of Commander-in-Chief should sufficiently satisfy his lust for position and power. At present Chiang is only chairman of the Military Council and he has at times acted in opposition to the Right. This affords [73] us an opportunity to be allied with some of the extremists of both the Right and Left and is very helpful to us.

It would naturally be unfortunate both for the Revolution and for himself if Chiang actually wants further to attack the Left. Yet Chiang can never destroy the Left for, warmly received everywhere, the Left has substantial force. For Chiang to fight such force is to seek self-extermination.

Chiang, a man of intelligence and ambition, will surely not resort to such a course. He claims he has learned an invaluable lesson from the incident of March Twentieth. His action was not influenced by the Left but was instigated by counterrevolutionaries of the Right. If we could inject into him a small dose of revolutionary ideology and surround him with the brave influence of the Left, we would ensure against repetition of the March Twentieth Incident. We are now creating conditions unfavorable to the occurrence of another such incident. We are trying to make Chiang cooperate with us again by satisfying his desire for glory and enabling him to achieve greater power and strength than he now enjoys.

Such is the general outline of our plan to utilize Chiang's characteristics for the cause of the National Revolution. It is permissible to make a few concessions to Chiang's political demands as the price we pay. The Central Committee of the Chinese Communist Party in Shanghai and the local [Kwangtung Regional] Committee here share the same view.

Since our policy is based on utilizing Chiang Kai-shek, the organization of the National [Revolutionary] Army should proceed in accordance with plans already formulated. These may be restated as follows:

1. Strengthen the centralization of military organs from the top down.
2. Continue to improve the organizational system of the Army.

[74]

3. Improve conditions within the Army, regulate discipline, and inspect Army service.
4. Elevate the standard of officers.
5. Improve the quality of the troops.
6. Centralize military supplies in the commissariat.
7. Expand the work of secret agents and unify communications in the Army.
8. Expand political propaganda work in the Army.
9. Expand aviation and the Navy.

The above are our tasks. The procedure of their execution depends upon the changing circumstances.

In accordance with instructions from the Committee, I shall issue orders to all members which they will observe in carrying out their duties. These orders will also serve as the temporary regulations of our work and of our contact with the Chinese.

DOCUMENT 24

This is a report presented by Stepanov at a meeting of Russian advisers in Canton. It is translated from Russian into Chinese under the title, "Stepanov's Report on the Present Situation of the Russians in Kwangtung Following Conflict between Chiang Kai-shek and the Russians" in Su-lien yin-mou..., III, "Canton," pp. 74-87. The report is followed by a record of the discussion held by the Russians at the meeting. The document is undated, but internal evidence indicates that the meeting took place between April 10, 1926, when Communist Party representatives withdraw from the First Army, and April 16, 1926, when the League of Military Youth was dissolved. See pp. 75 and 82 of Document 24.

[STEPANOV'S REPORT TO A MEETING OF THE
SOVIET GROUP AT CANTON]

[74] **There** seems to have been a slight turning-point in Canton since my last report. Chiang Kai-shek and Wang Ching-wei remain the central figures.

Chiang has issued a statement of self-condemnation. At the same time, he has relieved all Communist commissars and political workers [in the Army] of their duties and has demanded the right to investigate the Russians' residence and to restrict their activities.

[75] Nevertheless, he appears rather inclined toward the Left Wing. I presume you already know about his arrest of Ou-yang Ch'i [Ou-yang Chü] and demand for his dismissal by the Military Council. Chiang has also issued a telegram, strongly attacking the Right Wing's Congress at Shanghai, although the Congress is in favor of Chiang and actively opposed to the Communists and the Russians.

Chiang has never expressed his final opinion on the problem of political workers [in the Army], nor has he insisted on his own demands. However, the local [Kwangtung Regional] Committee has voluntarily recalled all Communist political workers from the First Army.

Chiang intends to keep check not only on Communist work in Army but on the Communist Party itself. On the surface, he appears amiable and intimate with the Russians. He often asks for suggestions during conversations and sometimes openly reveals his own views and intentions. With the generals, however, he maintains an attitude of unity against outsiders. He has taken from our ordnance store machine guns and cartridges for distribution among the military organs.

The foregoing is an account of past conditions in Canton and Chiang's individual actions. Departing from facts, we now discuss the conclusions to be drawn from the above.

There are two different conclusions. One is that Chiang intends sincerely to temper the incident of March Twentieth and to cooperate with the Left for the cause of the National Revolution. If this should be the case, it would be very profitable to us.

The second conclusion is that Chiang's actions are intended to deceive his opponents in preparation for a second move.

Should we adopt the first conclusion, we would then recognize that Chiang is basically continuing his efforts for the National Revolution and that we should in every way accept his ideas and give [76] him concessions. Should we adopt the second conclusion, we would have to be prepared to fight him.

Whichever conclusion we adopt, our basic policy is to cooperate with Chiang to the very end possible. We should not, however, overlook the second conclusion even if we adopt the first.

The Chinese Communist Party is in agreement with this view and completely approves this basic policy. According to the chairman of the Central Committee of the KCT [Ch'en Tu-hsiu], prior to his departure from Shanghai, the CC had passed a resolution to the effect that Chiang must be utilized by all means.

Although the KMT Left Wing has not completely revealed its attitude, it in fact maintains the same policy as ours. As for the Right Wing, it is reported here that it considers our policy of alliance with Chiang as detrimental to it, and that it will do its best to destroy our alliance.

Reference is again made to Wang Ching-wei. To this day, Wang has not yet returned. His confidential secretary came here a few days ago and said that Wang, now in Shanghai, has recovered from his illness and will soon be back to resume his duties. This statement is not to be relied upon because Wang has written Chiang, severely denouncing him (according to T'an Yen-k'ai). In T'an's view, there is room for reconciliation, although it cannot be expected that differences between Wang and Chiang can be completely avoided. Efforts toward the reconciliation of the two sides are now in progress.

To stabilize the situation in Canton, a plenary session of the Central [Executive] Committee of the Kuomintang will be convened in the middle of May, following the suggestion of Chiang Kai-shek. Previous to or during the session, the two parties, the KMT and the KCT, may reach some kind of agreement. In short, conciliatory moves are at present in progress in all quarters in the hope of achieving together the successful conclusion of the National Revolution.

The Kuomintang is now engaged in further studying the position of the Chinese Communist Party.

The foregoing discusses internal political conditions in Canton.
[77]   There are no special military developments. The armies are
continuing the task of bandit suppression. The Second Army has
been unsuccessfully engaged for the past month in besieging a
strategic point (I have forgotten the name) at Ying-t'a-k'o [Ying-te
hsien]. A representative was sent to request Comrade Remi for
planes to bomb the place. Bandit suppression is also in progress in
the South. The majority of the troops are undergoing general technical training in preparation for action.

You may have learned of conditions outside Kwangtung through
the press. In our cable of April 3, we reported that the Kuominchün
would not give up Peking because conflict between Wu [P'ei-fu]
and Chang [Tso-lin] was about to erupt as a result of mutual hatred
within the alliance. The Kuominchün wishes to utilize this situation
to negotiate with both sides. According to newspaper reports today, negotiations with Wu P'ei-fu have apparently been relatively
successful. Although the party in the negotiations is not the central
element of Wu's army, it is a part of Wu's army nevertheless.

These conditions in the North are favorable to the prospects of
the Northern Expedition.

Conditions in Hunan and Kiangsi will now be discussed. According
to a telegram from the commission sent to Hunan, T'ang Sheng-
chih is inclined toward an alliance with the National Government.
However, the Government (or more correctly, the Military Council)
insists that T'ang issue a declaration of formal alliance or it will
not conclude any agreement with him.

A representative of Fang Pen-jen has arrived at Canton from
Kiangsi with the report that Fang would ally with the National Government. According to the results of our investigation, Fang Pen-
jen still has a considerable number of troops. Reports in today's
newspapers about his visit to Shanghai, to the effect that the commissioner of Shanghai is a leader of Fang's clique, are mere fabrication and politically motivated. In the opinion of our generals, we
may utilize Fang when the Northern Expeditionary Forces are organized.

In addition, there are three divisions of the Kwangsi Army, totaling 9,000 men, which may also be used for the Northern Expedition.

Properly analyzed, the above conditions, are of benefit to us.

In discussing the Northern Expedition, the Chinese generals have
made such concrete suggestions as what troops should be sent to
[78] the North. A representative sent to Hunan has suggested to Ch'en
Ming-shu the dispatch of the First and Fourth armies for the
Northern Expedition. The problem has not been solved yet. Neither
Chiang Kai-shek nor the commander of the Fourth Army [Li Chi-
shen] has expressed any objection to this suggestion.

The problem of finance is the basic obstacle to the Northern

Expeditionary Forces. A financial campaign is now under way and in two or three months we may expect to move north. We only hope that political conditions in Canton will not deteriorate.

In view of general political and military conditions in Kwangtung and in China as a whole, our work in the National Revolutionary Army should still be divided into two categories, political and military.

Politically, we should strengthen the unity of the Kuomintang, strengthen in particular the KMT Left, and eliminate the counter-revolutionary elements of the Right. At the same time, we should pursue the task of allying with the KMT and the National Government.

There is a possibility of a split in the Sunyatsenist Society, which is composed of three groups, the negativists, reactionaries, and moderates. The Chinese say that a portion of the Society may be made to join the Left Wing or the Communists, another portion to remain neutral, but that the reactionaries must be weakened or attacked.

In our military work, we should stick to our former aim of strengthening our work and the organs we have already established in the armies. We should do our utmost to make the Army unite firmly with the present Government and the KMT Left Wing. In talking to military officers and political workers, we should urge them to pledge their loyalty to the Party and the Government.

The incident of March Twentieth may dishearten us, but we must forget it and keep up our efforts. We must look at all things from a broader point of view. In the presence of the Chinese we absolutely must not fight for seniority. We should observe etiquette 79] and the formalities. These are the most important things before us. Otherwise the incident of March Twentieth may be repeated. This point merits your special attention.

I have said previously that in two or three months we may be moving north. Accordingly, we should immediately study all data relative to the Northern Expedition, such as economic and military matters. Various reports should be prepared on an area basis to enable us to understand the situation in our Army and in neighboring provinces. Conditions in armies which may oppose us in the future require particular study.

Questions and Criticisms concerning Stepanov's Report

Q. What are Chiang Kai-shek's demands as to the work of the Russian advisers?

A. Chiang has made no definite indications or demands in his conversations with us. He did point out to Ivanovskii many mistakes of the Russian advisers. However, when I asked him exactly how the Russian advisers should work, he replied that they should work as before.

Q. Are there any connections between the National Government and the First Kuominchün?

A. The First Kuominchün recently sent a representative here who was entertained. The actual results, however, are not known. They may be revealed when the Northern Expedition starts.

Q. How should we deal with Yunnan?

A. With reference to Yunnan, Chiang reprimanded Kisanko for lending assistance to Yunnan and Kwangsi. True, this matter was kept secret from Chiang, but Chiang found out and suspected Kisanko of opposing the Northern Expedition. However, this matter is no longer a problem. The Chinese generals appear unanimously in favor of the Expedition. At the same time they are most interested in the internal political situation in Canton. The present situation in Yunnan would not endanger the Northern Expedition.

Q. How are relations with Sun Ch'uan-fang?

[80] A. Nothing definite at present. All we know is that during the fighting between Wu P'ei-fu and the Second Kuominchün, Sun allied himself with Fang Pen-jen. When the Second Kuominchün turned to [was defeated by] Wu, Sun dissolved his alliance with Fang. I believe this is the cause of Fang's flight to Shanghai.

Q. Has the local [Kwangtung Regional] Committee taken notice of the mutual relations between KCT and KMT members?

A. Yes.

Q. What is the KCT's policy towards the Sunyatsenist Society?

A. (answered by Nilov). The KCT now realizes the great mistakes they have committed, contrary to policy, in their work in the Kuomintang and in the Army. The Communists aimed only at the expansion of their own influence under cover of the KMT, without attempting to build up the KMT or pay any attention to the KMT Left. They openly took control of the highest KMT administrative organs and political organs in the Army and monopolized the labor and peasant movements. This has caused dissatisfaction among the majority of KMT members and a split between the two extremist groups within the KMT; The Right Wing and the Communists.

Currently, in setting up a preparatory committee for the National Peasant Conference, the Communists tried to place a few KMT members on the committee for the sake of appearances. They failed, for there are no KMT members working among the peasantry.

This is true not only of the KMT Right but the Left also. This is true not only of [work among] the peasantry but the Central [Executive] Committee and other departments of the Kuomintang. Our

comrades in the Chinese Communist Party seem to have the same
habit of monopolizing power typical of Chinese officials and generals who take on their own cliques and good friends as soon as they
obtain high office (as Li Ch'eng-lung [Li Chih-lung] did in the Navy).

The situation is even more pronounced in the Army, where [Com-
munist] political workers man the most important posts and appoint
[81] members of their own cliques to various posts. They secretly pursue tasks unknown to the respective commanding officers. This
arouses the jealousy and indignation of military officers of all
ranks as well as non-Communist workers. A great number of the
non-Communists are active elements of the Sunyatsenist Society
and many of them have been squeezed out of good positions.

Two facts to prove this: in each of the divisions of the Whampoa
[First] Army, four out of five commissars are Communists. (The
Chief of the Political Department of the Army [Chou En-lai] is
also a Communist). Of the sixteen commissars in each regiment,
five are Communists, eleven are KMT members. Kuomintang members are more in the majority in the companies, however.

I believe that with their progressive political ideas, the majority
of the active members of the Sunyatsenist Society could have been
affiliated with the Left Wing. Having been squeezed out, however,
they turned around and opposed the KCT. In view of their own rank,
the military officers feel they should be the directing organs of the
KCT [the military officers feel their own rank superior to Communist political commissars]. They also oppose the KCT because
they are dissatisfied with the commissar system.

If no basic solution is found to the problem of the mutual relations of the KMT and the KCT, it will be difficult to continue our
work in Canton. One solution is to call a joint conference of the
KMT C[E]C and the KCT CC at Canton to fix regulations for cooperative work. A preparatory meeting should first be convened with
the immediate objective of comforting Chiang Kai-shek.

We have received a circular order from the Central Committee*
stating that the chief duty of Communist Party is the organization of the Kuomintang Left and the strengthening of its position.
However, at the moment the KMT Left is absolutely empty. Not only
has it no leaders, it has no masses. It is difficult to say how the
CC's instructions can be carried out.

We have private duties as well as official duties, namely, to get
close to the KMT Left Wing and enable it to direct Party affairs
and the peasant movement. On the surface, we should take an inter-
[82] est in and not assume the attitude of neglecting Sunyatsenism and

---

* Probably the ECCI, which sent instructions to the KCT in April,
1926, calling on it to struggle against the Right Wing. See Stalin,
"The International Situation," p. 237.

the Three People's Principles. The KCT has, in fact, acquired a legal position in Kwangtung and it should not hereafter resort to unnecessary secrecy, thus arousing the KMT's suspicion and fear.

Recruitment for the armies should be temporarily suspended. Recall all Communists from the Second and Twentieth divisions of the First Army. This tactic will meet with the expressed wishes of Chiang Kai-shek. On the other hand, the organized and sudden withdrawal of over one hundred Communists should sufficiently indicate that the influence of the Chinese Communist Party is not weak and that the Party can still return to the First Army in the future.

In principle, the KCT should be entirely open in the Army and therefore it is proposed that complete lists of Communist members be handed over to the respective commanders, beginning with the Whampoa Academy in view of its large number of Communists. In the lower military units, Communists should form lecturing groups to emphasize that the KCT works in unison with the KMT in performing public duties and serving society. Under no circumstances should communism be stressed; this might arouse fear among the people.

The League of Military Youth is about to be dissolved voluntarily since political propaganda has been completed and secret alliances have been formed in the various armies. This move is intended to induce the Sunyatsenist Society to take the same step of voluntary dissolution.

At present, the Sunyatsenist Society is allied with leaders of the Right Wing (Wu Ch'ao-shu and Wu T'ieh-ch'eng) for destructive activities, beginning with labor unions and student associations. Due to their destructive activities in the student movement, a split has occurred in Canton's educational circles which formerly were unanimously opposed to the KMT. They are unable to achieve the unification plan under the direction of the KMT Youth Department.†

The Mechanics' Union and the reformist group in Kwangtung labor unions have also split. The Sunyatsenist Society attempted to obstruct the Kwangtung Labor Conference called for April 1st. Although its attempt was not successful, several hundred delegates out of the more than two thousand delegates present withdrew from the conference. They would not remain despite earnest persuasion. Wu T'ieh-ch'eng actively participated in this as in many other recent incidents.

[83]   Q. I have had contact with the Mechanics' Union and understand that it is taking part in all phases of the labor movement. For instance, when the workers of the "Small Third International" went on strike and got in touch with the union, the workers of the "Big Third

---

† This is a literal translation of the Chinese text, which is unclear.

International" insisted that it withdraw from the illegal organization. Consequently, the Mechanics' Union is not cooperating with the "Small Third International."‡ At present the union is still playing an important role, but I believe that if we take appropriate measures in dealing with it, it can be disbanded easily.

A. (answer of Nilov). You know more than I. The Mechanics' Union is one of the most important unions in Kwangtung. Its members are drivers and workers in arsenals, electric companies, and waterworks. Our duty as Communists is to join the union and to form a united front with its members against its reactionary leadership.

A. (answer of Ko-lei). The union is important also among seamen. I think our most important work now is to destroy the union. Craftsmen, such as blacksmiths, also are members of the union. At any rate, we should be able to persuade the seamen on gunboats to withdraw from the union.

Q. What is the scope of the Northern Expedition?

A. (answer of Stepanov). To the Chinese, Peking represents the highest objective of the Northern Expedition and the temporary occupation of Hupeh the lowest, depending much on circumstances.

Q. Our work at various places does not seem commensurate with the increase of our staff. Are there any obstacles?

A. I have not heard of any obstacles to our personnel. Efficiency is not low. Our people have perhaps been discouraged since the March Twentieth Incident. It is the belief among the Chinese generals that the scars of the incident have not been entirely healed. [84] T'an Yen-k'ai has said that even if we advisers were to revive our former relations with the top leaders, the effect of the incident will always remain in the minds of the people. We must constantly remember this.

Q. Are the conditions prevailing in the Mechanics' Union as described above caused by lack of Communist workers?

A. (answer of Nilov). Precisely. There are very few Communists among workers. Only about two thousand workers were recruited into the Party from among the workers involved in the Hongkong strike.

Q. What is known of the relations between Chiang and Wu Ch'ao-shu?

---

‡ The Peking Commission apparently mistranslated this passage. The terms, "Small Third International" and "Big Third International," are meaningless.

A. (answer of Stepanov). Wu is with Chiang nearly every day.
Chiang does not conceal this fact but claims that he merely listens
while Wu and Sun Fo talk. It is difficult to verify this statement.

A. (answer of Pei-tzu-szu-ch'a-szu-t'e-no-fu).** I should like
to refer to an incident at the Nan-ts'e [Nan-t'i] Club prior to our
departure for Hainan. When we arrived at the club, we saw Sun Fo,
Wu T'ieh-ch'eng, Wu Ch'ao-shu, and others, who betrayed extreme
uneasiness when the four of us appeared. Wu T'ieh-ch'eng forced
himself to greet us and one of them went to make a telephone call,
but he did not talk even with the receiver in his hand. This happened
on March 19th. They apparently thought that the Russians were
there to arrest them.

A. (answer of Ko-lei). The fact that the incident of March
Twentieth is not quite ended may be proved by the appointment
yesterday of General P'eng as commander of the Navy. P'eng
told me that no large-scale activities should be contemplated at
the present because the incident is not quite over. All in all, everyone and everything is dictated by Chiang. Take the Navy Department, where Chiang has four of his own appointees. None of them
would do a thing without his approval.

A. (answer of Stepanov). Ko-lei's words are too frightening.
You know that we all go to Chiang's place very often and he is
rather amiable to us.

[85]   A. (answer of Chi-lieh-fu).†† I should like to talk about our responsibilities. I feel that we should give priority to the kind of work
which can produce relative results. Military and political workers
should not be content merely with the fulfillment of their own duties
but should think from the standpoint of the organization as a whole.

** General Pei-tzu-szu-ch'a-szu-t'e-no-fu, whose Russian name
is unknown, was artillery adviser at the General Staff, adviser at
the arsenal, artillery adviser at commissariat headquarters, and
artillery adviser at the Central Military and Political Academy.
He had participated in the First Eastern Expedition. See "A
List of Names and Positions of Members of the Soviet Group in
South China" and "A List of Soviet Officers Who Participated in
the Eastern Expedition," Su-lien yin-mou..., III, "Canton," pp. 97,
105.

†† Colonel Chi-lieh-fu, whose Russian name is not known, was
adviser on military supplies at the Central Military and Political
Academy, adviser at commissariat headquarters, and artillery
adviser in the First Army. He had participated in the First Eastern Expedition. Chi-lieh-fu was his real name. See "A List of
Names and Positions of Members of the Soviet Group in South China"
and "A List of Soviet Officers Who Participated in the Eastern Expedition," Su-lien yin-mou..., III, "Canton," pp. 97, 100, 105.

For instance, Communists in the Whampoa Academy actually are of great help to us.

With reference to the Sunyatsenist Society, I learned about its leader through conversations with Communist comrades and with Wang Mei-yu [Wang Po-ling] at the Academy last year. After three months, I got a chance to talk to him. He conducted me to the office of propaganda workers of the Academy where I was shown a large portrait of Lenin and a small one of Sun Yat-sen. I told him that the portrait of Sun should be enlarged because both Lenin and Sun are great men. He later showed me a collection of political literature, Communist literature on a big shelf and Sunyatsenist literature on a small shelf. He told me that one third of the Academy students belong to the Left Wing and two thirds to the Right. He appeared to have had some advance knowledge of the March Twentieth Incident and cautioned me against it.

From casual conversations with Communist, Sunyatsenist, and nonpartisan cadets, I learned that many of the members of the Sunyatsenist Society are inclined to the Left. They asked me how the Communist Party is centralized and said that, in their experience, nothing can be decided after an organization has been formed. I explained to the utmost of my ability that there should be no distinction or discrimination within the KMT, that the KMT is unique, and that its duty is the National Revolution. Due to my inadequate Chinese, however, I was unable to explain fully. They apparently did not feel quite satisfied.

We should take note that the influence of the Right Wing is beginning to revive. Take, for instance, General Ch'en. At one time out of power, he is now in charge of the Hu-men Fort and strategic points at Whampoa, where he was once in command.

86] The Left Wing is gradually inclining toward the Right, even to the point of joining the Right Wing movement.

A. (answer of Karachev).‡‡ Our comrades foresaw that Wang Mei-yu wanted a coup d'etat to take place. I once engaged in conversation with him and asked about his attitude toward Borodin's telegram. On another occasion, he wrote me about Chiang Kai-shek's reply [to his letter], in which Chiang said that he was muddle-headed. Hence, he redoubled his efforts against the Russians and even tried to surround them. When he [Wang] came to Whampoa, he asked me why the Russian Communists lacked confidence in him and I replied that they did indeed have full confidence in him.

---

‡‡ Karachev was a political adviser at the Central Military and policial Academy. See "A List of Names and Positions of Members of the Soviet Group in South China," Su-lien yin-mou..., III, "Canton," p. 97.

I believe that Chiang Kai-shek is in fact a politician of no great consequence. When he was appointed Commander-in-Chief, he asked me with whom in the Russian Red Army he might be compared. I replied that he resembled Kamenev and he was much pleased. I consider it harmless to give him concessions.

A. (<u>answer of Pei-tzu-szu-ch'a-szu-t'e-no-fu</u>). Chiang is after all the man we are relying on. He is extremely fond of the Russian advisers, except Rogachev, towards whom he harbours very bad feelings because Rogachev is not [would not be?] his adviser.

A. (<u>answer of Hei-hsing</u>). The incident of March Twentieth cannot be considered a defeat for Chiang. It is incorrect to say that Chiang lacks understanding of the causes of events. He understands the causes of social conflict and is a very clever statesman. I believe that when the [KMT CEC] plenary session meets, all traces of the March Twentieth Incident will be wiped out and Chiang can be persuaded to lean to the Left.

A. (<u>answer of Stepanov</u>). The representative of the Central Committee of the KCT [P'eng Shu-chih?] said that Chiang is an individualist who does not rely on the masses. He said that if Chiang should be opposed by the Communists and the KMT Left Wing at Canton, he would be alienated and isolated.

However, under the present circumstances in China, Chiang will not be alienated. The Northern militarists, the students, and the merchants all attach great importance to him, and he himself realizes it. He is definitely not an ordinary militarist but a militarist with revolutionary interests. He has studied the success and failure of various military men. I have personally heard him speak of the achievements of Washington, Napoleon, and Lenin. He is filled with revolutionary ideas far superior to the other militarists. I believe that trivial details of his behavior are but signs of his weakness for self-aggrandizement and self-glorification. They may be overlooked.

The incident of March Twentieth is perhaps not entirely without benefit. I agree with Hei-hsing. The incident is like cancer, for which it is wise to have an operation. Sores remain, however, and we should by all means see that they are cured.

No one can guarantee at present that Chiang will always be one of us, but we must utilize him for the cause of the National Revolution. Chiang has the peculiar characteristic of not depending on the masses. The representative of the Central Committee of the KCT has referred to Chiang in the manner of hero-worship [referred to Chiang's desire to become a hero]. In China today, we must not scorn such a peculiarity. Napoleon at first also believed that the individual is the central figure in a revolution. Chiang is not yet as fearsome as Napoleon. We should do our utmost to alienate him from the Right Wing and persuade him to join the work of the KMT

[87]

Left. I am absolutely not afraid of Chiang's peculiar character, but we must try to remedy it in time.

Q. What is the reaction of the Second Army to the participation of the First and Fourth armies in the Northern Expedition?

A. According to Chiang, there is no one at present to fight T'an Yen-k'ai for political power in Hunan. This may be untrue. However, any movement of the Second Army at this time may furnish them grounds to attack Hunan. T'an Yen-k'ai, the Commander of the Second Army, shares this opinion.

Document 25 is a summary report by "Seifulin," Soviet Military
Attaché in Peking, dated June 3, 1926 and based on reports from
Borodin in Canton. The following is based on a Japanese trans-
lation of the Russian document which is available under the title,
"A Report to Moscow from Soviet Russia's Central Military Organ
in Peking on Strife within the Southern Government Centered
Around Chiang Kai-shek," in Pekin Ro-Taishikan ōshū himitsu
bunsho, Part V, pp. 1-11. The report is marked "Most Secret."

[SEIFULIN'S REPORT ON THE
SITUATION AT CANTON]

[1] Summary
The following report is based on Borodin's reports and concerns
events in Canton, May, 1926.

The Internal Situation
[2]   The Right Wing.—Following March 2nd [20th], the Right Wing interpreted Chiang Kai-shek's hostility toward the Soviet advisers
as a sympton of a sudden turn toward the Right. It therefore attempted to approach Chiang. After the dismissal of Wu T'ieh-ch'eng
on April 24, however, the Right discovered that it was hopeless to
attempt to bring Chiang into its fold and started approaching Li
Chi-shen and various other generals of Canton. The Right Wing
was able for a time to win over Li Chi-shen, who mustered his
army in the Canton area under the pretext of aiding Hunan. The
Right Wing got Hu Han-min as their "Chief Advance Commander"
and organizer.

    Taking advantage of Wang Ching-wei's absence, the Right Wing,
without informing the National Government, made plans for an
elaborate celebration in honor of Hu's arrival. They even planned
to erect a triumphal arch for him. Preparations were also made
[3] for a demonstration under the slogan of supporting Hu Han-min as
a representative of the Government.* Hu issued a declaration in
the newspapers and submitted a report to the National Government.
His report and declaration indicate he does not intend to cooperate
with us. He met secretly with Wu Ch'ao-shu, Sun Fo, Wu T'ieh-ch'eng,

---

* The mission on which the Right Wing wanted Hu Han-min to
represent the Government is not specified. Reference may have
been to the negotiations on the Hongkong-Canton Strike.

Ku Ying-fen, and other reactionaries and brought Li Chi-shen, Ch'en Ming-shu, and other Canton generals to his side. Furthermore, Hu told Chiang that Borodin was coming to make a settlement of the March Twentieth Incident and urged Chiang to arrest Borodin. This was an attempt to create a split within the Left Wing.

The negotiations between Hu and Chiang ended in the latter's refusal to meet Hu on May 8. The following day, Hu left for Hongkong. He is now staying in Shanghai.

As a result, the Right Wing has suspended plans to erect an arch, but it is spreading rumors to the effect that Communists are preparing to put their theories into action. It is also demanding that Hu Han-min should represent the Government and is inciting merchants and bankers to suspend business.

The local situation.—The conference of the four business associ-
4] ations opposed the appointment of Hu as a representative of the Government. Nevertheless, because of the rumors, the Central Bank met with a great loss. Withdrawal of money from the bank increased greatly and many people demanded that the bank exchange paper money for silver. After March Twentieth, this problem and the extraordinary disbursement disturbed the financial position of the Government considerably. At the same time, bloody fights broke out at various places between peasants and small landlords.

Looting by armed unemployed workers and prisoners took place and the looting of ships caused constant friction with consular officials. In addition, strikes broke out frequently and a split began to develop in the student movement. On May 7, Chinese Humiliation Day, two students [of the Whampoa Academy: P'an Yu-ch'iang and Yang Yin-chih] were beaten half to death at a demonstration staged by the two factions [the League of Military Youth and the Sunyatsenist Society]. Finally, the Whampoa Army took hostile action against the Communist faction in the name of the commanding officers and threatened Chiang Kai-shek himself unless he took action to purge Communist members from the Kuomintang.

On May 16, an anti-Communist demonstration was staged by the Whampoa Second Division and Students.

The Left Wing and the Left-Right struggle.—Chiang Kai-shek
5] demanded that restrictions be placed on the duties of Communist members (Communist political workers were ejected from the First Army following March Twentieth). The other commanders took a "wait and see" attitude.

Thus we were confronted with two alternatives:

1. Accept Chiang's demands in order to avoid a catastrophe which would otherwise be inevitable.

2. Adopt measures similar to those taken by Wang Ching-wei around the 20th of March in coping with the situation which we had

then considered inappropriate. In other words, form an anti-Chiang
alliance and, by the pressue of this alliance, force Chiang not to
yield to the demands of the anti-Communist faction in the KMT.
(Comrade Kuibyshev† supports this theory.)

The problem was solved by adopting a policy to satisfy Chiang
and to yield to his demands, which are as follows:

1. Communist members are not to head the departments of the
KMT's central Party headquarters.

[6]   2. A list of Communist members in the KMT is to be handed
over to the chairman of the KMT CEC.

3. KMT members are not allowed to become members of the
KCT.

A joint council consisting of five KMT members, three KCT
members, and one CI representative is to be formed to solve all
problems.

However, it was agreed that upon the CEC's acceptance of these
demands and the consequent satisfaction of the demands of the
Whampoa commanders and the KMT Center, Chiang Kai-shek
would take action to arrest, purge, and otherwise bring pressure
against the Right.

Following the CEC's acceptance of the resolutions, the following
situation was created. In Hongkong, it was believed that a revolution of the Right had occurred and they [the British] declared their
[7] unwillingness to negotiate with the Government. Hence, the Right
Wing lost ground for anti-Communist propaganda by which it had
been trying to intimidate the petty bourgeoisie.

The Right Wing was thus unable to gain political power and in
fact lost a great deal. Ch'en Yu-jen [Eugene Chen] was appointed
Minister of Foreign Affairs. Wu T'ieh-ch'eng was arrested on
May 30. Chiang intends to send Sun Fo to Moscow and Wu Ch'ao-
shu [former Minister of Foreign Affairs] was forced to go to
Shanghai. Furthermore, Fu Ping-ch'ang will probably be dismissed.
In short, the Right Wing has been severely hit and has had to
abandon its conspiracy.

Most people believe that the resolution on relations between KMT
and Communist members do not indicate a revolution of the Right
and that Chiang will probably be forced to oppose the Right. Borodin,
for instance, found that he could convince Chiang Kai-shek of the
necessity of having Wang Ching-wei join the conference on the

---

† According to Masayoshi Miyazaki, editor of the Japanese translation, the "Kuibyshev" mentioned in Document 25 was V. Kuibyshev, a member of the Central Committee of the Russian Communist Party. V. Kuibyshev was vice-chairman of the Council of
People's Commissars and concurrently Commissar of Economic
Affairs in the summer of 1926.

Northern Expedition scheduled for May 29, despite the fact that Wang had joined an anti-Chiang alliance around March Twentieth and thereafter and Chiang was aware of this. However, it was
8] rumored that Wang had gone to Paris.

Reforms.—A great number of measures have been adopted in order to win over the people, namely:

1. Sincere negotiations will be held on the [Hongkong-Canton] strike. In as much as the Right Wing has failed, Hongkong will probably not delay the negotiations unnecessarily.

2. The petroleum monopoly was abolished and a proclamation to this effect was issued on May 31.

3. It has been decided to establish an arbitration court which will attempt to settle disputes between peasants and small landlords and between capital and labor.

The present local situation.—As a result of the measures taken, the city has become very peaceful. All the business associations are taking great pains to express loyalty to the Kuomintang government.

9]   The situation in the Army.—A great secret enmity exists between Chiang Kai-shek and Li Chi-shen. Chiang thinks that, inevitably, there will be conflict between the revolutionary elements and Li Chi-shen's army (Chiang regards his own army as revolutionary and believes that Li's army is completely lacking in Leftist revolutionary elements. This is due to Chiang's conviction that Li is his rival and to his determination to get rid of Li. Although conflict is unavoidable, however, Chiang believes it should come after victory over Wu P'ei-fu.)

The External Situation
0]   No agreement between Sun Ch'uan-fang and the Canton Government has been concluded, although there has been an exchange of representatives and negotiations are in progress.

According to news from Shanghai, Sun is preparing against an attack by the Kwangtung Army which he expects to come through Kiangsi province.

In Fukien, Wu P'ei-fu's power is increasing. If circumstances turn to his favor, Wu would be able to apply pressure on Kwangtung from Fukien.

The Szechuan general, Yang Shen (number of troops, about 70,000), and [Kweichow general] Yüan Tsu-ming (number of troops, about 40,000) have sent representatives to Kwangtung for negotiations.

Yang Sen declared to the KMT that he would allow it to work among his troops and the people in his territory.

As for aid for Hunan, T'ang Sheng-chih's army has retreated to Hengchow [Hengyang, Hunan]. It is not engaged in heavy fighting and is suffering from ammunition shortages. Four divisions

have been dispatched to T'ang's rescue from Kwangsi. Around the
end of May, one division took part in a battle and the remaining
[11] three divisions are in the area between Kweilin [Chaling, Hunan]
and Yu-chou [Hunan]. The Twenty-fourth Regiment from Kwangtung
crossed the Hunan border on May 28. Ships were sent for around
the end of May to transport the Tenth and Twelfth divisions of the
Fourth Army from the South; the ships will probably arrive at Canton around the beginning of June. Five hundred thousand bullets
and $200,000 have been sent and it has also been decided to send
$200,000 worth of salt.

The translation of this document is based on the original Chinese text of the political report of the Chinese Communist Party's Central Committee, presented at the Second Enlarged Plenum, which met in Shanghai, July 12 to 18, 1926. It is published in <u>Su-lien yin-mou...</u>, III, "KCT," pp. 61-69.

POLITICAL REPORT OF THE CENTRAL COMMITTEE
[OF THE CHINESE COMMUNIST PARTY]

[1] 1. <u>Changes in the political situation and our Party's policies at each stage, from the Enlarged Conference of last year (October, 1925) to the present.</u>—During the nine months from the Enlarged Conference held in October of last year to the present, political changes may be classified into three periods, for each of which [2] we had a different policy. The three periods are: (1) the period from the Chihli-Mukden War [October 19, 1925] to Kuo Sung-ling's rebellion [October 22, 1925]: (2) the period from Kuo Sung-ling's defeat [December 24, 1925] to the withdrawal of the Kuominchün from Peking [April 15, 1926]; and (3) the period from the Kuominchün's withdrawal to the meeting of Chang [Tso-lin] and Wu [P'ei-fu] [June 28, 1926].

The first period witnessed the shaking of the political power of the militarists. During this period, the Mukden Clique was defeated, the Anhwei Clique was weak, and the Chihli Clique had yet to rise. The imperialists were unable to control the various militarist cliques and revealed unusual confusion. The government of Tuan [Ch'i-jui] had secret connections with the Kuominchün and Wu P'ei-fu showed good will toward the National Government. It appeared that the Kuomintang in the South and the Kuominchün in the North might join together to seize political power throughout the country and establish a relatively Red government.

During this period, our Party's policy was to make full use of the military action of Sun Ch'uan-fang against Mukden. We advanced the slogan, "Extend the nature of the war!" explaining that the anti-Mukden war should be a "war for the freedom of the people," and that it should enlist all revolutionary forces under its banner. This propaganda had a great effect on the masses and penetrated the troops of the militarists. Hence, the rebellion of Kuo Sung-ling. We also used such slogans as "Oppose the pro-Parliament movement of the Chihli Clique" and "Caution against alliance between the Mukden and Chihli Cliques," as we foresaw that the

Chihli Clique would certainly be pro-Parliament should it come to power, and that if the Mukden Clique were defeated, it would appease and join the Chihli Clique to establish a militarist regime. As we look back now, there was not a single mistake in our past policy.

During the Second period [December 24, 1925 to April 15, 1926], the imperialists attempted to suppress this high revolutionary tide by the formation of a military anti-Red united front of Britain, Japan, Wu P'ei-fu, and Chang Tso-lin and by the dissemination of anti-Red propaganda among the masses.

During this period, our Party's primary policy was destruction of the anti-Red united front. We proposed to set up a temporary "grey" government at Peking to absorb elements of both the Anhwei and Chihli cliques for the sole purpose of opposing Mukden. Before this policy could be executed, however, Wu P'ei-fu started [63] launching attacks on Honan from Hankow. We then proposed that Kwangtung [the National Government] should send forces to suppress Wu. Again, our policy could not be carried out. The reason was that our Party's political strength was not very great. Hence, despite good political strategy, we were not able to influence the Kuomintang and the Kuominchün to put it into effect.

The most important phenomena of the third period [April 15, 1926 to June 28, 1926] were the stabilization of militarist political regimes on the one hand and, on the other, the intensification of secret rivalry among the British, the Japanese, Chang, and Wu. At the time, the National Government in Kwangtung mobilized its forces for the Northern Expedition. Although secret conflict among Britain, Japan, Chang, and Wu was serious, Mukden and Chihli did not let this conflict lead to an open break because the Kuominchün was still a strong force.

During this period, our policy in the North was alliance with Mukden against Chihli and, in the South, aid to Hunan against Wu P'ei-fu.

Had the Northern anti-Red army (Mukden-Chihli-Shansi) cooperated and jointly attacked the Kuominchün, the latter would have found it difficult to survive. However, due to lack of sincere cooperation among them, each having its own selfish motives, the Kuominchün was able to avoid collapse. As long as relations between Mukden and Chihli remain unchanged, the Kuominchün will be capable only of defense. It will not be able to take the offensive.

In the South, the dispatch of the forces of the National Government signifies nothing more than a defensive war against the anti-Red army's penetration into Hunan and Kwangtung. It does not signify a real revolutionary Northern Expedition.

The present stabilization of militarist political regimes can be maintained temporarily in view of the static condition of the Kuominchün. Such stabilization, however, definitely cannot last.

2. <u>Imperialist policy toward China</u>.—The two most powerful imperialist countries are Britain and Japan. At present their one
common objective is suppression of the Reds in the North and
South. They differ, however, in their attitude toward the Tariff
Conference. Wanting increased customs revenues to be applied to
the reorganization of the Nishihara loans, Japan advocates continuation of the Conference. The British, fearing an increase would
affect the importation of British goods into China, want to delay
64] the Conference. The British are militarily more ambitious, attempting to annex all of China. The Japanese, on the other hand, concentrate their attention on the Three Eastern Provinces, advancing
when they can. They are not as boastful as the British.

Aside from the British and Japanese, the United States' imperialist policies in China are the most important. On the surface, it may
appear as if the Americans are trying to help the Chinese resist
the fearsome imperialist aggression of Britain and Japan by assisting Chinese capitalists in their efforts for peaceful industrial
development and by opposing the Tariff Conference, which cannot
satisfy the hopes of the Chinese people. Their actual objective,
however, is to take the place of the British and Japanese by utilizing the huge capital provided by the Dawes plan.

In coping with these imperialist policies, we emphasize opposition to Britain first, followed by opposition to Japan and then to
the United States. British influence in China is deeply rooted and
extends over great areas; Japanese influence is confined to a
limited sphere; the Americans have no definite sphere at all. It is
therefore our policy to utilize their differences and conflicts with
a view to destroying their alliance.

3. <u>The attitude of various social forces with regard to the National Revolution</u>.—In the development of the National Revolution
we must know the various social forces and their general trend.
The social forces in China today may be divided into the following
four categories:

The first is the anti-Red movement of the militarists, compradors, bureaucrats, and the old and new gentry (new gentry such as
college professors), a counterrevolutionary force allied with imperialist power.

The second is the revolutionary movement of the workers, peasants, and students. This is a new revolutionary force, counter-
acting the old reactionary force of the first category.

The third is the resistance movement of middle and petty merchants (such as resistance against taxes and levies).

65] The fourth is the reform movement of the bourgeoisie. The bourgeoisie have not completely abandoned comprador ideas. Bourgeois differentiation, however, will daily increase in the wake of
industrial development. The difference of attitude towards imperial-

ism between the bourgeoisie and the comprador class is this: One
wants conditional cooperation with imperialism, the other uncon-
ditional cooperation. In other words, the former [the bourgeoisie]
would cooperate with imperialism in return for certain concessions. The Chinese bourgeoisie find it difficult to develop independently since imperialism does not permit them to do so.

At this time, the bourgeoisie are a force which cannot be overlooked. In the future, however, they will be a reactionary obstacle.

Of the above four categories, which force should we employ to
further the revolutionary cause? The answer is, of course, the
second category, comprising workers, peasants, and students,
which is the only revolutionary force. The middle and petty merchants of the third category are economically oppressed by imperialism and by vexatious levies and excessive taxes. They feel
keenly the need for revolution and do not oppose it. The workers
and peasants must attempt to win over these groups in order to
avoid isolation.

The bourgeoisie of the fourth category suffer from foreign capitalist exploitation of China through foreign capital and importation
of goods. There is no escape from this oppression save by revolution. The bourgeoisie suffer also from vexatious levies and excessive taxes and the devastation of militarist wars. Thus, theoretically, they should be more revolutionary than the petty bourgeoisie.
In reality, however, the opposite is true.

First, the Chinese bourgeoisie do not acquire capital by accumu-
lating it from their own country. Capital comes from foreign
sources (e.g., comprador loans) or from exorbitant land rents. The
bourgeoisie cannot therefore sever their connections with imperialism. Secondly, seeing the development of the proletariat, the
bourgeoisie desire a few concessions from imperialism; on
the other hand, they fear to enhance the revolutionary strength
of the proletariat. Consequently they are in a dilemma between
advance and retreat and, being irresolute, do not go forward.

There are two alternatives for the bourgeoisie. One is to be
completely nonrevolutionary and to compromise with imperialism.
The other is to take into their own hands the revolutionary movement and prevent the proletariat from assuming revolutionary leadership. In the latter case, they would seek concessions from imperialism on the one hand and, on the other, suppress the proletariat and prevent proletarian action. Once concessions are secured
from imperialism, the bourgeoisie would then become nonrevolutionary. We know that the first path is not feasible and that the
[66] Chinese bourgeoisie are now taking the second road.

The question, then, is: Do we want the bourgeoisie to continue to
join us in the Revolution? Our answer is that for the time being
we must still utilize the bourgeoisie. The reason is that if attacked

too severely, the bourgeoisie would be drawn completely into the imperialist camp. This would further strengthen the enemy at the cost of the Revolution.

Our attitude toward the bourgeoisie should differ from our attitude toward the people of the first category—the militarists, compradors, bureaucrats, and the new and old gentry. We want thoroughly to eliminate the latter and struggle against the former for revolutionary leadership. The bourgeoisie have actually acquired for themselves considerable force; the May Thirtieth Movement in Shanghai was in reality led by the General Chamber of Commerce and not the General Labor Union (with reference to the later stage). The backward workers, filled with patriarchal ideas, are easily drawn into the ranks of the bourgeoisie. This is even truer of the petty bourgeoisie. We should build up the force of the workers and peasants, get hold of the petty merchants, and force the bourgeoisie to the Left.

4. Dissensions within the Kuomintang.—Dissensions within the Kuomintang reflect the forces of the above-mentioned four categories: The reactionary Right (Feng Tzu-yü, Ma Su, Sun Fo, Ku Ying-fen, etc.) represents the first category; the Communists represent the second category; the Left (Wang Ching-wei, Kan Nai-kuang, etc.) represents the third category; and the new Right (that is, the Center, Tai Chi-t'ao, Chiang Kai-shek, etc.) represents the fourth category. Our policy toward the Kuomintang is therefore the same as our policy toward the various classes in the country. We unite with the Left and force the Center to attack the reactionary Right. At the same time, we guard against the rise of the Center and force it to turn left against the Right. The victory of the National Revolution will be assured if our tactics of united front are successfully carried out.

5. The future of the national revolutionary movement.—As for the future of the national revolutionary movement, we foresee two courses: (1) The activation of the bourgeoisie by the petty bourgeoisie under the leadership of the workers and peasants to establish national capitalism by revolution; (2) The control of the petty bourgeoisie by the comprador-bourgeoisie and compromise between the comprador-bourgeoisie and imperialism, wiping out the revolutionary movement and realizing the Dawes Plan for capitalist aggression.

At the moment, it is even possible that a segment of labor would lean to the Right. The first course is revolutionary; the second tragic. Our duty therefore is to expand and strengthen the force of the workers and peasants, hold the petty bourgeoisie, and fight the big bourgeoisie for leadership of the national movement. We would be doomed to certain failure should the petty bourgeoisie be taken over by the big bourgeoisie for the reform movement. We can clearly see the Revolution's future. If we want to lead the Revolution, we must first have good Party organization. Otherwise, not only will we fail to hold the petty bourgeoisie, we may not even be able properly to organize the workers and peasants, much less expect to lead the Revolution.

As for the present condition of our Party, it may be true that our Party's nationwide propaganda has been effective. The actual strength of our Party, however, is far from enough to win control of the entire petty bourgeoisie of the country and to lead the Revolution. Greater efforts are needed in our work.

6. The development and work of the Party during the nine months' period. —Viewing the Party's development in the past nine months from the favorable side, we note the following: (1) Membership has increased threefold; (2) While we have not been able to exert complete control of the petty bourgeoisie organizationally, we have been able more or less to lead the mass movement throughout the country, particularly at such places as Peking, Shanghai, Canton, and Hunan; (3) The Party's influence during the country's political upheavals has been very great; for each political crisis, our slogans and policies have been able to guide the demands of the masses; (4) The labor movement in Shanghai, Tientsin, Tangshan, and Hunan enjoys a firmer foundation than in the past. The Shang-
[68] hai labor movement, in particular, has been gradually strengthened. Despite severe reactionary oppression, the foundation of the labor movement has not been completely destroyed at Tangshan and Tientsin.

It is clear from the above that our Party has developed. Many weaknesses, however, have been found in the process of development.

a) Although Party membership has increased in quantity, its quality has actually deteriorated. This may be witnessed from several angles.

(1) Our comrades lack theoretical and practical experience; they lack a definite revolutionary philosophy of life.
(2) Responsible workers among our comrades have a tendency to be mere employees; they lack the former spirit of hard struggle.
(3) A certain number of our comrades have a tendency toward corruption (there have been cases of squeeze and inaccurate accounting).

b) Party headquarters of all levels, from the CC down to Party cells, lack sufficient capacity for leadership and training.

c) The organization of Party cells is unhealthy. (However, the fact that we are now able to attend to the setting up of Party cells is itself an encouraging sign.)

d) There is a serious lack of theoretical propaganda. Our work

of agitation among the masses is not practical and fails to penetrate the masses.

e) The labor movement has become bureaucratic and lacks mass
substance. An exception is the Shanghai General Labor Union, which
is actually turning to the masses.

f) The peasant movement has developed the disease of left devia-
tion everywhere. Either the slogans are extreme or action is excessively Left-inclined. Consequently, the peasants themselves
often suffer great damage before the enemy has been hit.

In short, the present national political situation is characterized
by stabilization of the political power of the militarists. This definitely cannot last, however. The revolutionary movement will con-
69] tinue to develop. Whether the Revolution is to be led by the bourgeoisie or the proletariat depends entirely on whether the proletariat's party is well organized. We must have the organization of a
Bolshevik Party and be guided by the principles of Leninism in
order to seize leadership of the National Revolution.

DOCUMENT 27

Document 27 has been translated from the original Chinese text of the resolutions on relations between the Kuomintang and the Chinese Communist Party adopted at the Second Enlarged Plenum of the Chinese Communist Central Committee held from July 12 to July 18, 1926. The resolutions are published in Su-lien yin-mou..., III, "KCT," pp. 69-73.

RESOLUTIONS ON RELATIONS BETWEEN THE CHINESE COMMUNIST PARTY AND THE KUOMINTANG

[69] 1. Such events as the coup d'état in Canton on March 20, the meeting of the KMT Central [Executive] Committee on May 15, and the measures for dealing with Communists proposed by the Whampoa Academy on June 7 are part of a persistent anti-Communist offensive. The armed Center is now in power in Kwangtung; the anti-Red movement of the Right Wing prevails throughout the country. They are all taking the offensive against the Communist Party. Changes in the objective political situation (the Kuominchün's defeat and retreat to the North, the counter-revolutionary victory of the imperialists and militarists, Wu P'ei-fu's return to the political arena and conspiracy with the British, Japan's support of Chang Tso-lin and opposition to Soviet Russia on the pretext of the Chinese Eastern Railway incident, etc.) are of course partly responsible in making such attacks possible. Such attacks, however, are due also to errors committed by our Party.

We should launch a propaganda drive from the CC down to Party cells to explain that the present attacks on us by the reactionary Right and a segment of the Kuomintang Center are in harmony with, and in response to, the anti-Red movement of the imperialists and militarists and are in reality counterrevolutionary actions. Furthermore, we should also analyze the causes that have enabled the reactionary Right and Center to make use of the present political situation so readily for attacking us and to formulate plans for the removal of such causes.

2. One of the chief reasons the Kuomintang Right and even the Kuomintang Center were able to attack us easily and to demand that we withdraw from the Kuomintang is the incorrect formula we previously employed in directing the Kuomintang. Under that [70] formula, the Left was not able to participate in Party activities and in the fight against the Right. We ourselves created the situation of

a KMT-KCT struggle which overshadows what is actually a struggle between the Left and Right. At the same time, since we had caused the Left to crystallize politically and organizationally, the development of the Kuomintang was naturally hindered. It was not able fully to absorb the revolutionary intellectuals and the urban petty bourgeoisie. The Right and Center, however, fully utilized the opportunity and exerted their influence over these elements.

We have failed to execute the resolutions of the Enlarged Conference of last October on the necessity for our local Party headquarters to act with even greater independence and to ally with the Left against the Right in the ideological and organizational struggle. Hence, we have failed to lay a firm foundation among the masses (unions, peasant associations, student federations, and so on). Furthermore, we failed to utilize the revolutionary force of the masses to oppose the offensives of the Right and the armed Center following the deterioration of the political situation in the North.

3. The decisions regarding the Kuomintang adopted by the Enlarged Conference of the Central Committee last year are: (1) We stay within the Kuomintang and oppose the Right, but avoid taking the place of the Left ourselves; and (2) We try to achieve more political independence for our own Party. These resolutions were adopted because we recognized that the Kuomintang is a political party representing the alliance of various social forces (revolutionary intellectuals, the middle, industrial, and commercial national bourgeoisie, handicraft and small-enterprise petty bourgeoisie, peasants, and workers). We still recognized the development of the Kuomintang and our participation in directing the Kuomintang's work as prerequisites to a victorious Chinese Revolution.

Our policy in the National Revolution should be more precisely defined. We should make further efforts to achieve our own political independence. We should establish our own force among the workers and peasants in order to exert political influence over the revolutionary masses. We should organize the revolutionary tide of the 71] petty bourgeoisie and concentrate it within the Kuomintang to consolidate the Left Wing. We should bring the influence of the revolutionary force of the masses of workers and peasants to bear on the Kuomintang. We thus unite with the Kuomintang Left in a strong alliance and fight the bourgeoisie for the power of directing the national movement. Only thus can we insure seizure of leadership of the National Revolution by the proletariat's party. Hence, our policy within the Kuomintang at this time is: to expand the Left Wing and cooperate with it closely in order to deal with the Center and openly counterattack against the reactionary Right.

If some comrades hold that the KCT should completely divorce itself from organizational relationship with the Kuomintang and abolish this party which represents the alliance of all classes in the belief that the KCT is already capable of independently leading the proletariat and inducing other oppressed elements to follow it to finish the bourgeois democratic revolution, then they are completely wrong. Their view betrays absolute misunderstanding of the long-range view of the Chinese Revolution for national liberation. The reasoning behind the theory of immediate separation of the KCT from organizational relationship with the Kuomintang, to be followed by mere cooperation with that party, is the same as that held by the KMT Right Wing and New Right Wing (Center) in demanding Communist withdrawal from the KMT. This tendency reflects the bourgeoisie's increasingly apparent desire in the past year to seize leadership of the national movement.

If some comrades still hold that Communists should monopolize Kuomintang organs and develop independently the KMT's organization and the work of [KMT] Party headquarters, then the experience in Kwangtung can prove this view to be erroneous also. The reason is that it is not suited to the KMT's present organizational form and social foundation. Communist monopoly of the Kuomintang would reduce that party to a narrow organization through excessive concentration of power. The result would then be the diminution and loss of the strength of the great masses of the revolutionary petty bourgeoisie through dispersion and desertion.

Although these two views are diametrically opposed to each other, they are equally incorrect in terms of policy. They are equally [72] dangerous to the Chinese liberation movement, with the end result of the separation of the Chinese Communist Party and the proletariat from the great masses of the urban and rural petty bourgeoisie who would, to all practical purposes, fall under the direction of the big bourgeoisie.

4. The current erroneous tendencies within our Party are due in part to the recent extremely complicated objective situation. The respective crystallization of the proletariat and the bourgeoisie during the past year is naturally reflected in the Kuomintang. This is seen in the effect on the Center and Left of the conflict between Communists and the Right. Hence, it is more than ever essential for our Party to have a clearer long-range view of the development of the National Revolution and a more definite policy toward the Kuomintang. It is also important that the Central Committee's view of KMT-KCT relations be well understood by Party members and the masses so that they can formulate correct viewpoints.

Although this (July, 1926) Enlarged Conference of the Central Committee considers the solving of the problem of KMT-KCT organizational relationship as a question for the next Congress, the following decisions should take effect at once:

a) Carry out the resolutions adopted by the Enlarged Conference of last October for independent action by our Party in Kwangtung and elsewhere.

b) Positively develop the Kuomintang Left and correct our previous mistake of tying down the Left, thereby obstructing its full participation in Party work and in the fight against the Right.

c) Develop positively the Left's mass organizations outside the Party, particularly among the petty bourgeoisie (political clubs, etc.). Expand the foundation of the Kuomintang through these social organizations.

d) Convince the Kuomintang Left that the KMT organization cannot be one in which political power is concentrated in one class. The KMT should not have excessively rigid regulations and disci-
[73] pline. Due to the immediate necessity of taking in more members from the petty bourgeoisie and the revolutionary masses, the organizational system of the Kuomintang should be more flexible. To illustrate, the Kuomintang at lower levels may at least assume the characteristics of political clubs in order to be close to the masses. It is not necessary to stick to rigid and self-binding regulations. Furthermore, social organizations with revolutionary tendencies should be allowed to join the Party as a unit. In this way, the Koumintang would become a Party of the great masses.

e) Work together with the Left for a more realistic, daily struggle against the Right, to expose its compromises and treachery against the country and the people. Only thus can the center be alienated from the Right.

5. Our most pressing task with reference to the Kuomintang at this time is the anti-Right struggle. We naturally should still lend our active support to the National Government and the Kuomintang CEC in their current struggle against counterrevolutionary forces within and without Kwangtung even though they are directed by the Center. At the same time, we should maintain our own policy of supporting the interests of the laboring masses and use this policy as the basic condition of our aid to the KMT and the National Government.

PART V

THE CHINESE COMMUNIST PARTY'S POLICIES
IN THE MASS MOVEMENT, JULY, 1926

At the Second Enlarged Plenum held in Shanghai between July 12 and 18, 1926, the Central Committee of the Chinese Communist Party adopted a comprehensive set of resolutions on the labor movement, the peasant movement, the Red Spears movement, the merchant movement, the women's movement, the student movement, the relief movement, and the "military movement." The resolutions outline the CC's application of the united-front strategy to the mass movement. They are the Party's blueprints for executing among various groups and classes the basic Communist policy of simultaneously supporting the national revolutionary movement and strengthening the Communist Party's independent position among the masses.

In the resolutions on the peasant movement, the CC pointed out means of promoting a united front of all classes and groups in the National Revolution to over-throw imperialism and militarism. These include the calling of joint conferences of workers, peasants, and merchants, and conferences of representatives of all circles; the organization of such groups as associations to support the national assembly and local peace-preservation committees [Doc. 29, p. 101]. The relief movement, the CC declared, was a particularly effective device, since it could directly unite all classes and parties and indirectly arouse the sympathy and participation of the masses [Doc. 34, p. 117].

The policy of forming a united front of all mass movements was supplemented by Communist attempts to establish united fronts within certain groups: labor, students, women, and the Red Spears, peasant organizations active especially in the provinces of Honan, Shangtung, and Chihli. In each case, the CC spelled out the reasons for a united front, how Communists should work in it, and what the Party hoped to achieve thereby.

According to the CC, a student united front was necessary in order to centralize all available strength, so that the students could become an organized, powerful force in the National Revolution. The CC therefore called for the unification of student federations to achieve unity of action. Communists were instructed to raise only those slogans and demands which were acceptable to the majority of students. The CC cautioned Communists against monopolizing positions in student federations; together with Left KMT students, they were ordered to hold no more than a majority of such posts. The CC reminded them to maintain at all times a friendly attitude in order to avoid unpleasant feelings on the part of nonpartisans. They were told to refrain from lightly branding anyone as reactionary or counterrevolutionary [Doc. 33, pp. 112-14].

While working for unity of action in the student movement, however, Communists were not to seek unity of ideology. On the contrary, they were ordered to disseminate propaganda for their own revolutionary doctrines and policies in order to influence the masses of students to the Left. The CC declared simply: "It is necessary to influence the thinking of the masses of students in order to obtain political leadership." The CC explicitly defined the Communist objective in cooperating with other groups. Communist students should invite the cooperation of Right Kuomintang students, Christian students, and members of the Kuo-chia chu-i clique,1 but only in order to expose the incompetence of their leaders and encourage them toward the Left [Doc. 33, pp. 113-14].

Similar instructions were given in the resolutions on the Red Spears movement. Although the CC declared that the Red Spears Associations were full of superstitious and destructive tendencies, it called upon Communists to organize and strengthen the Red Spears as weapons against Wu P'ei-fu and Chang Tsung-ch'ang. Thus, a united front of all Red Spears groups, including those with "bandit characteristics," was justified as an auxiliary force for the National Revolution. The CC outlined tactics for seizure of control. Communists working in Red Spears Associations were to set up a secret central communications organ for all Red Spears groups. They were to man the important positions in this organ, which would later be transformed into a powerful directing organ [Doc. 30, pp. 106-7].

The CC advocated a different type of united front in the merchant movement, with the objective of splitting, rather than uniting, the various groups. Communists were instructed to organize middle and petty merchants in merchant associations and similar organs for the purpose of struggling against the "compromising and traitorous" actions of compradors and big merchants. The duty of Communists, the CC declared, was to steer the middle and petty merchants toward the Kuomintang Left Wing [Doc. 31, p. 109]. The resolutions thus mirror the Party's policy toward the Kuomintang: alliance with the Kuomintang Left (petty bourgeoisie) against the Kuomintang New Right Wing (bourgeoisie).

Flexibility was an outstanding characteristic of the Communist approach to mass organization. The resolutions reveal a shrewd ability to utilize varying circumstances to infiltrate groups where Communist influence was weak, or to strengthen the Party's leadership where its position had already been established.

Wherever the Kuomintang Left Wing had already gained influence among the merchants, the CC said, it was advisable for it to direct their organizations and activities. The CC added, however, that whenever there were Communists in merchant associations, Communist Party fractions should be organized to execute the Party's policies [Doc. 31, p. 109]. In short, where it was not possible or profitable for Communists directly to organize the masses, the task was to be performed indirectly or in the name of other groups. Communists working in the women's movement, for instance, were to try to reach the masses themselves while working through the Kuomintang Woman's Department, women's associations, and federations of women of all circles [Doc. 32, p. 110].

Among certain groups, Communists were instructed not to conduct their activities in the name of any political party. This was particularly the case in the peasant movement. The CC declared that peasant associations should not reflect the color of any particular political party or bear a distinctive class color. According to the CC, it was even unnecessary to bring up the peasantry as a class [Doc. 29, pp. 98-99, 103].

The CC criticized excessive emphasis on organizational form. In organizing workers, it said, it was unnecessary to stick to labor unions. Wherever unions were illegal, all forms and names, such as those of athletic associations and clubs, should be utilized for organizational purposes. Communists were reminded that labor organizations would become dead and mechanical if organizational rules were too strictly adhered to [Doc. 28, p. 91]. Similarly, in the resolutions on the peasant movement, the CC asserted that organization of the peasantry should not be confined to peasant associations, but that existing rural groups should be utilized. These organs should be allowed to join Communist-organized hsien peasant associations, which would control and absorb them as far as possible [Doc. 29, pp. 98-99].

Utilization of local resources characterized the Communist attitude. The CC instructed Communists to use village school teachers and urban workers and students returning to the villages on vacation to begin organizational work among the peasantry. The CC declared that the peasants' fairy tales and legends, adapted to Party propaganda, should be employed. It ordered unusual tolerance on the part of Communist organizers. They were told not to oppose the superstitions and clan relationships to the peasantry. They were in fact instructed to follow such superstitions themselves for the time being in order to develop Party work. The CC declared: "Persons working in the peasant movement must first do as the peasants do in speech and action. Their living conditions and clothing must also be similar to those of the peasants. Only thus can they gain close contact with and disseminate propaganda among the peasants." [Doc. 29, pp. 99-100, 103-4].

The need to get close to the lowest level of the masses is a dominating theme throughout the CC's resolutions. Getting hold of the masses, Communists were repeatedly reminded, did not mean mere control of organizations. They were warned against the evils of bureaucratism as manifested in excessive attention to organizational form and emphasis on high-level work. As an antidote to such evils in the labor movement, for instance, the CC stressed attention to work in low-level labor organs [Doc. 28, p. 91].

By the summer of 1926, the Communist Party was entrenched in the position of leadership of the labor and peasant movements. According to a manifesto issued by the Second Enlarged Plenum, the Party had succeeded in organizing a total of 1,200,000 workers and 800,000 peasants.[2] It was the desire to preserve the opportunity to strengthen the Communist position among the masses while supporting the national revolutionary movement which contributed to the decision to retain membership in the Kuomintang. As the author of the "Brief History" points out, the severing of relations with the Kuomintang would result in the alienation of the Communist Party from the masses through the loss of opportunities to carry on work among them [Doc. 1, p. 45]. However, the preponderant Communist strength among organized labor and peasantry became an increasingly serious source of friction between "pure" Kuomintang members and Communists. The Communist Party was thus confronted with a difficult dilemma, expressed in simple terms in the CC's resolutions on the labor movement. Fear of a split in the united front, the CC stated, would result in neglect of labor's interests. Conversely, excessively radical demands and slogans would obstruct the united front [Doc. 28, p. 89].

Since the overriding Communist policy was continuation of the entente with the Kuomintang, the Central Committee sought to resolve the dilemma by curbing the mass movement wherever it showed signs of excessive radicalism.

This approach was most apparent in the Party's peasant policy. In the political report to the Second Enlarged Plenum, the CC declared that the peasant movement had developed the disease of left deviationism everywhere. Either the slogans were extreme or action was excessively Left-inclined. Thus, the peasants themselves had suffered greatly before the enemy had been hit [Doc. 26, p. 68]. To counteract this tendency, the CC formulated the policy of the agrarian united front, to be composed of peasant self-cultivators, hired farm laborers, tenant farmers and small and middle landlords to struggle against reactionary big landlords, the bad gentry, and local bullies. The CC called for neutralization of big landlords who were not actively engaged in oppressing the peasantry [Doc. 29, pp. 99-100].

The agrarian united front was thus unlike the united fronts in other groups, since it allied one class with certain elements of another class by differentiation of the latter. While the Party had previously classified all landlords as oppressors of the peasantry,[3] in July, 1926, it differentiated landlords according to the size of their holdings and their conduct toward the peasantry. Opposition was thereby restricted to reactionary big landlords. Bandits were similarly differentiated. The CC called for opposition to those bandits who oppressed the peasantry, and neutralization of those who did not [Doc. 29, 102].

Caution likewise characterized Communist policy toward the Christian Church. The CC declared that it was necessry to carry out propaganda against the Church as the vanguard of imperialism. However, the CC warned that it was imperative not to create opportunities of actual conflict with the Church. This attitude was the only one possible, the CC explained, because the Church was backed by imperialist and militarist power. Communists were ordered, however, to stir up popular sentiment against the Church in the event of any obviously aggressive act on its part [Doc. 29, pp. 101-102].

In addition to limiting the targets of peasant opposition, the CC took preventive measures against the adoption of militant tactics by the peasantry. This approach is illustrated by the CC's policy toward the min-t'uan (People's Corps). The CC stated that the min-t'uan was an instrument used by landlords, bad gentry, and local bullies to oppress the peasantry. However, it was impossible to hope that the min-t'uan could be destroyed. Thus, the CC's objective was not the overthrow of the min-t'uan, but the tansfer of leadership of the min-t'uan from the bad gentry to the honest gentry. To this end, Communists were instructed to disseminate propaganda among min-t'uan members, urging them not to cooperate with the bad gentry, and to encourage the election of min-t'uan chiefs at peasant assemblies [Doc. 29, p. 100].

While the CC recognized the necessity of armed self-defense by the peasants, it cautioned against the danger of exceeding its limits. Peasant self-defense corps must not become permanent organizations, said the CC, for fear of possible conflict with other groups, such as landlords, the min-t'uan, and local garrisons. The CC warned that the peasantry, once armed, could easily exceed the limits imposed by the objective situation because of their total lack of organization and training [Doc. 29, p. 102]. Similarly, the CC declared that while the Red Spears should participate in local government, under no circumstances should they be allowed to seize local political power [Doc. 30, p. 107].

Fear of disrupting the entente with the Kuomintang likewise underlies the CC's resolutions on the "military movement." The CC chastised Communists for not understanding the meaning of systematic preparations for armed uprisings, for failing to secure close contact with low-ranking officers and the masses of soldiers, and for emphasizing only the maneuvering of high-ranking officers. Yet it refrained from organizing Communist cells in revolutionary armies (the National Revolutionary Army and the Kuominchün), although it decided to organize cells in reactionary militarist armies. The CC declared in fact that the duty of Communists in revolutionary armies was to see that they became gradually more consolidated and revolutionary; they must studiously avoid premature differentiation of the revolutionary armies [Doc. 35, pp. 120-21].

Despite the CC's cautious policies, the dilemma which it recognized so clearly grew more pressing during the ensuing months, as the Northern Expedition extended the Kuomintang's authority from Kwangtung to the Yangtze valley. The task of reconciling the expansion and increasing militancy of the mass movement with the political necessity of remaining within the KMT was to become one of the most difficult problems confronting the Chinese Communist leadership.

DOCUMENT 28

Document 28 has been translated from the original Chinese text of the resolutions on the labor movement adopted by the Central Committee of the Chinese Communist Party at the Second Enlarged Plenum in Shanghai, July 12 to July 18, 1926. See Su-lien yin-mou..., III, "KCT," pp. 87-96.

RESOLUTIONS ON THE LABOR MOVEMENT

[87]   1. Following the May Thirtieth Movement, the workers have proved that they are the principal force in the national anti-imperialist movement. With the rising angry revolutionary tide, they have greatly developed class and national consciousness and initial organizational ability. Despite repeated slaughter and destruction by the imperialists and militarists, the workers have unceasingly carried on resistance and have repeatedly participated in an organized fashion in the struggle against reactionary militarists in Kwangtung and the Mukden militarists in the North. This proves the great advance in the workers' consciousness.

Militarist strife and oppression, natural calamities, and loose trade restrictions recently combined to bring about a national economic crisis, as is evident in the depreciation of paper money, the forced circulation of military notes, the soaring prices of rice and other commodities, and the arrears in government salaries, etc. The workers, whose real wages have dropped, have been hard hit. Hence, a wave of economic strikes has been spreading everywhere. Even the unorganized silk workers and handicraftsmen held determined strikes.

The strike wave will daily grow stronger as the economic crisis
[88] worsens. The workers' hard-pressed condition can lead only to revolution. On the other hand, weakly organized strikes are easily suppressed by the imperialists, militarists, and Chinese and foreign capitalists. We must do our utmost not to lose any opportunity for leadership in resisting the enemy, so that the movement of economic strikes will ultimately strengthen the force of the Chinese proletariat.

2. From its inception to the present day, the Chinese labor movement has been under the direction of our Party. This fact was reflected most strongly during the May Thirtieth strikes in Canton and Shanghai. Therefore, with reference to the labor movement, our Party's problem is not whether or not the Party should maintain close relations with labor unions, but how to enable our

Party at all levels to guide and train, through the form of unions, the broad masses of workers.

a) In guiding the labor movement, our Party does not aim at the monopoly of labor unions but the ability continuously to bring up practical political and economic demands for the workers and the capacity of Party members to struggle for their benefit and interests.

b) We exert our influence over the masses of workers through our Party cells in factories. Because Party cells in factories are organizations closest to the masses, they must instantly rise to struggle on behalf of workers as a whole in the event of any factory incident affecting the welfare of workers. (It is necessary to abide by the form of going through the union.) Thus, we organize and train workers on the one hand and, on the other, develop the consciousness of the masses of workers and guide their participation in the work of unions by utilizing these concrete day-by-day struggles. Unions are the schools of communism: we should further utilize the work of unions and day-by-day struggles to educate the masses of workers. In this way, we should be able to progress from the former monopoly of union work by our Party fractions to a labor movement in which the masses of our Party members exert an influence over the workers.

[89]   3. The present important duty of Chinese workers is to lead the national struggle for liberation. The united front against imperialism and militarism set up by the unions and by the mass organizations of other classes is the only strategy for realizing this duty. Hence, labor unions should issue statements of policy from time to time on the common interests of the people of all classes and lead the masses of workers to actual participation in the national revolutionary movement.

Weaknesses are often likely to develop in carrying out this policy. Either labor's interests are overlooked for fear of splitting the united front, or the slogans and demands of class struggle are extreme, thus obstructing the united front. We must realize that the firmer the unity of labor, the stronger the force of the united front. The collective strength of labor must be developed gradually in class struggle. Hence, neglect of the interests of labor results not only in the danger of its alienation from us, but shakes the foundation of the United front. At the same time, extreme slogans and demands of class struggle can easily give the bourgeoisie good propaganda material in order to separate and isolate labor.

There is a third weakness. In the execution of our policy, too much emphasis has been laid on superficial and abstract national political slogans and demands which cannot be applied to practical daily struggles. This weakness, which has become very widespread, accounts for the failure of our policy to produce practical action, with the exception of Shanghai during the days of the May Thirtieth Movement and Kwangtung at the present time. To realize our policy, we should begin with the acute problems of daily life of the masses, that is, local political and economic problems, such as exorbitant taxes and irregular levies, the price of rice, and the disturbance caused by armies. It is not sufficient for labor unions merely to issue a few prolamations in executing our policy. Labor should be the nucleus to call forth people of all classes to participate in practical resistance movements so that the united front may penetrate the masses and become gradually strengthened.

[90]   4. All central and local Party publications should truthfully publish articles and news on the labor movement. (Although several resolutions have been passed on this subject, they have not been carried out in earnest.) In the past, our Party's regular periodicals have had one common defect. Either the writing was too complicated and difficult or the discussions were abstract and vague, not based on reality. Articles contributed by workers were very seldom published. There has been some improvement recently, but the publications are still far from genuinely popular. Past experience tells us that only illustrated papers can exert wide influence among the masses of workers. Hereafter, Party headquarters of all levels should stress publication of pictorial papers for workers. Pictorial sections should also be inserted in all our other publications.

5. In the one year since its establishment at the second National Labor Conference, the All-China Federation of Labor has gained the confidence of Canton labor unions, particularly workers of the Canton and Hongkong strike. The Federation has not been able, however, to exert influence over workers throughout the country. Although the third [National] Labor Conference held on "May First" this year failed to produce great influence among the masses of workers throughout the country, it was very significant in terms of education and propaganda. The best sign is that all labor unions in the country which have masses have joined the Federation (with the exception of a minority of Canton labor unions). The directing organ of the Federation is also quite healthy.

In the nearest future, attention should be directed to the work of the Shanghai office of the Federation. First, close organizational relationships should be developed with labor unions throughout the country. Secondly, a regular periodical should be published in Shanghai to lead the national labor movement. Thirdly, a system of rotating inspectors should be established for the direction of workers' struggles everywhere. If the highest directing organ of the Federation can be established in the North to unify the national labor movement, the CC's committee on the Labor Movement should direct its attention to guiding and utilizing this organ of the Federation.

[91]   6. It is a good thing to have many high-level organs to unify the
labor movement. At the same time, however, our labor movement
is faced with the danger of bureaucratism. We should try to adapt
labor unions to the masses, that is to say, we should pay attention
to lower-level labor union organizations. We have made two mistakes in the past in union organization: excessive emphasis on
bureaucratic forms of organization, and failure correctly to utilize
basic organizations [cells], although we did pay attention to them.

Wherever union organization is illegal, the basic organizations
need not stick to the name or formal organization of labor unions.
We should employ all types of organizations and names to organize
workers (such as schools, clubs, dining-halls, hospitals, music
and athletic associations, cooperatives, and boxing clubs). Such
organizations require only two conditions: the masses, although
the number may be small, and class [nature]. Our past error in
utilizing basic organizations in labor unions (Party cells or small
units in factory departments) is excessive emphasis on form and
strict, almost mechanical, [organization].

In fact, the main significance of the basic organization is its being the unit of activity of the masses of workers. Basic organizations should stress not uniformity of form but actual capacity to
be the nucleus of the masses and, further, to be the active unit in
absorbing workers and organizing unions. If basic organizations
are too strict, they will become dead and mechanical and the significance and function of Party cells or small units of factories
would be lost. (For example, a certain department in a factory has
100 workers, 20 of whom are members of the union. In case of
mistreatment or oppression of any one of the workers by either
the factory manager or foreman, the basic organization of the 20
union members should at once assemble all the 100 workers to a
meeting for discussion and decision on a suitable line of action to
oppose this particular incident of oppression. Should it be impossible to hold a meeting, the union members should proceed with
the work of propaganda and agitation both inside and outside the
factory so that the entire labor force of the department would
sympathize with and join the union. They also should enable the
laboring masses to learn the methods of daily [struggle]. This
is the chief significance of basic organizations.)

[92]   At the same time, we must also pay attention to the training
and education of low-level union committees and factory workers'
representatives. Most of these workers' committee members and
representatives are strong elements of the factories. They must be
given suitable training before we can properly push the organization of Party cells or small units in factories. This is the realistic
method of organizing labor unions.

    7. Due to China's political chaos and economic complications, it

is very difficult to achieve uniformity of labor demands throughout the country. With the exception of Kwangtung, the demand of workers of the entire country is to obtain their rights and freedom. We should formulate such minimum demands as that for improved treatment on the basis of actual local conditions of workers. Although we may not be able to attain our goal immediately, we should start the work of propaganda. We should carry out propaganda for the maximum ten-hour working day and one holiday each week. Central and local Party headquarters should outline national and local labor demands for propaganda among the laboring masses and society in general.

8. In such light industries as textile, tobacco, and silk factories, young and female workers form a very important group numerically. They have been most active, participating in the union movement, strikes, and other mass movements. In order to encourage them to participate more energetically in the class struggle and the revolutionary movement and to train personnel for proletarian struggle, we should guide them to fight and give them the necessary education and training. In all economic strikes, we should bring up their special conditions. In labor unions where there are young and women workers, we should select the able elements to be elected as members of union committees. [CY] representatives should participate in Party fractions of labor unions so that the CY can take uniform steps in its activities among the laboring masses.

[93]   9. In accordance with actual local conditions in the labor movement and the local minimum demands of the workers, the regional and local committees of the Party should draft practical immediate plans for the labor movement and submit them to the Central Committee for approval. They should also hasten and supervise the execution of these plans by our Party cells in factories and Party fractions in labor unions. In the national Labor movement, the most important industries are railroads, seamen [shipping], and mines, and the most important places are Shanghai, Canton, Hankow, Tientsin, and Tsingtao. The labor movement in different industries and cities all have their respective points which merit our attention.

a) With the exception of the Peking-Suiyuan Railway Union, the railway unions in the North are suppressed, unable to function openly or half openly. Railway unions have failed to build a foundation on the masses and our Party cells on the railways have not been developed. Moreover, among the railway workers the difference between experienced and inexperienced workers is too great. Objectively, there are also many organizational difficulties. Henceforth, we should employ open or half-open methods, regardless of form or name as well as secret methods to organize railway

workers at major stations, from enginemen and firemen to main-
tenance crews and porters. On the one hand, the railway workers
should find means to oppose the treacherous militarists. On the
other hand, they should unite on the basis of their most acute
daily sufferings and develop close relations with other workers and
peasants along the railways. To attain the above objectives, local
Party headquarters should devote efforts to developing our Party
cells on railways and recognize that the work of railway unions is
of foremost importance in their work in the labor movement.
Hereafter, the Federation of Railway Unions appoints only rotating
inspectors to guide and inspect railway work; it is not to appoint
regular officials stationed at various railway stations. The work
of developing railway unions at each station is the responsibility
of local Party headquarters. The Federation of Railway Unions
only has official relationships with railway unions at railway
stations. Each railway station, in turn, should maintain close re-
[94] lations with the Federation of Railway Unions in order to strengthen
the unification of railway unions. It should also report to the Federation on the conditions of its work to facilitate publication of
regular periodicals to guide the railway workers' movement.

b) The Seamen's Union has built a foundation only among a group
of seamen on ocean liners. Very few seamen of inland steamers
have joined the Union. Since the Canton-Hankow [Hongkong] Strike,
a group of the most revolutionary seamen have left their jobs.
Hence, in the seamen's movement, secret work should be initiated
immediately on ocean liners. Attempts also should be made to get
the seamen of inland steamers to join the Union and to extend the
Seamen's Union organization to all major ports. Of course, the
development of Party organizations should follow the development
of labor unions. All local Party headquarters should henceforth
pay special attention to the seamen's movement.

c) The miners' movement in Anyuan [Kiangsi] has been totally
destroyed and no possibility of revival is in sight. There has been
some organization at such places as Kailan [Hopeh], Tzu-chou
[Tzechwan, in Shantung?], Poshan [Shantung], Tsiaotso [Honan],
Tayeh [Hupeh], Shuikoushan [Hunan], and Sikwangshan [Hunan].
Henceforth we should continue to develop the miners' movement
at the above places and dispatch people to initiate the movement
at such places as Fushun [in Liaoning, now Liaotung], Tsingsing
[Hopeh], Linch'eng [Shantung], and Tzu-liu-lin [Tzeliutsing,
Szechwan?].

d). Although the Shanghai General Labor Union is supported by
all Shanghai workers, its foundation is built only on a portion of the
printers and textile workers. Henceforth, our most important task
is the organization of seamen, railway, postal, telephone, and telegraph workers, longshoremen, and street transportation workers.

Due to hard living conditions or their relatively strong class consciousness, the workers of Shanghai are most apt to stage unorganized strikes and riots. It is necessary for our Party cells in factories and low-level unions to become strong and developed before the action of Shanghai workers can be organized and planned. At the same time, we should fight for the open existence of Shanghai labor unions and disseminate widespread propaganda on the general demands of Shanghai workers. Our Party headquarters in Shanghai [95] should, in particular, guide Shanghai workers to participate in the local movement for political and economic reforms, so that the workers of Shanghai may accumulate revolutionary experience and acquire their [proper] social status.

e) The labor movement in Canton has two shortcomings: (1) a portion of the industrial workers is still under the influence of a small number of reactionary leaders; (2) the long-standing traditions of the old guilds are still strong in the labor unions, In our Party's work in the labor movement in Canton, primary attention should be paid to enlisting the support of the masses of workers of arsenals, railways, post, telephone and telegraph, and waterworks. Our Party should also establish a small number of model unions which are free from the old traditions of the guilds. It must not emphasize only the so-called movement for the unification of unions. We must urgently find a solution to the Canton-Hongkong strike. The revival of the Hongkong labor movement is one of the principal tasks of the Kwangtung Regional Committee. Our Party cells in factories should pay attention to absorbing the masses and workers. Strict screening, however, is necessary in selecting union officers to join our Party.

f) Under severe oppression, the majority of workers at such places as Tientsin, Hankow, Dairen, and Tsingtao are still unorganized. Positive steps should be taken to organize the workers of these places. At the same time, we must avoid the mistake of excessively strict and mechanical utilization of Party cells or small units in factories. We should use the facts of daily struggle and employ all kinds of open or secret formulas to organize workers' organizations and basic organizations of labor unions. Special attention should be given to the development of Party cells in factories for the purpose of absorbing the strong elements of the masses of workers in preparation for the development of all types of struggle.

g) Special attention should also be given the workers of small factories, shops, and handicraftsmen in various cities because they represent workers of big industries and therefore constitute [96] a strong group in the national movement. Although the organizations of these workers cannot be very strict, we must first of all see that they are class organizations, without mixed bourgeois elements. This point deserves special attention.

10. During the past year, the working class of the country has been in a situation of heated struggle. Our Party has been busily engaged in directing this struggle. Consequently, responsible personnel of the CC's Committee on the Labor Movement were frequently dispatched to various places and unable to attend to their regular duties or to proceed systematically with the development of the national labor movement. Henceforth, the Central Committee should designate a responsible person in the Committee on the Labor Movement to exercise regular direction over all local Party headquarters in the execution of policy on the basis of the practical methods outlined in the above plans.

11. At present, we face a grave shortage of personnel for the labor movement, particularly low-level cadres. We should immediately establish at such places as Shanghai, Hankow, Tientsin, and Canton, training classes to cultivate personnel to serve as low-level cadres in the labor movement. We should also establish an advanced training class in Shanghai or Canton to train high-level leaders for our Party.

DOCUMENT 29

The following translation is based on the original Chinese text of
the resolutions on the peasant movement adopted by the Central
Committee of the Chinese Communist Party at the Second Enlarged
Plenum in Shanghai, July 12 to July 18, 1926. The resolutions are
published in Su-lien yin-mou..., III, "KCT," pp. 96-105.

RESOLUTIONS ON THE PEASANT MOVEMENT

[96] Tendencies in the Peasant Movement

The growing imperialist encroachment, militarist oppression
and extortion, and the frequent and expanded militarist wars of
recent years have created the currently widespread peasant uprisings, such as the uprisings of the Red Spears in Honan and
Shantung, the movement to oppose [oppressive] taxes and reduce
rent in Szechuan, Shensi, and Chihli, and the peasant association
movement in Kwangtung and Hunan.

These movements are marked by a number of common characteristics: opposition to exorbitant taxes and irregular levies, advance collection of money and crops, corrupt officials, oppression
by the min-t'uan and the devastation of civil wars. At the same
[97] time, positive demands have been expressed: demands for self-
organization, armed self-defense, and clean and orderly government. In Kwangtung, where the peasant movement is relatively
advanced, certain local political rights have been demanded
(popular election of hsien magistrates, etc.).

In short, the peasants have become conscious of their own sufferings and cannot endure them any longer. They have, on their
own initiative (whether consciously or unconsciously, in a primitive or organized fashion), risen to revolt against the classes which
oppress and encroach upon them (landlords, local bullies, bad
gentry, compradors, imperialists). In other words, the peasants
have risen to participate in the National Revolution and have proved
highly functional in actual politics (for instance, the success of the
National Government in Kwangtung and the defeat of the Second
Kuominchün in Honan). They occupy an extremely important position in the Chinese national liberation movement.

In view of the foregoing tendencies, we may safely say that the
people's political consciousness and position in political life will
continue to develop and will become the principal force in the national liberation movement. In order to guide the smooth advance
of the Chinese national liberation movement, our Party must

secure the force of the peasantry and the directing power in the
peasant movement. Therefore, the following resolutions are
adopted by the Enlarged Conference.

Economic and Political Demands

The peasant movement in Kwangtung is already in need of a
minimum political platform. From a national point of view, however, it is still premature to decide on an organized political
platform. The present resolutions are not intended, therefore,
as a systematic exposition of peasant demands, but merely to
point out the most pressing demands in the country which require immediate action. As for a complete peasant political
platform, it will have to await discussion at the Fifth Congress.

1. Economic [demands]:
   a) Rent ceilings to be fixed by the government. Peasants to
   [98]   receive at least 50 percent of the crops.
   b) Fix the maximum interest at 3 percent.
   c) Oppose advanced collection of money and crops, exorbitant
      taxes, and irregular levies.
   d) Demand freedom from graft; all levies should be computed
      according to market prices.
   e) Unify the system of weights and measures.
   f) Prohibit hoarding. Promote the movement for agrarian con-
      sumers cooperatives.
2. Political [demands]:
   a) Freedom of assembly for the peasantry.
   b) Popular election of hsien magistrates.
   c) Popular election of self-governing organs in the villages.
   d) Open local finance.
   e) Opposition to execution by the min-t'uan of the judicial pow-
      ers of arrest and trial.

The Problem of Organization

1. Peasant organizations should not be too strictly confined to
the form of peasant associations. If, in certain villages and towns,
there already exist such groups as Village Federations or "Watch
and Guard Associations," organizations which truly represent the
masses of peasants and their interests, and which cannot easily
be transformed, they should not be forced to change into peasant
associations. Furthermore, they should be permitted to join hsien
[99] peasant associations which unify the peasant associations of the
entire hsien.

2. The organization of peasant associations cannot yet have a
distinct class color. We should propose the organization of hired
farm laborers and tenant farmers. We cannot exclude persons
from membership simply on the basis of ownership of a certain

amount of land. Owing to the difficulty of setting up a suitable standard, we may only place a relatively general limitation and disqualify the following two categories for membership in peasant associations:

a) Those who own a large amount of land but do not till it.

b) Those who extort high interest.

3. Toward old established peasant organizations, the policy of our peasant associations is to control and absorb them as far as possible so that the bad gentry and local bullies may not utilize their so-called legal organs to oppress the peasants. In case of conflict between landlords and poor peasants, we should find means to utilize the old peasant organizations as the mediating party.

The Problem of Propaganda

1. Agitation and propaganda should be based on the actual sufferings of the peasantry as the point of departure. Avoid the use of broad, vague propaganda and mechanical, preaching lectures.

2. Avoid active opposition to the superstitions and clan relationships of the villages. We should elevate the cultural level of the villages in a gradual and methodical manner. At times, we may lower our own standard of living to meet that of the peasants in order to gain close contact with them. We may at times even find it necessary to follow for the time being the superstitions of the masses in order to develop our work.

3. Class relationships in the villages are extremely complicated. Therefore it is not necessary to bring up the term "the peasant class." Our propaganda should be based on the opposition of the [100] entire peasantry to the bad gentry and local bullies.

4. Means of propaganda are pictorial papers and magazines, slogans, folk songs, slides, and stories. It is advisable to utilize and adapt to our propaganda the fairy tales and legends of the villages. In any event, uninteresting, mechanical, and preaching lectures are not to be employed.

Policy toward Landlords, the Min-t'uan, and Local Government

1. Our policy toward landlords is to unite self-cultivating peasants, hired farm laborers, tenant farmers, and middle and small landlords in a united front. Those big landlords who do not actively engage in oppressive activities are to be neutralized. Attacks should be concentrated on the most reactionary big landlords. In case of big landlords who are members of the bad gentry or local bullies, we should not simply propose the slogan, "Down with the landlords," for slogans attacking the bad gentry and local bullies in reality work toward overthrow of big landlords also.

2. Our policy toward the min-t'uan. Although the min-t'uan is the machinery by which the landlords, bad gentry, and local bullies

protect their own interests at the expense of the common people, it is impossible to hope that this system can be destroyed at the present time. Our policy is to disseminate propaganda among members of the min-t'uan not to cooperate with the bad gentry (members of the min-t'uan are all peasants). We should suggest that the min-t'uan chieftains should be elected at peasant assemblies or through other suitable means, so that honest members of the gentry may assume min-t'uan leadership instead of the bad gentry and local bullies. The purpose is to place the power of the min-t'uan in the hands of the enlightened petty bourgeoisie as the initial step, so that the min-t'uan may not obstruct the peasant movement.

3. The problem of [policy toward] local governments should be discussed separately.

a) We should employ the formula of revolt or internal splits to attain our objective in dealing with [local] governments under militarist rule.

b) We should employ the formula of the masses' demands for their rights and interests in dealing with local [governments] under 101] the rule or influence of the National Government.

The Problem of the Agrarian United Front

Our principal policy is not to let the peasantry be isolated; we should avail ourselves of all opportunities and the so-called public social welfare to cooperate with the rest of the masses in a united movement. There are the following kinds of alliances:

1. In normal times, we may utilize joint conferences of workers, peasants, and merchants, or conferences of representatives of all circles.

2. At the high tide of [the movement for a] national assembly, we may organize associations for the promotion of the national assembly and set up branches in cities and villages.

3. In times of local emergency, we may organize people's peace-preservation committees. The policy and attitude toward various groups which should be adopted in the peasant movement are embodied in the various sections of the resolutions.

Attitude toward the Church

In our verbal propaganda, we should do our utmost to depict the [Christian] Church as the vanguard of imperialism. On the one hand, the Church acts as espionage agent for imperialism, investigating conditions in the interior of China: politics, economics, popular sentiment, and customs. On the other hand, it uses such high-sounding words as "peace" and "universal love" and occasionally even spends money to buy the people's confidence. The Church wishes to deceive all oppressed peoples and lead them to forget their own actual sufferings in order to insure a strong and lasting foundation for imperialist oppression.

We must not at this time create any opportunity of actual conflict with the Church. This condition is imposed by our present situation (the Church is allied with militarists everywhere under the [102] pretext of treaty protection). In case of obviously aggressive acts such as the occupation of land and forced purchase of people's houses, however, we should take action and stir up popular sentiment against the church.

Policy toward Bandits

We should of course firmly oppose those bandits who oppress the peasantry. As for those who do not, we still should not allow them to join the peasant associations, thereby creating an organizational relationship. We should make them remain in a neutral position without being utilized by the bad gentry and local bullies in case of struggle between the latter and the peasants. If bandits are allowed to join peasant associations, peasants' organizations might easily be corrupted and invite outside criticism and attacks.

Armed Self-Defense

1. The peasants' present demand for armed self-defense is necessary, but the following two points must be taken into consideration:

a) Avoid exceeding the limits of self-defense. Such actions as interference with [local] administration and confiscation of the arms of the min-t'uan are defensive, not offensive, self-defense.

b) It is not permissible to establish organizations of a permanent nature because it would inevitably give rise to conflict with other groups (such as landlords, min-t'uan and military garrisons).

2. The name "self-defense army," can easily be changed to "self-defense corps" or some other title to avoid misunderstanding and jealousy.

3. The organization of the self-defense corps should not be complicated, but simple and expedient in action.

4. Political training is even more important for the self-defense corps, than military training, because the totally disorganized and untrained peasants, once in possession of arms, could easily [103] exceed the objective limits of action.

Relations between the Peasant Movement and the Kuomintang

Peasant organizations need not reflect the coloring of any political party. The work of organizing the peasantry need not be undertaken in the name of any political party (it may be done in the name of labor unions). Where the peasant movement has been initiated by the KMT, we should cooperate with the KMT. However, with reference to relations between peasant associations and the KMT, the associations must be kept organizationally independent and not become an appendage of that party.

The Party's Development in the Villages

Our Party must devote the utmost effort to gaining the position of leadership in all peasants' movements. Party cells should be organized in every single lowest-level peasant association to be the nucleus in guiding the activities of the peasant association.

Methods of Work

We have not devoted a great deal of time to work in the peasant movement, and, with the exception of Kwangtung, we have only just begun this work at most places. Although we have committed many mistakes, a good deal of experience has been gained. The following points should be noted with regard to our future methods of work.

1. General points:

a) Persons working in the peasant movement must first do as the peasants do in speech and action. Their living conditions and clothing must also be similar to those of the peasants. Only thus can they gain close contact with and disseminate propaganda among the peasants.

b) It is necessary thoroughly, to understand the sufferings of the people in order to express the demands of the peasantry; to know the objective limits of action in order to lead the peasantry to 104] struggle; and to utilize the tactics of united fronts in order to prevent the peasants from being isolated and defeated.

2. Where there has hitherto been no work:

a) Use should be made of village primary school teachers, comrades and city workers who are natives of villages and students returning to the villages for holidays to initiate organizational work. Primary school teachers are, in particular, the natural leaders of the villages. We should earnestly enlist this group in our ranks.

b) We should utilize various important events for propaganda tours in the countryside (such as propaganda on May Thirtieth and the Northern Expedition). At such times, we should take the opportunity to organize peasant associations or similar organizations.

c) We should find means of establishing village supplementary classes, village clubs, mobile lecture groups, and consumers' cooperatives to penetrate the villages and begin organizational work.

d) Investigate the living conditions, customs, and habits of the local peasantry for formulating the best methods to get close to and organize them.

e) Attempt to organize the many unorganized peasant rioters in the course of insurrections.

3. At places where there has been work:

a) Attention should be given to low-level and secret work. Peasant associations of the villages or large villages are the foundation of peasant organization. Conferences of peasant representatives of villages or large villages should be held regularly. Sufficient preparation should be undertaken prior to such meetings, at which peasants should be encouraged to express their opinions to the utmost. Mechanical or preaching propaganda should be prohibited.

b) We should conduct frequent surveys of the sufferings and all [105] other conditions relative to the peasantry. To maintain the peasants' confidence and faith in organization, it is essential constantly to find out the peasants' demands and guide them in systematic action to gain their own interests.

c) We should find means to know and bring up the demands of the peasantry. When the objective situation does not allow the raising of such demands, a full explanation [to the peasants] is necessary. We should inspire them so that they will not be disheartened. We must absolutely avoid resorting to outright suppression of their demands.

d) In order to strengthen the foundation of the peasant movement, we must develop our Party among the peasantry, so that it will become the nucleus in the development of the peasant movement.

e) Do not rely on political influence for the sake of expediency. Peasants should be taught in every way to have confidence in the capacity of their own organization.

DOCUMENT 30

Document 30 has been translated from an original Chinese document. It consists of resolutions on the Red Spears movement adopted by the Central Committee of the Chinese Communist Party at the Second Enlarged Plenum held in Shanghai, July 12 to July 18, 1926. See Su-lien yin-mou..., III, "KCT," pp. 105-8.

RESOLUTIONS ON THE
RED SPEARS MOVEMENT

[105] 1. The Red Spears Association is a product of militarist political regimes. It is a primitive organization for the self-defense of the middle and petty peasantry who can no longer tolerate the extortionist practices of corrupt officials, the burden of oppressive taxes and levies, the devastation of civil wars, the menace of bandits and defeated soldiers, the economic aggression of imperialism, and the squeeze of the bad gentry and local bullies. It may be true that a considerable number of vagabonds have slipped into the organization and that leadership has fallen into the hands of some bad gentry. Nevertheless, we can hardly regard it as an organization of bandits.

The Red Spears in Chihli, Shantung, and Honan have proved and are proving now that their demands and actions directly or indirectly oppose militarist rule. The organization has become the real armed force of the people and an important anti-militarist force in the National Revolution. We should do our utmost to guide this force and to see that it is not utilized by the militarists and local bullies.

[106] 2. The Red Spears Association is not only an important force in the National revolutionary movement, but merits our close attention in our work of developing peasant associations. In the provinces of Honan, Shantung, and Chihli, where the Red Spears Association is most active, it is impossible to distinguish very clearly the Red Spears movement from the peasant movement. We should, however, see to it that peasant associations are made the general peasants' organization and the Red Spears Association is made the armed peasants' organization. In the immediate future, we must utilize the Red Spears Association to develop peasant associations. When peasant associations have become widespread and fully developed, the Red Spears Association should become the armed force of the peasant associations.

3. The Red Spears Association is a force in the people's opposi-

tion to militarism, but this force must be consolidated with and
influenced by other revolutionary forces in order to minimize the
possibility of defeat and the danger of its reactionary character.
(In view of its loose organization and addiction to superstition, it
cannot stand the test of battle. Furthermore, it is full of destructive tendencies and lacks constructive tendencies).

4. We should assist the Red Spears Associations in methods of
organization and principles of action; such methods and principles
should be clear, simple, and easily understood.

With reference to methods of organization, we should first carry
out propaganda to the effect that all local Red Spears groups should
join together to form a secret communications organ for exchanging
information and mutual assistance. The work [of this organ] should
be undertaken by our comrades in the Red Spears Association.
Originally an organ of information and communication, it should
gradually become a powerful directing organ.

The second step after the establishment of the communications
organ is to find means of convening a conference of representatives
of leaders of the Red Spears and Black Spears Associations to form
a simple organization and formulate a political platform for common action. This common political platform should include the
following:

    a) Resistance to bandits

[107]   b) Resistance to molestation by undisciplined troops

    c) Resistance to exorbitant taxes and irregular levies

    d) Resistance to forced conscription for military service and
       labor squads

    e) Resistance to circulation of military notes. Demand that
       government paper currency be used in payment of taxes

    f) Protection and preservation of local peace and order (that is,
       participation in the work of local self-government)

    g) Supervision of and making public local finance

    h) Opposition to corrupt officials

The above slogans should be conveyed in language that is most
easily understood by the local people.

The Red Spears Associations' actions should at present be
limited by the above principles as self-defense organizations. It is
permissible to demand participation in local self-government, but
seizure of local political power by force is absolutely not allowed.

5. It is unnecessary actively to oppose the superstitious dogmas
of the Red Spears Association because they are the essential
factor in bringing these people together to struggle and are unavoidable phenomena among backward peasants. We only want their activities to benefit the development of the Revolution.

6. Under the present peculiar situation in Honan and Shantung,
the genuine Red Spears Associations of the peasants, those with

bandit characteristics, and those utilized by local bullies have one common objective: opposition to Chang Tsung-ch'ang and Wu P'ei-fu. We should therefore see that they are welded into a united front for opposing local militarist governments. At the same time, we should strengthen the genuine organizations of the peasants.

108]   7. The directing power of the Red Spears Association falls easily into the hands of the local bullies, the Red Spears becoming their tools. Furthermore, since they have the strongest force, the Red Spears Associations with bandit characteristics frequently become the basic mass fighting force of the local bullies.

Our policy toward them is as follows: if we fail to bring them under the banner of opposition to the local militarist government, we should first of all try to take over their masses. The first step is to see that the genuine Red Spears Associations of the peasants stand independently and unintimidated by them. The second step is to see that the Red Spears Associations with bandit characteristics are not utilized by others, but stand on the side of the peasantry to attack the local bullies.

Document 31 has been translated from the original Chinese text of the resolutions on the merchant movement adopted by the Central Committee of the Chinese Communist Party at the Second Enlarged Plenum held in Shanghai, July 12 to July 18, 1926. See Su-lien yin-mou..., III, "KCT," pp. 108-9.

RESOLUTIONS ON THE MERCHANT MOVEMENT

[108] In the course of the national movement, Chinese merchants have three tendencies.

The most reactionary are the compradors of foreign firms, banks, and big stores. This pure comprador class has virtually lost all national consciousness.

Next come the merchants who have advanced from the position of compradors to become rising industrialists in textiles, silk, and shipping. Since they desire political assistance in expanding their enterprises, they appear to have a little political consciousness. They cannot rid themselves of the comprador outlook, however, and are antagonistic to the labor movement. They hope to gain a few benefits from the imperialists and militarists through compromise tactics. Furthermore, they are afraid of getting close to the masses and oppose revolutionary tendencies.

The middle and petty merchants are the only group that is revolutionary, or at least not counterrevolutionary. They have no direct economic connections with the imperialists and are subject to the double oppression of exorbitant taxes and irregular levies imposed by militarists and unfair competition at the hands of big merchants. Thus, they are in constant fear of bankruptcy. Since they own no factories, they are not afraid of strikes. Hence, they can be brought to close contact with the masses of revolutionary workers and students. Furthermore, they themselves constitute a great portion of the masses.

Our objective in the merchant movement is the masses of middle [109] and petty merchants. They are an important element of the united front in the national movement. In the city, they are necessary to save the workers and students from isolation; in the village, they are necessary to save the peasants from isolation.

The method of organization in the merchant movement is to organize the masses of middle and petty merchants in merchant associations and similar organizations in order to transform, and not merely to unite with, existing chambers of commerce. The latter (especially in big cities) are not only monopolized by big merchants and are therefore unable to represent the middle and petty merchants, but are superficial organizations without mass support.

The important objective of our merchant movement is the organization of the middle and petty merchants against the compromising and traitorous actions of the big merchants and compradors in the national movement. We should oppose contributions by middle and petty merchants to the Merchants' Corps which protects big merchants. Instead, middle and petty merchants should propose the organization of defensive units composed of the city populace in general.

Merchant associations should be organizations composed exclusively of middle and petty merchants, without the participation of big merchants. In big cities, it is desirable not to allow the participation of small shop workers who should properly belong to organizations of the commercial workers. The small shop workers occupy a special status in relation to other merchants, with whom there are grounds of serious conflict.

In terms of the relationship of political parties, the revolutionary middle and petty merchants are the masses of the Kuomintang Right. We should attempt to steer them toward the Kuomintang Left. Where the Kuomintang Left has already gained influence among the masses of merchants, it may be well for it to direct the organization and activities of the merchants. However, whenever we have comrades in merchant associations, the work of our Party fractions must not be abandoned in order that our political policy may be realized.

DOCUMENT 32

The following translation is based on an original Chinese document, giving resolutions on the women's movement adopted by the Central Committee of the Chinese Communist Party at the Second Enlarged Plenum held in Shanghai, July 12 to July 18, 1926. See Su-lien yin-mou..., III, "KCT," pp. 110-12.

RESOLUTIONS ON THE WOMEN'S MOVEMENT

[110] Having studied the report of the Women's Department of the Central Committee, we note a certain amount of achievement in the women's movement, which has demonstrated considerable usefulness in the national liberation movement. On the other hand, many weaknesses have come to light, such as failure to penetrate the masses and excessive emphasis on bureaucratic activities. [Party members working in the women's movement] in Kwangtung and Peking have neglected the Party's development. Publications are too monotonous and political. Hereafter, the following points should be given special attention in our women's movement.

1. Emphasis on the masses.—We have in the past utilized such organs as the Woman's Department of the Kuomintang, women's associations, and federations of women of all circles in many places to activate and "summon the masses." Frequently, however, the result has been neglect of the masses. We have failed to penetrate the masses and merely control these organs. Upon the outbreak of certain incidents, we issued manifestos and pamphlets and dispatched telegrams in the name of these organs. Such practice has created increasing fear and suspicion among the masses, separating us further from them and placing us in an increasingly isolated position. This is a very serious mistake.

In our future work, we should not, naturally, refrain from using such organs as women's associations and the Woman's Department of the people's school [KMT] to summon the masses. Our primary duty, however, is to summon the masses. To get hold of the masses, it is not enough merely to control certain organs, creating thereby a bureaucratic kind of movement. We must lay primary emphasis on work among the masses.

2. United front.—At present, a number of cliques have developed among the masses of women as a result of class differentiation, especially in Kwangtung. Hence, a united front of all women's cliques has become a serious problem. We have been too subjective on this point in the past. We have too often merely aimed at our own

activities and brought up our own slogans, paying little attention
to the interests of women of all classes and the views of women's
organizations of all cliques. The result was that our activities
were monotonous and isolated and we have lost the sympathy of
the majority of the masses. This is one of our past mistakes. We
should hereafter pay special attention to the united front of women
[111] of all classes and all women's organizations. In order to establish
this united front, we must emphasize: (1) more attention to
women's own interests; (2) a certain amount of respect for the
views and policies of other women's organizations when certain
movements occur; and (3) avoidance of monopoly situations and
other unnecessary conflicts.

3. Female labor and women students.—Resolutions on the
method of dealing with female labor and students were adopted at
the Fourth Congress and at the Enlarged Conference of last year.
To this day, however, very little has been done. Little attention
has yet been given to this problem at certain places, such as
Kwangtung, Peking, and Hupeh. This is a very bad situation. We
must realize that the labor movement is the essence, and women
students a tool, of the women's movement. If we fail to achieve results among these two groups, it is senseless to speak of all other
women's movements.

4. Peasant women's movement.—This has just been initiated.
With the peasant movement suddenly and rapidly developing, however, the future peasant women's movement will occupy a very
important position in the Chinese women's movement. Although
we cannot as yet formulate concrete plans, we should at least
begin to give our serious attention to the problem and prepare
personnel for the peasant women's movement, especially in
Kwangtung and Hunan.

5. Popularization of women's publications.—It is a sign of
progress that there has been an increase in local women's publications. Their contents, however, are not satisfactory. Either
there is excessive duplication and redundancy, or the writing is
too political and theoretical. Very few can really speak on behalf
of women, representing their sufferings and actual demands.
In the future, our own publications and those under our control
should institute improvements, avoid empty political and theoretical discussions, and concentrate on articles on women's own
[112] sufferings and practical demands, so that women readers will
feel that the articles speak on their behalf. Only thus can we
achieve results in propaganda and agitation among the majority
of women who are numb and unconscious.

6. Reform of local women's departments and committees on
the women's movement.—Although these organs have been organized, they are for the most part ineffective and unable to guide

the work of the women's movement. Reform of these organs is
prerequisite to spurring the progress of the women's movement.
The Party at all levels should take special note of this point.

7. Expansion of Party membership and training of personnel for
the women's movement.—Since the last Enlarged Conference, the
number of female members has increased considerably. It is still
a very small figure, however, when compared with the number of
male members. Furthermore, female membership is confined to
Shanghai and Hunan. In Kwangtung, Hupeh, Peking, and other areas,
expansion of female membership has been extremely slow. This is
indeed a very bad situation! Hereafter attention should be given
to the development of female membership everywhere.

The shortage of personnel for the women's movement is even
more acute, and consequently local work has been much retarded.
The training of personnel for the women's movement (especially
personnel for the female labor movement and the peasant women's
movement) is the most important immediate task of the Party at
all levels. As far as possible the Party at all levels should sponsor training classes for the women's movement, special discussions of the women's movement, or gather and regularly train
responsible and promising women comrades.

DOCUMENT 33

Document 33 is based on the original Chinese text of the resolutions on the student movement adopted by the Central Committee of the Chinese Communist Party at the Second Enlarged Plenum held in Shanghai, July 12 to July 18, 1926. See Su-lien yin-mou..., III, "KCT," pp. 112-14.

RESOLUTIONS ON THE STUDENT MOVEMENT

12] Students are an important group in the national revolutionary movement. This was clearly revealed in the May Fourth and May Thirtieth movements. From the objective point of view, the majority of students are bankrupt petty bourgeois youths and, from the subjective point of view, they are susceptible to the revolutionary
13] propaganda and knowledge to which they are exposed in the schools. They are an extremely important group in the national revolutionary united front, second only to the workers and peasants. However, the students must themselves form a united front to centralize the strength of the masses of students in order to become a force in the national revolutionary united front.

We have in the past paid attention to the policy of a student united front in our student movement. By this we mean the unification of student federations. We have gained considerable results in Peking and Shanghai; elsewhere, we have either failed to adopt this policy or endorsed it only on the surface, lacking proper means of execution in order to obtain positive results.

Our policy to expand and strengthen the student united front should hereafter be based on the following principles, adapted to actual local conditions:

1. We should stress the slogan of the unification of the student movement, with unity in organization, policy, and action, and without discrimination on the basis of religion, party, or ideology, in our propaganda among the masses of students in the schools.

2. By the so-called student united front and the so-called unification of the student movement, we do not mean the unification of students of all cliques under our doctrines, policies, and slogans. Our policy is to present to the masses of students minimum revolutionary slogans and policies which are acceptable to the majority of students of all cliques in order to unify the student movement.

3. By the so-called unification of policy, we mean the unification of policy in terms of action rather than ideology. Hence, in concrete situations, we may bring up only those slogans and policies

which are acceptable to the majority of students in order to expand the student united front and unify the student movement. At the same time, in our daily political and ideological propaganda, we should bring up as far as possible concrete facts to stress [114] the necessity of our revolutionary theories and policies. It is necessary to influence the thinking of the masses of students in order to obtain political leadership.

4. We should cooperate very closely with students of the KMT Left Wing, but we should also earnestly invite the cooperation of students of the KMT Right, the Kuo-chia chu-i Clique, and Christian students in political struggle as well as struggle for the students' own interests, in order to expose the incompetence of their leaders and encourage them toward the Left.

5. Our strength should be built on the masses of students in schools. As for the officers of student federations, we need only ally with the Left to secure the majority. We should not monopolize the organizations.

6. In our daily political and ideological propaganda, that is, analysis of facts and theoretical debates, we must not betray any sign of retreat from the students of the KMT Right Wing, the Kuo-chia chu-i Clique, and Christian students. However, we must not lightly brand anyone as reactionary and counterrevolutionary. Furthermore, we should at all times maintain a friendly attitude in our personal relations with them in order to avoid unpleasant feelings on the part of nonpartisan students.

7. In our attitude toward mission schools, we may attack only religious education but not the entire student body of mission schools.

8. Our comrades in various schools should concentrate their efforts on studies but they must also pay attention to student activities, such as student clubs and oratory societies. They must do their utmost to avoid deviating from the masses of students in any given school. Only thus can we establish leadership among the masses of students.

DOCUMENT 34

This translation of Document 34 is based on the original Chinese text of the resolutions on the relief movement adopted by the Central Committee of the Chinese Communist Party at the Second Enlarged Plenum held in Shanghai, July 12 to July 18, 1926. See Su-lien yin-mou..., III, "KCT," pp. 116-19.

RESOLUTIONS ON THE RELIEF MOVEMENT

[117] The relief movement is a tool for the realization of the united front. It can directly unite all classes and parties to oppose militarist and imperialist oppression and indirectly arouse the great masses to participate in and sympathize with the revolutionary movement. The Party at all levels should pay great attention to relief work and earnestly carry out the following tasks:

1. The Party at all levels should help in every way to organize relief associations and establish and develop branch organizations at various places.

2. All Party members are urged to join the membership of relief associations and as far as possible shoulder the responsibility for their work.

3. All organizations under our Party's direction are urged to join relief associations as member organizations; their members are urged to join as individual members.

4. Party headquarters at all levels should appoint a committee on the relief movement, its members to be selected from among Party members or members of Party committees. Party headquarters may also appoint a special commissioner to be responsible for the relief movement within their jurisdiction.

5. Party cells in schools, factories, offices, municipalities, and districts should appoint at least one comrade, or whatever number is suitable, to be responsible for the work of branch organizations of relief associations.

6. In big cities and industrial areas, various committees on mass organizations should be set up under committees on the relief movement or special commissioners, to be responsible for organizing relief units among various groups, such as workers, students, peasants, merchants, women and children. The committees on mass organizations should maintain an intimate relationship with the various movements of the Party. When necessary, responsible members of committees on mass organizations are to attend meetings of the responsible comrades of the various movements.

[118]   7. The Party at all levels should work with committees on the relief movement or special commissioners to draw up comprehensive plans for the local relief movement and a budget to be submitted to the Central Committee for approval. Such plans and appointments of responsible persons are to be submitted within the month of August of this year, in any case not later than the end of August.

8. Committees on the relief movement or special commissioners should be entirely under the Party's direction in terms of policy. The special commissioner of the relief movement of the Central Committee should direct local developments through local or regional committees. Where Party organs are lacking, activities should be temporarily placed under the direct supervision of the Central Committee's special commissioner.

9. Party headquarters should convene regular conferences of responsible personnel in the relief movement to acquaint them with the entire plan of activities of the Party as frames of reference for the relief movement. Party headquarters should refer all policy matters pertaining to the relief movement, solutions to important problems, and appointments to the special commissioners or committees on the relief movement for discussion before decision.

10. Party members shouldering the work of relief associations should bear official titles and receive appointments from official organs, preferably by election at meetings.

11. Our comrades should shoulder the duties of actual work in official relief organizations. It is not necessary for them to hold the highest positions. Relatively high positions should be manned by nonpartisan Leftist elements.

12. The Left and our comrades together should hold the majority of the positions in official relief associations. Our comrades alone should not comprise more than one third of the staff.

13. Our comrades working in relief associations should earnestly cooperate with nonpartisan elements and avoid monopolizing [119] everything. As far as possible, they should report publicly on the work of the relief associations.

14. Responsible comrades in the relief movement should submit monthly reports on the condition of activities to Party headquarters for communication to the Central Committee.

15. Responsible comrades in the local relief movement should maintain a "grey" attitude in propaganda on the relief association. Their writings should be simple and popular and concerned particularly with local problems.

16. In the event of the outbreak of reactionary oppression at any given place, the name of the relief association should be used to assemble all circles and organizations to put up strong resistance.

At the same time, it is necessary to report on the true circumstances of the incident, together with photographs, to the National Committee of the relief association for extensive propaganda purposes.

17. Comrades responsible for the local relief movement should help collect data and material for the national propaganda publications of the relief association (Kuang-ming pan-yüeh k'an [Brightness Semi-monthly] and Chi-nan hua-pao [Relief Pictorial Review]). Emergency news, propaganda, and circular telegrams of the National Committee of the relief association should be published in local papers.

18. Our comrades should carefully investigate the condition of victims and refugees everywhere, regardless of party, class, and religion. This information should be reported to the higher organs of relief associations along with requests for appropriate remedial measures.

19. Our comrades should everywhere respect and abide by the official regulations of the relief associations. They are not to make changes at will which may lead to the concentration of our enemy's [forces].

The following translation is based on the orginal Chinese text of
the resolutions on the military movement by the Central Committee of the Chinese Communist Party at the Second Enlarged
Plenum held in Shanghai, July 12 to 18, 1926. The resolutions are
published in <u>Su-lien yin-mou</u>..., III, "KCT," pp. 119-20.

RESOLUTIONS ON THE MILITARY MOVEMENT

[119] 1. China is at present embroiled in a period of violent armed
conflict between military forces bearing the colors of the National
Revolution and the reactionary militarists. From the objective
standpoint, we should at least carry out suitable political propaganda among the national revolutionary forces. At the same time,
[120] it should be easy for us to work within the armies of the reactionary militarists in view of militarist rivalry and hostility, internal
conflicts within the armies, and the excessive mistreatment of
mercenary soldiers in the militarist armies.

In the villages, a great number of the poor peasants have
secretly organized armed organizations. Furthermore, they are
beginning to organize armed uprisings of political significance,
such as those of the Red Spears in Honan and Shantung.

The class struggle of the urban proletariat has been marked
by many incidents of armed conflict between the workers and
scabs. Railroad workers in both North and South China are
gradually demonstrating their capacity in civil war.

Our Party is a proletarian revolutionary party, prepared at all
times for armed uprisings. In the course of the National Revolution, we should participate in armed struggles to help strengthen
progressive military forces, smash the power of reactionary
militarists, and gradually expand the armed force of the masses
of workers and peasants. This type of work provides our Party
with the experience of systematically preparing for armed uprisings.

The military movement has been largely neglected by our
comrades. Our organization appears to be a study group. Although
our comrades' attention has recently been directed to the military movement, they tend to emphasize maneuvering high-ranking
military officers. This shows lack of understanding of the responsibility of our Party in immediate military work and the meaning
of gaining the experience of systematically preparing for armed
uprisings.

2. As a result of six months' work, we have succeeded in setting up various central and local Party organs and their mutual relationships. We have made proper progress in collecting data and promoting workers' self-defense corps. Aside from appropriate political propaganda work in progressive armies, our work in enemy armies is largely characterized by attention to conflicts between high-ranking officers. We have failed to establish close contacts with low-ranking officers and the masses of soldiers. We have not begun systematic work with reference to

121] armed peasant organizations (such as the Red Spears).

3. Henceforth we should try to organize soldiers' cells under our direction in reactionary militarist armies, and secure close contact with the masses of soldiers. We should utilize daily events in the army for oral and written propaganda among the soldiers. At the same time, we should devote all our efforts to agitation and organization of Party cells in arsenals and ordinance bureaus to cut the supply of weapons to reactionary militarists.

With reference to armed peasant organizations, emphasis should first be placed on the training of low-level leaders, particularly political training. With reference to workers' self-defense corps, emphasis should be on military and political training of the firm central elements of the corps rather than on the increase of persons.

4. When we send personnel to do political work in the National Revolutionary Army and the Kuominchün, it is necessary to employ (few but good) principles. If a person [sent by us] becomes an officer, his duty is to see that the army becomes gradually more consolidated and revolutionary. He should studiously avoid premature differentiation of the revolutionary armies and his actions should be in complete accordance with instructions of local Party headquarters.

5. Military work is a part of the Party's work. Our comrades responsible for military work should maintain intimate relations with local Party secretaries. They should report to and consult with the local Party secretaries on the situation of their work.

PART VI

KUOMINTANG AND SOVIET RELATIONS WITH
FENG YÜ-HSIANG, OCTOBER, 1924, TO SEPTEMBER, 1926

By the spring of 1925, Soviet advisers had achieved considerable success in Kwangtung. The Kuomintang Left Wing, which cooperated closely with the Russians, was in power. The First Eastern Expedition against Ch'en Ch'iung-ming was being successfully carried out. A Party army was being organized. It was then that Soviet interest was increasingly drawn to Feng Yü-hsiang in North China.

Feng Yü-hsiang's Coup d'État, October 23, 1924

Feng Yü-hsiang catapulted into national prominence during the Second Mukden-Chihli War. Two days after the outbreak of war on September 16, 1924, Sun Yat-sen launched the Second Northern Expedition against Wu P'ei-fu. The KMT thus became an ally of Chang Tso-lin against Wu. On October 23, Feng Yü-hsiang, commander of the Third Chihli Army, who had been ordered to encounter Chang Tso-lin's forces in Jehol, suddenly turned back and took over the city of Peking. Three days later, on October 26, the Kuominchün (the People's Armies) was organized. Feng was named Commander-in-Chief and concurrently commander of the First Kuominchün (First People's Army). Hu Ching-yi became Deputy Commander-in-Chief and concurrently commander of the Second Kuominchün. Sun Yüeh assumed command of the Third Kuominchun.[1]

What was the nature of Feng's coup d'état? Was it executed in support of the Kuomintang and its platform? What were the distinguishing characteristics of the Kuominchün? Was it an ordinary militarist army, or an army dedicated to the principles of the National Revolution?

In his autobiography, published in 1944, Feng Yü-hsiang presents his interpretation. The coup, he asserts, was conceived from the start as a revolution in support of the Sun Yat-sen's principles. It was staged for the express purpose of inviting Sun to Peking to establish Kuomintang authority over North China.[2] Contemporary

documents contradict Feng's account, however. They indicate that
during the period from October, 1924, to September, 1926, when
Feng formally joined the Kuomintang, his relations with the Party
were at best uncertain. They reveal also that the Russians played
a substantial role in finally linking Feng with Kuomintang.

The Kuomintang, the Chinese Communist Party, Feng Yü-hsiang, and Tuan Ch'i-jui, November, 1924, to March, 1925

Relations between Feng Yü-hsiang and the KMT were complicated immediately after the coup d'état by the policies of Tuan
Ch'i-jui. Feng had deposed President Ts'ao K'un and, with the
concurrence of Chang Tso-lin, supported Tuan to head the provisional Peking Government. Tuan Ch'i-jui took office on November 24, 1924.[3]

Meanwhile, Sun Yat-sen had left Canton (on November 13, 1924)
for Peking in response to the invitation of Kuominchün leaders
and Tuan Ch'i-jui.[4] Three days before his departure, Sun issued
a declaration setting forth his policies. The most important
item was his proposal for convening a national assembly. As a
preliminary step, he proposed the organization of a preparatory
conference of delegates of the following types of organizations:
industrial associations, chambers of commerce, educational associations, universities, provincial student associations, labor
unions, peasant associations, political parties, and all armies
opposed to Wu P'ei-fu.[5]

Sun Yat-sen arrived at Peking on December 31, 1924, having
traveled via Japan and Tientsin.[6] His negotiations with Tuan
Ch'i-jui were soon deadlocked. In place of Sun's plans for a
preparatory conference, Tuan advocated convening a "reconstruction conference." This was opposed by Sun on the ground that
delegates of mass organizations would be excluded and that the
conference would be weighted in favor of the militarists.[7] The
reconstruction conference was convened, in the face of Sun's
opposition, on February 1, 1925. This led to an open break between Tuan and the Kuomintang. The KMT issued a circular telegram making clear it would not join the conference.[8]

As early as July, 1923, the Chinese Communist Party had called
on the Kuomintang to summon representatives of student associations, labor unions, and other organizations to organize a national
assembly. It declared that should the KMT fail to carry out this
historical task, the people themselves should take the initiative.[9] In
November, 1924, when Sun left Canton for Peking, the Communist
Party restated the belief that only a national assembly could serve
the country's needs. The Party proposed that the preparatory conference for a national assembly serve as a provisional government
prior to the establishment of a formal, legal government.[10]

While supporting Sun's plans for a national assembly, the Communists were far from enthusiastic about his negotiations with Tuan Ch'i-jui. According to Ch'en Tu-hsiu's political report to the Fifth KCT Congress, held in late April, 1927, the Central Committee had opposed Sun's decision to journey to Peking, because the committee's belief was that he should remain in Canton to exterminate the counterrevolutionary forces and consolidate the revolution in Kwangtung province.[11] Once the negotiations were under way, they resorted to open criticism of Sun Yat-sen. On January 7, 1925, the Hsiang-tao chou-pao published an article, "The Question of Dr. Sun's Attitude," by P'eng Shu-chih. P'eng, who was a close follower of Ch'en Tu-hsiu, accused Sun of weakness and ambiguity in dealing with Tuan and urged him to stand firm for a preparatory conference or risk losing the people's confidence.[12] The Communists were of course even more critical of Tuan Ch'i-jui. Furthermore, at the Party's Fourth Congress, held in January, 1925, the Communist Party denounced Feng Yü-hsiang together with Tuan for playing the "same old game of militarist politics" and fighting for power.[13]

How responsible was Feng Yü-hsiang for Tuan Ch'i-jui's policies in early 1925?

In September, 1926, Feng bitterly denounced Tuan Ch'i-jui and accused his government of oppressive acts against the people.[14] In his autobiography, Feng further defends his own position by explaining that the Peking Government was completely controlled by Tuan and members of the Anfu Clique and that it was precisely for this reason that he retired to the mountains near Peking at the end of 1924.[15]

It is clear, however, that Feng held effective control of military power in the North, particularly after the Mukden Army began to withdraw into Manchuria on January 11, 1925. Tuan Ch'i-jui was to a great extent dependent on Feng's sponsorship. On January 4, 1925, shortly after his formal retirement, Feng was appointed military governor of the Northwestern Border Areas by Tuan's government. His followers were named to important posts: Lu Chung-lin was appointed garrison commander of Peking, Li Ming-chung military governor of Suiyuan, and Chang Chih-chiang military governor of Chahar. Ten days later, on January 14, Tuan Ch'i-jui appointed Sun Yüeh as commander-in-chief of bandit suppression in Honan, Shensi, and Kansu. The expansion of the Kuominchün's authority into these provinces was later formalized by another series of appointments. On April 24, Yüeh Wei-chün, who had just succeeded Hu Ching-yi as commander of the Second Kuominchün, was appointed military governor of Honan. Sun Yüeh was named military governor of Shensi on August 29, 1925. Feng himself was appointed military governor of Kansu on September 4.

He remained at Kalgan, however, and dispatched Liu Yü-fen as his deputy to Lanchow, Kansu.[16]

In view of Feng Yü-hsiang's military supremacy, could he have intervened on behalf of Sun Yat-sen in the latter's conflict with Tuan Ch'i-jui? According to Feng's own testimony in 1944, Sun had tried unsuccessfully to enlist his support. Feng recalls that on Sun's instructions, Wang Ching-wei, Wu Ch'ih-hui, and Sun Fo visited him frequently and pleaded with him not to take a passive attitude.[17] Feng, however, was noncommittal. He confesses in his autobiography (although it contradicts his interpretation of the coup d'état as a KMT revolution) that his mind was still filled with the traditional Chinese political philosophy in early 1925. He was thus unable to understand the significance of political parties and had serious misgivings about the wisdom of organizing political parties. Much as he admired Sun Yat-sen, he feared the dangerous tendency of political parties to place personal interests above national interests. Feng aptly describes his position in early 1925 as that of a disciple of Sun Yat-sen outside the Party.[18]

Furthermore, Feng's diary, published in 1932, reveals that he in fact gave full support to Tuan Ch'i-jui. As early as January 7, 1925, Feng criticized Hu Ching-yi and Sun Yüeh for disobedience to Tuan Ch'i-jui.[19] On March 27, 1925, about two weeks after Sun Yat-sen's death, Feng ordered his followers to render full obedience to Tuan.[20]

Soviet Negotiations with Feng Yü-hsiang, April to June, 1925

In view of Feng's equivocal attitude, the attempt to bring him into the Party fold became a major Kuomintang policy. The Party was greatly aided in this attempt by the Russians, who had material and technical aid to offer as bait.

An interesting account of the early negotiations between Feng and the Russians is given in Document 36, a letter to Frunze, Minister of War of the USSR, from a Russian agent working under the Chinese alias "Jen Te-chiang."[21] Dated May 22, 1925, the document reveals that the Russians had first contacted Hu Ching-yi, commander of the Second Kuominchün, with plans for a Soviet advisory mission. When Hu died on April 10, 1925, there was uncertainty as to whether the Russian plan would be accepted by his successor, Yüeh Wei-chün. Hence Karakhan decided to dispatch the group to work in Feng's First Kuominchün at Kalgan [Doc. 36, pp. 23, 24].

Headed by Jen Te-chiang, the group had arrived at Peking in the middle of April, 1925. It included twenty-nine military experts, two military-political experts, one doctor, and four interpreters.[22]

The original Russian decision to approach Hu Ching-yi may have been influenced by the fact that Hu was a member of the KMT.[23] Furthermore, in the spring of 1925, the Second Kuominchün was by far the strongest army in the Kuominchün combination. It boasted a force of 150,000 men, compared with 50,000 in the First Kuominchün and 30,000 in the Third Kuominchün.[24]

According to Jen Te-chiang, initial discussions with Feng Yü-hsiang were held on April 21, 1925, by Borodin, A. I. Gecker, Soviet Military Attaché,[25] and an unidentified member of the KMT Central Executive Committee. The talk was extremely tentative in nature and the resulting agreement resembled a business deal: there was to be an exchange of Russian supplies and military instructors for Feng's acceptance of the Russians' services and obligations to the KMT. The latter consisted of a promise on Feng's part to admit KMT political workers into the Kuominchün and to oppose imperialism. However, the exact nature of these obligations and of the Russians' services were not clearly defined [Doc. 36, p. 24].[26] Feng Yü-hsiang confirmed in 1944 that there were no definite commitments on either side.[27]

The lack of a clear definition of the Russians' role at Kalgan immediately produced confusion. The principal issue was whether they were to serve merely as technical experts or as political-military advisers. Karakhan and Jen Te-chiang apparently disagreed on this point. On his part, Feng appeared most unwilling to accept the Russians as his personal advisers [Doc. 36, pp. 27, 28].

The Soviet mission was in a dilemma over the character of Feng himself. They were uncertain as to whether he was a pillar of the national revolutionary movement or an ordinary militarist. Therefore, Borodin suggested as a precautionary measure the cultivation of elements in Feng's army which could be counted on to bring about his collapse should he turn against the Russians. On the other hand, Jen Te-chiang emphasized using material aid as a lever to extract promises from Feng and as a means to bolster his wavering revolutionary determination [Doc. 36, pp. 25, 28].

Soviet indecision is revealed also in Document 37, a letter to Karakhan dated June 6, 1925, written probably by Jen Te-chiang. The letter cites evidence indicating that Feng Yü-hsiang was not a man of principle but an ordinary militarist. It stresses the fact that Feng had not joined the KMT and points to his open refusal to allow KMT members to work in the First Kuominchün, although this was one of the obligations he had undertaken in exchange for Soviet weapons. The writer of the letter points out also that Feng refused to recognize the independence of Outer Mongolia.[28] He suggested to Karakhan that certain concrete demands be presented to Feng in order to test his attitude [Doc. 37, pp. 20-22].

As in Canton, the Russians turned first to the establishment of military academies in the Kuominchün. Detailed information on the objectives and results of such work is provided in Document 38, a record of a meeting at the Soviet Embassy in Peking on

December 2, 1925. The meeting was attended by Soviet Ambassador Karakhan, Soviet Military Attaché Voronin, Egorov,[29] and the chief of the Kalgan Soviet group, who worked under the alias "Henry A. Lin."[30] Lin reported fully on the military academies and other aspects of the group's activities.

In addition to organizing schools in the First Kuominchün, the Russians made arrangements to send students from the First and Second Kuominchün to Russia.[31] They also established military academies in the Second and Third Kuominchün.[32]

Feng Yü-hsiang and the National Revolutionary Movement, to October, 1925

While Feng persisted in supporting Tuan Ch'i-jui, he did have tenuous ties with the Kuomintang. He subsidized a Peking newspaper edited by Eugene Chen which supported the Kuomintang's policies.[33] Although he at first refused to allow KMT members to work in his army, he later relented and permitted activities on a limited scale. Shortly after the May Thirtieth Incident in Shanghai, a political club was established at Feng's headquarters. Political clubs were organized at divisional headquarters and at the schools. Under the leadership of Hsü Ch'ien, KMT members delivered anti-imperialist lectures and organized rallies. At Paotow, Suiyuan, a school was organized to train personnel in propaganda techniques. Feng also allowed the Russians to give political lectures to men of the guard brigade and students at the advanced military academy.[34]

KMT headquarters at Kalgan served as the center of Party operations. In August, 1925, a conference of KMT delegates was held at Kalgan, at which Shao Li-tzu was a delegate of the KMT Central Executive Committee.[35] A prominent member of the KMT CEC, Pai Wen-wei, served as adviser to the Second Kuominchün.[36] On August 4, 1925, a group of Whampoa cadets was dispatched from Canton to serve as instructors and concurrently as political workers in the Sixth Mixed Infantry Training Regiment of the Second Kuominchün.[37]

As KMT members, Communists were active in the Kuominchün. The first propaganda team sent out to tour Suiyuan and Chahar was composed exclusively of Communists [Doc. 38, p. 10]. Communists were particularly active in propaganda and liaison work among peasant and bandit groups in Kuominchün territory. Han Lin-fu, a Northern Communist leader, worked among the masses in Jehol, Chahar, and Suiyuan, organizing armed self-defense units to support the Kuominchün and the revolutionary movement.[38] Another top leader of the Northern Communists, Yü Shu-te, worked with the Red Spears Associations in Honan. Wang Jo-fei concentrated his efforts among the workers of the Peking-Hankow and

the Lunghai railways. P'eng Tse-hsiang worked among Second
Kuominchün units in Honan.[39] Hsiao Ch'u-nü gave speeches in
the Kuominchün armies.[40] An T'i-ch'eng was active in the Third
Kuominchün in Shensi and established a club at Sian for propaganda
purposes.[41]

The Kuominchün garrison commander in Peking, Lu Chung-lin,
appeared to be sympathetic to the student movement. In May, for
instance, he arranged the release of students who had been arrested by the Provisional Government.[42]

In short, Kuomintang and Communist members were able to
engage in propaganda and organizational activities with far greater
freedom than under the previous regime of Ts'ao K'un. Thus,
optimism regarding closer Kuomintang-Kuominchün collaboration
prevailed in certain segments of the Kuomintang and the Chinese
Communist Party. The Communists appear to have been particularly sanguine. This hopeful mood reached a height when, in the
fall of 1925, Feng Yü-hsiang began to form alliances against the
Mukden Clique led by Chang Tso-lin.

Outbreak of the Anti-Mukden War, October, 1925

Chang Tso-lin had incurred the wrath of revolutionary Kuomintang and Communist elements by suppressing the labor movement
in Shanghai and other cities following the decline of the May
Thirtieth strike wave. In September, the Shanghai General Labor
Union was ordered closed; its chairman, Li Li-san, was arrested.
Similar measures were carried out in other cities controlled by
members of the Mukden Clique.[43] The Communist press played up
Feng Yü-hsiang as a revolutionary force and Chang Tso-lin as
the arch counterrevolutionary. An article in the Communist International written shortly before the outbreak of war asserts that
Chang Tso-lin was openly hostile to the national revolutionary
movement, whereas Feng Yü-hsiang had from the first sided with
the people; Feng had openly placed his army at the disposal of the
revolutionary movement, although the commanders of the Second
and Third Kuominchün were more cautious. Finally, the article states
that the labor movement had already helped to transform the
Kuominchün into an instrument of struggle against Chang Tso-lin
and imperialism.[44]

The Russians were quite as intent upon strengthening Feng
Yü-hsiang as a bulwark against Chang Tso-lin as in linking him
with the Kuomintang. According to the Comintern's estimate of
the Chinese situation, Japanese influence, as represented by Chang
Tso-lin, had been in the ascendancy since the end of 1924 with the
defeat of Wu P'ei-fu, representative of Anglo-American influence.[45] Thus, it was in the national interest of Soviet Russia to
weaken Chang Tso-lin. This aspect of Soviet policy is fully

discussed in Jen Te-chiang's letter of May 22, 1925, to the Minister of War, Michael Frunze. Jen reported that he had already started efforts to bring about conflict between Feng and Chang. Even if Chang could not be destroyed, Jen said, he should at least be weakened [Doc. 36, p. 25].

An optimistic approach to the impending war against Mukden underlined the resolutions adopted by the Chinese Communist Party's Central Committee at an enlarged plenum held in Peking at the beginning of October. The CC recognized the existence of reaction in the country, but resolved that it was temporary and that the situation remained revolutionary. The national revolutionary movement had not been liquidated or suffered any defeat, the CC declared; in fact it was likely to experience a fresh revival. The CC stated that an armed collision between militarist groups was possible in the near future, and that this would develop into a struggle between the national revolutionary movement and forces opposed to it which would be on a considerably larger scale than before. The approaching conflict would produce tension of forces in the country and absorb imperialists into the struggle. National revolutionary energy would thereby be let loose to such an extent that the war might become the beginning of a movement to crown the 1911 Revolution.[46] In short, the Central Committee viewed the approaching war between Feng Yü-hsiang and his allies on the one hand, and Chang Tso-lin on the other, as the signal for the rise of a fresh revolutionary wave. The CC resolved that the formation of the Kuominchün was already a victory of the Chinese liberation movement.[47]

On October 14, the first phase of the war began when Sun Ch'uan-fang assumed the post of Commander-in-Chief of the Allied Armies of Five Provinces (Kiangsu, Chekiang, Kiangsi, Anhwei, and Fukien). His army marched into Nanking and Shanghai and drove out Mukden's forces.[48] On October 19 Wu P'ei-fu declared support for Sun Ch'uan-fang. Two days later he arrived at Hankow and took the title of Commander-in-Chief of the Allied Anti-Mukden Armies.[49]

These developments were followed by Kuo Sung-ling's rebellion against Chang Tso-lin on October 22. Kuo renamed his army the Northeastern Kuominchün and allied himself with Feng Yü-hsiang. On October 25, Feng issued a circular telegram demanding the retirement of Chang Tso-lin.[50]

The Chinese Communist Party and the Kuomintang immediately declared support for the anti-Mukden forces. On October 20, the KCT issued a "Manifesto on the Anti-Mukden War" which called on the people of the country to support the forces opposing Mukden and to develop the war into a war for their own freedom.[51] A similar position was announced by the Kuomintang, which denounced Chang Tso-lin and Tuan Ch'i-jui as "running-dogs of imperialism" and pledged to support the Kuominchün and other anti-Mukden armies.[52]

The November Twenty-eighth Demonstration, 1925

Agitation for the overthrow of the provisional Peking government reached a peak during the war. On November 28, 1925, Peking students and workers staged a huge demonstration against the government. They surrounded government offices, demanded Tuan Ch'i-jui's resignation, and mobbed the residences of Chang Shih-chao and other cabinet members. On the following day, they held a mass meeting at T'ien-an Men (Gate of Heavenly Peace) and resolved to overthrow Tuan Ch'i-jui and punish the "traitors."[53]

A year later, Katsuji Fuse recalled that in Peking on the eve of the demonstration rumors were prevalent to the effect that the Left KMT leaders Hsü Ch'ien and Li Shih-tseng were planning to overthrow Tuan Ch'i-jui with the connivance of Feng Yü-hsiang.[54] There was actually no such accord between Feng and the Kuomintang. In fact, on the very day of the demonstration, the KMT issued a declaration severely criticizing the Kuominchün leaders. The first objective of the Kuominchün, it stated, should be to unite closely with the national revolutionary movement. Otherwise, it would inevitably become a militarist force opposed to the people and its future would be as short-lived as the Mukden Army's. The Kuominchün could either become the people's ally or the people's enemy, the KMT warned, there was absolutely no room for neutrality.[55]

In the days immediately following the demonstration, Feng's Kalgan headquarters was the destination of representatives of diverse groups all seeking his support. Henry A. Lin was among the first to arrive, apparently on the morning of November 29. According to Lin's report to Karakhan on December 2, 1925, he tried to impress upon Feng the revolutionary character of the Peking demonstration. To produce the desired effect, Lin said, he deliberately exaggerated the number of demonstrators and attempted, as instructed, to persuade Feng to utilize the revolutionary demonstration, presumably to overthrow the Tuan government. Feng's answer, according to Lin, was that he had not heard anything at all about the demonstration [Doc. 38, p. 14].

Feng's diary does not mention Lin's visit, but reveals that on the afternoon of November 29 Hsü Shih-ying, premier of the Peking Government, arrived at Kalgan to request support; Feng's answer was that he would "from beginning to end" support the Government. This position was reiterated on December 2 when he instructed the Peking garrison commander, Lu Chung-lin, always to support the Government. The Kuominchün, Feng declared, would not antagonize,

or be assimilated by, any party or clique. Four days later, on
December 6, Feng told the Chief of Staff, Liu Chi, that the
Kuominchün would publicly proclaim support for Tuan Ch'i-jui.[56]

Meanwhile, the Kuomintang and the Chinese Communist Party
were openly calling for the overthrow of Tuan Ch'i-jui. On December 1, 1925, the central committees of the KCT and CY called on
all revolutionary people of the country, the Kuomintang, and revolutionary military men to respond to the Peking demonstration for
the overthrow of Tuan Ch'i-jui's government and the establishment
of a national government throughout China.[57] In a manifesto issued
one week later, the Kuomintang hailed the revolutionary people of
Peking as leaders of the oppressed people of North China. The
Party expressed the hope that the Peking people would assemble
under the Kuomintang's banner and immediately organize a
committee government to replace Tuan's government.[58]

Feng Yü-hsiang's stand regarding the November 28 demonstration strained his relations with the Kuomintang to the breaking
point. It also deepened the suspicions of his Russian advisers.
Henry A. Lin reported to Karakhan on December 2 that the Russians were able to influence the Kuominchün's strategy and policies.
He claimed that Soviet influence at the staff headquarters was
particularly strong and that Liu Chi, the chief of staff, cooperated
closely with the Russians. Yet, Lin admitted that Feng had no
genuine intentions of being friendly with Soviet Russia. Despite
his frequent assurances of good will, Lin said, there was no real
friendship between Feng and the Russians [Doc. 38, pp. 5, 11-12].[59]

Feng Yü-hsiang's Retirement and Relations with
Soviet Advisers, December, 1925, to February, 1926

The Russians got their first chance to participate in battle with
Kuominchün forces at the end of December. Eighteen Soviet advisers joined in the battle for Tientsin, which was captured on
December 24.[60] Jen Te-chiang had stressed the need for Russian
advisers to join in battle, but their participation in the Tientsin
War apparently failed to bolster their position. Disappointment
characterized a report written on January 27, 1926 by a Russian
who used the name Ya-en. Ya-en was a member of an inspection
team sent out by Moscow to review the work of the Kalgan Soviet
Group.[61] He declared that close relations between Russian advisers and Chinese commanders were completely lacking. During the war, he said, most of the advisers were idle in the rear and
their suggestions were generally ignored. Ya-en concluded that all
Soviet hopes "had vanished like bubbles." Members of the Soviet
group, he reported, were so disappointed with the results of their
work that they proposed winding up everything and returning to
Russia [Doc. 39, p. 79].

Ya-en was extremely critical of the Russians' tendency to approach Feng Yü-hsiang indirectly through his subordinates rather than directly. How could they win confidence and influence among Feng's followers, he asked, when the latter could see that their influence over Feng was so weak that they even appeared to be afraid of him? Ya-en also questioned the basic policy of concentrating on work in the military academies which, he said, had been designed as a compromise means of infiltration. His opinion was that junior Kuominchün officers graduated from the schools were unable to exert any appreciable influence in the Army. Therefore, he proposed giving up broad training plans and advocated organizing a model division which could be relied upon in times of war and political crisis and which could serve as a nucleus in reorganizing the Kuominchün [Doc. 39, pp. 77-81].

The extent of Soviet distrust of Feng Yü-hsiang is illustrated by Document 40, a set of plans for the organization of a civilian volunteer militia in Peking. It was drafted by a Russian who used the name K'o-erh-te. The objective was the formation of an armed force, obedient only to the Kuomintang, which could be relied upon to fight under KMT orders in a political crisis. K'o-erh-te stated, however, that to the Kuominchün authorities, the militia was to be represented merely as an organization for the preservation of local peace and order [Doc. 40, pp. 17-18].

Meanwhile, on January 1, 1926, Feng Yü-hsiang resigned abruptly. He delegated his authority to Chang Chih-chiang and retired to P'ing-ti-ch'üan, Suiyuan.[62] Feng asserts he did so to prevent bloodshed which might result from internal conflicts in the Kuominchün combination, and because he desired to go abroad to study.[63] His retirement made possible a postponement of a choice between continued support of Tuan Ch'i-jui or support of the Kuomintang's program, including its declared objective of overthrowing Tuan. It had become increasingly difficult for Feng to reconcile his frequent declarations of admiration for Sun Yat-sen and his promise to carry out the Three People's Principles[64] with his practical policy of supporting the provisional government.

For three months Feng remained somewhere between P'ing-ti-ch'üan and Paotow, Suiyuan.[65] According to Henry A. Lin, however, he retained actual control of the First Kuominchün.[66]

His retirement came at a time when the Kuominchün armies were experiencing a series of military reverses. Kuo Sung-ling, Feng's ally, was captured and executed by the Mukden Army on December 24, 1925.[67] Furthermore, developments pointed to the formation of an alliance between Chang Tso-lin, Chang Tsung-ch'ang, the Shantung militarist, and Wu P'ei-fu, which was consummated January 23, 1926.[68] On February 17, the Second Kuominchün, commanded by Yüeh Wei-chün, was decisively defeated in

Honan.69 A month later, the First Kuominchün itself was defeated
in the "Second Tientsin War."70 On March 24, 1926, representatives of the victorious Chihli and Mukden armies met at Tientsin
to outline strategy in the continuing offensive against the Kuomin-
chün.71

The March Eighteenth Incident, 1926

On March 18, three days before the loss of Tientsin, an incident
occurred which marked a change in the complicated relationships
within the triangle formed by the provisional government, the
First Kuominchün, and the Kuomintang.

The immediate cause of the incident was the "Taku Ultimatum"
presented to the Government by the signatory powers of the Boxer
Protocol, demanding immediate removal of Kuominchün artillery
installations at Taku harbor outside Tientsin. The Powers gave
the Government forty-eight hours for compliance.72 As the
Government prepared to submit, opposition arose among students
and other groups under the leadership of the KMT Left Wing and
the Communists. On March 17, representatives of various Peking
groups petitioned the Government to reject the ultimatum. Government guards opened fire and wounded several persons. The
following day, March 18, a mass protest meeting was held at
T'ien-an Men. The demonstrators headed for the premier's office.
There they were surrounded by government guards who reportedly
killed more than forty demonstrators.73

On March 19 Tuan ordered the arrest of KMT members Hsü
Ch'ien, Li Shih-tseng, Ku Meng-yü, and I P'ei-chi, and the Communist Li Ta-chao for agitation and dissemination of Communist
propaganda and for instigating the incident.74

The incident, known as the "March Eighteenth Massacre" or the
"Tragic Incident of March Eighteenth," raised in a dramatic fashion the question of the Kuominchün's responsibility for the actions
of the Provisional Government. A vivid picture of the stunned
reactions of the Chinese Communists is given in Document 41,
"Resolutions on the Question of Cooperation between our Party
Members and the First Kuominchün." The resolutions were apparently adopted immediately after the shootings by either the
KCT's Northern Regional Committee or the Peking Local Committee. The Communists laid the responsibility for the massacre
squarely on the First Kuominchün and called for the severing of
all relations with it. In return for continued cooperation, they
demanded the arrest of Tuan Ch'i-jui and other members of the
Provisional Government and thorough reorganization of the
Government [Doc. 41].

Though retired, Feng Yü-hsiang was the center of interest and
speculation. He had previously supported Tuan Ch'i-jui against all

attempts to oust him. What effect, if any, would the incident have
on Feng's attitude? How responsible was Feng himself, whose
troops garrisoned Peking, for the massacre?

According to Feng's diary, he was still at P'ing-ti-ch'üan,
Suiyuan, at the time of the incident. He left there for Moscow on
March 20, arriving at Urga (Ulan Bator) via the Kalgan–Verkne-
Udinsk (Ulan-Ude) road on March 22, 1926.[75] It was on March 26,
1926, while he was at Urga, according to Feng, that he first
learned of the March Eighteenth Incident from the newspapers. On
hearing the news, he asserts, he exclaimed that the Government
was bringing about its own downfall by slaughtering the people.[76]
But he made no public declaration denouncing Tuan's action.

In a report written on the same day, Henry A. Lin, who accompanied Feng on the journey to Moscow, makes some interesting
observations on Feng's political tendencies. Feng's policies are
subject to sudden changes, Lin remarked, despite his connections
with the national revolutionary movement. When the national revolutionary movement appeared strong, Lin said, Feng would allow
political work in his army. When it appeared to be subsiding, he
would prohibit political work and pursue conservative policies. To
remedy the situation, Lin urged the appointment of a prominent
Kuomintang member or a Russian of Borodin's stature as Feng's
political adviser. Someone like Borodin, said Lin, could surely win
his personal friendship. Lin emphasized also the need for a more
definite agreement between Feng and the KMT Central Executive
Committee on political work in the Kuominchün. At the same time,
he reported that a group of officers in the First Kuominchün, had
signed secret pacts to cooperate with the Kuomintang under any
circumstances.[77] As previously discussed, as early as April,
1925, Borodin had advocated cultivating certain elements in Feng's
army as insurance against possible disloyalty.

Feng Yü-hsiang's Change of Attitude, April to Early May, 1926

According to his diary, Feng's political education was greatly
accelerated during his stay at Urga, where he remained until
April 27, 1926. He took Russian lessions and engaged in frequent
discussions of communism, the Bolshevik Revolution, and the world
situation with leaders of the Mongolian People's Republic, the Soviet Ambassador, and Henry A. Lin. As early as April 2, 1926,
according to his diary, Feng had come to the conclusion that Lenin
and Confucius were equals as champions of humanity. Lenin respected weak and oppressed peoples; Confucius respected the
Emperor. This difference, Feng said, was merely the product of
difference in time and circumstances.[78]

Apparently a further stimulus was provided by a series of meetings with Borodin who arrived at Urga with a party of thirty on

April 3, 1926.[79] Included in the party were Eugene Chen, Ku Meng-yü, Ch'en Ch'i-hsiu and Hsü Ch'ien.[80] Feng's diary records a meeting on April 5 between Borodin, Yü Yu-jen, and Feng Yü-hsiang on the subject of cooperation between the Kuomintang and the Kuominchün. Feng spent nearly all of the following day with Borodin and his wife and saw Borodin's party off the afternoon of April 7.[81]

Details concerning these conversations are not available. It may be assumed on the basis of over-all Soviet and KMT policies, however, that Borodin's prime objective was a definite commitment on Feng's part to enter the Party. Feng recalls that after Borodin and the others had left for Vladivostok, Hsü Ch'ien stayed behind, determined to accompany him to Moscow, and strongly urging him to join the KMT.[82]

From Urga Feng headed for Verkne-Udinsk, arriving on April 30. Both he and Hsü Ch'ien were invited to give speeches at a May First celebration two days later.[83] On May 3, Feng sent a telegram to Chang Chih-chiang, Li Ming-chung, and Lu Chung-lin, informing them that he had asked Henry A. Lin to invite one Karpenko to proceed to Kalgan. Karpenko was not only a great statesman, Feng told his subordinates, but an expert Party organizer. He ordered them to revere Karpenko as their teacher and to heed his advice. Feng said also that the work of agitation was most important and that the KMT's Kalgan headquarters should be entrusted with directing the work of propaganda. It was most necessary, Feng said, for Kuominchün officers and men to understand the significance of ideology.[84]

This was a marked change from Feng's previous attitude. As late as April 19 the Russian advisers had complained about the Kuominchün's policy on political work in the Army. At the outbreak of the Anti-Mukden War in October, 1925, Feng had ordered the closing of all political clubs in his army and had not allowed them to reopen when the military academies resumed functioning. Political lectures and even political discussions among the troops were forbidden and punishable by death. Furthermore, a group of KMT political workers had been dismissed shortly before April 19.[85]

Document 42, a Soviet report written soon after April 15, 1926, is extremely critical of the political tendencies of Feng Yü-hsiang and generals of the First Kuominchün. It points out that the First Kuominchün had not yet clarified its political position and concludes with the opinion that its policies had become increasingly contradictory to the slogans of the National Revolution which it had adopted. Nevertheless, the author of the report did not advocate immediate rupture of relations between the Russians and the Kuominchün, or between the Kuomintang and the Kuominchün.

He pointed out that a group of Kuominchün officers who were dissatisfied with the conservative policy of Feng Yü-hsiang and
Chang Chih-chiang could be relied upon to seize control of the
Kuominchün should Feng and Chang continue their policy or should
they break completely with the national revolutionary movement.

Thus, despite intense distrust of Feng, the Russians were still
determined to induce him to align himself definitely with the
Kuomintang. At the same time, in the wake of the March Twentieth
coup d'état at Canton, Russian advisers sought to conciliate Chiang
Kai-shek in the hope of preserving the Kuomintang-Communist
entente.

The suspicions of the Russian advisers at Kalgan were echoed in
the international Communist press. In the April 15 issue of the
International Press Correspondence, Tang Shin She criticized the
First Kuominchün as extremely vacillating. It was threatened with
the loss of the people's sympathy, Tang said, for doing nothing
after the March Eighteenth shootings. In fact, the Kuominchün had
been accused of cooperating with Tuan, he declared. However,
Tang also revealed the Communists' willingness to continue relations with the Kuominchün. While the character of the Kuominchün
armies was of course not the same as the Canton armies, he said,
they had no connections with imperialism and had frequently taken
an anti-imperialist position. While the Kuominchün armies did
not definitely support the mass movement, workers and peasant
organizations could freely develop in their territories. Furthermore, Tang pointed out, the Kuominchün armies were in constant
touch with the Canton Government.[86]

The following week, Gregory Voitinskii, chief Comintern representative to the Chinese Communist Party, attacked Feng Yü-hsiang
for his silence. Feng and the Kuominchün armies did not understand the significance of political struggle, he said, and devoted
all their attention to military problems. Although the Kuomintang
and the Chinese Communist Party had long ago requested the
Kuominchün to declare its political platform, it refused to comply.
The Kuominchün armies, said Voitinskii, remained primarily military groupings. The silence of Feng Yü-hsiang and other leaders
was being interpreted by the imperialists as an adroit political
move, while the broad masses were compelled to think that Feng
was merely following his old policy of strengthening his military
power. Voitinskii concluded: "We consider that one of the causes
of Feng's subsequent defeat was his policy of silence. Not only
did it help to isolate the National Armies [Kuominchün] from the
people of the country in general, but it had also a bad effect on
the morale of the army itself."[87]

Even though Feng made increasingly enthusiastic statements
about Leninism and the Kuomintang, he did not decide to join the

Kuomintang until May 10, 1926. He had arrived at Moscow the day before amidst impressive ceremonies led by high Soviet leaders. According to his diary, the decision to join the KMT followed a visit to Lenin's tomb, after which Feng records: "Today, I have determined to join the Kuomintang, to become a Kuomintang member and [work] for the National Revolution."[88]

Why did Feng Yü-hsiang decide at that particular time to join the Kuomintang? If, as he asserts in 1944, his coup d'état was in effect a KMT revolution, why had he not entered the Party earlier?

One answer, it appears, lies in the series of defeats sustained by the Kuominchün at the very time Feng Yü-hsiang's attitude seemed to undergo a profound change. During his stay at Urga in April, 1926, the allied armies of Mukden, Chihli, and Shantung were conducting a successful offensive against the Kuominchün. A general offensive was launched against Peking on April 7, 1926. On April 15 the Kuominchün withdrew to Nankow and Peking was occupied by the Mukden Army five days later, on April 20, 1926.[89]

Prior to the withdrawal from Peking the Kuominchün had attempted to come to terms with Wu P'ei-fu. On March 31 Kuominchün representatives met Wu's field commander, T'ien Wei-ch'in at Paoting, Chihli, in an effort to negotiate an agreement. On April 9, two days after the launching of the general offensive against Peking, Kuominchün units led by Lu Chung-lin surrounded the residences of members of Tuan's government and denounced Tuan as a traitor. Ts'ao K'un, the former president and close collaborator of Wu P'ei-fu, was released and the Kuominchün officially wired Wu P'ei-fu to enter Peking.[90] Wu, however, rejected the overtures for peace.[91]

Thus, Feng's decision to join the Kuomintang was made after futile attempts to form an alliance with Wu P'ei-fu, his former chief, and against the background of a steadily worsening military situation. According to his diary, on May 9, 1926, the eve of his decision, Feng learned that the Kuominchün was suffering from serious shortages of ammunition.[92] With Tientsin in enemy hands, the Kuominchün was entirely cut off from overseas supply. The only supply route open was the Ulan-Ude—Kalgan highway, which connects with the Trans-Siberian Railway. In the eleven months between April, 1925, and March, 1926, the Soviet Union had supplied Feng with 6,000,000 rubles' worth of weapons and ammunition.[93] In view of the critical military situation, therefore, Soviet military supplies must have seemed ever more attractive to Feng Yü-hsiang.

Feng Yü-hsiang in Moscow, Summer, 1926

While in Moscow, Feng Yü-hsiang gave a series of radical speeches to dramatize his new position. At a reception given in

his honor by Chinese students of Sun Yat-sen University, he
reportedly gave an extremely revolutionary address, concluding
with the slogans, "Long live Leninism! Long live the proletariat!
Long live the World Revolution!"[94] Feng, in fact, sent his son
to study at the University.[95]

In a speech on July 19, Feng declared that the Kuominchün in
the North and the National Revolutionary Army in the South would
soon bring about victory for the National Revolution. In an interview published in Pravda, he said that the alliance of the Kuominchün and the National Revolutionary Army had created a firm and
powerful revolutionary force and that victory was certain. He
said that although the Kuominchün had to fight against superior
armies, it never surrendered because it was united with the people
and fought for the country.[96]

Feng met many important leaders of the Party and government in
Moscow, including Chicherin, Zinoviev, Kalinin, Radek, Voroshiloff,
Trotsky, and Mrs. Lenin.[97] He had several meetings also with
Gregory Voitinskii.[98]

Apparently Henry A. Lin's suggestion that Feng's adviser should be
a man of Borodin's stature was heeded, for the Soviet Government immediately appointed Usmanov, at one time Chief of Staff to General
Galen,[99] as adviser to Feng. According to Feng, he began to have daily
discussions with Usmanov on such subjects as dialectical materialism
as the beginning of his study of the new philosophy.[100]

After several trips to other points in the Soviet Union, Feng
left Moscow on August 17, 1926. According to Feng, he could no
longer remain in Moscow when news arrived of the Kuominchün's
loss of Nankow (on August 14) and the departure of the National
Revolutionary troops from Canton on the Northern Expedition.[101]

Feng Yü-hsiang's Entry into the Kuomintang, September 16, 1926

After his decision to enter the Party, Feng had ordered Liu Chi
and Li Ming-chung to Canton to serve as his envoys plenipotentiary. They arrived at Canton on August 22.[102] That same day,
the National Revolutionary Army captured Yoyang (Yochow), Hunan, on
the Hunan-Hupeh border. From the front Chiang Kai-shek wired
the following day, suggesting that the Kuominchün occupy Peking
when the National Revolutionary Army occupied Wuhan and then
that the armies join together in Honan.[103]

On August 23, Feng Yü-hsiang was formally appointed KMT
Party Representative in the Northwest and member of the Military
Council and the National Government Council.[104]

Feng received news of his appointment at Urga on his return
journey to China. On September 15 he reached Wuyüan, Suiyuan,
and issued a declaration the following day. The duty of the Kuominchün, announced Feng, was to awaken the masses, overthrow

militarism and imperialism, and, in accordance with KMT principles, to struggle for the independence and freedom of China and
to ally with all peoples willing to treat China as an equal. Feng
then injected a note of caution and declared that although he had
undertaken revolutionary tasks, he lacked a clear revolutionary
policy and was not worthy to be known as a Chinese revolutionary
or a Sunyatsenist. He would be even more ashamed to be called
a Marxist, Leninist, or World Revolutionary, since he did not
even understand the meaning of those terms. Then, having made
a pointed denial of rumors that he had become "bolshevized,"
Feng confirmed his ties with Soviet Russia, the only country,
said Feng, which had volutionarily abolished the unequal treaties
and was willing to help all oppressed peoples in their struggle
for liberation.[105]

Document 36 is a letter, dated May 22, 1925, addressed to Michael Frunze, Minister of War, of the USSR, from Jen Te-chiang, chief of the Soviet advisory group attached to Feng Yü-hsiang. The Peking Commission based its Chinese translation on a copy of a Russian document which was seized in the raid on the Soviet Military Attaché's office. The Chinese translation is available under the title, "A Letter from Jen Te-chiang to Frunze, Chairman of the Revolutionary Military Council of the Soviet Union, on Liaison with Feng Yü-hsiang and Various Observations, with a Copy to Voronin," in Su-lien yin mou..., III, "Kuominchün," pp. 23-29. The letter is marked "Most Secret."

[JEN TE-CHIANG'S LETTER TO FRUNZE ON ALLIANCE WITH FENG YÜ-HSIANG]

[23] In compliance with your verbal instruction to send all reports direct, I am submitting this report to inform you of the reasons for changing our place of work, the results obtained, and the difficulties confronting us in our present position.

Three days before our arrival at Peking on April 13, 1925, Hu Ching-yi died of illness. Considerable dispute arose over the question of succession. It lasted for two weeks and there was some uncertainty as to what attitude his successor would take toward our plans previously approved by Hu. Hence, Peking decided not to send us there [Second Kuominchün in Honan].

The Military Attaché, Gecker, suggested that members of the
[24] group be distributed to different places in accordance with needs, a few of them to be attached to other groups at such places as Canton and Hunan [Honan?]. (There is only one [Russian] at the latter place.) The rest were to remain in Peking. However, in view of the money and effort it had cost you to have our group organized, I stated various reasons why we should not be scattered. My suggestion was accepted by Karakhan.

We then considered which part of China would be most suitable for our work. From the standpoint of our country's influence, as well as the general military and political situation, Feng Yü-hsiang, commander of the First Kuominchün, whose army now occupies Peking, Suiyuan, and Chahar, was considered the closest to our country, with the exception of Kwangtung and Hu Ching-yi. Hence, Peking [Soviet Embassy] decided to send us to Feng.

On April 21st, Borodin, Gecker, and a member of the Central Executive Committee of the Kuomintang went to see Feng. As a result

of the negotiations, Feng expressed willingness to accept our services and to undertake various tasks for the Kuomintang (such as
allowing Kuomintang political workers to enter his army and to
oppose imperialism) in exchange for ammunition.

On the 22d, T'a-hsin, Nikitin,* and I again called on General
Feng. Following Borodin's instructions, we avoided any discussion
of the condition and nature of our work, since we had failed to make
Feng really sincere in receiving our country's political aid.

The actual result of our negotiations is an agreement somewhat
resembling a business deal: an exchange of ammunition and instructors for Feng's obligations to the KMT. Fundamental problems
relative to the work of our group remain unsolved. These include
the question of our position in Feng's army, whether we are to be
ordinary technical instructors or Feng's personal advisers.

We have decided, however, that while working in Feng's army
we would conduct a careful investigation of political and military
relations between the various cliques. We will also collect up-to-
date information on all important armies, and statistical and geographical data, so that we will have complete and accurate information on everything. The military attaché's office (organized with
one Military attaché and one commissar) is not able to furnish us
25] with sufficient information, but when Voronin arrives he will put
all things in order with the help of our comrades. (A graduate of
the Military Academy has been appointed to work in his office.)
This will greatly facilitate the work of our group.

A conference was held by the senior personnel of the group at
Karakhan's place on April 28th to discuss problems concerning
our work. Borodin and Gecker were also present. Karakhan expressed the belief that Feng's army is a pillar of the national revolutionary movement in North China and that we should help to build
up its fighting capacity so it will be strong and lasting. In Borodin's
view, we should simultaneously develop elements in Feng's army
which will be capable of bringing about his collapse, as insurance
against his possible opposition to our country. Karakhan also remarked that it was too early to speak of united action on the part
of Feng's army, the Honan Army [Second Kuominchün], and the

---

* There were apparently at least two Russians by the name of
Nikitin in China in 1925-1927. The one mentioned here also worked
under an assumed name which was rendered by the Chinese as Hsi-
lin. He later became adviser to Yü Yu-jen in Shensi in late 1926
and the beginning of 1927. See "List of Persons Working in the
Northwestern Army" and "List of Names and Positions of Persons Sent by the Soviet Union to Serve in Feng Yü-hsiang's
Army," Su-lien yin-mou..., "KMC," pp. 104, 106. See also Doc. 44,
p. 415.

Southern armies. We failed to arrive at any basic direction for our work during the course of the meeting.

I personally consider most important the problem of whether Feng's army is indeed a pillar of the national liberation movement. If Feng is consistent and of permanent benefit to us, we should see that his influence grows strong and lasting. On the other hand, if we wish to ally with him merely because he is an enemy of pro-Japanese and conservative groups, we need only build up his fighting force in order to attain our objective, after which we may destroy the "deceitful fellow."

Since I have not received basic instructions, I have had to solve this problem on my own. I have started efforts to bring about conflict between Feng Yü-hsiang and Chang [Tso-lin] of Mukden. A victory for Chang would mean a victory for the conservatives and imperialists (Japan in particular), and would be dangerous for the Soviet Union. Even if we cannot destroy Chang, we should at least weaken him. At present, the important enemy of Chang is Feng Yü-hsiang, but Feng's capacity (skill and technical strength) is small and he has insufficient troops. If we extend our help at these points, Feng would probably accept the Kuomintang's demands for Left KMT elements to work in his army. Since Feng owes us no moral obligations, this is all we can count on.

Whether Feng is actually our comrade in the national liberation [26] movement, how much he can be trusted, and whether he is an irreconcilable enemy of Chang and will fight him to the end—these are questions which must be solved before we begin our work. However, we lack accurate military and political data. Information obtained from organs of the General Staff, newspaper reports, and individual investigations and incidental reports from our secret agents constitute our only sources of news. As yet, we have not established intelligence organs and are therefore unable to obtain sufficient data to aid in the solution of our problems. Yet, these problems must be solved.

For the present there are only two alternatives: ally with Feng, at the same time insuring against his endangering the interests of our country, or break off all relations with him in order to avoid taking risks.

The following is Borodin's description of Feng's character which I am presenting for your reference.

The fact that we have already gained Feng's confidence is proved by his permission for us to join the various parts of his army. He has ordered the artillery to be assembled for our inspection; the cavalry is already assembled. His army here is divided into regular companies, half companies, and engineering companies, and we have inspected them all.

My summary report to the higher officers based on notes we took

in the various units of the army have been circulated by General
Feng with orders to expedite execution [of points made in my re-
port].

With their plans on armored cars, our engineers and armored-
car experts have won the praise of the technical personnel and
their complete confidence in our technical knowledge. The plans
will be carried out by the army's technical staff.

General Feng has said he is willing to send officers to study in
our country's schools. He permits us to wear Chinese uniforms.
The General asks us to write frequent reports on army administration and various basic problems of war. All the officers listen very
carefully to what we say.

[27]   Judging by the above, it would seem our work has opened up a
far-reaching and great future. Tangible results are not great, however. I believe that we should strengthen Feng's army, not only by
improving its training and organization but by getting permission
to participate in battles and to carry out military-political work.
[The latter should consist of:] (1) improvement of the army's strategy and methods of supervision to fit in with our military-political
plans; (2) Investigation of the [army's] fighting capacity with a
view to determining how it may be utilized in the interest of the
Chinese national liberation movement.

The reason why we cannot proceed quickly or thoroughly with our
military-political work may be the fact that Feng has actually received very little of the material aid promised him. According to
Feng, all the supplies previously prepared for Honan [Second
Kuominchün], excepting a few remnant pieces, have been shipped to
his place. We have told him that fresh supplies will soon arrive,
but that since they come from afar and require a great deal of time
for transportation (due to poor facilities), they may fall short of his
expectations. Feng feels that our aid has been very meager. Recent
events too have placed him in a very difficult position. There are
two possible conclusions about Feng Yü-hsiang.

1. Feng has not expressed willingness to let us serve as military
and political advisers.

2. Feng treats us in this manner because Karakhan does not allow
us to take the initiative freely or to work independently. Acting on
special instructions of the Foreign Commissariat of the USSR,
Karakhan directs his subordinates with strict orders. It is perfectly
clear that he wishes to be personally responsible for everything.
He selects work for his subordinates and determines how it is to be
carried out to such an extent that they need only act blindly. The
Foreign Commissariat is a model government department. Karakhan
is an envoy plenipotentiary of the USSR. While his methods may suit
[28] the interests of the Foreign Commissariat, we cannot do our best
under his direction because it is not suited to our work. Of course,

it may be that the job of directing us is not an easy one. (To clarify
the situation, I am sending herewith selected copies of correspondence between Peking [Soviet Embassy] and myself.)

I have been summoned to Peking because of this problem. Peking
has told me that the establishment of Kuomintang influence in
Feng's army is no concern of mine and that I am not to negotiate
with Feng on our arms supply. Although all of their negotiations
with Feng had previously been conducted through me, I am not permitted to take up any of Feng's questions regarding supplies. This
situation has continued to this day.

Since I answer "I don't know" to all of his important questions,
Feng naturally cannot belp treating me as an ordinary technician.

As the present situation is urgent, it is necessary to make a definite decision according to the following:

1. If we consider Feng Yü-hsiang an unreliable ally and alliance
with him too risky, it is not too late to sever relations with him.
On the other hand, if we believe his attitude to be firm and consider
him a natural ally of our country, as well as an enemy of Chang
Tso-lin, we should spare no effort to give him abundant material
support. Time flies and opportunities must not be lost. Our supplies
so far amount to "a grain in the granary" and transportation is
poor. Since he has not received real support, Feng is wavering and
losing determination. His confidence in our country is gradually
weakening. Of course, as an individual without the support of the
army and other organizations, Feng Yü-hsiang is not worthy of
attention.

Our political work must not be delayed. We have two objectives:
(a) build up Feng's army as an army of the KMT, with a view to
implanting this concept in the minds of Feng's officers and the
people; and (b) make Feng firm and lead him into definite party
connections [with the Kuomintang].

[29]   2. As for ourselves, it is not appropriate merely to make use of
us as technical instructors. This does not fit the nature of our
group, nor is it consistent with its original purpose, particularly in
view of the great expense involved in organizing the group. Peking
should adopt a definite policy toward Feng and change its ways of
supervising us. They should request Feng to appoint us as political
and military advisers at his headquarters. Otherwise we should
immediately give up ambitious schemes. As ordinary technicians,
instructors, and military secret agents, we can be of use to other
armies and need not be confined to Feng's army, ignoring the others.
Peking may be fully aware of the situation regarding Feng and our
tasks in connection with him. However, I am not clear about the inside situation. This is why I am presenting my considerations to you.

Kindly decide whether my opinions, the problems I raised, and my
conduct are proper. If they are, please extend me your prompt support.

Document 37, a letter to Nikolayev (code name for Ambassador Karakhan), dated June 6, 1925, is translated from Russian into Chinese and published under the title, "The Soviet Union's Conspiratorial Plans for Utilizing Feng Yü-hsiang," in Su-lien yin-mou..., III, "Kuominchün," pp. 19-23. Our translation is based on the above, checked against brief excerpts of the same document in English in Mitarevsky's World-wide Soviet Plots, pp. 19-20. According to Mitarevsky, the letter is signed with the initial J. This clue, in addition to the general character of the document, suggests that it was written by the Soviet adviser Jen Te-chiang. The Peking Commission deleted a section toward the end of the document.

[LETTER TO KARAKHAN ON FENG YÜ-HSIANG]

[19] There are extremely close connections between Feng Yü-hsiang's political attitude and our work. As I have repeatedly reported to you in person and in writing, we cannot have firm policies and clear objectives in our work unless the problem of Feng's political attitude is clarified. I am thus compelled to draw your attention again to the question: is Feng Yü-hsiang a political figure who is of benefit to us?

Two alternative answers may be given in this question:

1. Feng is a man of definite principle, allied with the various movements in China and a symbol of the anti-imperialist national revolutionary movement in North China.

2. Feng is an ordinary militarist who is forced by circumstances and geographical location to act temporarily in the interests of [20] Soviet Russia, since Russia is a nation which wishes to see the weakening of all imperialist countries (particularly Japan).

[If we adopt] the first estimate, we would strengthen Feng's military force at every opportunity without fearing possible danger or failure in the belief that Feng will definitely act in the interests of the Chinese and world revolutionary movements and will make of China an ally of the USSR. The basic factor then would be tactics of revolutionary struggle. It would not be necessary to use our material aid as a decisive factor in settling our relationship. The primary objective of our Party would be to strengthen Feng's fighting capacity and [capacity for] independent work.

[If we adopt] the second estimate, we would carry on our work through other means. On the one hand, we would assist Feng in order that he might carry out the tasks we assign him. On the other hand, we would ensure against the possibility of his contradicting our interests. Material aid would then be of primary importance. [We would plan our aid] in such manner that should we refuse it Feng would be reduced to a secondary position if not completely defeated. We would therefore direct our assistance so that once our support is withdrawn, his army would revert to its original state.

In view of the above alternatives, I feel it necessary to clarify Feng Yü-hsiang's political attitude. The following are several points I am presenting in the hope that they may be helpful in arriving at a solution to the problem.

In point of fact, we lack data which might induce us to form a favorable judgment of Feng. On the contrary, there is abundant evidence, such as the following, to support the opposite point of view:

1. Feng's inconsistent political attitude.

2. Feng's vacillating attitude in his relations with the Kuomintang. Despite the Kuomintang's efforts to appease and compromise with him, he has not joined the Party. It is obvious also that not even [21] one of Feng's close subordinates has joined the KMT. (We cannot accept as accurate the report that he has secretly joined the KMT.)

3. Feng's open refusal to allow the KMT to carry on political work in his army.

4. Feng's alliance with the provinces of Chekiang and Fukien, which today remain enemies of the Kwangtung Government.

5. Feng's [friendly] attitude toward imperialism:

a) A "National Humiliation Map" is used for propaganda in the army; it is marked with territories to be returned to China. These include the Baikal and Amur provinces and Vladivostok, although no mention at all is made of Japanese occupied Manchuria or American economic interests in central China.

b) There are frequent newspaper reports of negotiations between Feng and Chang [Tso-lin], particularly about Outer Mongolia.

c) Feng refuses to recognize the independence of Outer Mongolia. (The visit of prominent Mongolians to Kalgan and their reception by Feng are merely routine matters.)

6. Feng's obviously friendly relations with the United States (indicated by the special protection he accords American missionaries).

7. Feng's refusal to allow trade-union activies on the Peking-Suiyuan Railway. (This has not been confirmed yet.)

These facts suffice to convince us that it is necessary to resort to the second plan in dealing with Feng and to conduct a careful investigation.

Should we still wish to follow the first plan, I feel that answers to the following are necessary in order to secure sufficient guarantees for the plan.

[22]   1. We should clearly put up to Feng the question of his actual relations with the Kuomintang and demand that the KMT be allowed to organize and carry on political work in Feng's army.

2. We should demand that Feng accept and carry out in his territories the minimum political program already formulated.

3. We should demand, as the final result of the above, that Feng accept joint control of his army with the commissioners' group appointed by the Kuomintang Central [Executive] Committee.

Should Feng accept and promise to realize the above demands, our greatest gain would be the attainment of our goal, which has hitherto eluded us. This is the goal of participating in Feng's military and political work and in actual battles. Should he reject our demands, his political attitude would be amply clarified and we could then conclude that we should cooperate with him merely as one of the militarists who are of relative benefit to us at the present time.

Judging by Ko-lei's report, we know it is not likely that Feng will agree to the above demands, and that Feng lacks strong determination. Clearly, then, we should carry out some sort of secret political plan in his army. Without affecting his actual strength we should see that he is not dominated by the imperialists. In other words, we should prevent his army from being a tool of the counter-revolution. [section deleted].

Should Feng refuse to grant the aforesaid guarantees, two alternative measures are open to us:

1. We may immediately cut off all relations with Feng (this is feasible) and shift the activities of our group to proletarian centers.

2. We may make Feng completely dependent on our country's aid in accordance with plans outlined above. In this event, the following measures are necessary:

a) Equip Feng's army with our arms and impress upon him his utter dependence on our supplies.

b) Establish a large ammunition warehouse at Urga [Ulan Bator]
[23] and repair the highway between Kalgan and Verkne-Udinsk [Ulan-Ude] for the transportation of needed supplies and reserves.

c) Reduce our plans for training Feng's army by concentrating on low-ranking officers and soldiers, so that they will be able to carry out our orders. At the same time, we should leave high-ranking officers at such a level of efficiency that lacking our assistance, Feng's army will suffer from lack of direction.

d) Incite to the best of our ability Feng's hostility toward those forces which are hostile to our country so that they cannot ally themselves with him.

DOCUMENT 38

Document 38 is the record of a meeting held at the Soviet Embassy
in Peking on December 2, 1925. Among the participants were
Soviet Ambassador Karakhan, Soviet Military Attaché Voronin, and
Henry A. Lin, chief adviser to Feng Yü-hsiang. The following is
based on a Chinese translation of the Russian document published
under the title, "Record of a Meeting Attended by Karakhan and
Others at the Soviet Embassy on December 2, 1925, concerning
Interference with China's Internal Political Affairs and Other Problems," in Su-lien yin-mou..., III, "Kuominchün," pp. 1-16. Short
extracts of the document are given in English in Soviet Plot in
China, p. 100, and Mitarevsky, World-wide Soviet Plots, pp. 29,
31-32. The original document is marked "Most Secret."

[RECORD OF A MEETING AT THE
SOVIET EMBASSY IN PEKING]

[1] [Henry A.] Lin: In view of the small number of available instructors
and lack of translators, we have centralized our efforts in the
schools. Greater results have been obtained in such work than in
other kinds of work. It is truly the most effective way to utilize our
resources.

During this period, an artillery school has been established with
114 students, all of whom qualified to become platoon and company
commanders. They have in fact registered for such positions. The
other day when we tested their ball-firing, we found the average
infantry artillery student definitely inferior to students in Russian
schools. However, they rank high in China and the school's reputation is firmly established. Although the majority of the students
were recruited from the ranks and only a few had been officers,
they are appointed captains or battalion commanders upon graduation. A few have been appointed platoon commanders. All platoon
and company commanders in the artillery units at this time are
graduates of the school. Thus, the reputation of the school has
affected the Army also. Before the war, the school had recruited
cadets by examination and had sought to train battalion and company commanders (that is, high officers). The outbreak of the war,
however, resulted in dissolution of the school. Eighty students
from the Second Kuominchün attended the school.

The advanced infantry school was established later. Altogether
38 students studied at the school. One group received appointments
before graduation. Therefore, only 30 actually graduated. Of these,

some were appointed brigade and regiment commanders; others
[2] were given good positions also. They are treated well in the various armies and are known for their real capabilities among high-
ranking army officers.

A cavalry school has been set up with 240 students, 70 of whom
are officers and the others low-ranking officers. They suffice to
meet our immediate cavalry needs. The other day, when Governor
Chang [Chih-chiang] of Chahar came for inspection, they displayed
high jumps for him. The fact that he established the Sixth Cavalry
Brigade in such a short period has been attributed to the jumps!
The training of his Second Cavalry Brigade is being carried on
simultaneously with courses in the school. A group has received
swords, some Russian swords, and swords of various types. The
cavalry at present totals about four thousand men, half equipped
with swords and the other half, spears.

Karakhan: How many swords have you received?

Lin: We have received a total of 1,000 Russian swords. Only a
portion of the Army has swords. We have proposed the organization of one cavalry division out of the two divisions which are
composed of four regiments each. There are good officers in certain portions of the divisions. We also proposed the appointment of
a brilliant man as cavalry commander and left the appointment
of two others to General Feng himself under certain conditions.
I once said to General Feng that since we had nominated General
Sung, the other two men should be appointed by him on condition
that they accept the views of the Russian advisers. Feng then
appointed General Sung [Che-yüan] commander of the Cavalry Division. Sung was formerly commander of the Eleventh Division and
is presently Military Governor of Jehol.

We have established a machine-gun school with an enrollment
of 180 students. About 140 students have graduated. They have been
trained not only in ballistics but in loading and unloading machine
guns. The other day when I visited the Army with the inspection
group, I noticed that the ballistics record of some of the students
[3] was excellent but that the loading and unloading of Maxim machine
guns required approximately seven minutes. This is about the
same as loading and unloading ordinary machine guns.

Karakhan: What is the speed of loading and unloading machine
guns in our army?

Lin: Only forty seconds. Our aim is to enable them to finish
loading and unloading within one minute. The Russian machine guns
received at the same time as the old-model Chinese machine
guns are the most suitable. This is the type used exclusively at
present.

There is also an engineering school in addition to the above
schools. The work of this school is not well regulated and although

it has 40 students, its organization is loose. The students have received some basic training in fort construction.

Elements from this loose organization have been sent to the mixed school, where we have also performed some work.

The above pertains to the problem of the schools. Attention should be drawn to the fact that there is no uniform system within the schools. We can only proceed gradually as the situation warrants.

There is an intelligence school with 60 students. A guard school has also been established with 14 students, although it had originally been planned to admit 100 students. The students have already been sent to the rear of Chang Ch'iung-ming [Chang Tso-lin] and have been registered with us. We formulated plans for the work of the schools which were enclosed in the detailed report submitted to the [Soviet] inspection group during its trip. Such plans contain critical comments on the current condition of Feng's army and explanations of its training program. The Chinese armies have all received orders in accordance with our plans. The orders include entrusting you [Karakhan] with certain matters. The basic objective is to realize our plans.

We mapped out working plans for the schools with an eye to the future. Although high-ranking infantry officers have already been trained, they should be supplemented by lower officers who are relatively better educated and qualified. We should proceed with this
[4] matter by organizing a school to train 100 captains who will later serve as battalion commanders. There will then be 100 battalions altogether. General Feng has agreed to establish an advanced infantry school (captains' school) for training infantry officers. This school should have machine-gun, cannon, and cavalry departments. There should also be an advanced artillery school. Artillery requirements are opposite to those of the infantry. The artillery needs high officers, whereas the infantry needs low officers. General Feng has promised to turn over to us all battalion and company commanders so that high and low artillery officers will be given centralized training. General Feng has agreed completely to the principle of centralized training and in our opinion will certainly not hinder its execution. I once asked him whether this particular school is intended to train only his armies, or other armies as well. He replied that a general school should be established to train officers of all armies of the Kuominchün and officers of those armies which wish to ally with the Kuominchün.

The above pertains to working plans for the schools. I will now discuss the question of political work.

Karakhan: You have not quite finished the military part, nor have you mentioned the condition of the college.

Lin: I particularly stress the importance of the cavalry. In my opinion, 70 high cavalry officers and 120 low cavalry officers should be sufficient for the moment. All types of work should be undertaken within each division. As for the infantry, I believe that the training of high officers and the [personnel of] machine-gun units has been completed, but not the training of captains. There is no system within the companies. The same situation prevails in the artillery. Looking forward to future reorganization, General Feng intends to promote platoon commanders to battalion [?] commanders. The more high officers trained, the better the system.

Karakhan: These plans have not been carried out because of the war. All the schools have been closed.

[5]   Lin: Now let us take up again the matter of the college. The situation in this. The college existed for about two months. When the war started, General Feng ordered it closed because the college carried out some propaganda. The students were distributed among the infantry, artillery, and machine-gun units. We cannot help suspecting that the closure was due to his fear that the college might become the center of propaganda.

About the General Staff. Upon the outbreak of war, we utilized the confidence we enjoyed (various facts can prove there is confidence in our work) to obtain considerable results by working at the office of the General Staff. Our advisers work together daily with General Liu Chi, on routine matters every three days and in conference also every three days. The General Staff is composed of administrative and intelligence departments. It has devised means to estimate the number of troops known to belong to Marshall Chang Tso-lin. As for relations between our nationals and the Chinese at the General Staff, I can say for sure that our conversations have been most cordial. I believe that our participation in the work of the General Staff should proceed not only through formal means but also through personal contacts. As an indication of the results obtained through our technical influence with the General Staff, one current fact should be noted. The withdrawal of the Army from Peking to Nankow when Peking was threatened was carried out in accordance with our proposal.

Karakhan: Was that our suggestion?

Lin: When they withdrew to Nankow, they had all kinds of ideas about the movement of troops. The withdrawal was carried out in accordance with their own plans. However, in times of crisis, such as when they had to put up defense, they completely followed our direction. According to their original plan, all trenches were to be connected in one line, but they accepted our suggestion to dig [6] trenches in a zigzag line. The trenches are about three Russian miles from Jehol.

Karakhan: Was the artillery sent there also?

Lin: I believe that all technical decisions were made according to our directions. The withdrawal to Nankow, for instance, indicates our influence and acceptance of our plans. Furthermore, we entirely directed the dispatch of two divisions to Nankow and other troop movements. It was our original plan to concentrate the Army around Nankow, but they changed the plans and instead concentrated the troops in the center. This decision was correct, because their prediction of the attitude of Shansi exceeded our capacity for political predictions. The movement of the cavalry, that is, its dispatch to Nankow, the troop movements, and the organization of the cavalry into divisions and regiments were all accomplished under our technical influence. They are concrete manifestations of our influence at the office of the Chief of Staff.

Routine matters at the office of the General Staff are handled according to the following procedure. At 9:00 o'clock every morning, all personnel are assembled (the same during wartime) and a technical conference is immediately convened by their chief of staff and our chief of staff [chief adviser]. This procedure has recently been changed to that of calling on one another for consultation on the work of the General Staff. They have thereby gained quite a bit in knowledge and will continue to gain more in the future.

Karakhan: How is the General Staff organized?

Lin: It is headed by General Liu Chi, who has great respect for the Russian Army. He is a brilliant man. Although he says he has never studied military science, my impression is that either he has engaged in advanced self-study or he did study somewhere. I recall a certain major who was General Liu's guard and whose services were at Liu's disposal. The major also said that he had never studied anywhere, but had in fact studied and graduated from a school in France. There are two deputies to General Liu:
[7] one is General Ts'ai [Ts'ao Hao-shen?] and the other, General Ch'en. Ch'en was once president of a college but I cannot remember offhand where Ts'ai was graduated. There is another colonel who is also well versed in military knowledge. Aside from these men, six officers assist in handling work which is done by one deputy chief of staff in our country. The office is staffed with a total of eighteen persons, of whom only General Liu Chi and General Ch'en are really hard working and willing to accept our opinions.

Karakhan: How many departments and sections are there at the office of the General Staff?

Lin: The technical section is the most important. There are also administrative and financial sections and an ordnance section, which came to my knowledge purely by accident. General Feng used to handle personally all matters concerning military equipment. When I talked with him about the condition of the Russian Army he paid great attention to the question of arms management in Russia. Subsequently, a certain officer came to my place, introducing himself as Chief of the Ordnance Section. His assistant, who is in charge of rifles and cartridges, accompanied him on that occasion. Thus, I learned of the existence of the Ordnance Section. There is also a commissariat section. Altogether there are five sections, all having connections with us.

Karakhan: Is there an accurate and detailed account of the quantity of arms?

Lin: The list sent to you a few days ago has been checked on the spot and corresponds with the actual quantity.

Egorov: What is the actual number?

Lin: There is a detailed account in the list. The total number of rifles is 46,000. With the addition of 13,600 received later, the final total is 59,000.

Voronin: They do not have as many as 55,000 rifles.

[8] Lin: They do have 55,000. We have a map indicating troop concentration and it lists 59,000 rifles, 320 machine guns (including our Maxim-type machine guns), 158 cannons, 4 heavy cannons (they are old-type mortars with a firing range of twenty kilometers). I feel that if we can also add the two heavy cannons stored in the Military Attaché's house, it would be most helpful. As for the troops, they have six infantry divisions—the First, Second, Third, Fifth and Sixth divisions—two cavalry divisions, two guard brigades, and the garrison force in Peking.

Karakhan: How many troops are there in Peking?

Lin: Besides the First Division, half of a brigade of the Third Division and two guard brigades, totaling approximately seven brigades.

Karakhan: Are these the troops transferred during the last two weeks?

Lin: They have been moving within the last four days.

Karakhan: Can you tell us something about armored cars [tanks?] and airplanes?

Lin: There is a group of armored cars manufactured by us. The officers who operate them are very well trained. There are three cannons, twelve Chinese Maxim-type machine guns which can be moved freely and four machine guns attached to the sides of the cars.

Karakhan: Are the cannons also movable?

Lin: The cannons are movable in four directions. There are two armored cars, one fully equipped and the other is now being equipped. [9] They are now manufacturing cement-armored trains. The cement is so strong that even bullets cannot penetrate it. The officers have been trained by us and they had good records. They have now left the school. There is only one armored column, and General Feng wants it divided into two columns, separating our cannon-equipped armored cars from cement-armored trains. In short, the column of armored cars can be divided into two at any time.

Voronin: They have altogether three armored cars; the rest are open armored cars. [?]

Lin: They have altogether eight airplanes, some of which are old and two unfit for use. The planes are all two-seaters.

Karakhan: Can they provide six more airplanes?

Lin: They have an airfield suitable for use and they have set a time limit for expanding its site.

Now, let us take up political work. When I drafted plans for our work, I suggested that it was necessary to organize two important types of work, military and political. Some results, I believe, have been achieved in military work. The personnel of various departments have undergone thorough training in the schools and the schools have gained in prestige. Political work also has been in progress all the time. For instance, there is evident expansion of our work when our country's propagandists went to Kiangsi [Kansu] province. Numerous letters from cities and counties indicate that our propagandists were received with great warmth by the people. We are now assembling various groups and sending them out on the road. Each propagandist is given a propaganda outline. This is the outline you approved before your trip. It seeks to publicize conditions in Soviet Russia. The propaganda teams will make speeches to the troops in Suiyuan and Chahar according to the outlines. They left on the 15th. We have not received any report on the results of their work, since we do not maintain constant contact with them. I [10] feel, however, that they will carry out their mission satisfactorily. They were well trained in this type of work while at the school.

Karakhan: Are they all Communists?

Lin: Yes.

Karakhan: Are they the thirteen Communist members who were sent out by you?

Lin: Yes, they are the first group, We have proposed organizing a propaganda school with the aim of establishing a propaganda battalion to administer propaganda work. The plan is to assign its members to different regiments for liaison work with other armies and divisions. The propaganda battalion may be attached to the Army. There should be five propagandists from the battalion to work in each regiment. I have talked with General [Feng] about this and suggested that more propagandists are needed. This good suggestion, after minor modifications, will probably be accepted. The school is now working on a plan which may be adopted.

Karakhan: Are there 90 propagandists?

Lin: Yes, the school is entirely administered by Fu-lin-t'e. General Feng selected 90 persons from the Army with whom the school was organized.

Karakhan: Did he select them himself?

Lin: Yes. Two weeks are required for graduation from the school.

The graduates were the first group of propagandists assigned to work against Marshall Chang [Tso-lin]. We are contemplating giving three months' training to the second group of new students so that they can be better prepared for service. They are expected to leave the school next spring. After that, the first group of students may be called back to the school for advanced training. This plan will surely be carried out in the future.

[11]   Now I am going to discuss briefly several matters related to the expansion of our country's influence among military circles and the record of our political work. In this connection, the trip of General [Hsiung Pin] brought good results. One important result is the repudiation of rumors. The Chinese and the Orientals have an entirely erroneous conception of Soviet Russia. General Kao, for instance, once said that such things as the system of communal wives and the compulsory sending of children to kindergartens exist in Russia. Our propagandists have to explain carefully that Russia is not the country they imagine it to be. Here is one result of his trip.* Among our projects, the model village attracted the General's attention more than anything else. He [Feng] will soon make a decision to establish a model village.

Karakhan: Did you draw his attention only to the matter of the model village?

Lin: For two days he asked me what is the model village and the method of construction. I explained to him in detail. He said it was a good project and should be carried out at once. He immediately called in a man, a so-called adviser, and instructed him to get the materials ready, explaining how the matter should be done and how the model village should be constructed. He has also accepted one of our plans relating to the style of uniforms. This is another good result.

Karakhan: Did he give serious attention to our military uniforms such as helmets, etc.?

Lin: Yes. He requested the dispatch of one Russian cavalry brigade to serve as a guard brigade in order to indicate his confidence in Russia. I explained that this matter should be referred here [Soviet Embassy] for an answer. He is now recruiting bodyguards at a monthly pay of eighteen dollars. I told him that I would report the matter to you. He has often asked about it and a reply must be given him soon.

Among other miscellaneous incidents which indicate our influence is Feng's request for the establishment of an organ of Russian advisers on financial, industrial, political, military, and agricultural matters. In short, he requests advice on each and every ques-

---

* Probably referring to the visit of General Hsiung Pin to Soviet Russia. Hsiung reported to Feng Yü-hsiang the results of his inspection trip on November 11, 1925. He discussed the Russians' hospitality and the results of his negotiations with important Soviet leaders. See Feng Yü-hsiang, Feng Yü-hsiang jih-chi, II, 126.

tion. Nevertheless, we have no real and true frienship with him.
Even I have hardly any friendship with him to speak of. He considers
himself a great star for the good of China and has no genuine inten-
[12] tions to be friendly with our country. As for the question of confidence and personal contact, the situation has been good. Feng treats
us not only with confidence but also very informally. He has always
told us to do away with the formalities.

Karakhan: In view of the critical war situation, what is the degree of his confidence in our country and how does he account for
such current events as the actions of Kuo Sung-ling?

Lin: Feng discussed the movement [rebellion] of Kuo Sung-ling
ten days before it occurred. He was also very frank and forthright
concerning Sun Ch'uang-fang.

Karakhan: Why did Sun Ch'uan-fang start out first? Did it take
General Feng by surprise? They had agreed on maintaining the
status quo and, judging by the time factor, was his action [march
into Shanghai and Nanking] entirely unexpected by General Feng?

Lin: The action of Sun Ch'uan-fang was really unexpected. Plans
had been formulated but Sun, being over-anxious, started out much
earlier than we had expected. Efforts were made to stop him, but
General Feng received the telegram informing him of Sun's movement after it had already started.

Karakhan: You have just said that he received this telegram. Are
his telegraphic facilities able to reach Shanghai?

Lin: Yes.

Karakhan: What is his reaction to events these few days? I do not
want his reaction as gathered from your conversation with him, but
the remarks and hopes he has currently expressed. Please state.

Lin: He has made quite lengthy remarks.

[13]   Karakhan: Was it a declaration?

Lin: Yes. He declared that his personal relations with the people
of Japan and Britain have caused concern to many people and asked
us to inform all that he maintains friendship with Japan on the same
grounds that we send an ambassador to Japan. He said that real
friendship can only exist between him and our country. Feng said
the Japanese are fond of exaggeration and a lengthy, elaborate essay
would ensue once the word "friendship" is mentioned. I said to him
that I was surprised that the Swiss lady at his home, his son's teacher,
seems to know a great many things and maintains frequent correspondence with Matsumura.† He then said, "Ah! Correspondence

---

† A Japanese adviser by the name of Matsumuro is mentioned in
Feng's diaries at this time. See, for instance, Feng Yü-hsiang,
Feng Yü-hsiang jih-chi, II, 50. The difference between the two names
may be due to errors made in the double transliteration from Japanese to Russian, and then from Russian to Chinese.

with Matsumura! Curious! This is a serious matter!" He again reassured me of his friendship with our country.

Karakhan: What is the Japanese adviser Matsumura doing?

Lin: He does nothing, but draws a salary.

Karakhan: He must be an espionage agent without question. Does he have any contact with the people?

Lin: As far as I know, although he often talks with General Feng, his friendship with him is not really very deep.

Karakhan: Is Matsumura all by himself or does he have assistants?

Lin: That I don't know. About eight of them came together, and they all stay at the hotel. They once said to us in English that they will not bother us, that they only attack the Chinese[?]. In short, many jokes are made at the hotel.

Karakhan: Has Feng ever mentioned his future plans?

[14] Lin: Yes. He said earnestly that Chang Tso-lin can be defeated soon without need of a large armed force. However, fighting with Wu P'ei-fu would have to follow. I told him that it would be a good idea to present a brief statement on his future plans and those of the Kuominchün in Peking. This he did two weeks ago. He informs me of the troop movements at the front. On important matters, what others know today, I know the night before.

Karakhan: Did he talk about political problems?

Lin: His policy is very firm. Once a certain person and I received letters from him asking us to investigate the current situation. We then made an appointment to meet at the Japanese adviser's place. When I arrived at the appointed time, I tried to say to the Japanese adviser that Karakhan's comrade was here. He said, "No he is not here," and broke into a laugh. I told him that the [November 28, 1925] demonstration being held then in Peking was unprecedented and that it must be a continuance of the [May Thirtieth] Shanghai incident. I added that I had orders to persuade General Feng to utilize the demonstration to his advantage, as the revolutionary tide was at its height. I had arrived the night before [from Peking] and had gone to see Feng the following morning.

During my conversation with him, I stated my personal impressions and told him that I saw several hundred thousand people at the demonstration (deliberately exaggerating the situation), demanding the overthrow of Tuan's government and the immediate establishment of a national revolutionary government. The Japanese adviser interrupted to the effect that General Feng himself might have taken part in the demonstration. He said this earnestly. I asked, "How could General Feng take part in it?" and he answered, "General Feng took part in it because China needs a strong government. As for the situation after the demonstration, I don't know." I said I did not know the situation after my departure, except that the people were dissatisfied.

General Feng said that he had not heard anything at all about the demonstration. I then suggested that he make a trip under any circumstances.

Feng informed me that he was negotiating with various provinces [15] and, although no definite arrangement had been made, all were agreed on the necessity of building a strong and firm political foundation. He promised to inform me of the results of his negotiations tomorrow noon.

Karakhan: Has he been negotiating with other provinces?

Lin: Yes. He hopes to organize a strong government.

Karakhan: Did he say that he had to negotiate with the provinces about the organization of the government?

Lin: Yes, he has been negotiating with the four provinces of Honan, Hunan, Hupeh, and Anhwei.

Karakhan: Negotiate with Wu P'ei-fu or Sun Ch'uan-fang?

Lin: He only said he was negotiating with different provinces.

Karakhan: Whose agreement has he obtained?

Lin: He has obtained the agreement of Shansi. As for other matters, he promised to inform me of them tomorrow noon. He talked with great spirit and said that no effort should be spared to bring the matter to a successful conclusion, for he regarded it as a fine thing. He also said he had someone to act on his behalf but would not say any more. When he learned of my coming here, he wrote a letter to General Liu Chi. He used to address me as "elder brother" and our conversation was usually short and simple, but not this time. I asked him "What is your opinion"? He replied that, while they [?] advocate freedom of the press, they themselves arrest newspapermen and later release them. He said it was most inconsistent. My personal impression is that our propaganda and political work have brought closer relations between us and they desire our help. Before his departure, Feng again reassured me of his friendship and we left together.

Karakhan: What is their opinion of Wang Hu? What is his actual position in the Kuominchün or is he simply a follower of General [16] Feng? What sort of person is he anyway?

Lin: He seems to be a reserve official of the government.

DOCUMENT 39

The following is a report on the work of the Soviet group at Kalgan
written by a member of a Soviet inspection team by the name of
Ya-en. Our translation is based on a Chinese translation of the Russian document which is published under the title, "Inspection of the
Work of the Kalgan Soviet Military Group and Plans for dealing
with Feng Yü-hsiang," in Su-lien yin-mou..., III, "Kuominchün," pp.
76-82. In that source the document is undated. According to
Mitarevsky, the document is dated January 27, 1926 (World-wide
Soviet Plots, p. 29). This date appears to be correct.

[YA-EN'S REPORT ON THE KALGAN SOVIET GROUP]

[76] I have been inspecting the work of the Kalgan group since August,
1925. The group concentrates all its efforts on specialized schools,
as follows:
1. Advanced Military Academy
2. Artillery School
3. Cavalry School
4. Machine-gun Corps School
5. Engineering Corps School
6. The General School
[77]   7. Intelligence School
The schools are scattered at various places and it is quite difficult to direct all the personnel working in them. It had been planned
to establish a school for lower officers, but the war interrupted the
realization of this plan.

We often think that, lacking means to control Feng's entire army,
we should begin our work in the schools, that we should first inject
propaganda into Feng's army and then surround it ideologically.
We think that by using officers graduated from the schools to control Feng's army we are executing a compromise method of infiltration of Feng's army, and that we should consider this task as
a prerequisite of all military work.

It is difficult, however, to say to what extent this plan can be
carried out. Most of our workers are kept busy running back and
forth between the various schools, and they are exhausted by the
heavy work load. Moreover, we lack interpreters and reserve personnel. It is therefore most difficult to attain the above objective,
though it may be very appropriate and important.

Furthermore, it is debatable whether the above objective is indeed correct. The majority of officer graduates are appointed to

army posts after a period of three months. Although they have considerable knowledge and new methods of work, they are placed in
pre-arranged positions and are unable to act independently. As we
have known for a long time, only orders of high-ranking officers
are acted upon in Chinese armies. (This is particularly true of the
First Kuominchün). It is considered almost an offense to express
individual opinions, no matter where or what. We are further convinced of this following our inspection of the Army at the front.

Nevertheless, since it is inexpedient to change our set policy, we
are continuing our work as before.

I do not deny that the officers are benefited by the schools, particularly the artillery and secondly, the cavalry officers. The machine-
gun corps and the infantry have been affected the least, since officers in these groups have not yet graduated. While the officers themselves have gained more or less, however, they have failed to introduce new ideas to the Army. Even if they had, their contributions
[78] have been so minute that they have had no effect at all during the
war. Furthermore, many good graduates have not been assigned
any work and they are idle and scattered in the rear.

Our advisers should have frequent contact with high officers
commanding the allied armies, especially at this time, when the
military situation is serious. Although such contact exists at present,
the advisers serve merely in a supervisory capacity. Close cooperation between Chinese officers and Russian advisers is completely
lacking. Furthermore, it is only during the war that the advisers
were able to begin working together with Chinese commanders.

Military action depends on preparations during peacetime. That is
when the advisers are most needed. There is indeed a wide margin
between the influence we had expected to wield and the actual results! We had not been acquainted before the war with the Chinese
officers commanding the allied armies. Thus, working with persons
we hardly know, we have often found ourselves in situations at the
front which are beyond our expectations. Occasional advice from us
has generally been ignored.

What are the causes of this situation? They may be stated as follows:

1. The Chinese are a practical people. They must be shown actual
results before they have confidence in anyone.

2. The Russian advisers lack personal and public friendship with
the commanders to whom they are assigned.

3. There has been no discussion at all between the Chinese and the
senior members of the Russian group as to the wartime status of
the Russian advisers.

Attention has never been paid to these points. Our efforts have
been concentrated on installing members of the group in advisory
positions for fear that there would be no room for them after the
closing of the schools.

We will state again the results thus produced.

79]   For one thing, the majority of the members of the group have nothing to do and are idle in the rear.

Secondly, since the Chinese generals grasp full authority, our advisers who follow them to the front have no chance to demonstrate their ability.

In short, our hopes have vanished like bubbles. This is because all our proposals and plans have been entirely incorrect, and they inevitably produce failure when executed. Furthermore, the limited power and influence which we had built up through our peacetime work have also been completely destroyed.

What conclusions may be drawn from our experience of failure as described above?

Some comrades may feel that it is a mistake in the first place to help militarists. Some may be disappointed because of the futility of their own work. Hence, the idea of winding up our work and returning to Soviet Russia. I regard these people as the real hindrance to the progress of our work. It may be recalled that in 1924 a few of our comrades were disappointed in Canton, the birthplace of the Chinese revolutionary movement, and decided it was useless to work there. They demanded transferring the center of our work to the North or the Yangtze valley. Shortly after their departure, however, our work in Canton developed greatly and became very effective. We must therefore absolutely dismiss this idea of winding up everything here. We should have a strong determination to correct the mistakes of individuals and of the group, in order to clear the atmosphere and handle our work in due order. In purely military work we should, in my opinion, give up broad school plans and concentrate instead on a relatively smaller foundation. The smaller our scale of operations, the better the results. I shall state my opinion as follows:

1. Establish a military academy and instill in the students the qualities of a model army (a mixed regiment or smaller unit). When necessary, they may be used to reorganize the Army.

80]   2. Establish a review class for the artillery and machine-gun corps.

3. Organize a three-regiment mixed brigade or mixed division (the name is of no consequence), based on the newest system in Canton.

4. Locate this army in one place.

The utmost attention should be given the training of this army so that it will become the model of all armies. Plans need not be confined to this army, but actual work should be concentrated in it.

The results of such work may be stated as follows:

1. A group of model officers to serve as a nucleus in future army reorganization (referring to the military school).

2. Improvement and expansion of technical knowledge (referring to the review class).

3. A small but strong army which can be relied upon not only in time of war but also during political crises (referring to the new brigade or division)

4. Proof that our military system is superior to the Chinese system in war or peace.

5. Economy in the size and work of our group.

6. A model for other armies.

7. The ability of our personnel to work in the army to which they are assigned and in other armies during wartime.

My report has not thus far discussed Feng Yü-hsiang and his close followers. From the very beginning we have avoided direct contact with Feng. The members of the group often say that Feng is a "big star," that it is impossible directly to gain his friendship and confidence, and that we must therefore approach his subordinates and people around him in order to create influence and power. [81] When [our] directing capacity is weak, this approach may be appropriate. Judged by the nature of the matter, however, it is not entirely appropriate, for the various generals under Feng Yü-hsiang perceive the weakness of our influence over Feng, so much so that we appear to be afraid of him. How, then, can we win their confidence or influence them? This is obviously a doubtful point. We see this with particular clarity during wartime.

Such subordinates of Feng Yü-hsiang as Governor-General Chang [Chih-chiang] and Hsiung Pin are very close to us. They accept our direction at the front. As for those generals who have no friendship for their Russian advisers, we have nothing to say.

Let us again discuss the question of selecting personnel for the group.

The majority of the group had held high positions in Soviet Russia before coming here and they had assumed that they would be assigned important posts. Actually, however, they are working as very ordinary officers. Hence, the current view that we should send here low-ranking officers, technical personnel, and ordinary military technicians. This opinion is not at all correct. The Cantonese were at first antagonistic toward the infiltration of our propaganda. Now, aware that we are of benefit to them, they compete in inviting us, especially in times of war. This may serve to prove [the correctness of my opinion].

Our greatest disadvantage is lack of officers who can work as advisers at regimental and brigade headquarters, although we have here a sufficient number of military technicians.

My personal view is that it is necessary to send here men

thoroughly trained as regimental commanders or commanders of higher rank. In addition, send a number of technical men who can coordinate their activities with the high officers.

These officers may be appointed at the start as the most ordinary officers. After a sufficient period of time, however, they should be able to assume command both in times of peace and war. However, if they lack proper theoretical and practical training, they would not be fit even as company or battalion commanders.

The organization of the Army should have its foundation in the military academy, the artillery school, and the specialized schools. A number of officers of the Red Army may be transferred here.

82]   Those sent here should work not only as advisers on army administration, but also as commanders. There is very little need here for "pure" advisers or commanders.

Aside from the above, the following principles should be observed in selecting personnel to be sent here: (1) men willing to serve more than three years; (2) men in good physical condition who can be so certified by physicians; and (3) men who must be accompanied by their families[?].

Those previously sent here have frequently been criticized for ignorance of the situation and the requirements of the life and work here. In order to avoid such criticism, we are in need of a comrade who is well acquainted with the conditions of life and work in China and have him undertake responsibility for employing competent personnel to be sent here. He should provide persons sent here with various types of necessary material, explain to them their place of work, and draw up regulations concerning their rights and duties.

DOCUMENT 40

Document 40 is a plan for the organization of a volunteer militia in
Peking. It was drafted by a Russian adviser, going by the name
of K'o-erh-te during the period from October, 1924 to April, 1926,
when Peking was garrisoned by the Kuominchün. A Chinese translation of the Russian document is available under the title, "An Outline Drafted by K'o-erh-te on the Organization of a Local Civilian
Volunteer Militia in Peking to Serve as a Secret, Armed Army of
the Kuomintang," in Su-lien yin-mou..., II, "Military," pp. 17-24.
In the following translation we have omitted the second part of
the document, which gives detailed plans on the organization of the
militia.

[DRAFT OUTLINE ON THE ORGANIZATION OF A
VOLUNTEER MILITIA IN PEKING]

[17] With reference to the establishment of a civilian volunteer militia
in Peking as the clandestine armed force of the Kuomintang:
    1. Objectives in the establishment of a volunteer militia. —In view
of the recent situation, there is evident need for organizing a concealed armed force of the KMT which may be mobilized for action
and appropriate struggle by order of the Kuomintang in the event of
a political crisis. It is politically necessary to establish a strong
national army in order to meet the present situation.
    a) Organize into the armed militia all civilians in Peking who
favor support of the Kuomintang (priority to Kuomintang members).
    b) Organize the Left elements of the Kuominchün and ally them
with the revolutionary masses to build a strong foundation for
socialism and to organize a militia.
[18]   c) Organize a fighting force equal to that which opposes the
Kuominchün. When reaction sets in, this force can hold a position
of neutrality, offer services of mediation, or carry out a policy of
division of strength from within (the reactionary forces).
    2. General requirements and results in the organization of a
volunteer militia. —Clearly, this type of armed force cannot be incorporated openly into the Kuominchün. (It would be a different situation if and when in the future the Kuominchün leans toward the
Kuomintang.) On the other hand, under the present circumstances in
China, it is impossible to prevent the Kuominchün, the government,
and the foreign powers from learning of the existence of such an
organization. Therefore, the volunteer militia should be organized
in the following manner:

a) We should present the organization of such an armed force to the Kuominchün authorities as experimental work in the preservation of local peace, comparable to the establishment of a "model division" in peacetime. We should employ the following arguments:

(1) The only task [in connection with] the organization of a volunteer militia during peace time is the training of this volunteer army.

(2) It is necessary to organize a large reserve army which can rise in armed struggle in times of danger to strengthen the Kuominchün's fighting capacity within the shortest period.

(3) According to the needs of the current war (such as the anti-imperialist struggle), it is necessary to create a potentially powerful Chinese national army.

b) For public announcement and publicity, the following points should be stated:

(1) The experimental organization of a truly strong Chinese army (civilian soldiers to replace conscripts).

[19]   (2) The adoption of the methods of the European countries for the purpose of giving the Chinese people (such as students and other revolutionary elements) military training in a very short period of time without interrupting their daily work.

(3) Giving the people of Peking proper physical training, etc. (such as artillery training, athletic meets, etc.).

c) We should persuade the Kuominchün to assume secret responsibility for providing material supplies (military supplies required by the volunteer militia) in the following manner:

(1) Expansion plans should be made in accordance with the number of persons who have completed our training. All those who have completed our training may become volunteers. The first important thing is to furnish the militia with all the necessary equipment, so that there will be no deficiency in military supplies (such as airplanes, tanks, etc.). Instructors will be appointed by us without salary.

(2) The Kuomintang should take an active part in organizing and training the volunteers. KMT Party headquarters should handle the organization of the political department and the committee for recruiting volunteers and appointment of the training personnel.

The nucleus of the volunteer militia should be composed of 700 students from the Kalgan Military School (low-ranking officers), 300 Whampoa officers from the Kwangtung army, newly recruited students, volunteers recruited by the Kuomintang, and commanders appointed by the Kuomintang.

[20]   (3) Regular expenses of the volunteer militia should be borne by commanders of the Kuominchün (about 8,000 men, 600 horses, and 20 automobiles).

d) See to it that the Kuomintang clearly orders all KMT members to be trained by the volunteer militia. Training is necessary for even the most ordinary militia member. The KMT should encourage in every way those who support the Revolution to join the militia and to undergo proper training. Even if there are not many volunteers, the first group of the volunteer militia should receive sufficient technical training to become a powerful army, loyal to the Kuomintang.

3. The system of organization of the volunteer militia. —The development of the national movement of any country depends very greatly on the organization of volunteer armies. It is necessary to find the proper solution to the above-mentioned problems immediately. It should not be very difficult to organize a volunteer militia within the shortest period. When it is necessary to carry on the Revolution, it can serve not only within the limits of Peking but provide a basis for organizing a revolutionary army of North China. This point should not be overlooked.

[Omitted: second half of the document, pp. 20-24.]

DOCUMENT 41

The following translation is based on an original Chinese document published in Su-lien yin-mou..., III, "Kuominchün, pp. 70-72. The catalogue of seized documents compiled by the Peking Commission identifies it as a document of the Chinese Communist Party (see Su-lien yin-mou..., I, 3). It is undated, but was apparently written immediately after the March Eighteenth Incident of 1926. It appears to be a document either of the Peking Local Committee or the Northern Regional Committee.

RESOLUTIONS ON THE QUESTION OF COOPERATION
BETWEEN OUR PARTY MEMBERS
AND THE FIRST KUOMINCHÜN

70] Our Party considers the First Kuominchün's attitude for the past year as insincere, and that it is difficult to cooperate with it. The responsibility of the recent massacre should be laid on the First Kuominchün on the basis of the following facts.

1. The three telegrams of Chang Chih-chiang on the reform of learning are entirely contrary to our Party's policy and precipitated the massacre. Chang has extremely close relations with Chang Shih-chao and his telegrams were intended to support Chang.

2. On the 17th [of March], after more than ten persons had been injured, Li Ming-chung asked T'ang Yüeh-liang to telephone Comrade Hsü Chi-lung [Hsü Ch'ien]. T'ang expressed regret over the incident and gave assurances that the government guards had been withdrawn and that the people would be properly received. He said there would definitely be no danger.

3. On the 17th, Li Ming-chung sent Li T'ai-fen to contact the Peking Student Association and the Women's Normal College and conveyed apologies for the incident before the premier's office. Li T'ai-fen told a member of the Student Association that he represented the Kuominchün in coming to express regrets and to

71] explain that the Kuominchün knew nothing of the incident in front of the premier's office that afternoon. He said there would definitely be no risk of an untoward incident when the demonstration took place the next day, since the government guards had been withdrawn and the Kuominchün would extend protection.

4. On the morning of the 18th, at the mass meeting at T'ien-anmen, the presidium of the meeting received a letter from Li Ming-chung saying that police forces had been dispatched to maintain

order at the meeting. However, Li later denied the dispatch of this letter and claimed it had been forged by Comrade Hsü.

Following the massacre of the 18th, public opinion throughout the country, whether expressed in our Party organs or organs of our opponents, unanimously denounced the tyranny of Tuan Ch'i-jui's government. The First Kuominchün, however, kept quiet. Li Ming-chung told Comrade Wang Li-chai after the incident that he was unable to prevent it and that such actions of the students were detrimental to the Kuominchün.

5. Tuan's government arrested five of our Party members. The arrests were carried out by Li Ming-chung.

The above facts sufficiently prove that Li Ming-chung is under suspicion of encouraging the massacre of the 18th. The incident has in fact placed our Party in open opposition [to the Kuominchün].

In view of the above, our Party has decided to break off friendly relations with the First Kuominchün.

Should the First Kuominchün realize the critical state of its own position and wish to cooperate sincerely with our Party, we demand that it first fulfill the following conditions:

a) Reorganize the present government.

b) Arrest the principal instigators of the massacre, Tuan Ch'i-jui, Chia Te-yao, Chang Shih-chao, and other criminals.

[72]   Until the Kuominchün assumes responsibility for carrying out by force these two conditions, we refuse to engage in any kind of negotiations with the First Kuominchün and we publicize its crimes.

DOCUMENT 42

Document 42 is a report on the attitude of Feng Yü-hsiang and officers of the First Kuominchün which was prepared by an unidentified Russian adviser. It was apparently written in the spring of 1926, shortly after April 15, 1926, when the Kuominchün withdrew from Peking. The following is based on a Chinese translation of the Russian document which is published under the title, "A Russian's Observations on the Political Attitude of Feng Yü-hsiang and Officers of the First Kuominchün, in Su-lien yin-mou..., III, "Kuominchün," 52-53.

[SOVIET REPORT ON THE POLITICAL ATTITUDE OF FENG YÜ-HSIANG AND FIRST KUOMINCHÜN OFFICERS]

52] All low-ranking officers of the First Kuominchün rose from the ranks. Most of them were formerly peasants. While long military service has caused them to lose contact with the peasantry, they are gradually getting closer to the masses through their present position of service. They may be utilized in the movement to liberate China from the imperialist yoke and the movement of the oppressed workers and peasants.

The majority of middle and high-ranking officers are not graduates of military academies (a few graduated from officers' training departments run by military governors). Having risen from the ranks, they have not lost contact with their native villages and are very much concerned with local politics. They can be used most effectively to disseminate propaganda on the principles of the National Revolution.

For various reasons, the work of the Left Party in Feng's army is poorly organized. Feng sets severe restrictions on political work in the army. It is allowed only when necessary and in the interests of Feng.

The generals of the First Kuominchün have not yet clarified their political attitude. The Kuominchün policies appear increasingly
53] contradictory to the slogans of the National Revolution which it has adopted. Although Peking was at that time garrisoned by the Kuominchün, there yet occurred the [March Eighteenth] incident in which the revolutionary youths of Peking were killed! Feng Yü-hsiang's anti-Red intentions and the reform of learning sponsored by Chang Chih-chiang and Li Ming-chung offer further proof of the Kuominchün's inconsistent attitude.

Because of economic difficulties, Feng's army has allowed the infiltration of Japanese capital into territories under its jurisdiction (e.g., the establishment of the Sino-Japanese Bank at Kalgan). This has of course affected the Kuominchün's policies.

A group of Kuominchün officers are rather dissatisfied with the conservatism of First Kuominchün generals. They intend to build within the Kuominchün a nucleus of a truly national army. The influence of these officers is very weak at the moment and they are not yet fully organized. Nevertheless, they are deeply rooted in the Army and can be expected to have a great future. Should Feng, Chang Chih-chiang, and others continue to espouse conservative policies and break off completely with the national revolutionary movement, these dissatisfied officers could at once assume leadership of the truly national elements of the Army.

There were 60 students in the military intelligence school established by Feng Yü-hsiang and 100 students in the infantry tactics school. Fourteen of the graduates have been sent to the rear of the Mukden Army. The schools were open only for two months and were closed by Feng upon the outbreak of the war. Students who had not yet finished their courses were assigned to infantry, artillery, and machine-gun units. The real cause of Feng's closure of the school was his fear that it would become the birthplace of propagandists who would work against his interests.

KUOMINTANG-COMMUNIST RELATIONS DURING THE
NORTHERN EXPEDITION, JULY, 1926, TO APRIL 6, 1927

Victory in Hunan and Hupeh and the Emergence of
T'ang Sheng-chih, July to October, 1926

The Northern Expedition started as a campaign to aid T'ang Sheng-chih in Hunan. The unit sent to rescue T'ang in May, 1926, was followed by two divisions of the Fourth Army. On June 28, Ch'en Ming-shu, vice-commander of the Fourth Army and concurrently commander of the Tenth Division, was ordered to proceed to Hunan with the Twelfth Division under Chang Fa-k'uei.[1] On July 1, the National Revolutionary Army was mobilized and strategy was determined. It was planned first to pacify Hunan, occupy the Wuhan cities, and then joined with the Kuominchün to unify the country.[2]

With T'ang Sheng-chih's Eighth Army, the KMT forces sent to Hunan were to win a series of victories in the following three months until they were entrenched in Wuhan, the base of Wu P'ei-fu's power.

Their first prize was Changsha, Hunan, which fell on July 10, 1926. By the end of the month, a Hunan provincial government had been established, headed by T'ang Sheng-chih.[3] On August 22, 1926, Yochow [Yoyang], Hunan, at the gateway to Hupeh, was captured. Ting-szu-ch'ao, Hupeh, fell on August 27. By September 1, 1926, the Fourth and Seventh armies were outside the walls of Wuchang.[4] Hanyang fell on September 6, followed by the fall of Hankow the next day. Wuchang, however, was not captured until October 10, 1926, after a prolonged seige.[5] Its fall marked the end of Wu P'ei-fu's power in Hupeh, although his army had still to be accounted for in the western and northwestern parts of the province. By the end of October, the Kuomintang's forces had occupied Sinyang, southern Honan,[6] ready, according to strategy, to link up with the Kuominchün.

Meanwhile, military action in Kiangsi had been delayed by political negotiations with Sun Ch'uan-fang. As Commander-in-Chief of the Allied Armies of the Five Provinces with headquarters at Nanking, Sun controlled Kiangsi, Anhwei, Fukien, Kiangsu, and Chekiang. As early as February 3, 1926, Chiang Kai-shek had met with a representative of Sun Ch'uan-fang. While the meeting apparently failed to produce any agreement, the KMT's strategy outlined on

July 1, 1926, significantly excluded plans for an offensive in
Kiangsi.7 On August 12, 1926, the day following his arrival at
Changsha, Chiang again received a representative of Sun Ch'uan-
fang. After the meeting, Chiang wired Sun and promised to use
his good offices with the National Government to appoint him Commander-in-Chief of the Five Provinces, provided he accept the
jurisdiction of the National Government. That same day, at a military conference attended by T'ang Sheng-chih and Chiang Kai-shek,
it was decided to send troops to the Kiangsi border. The invasion of
Kiangsi, however, was not to begin until after the fall of Wuhan.8

On August 18, 1926, Sun Ch'uan-fang issued a circular telegram
announcing the dispatch of troops to defend Kiangsi against invasion.
The National Government then decided that Kiangsi would be attacked in three directions. The targets were Kung-chou in the
south, Nanchang in the west, and the Nanchang-Kiukiang railway to
the north.9 Efforts to persuade Sun Ch'uan-fang to withdraw his
army from Kiangsi were nevertheless continued in the following
two months.10

The Sixth Army under Ch'eng Ch'ien succeeded in capturing
Nanchang with the help of Nanchang students and workers and the
local garrison on September 19, 1926, but was forced to give up the
city two days later. These events were followed by the retreat of
two divisions of the First Army under the command of the Army's
vice-commander, Wang Po-lin, at the beginning of October.11 On
October 15, Chiang Kai-shek wired the Fourth Army at Wuchang to
proceed to Kiangsi to aid the First, Second, Third, Sixth, and
Seventh armies in the Kiangsi campaign. Preparations were made
for a general offensive in Kiangsi.12

Nevertheless, negotiations with Sun Ch'uan-fang were still not
abandoned.13 The last attempt at a negotiated settlement took place
on October 28, when Chiang again met with Sun's representatives
at Kaoan, Kiangsi. The meeting apparently failed to achieve results,
for on the following day the National Government launched a general
offensive against Sun Ch'uan-fang in Kiangsi.14 All efforts towards
a negotiated settlement were finally abandoned.

The swift advance through Hunan and Hupeh and up to southern
Honan, contrasted with the relatively slow progress in Kiangsi,
introduced a new factor in the contest for power among Kuomintang
leaders. As commander-in-chief of the forces in Hunan and Hupeh,
T'ang Sheng-chih was able to make political capital out of the series of military victories and emerged as a powerful figure vis-à-
vis Chiang Kai-shek.

Document 43, a Soviet report on the Eighth Army dated August 9,
1926, reveals that the Russians were aware of T'ang Sheng-chih's
increasing power and its possible consequences. Pavlov, the writer
of the report, was apparently an intelligence agent or unofficial

Soviet representative in the Eighth Army. (Soviet advisers had yet to be appointed to the Eighth Army.)

Regarding T'ang with suspicion, Pavlov expressed fear that he would sever relations with the National Government should it fail to appoint him to a position of the highest importance. In fact, Pavlov reported, T'ang had already started talking along this line. Pavlov's appraisal of T'ang is particularly interesting in view of the fact that T'ang had been allied with the Kuomintang for barely two months at the time of the report.

Pavlov apparently conducted his investigation with great thoroughness. He reported, for instance, that T'ang was hypocritical in saying he did not smoke, since his fingers were "stained as dark as smoked sausages." While apprehensive about T'ang's motives, however, Pavlov did not suggest opposing him actively. He pointed out that Soviet policy toward T'ang was not at all clear and that the Russians should define their objectives at the first opportunity.

On August 11, 1926, Chiang Kai-shek arrived at Changsha and met T'ang Sheng-chih.[15] Apparently Pavlov's uneasiness about T'ang was shared by Chiang and his staff. On August 23, 1926, the day following the capture of Yochow [Yoyang], the Fourth, Seventh, and Eighth armies were ordered to press the enemy immediately at Ting-szu-ch'ao, Hupeh.[16] According to Kuo Mo-jo, then chief of the Propaganda Section of the General Political Department, this decision was taken to prevent a "newly-recruited KMT general," presumably T'ang Sheng-chih, from seizing control of Hupeh province. The Fourth Army was in effect entrusted with the mission of speeding to Ting-szu-ch'ao in a race against T'ang Sheng-chih. Thus, as Kuo puts it, the struggle for Wuchang was waged against Wu P'ei-fu on the military level, and against the "newly-recruited general" on the political level.[17]

Following the capture of Hankow and Hanyang, the question of political control of Hupeh province assumed great importance. As early as September 9, 1926, Chiang Kai-shek wired Chang Ching-chiang and T'an Yen-k'ai to dispatch members of the CEC Standing Committee to Hupeh to take charge of political affairs. Again, on September 18, Chiang requested members of the CEC and the National Government Council to proceed immediately to Hupeh. Otherwise, he declared, political affairs in Wuhan would be complicated and difficult to manage.[18]

Document 44, a Soviet report dated October 30, 1926, from Wuchang, throws an interesting light on the complex relationships between Chiang Kai-shek, T'ang Sheng-chih, and the Russians. It was drafted by Teruni, chief Soviet adviser to the General Political Department of the National Revolutionary Army who had accompanied the KMT forces on the Hunan and Hupeh campaign,[19] and was addressed to Borodin, who was still in Canton.

According to Teruni, T'ang Sheng-chih had been engaged in efforts to overthrow Chiang Kai-shek and to take over Chiang's position of commander-in-chief ever since he had met Chiang at Changsha in mid-August. T'ang had even tried, said Teruni, to enlist his help in this maneuver, which was apparently serious enough to warrant considerable countermaneuvering by Teruni. When Chiang ordered the Fourth Army to Kiangsi, for instance, Teruni was instrumental in maintaining through Teng Yen-ta the headquarters of the Fourth Army at Wuchang as a counterpoise to T'ang's power. Teruni also sought to strengthen the power of Ch'en Ming-shu, commander of the Fourth Army and garrison commander of Wuchang, vis-à-vis T'ang [Doc. 44, pp. 9, 7, 5].

In Teruni's opinion, T'ang Sheng-chih probably would have succeeded in his anti-Chiang maneuvers had the Russians not supported Chiang. Teruni informed Borodin that he had been pursuing the policy of supporting Chiang and manipulating T'ang, and that this policy had been approved by Ambassador Karakhan. The Russians, however, were not unanimously in favor of continued support to T'ang Sheng-chih. Teruni said he disagreed with those who advocated withdrawing help from Chiang because T'ang was not a real revolutionary but only an ambitious opportunist. Nevertheless he did not propose severing all relations with T'ang [Doc. 44, pp. 10-11].

In view of T'ang's power and prestige, Teruni was most distressed at the lack of a central political organ in Wuhan. He complained that the KMT Hupeh Provincial Committee was weak and, as did Chiang Kai-shek, urged the immediate establishment of the KMT Central Executive Committee in Wuhan. Otherwise, he said, it would be difficult to implant KMT power firmly in Wuhan. This was a question of such magnitude, said Teruni, that he found the National Government's attitude incomprehensible [Doc. 44, pp. 21-22].

Communist Policy and the Kuomintang Joint Conference, July to October, 1926

Teruni may have been referring to the failure of the Kuomintang to decide to move to Wuhan. This question was discussed at a Joint Conference of the Kuomintang CEC and Provincial Party Headquarters which was held at Canton from October 15 to October 28, 1926. On October 22, in a wire to the delegates, Chiang Kai-shek proposed a resolution to transfer the CEC to Wuchang.[20] Although the Chinese Communist Party later claimed that the conference voted to transfer both the Party and Government to Wuhan, no decision was actually reached.[21] It was not until November, after the Joint Conference had adjourned, that the National Government appointed Sun Fo, T. V. Soong, Sung Ch'ing-ling (Madame Sun Yat-sen), Eugene Chen, and Borodin to proceed to Wuhan to investigate

the possibility of a transfer. The appointments followed the arrival
of Teng Yen-ta and Chang Fa-k'uei at Canton from Hankow to plead
for immediate removal.22

Wu Yü-chang, a Communist, was one of the five members of the
presidium at the Joint Conference. According to KMT and independent sources, the Communists attempted to dominate the meeting.
They reportedly raised such slogans as "Down with personal dictatorship!" "Democracy within the Party!" and "Supremacy of the
Party!"23 Communist sources tend to confirm these charges.
Hu Hua, for instance, asserts that under the leadership of Wu
Yu-chang and others, the delegates adopted a number of important
resolutions which displeased Chiang.24

The most important Communist gain at the Joint Conference was
passage of the resolution to recall Wang Ching-wei from abroad.
Although Chiang Kai-shek himself proposed the resolution in a telegram to the conference, he was disturbed by what he considered to
be Communist sponsorship of the "Movement to Welcome Wang
Ching-wei" (Ying Wang yün-tung). On August 20, 1926, his diary reveals, he had been informed by certain persons in Canton that the
Communists were conspiring to "welcome" Wang in order to overthrow him.25

The great importance which the Communists attached to Wang
Ching-wei tends to confirm assertions of the KMT and other anti-
Communists that the "Movement to Welcome Wang Ching-wei"
had Communist backing. Contemporary Communist sources provide
ample evidence that recall of Wang was conceived as an integral
part of the Communist strategy to organize and strengthen the Left
Wing. Ch'ü Ch'iu-pai, in his report to the Sixth KCT Congress, asserts that the "Movement to Welcome Wang Ching-wei" was initiated
shortly after May 15, 1926. The Left Wing began to be assembled
around this movement, according to Ch'ü, and later adopted a definite anti-Chiang attitude.26 Mandalyan, representative of the Russian Communist Party in China, declares that Wang's retirement
following the Coup of March Twentieth demonstrated the Left Wing's
weakness on the one hand and, on the other, provided an opportunity
for uniting the forces of the Left. Mandalyan in fact interprets Wang's
retirement as the opening phase of the Nanchang Uprising of August 1,
1927.27

At the Second Enlarged Plenum in July, 1926, the KCT Central
Committee had Wang Ching-wei and Kan Nai-kuang specifically
named as leaders of the Left Wing [Doc. 26, p. 66]. As the "Movement
to Welcome Wang" gained momentum, however, the CC singled out
Wang Ching-wei as the supreme leader of the Left. At the special
conference held in Hankow in December, 1926, the Central Committee declared that upon Wang Ching-wei's return the Left would
have an organization even stronger than that of the Right. The CC

repudiated the Kwangtung Communists' view that the Left did not exist at all with the exclamation "Wang Ching-wei is not yet dead!"28

The CC viewed the KMT Joint Conference in October as a significant landmark in the organization of the Left Wing. Following the Joint Conference, the CC declared, the Left began to have a concrete political platform. Members of the Left, many of them provincial delegates at the October Joint Conference, began to organize under the leadership of Kan Nai-kuang. Although the Left's organization still lacked an official name and constitution, the Left Wing espoused the following basic policies: (1) alliance with the Communists and Soviet Russia; (2) opposition to the Western Hills Group; (3) support of the labor and peasant policies of Sun Yat-sen and Liao Chung-k'ai; and (4) support of Wang Ching-wei as leader of the Left.29

According to Ch'ü Ch'iu-pai, the KMT Joint Conference, under the influence of the Communist fraction, also adopted a resolution to grant political power to mass organizations.30

At the Second Enlarged Plenum in July, 1926, the CC had emphasized the necessity of developing mass organizations of the Left Wing outside the Party. The CC also emphasized expanding the KMT and loosening its structure in order to absorb Left elements into the KMT [Doc. 27, p. 72]. According to Ch'ü, the first circular issued by the CC following the Second Enlarged Plenum had introduced the slogan "All political power to conferences of mass organizations!" The objective, Ch'ü asserts, was to utilize the revolutionary movement of the masses to expand the Party power of the KMT into the people's political power. This was of course designed to counteract the dominance of the KMT Center. Thus, according to Ch'ü, dating from the October Joint Conference, the issue of "Party power" began to be a bone of contention between the Left Wing and Chiang's faction.31

In short, between July and October, 1926 the Communists made considerable progress in organizing and strengthening the Left Wing in the absence of Chiang Kai-shek, who was at the front. Although the Communists undoubtedly played a major role in fostering the Left's organization and promoting Wang's return, it is clear that certain KMT leaders were independently opposed to Chiang. Following the March Twentieth coup, for instance, there was apparently an abortive attempt to form an anti-Chiang alliance.32 It was this current of opposition which the Communists were able successfully to exploit and organize.

Victory in Kiangsi and Fukien and Relations between Chiang Kai-shek and the Communists, November to December, 1926

Shortly after the Joint Conference, the military situation began to undergo considerable change. Prior to October 29, the Kiangsi

campaign had been delayed by attempts at negotiation with Sun
Ch'uan-fang. The general offensive launched on October 29, however, brought swift results. Kiukiang was captured on November 3,
1926, and Nanchang six days later. The whole province of Kiangsi
was shortly afterwards pacified.[33]

Fighting had in the meantime been going on in Fukien province.
Chaochow (Chaoan) and Meihsien in northern Kwangtung had been
invaded by an army loyal to Sun Ch'uan-fang and, in retaliation,
Chiang Kai-shek had ordered Ho Ying-ch'in, commander of the
First Army to attack Fukien. Efforts were made at the same time
for a peaceful settlement.[34] The negotiations apparently fell
through and reinforcements were rushed to Ho Ying-ch'in from
Canton during October. By the beginning of December, the Fukien
navy and provincial garrison had defected to the KMT, and Ho was
in Foochow, capital of Fukien, by December 20.[35]

With Kiangsi and Fukien in the KMT fold by the end of December,
the center of attention shifted to Chekiang.

Prospects for a bloodless occupation of Chekiang had been
bright in October with the defection of Hsia Ch'ao, governor of
Chekiang, to the National Government.[36] Sun Ch'uan-fang, however, took measures to suppress the autonomous movement which
had been making headway in Chekiang.[37] In early December,
Chiang ordered the launching of the Chekiang offensive. Wang
Chün and Hsüeh Yüeh were instructed to capture Chuchow (Lishui)
near the southeastern border of Chekiang, where they were to
await the forces of Ho Ying-ch'in driving north from Fukien. Chuchow fell on December 11, 1926.[38]

Meanwhile, Sun Ch'uan-fang had gone to Tientsin on November
20, 1926, to plead with Chang Tsung-ch'ang for immediate support.
Four days later, on November 24, Chang Tso-lin, Sun Ch'uan-
fang, and Chang Tsung-ch'ang met at a conference and organized
the Ankuochün (Army of National Pacification). Chang Tso-lin
assumed the position of commander-in-chief; Sun and Chang became vice-commanders.[39] Shortly after the conference, Chang
Tsung-ch'ang sent his army from Shantung to reinforce Sun's
forces. Chang himself arrived at Nanking on December 25, 1926.[40]
In view of Chang Tso-lin's alliance with Sun Ch'uan-fang and Chang
Tsung-ch'ang, policy toward Chang Tso-lin became an immediate
and urgent problem for the Kuomintang.

Negotiations between the KMT and Chang Tso-lin had been in
progress. On October 3, 1926, Chiang instructed T'ang Sheng-chih
to open negotiations with Chang Tso-lin's representatives at
Changsha.[41] Apparently they arrived at an understanding whereby
Chang Tso-lin agreed not to dispatch troops to the South, for on
November 29, Chiang himself met with Chang's representatives
and rebuked them for violating the aggreement.[42]

According to Chiang's diary, it was decided at a conference at
Lushan on December 7 to adopt the policy of destroying Sun Ch'uan-
fang and allying with Chang Tso-lin. Those who attended the
conference included, besides Chiang, Sung Ch'ing-ling, Sun Fo,
T. V. Soong, Hsü Ch'ien, Eugene Chen and Borodin, who had arrived
at Kiangsi enroute to Wuhan.[43] In line with this decision, Chiang
informed Ho Ying-ch'in on December 24, 1926, that the National
Government was assuming for the time being a "mild" attitude toward Chang Tso-lin, pending evidence of the latter's attitude upon
the occupation of Chekiang by the National Revolutionary Army.[44]
Five days later, Chiang wired Feng Yü-hsiang that it had been
decided to deal first with Sun Ch'uan-fang, before coping with
Chang Tso-lin and Chang Tsung-ch'ang.[45]

There were a number of other important decisions at the Lushan
conference. A proposal to abolish the chairmanship of the CEC
was seconded by Chiang who held that powerful position. Chiang
also proposed that Wang Ching-wei be recalled from abroad. Both
proposals were accepted.[46] According to Chiang's diary, it was
also decided to "retard" the labor movement, while pushing forward the peasant movement as a basis for solving the land question.[47] Borodin apparently concurred in these decisions.[48]

The decisions at Lushan were primarily compromise solutions.
During this period friction was evident between Chiang's faction
and the Communists. Ch'en Kuo-fu recalls that the Communists
in Canton attacked Chang Ching-chiang as early as July, 1926, but
did not attack Ch'en himself until shortly after the October Joint
Conference. At that time, they raised the slogan of "Down with
Chang Ching-chiang and Ch'en Kuo-fu!"[49] Numerous conflicts
resulted from the efforts of Chang and Ch'en to weed out Communists from the KMT Organization Department and to defeat Communist attempts to infiltrate the Political Training Institute.[50] The
area of conflict steadily widened as the Northern Expedition advanced. In Shanghai, for instance, suspicion between the Communists
and Niu Yung-chien, chief KMT representative in Shanghai, developed during preparations for the First Shanghai Insurrection
of October 24, 1926.[51]

Chiang Kai-shek's diary contains increasingly frequent complaints about Communist agitation and intrigue.[52] In a speech at
Kiukiang on December 8, 1926, Chiang declared that Kuomintang-
Communist conflict was growing daily more apparent and that he
greatly regretted this state of affairs.[53]

Although friction mounted, the Communists appeared determined
to avoid direct conflict with Chiang. The Central Committee
addressed a letter to Chiang in December in which it again assured
him of Communist support and good-will, and denied that Communists approved of Wang Ching-wei's return in order to overthrow

Chiang. The Communists approved of Wang's return, said the CC, only because it would mean greater advantage for Chiang. However, the CC accused the Sunyatsenist Society and "greedy and covetous Chekiang officials" of disseminating rumors of a Communist conspiracy against Chiang. The behavior of these men in Kwangtung, said the CC, had already aroused the "wrath of heaven and the anger of men." Everyone knew, however, that they were men attached to the Commander-in-Chief, and this had caused the masses and the Left to lose confidence in him. The CC warned Chiang that unless they were expelled, he would find himself in a highly undesirable position from which the Communists, though willing, would be unable to extricate him.[54]

Since Chang Ching-chiang and Ch'en Kuo-fu were natives of Chekiang and leaders of the movement to strengthen "pure" KMT elements against the Communists, there is little doubt that they were the "Chekiang officials" attacked by the CC. Shortly after the CC's letter, the slogan, "Ta-tao hun-yung lao-hsiu!" "Down with old, confused, mediocre, and rotten elements!" was coined in the Communist propaganda offensive against Chang Ching-chiang and Ch'en Kuo-fu.[55]

Relations between Chiang and the Soviet advisers during this period were cordial. Judging by Teruni's report, the Russians were still supporting Chiang against T'ang Sheng-chih's maneuvers as late as the end of October. Chiang's diary reveals the holding of frequent conferences with Galen, who had accompanied him on the campaign.[56] On his part, Chiang appeared courteous and friendly. On November 7, he wired congratulations to Stalin and Kalinin on the ninth anniversary of the Russian Revolution. Chiang expressed the hope that the two countries would continue their alliance in the struggle for the World Revolution.[57]

Communist Policy, December, 1926

When the Central Committee of the Chinese Communist Party convened at a Special Conference at Hankow on December 13, 1926, it noted the progress the Left Wing had made in defining its organization and platform. Since Communist policy was based on alliance with the Left Wing, the strengthening of the Left indirectly bolstered the Communists' own position. Actually, however, Communist strength was much more effectively increased as a result of the expansion of the Communist-controlled labor and peasant movements.

The Communists already enjoyed an unchallenged position in the labor and peasant movements at the outset of the Northern Expedition. They were particularly active in indoctrinating the masses and mobilizing their support for the Northern Expedition in advance of the Army, and utilized this advantage to develop labor and peasant organizations in areas occupied by the Kuomintang. Within the three months between September and December, 1926, for instance, two hundred new labor unions were organized in Wuhan alone.[58]

The development of the peasant movement was even more startling, particularly in Hunan. By January, 1927, according to Mao Tse-tung's "Report on an Investigation of the Hunan Peasant Movement," 2,000,000 Hunanese peasants had been organized in peasant associations. The number of persons under the direct command of peasant associations totaled 10,000,000. The bad gentry, local bullies, and illegitimate landlords, reported Mao, were deprived of the right of free speech. The slogan "All power to the peasant associations!" was actually realized and every word of the peasant associations passed as command. The peasants had even raised the slogan "All who own land are bullies and all gentry are bad!"[59]

These slogans are symbolic of the militancy of the peasant movement in Hunan and directly contradict the Chinese Communist Central Committee's agrarian united-front policy formulated in July, 1926. This restricted opposition to the bad gentry, local bullies, and reactionary, big landlords, and called for the united front of peasant self-cultivators, hired farm laborers, and tenant farmers with the small and middle landlords.

The Party's attitude toward increasingly radical tendencies in the mass movement emerged as a central issue at the CC's Special Conference. The CC resolved to maintain the cautious approach typified by the agrarian united-front policy. The resolutions on the CC's report adopted at the Special Conference declared that the greatest danger confronting the Party was the development of the mass movement toward the Left, while political and military authorities, seeing the swift growth of the mass movement, were seized with panic and were inclining to the Right.[60] In another set of resolutions, the CC declared unequivocally: "The land [peasant confiscation of the land] is not yet a problem! The immediate problems of the peasantry are [to raise] pressing demands for the reduction of rent and interest, freedom of organization, armed self-defense, resistance against local bullies and the bad gentry, and opposition to excessive taxes and irregular levies. To lead the peasantry away from actual struggle for these demands to study the blocked land problem is to stop struggling."[61]

The resolutions were adopted against considerable internal opposition. According to Mao Tse-tung, he had begun to disagree with Ch'en Tu-hsiu's peasant policy as early as the second half of 1925. In place of the CC's cautious approach, he advocated radical land policies, particularly after his inspection tour of Hunan in early 1927.[62] Opposition came also from the Kwangtung Communists, who had been denounced in July, 1926, for advocating immediate struggle for leadership of the KMT in disregard of the Left Wing. They persisted, however, in advocating direct struggle. In a report dated November 23, 1926, the Kwangtung Regional Committee declared that the period of confrontation of the masses and the National Government was approaching. While the Communists should not heedlessly provoke clashes and should avoid senseless struggles, they must nevertheless exert every effort to prepare united forces for a great uprising.[63]

As in Hunan, the peasant movement in Kwangtung had assumed militant characteristics. Karachev, a political adviser at the Central Military and Political Academy, reported to the Soviet Military Attaché, Longva,[64] on November 15, 1926, that the peasant associations had acquired considerable force and had become the most thorny question in the province. They had developed to such an extent, said Karachev, that in certain areas they imposed their will and policies on others. He expressed alarm at the outbreak of fights not only between the gentry and the peasantry, but between the men of the Twentieth Division of the First Army and the peasantry. The real nature of the Revolution, said Karachev, was more evident in Kwangtung than elsewhere. In Kwangtung, it was not confined to general anti-imperialist and antimilitarist slogans; one could clearly see its real foundations were the agrarian and labor problems.[65]

The policies of the Kwangtung Communists produced such alarm within the Chinese Communist Party that a great portion of the "Resolutions on the Problem of the KMT Left Wing" adopted at the Conference was devoted to an attack on their views.

The majority of the Kwangtung Communists, the CC declared, denied the existence of a Kuomintang Left Wing. They believed that the present Left Wing consisted merely of high-level personalities; that only oppressed workers, peasants, merchants, students, and masses of all circles were truly of the Left; and that in the future only those who approved of solving the land question could become the Left. This policy of denying the Left, said the CC, admitted of only two alternative courses of action: (1) The Communists would have to cooperate with the Right and follow the Right to oppress the masses of workers and peasants; or (2) They would have to struggle directly against the Right. If the existence of the KMT Left were denied, this struggle would be between the Chinese Communist Party and the entire Kuomintang, which was precisely what the reactionaries and imperialists wanted. The CC declared: "The comrades of the Kwangtung Regional Committee are taking exactly these two paths....Evil results have already been reaped through the erroneous conception of the denial of the Left Wing. Should the comrades of the Kwangtung Regional

Committee fail to correct their error at once and should other
local Party headquarters fail to take precautionary measures, the
situation will lead to extremely great and irreparable losses!"

Why was it necessary to admit that there was a Left Wing? The
CC's answer reveals the essence of Communist policy. "Not only
is it a fact that the Left exists, it is the pivot of our cooperation
with the Kuomintang. We cannot of course believe that there is
already a strong and responsible Left Wing. However, a Left
which is different from and cannot cooperate with the Right can
still perform an extremely important function as a buffer between
the Right and ourselves."

The CC defined the KMT Left in detail: The Left represented the
peasantry and the urban petty bourgeoisie. It stood for democracy
and opposed feudal power. The Left and Right were, however, relative terms. Those who were relatively Left-inclined, declared the
CC, were the Left. "Since we cannot confuse the Right and Left
Wings of society with the Right and Left Wings of a political party,
and since a KMT Left which would favor solving the land question
has not yet materialized, we can only recognize as the Left those
elements who approve continuation of the three policies of Sun
Yat-sen and Liao Chung-k'ai: alliance with Russia, alliance with
Communists, and support of workers and peasants. Those who are
opposed are the Right."66

One year earlier, Ch'en Tu-hsiu had declared that the Left must
support the policies of alliance with Russia, cooperation with the
Communists and nonopposition to the class struggle in order to
realize the Three People's Principles.67 It was only in December,
1926, however, that the Central Committee decided to characterize
these policies as "The Three Policies" and attributed them to Dr.
Sun Yat-sen. This is confirmed by Document 50, a report of the
Communist Peking Local Committee, dated February 10, 1927,
which states: "To ascertain whether any particular member of the
People's School [KMT] belongs to the Right or Left, it is only
necessary to observe whether his actions and thoughts violate Dr.
Sun's Three Great Policies," recently adopted by the Central Committee as the criterion of the Left [Doc. 50, p. 162].

The CC emphasized the urgent need of strengthening the Left
by the following means:

First, Communists should help top Left leaders in the KMT's
central and local Party organs to be united and strong. Communists
were to help Left leaders to obtain, but not to monopolize, political
and Party power. The condition of such support was continuation of
"The Three Policies." However, Communists must take into consideration the Left's petty-bourgeois outlook and make concessions to it. They must not imagine, said the CC, that the Left
could adopt the same attitude as their own, particularly with

regard to actual struggle in the peasant and labor movements.

Secondly, Communists should work among the lower levels of society, such as handicraft workers, shop employees, and the peasantry, in order to organize the Left's masses. This was necessary so that the masses could rise on their own to oppose the Right. It would also reduce envy and suspicion of Communists and lessen the weakness and vacillation of Left leaders.

Thirdly, Communists should help build up the Left's middle-level forces to cement the top Left leaders and Left masses, by helping the Left to establish Party schools and other organs to train Left personnel.

The Central Committee adopted the following policies in helping the Left to organize:

First, the CC declared it was in favor of the Left having an independent platform.

Secondly, Communists were to help Left leaders seize Party headquarters wherever differentiation of the Left was not great and the Right was weak. These Left leaders would then execute the Left's policies under the direction of Left leaders in the KMT's Central Executive Committee.

Thirdly, where there was Right-Left conflict, Communists should help organize small groups of the Left's masses in clubs, research societies, and schools. Left leaders should periodically call joint conferences of delegates of these small organizations, to which the Chinese Communist Party could formally send representatives. Communists were not to join these small organizations openly.68

Thus, as in July, 1926, the Central Committee outlined two basic methods of strengthening the Left Wing: organization of the Left's mass organizations and strengthening of the Left within the KMT. There is one major difference, however. In July, 1926, the CC had emphasized loosening the KMT structure [Doc. 27, pp. 72-73]. In December, 1926, it ordered Communists to help Left leaders to seize KMT Party headquarters where the Right was weak.

Alliance with the Left Wing was thus the core of Communist policy, the determining factor in the Party's position on all major issues, including policy in the peasant movement.

Orthodox Communist histories accuse Ch'en Tu-hsiu of neglecting the land problem. Ts'ai Ho-shen, for instance, denounces him for executing the agrarian united-front policy to obstruct the land revolution in Kwangtung and later in Hunan.69 However, given the premise that a Left Wing which would approve solving the land question could not materialize and, simultaneously, that it was necessary to give the Left concessions in return for continuation of the Three Policies, the only conclusion the CC could and did reach was that the land question did not exist at all. The policy of alliance with the Left may therefore be considered the fundamental cause if, as orthodox Communist histories assert, the CC's neglect of the land revolution was largely responsible for Communist defeat in 1927.

A comparison of the CC's December resolutions with the ECCI's "Theses on the Chinese Question," adopted at the Seventh Enlarged Plenum which was convened in Moscow on November 22, 1926, indicates that the CC's insistence on alliance with the KMT Left and the consequent decision to curb the peasant movement were fully in line with Comintern policy.

The ECCI described the Chinese Revolution as entering a stage in which a revolutionary block comprised of the proletariat, peasantry, and petty bourgeoisie would become the motive force of the Revolution. The state which would emerge would be a democratic dictatorship of the proletariat, peasantry, and other oppressed classes. While the gradual secession of the big bourgeoisie from the Revolution was inevitable, and leadership would pass gradually into the hands of the proletariat, it was still necessary to continue cooperating with certain elements of the bourgeoisie which would continue for a time to participate in the Revolution. Hence, the ECCI stated that it was necessary for Chinese Communists to remain within the Kuomintang. Furthermore, they were instructed to enter the National Government in order to support the revolutionary Left Wing in the struggle against the Right. This was all the more necessary, the ECCI stated, in view of the extention of the National Government's territory.

With the aim of developing the KMT into a real people's party, the Communist Party was instructed to execute the following policies: (1) struggle against the KMT Right; (2) give proper form to and collaborate closely with the Left without trying to substitute in it Communist members in the work of leadership; and (3) persistently criticize the Center (Chiang Kai-shek), which was vacillating between the Right and the Left.

Communist penetration of the National Government in order to steer it to the Left in alliance with the Kuomintang Left Wing was thus a key Comintern policy. Communists were to use the government apparatus for the gradual execution of such policies as the confiscation of land and reduction of taxes. The ECCI advocated confiscation of lands belonging to monasteries, churches, reactionary militarists, compradors and the gentry. This was indeed more radical than the CC's agrarian united-front policy (opposition to the bad gentry, local bullies, and reactionary big landlords). However, the ECCI stipulated that confiscation must be extended by the Government. Thus, despite the ECCI's view that the development of the National Revolution rested upon the agrarian revolution and its recognition of the necessity of demanding nationalization of the land, realization of such policies hinged upon the attitude of the National Government.[70]

The ECCI's policies were endorsed by the Executive Committee of the Young Communist International which convened its Sixth Plenum in Moscow at about the same time.[71] It adopted a set of resolutions on the Chinese Communist Youth Corps which ordered members of the CY to struggle together with the Chinese Communist Party to strengthen the Kuomintang Left Wing. CY members were instructed to utilize the Kuomintang Youth Department to organize and train revolutionary elements of the middle bourgeoisie and the intelligentsia [Doc. 45, p. 20].

A major difference between the CC's resolutions and the ECCI's "Theses" concerns the capacity and revolutionary determination of the Left. Although it recognized that the Left Wing had made some progress, the CC still regarded it as weak, disunited, and wavering. It still believed the Left had not yet become a political group with definite policies. The Left was only a tendency and not an organization, the CC said. It was only Left-inclined in words and unable to carry through its policies.[72] The ECCI revealed no comparable anxiety over the Kuomintang Left.

Development of Wuhan-Nanchang Conflict, December, 1926, to January, 1927

On December 13, 1926, the day the CC's Special Conference began, a further advance in organization was made by the Left Wing with the organization of the Joint Council at Wuhan. The Joint Council was composed of members of both the Kuomintang CEC and the National Government who had already moved to Wuhan. It was designed as a temporary organ to function until the arrival of the main body of Party and Government leaders and staff members.[73] Hsü Ch'ien was elected chairman. Other organizers of the Joint Council included Sun Fo, Sung Ch'ing-ling, Eugene Chen, Teng Yen-ta, the Communists Wu Yü-chang and Lin Tsu-han, and Borodin.[74]

The Joint Council began immediately to serve as the nucleus of Kuomintang leaders at Wuhan, who were beginning to be known as the "Wuhan Left Wing." According to the CC, it was only after the Kuomintang Joint Conference in October that the Left Wing began to have an organization and platform. Now, the Left began to entrench itself in an official, though temporary, organ of the Party and Government.

The Joint Council was confronted with a multitude of problems. Document 46, minutes of a meeting of the Council on December 29, 1926, for instance, illustrates the difficulty of coping with armies which had defected to the National Government during the Northern Expedition. The magnitude of this problem may be suggested by the fact that in July, 1926, the eight armies of the National Revolutionary Army had totaled 100,000 men.[75] By

December, 1926, some 260,000 men owed allegiance to the National Government.76

The greater part of Document 46 consists of T'ang Sheng-chih's report to the Joint Council following a personal investigation of the conduct of the Ninth and Tenth Armies in Ichang and Shasi, western Hupeh.77 T'ang reported that the poor discipline of the troops had caused considerable discontent among the people. The progress of revolutionary undertakings, said T'ang, depended not only on military force but on the force of the masses. He reported the existence of serious friction between officers of the Ninth and Tenth armies and KMT Party headquarters in Western Hupeh [Doc. 46, p. 8-9].

Conflict developed almost immediately between the Wuhan Joint Council and Commander-in-Chief Chiang Kai-shek, whose head-quarters were at Nanchang, over the question of army funds and sup-plies. On December 24, Chiang wired T. V. Soong, Minister of Fi-nance at Wuhan, informing him that troops of the Seventh Army had mutinied for lack of pay. He requested Soong to reorganize the finan-cial setup in order to maintain regular payments to the Army. On the following day, Chiang twice wired Soong, and implied that the delay in sending funds was intentional. On December 31, 1926, Chiang again wired T. V. Soong, urging him immediately to supply funds for the current month as well as the funds in arrears. Chiang pointed out the gravity of the situation and urged Soong not to base his attitude toward the Army on his personal attitude towards Chiang himself.78

Two other issues almost immediately emerged—the southeast-ern campaign and the location of the seat of the Party and Govern-ment.

At the conference of army commanders and vice-commanders which convened at Nanchang on Chiang Kai-shek's orders on Jan-uary 1, 1927,79 Chiang proposed the strategy of attacking the Southeast in the direction of Nanking and Shanghai. According to Ch'en Ming-shu, this was opposed by Galen and other Russian ad-visers, by Teng Yen-ta, chairman of the General Political Depart-ment, and by T'ang Sheng-chih.80 Teng and T'ang were important Wuhan leaders and may be regarded as spokesmen of the Wuhan Kuomintang leaders.

The record tends to corroborate Ch'en Ming-shu's assertion. T. C. Woo, spokesman of the Left Wing led by Sung Ch'ing-ling and Eugene Chen, stated one year later that the development of the campaign from Wuhan in the direction of Shanghai, instead of northward toward Peking, was a serious mistake. It was the be-lief of many that the Party's plan was for a continuous drive to-wards the north, Woo said, and the change of plans was effected by the military authorities in defiance of party authority.81 It seems certain that the Communists, both Russian and Chinese, were at first opposed to Chiang's strategy.

In his report of October 30, 1926, Teruni had declared that it was imperative to cease all military operations following the Fukien campaign because casualties were great and the army exhausted. Teruni stated that it would be extremely dangerous to move any farther along the Yangtze River and that it was absolutely necessary to set up a buffer zone between Shanghai and the territory of the National Government [Doc. 44, p. 20]. M. N. Roy, the Comintern delegate who arrived in China in early 1927, later confirmed that Galen was opposed to Chiang's strategy of heading for Shanghai.[82] According to KMT sources, Borodin also opposed the southeastern campaign. Wu Ch'ih-hui asserts that while in Canton Borodin had suggested postponing military operations in Kiangsu and Chekiang.[83] Borodin reportedly opposed even the Kiangsi campaign. Following the occupation of Wuchang, Ch'en Ming-shu asserts, Borodin thrice wired Galen, urging him to take every measure to obstruct the Kiangsi offensive.[84]

Document 47, a political report of the Central Committee of the Chinese Communist Party dated January 8, 1927, indicates that the Chinese Communists were opposed to the southeastern campaign. The CC insisted on pushing north against Peking. It was necessary, said the CC, to emphasize anti-Mukden action and to concentrate all forces on the Peking-Hankow Railway [Doc. 47, p. 42].

The southeastern campaign was linked by Chiang Kai-shek to the controversy over the location of the capital. On December 31, 1926, the Party and Government staff arrived at Nanchang enroute to Wuhan.[85] In a speech in February, 1927, Chiang dated the conflict over the location of the capital from the time of their arrival. There had previously been no question about the transfer to Wuhan, he said. However, the arrival of the Party and Government staff at Nanchang coincided with the development of military operations in the Southeast. Thus it was Chiang's opinion that while Wuhan was suitable from the standpoint of foreign relations and finance, Nanchang was more suitable from the military point of view.[86]

By January 7, the Party leaders at Nanchang reportedly agreed that the Party and Government would remain there temporarily, pending further discussion of the question at the Third Plenum of the CEC to be convened at Nanchang.[87] The Wuhan Left Wing, however, insisted on immediate transfer of the staff to Wuhan. In an effort to win support for his views, Chiang made a trip to Wuhan on January 11, remaining there until January 18.[88] Failing to win the Wuhan leaders over to his stand, he returned to Nanchang.

According to pro-Chiang sources, the decision to remain at Nanchang was officially passed by the Party and Government. The

Left Wing was therefore guilty of violating Party discipline in ignoring the decision and threatening to establish another central executive committee at Wuhan. The Left Wing, according to these sources, adopted this attitude upon Borodin's orders. Borodin in fact had led the group of "Communist" and "quasi-Communist" politicians to Wuhan for the express purpose of seizing power there. These sources assert that Communists controlled Wuhan's financial resources and instigated the stopping of funds to Chiang's army in Kiangsi, that they dominated the Hanyang arsenal and organized strikes at the Canton arsenal to prevent shipment of military supplies to Chiang.[89]

The Left Wing, on the other hand, regarded Chiang's policy of establishing the capital at Nanchang as a violation of Party authority by the military. According to T.C. Woo, the question of location was not looked upon seriously except in the light of the struggle between military and Party authority.[90]

Communist Policy, January, 1927

The Chinese Communists backed the position of the Left Wing and insisted that the Joint Conference of October, 1926, had definitely decided to move the capital to Wuhan.[91] According to a letter written on March 17, 1927, by Nassonov, representative of the Russian Young Communist League, and two Comintern representatives, Borodin was primarily responsible for bolstering the Left against Chiang. They reported that during Chiang's trip to Wuhan, Borodin had delivered a speech at a banquet in which he denounced personal dictatorship and, indirectly, Chiang Kai-shek. It was under Borodin's influence that the Left Wing consolidated itself and took a firm stand against Chiang's proposal to transfer the capital to Nanchang. The three delegates attributed the determination of the Left Wing and Borodin to the "revolutionizing effect" of the Hankow Incident.[92]

On January 3, 1927, crowds of Chinese staged a demonstration and took over the British Concession at Hankow. The British government took no retaliatory action and the incident was settled by negotiation. The Ch'en-O'Malley notes of February 19 and March 2, 1927, returned to Chinese jurisdiction the Hankow concession and the Kiukiang concession, which was also seized.[93] This diplomatic victory, which was negotiated by Foreign Minister Eugene Chen, considerably strengthened the Left's position vis-à-vis Chiang Kai-shek.

While the Hankow Incident encouraged Borodin and the Left Wing to stand firm against Chiang, Nassonov and his associates charged that it had the opposite effect on the chief Comintern delegate, Voitinskii, and the Chinese Communist Central Committee. The CC "did not want to react at all," they asserted. They reported that Ch'en Tu-hsiu declared at a conference of the CC: "Why should we clamor over it and what kind of agitation should we develop when the aggressors were not the English but the Chinese?" They accused the CC of insisting that the foreigners and the petty bourgeoisie should not have been incensed. In short, they complained that the CC and Voitinskii did not want to participate in the struggle against Chiang, but on the contrary wanted only to appease him.94

Document 47, a political report made by the CC on January 8, 1927, five days after the Hankow Incident, substantially confirms the assertions of the three representatives. It reveals the extremely cautious attitude of the CC. The mass movement had entered the revolutionary path in the provinces of Hunan, Hupeh, and Kiangsi, the CC declared. Revolutionary work had deeply penetrated the villages, and assassinations of the bad gentry and local bullies were taking place without end. However, the CC warned that it would be inappropriate even to issue the slogan "Reduce the people's burdens!" while military action was still in progress. It emphasized the need to continue efforts at reconciliation between leaders of the National Government. It considered reconciliation between Chiang Kai-shek and Wang Ching-wei as the most important problem of all and resolved to continue support for the slogan "Wang-Chiang cooperation."

Document 48, the CC's political report of January 28, 1927, reveals the reasons for the CC's caution. Jealousy and fear of Communist control of the labor and peasant movements had contributed to the rise of Rightist tendencies, the CC declared. It betrayed apprehension over the development of an anti-Red united front, comprised of the Right Wing, the moderates (Center), and foreign imperialists. The bourgeoisie must not under any circumstances be considered revolutionary, the CC declared. The Right Wing was growing daily and there was a strong tendency to oppose Soviet Russia, the Chinese Communist Party, and the labor and peasant movements. Furthermore, the CC expressed anxiety about the attitude of the Left. The Communists, the CC reported, had neglected to make concessions to the petty bourgeoisie, and hence even the Left did not show good feeling toward them. In fact, the CC declared, the anti-Communist movement involved a portion of the Left as well as the Right and Center [Doc. 48, pp. 30-32].

The CC maintained the policy of differentiation of the gentry; landlords, bad gentry, and local bullies were to be considered as counterrevolutionary forces in the villages. The CC stressed the need of allaying the KMT's suspicion of Communist influence among the masses and its fear of a Communist revolution. Communists must convince the Kuomintang, the CC said, that the National Revolution was still far from victory, that it was still in a period of difficult struggle and needed mass support. It called

for a vigorous campaign against Taichitaoism. Most important, the
CC re-emphasized alliance with the Left Wing. Although conflict
between the petty bourgeoisie and the proletariat was unavoidable
and would continue to expand, the CC said, it was absolutely necessary to give the petty bourgeoisie further concessions [Doc. 48,
pp. 30-32].

Thus, the CC's chief tactic was to stem the anti-Communist tide
by appeasing the Left and steering the KMT away from Rightist
tendencies.

The CC's apprehension stemmed in part from the suppression
of mass organizations in Canton and other areas controlled by
Kuomintang leaders opposed to the Wuhan Left Wing. A number of
Communist sources date the beginning of suppressive measures
against labor organizations and Communists in Kiangsi from
Chiang Kai-shek's return to Nanchang from Wuhan on January 18.[95]

The Wuhan-Nanchang Controversy, February to March, 1927

Chiang Kai-shek's return to Nanchang ushered in a period of intensification of the Wuhan-Nanchang controversy. The Left Wing
rallied under the banner of the "Movement to Restore Party Power"
(Hui-fu tang-ch'üan yün-tung). On February 24, 1927, a conference
of 15,000 KMT members of Wuhan, Hanyang, and Hsia-k'o was
convened. The chairman of the conference declared that the salva-
tion of the Party was the supreme objective. Military strength
superseded Party strength, he said, and the will of individuals
overshadowed that of the Party. The Government had failed to
move to Wuhan and Wang Ching-wei was still unable to resume his
duties. All these were symptoms of the ills of the Party which were
caused by the manipulations of reactionaries. Hence, he declared,
it was necessary to carry out a program of democratization of the
Party to strengthen Party power and elminate feudal influence.
According to a record of the meeting, at that point the audience
shouted such slogans as "Down with the old, confused, mediocre
and rotten elements!"

Hsü Ch'ien made essentially the same points, adding that it was
necessary to centralize the revolutionary forces by enabling Communists to participate in the CEC of the KMT and in all other political and mass organizations. He favored reviving the Military Council in order to subordinate military leaders to Party direction. Hsü's
speech was interrupted by shouts of "Overthrow Chang Ching-chiang!"
"Oppose military dictatorship!" and "Oppose the reactionaries!"

The conference adopted resolutions to: (1) Strengthen the CEC's
power and unify the Party's directing organ; (2) Convene immediately a plenary session of the CEC at Wuchang to solve Party
problems; (3) Urge Wang Ching-wei to cancel his leave of absence
and resume his duties at once; (4) Eliminate the "old, confused,

mediocre, and rotten elements" from the Party; and (5) Support the foreign policy of the National Government and crush all reactionary elements in the Party who were attempting to compromise with the imperialists.[96]

The resolutions of the conference were elaborated in a pamphlet, "Essential Points of Propaganda on Party Affairs," published by the Central Propaganda Department of the KMT. The policy of strengthening the CEC's power and unifying the Party's directing organ was expanded into the following three points: (1) Strengthen the Party's authority; all power belongs to the Party. The CEC is the supreme Party organ and there must not be any other organ to challenge its authority; (2) Unify the Party's directing organ and render absolute obedience to the CEC. Lack of unification invites counterrevolutionary and feudal tendencies; and (3) Realize political democracy and eliminate all feudal forces.[97]

On February 21, 1927, Chiang retaliated by accusing the Joint Council of usurping power and utilizing the "Movement to Restore Party Power" as a tool to seize control. Chiang said he believed that Party power was already centralized and supreme. He did not think that there was any other organ competing with the CEC; if there was, it was the Joint Council, which was without foundation; the Commander-in-Chief (Chiang himself) on the other hand, was legally empowered by the National Government and the Central Party Headquarters. Hence, Chiang declared, it was Hsü Ch'ien who was actually guilty of dictatorship.[98]

Six days later, Chiang pointed out that the chairmanship of the CEC was established at the Second Plenum of the CEC in May, 1926, as a temporary office, and that he himself had already proposed its abolition.[99]

Chiang vehemently denied that he did not wish Wang Ching-wei to return from abroad. He and Wang, Chiang said, were loving and intimate comrades. "If I have the desire to seize personal control of the Party and do not wish Comrade Wang Ching-wei to return," Chiang declared, "I would be totally devoid of character. Anyone can come and kill me! I believe Comrade Wang Ching-wei and I can be united to the end." Chiang added that there was no obstacle at all between them, save for the atmosphere created on purpose by people who wished to destroy him by utilizing Wang Ching-wei.[100] On February 27, Chiang declared that should Wang fail to return immediately, Chiang himself would be forced to resign.[101]

Those who denounced KMT members as "old, confused, mediocre, and rotten" merely because they were old, said Chiang, were guilty of wishing to destroy the Party.[102] In a subsequent letter, Chiang specifically defended Chang Ching-chiang and Ch'en Kuo-fu. Chang Ching-chiang, said Chiang, was one of Sun Yat-sen's most trusted associates.[103]

Having answered Wuhan's challenge, Chiang proceeded to raise
two issues of his own: the Chinese communists and the Russian
advisers.

He was not opposed to the Communists, said Chiang, but they
were oppressing KMT members and were guilty of tyranny. He
hoped, however, that they would genuinely cooperate with KMT
members. Should they continue their attitude, he warned, not only
would the Chinese revolutionary forces be disunited but they would
be extinguished by the enemy.[104]

On March 7, 1927, Chiang accused Soviet representatives of
tyranny. He had no thought of abandoning the alliance with Soviet
Russia, said Chiang, since Russia had not abandoned the spirit
of equality in dealing with China. Nevertheless, it was important
to associate with a friend who would remain true to the end. Soviet
Russia, he declared, was incapable of oppressive conduct toward
China, although her representatives employed oppressive tactics
against KMT leaders and scorned the Party's activities. Nevertheless, their conduct was an individual matter and must not be allowed to interfere with friendship between the KMT and Soviet
Russia.[105]

The test issue in the Wuhan-Nanchang schism was the convocation of the Third Plenum of the KMT Central Executive Committee.
The Left Wing, supported by the Communists, insisted on convening the plenum at Wuhan; Chiang's group insisted that it be called
at Nanchang.

The Communist Propaganda Offensive, February to March, 1927

The deepening of the Wuhan-Nanchang crisis coincided with
the advance of the Northern Expeditionary Forces towards Nanking
and Shanghai. At the same time, there was a noticeable increase in
the Communists' anxiety.

In the political report of January 26, 1927, the Central Committee of the Chinese Communist Party had expressed concern over
what they alleged to be British attempts to organize international
opposition to the Chinese Revolution and to woo the KMT moderates. Thus, it advocated concentrating on the anti-British movement [Doc. 48, pp. 29, 32]. Then, as the Eastern Route Army
neared Hangchow, Chekiang, toward middle February, the
Central Committee's fear grew more pronounced. Japan, instead
of Britain, had become the principal source of anxiety. In a letter
to the Northern Regional Committee on February 13, the CC
stated that under Japanese leadership, the moderates and Mukden
had begun a movement for compromise between North and South.
Should this movement succeed, warned the CC, it would mean a
blow not only to the Kuomintang Left Wing and the Chinese Communist Party but to the Chinese Revolution itself.

To counteract this situation, the Central Committee called for propaganda against Chiang Kai-shek who, it said, had become the hub of Right counterrevolutionary forces. It added, however, that caution must be exercised in disseminating anti-Chiang propaganda, which was to be carried out by word of mouth. In printed matter, Chiang's name was not to be mentioned, but his identity should nevertheless be obvious.

Among Chiang's "principal misdeeds" which the CC instructed local Party organizations to publicize was his alleged connections with the Japanese and Chang Tso-lin of Mukden. Huang Fu, said the CC, had introduced Sadao Saburi to Chiang Kai-shek and the two had held a long secret conversation at Kuling, Kiangsi. Furthermore, said the CC, prominent members of the Japanese government were constantly saying that a compromise between the moderates and Mukden was possible.[106] In the March 6, 1927, issue of Hsiang-tao, Ch'en Tu-hsiu accused the moderates of conspiring with the Japanese imperialists and Mudken.[107] On the following day Chiang Kai-shek pointedly denied that he was negotiating with Japan and Mukden. Japan was an imperialist nation, said Chiang, and unless she abandoned imperialist policies, it was impossible to compromise with Japan. As for negotiations with Mukden and Shantung, Chiang asserted they were merely rumors created by Wuhan Party members to destroy the National Revolutionary Army and defeat the Chinese Revolution.[108]

While the Communists themselves were undoubtedly disseminating rumors of secret negotiations between Chiang, the Japanese, and Chang Tso-lin, their alarm was, it appears, genuine.

Evidence is lacking on the controversial question whether Chiang did enter into negotiations with the Japanese and Chang Tso-lin. The record suggests, however, that the Japanese government assumed a noticeably friendly position toward Chiang around the beginning of 1927. It further suggests that this attitude was influenced at least in part by the views of Sadao Saburi who, the Communists allege, visited Chiang in Kiangsi.

Sadao Saburi, chief of the Treaty Bureau of the Japanese Foreign Office, was a delegate to the Chinese Tariff Conference. He traveled widely in China in late 1926 and early 1927. According to a Japanese biographical dictionary, he undertook these journeys in the hope of making "readjustments" in Chinese-Japanese diplomatic relations.[109] Huang Fu, whom Communists accused of being the go-between for Saburi and Chiang, also attended the Tariff Conference as a Chinese plenipotentiary delegate. A Japanese Foreign Office source asserts that, in response to Chiang's request, Huang went to South China at the beginning of 1927 to serve as liaison officer between Chiang and the Japanese.[110]

Contemporary dispatches from the American Ambassador and the

Chargé d'Affaires in Tokyo throw interesting light on Saburi's travels in terms of Japan's China policy. On Januarary 18, 1927, Ambassador MacVeagh sent to Washington a memorandum on a conversation held three days earlier between himself and Japanese Foreign Minister Shidehara. According to the memorandum, Baron Shidehara expressed the opinion that the generals of the National Revolutionary Army were dissatisfied with the increasingly open control exercised by Borodin, and that Chiang Kai-shek was not in favor of anti-British policies. Chiang's real feelings were far from radical, Shidehara said, despite his many radical speeches, which were necessary in order for him to keep his place. Ambassador MacVeagh suggested to the Secretary of State that Shidehara's remarks about the political sympathies of the Southern leaders, notably Chiang, were based on reports from Sadao Saburi.[111]

In a dispatch on May 25, 1927, the American Chargé d'Affaires in Tokyo, Norman Armour, expressed certainty that Saburi's visit to South China in November and December, 1926, was for the purpose of studying the situation at first hand, and that the Japanese government's confidence in Chiang dated from the time of Saburi's return to Tokyo. Armour pointed out that from the beginning of January, coinciding almost exactly with Saburi's return, the Japanese government had maintained a consistently friendly attitude toward Chiang and singled him out for support.[112]

The State Department's files on the Nanking Incident tend to confirm Armour's observations on the Japanese attitude toward Chiang. As early as March 28, 1927, four days after the Nanking Incident, Baron Shidehara told Ambassador MacVeagh that he believed Chiang Kai-shek was strongly opposed to the antiforeign outrages and would exert every effort to maintain order. The incident, said Shidehara, was instigated by the radicals in order to discredit Chiang. He warned that it would be a mistake for the foreign powers to take drastic measures lest they play into radical schemes to destroy Chiang. On the same day, Vice-Minister Debuchi informed the Councillor of the American Embassy that Chiang Kai-shek represented the only responsible element in South China and that he should be given a free hand to show what he could do.[113] In subsequent discussions between the British, Americans, and Japanese, the Japanese government consistently urged giving Chiang every opportunity to take the initiative in restoring order and meeting the Powers' demands and avoiding any action which might embarrass Chiang and thus lead to his downfall.[114]

It does not necessarily follow from this, however, that Saburi actually met with Chiang, or that secret agreements were reached or even discussed by them. Of this we have found no conclusive evidence in the available historical record. It is equally difficult to draw conclusions on the validity of the persistent rumors of negotiations between Chiang and Mukden. By early April, 1927, of course, Chiang and Chang Tso-lin were in opposing campus. Chang Tso-lin's raid on the Soviet Military Attaché's office in Peking on April 6, 1927 was directed against Chiang as well as the Wuhan Left Wing, the Communists, and the Russians. The seized documents, after all, compromised Chiang with their revelations of his close cooperation with the Russian advisers at Canton. The fact that there was an open break between Chiang and Chang in early April, 1927, however, still leaves open the possibility that negotiations were held prior to that month.

In this connection, it is interesting to note a dispatch from the American Minister at Peking to the Secretary of State, dated April 9, 1927. Minister MacMurray reported the following information supplied him by Liang Shih-i, a prominent member of the Northern government. Liang, according to MacMurray, had been active in seeking an agreement between Chiang and Mukden but had just informed MacMurray that efforts toward a settlement had finally been abandoned following a sudden unfavorable turn of events. Liang said there had previously been such progress, however, that Chiang had asked that a plenipotentiary representative be sent to Shanghai to conclude negotiations and Wang Ch'ung-hui was dispatched there for this purpose.[115]

Whether or not the rumors of negotiations were entirely baseless, the Central Committee sought to forestall a Chiang-Mukden rapprochement. The CC's tactics included, besides an anti-Chiang propaganda drive, continued insistence on pushing north against Chang Tso-lin in Peking. As previously noted, the CC urged concentrating all forces on the Peking-Hankow Railroad in early January, 1927, although the Chekiang offensive had already been launched in early December. In mid-March, 1927, as the Right Bank Army neared Nanking, Ch'en Tu-hsiu demanded again that the Mukden Clique be the main target of attack.[116]

Throughout the Southeastern campaign, according to KMT sources, the Communists, aided by the Left Wing, attempted to obstruct the progress of military operations. Ch'en Ming-shu accuses them of cutting off ammunition supplies to the front and agitating among workers in the rear to obstruct the campaign.[117] Ho Ying-ch'in made similar charges in May, 1927. The Joint Council at Wuhan, according to Ho, exerted every effort to obstruct the progress of the Right Bank Army. Ho said that Lin Tsu-han, the Communist chairman of the Political Department of the Right Bank Army likewise sought to frustrate the advance towards Nanking.[118]

Another major point of anti-Chiang propaganda which the CC instructed local organizations to elaborate was the charge that he was organizing a movement against the Russians, the Communists, and the workers and peasants.[119] The CC had previously expressed misgivings over what it regarded as an extremely strong tendency within the KMT to oppose Soviet Russia, the Chinese Communist Party, and the labor and peasant movements [Doc. 48, p. 30]. Apparently, it was the fear of such tendencies which prompted the CC to decide in December, 1926, to support the KMT Left Wing on the sole condition that it uphold "The Three Policies"—alliance with Soviet Russia, alliance with the Communists, and support of the labor and peasant movements.

In line with the CC's instructions, the Communist propaganda offensive was dominated by the theme of violation of the Three Policies. In an article, "Sorrow on the Second Anniversary of Dr. Sun's Death," published in the March 12, 1927, issue of Hsiang-tao, Ch'en Tu-hsiu denounced the moderates for allegedly abandoning "The Three Policies." Ch'en stated: "It is true that the Chinese Revolution was developed considerably following the death of Dr. Sun, particularly during the May Thirtieth Movement and the Northern Expedition of the National Revolutionary Army. There is still a long road ahead, however, before the National Revolution can be completed. The revolutionary movement must be further developed in order to fulfill Dr. Sun's unfinished tasks. Some of the so-called stable elements [moderates], however, lack strong revolutionary determination and presume to be middle-of-the-road revolutionary leaders. Through fear of the further development of the Revolution, they have thrown away Dr. Sun's Three Great Revolutionary Policies, namely, alliance with Soviet Russia, alliance with the Communist Party, and support of the workers and peasants. They have abandoned Dr. Sun's will and ceased working for the Revolution. Is this not a cause for great sorrow and anguish while we commemorate the second anniversary of Dr. Sun's death?....Is it not a cause for anguish that, barely two years following his death, Dr. Sun's policies should be secretly repudiated and even frankly regarded by certain elements as unsuitable for execution?"120

The Communist campaign to attack Chiang's group on the charge of violation of "Dr. Sun's Three Great Policies" was so successful that, with the exception of Kuomintang sources, most of the writings on the Chinese Revolution accept the Communist identification of "The Three Policies" with Sun Yat-sen and trace their formulation to the First Kuomintang Congress of January, 1924. Beginning in the summer of 1922, Dr. Sun did indeed decide to ally with Soviet Russia, admit Communists into the Kuomintang (not ally with Communists), and support the interests of workers and peasants, but there is no evidence that he ever referred to them as "The Three Policies" or set them apart from other policies adopted about the same time (see Part III, pp. 140-148). In fact, in December, 1925, the Kuomintang CEC declared that five fundamental policies had been adopted by Sun Yat-sen at the First Kuomintang Congress.121 The very term "The Three Policies" is a Communist creation.

Although Ch'en Tu-hsiu did not name Chiang Kai-shek in his article, he was clearly the target being attacked. Thus, by the middle of February, 1927, the CC had definitely adopted an anti-Chiang stand, although it did not openly attack him.

Orthodox Communist histories accuse Ch'en Tu-hsiu, P'eng Shu-chih, and other CC members in Shanghai of pursuing a policy of retreat in dealing with Chiang Kai-shek. Pavel Mif contrasts their negative position with the active anti-Chiang policy of the majority of CC members who had moved to Wuhan. Under the leadership of Ch'ü Ch'iu-pai, Chang Kuo-t'ao, and Li Li-san, said Mif, the Wuhan Communists conducted an intensive anti-Chiang campaign. They issued such slogans as "Down with Chiang Kai-shek!" and "Overthrow the Traitors!" They organized innumerable demon-strations, and succeeded, according to Mif, in concentrating Kuo-mintang masses around anti-Chiang slogans and in drawing many wavering KMT leaders to their side.122 In his report to the Fifth KCT Congress later in the spring, Ch'en Tu-hsiu confirmed that the CC had indeed been criticized by the Hupeh Communists for lacking courage.123 The vigor of the Wuhan Communists' anti-Chiang campaign is attested to in Kuomintang sources. Ch'en Kuo-fu, for instance, recalls that by early March, 1927, the slogans "Down with Chiang Kai-shek!" and "Oust Ch'en Kuo-fu!" were prominently displayed in the streets of Wuhan.124

There were considerable differences, however, between the respective positions of the Wuhan Communists and the CC at Shanghai. As the Party's General Secretary, Ch'en Tu-hsiu was committed to the policy of the Comintern, which remained geared to the decision of the Seventh Enlarged ECCI Plenum to continue cooperating with those elements of the big bourgeoisie which were still on the side of the Revolution. Chiang, of course, was included in this category. Furthermore, while the Shanghai Communists had to cope with an increasingly oppressive militarist regime, the Wuhan Communists enjoyed complete freedom of action. They found Wuhan to be fertile soil for anti-Chiang propaganda. They also found a powerful sponsor in the person of T'ang Sheng-chih, who had already initiated an anti-Chiang campaign of his own.

Anti-Chiang Military Alliance, to March, 1927

Friction had developed between T'ang Sheng-chih and Chiang Kai-shek as early as August, 1926.125 As a counterpoise to the Whampoa Alumni Association which backed Chiang, T'ang organ-ized the Alumni Association of Four Military Academies, led by the Paoting Clique.126 Pavlov reported in August, 1926, that the

Paoting Clique was formed as a result of jealousy of Chiang. He expressed fear that T'ang might sever his ties with the National Government and suggested that an important factor in determining whether he would was the speed with which he would be able to form alliances [Doc. 43, p. 89].

T'ang Sheng-chih apparently began to cultivate the Communists immediately after the occupation of Wuchang. According to Teruni's report of October 30, 1926, T'ang expressed a strong desire to meet Ch'en Tu-hsiu, and he consulted Communists when he organized the Hupeh Provincial Government [Doc. 44, pp. 13, 23]. Nassonov and others reported that T'ang Sheng-chih offered to the Wuhan Communists the suggestion that he recruit members of peasant associations into his army.[127]

In a letter dated October 10, 1926, the executive committees of the Hupeh regional committees of the KCT and CY outlined the strategy of aiding those who desired to become "new militarists." Since the Communists' enemies had not yet been destroyed and the Communist force was inadequate, the letter states, it was necessary to utilize the psychology of those who desired to become new militarists and support them.[128] Although the document does not mention either Chiang Kai-shek or T'ang Sheng-chih, it seems possible that local Hupeh Communists began to support T'ang against Chiang even before the arrival of Chang Kuo-t'ao, Ch'ü Ch'iu-pai, Li Li-san, and other CC members at Wuhan.

At any rate, an alliance between T'ang Sheng-chih and the Wuhan Communists, cemented by mutual opposition to Chiang, had definitely materialized by the early part of 1927.[129] T'ang Sheng-chih's personal campaign against Chiang was intensified by the Communists. In later years, M. N. Roy bitterly criticized the Communists for playing "second fiddle" to T'ang and failing to organize an anti-Chiang campaign of their own.[130]

Document 49, a Soviet report dated March 5, 1927, reveals the success T'ang Sheng-chih enjoyed in forming an anti-Chiang military alliance. The report states that T'ang had succeeded in getting the Fourth Army under Chang Fa-k'uei and the Eleventh Army under Ch'en Ming-shu[131] to turn against Chiang. T'ang had also persuaded Li Tsung-jen, commander of the Seventh Army, to assume a hostile attitude toward Chiang. Furthermore, according to Document 49, Chu P'ei-te, Commander of the Third Army, no longer supported Chiang, and the Ninth and Tenth armies had also joined the anti-Chiang combination. Thus, according to the document, the only units participating in the Northern Expedition which were loyal to Chiang were his own First Army and the Second and the Sixth armies.[132] The report concludes with the opinion that Chiang had definitely lost control of the best elements of the National Revolutionary Army [Doc. 49, pp. 65-66].

Ch'ü Ch'iu-pai later agreed with the Soviet estimate of the military line-up against Chiang and asserted that the Second and Sixth armies were also opposed to Chiang. Prior to his entry into Shanghai on March 26, 1927, according to Ch'ü, Chiang was in a position of isolation or near-isolation.[133] Mandalyan, asserts that the Left Wing had a good chance to destroy Chiang at the time of the occupation of Shanghai and Nanking. The Second and Sixth armies which took Nanking stood on the side of the Left. Hence, the Left could have destroyed Chiang's army at Nanking.[134] While sources disagree on the alignment of individual generals, the evidence suggests that Chiang's military position in February and March, up to the anti-Communist coup of mid-April, 1927, in Shanghai, was far from strong. Communist sources assert that Hsüeh Yüeh, commander of the units of the First Division of the First Army which entered Shanghai on March 21, 1927, was sympathetic to the Communists and offered to turn against Chiang.[135] Contemporary dispatches to the Secretary of State from American foreign service personnel frequently express doubt of Chiang's ability to control the troops, and estimate that only small numbers of the men were loyal to him.[136] According to an anti-Communist source, T'ang Sheng-chih considered Chiang's position in February, 1927, so precarious that he sought to interest Borodin in a plan for a surprise attack on Chiang at Nanchang.[137]

By this time, Borodin and other Russian advisers had reversed their former policy of supporting Chiang against T'ang Sheng-chih. M. N. Roy later criticized Borodin severely for what he called the "T'ang Sheng-chih orientation." It is significant for instance, that Soviet advisers did not take part in the drive for Shanghai and Nanking. Galen, who had been attached to Chiang's headquarters from the outset of the Northern Expedition, left it during the campaign and headed for Wuhan.[138] According to Nassonov and others, Galen believed that the march on Shanghai was doomed to failure, and Borodin and the other Russians wanted Chiang to "break his neck" on Shanghai.[139]

T'ang Sheng-chih and the Communists apparently eyed Feng Yü-hsiang as a potential ally against Chiang. Feng's Kuominchün forces had occupied Sian, Shensi, in October, 1926, and had proceeded eastward along the Lunghai Railway toward Honan, crossing the border into Honan on December 1, 1926.[140] Feng Yü-hsiang later recalled that at this juncture, a representative of T'ang Sheng chih began to publicize anti-Chiang slogans in Kuominchün territory and sought in vain to persuade Feng to turn against Chiang.[141]

The Russian and Chinese Communists had by that time drastically revised their estimate of Feng Yü-hsiang. Though they had been exceedingly suspicious of Feng, they began to regard him as a genuine revolutionary following the trip to Moscow in the summer of 1926.

A number of reports made by the Central Committee of the Chinese
Communist Party in December, 1926, assert that Feng had made
progress in his revolutionary convictions and had inclined much to
the Left. He was cautious, studious, and thrifty, the CC declared, in
contrast to members of Chiang Kai-shek's staff who were bent on
personal advancement. In the CC's opinion, Feng understood better
than anyone else the needs of the masses and supported their interests. Hence, the CC reports predicted, his army was destined to
play a very great part in the future revolutionary struggle.[142]

According to orthodox Communist histories, Ch'en Tu-hsiu and
Borodin advocated joining forces with Feng Yü-hsiang in the
Northwest during the Wuhan period (mid-April to mid-July, 1927).
Ch'en and Borodin, it is asserted, espoused the "Northwest Theory,"
holding that the Revolution could not be developed in industrial
areas because of the power of imperialism and the bourgeoisie.
They therefore advocated heading toward the northwestern prov-
inces of China and establishing there a revolutionary base in con-
cert with Feng Yü-hsiang. According to Pavel Mif, the "Northwest
Theory" was decisively defeated at the Fifth Congress of the
Chinese Communist Party held at Wuhan in late April and early
May, 1927.[143] Thus, if orthodox Communist charges are true, the
"Northwest Theory" was at least discussed, if not formally proposed, at some time before late April, 1927. In this connection it is
of interest to note a telegram to the Secretary of State from Douglas
Jenkins, the American Consul General at Canton, dated March 24,
1927. Jenkins reported that he had been informed by a source close
to high Kuomintang leaders that certain KMT leaders at Wuhan
believed it possible that Borodin might shortly move to Feng Yü-
hsiang's headquarters.[144]

Communist Alliance with the Wuhan Left Wing,
February to March, 1927

In addition to promoting an anti-Chiang propaganda campaign and
forming anti-Chiang military alliances, the Chinese Communist
leadership called for more aggressive tactics in dealing with the
Kuomintang Left Wing and leading it to struggle against the Right.
The Communist Kiangsu-Chekiang Regional Committee warned
against the growing tide of Rightist tendencies and exhorted Party
members not to retreat in any direction. It was first of all
necessary to win the struggle within the KMT, the Committee
stated. For this purpose, Communists must take the offensive
against the Right. However, this struggle must not become a simple struggle between the Chinese Communist Party and the Kuomintang. Communists were told that they must give prominence to the
Left and ally with it to advance. The appropriate Communist-Left
Wing relationship was defined as follows:

"The so-called cooperation with the Left does not mean that we should let the Left Wing become the central element and the Communists its supporters. We should be the central element and force the Left to help us. The Left's capacity is still scattered and weak. Hence, it is necessary for us to lead it in struggle and become its vanguard. In past intra-KMT struggles, we let the Left Wing handle the situation, we merely suggesting things at the rear. The Left was weak and it was often defeated. This has not only affected revolutionary work but has caused the Left to resent us. We must henceforth correct this error. The form of struggle should be a Right-Left struggle and not simply a struggle between the Chinese Communist Party and the Kuomintang. Actually, however, we should be the vanguard, leading the Left to advance."[145] A letter from the Communist Central Political Bureau to Party members in Hunan, Hupeh, and Kiangsi declared that if Communists were unwilling to serve as the Left's vanguard and allowed the Left to become the vanguard, it would mean letting the petty bourgeoisie lead the Revolution. The petty bourgeoisie, said the Central Political Bureau, could never lead the Revolution![146]

The test case in the Wuhan-Nanchang controversy was the choice of a location for holding the Third CEC Plenum. The Central Committee of the Chinese Communist Party regarded this struggle to be of the utmost significance. In a letter to the Northern Regional Committee on February 13, 1927, the CC declared that the outcome of the struggle over whether the plenum was to be convened at Wuhan or Nanchang would determine who was to be the victor in the struggle between revolutionary and counterrevolutionary forces. Therefore, besides launching a vigorous anti-Chiang propaganda campaign, Communists should do their utmost to help the Left convene the plenum at Wuhan.[147]

The Left Wing, supported by the Communists, won the test. As Hu Hua puts it, the revolutionary force was superior in the KMT Central Executive Committee, with Communist CEC members supplementing the Left Wing which supported "The Three Policies."[148] In early March, Chiang Kai-shek asked those CEC members who were at Nanchang to proceed to Wuhan to attend the Third Plenum.[149]

The decisions of the Third CEC Plenum, held between March 10 and March 17, 1927, further consolidated the position of the Left Wing vis-à-vis Chiang Kai-shek.[150]

The first session of the Plenum opened with a report by Hsü Ch'ien on the formation and history of the Joint Council. This was followed by passage of a resolution stating that the Joint Council had been an indispensable organization for the Revolution and that it had represented the authority of the government. The resolution expressed praise of the Joint Council's work and declared that all

its resolutions were still valid although it had ceased to function.
This endorsement of the Joint Council, one of Chiang's chief targets
of attack, indicated that the Left Wing was in control of the situation from the start.

The adoption of two important resolutions, drafted in accordance with
the principles of the Movement to Restore Party Power, followed. The
first, the resolution on the unification of the directing organ of the Party,
revised Party organization. Its central provision was establishment of
the seven-man Presidium of the Political Council, invested with supreme
Party authority. This decision in effect abolished the chairmanship of
the CEC and reversed the trend toward concentration of power within the
KMT which had culminated in May, 1926, in centralizing authority in the
chairman of the CEC. The immediate outcome was of course the elimination of the unique political power of Chiang Kai-shek, chairman of the CEC,
and of Chang Ching-chiang, the deputy chairman.

The second resolution outlined the organization of the Military
Council. The Military Council, which had been abolished in the
summer of 1926, was re-established as the highest organ for administer-
ing the military affairs of the National Government and was given
full jurisdiction over all things military. It was stipulated that six
of the members of the Military Council were to be CEC members,
the rest high military officers (from three to seven members). The
resolution was thus designed to strengthen Party authority over the
military, in particular over Chiang Kai-shek. In the interest of
further bolstering Party authority against Chiang, the Plenum
adopted separate statutes on the Commander-in-Chief. The most
important point was that the Commander-in-Chief should be entirely
responsible to the Central Executive Committee.

The outcome of the elections to Party and government posts on
the following day was fully in line with the spirit of the resolutions.
Although Chiang Kai-shek was elected to the Standing Committee of
the CEC, the Political Council, the Military Council, the Presidium
of the Military Council, and the National Government Council, he
was left out of the all-powerful seven-man Presidium of the Political
Council. Furthermore, he was replaced by Wang Ching-wei as head
of the KMT Organization Department. Chang Ching-chiang and
Ch'en Kuo-fu were completely by-passed at the elections. Neither
was even elected to the twenty-eight-man National Government
Council.

The Left Wing won controlling positions in all organs. Its dominance was reflected most strongly in the Presidium of the Political
Council, composed of the following members: Wang Ching-wei,
T'an Yen-k'ai, Sun Fo, Ku Meng-yü, Hsü Ch'ien, T. V. Soong, and
the Communist, T'an P'ing-shan.

The elections left no doubt as to who was the leader of the Left
Wing. The name of Wang Ching-wei, who had not yet returned from

France conspicuously heads the lists of members elected to all
Party and Government organs. Aside from the Presidium of the
Political Council, Wang was elected to the Standing Committee of
the CEC, the Military Council, the Presidium of the Military Council, and the National Government. He was also named to take charge
of the KMT Organization Department. Thus, in the absence of both
men, the Third CEC Plenum in effect reversed the balance of
power between Chiang and Wang affected by the March Twentieth coup
d'état.

Membership on the Presidium of the Political Council distin-
guished T'an Yen-k'ai, Sun Fo, Ku Meng-yü, Hsü Ch'ien, and T. V.
Soong as the most important KMT leaders at Wuhan at that time.
Eugene Chen and Teng Yen-ta also held leading positions in the
Party and Government. Other influential Left leaders included Sung
Ch'ing-ling and Ho Hsiang-ning.

The Left Wing's ascendancy over Chiang Kai-shek's faction is
further indicated by the Plenum's decision to invalidate elections
to the Kiangsi and Kwangtung Provincial Party Headquarters and
the Canton Municipal Party Headquarters, which had been reorganized under the auspices of Chang Ching-chiang and Ch'en Kuo-fu.151

The Plenum marked the height of KMT-KCT collaboration with
passage of the resolution on unification of the revolutionary forces.
This called for a joint conference of the KMT and KCT to meet at
once to discuss problems of cooperation, including the following:
(1) unification of the mass movements, especially the peasant and
labor movements, which should be led jointly; (2) the question of
the minority races of the country; (3) the question of jointly assuming political responsibility; the sending by the Chinese Communist
Party of responsible members to participate in the National Government and provincial governments; (4) the press organs of the
Third International, the Kuomintang, and the Chinese Communist
Party should not violate the spirit of cooperation in their reports
and criticisms of one another; and (5) in response to the invitation
of the Third International, the Kuomintang was to send immediately
three representatives to discuss with it the problems of the Chinese
Revolution, especially the relationship between the Chinese Revolution and the World Revolution.

The outstanding provision of the resolution on unification of the
revolutionary forces was Article Three, which called upon Communists to participate in the National Government. Following its
passage, the Plenum voted to create five new government ministries.
Communists were named to head two of the new ministries;
T'an P'ing-shan became Minister of Agriculture and Su Chao-cheng,
Minister of Labor. The appointment of Communists to cabinet posts
pushed the original KMT policy to admit Communists into the
Kuomintang further toward the concept of two-party coalition,

particularly because the resolution specifically called on the Chinese Communist Party to <u>send</u> men to the National Government. T'an and Su in effect became the KCT's representatives in the National Government rather than KMT members who also belonged to the KCT.

This development was completely in line with Comintern policy. The "Theses" of the Seventh Enlarged Plenum of the ECCI had called for Communist penetration of the National Government to steer it to the Left in alliance with the Left Wing. The Plenum, which T'an P'ing-shan attended, had declared that Communists should utilize the government apparatus to carry out such policies as land confiscation and tax reduction. Communist influence is discernible in a number of other decisions of the Plenum—the resolution to establish a revolutionary court for the suppression of counterrevolutionaries and the statutes on punishment of the bad gentry and local bullies.

Despite their influence, the Communists failed to deepen their penetration of top KMT organs. Two Communists, T'an P'ing-shan and Wu Yü-chang, were elected to the nine-man Standing Committee, as compared with the election of three Communists to the same committee in January, 1926. Not one Communist was elected to the sixteen-member Military Council. Communists were still barred from heading KMT departments in accordance with the resolutions of the Second CEC Plenum.

The available evidence in fact suggests that certain elements of the Left Wing had become weary of the Communist influence.

On March 4, 1927, Takao, the Japanese Consul General at Hankow, reported to Tokyo that Eugene Chen had called on him in connection with the arrest of Mrs. Borodin by Chang Tsung-ch'ang's men on board the S.S. "Pamiat Lenina." Chen confidentially informed him, Takao said, that the KMT had decided to dismiss Borodin, who was to return immediately to Soviet Russia. Chen then requested that the Japanese authorities intercede with Chang Tsung-ch'ang for Mrs. Borodin's release. According to Takao, Chen was chiefly worried lest Mrs. Borodin's continued detention should delay Borodin's departure from Hankow. Such a turn of events, Chen reportedly told Takao, would in turn lead to numerous complications.152

Takao's report is partially confirmed by a dispatch to the Secretary of State from Lockhart, the American Consul General at Hankow, enclosing a memorandum on a conversation he had had with Lo Ch'eng, a confidential aide and adviser to T'ang Sheng-chih, on March 16, 1927. According to the memorandum, Lo informed Lockhart that T'ang Sheng-chih was not in the radical camp but was only temporarily allied with the radicals to oppose Chiang Kai-shek. Lo further told Lockhart that Chiang had threatened to attack

T'ang Sheng-chih unless the latter forced Borodin and Hsü Ch'ien
to leave Hankow. T'ang had agreed to Chiang's demand, said Lo
Ch'eng, but Borodin and Hsü were unwilling to leave and were doing everything to resist. Lo added that Eugene Chen was trying to
occupy the middle ground in this dispute in an attempt to achieve
a compromise between the two factions.[153] On March 19,1927,
the American Consul General at Canton reported that a source close
to certain KMT leaders had informed him that Eugene Chen and
T. V. Soong were definitely sympathetic to Chiang. His informant
believed that Sun Fo was Borodin's main supporter but that he would
probably join Chiang's camp if convinced of the good will of the
Powers. He then urged the American Consul General to do his best to
make the American government see the situation as it really was.[154]

Though unconfirmed, these reports suggest that the Wuhan leaders' solidarity and triumph over Chiang Kai-shek were in reality
not quite as impressive as they would appear from official Party
resolutions. Furthermore, Wang Ching-wei himself later admitted
that he was ready to re-examine the policy of cooperating with the
Communists when he returned from abroad at the beginning of
April, 1927.[155] In short, opposition to Chiang Kai-shek appeared
to have been the dominant motive behind the triple alliance of the
Communists, the Left Wing, and T'ang Sheng-chih, who utilized one
another for their own divergent purposes.[156]

The Chinese Communist Central Committee and Moscow, January to April, 1927

The Communist policy of forming alliances, particularly within the
Army, was cited as proof of Communist conspiracy during the Kuomintang's Party Purification Movement.[157] In orthodox Communist
histories, Ch'en Tu-hsiu is held responsible for relying on alliances to
achieve Communist objectives. He is accused of concentrating exclusively on "utilizing A against B and B against A," in the manner of petty politicians.[158] Orthodox histories assert that he failed to build an independent
Communist armed force and neglected the task of seizing power. He is in
particular denounced for pursuing a policy of retreat at Shanghai following
the Third Shanghai Insurrection on March 21, 1927, thus paving the way
for the anti-Communist coup of April 12.[159]

In his political report to the Sixth KCT Congress, which was held
in Moscow in the summer of 1928, Ch'ü Ch'iu-pai, Ch'en Tu-hsiu's successor as Party leader, emphasized that the CC had made no preparations for armed struggle.[160] However, Ch'ü himself and the other Communists at Wuhan apparently also refrained from organizing an independent Communist armed force. Pavel Mif, who applauds their anti-
Chiang campaign, makes no mention of any attempt to arm the workers
and peasants. Mif in fact praises them for persuading wavering Kuomintang leaders to join their stand.[161] Thus, the Wuhan Communists

themselves evidently stressed alliance with elements of the KMT
rather than preparation for seizure of power.

On the other hand, according to Ch'en Tu-hsiu's testimony, Ch'en
himself, P'eng Shu-chih, Lo I-nung, and other Communist leaders
in Shanghai were in fact dubious about this course of action. At an
enlarged conference of the CC which was convened at this time,
Ch'en asserts, he proposed that Communists should seize leadership of the Chinese Revolution. He pointed out that there were only
two alternatives: either the Revolution was to be led by the proletariat and would achieve victory, or it would be led by the
bourgeoisie, which was sure to betray it halfway. This opinion, he
said, was opposed unanimously by members of the Comintern's
Far Eastern Bureau in Shanghai (which included Voitinskii), who declared that such action would bring about premature opposition by
the bourgeoisie. Thus, he failed to maintain his position.

According to Ch'en, it was Ch'ü Ch'ui-pai who emphasized allying
with the petty bourgeoisie to oppose the big bourgeoisie in Shanghai.
On the other hand, he himself and other Shanghai Communists were
convinced that the proletariat must overcome Chiang Kai-shek by
force. According to Ch'en, P'eng Shu-chih was sent to Hankow to
state this opinion before the CC members in Wuhan and the Comintern delegates, but they showed little interest in the CC's proposals.
Furthermore, Ch'en asserts, in late March, 1927, the CI telegraphed
the Shanghai CC to avoid at all cost military conflict between the
workers and Chiang's forces and instructed it to hide or bury all
weapons of the workers.[162] Thus, according to Ch'en Tu-hsiu, the
ECCI was responsible for the Communist debacle at Shanghai.

The letter of Nassonov, Fokine, and Albrecht, written on March
17, 1927, four days before the Third Shanghai Insurrection, substantially corroborates Ch'en's account. On the issue of Communist
policy in Shanghai, the delegates confirmed that certain Chinese
Communists advocated unleashing the mass movement in Shanghai
as a counterpoise to the Kuomintang Right Wing, thereby creating
a democratic people's regime. Although they criticized Ch'en Tu-
hsiu throughout the letter, it is clear that they held Voitinskii chiefly
responsible for the policies executed by the CC. They declared
that it was Voitinskii who opposed drawing workers, peasants,
and Communists into the army on a mass scale and who obstructed the organization of Communist cells in the National Revolutionary Army.

Although they accused both the CC and Voitinskii of passivity in
the struggle against Chiang, they stated: "This line, if it can be
called a line at all, was not so much the course of the CC, as it was
of Comrade V." Voitinskii, they asserted, feared that Borodin was
pushing the Left Wing too far in the dispute with Chiang and requested Moscow to recall Borodin. Finally, they held Voitinskii

chiefly responsible for Communist insistence on alliance with the
Left Wing and the recall of Wang Ching-wei. They declared: "Our
Party has bound up all its work within the national revolutionary
movement with the return of Wang Ching-wei. All talk of the Left
Kuomintang, of connection with the Left Kuomintang, leads in the
end to Wang Ching-wei."163

Voitinskii, of course, was merely following orders from the
Comintern leadership, which consistently maintained that the key
Communist policy was alliance with the Kuomintang Left Wing,
and rejected plans for an independent Communist struggle. Even
a document cited by Stalin to defend his policies on August 1, 1927,
offers confirmation that the ECCI's plans did not include preparations for Communist seizure of power. According to Stalin, the
document contained instructions which the ECCI sent the Chinese
Communist Party in late March, 1927, calling on it to steer a
course toward the arming of workers and peasants. The ECCI instructed the Chinese Communists not to shield the traitorous and
reactionary policies of the KMT Right Wing, Stalin said, but to expose them by mobilizing the masses around the Kuomintang and the
Chinese Communist Party.164 Thus, the ECCI was still committed
to the policy of continued cooperation with the Kuomintang, and
restricted Communist struggle to the struggle against the KMT
Right Wing. As late as April 5, 1927, Stalin was still calling for
continued cooperation with Chiang Kai-shek. While Chiang perhaps had no sympathy for the Revolution, Stalin said, he was leading the Army and could not do otherwise than lead it against imperialism. Furthermore, Communists still needed the Right Wing,
which had capable people and valuable connections. The Right
Wing should therefore be utilized to the end, Stalin declared,
"squeezed out like a lemon," and then flung away.165

The documents of the Chinese Communist Party prove that the
Central Committee had consistently doubted the capacity and revolutionary determination of the Kuomintang Left Wing. The CC had
repeatedly warned of the disunity and weakness of the Left and of
the growing power of the Right.166 This points strongly to the conclusion that the Chinese Communist Party adjusted its tactics to
the policy of alliance with the Left under Comintern direction.

Communists and the Left Wing at Peking, to April 6, 1927

The Communist policy of alliance with the Left Wing achieved the
greatest results at the lower levels of the Kuomintang Party
hierarchy. The victory of the Left Wing at the Third CEC Plenum
was due in no small measure to Left Wing and/or Communist
strength in local Party headquarters. According to Ch'ü Ch'iu-pai,
Communists controlled many local low-level Party headquarters
because true Left KMT members were actually Communists. Com-

munist-controlled KMT Party headquarters of various levels,
Ch'ü states, established local "Party government." The Kuomintang
Left Wing was in control only of the Central Executive Commit-
tee.167

Document 50, a report written by Po Hai, secretary of the
Committee on the National Movement of the Chinese Communist
Peking Local Committee,168 dated February 10, 1927, reveals
how Communists built up the Left Wing against the Right and how
they infiltrated and controlled the Left Wing at Peking.

An unusual set of circumstances existed in Peking, headquarters of
the Ankuochün. There, Kuomintang members and Communists found
their area of activity increasingly narrowed under the repressive measures imposed by Chang Tso-lin's regime. In contrast to the period from
October, 1924, to April, 1926, when the Kuominchün garrisoned the city,
they were unable to stage mass demonstrations. They found it increasingly difficult even to pursue the task of secret propaganda and organization. These circumstances in effect isolated the Kuomintang and the
Chinese Communist Party from the masses and concentrated attention
on Intra-Party struggles in the KMT. Thus, to a greater extent than
elsewhere, the Peking Communists, in alliance with the Left, were im-
mersed in the struggle against the New Right Wing.

Despite the local character of Po Hai's Report, the information
it gives on Communist methods has wider areas of application and
contributes to an understanding of Communist success in low-
level Party organs of the Kuomintang.

According to a Communist document dated November 25, 1925,
two days after the opening of the Western Hills Conference, there
were few Left Wing members in Peking. Communists were warned
that it was extremely dangerous to fight the Right Wing singlehandedly. They were instructed to form a Left Wing of the masses
and a united front of the Left Wing and the Communists to struggle
against the Right [Doc. 21, pp. 148-49]. By the time of elections of
the Peking KMT Municipal Party headquarters in January, 1927,169
the balance of forces within the Kuomintang had completely changed.
The Left Wing and Communists won a solid victory over the New
Right Wing; Communist strength was particularly impressive.
Communists won four of the nine executive committee seats and
received 70 percent of the votes cast, although there were altogether only twelve hundred Communists out of a total of 4,300 members registered at the KMT's Peking Municipal Party headquarters
[Doc. 50, pp. 158, 177-78].

The Communist position was even stronger at the 17 district
Party headquarters subordinated to the Municipal Party Headquarters. In these Communists won 37 of a total of 51 executive committee seats. They occupied an even greater portion of the positions
at subdistrict Party headquarters. As Po Hai writes, the Peking

Communists had planned only to control but not monopolize low-level Party organs. For various reasons, however, they practically monopolized all low-level Party headquarters. [Doc. 50, pp. 175-76].

Many explanations can be found for the Communists' success in winning a controlling position for themselves at KMT Party headquarters. There is one, however, which appears to be particularly pertinent. It is the Communist method of encouraging the establishment of many Left Wing organizations, then infiltrating and bringing them under Communist control through Communist Party fractions. In September, 1926, a United Council of the Left was formed, composed of nine Left Wing organizations, six of which had come under Communist domination by February, 1927 [Doc. 50, pp. 162-63].

An example or two many serve to illustrate how a small Communist minority, effectively organized into a Communist Party fraction, was able to seize control of Left Wing organizations.

There were only 75 Communists out of a total of 264 members in the New Army Society. In numerical strength, therefore, they constituted less than 30 percent of the total membership. However, Communists won 3 of the 5 seats on the executive committee of the New Army Society and were able completely to control it. The secretary of the Communist fraction, T'an Tsu-yao,[170] was recognized as the Society's leader and was elected as the Society's representative to the Peking Municipal Party Headquarters [Doc. 50, pp. 165, 168, 175]. The Communist Party fraction was highly developed, with four departments—the organization, propaganda, workers' and peasants', and women's departments—and a secretariat.[171]

According to Document 50, the Soul of Hainan Society was completely controlled by six Communists, although they constituted less than 5 percent of the total membership. Communist infiltration of this organization was accomplished when the leader of the Society, Mo T'ung-jung, was induced to join the Communist Party. A Communist Party fraction was then established within the Society, headed by Mo.[172] Mo was elected to the Peking KMT Municipal Party Headquarters as the representative of the Soul of Hainan Society [Doc. 50, pp. 165, 172].

Both Mo T'ung-jung and T'an Tsu-yao were thus elected, not as Communists, but as representatives of Left Wing societies. Only two of the four Communists on the executive committee of the Peking Municipal Party Headquarters were elected as Communists. In this fashion, Communists were able to bypass the May, 1926, regulation prohibiting them from holding more than one third of executive committee posts at Kuomintang central and local Party headquarters.

Another effective way of bypassing the regulation was for some of the Peking members to keep secret the fact that they were Communists. According to Po Hai, Communists were sometimes elected to district Party headquarters without their Party affiliation being known [Doc. 50, p. 176].

The KMT Municipal Party Headquarters itself was controlled by an effective nine-man Communist Party fraction. The secretary of the fraction, Hsieh Pai-yü, held the important post of chief of the Organization Department. Other Communist members of the fraction headed the Labor and Peasant Departments and served on the Standing Committee.[173] The Communist fraction held weekly meetings and gave detailed instructions to Communists serving as department heads [Doc. 50, p. 178].

Communist control of Left Wing organizations also facilitated the expansion of Communist influence in the universities of Peking through the activities of branch organs of these societies. The New Army Society, for instance, established basic organizations in all the universities of Peking. These basic organizations met biweekly for discussions and reports. According to Po Hai, the spirit at the meetings was extremely good and positive work was being done by basic organizations which were led by Communists under the direction of Communist Party cells [Doc. 50, p. 168].

Since infiltration and control of Left Wing organizations was the basic technique with which Communists proceeded simultaneously to dominate KMT Party headquarters and absorb the Peking intelligentsia, it may be of interest to note some of the major characteristics of the KCT's policy toward Left Wing organizations.

First, Communists disapproved of a centralized Left organization and emphasized the need for establishing many types of Left organizations. It was hard for the petty bourgeoisie to form a strict organization, Po Hai states. Hence, in unifying Left masses, Communist policy was not one of mixture but alliance. The Peking masses were extremely complicated and it was necessary, therefore, to have all kinds of organizations under different names and with different characteristics in order to include all groups [Doc. 50, pp. 164-65].

Secondly, Communists emphasized the need to adopt the same public attitude toward all Left organizations. Po Hai writes, for instance, that Communists were actually closer to the Soul of Hainan Society than to its rival organization, the Ch'iung-yai Association. On the surface, however, Communists maintained exactly the same attitude toward both [Doc. 50, p. 172]. The KCT stressed politeness and tolerance in dealing with Left Wing groups, as well as a just and unbiased attitude towards all organizations.

Thirdly, Communists sought to strengthen certain Left organizations in order to counteract the influence of other organizations which they had failed to infiltrate. According to Po Hai, for instance,

Communists sought to build up the New Army Society, which they controlled, as the leading organization of the KMT Left in Peking. At the minimum, Po Hai writes, it should have a standing equal to that of the Practical Society, which Communists were unable to penetrate because the Society's leaders refused to admit them into the organization [Doc. 50, pp. 167, 169].

Fourthly, Communists stressed the necessity for contracting temporary alliances. Although they distrusted the Practical Society, Communists emphasized the need to continue cooperating with it. Some Communists, Po Hai writes, believed that the Society would form a "New New Right Wing," and therefore suggested discontinuing cooperation with it. This was a mistaken view, he states. Although the Practical Society would surely turn Rightist and reactionary, Communists must not for the time being break off relations with the Society. It might be said, Po Hai concludes, that alliance with the Society was one of the Chinese Communist Party's historical tasks [Doc. 50, pp. 167-68].

Fifthly, Communists tried to avoid monopolizing Left Wing organizations, and to correct it where such a situation had arisen. Po Hai was extremely critical of the Communist position in the New Army Society, which he regarded as "unhealthy." Communists often hampered the work of the Society, he writes, by doing work of the Communist Party. Past errors had caused the New Army Society to appear excessively "Red," and Communists should henceforth assume a "grey" attitude. The New Army Society should absorb enlightened elements to take charge and Communists must not monopolize the Society. In discussing another Communist-controlled organization, Po Hai expressed relief that the Communists in the organization were not excessively Red, although there, again, they had taken too many of the organization's posts [Doc. 50, pp. 169-70].

While Communists stressed flexibility in Left organizations, they themselves were tightly organized and disciplined. The effectiveness of Communist fractions stemmed principally from the solidarity of their membership. Members of Communist Party fractions were bound to act collectively at all times to execute the policy of the Party [Doc. 4, p. 78].

Communists in Peking, as elsewhere, were well aware of their numerical weakness. They made up for it, however, by individual diligence. According to Po Hai, each Communist was told a few months before the elections that he was responsible for leading five Left Wing members [Doc. 50, p. 163].

Communist success in seizing control of Kuomintang organs in Peking cannot be attributed entirely to skillful maneuvering, good organization, and individual diligence. The Communist program of domination was facilitated by the departure of most of the top KMT leaders from Peking. Following the Western Hills Conference of November, 1925, the Right Wing sponsors of the conference left Peking for Shanghai to convene their so-called "Second Kuomintang Congress." Another exodus of Kuomintang leaders, this time Left KMT leaders, took place following the March Eighteenth Incident of 1926.[174] Their departure in effect left the field to the Communists.

The Peking Communists had another asset in the sanctuary offered by the Soviet Embassy. As the "White Terror" was intensified, the Soviet Embassy compound served as the base of operations not only for Communist but for Kuomintang organs. There can be no question of the validity of the Peking Government's charge that Kuomintang members functioned within the walls of the Soviet Embassy.[175] This is proved by an urgent circular notice to district Party headquarters issued by the Peking KMT Municipal Party Headquarters on November 8, 1926, advising them of the arrangements made with the Soviet Embassy guards for admitting committee and staff members.[176] Moreover, six of the nine members of the Executive Committee of the KMT Municipal Party Headquarters were arrested in the premises of the Soviet Embassy on April 6, 1927.[177]

The raid on the Soviet Embassy greatly disrupted the work of both the Communist Party and the Kuomintang in Peking. The Peking Government, however, justified the action on the ground that all the revolutionaries harbored by the Soviet Embassy were engaged in disseminating Communist doctrines.[178] The death sentences of twenty prisoners and imprisonment of ten other prisoners were based on the charge that they were all Communists. The announcement of the executions signed by Chang Tso-lin declares that Li Ta-chao and the others were all members of the Red Party and guilty of disseminating Communist propaganda and of plotting the overthrow of the Government.[179]

An examination of the execution list reveals names of KMT members who not only were not Communists but were enemies of the Communists. The most prominent of these was Lu Yu-yü, whom the Communists had considered one of the most important and influential leaders of the New Right Wing in Peking. Po Hai refers to Lu as the person who had done the most to break the union between Communists and the Left Wing. Lu Yu-yü was in fact one of the major targets of Communist attack [Doc. 50, pp. 160-61].

The execution list includes Hsiao Chung-chen and Teng Wen-hui, leaders of the Practical Society, whom the Communists had distrusted. Communists had been extremely critical of some of the other less important KMT leaders who were executed as Communists on April, 28, 1927. Po Hai writes of Yao Yen,[180] for instance, as a person of vanity and lust for power, and accuses him of having dealings with the New Right Wing [Doc. 50, p. 173].

The government accused the Peking Communists of planning an immediate insurrection.[181] Ch'en Tu-hsiu reported to the Fifth KCT Congress that the Peking Communists had considered plans for a revolution during the period from December, 1925, to March, 1926.[182] It appears doubtful, however, that they had any such plans in the spring of 1927.

The strength of the Kuomintang and the Chinese Communist Party in Peking was greatly exaggerated in the contemporary press. According to a Toho News Agency dispatch dated April 7, 1927, the Peking authorities found a list of 40,000 Peking KMT and Communist members during the Embassy raid.[183] Actually, however, we now know that there were only a few more than a thousand Communists and a few more than four thousand KMT members (including Communists) in Peking just three months prior to the time of the raid.

Document 43 is a Russian report translated into Chinese under the title, "Report of a Soviet Russian Military Intelligence Group on Its Investigation of Conditions in Kwangtung's Eighth Army." In Su-lien yin-mou..., III, "Canton," pp. 87-90. It is signed by a Russian named "Pavlov" and is dated August 9, 1926 in Changsha. T'ang Sheng-chih, the subject of the report, is referred to interchangeably as "T'an Yen-k'ai." We have corrected this error in our translation. Other errors in names are corrected in brackets.

[PAVLOV'S REPORT ON THE EIGHTH ARMY]

[87] This is a brief report on military intelligence in the Eighth Army.

There is actually no Kuomintang work in the Eighth Army. Li Wan-tao [Liu Wen-tao], who was appointed to take charge of KMT work, has been engaged in affairs other than political work. (T'ang [88] Sheng-chih once said that Liu is very interested in activities outside his jurisdiction and neglects his own duties.) Buddhism is very popular in the Army, supported chiefly by T'ang and followed by the officers.

The various cliques in T'ang's civil organization are as follows:

1. Commissioner of Finance, Liu Liang-chen [Liu Yüeh-chih]; Commissioner of Education, Chou Hao-shan [Chou Ao-shan]; Commissioner of Civil Administration, Fei Kuo-cho [Feng T'ien-chu]; and the representative at Kwangtung, Lei Chen-huang [Lei Chu-huan]. All of these men are of good repute in the province for their sound character. They are all friendly with T'ang Sheng-chih.

2. Chief of the construction department, Tan Shou-sui [Teng Shou-ch'üan] (formerly director of the Mining Bureau at Sui-k'o-shan [Shuikowshan]); Director of the Intelligence Bureau, Liu Chia-hsin; and Director of railways, Liu Jung. While they do not stand for any definite political policy, they are connected with the compradors and are hostile to the first group and the Chinese Communist Party. They exert considerable influence over T'ang Sheng-chih.

3. Liu Wan-tao [Liu Wen-tao], a native of Hupeh, studied at the Pao-ting Military Academy and in Japan and France. He is a man of self-esteem and eloquence, and has the characteristics of a politician. His slogan is: "Down with Militarism and Imperialism!" He is not really closely connected with the Kuomintang and is extremely hostile to the Chinese Communist Party. He has no confidence in the work of the Political Department and does not trust its personnel, for he suspects there are many Communists in the Department.

The construction department chief, T'ang Shou-sui [Teng Shou-ch'üan], is a close friend of his; Liu therefore has connections with the second group. T'ang rather looks down on him and calls him "dirty stuff" (This is very hard to understand. It may be a tactic of T'ang's).

The various military cliques are as follows:

1. Chang Tzu-p'ing group: Chief of Staff, Li Ling-yung, and Commander of the Second Division, Ho Chia [Ho Chien].

2. Yi Yang-ts'ai's group: A student [graduate] of the Military [89] Academy and formerly Chief of Staff to Kuan Hao [Kung Hao].

3. The Kwangsi group: Commander of the First Division, Yeh Ch'i [Yeh Chi], and commander of the Third Division, Li P'in-hsien, etc.

4. The Hupeh group: Commander of the Hupeh First Division, Hsia Tou-yin.

The various military cliques are of no great importance. They are all obedient to T'ang Sheng-chih and they hold moderate opinions. T'ang Sheng-chih himself is lively, resolute, and radical in speech. He acts with great determination. Since he himself does not smoke, he forbids others to smoke. However, he must be hypocritical about this, because two fingers on his right hand are stained as dark as smoked sausages. It is reported that he used to smoke opium. He is a Buddhist and often brings a Buddhist statue to the front. There is always a statue of Buddha in his room and he often burns incense. He even plans to build a Buddhist temple.

T'ang believes that Buddhism points out the objectives of war, whereas Sunyatsenism is merely the means of obtaining such objectives.

Now let us talk about the Pao-ting Clique again. The Pao-ting Clique absorbs men who have not received any formal education, such as Li Tsung-jen.* Like other groups, it is not a strong organization. It was actually formed as a result of jealousy of Chiang Kai-shek. The Clique is divided into those who are leaders and those who are followers (as in the Kwangsi Clique). The leading elements are T'ang Sheng-chih and his armies, and Ch'en Ming-hsiu [Ch'en Ming-shu].

T'ang has already realized the plan to organize twenty-eight regiments. Should the National Government fail to appoint him to the highest position, T'ang would sever connections with it. Already, he has been talking about the idea of separation. It is difficult to foresee at the moment whether this would take place

---

* Apparently a mistake in translation from Russian to Chinese. Members of the Pao-ting Clique, such as Li Tsung-jen, were graduates of the Pao-ting Academy.

at Wuchang or Hankow,[when the cities fall to the National Revolutionary Army]. Such a possibility depends first on the reaction of parties who are opposed to T'ang and, secondly, on T'ang's strength and speed in organizing alliances. I believe that, barring unforeseen circumstances, a split will not occur at Wuhan, for the relative strength of all parties concerned does not favor such an eventuality.

[90]   Our present policy toward T'ang is not at all clear. We should not miss any opportunity to define our objectives.

DOCUMENT 44

The following is a report submitted to Borodin by Teruni, chief
Soviet adviser with the General Political Department of the National
Revolutionary Army. It is based on a Japanese translation of a copy
of the Russian document which was seized in the raid. The Japanese
translation is published under the title, "A Report to Borodin from
Teruni, a Red Russian Military Adviser, Following the Occupation
of Wuhan by the Revolutionary Army," in Pekin Ro-Taishikan ōshū
himitsu bunsho, Part XIII, pp. 1-24. Teruni's report, numbered
191 and enclosing a map, is dated October, 1926, from Wuchang.
It was apparently written on October 30, the day after the launching
of the Kiangsi offensive (see p. 7 of Document 44). The copy seized
in the Soviet Military Attaché's office was badly damaged by fire.
All illegible passages have been omitted in our translation. The
Japanese translators were unable to identify some of the Chinese
names and rendered them by sound in Japanese katakana. We identify
such names in brackets.

[TERUNI'S REPORT TO BORODIN ON THE
SITUATION AT WUHAN]

[1]   1. For various reasons, especially lack of time (the courier is
staying in Hankow only one day), I am unable to report to you in detail about the political situation in the North and the discord existing
between generals of the Northern Expeditionary Army. Have you re-
[2] ceived reports from the front? Up to this day, I have not received any
word from you. Lack of communication and coordination makes my
work 80 percent more complicated because I cannot comprehend
what is going on elsewhere. I am therefore unable to report much
to you. The following report discusses only my contacts with Chiang
Kai-shek, T'ang Sheng-chih, and others, and the situation at Wuhan.
   2. Considerable Chinese blood was shed over the Wuchang Problem [battle for Wuchang], so much, in fact, that it caused us Russian
comrades a good deal of concern. Finally, the issue was settled on
the 10th of October. It was actually possible to have seized Wuchang
earlier had we been willing to ignore circumstances peculiar to
China. The fundamental cause [of the delay] was the unwillingness
of General T'ang Sheng-chih to see Wuchang occupied by the Kwangtung Army. The Kwangtung Army (the Fourth Army) was actually
before the walls of the city, but T'ang regarded and still regards it
as Chiang Kai-shek's army.
[3]   Up to the 10th of October, T'ang was most anxious to drive off

the said army, specifically the Twelfth Division, and devised various measures to this end. However, the Tenth Division under Ch'en Ming-shu ordered it to remain.

On the 2d of October, the Twelfth Division had left for Chin-niu [Hupeh], to the east of Kan-ning [Sienning or Hsien-ning, Hupeh], and had moved farther toward Kiangsi. We informed Chiang Kai-shek of this and Chiang wired Teng Yen-ta, asking him for the condition of his agreement to dispatch the Twelfth Division [to Kiangsi]. Subsequently, I obtained definite information that a demand was made for the immediate return of the Twelfth Division to Wuchang. T'ang was not agreeable to this, however, as he wished to occupy Wuchang himself...[burned]. Under our pressure...[burned]. Ch'en K'o-chüeh [Ch'en K'o-yü], deputy commander of the Hupeh Army [Eighth Army], and the deputy commander of the Fourth Army [Ch'en Ming-shu] led the Twelfth Division to Wuchang without obtaining T'ang's consent.

Between 10 p.m. on October 9th and 4 a.m. [October 10th], the Twelfth Division, together with the Tenth Division and two of T'ang's regiments, entered the city of Wuchang. The Fourth Army took half of the large amount of booty: 7,000 rifles, 12 cannons, and a great number of machine guns.

[4]   It is generally acknowledged that Wuchang was captured by the Kwangtung [Fourth] Army of the National Revolutionary Army and therefore comes under the jurisdiction [of the National Government].

Although it is true that the military situation did demand the dispatch of the Fourth Army to Kiangsi, the action was taken also for political reasons.

T'ang removed the Twelfth Division following the occupation of Wuchang and replaced it with two regiments under Liu Tso-lung. T'ang also tried to appoint Liu as commander of the Wuchang garrison to replace Ch'en Ming-shu. Teng Yen-ta opposed this in accordance with my advice, and Ch'en Ming-shu is still garrison commander. T'ang's attempt to appoint Liu as garrison commander is most significant for us for, since then, Ch'en Ming-shu is no longer in full accord with and tends to be rather aloof to T'ang. Things have now come to such a point that when T'ang recently offered to appoint Ch'en as Chief of Staff in his own army [the Eighth Army], Ch'en rejected the offer.

On the 15th of October, due to the deterioration of the situation at the [Kiangsi] front, Chiang Kai-shek ordered the Fourth Army to [5] proceed to Kiangsi. However, if the entire Army were to be sent, it would have been equivalent to losing Wuchang, our only base in the Wuhan area. I therefore gave the following advice through Teng Yen-ta.

a) Only four and a half regiments, totaling 4,500 to 5,000 men, should be sent.

b) The Fourth Army's headquarters should remain in Wuchang.

c) Ch'en Ming-shu should remain in Wuchang.

My advice was accepted. Today, after most of the men of the Fourth Army have been sent, "we" are still holding a commanding position here in Wuchang, although T'ang Sheng-chih does not realize it.

It is my opinion that many people (such as Teng Yen-ta, Ch'en Ming-shu, Ch'en K'o-yü, and others), having observed his actions in connection with the occupation of Wuchang, have come to realize just what kind of person T'ang really is.

[6]   3. Around the middle of the month [October]...[burned] we were forced to prepare for a new general offensive [in Kiangsi].

In order to rest and reorganize, the units at the front were ordered to withdraw to a point 60 li from the range of enemy fire. They were replaced by units of the Fourth Army and one division under Ho Yao-tsu.

It was planned to begin the general offensive on the 28th of October. According to strategy, it was necessary to advance troops to the northern bank of the Yangtze River and make a clean sweep of the enemy at Wusüeh [in Hupeh] (on the northern bank of the Yangtze, 60 li west of Kiukiang [in Kiangsi]). This operation could be accomplished only by the troops of T'ang and Liu Tso-lung. However, neither T'ang nor Liu even considered performing this task or attempting to do so. Realizing that such action would help Chiang obtain victory in Kiangsi, they not only did not wish a victory for Chiang but even wanted him destroyed. T'ang spoke to me on several occasions as [7] follows: "Chiang Kai-shek is fatigued. It would be better for him to take a rest, since he will not be able to accomplish anything in Kiangsi. If I were to take command, I would attack not only Kiangsi but Nanking." Up to the 29th of October, T'ang did not want to fight Sun Ch'uan-fang, because it was not evident whether Sun or Chiang would be victorious. Should Chiang be defeated in Kiangsi, Sun Ch'uan-fang would make an ideal partner for T'ang.

It is clear now that Sun Ch'uan-fang will ultimately be defeated in Kiangsi and Fukien, if not in all of the provinces under his control. Therefore, T'ang has come to agree, but only after Sun's eventual defeat became obvious, to advance his own troops along the northern bank and to attempt to defeat the enemy, who recently advanced a considerable distance in the direction of the Wuhan area.

Yesterday, October 29th, I left Hankow with him [T'ang] and sent [8] Nikitin* to the combat area. At present, it is still difficult to say

---

* There were apparently at least two Russians by the name of Nikitin in China in 1925-1927. The name mentioned here is an assumed name of a person whose real name is rendered in Chinese as Kuo-lieh-fu (Guryev?). He served as an intelligence agent and Chief of the Information and Intelligence Bureau of the General Staff at Canton, early in 1926. In the fall of 1926 he served as an adviser to the Eleventh National Revolutionary Army. For the other Nikitin, see Doc. 36, p. 337.

how sincere T'ang is in finally deciding to advance his own units
along the northern bank. He has told me in a very spirited manner
that he will positively defeat Sun Ch'uan-fang. Nevertheless, he is
an opportunist. Seeing that Sun is gasping for breath, he wants a
share in winning the victory over him.

On the question of Anhwei...[burned]

The same job has been given Chan Hen Fan [Ch'ang Heng-fang]
in Anhwei as was given Fan Puin Jein [Fang Pen-jen] in Kiangsi...
[burned]

4. Until recently, Sun's representative has been staying at
T'ang's place, attempting a conciliation between T'ang and Sun.
T'ang Sheng-chih concludes a peace when his allies are in a bad
position.

[9]   Chiang Kai-shek stopped fighting (because of cowardice). In
order to negotiate peace with Sun Ch'uan-fang, Chiang was willing
to let him remain in Chekiang and Anhwei. When he discovered this,
T'ang reversed his attitude toward Sun. (Chiang's telegram in
reply to Sun Ch'uan-fang has already been sent to you.) T'ang is
planning now to defeat Sun severely and has ceased all negotiations
with him. This is most significant for us, since T'ang's offensive
against Sun will cut off the road of retreat into Anhwei for Sun's
army, now in Kiangsi.

I believe that T'ang's attitude of the past several months is as
follows. After T'ang met Chiang Kai-shek at Changsha, he found
that Chiang was a person of neither military nor political importance. On the other hand, when Chiang saw that his two divisions
(the First and Second) [under Wang Po-lin's command] were completely disorganized, he became confused, took wrong measures,
and became a mere shadow of his former self. In other words,
Chiang was only living in his memory of the past and on his vanity
[10] as a former dictator in Canton.

T'ang decided to take the following measures and devised all
means to defeat Chiang in order to assume the position of Commander-in-Chief himself. Had we not provided support for Chiang,
T'ang's plan would probably have been successful. Actually, Chiang's
actions had all been foreseen by us.

Following March 2nd [20th, 1926], Chiang had exclaimed, "What
stupid steps I have taken!" T'ang could not help but observe all
these happenings...[burned]. Some people believe that our support
of Chiang should be withdrawn...[burned].

[11]   I cannot agree with this opinion because T'ang fails to represent
himself as a revolutionary general. On the contrary, he has revealed himself as a general who is not in full accord with the Revolution. However, this does not by any means imply that we should
sever all relations with T'ang. Indeed I have given T'ang moral
support and have shown good will towards him. I say that only moral

support has been extended because we have not supplied an adviser for T'ang despite his requests. The wishes he has expressed and the requests he has made are numerous, as follows.

a) Borodin, or Galen, if Borodin is not available, but not any person of lower rank than they, should be his adviser.

b) The Soviet Union should communicate directly with him concerning the supply of arms (without going through the National Government).

c) The Soviet Union should provide him with financial aid (T'ang made this request in Hankow in September), etc.

The above requests have been conveyed to you several times.

[12]   T'ang realized that I was objectively opposing his expansion by withholding actual help because I was supporting Chiang Kai-shek. He finally stopped talking about an adviser and our relations became such that T'ang began to look around for a new friend.

T'ang began to open negotiations with the Japanese in Hankow (even the captain of a Japanese gunboat visited him, and T'ang returned the call). He also negotiated with Sun Ch'uan-fang. Sun sent derogatory letters to Chiang Kai-shek and to various other generals of the Canton Government, but not to T'ang. Instead he sent two delegates. Hence, we may assume why until recently T'ang had failed to agree to advance his troops along the northern bank of the Yangtze River to fight Sun. In short, T'ang is like a beautiful woman who shows off her beauty, that is, the force of arms, and

[13] gives herself to whoever gives her the most. Within the last few days, T'ang has begun to realize that Sun's defeat is inevitable and, though very cautiously, has begun to resume dealing with us...[burned]

T'ang told me he wanted to meet Ch'en Tu-hsiu and said also that he wished to draw up a list of members of the Provincial Government with us. I cannot trust his sincerity. (The list of members has already been conveyed to you by telegraph.)

When I saw T'ang three days ago, I recommended a military adviser for him. I told him, however, that for the time being, although the adviser is an outstanding military expert, he is not a political adviser. A senior political adviser has been requested of Moscow

[14] and he will arrive in the near future. T'ang agreed to this. After the Kiangsi battle is over, I am thinking of sending Orishevskii† to him. It would be suitable to send Sinani‡ as a political adviser,

---

† Orishevskii was appointed adviser to T'ang Sheng-chih late in 1926.
‡ Sinani was chief of a Soviet group assigned to the Second Kuominchün early in 1925 and Chief of the Soviet Intelligence Branch (in Peking?) late in the same year. After the defeat of the Second Kuominchün by Wu P'ei-fu in February, 1926, Sinani was sent to Canton. In November, 1926, after Borodin had left Canton for Wuhan, Sinani was Borodin's deputy in Canton.

but Sinani should be placed under Galen as Peking wishes. I have conferred with Galen about this and he has agreed. If you agree also, will you send him here immediately?

My relationship with the two generals is as follows: I have been working together with Chiang Kai-shek and simultaneously manipulating T'ang. I should like to inform you that Karakhan has expressed his approval of this relationship.

6. I have already reported to you in detail about the Pao-ting Clique. In the past several months I have noticed symptoms of discord among the various leaders (T'ang Sheng-chih, Ch'en Ming-shu, Pai Ch'ung-hsi, Chief of Staff of the Commander-in-Chief's headquarters and a Kiangsinese [Kwangsinese], and Hu Tsung-to, commander of the Seventh Division [commander of a division in the Seventh Army] and a Hupehnese).

[15]   a) Subsequent to our propaganda and maneuvers with Ch'en Ming-shu, the Wuchang Incident took place. This event helped to create friction between Ch'en and T'ang to some degree and has drawn Ch'en much closer to us. Ch'en Ming-shu has requested [additional] advisers and I have decided to send them after Kiangsi is settled. At this point it is quite obvious that Ch'en is not entirely an ally of T'ang's.

b) Pai Ch'ung-hsi is discontented. He feels that T'ang is holding full authority without granting even partial authority to other leaders of the Pao-ting Clique...[burned]. Pai Ch'ung-hsi is asking for a conference of the Pao-ting Clique in order to discuss the problem of organization of the National Revolutionary Army, in particular the organization of the General Staff of the National Revolutionary Army.

[16]   Prior to the fall of Wuchang, we had noticed that the above-mentioned leaders were in agreement and their actions were in the open. It is clear now, however, that unity among them is completely lacking. (The fact that China is so full of contradictions helps our work a great deal).

7. With the capture of Hankow, the National Revolutionary Army got another scoundrel. (This is Liu Tso-lung, commander of the Fifteenth Army). I think it would have been possible to capture Hankow without him and regret that his surrender occurred at such a propitious time. Now he is just someone who is in our way. One might say that Liu Tso-lung is the Li Fu-lin of Wuhan. However, Li is harmless whereas Liu is aggressive and tries to play an important part. In addition, he advocates the principle of "Hupeh for the Hupehnese." T'ang himself seems to sense this but still draws himself to Liu. He still retains Liu as the military governor of Hupeh.

[17]   Liu is said to be a very wealthy man, possessing ten million dollars and a vast amount of real estate. Wealthy merchants support

him; he in turn protects them. For instance, after Wuchang fell, he sent two regiments there and placed flags on the roofs of homes of wealthy merchants and the Chamber of Commerce building, with signs in big letters: "This building is under the protection of Liu Tso-lung. No man, whoever he may be, may enter." As garrison commander, Ch'en Ming-shu could not help interfering and demanded the withdrawal of Liu's units from Wuchang. Ch'en declared that he would resign from the position of garrison commander if his demand were not accepted. It was due to this firm attitude that T'ang finally gave in.

Liu Tso-lung is a general who should eventually be disarmed and even T'ang recognizes this. The time, however, is not yet right. The matter should be reconsidered at a later date.

[18]   8. A suggestion has been made to Yang Shen to issue a declaration of alliance with the National Revolutionary Army. He has been appointed commander of the Twentieth Army.

9. Ban Han Han [P'eng Han-chang], Wan Tin Pei [Wang T'ien-p'ei], and Ho Run [Ho Lung] are at Ichang and Shasi [in western Hupeh] fighting the enemy under the command of General Ru Ji Jan [Lu Chin-shan]. The battle is still not yet won.

10. Fan She Min [Fan Hsing-ming] is at Sinyang, southern Honan. His army numbers not over 5,500. The other day, Teng Yen-ta and T'ang Sheng-chih paid Fan a visit. Teng was favorably impressed by the situation. There is no reason to fear that a grave situation will develop in northern and western Hupeh, particularly if Sun Ch'uan-fang is defeated in Kiangsi.

[19]   11. It may be said that the Northern Expeditionary Army will have achieved its purpose if Sun Ch'uan-fang is defeated in Kiangsi. If the battle of Kiangsi is lost, it would mean the defeat of the National Revolutionary Army and the National Government. T'ang would make peace with Sun. Even Chiang Kai-shek has begun to realize this.

In deciding to let T'ang's army move to the northern bank of the Yangtze River, we were influenced by the plan to start military operations in southern Anhwei. As I have already explained, the objective is to sever the line of communications between Sun's army and the northern bank of the Yangtze.

It is clear that a crisis will occur as the battle moves towards Anhwei. By moving toward southern Anhwei, we hope to capture the entire province of Anhwei. We believe this to be possible if the situation is still favorable to us after Sun's army is defeated in Kiangsi.

Since it is necessary to occupy Fukien, decisive action should [20] be taken there after obtaining victory in Kiangsi. Thereafter, we should put an end to military operations, because casualties in the Army are great and the troops are terribly exhausted. It would be dangerous to advance farther north from the Yangtze River.

If the situation is unfavorable...[burned] the Chekiang problem must be settled peacefully (although the recent situation suggests this would not be easy). Chekiang should voluntarily ally itself with the National Government. A buffer zone should be created between Shanghai and the sphere of influence of the National Government. Such a buffer zone is absolutely necessary. It may be set up in Anhwei province. Your advice on this matter is requested.

12. Even after the arrival of the National Revolutionary Army in the Wuhan area, the residents seem to show no significant change [21] in their political views. The responsibility for this should be borne by us. The Army came to Wuhan without a central political organ. Although we had insisted while at Changsha that it was desirable to have such an organ, nothing has yet been established. The Kuomintang Provincial Committee lacks power and the ability to handle political affairs properly. T'ang Sheng-chih alone is in command of the situation, with only Chen Gu Po [Ch'en Kung-po] (a lazy fellow) and Teng Yen-ta to challenge him.

Teng Yen-ta is a genuinely good Leftist, but he is young and lacks authority. Furthermore, he is overawed by T'ang's power and often loses prudence. Aside from Ch'en Kung-po and Teng, there is virtually no one else. Although Teng at times loses prudence, he is the "leader" of the Left and possesses more influence than the others. (We, that is, Teng and I, cooperate closely and are very intimate. We live together; in fact, I live at his house.)

[22]   In view of the importance of this problem, it is difficult for me to understand the Canton Government's attitude. It is necessary that two or three Central [Executive] Committee members should come and set up the Committee here, since it is impossible to begin serious business or to establish the Party's power without it.

In my opinion, it is necessary to settle all important problems (finance, organization of a central military organ, organization of the Provincial Government, etc.) after the Kiangsi battle...[burned]. As for a conference or congress, I should be able to do something about it. I should also be able to subdue the various generals since I do have considerable power to exercise. After the National Revolutionary Army wins complete victory, it would be most significant politically and for propaganda purposes to hold a Kuomintang conference or congress.

[23]   This may be only a mistaken idea of mine (I don't think so, however) or an observation based exclusively on the situation at the front. It is very easy to make mistakes, especially in my situation. I have always tried to follow the dictates of reason in making decisions. However, since I have not received a single letter of instruction, I could have made mistakes. I discussed this matter with Karakhan in Shanghai.

13. For the past few days, T'ang Sheng-chih has been talking

frequently about the organization of the Hupeh Provincial Government. He ended up by holding a conference on this problem with
members of the Chinese Communist Party. This has been reported
to you in detail by telegraph. I shall await the arrival of the Central
[Executive] Committee members (Hsü Ch'ien and others). Through
certain Chinese persons, I will try to delay a solution to this problem as long as possible. I should like to have your instructions on
this.

14. The courier is getting impatient. Since I have already written
[24] a great deal, I shall close here. This letter is not in good order,
I realize, but circumstances prevent my rewriting it. Please for-
give me. Please let Abumori and Karachev read this letter and
give my regards to everybody and Fanny [Mrs. Borodin].

P.S. I am waiting for your instructions.

P.S.S. Please remember that I am in Wuchang and Galen in
Kiangsi and that it is only through me that Galen can send confidential letters. Leaving Galen, I arrived Wuchang on October 25th.

I am enclosing the most recent letter from Galen, written on
October 17th, before the current offensive.

The following is based on a Chinese translation of a copy of a Russian document published in <u>Su-lien yin-mou...</u>, III, "Party Affairs," pp. 18-32. The date, March 30, 1927, is given in the Chinese translation, apparently indicating either the date on which the document was received from Moscow or the day on which it was copied and checked by Kiselev in Peking. The Sixth Plenum of the Executive Committee of the Young Communist International was convened on November 12, 1926. We have translated the first two resolutions concerning the Chinese Communist Youth Corps adopted at the Plenum, omitting the following resolutions: No. 3, on the CY's economic and labor work; No. 4, on work among peasant youths; No. 5, on the question of work; No. 6, on the CY's political training work; No. 7, the CY's work and tasks in the student movement; No. 8, on the problem of organizing a Kuomintang youth organization and occupational organizations; No. 9, on the CY's tasks with reference to the Y.M.C.A. and the anti-Christian movement; No. 10, on the organization of athletic organizations; and No. 11, on the CY's tasks in the children's movement.

RESOLUTIONS ON THE CHINESE COMMUNIST YOUTH
CORPS ADOPTED AT THE [SIXTH] PLENUM
OF THE YOUNG COMMUNIST INTERNATIONAL

[18] The Plenum of the Executive Committee of the Young Communist International endorses the resolutions on the Chinese question adopted by the [Seventh Enlarged] Plenum of the Executive Committee of the Communist International.

Since the close of the last plenum, the Chinese Communist Youth Corps has established close connections with the majority of young workers. It has made greater efforts to help them and has reaped better results than formerly. The Plenum of the Executive Committee of the Communist Youth International takes note of this fact with great pleasure and satisfaction.

The CY's decision to transform itself into a real organization of the majority of young workers in order to improve its work and [19] to cope better with current problems is correct. The Plenum believes, however, that certain aspects of the CY's work has yet to be corrected (for instance, slow progress in establishing CY cells and failure to exert every effort to enlist peasants into the CY).

In view of these shortcomings, the CY should proceed in accordance with the following.

The Nature and Actual Condition of the Corps

a) For many reasons, Chinese labor youths cannot but participate in the struggle of the Chinese National Revolution (such as strikes, the anti-imperialist movement, enlistment in the National Revolutionary Army and peasant associations) in order to obtain liberation. By leading the masses and demonstrating methods of revolutionary struggle, the CY can daily increase the proletariat's influence. This in turn strengthens the influence of the Chinese Communist Party and the Chinese Communist Youth Corps and facilitates the expansion of the revolutionary movement of Chinese laborers throughout the country. The CY's work must proceed from this premise.

b) Due to various circumstances the Chinese Communist Youth Corps has been primarily an organization of intellectuals. This has already affected its work (such as economic struggle, contact with peasant youths). The CY should be truly an organization which unites urban and agrarian proletarian youths. All peasant or intellectual youths who are loyal to and enthusiastic about revolution should be enlisted into the Corps. Special care, however, should be taken to guarantee that the workers' cadres of the CY can realize proletarian leadership. The Plenum of the Executive Committee of the Young Communist International earnestly declares that it is necessary for the CY to exert every effort to carry on work among Chinese labor youths in order to strengthen its own organization. [20] At places occupied by the National Revolutionary Army, such as the industrial cities of Wuchang and Hankow, the Communist Youth Corps should pay particular attention to expanding the scope of its activities and carrying out all kinds of work in the interest of self-development. The Plenum believes it necessary to expend a great amount of energy and money in proceeding according to the above until the goal is achieved.

Political Tasks of the Communist Youth Corps

a) The Plenum of the Executive Committee of the Young Communist International concurs in the ECCI Plenum's estimate of the strength of the Canton Government and the Kuomintang army. The CY should strive to execute tasks [connected with the Government, and the KMT Army] which are advocated by the KCT. The Plenum considers the execution of various kinds of work in the National Revolutionary Army as an extremely important duty of the CY.

b) Since the Communist Youth Corps struggles together with the Communist Party to strengthen the position of the Kuomintang Left Wing with a view to developing the Left and pushing forward

the Revolution, it should give special attention to and establish relations with middle bourgeois revolutionary youths of different circles. On the other hand, the Communist Youth Corps should promote propaganda emphasizing the strength of the proletariat in
order to help enhance it. The Chinese national revolutionary movement must proceed without delay. The CY should take an active part
in directing the activities of the Youth Department of the KMT as a
weapon for training middle bourgeois revolutionary youths of all
circles. The Kuomintang Youth Department is one of the safeguards
of the Kuomintang Left Wing. The Communist Youth Corps should
support and find means to organize revolutionary elements of
the middle bourgeoisie and the intelligentsia in the Youth Departments. The CY must strive in every way to promote the interests
of workers and peasants.

[21]   c) Half of the CY organs in Canton were formerly secret organizations. Even work which should very properly be done was not
carried out openly in the name of the CY. This was indeed a deficiency in the past work of the Communist Youth Corps and it has
resulted in many mistakes. The idea was that open work might
arouse the fear of bourgeois youths who would thus hesitate to go
forward, and the actual result has been the failure of the laboring
class, the KCT, and the CY to develop and to assume leadership
of society. Even the program of giving revolutionary training to
the Chinese laboring class cannot be carried out. While recognizing
the general soundness of the CY's policies, therefore, the Plenum
cannot consider as suitable the secret manner in which CY organs
carried out their work in Canton. The Plenum believes that all
necessary work should be done openly and positively in the name of
the CY. All activities conducted in secret and under cover among
the laboring class in cities and villages under the jurisdiction of
the Canton Government should now take the form of open struggle.
However, the CY's secret setup and communications, liaison with
persons working in the Army and means of secret direction should
still be kept intact and strengthened. It is absolutely necessary to
plant several persons secretly in every organ. They are not to
participate in any public or open activities so that they may continue to perform their tasks should a change in the situation occur.
     [Pages 21-32 omitted.]

Document 46, minutes of a meeting of the Wuhan Joint Council on December 29, 1926, "Minutes No. 7," was originally a Chinese document. It was translated into Russian and checked by Kiselev. For publication it was retranslated into Chinese in Su-lien yin-mou..., III, "Canton," pp. 8-10. The Peking Commission deleted the first part of the minutes.

MINUTES OF A MEETING OF THE PROVISIONAL JOINT COUNCIL OF THE KUOMINTANG'S CENTRAL EXECUTIVE COMMITTEE AND THE NATIONAL GOVERNMENT COUNCIL

[8]   Report by T'ang Sheng-chih on military movements and conditions in Western Hupeh. —The troops stationed at Ichang and Shasi have complicated names. Their discipline is poor. By replacing tyranny with tyranny, they have caused dissatisfaction among the people. Several units originally belonging to the Provisional Special Army have become part of the regular Army. They do not have sufficient numbers of men, however, and are called divisions or brigades with merely a little over a thousand or a few hundred men. In view of such difficult conditions, a military conference was held, the details of which have already been reported. General Headquarters should immediately take measures to relieve the people's suffering so they will not be subject to the oppression and robbery typical of the militarist era.

If the troops completely lack discipline, it would be impossible to raise military funds.

[9]   The strength of an army is determined not by quantity but by quality. The Army must not replace tyranny with tyranny. The progress of revolutionary undertakings does not depend merely on military force but, even more important, it depends on the force of the people.

The Government should have the kind of power which commands the respect of the Army and the people.

Although the troops at Ichang and Shasi are supposed to number 50,000, this far exceeds the actual number. Excepting the First, Second, and Third Divisions, which have received regular training, the others merely bear various names and incur unnecessary costs. Moreover, these troops are of no use whatever except in soliciting contributions and resorting to robbery. Undisciplined troops cannot have combat ability. Failure to provide adequate revenues to maintain the Army will cause the people to lose faith in our revolutionary principles.

At an officer's meeting at Ichang, shouts of "Down with the Bogus Revolution!" were raised. On the other hand, [KMT] hsien and district Party headquarters have issued the slogan, "The Army is Cutting the People's Lives!" I have already reported the above to the Central [Executive] Committee for remedy.

It is difficult to fix the amount of necessary expenditures for the Army, since accounts are lacking for checking purposes.

There is only one enemy division left. After being disarmed and reorganized, it consists of only a few thousand men with no fighting capacity at all.

The Chairman stated: Since Commander-in-chief T'ang Sheng-chih reported last time on the bad discipline of the troops at Ichang and Shasi, and their oppressive acts against the people, a telegram in the name of the Joint Council has been sent asking the commander there to take remedial measures. Telegrams have also been sent to the headquarters of the Ninth and Tenth armies, ordering them to conduct a strict investigation and to take proper remedial measures.

The attention of all will please be directed to the slogans "Down with the Bogus Revolution!" and "The Army is Cutting the People's Lives!"

The question of the distribution of military funds in the future should also be discussed.

T'ang Sheng-chih: This question is a military one and, in my opinion, should be referred to the Office of the Chief of Staff for investigation and action.

Adviser Borodin: The special attention of the Commander-in-Chief should be drawn to the fact that financial unification is en-
[10] dangered by the Ninth and Tenth armies. We have been busy day and night, with considerable sacrifice of time, trying to protect the people's life and property. Should security be destroyed by the bad discipline of the Ichang troops, we will not only lose the confidence of the people but also face adverse effects in our financial policy.

The following resolution was adopted: [To] dispatch an urgent telegram to Commander-in-Chief Chiang Kai-shek drawing his attention to the tyrannical conduct of the Ninth and Tenth armies in western Hupeh and requesting him to take proper measures to maintain the discipline of the said troops.

Document 47, a political report made by the KCT's Central Committee on January 8, 1927, had apparently been translated from the
original Chinese into Russian. It was retranslated into Chinese
by the Peking Commision. The following is based on the Chinese re-
translation in <u>Su-lien yin-mou...</u>, X, "Military-Political Conspirary,"
pp. 41-43 (the set with Chinese pagination and binding). Large
portions of the document were deleted by the Peking Commission.

POLITICAL REPORT OF THE CENTRAL COMMITTEE
OF THE CHINESE COMMUNIST PARTY

[41] [Deleted] 1. Marshal Chang [Tso-lin] has been moving toward an
agreement within the last few days on Yang Yü-t'ing's plan...
[deleted]. The Mukden Army is still trying in every way to avoid
a direct clash with the Northern Expeditionary Forces.

a) The Mukden Army hopes to encourage other discontented anti-
Red armies to be destroyed...[deleted]. no matter which side in
this war emerges victorious, it will still remain a powerful force
in the country.

b) Hence, Marshal Chang [Tso-lin] is currently utilizing Chang
Tsung-ch'ang and Sun Ch'uan-fang to resist the Northern Expeditionary Forces in the Southeast and sacrificing their armies in key
positions. Chang is trying to make arrangements in Honan...[de-
leted] planning to hand Honan over to Chin Yün-e and to let Chin
Yün-p'eng form a cabinet. Chang wants to make use of the 200,000
crack troops commanded by the two Chin brothers and await
quietly an opportune time for action...[deleted]. However, Chang
fears that the Kuominchün in central Honan may align itself with
the revolutionary forces to attack the Mukden Army...[deleted].
The attitude of Yen Hsi-shan also engages Mukden's attention.

2. Under pressure from the Mukden forces, the Kuominchün has
evacuated Paotow [in Suiyuan] [December 25, 1926]. The plan of the
Mukden forces is still to capture Wuyüan [in Suiyuan] in order to
cut off the Kuominchün's source of ammunition supply.

...[deleted] the Kuominchün suffers shortages in cartridges and
military supplies. Moreover, as a result of the defeat at Nankow
[Hopeh] [August 14, 1926], it has lost almost all its artillery and
cavalry. Hence, the Kuominchün finds it difficult to fight Mukden's
well-equipped crack forces...[deleted].

3. Since the occupation of Western Honan by the Kuominchün
[December, 1926], the situation in Honan has become very tense...

[deleted]. Both Chang and Wu [P'ei-fu] have been unable to command the Honan Army to resist the Southern forces. Although re-
[42] peated orders for a major offensive have been issued, they have
been of no avail.

4. The attitude of Yen Hsi-shan toward this war plays an important role. Final victory in the war between Mukden and the
Party forces will go to the side which can unite with Yen Hsi-shan.
Yen has recently revealed close contact with the National Government. He has expressed a desire for Kuomintang membership and
to organize the northern Kuominchün against Mukden. The National
Government naturally wishes to cooperate in every way with Yen.
On the sole condition that Yen resists Mukden, all his demands can
be accepted.

The independence of Yen must also be respected so that he will
not be under Feng's [Yü-hsiang's] control. Even if Yen is not
prepared to be subordinated to the National Government for the present and wishes only to enter into an anti-Mukden military alliance,
the National Government would be willing to be allied with him for,
upon the defeat of Mukden, Yen will not be able to get out of the
jurisdiction of the National Government...[deleted].

5. Under the severe military pressure of Sun Ch'uan-fang, the
autonomous movement in Shanghai has temporarily ceased...[de-
leted].

Our views on the Shanghai problem are:

a) Recognize Shanghai as the place where serious conflict with
imperialism will be encountered. This problem will not be easily
solved.

b) Mukden and Shantung will have conflict over this problem also.

c) The Peking-Hankow Railway has now become the center of military movement and we should concentrate all our forces on this line.

d) We should support the autonomous movement in Shanghai in
order to create a buffer zone in the clash between the Northern Expeditionary Forces and the Mukden-Shantung forces.

6. With reference to the National Government:

a) In the provinces of Hunan, Hupeh, and Kiangsi now occupied by
the Northern Expeditionary Forces, the mass movement has entered
the revolutionary path and revolutionary work has penetrated deeply
into the villages...[deleted]. Assassinations of local bullies and the
bad gentry continue to occur without end. The current social movement of the people is much more far-reaching than during the Revolution of 1911 or the May Fourth Movement [deleted]. A violent
reaction would ensue should there be a military setback.

b) In the military situation...[deleted].
   (1) Considerable rest is necessary;
   (2) There is lack of military funds...[deleted] the Seventh and
      Third armies mutinied in Kiangsi...[deleted].

c) Upon the transfer of the National Government and the Kuomintang to Hankow, a provisional committee [Joint Council] was immediately organized to support the Government. We cannot but approve of this. Even Chiang Kai-shek does not express any opposition to it. However, local Hupeh Kuomintang members insist on self-government by the people of Hupeh...[deleted].

d) Conflict of opinion among the leaders constitutes a very serious internal problem of the National Government...[deleted]. The conflict between Wang [Ching-wei] and Chiang [Kai-shek]...[deleted] we consider the problem of reconciliation between Wang and Chiang and among other leaders as the most important of all problems...[deleted].

e) The two most important countries, Britain and Japan...[deleted] have come to the point of discussing recognition. One [Britain] favors a division of government between the North and South; the other [Japan] continues to render active support to Mukden to resist the South...[deleted].

f) On the basis of the above analysis, the most important tasks are as follows:

(1) Continue the anti-Mukden military action...[deleted]. Since the fortunes of Wu P'ei-fu and Sun Ch'uan-fang have been receding, a direct clash with Mukden-Shantung will be inavoidable.

[43]

    a) Expedite military preparations. Particular attention should be given the Peking-Hankow Railway.

    b) ...[deleted]. Quickly crush the main forces of ...[deleted].

    c) A defensive position should be taken in eastern Hupeh and Kiukiang [Kiangsi] to guard against a sneak attack from Shantung.

    d) Under the KMT's influence, the people of Shanghai have been engaged in the autonomous movement. They oppose the stationing of troops in the city. The defense of Kiangsu has been turned over to the forces of Li Pao-chang and Feng Shao-min.

    e) The National Government and the National Revolutionary Army should endeavor to make contact with Yen Hsi-shan and established an anti-Mukden alliance with him.

    f) The National Revolutionary Army should contact the [Kuominchün] armies in Central Honan and connect them with the Party's army to occupy the southern bank of the Yellow River...[deleted] to obstruct the southern route of the Mukden Army. In the East, the National Revolutionary Army should withdraw to the South and threaten the Mukden-Shantung Army.

(2) ...[deleted] continue efforts at reconciliation between the leaders of the National Government and continue to support the slogan, "Wang-Chiang Cooperation"...[deleted]

(3) Disseminate intensive propaganda among the masses, awakening them to support and aid the National Government in solving the many difficult financial problems. Arouse an enthusiastic spirit in the army. ...[deleted] issue the slogan, "Down with corrupt and greedy officials!" The slogan "Reduce the people's burdens!" is not appropriate at the moment, particularly when military action is still in progress.

DOCUMENT 48

The political report of the Central Committee of the Chinese Communist Party dated January 26, 1927, was presumably translated from Chinese into Russian. It was retranslated into Chinese in Su-lien yin-mou..., II, "Political," pp. 28-33. Short extracts of this document are given by Mitarevsky in World-wide Soviet Plots, pp. 148-49.

POLITICAL REPORT OF THE CENTRAL COMMITTEE
[OF THE CHINESE COMMUNIST PARTY]

[28] Since the Hankow Incident [January 3, 1927], the British imperialists have been exerting every effort to bring about opposition to the Chinese Revolution internationally and within their own country. However, they have had little success so far.

1. The conflict arising from the 2.5 percent surtax has led Great Britain to consider her tactics as very clever, particularly since the surtax was already in effect in the South. She was pleased to think that she would thus appease the Chinese while at the same time the surtax would in fact result in greater revenues for the Northern militarists. Furthermore, Japan suffers the most from increased tariffs while British losses are comparatively small. In short, the
[29] surtax would render considerable aid to the Northern militarists (about 80 percent of the increased tax revenue goes to the North; only approximately 20 percent to the South), and win the good will of the Chinese people. Actually, however, this problem can only intensify the conflict between Japan and Britain.

2. Italy and France, their interests not yet affected, are maintaining for the moment a watchful attitude and have not actively aided the British.

3. [Senator William E.] Borah of the United States still maintains his policy of respecting the Chinese national movement for equality and the demands of this movement.

4. The British Manchester clique [?] still believes in giving concessions to the Chinese. The Liberals also maintain a very calm attitude. Only the attitude of the Labour Party leader [Ramsay MacDonald] is relatively bad.

British imperialism has not been able to achieve the unity it desires at home or abroad. Its recent policy in China is to induce the moderate elements of the Kuomintang to lean towards it on the one hand and, on the other, to stage demonstrations with gunboats.

As for the militarists, they also use force for demonstrations

against the South and simultaneously seek to absorb the moderate
elements of the Kuomintang. They spread the idea that Sunyatsenism
is acceptable on condition that relations with Red Russia be broken
and the radicals driven out. Furthermore, they raise such slogans
as the return of the settlements, abolition of unequal treaties, and
convening of a national assembly, in order to appease the masses.
Their tactics are identical with those of the imperialists. The imperialists and the militarists are watching the effectiveness of their
tactics carried out from both directions.

When the National Government and the Kuomintang are united,
such tactics would definitely not yield results. It is regrettable,
however, that present internal conditions are not good.

The Right Wing of the Kuomintang is daily becoming more powerful. Although it has failed organizationally since the Western Hills
[30] and Shanghai Conferences, it has been successful in terms of
ideology and policy. There is currently an extremely strong tendency within the KMT to oppose Soviet Russia, the Communist Party,
and the labor and peasant movements.

The tendency toward the Right is due first to the belief of Chiang
Kai-shek and Chang Ching-chiang that only one party should exist
in the country, that all classes should cooperate, that class struggle
should be prohibited, and that there is no need of a Communist
party. Many of the bourgeois class have been influenced by this
belief, since they do not realize their own sufferings.

The second reason is their idea that the National Revolution will
soon succeed, that there will soon be a movement for class revolution, and that the greatest enemy at present is not imperialism or
militarism but the Communist Party. Hence, the tendency to oppose
Russia, the KCT, and the peasant and labor movements.

The third reason is jealousy and fear on the part of a third group,
which sees that the development of the Northern Expedition and of
the labor and peasant movements is controlled and directed by the
KCT.

For these reasons, a great anti-Communist tide has developed
within the Kuomintang. Personal conflict is negligible. These
three factors stem from a common source, the class problem, for
the interests of the bourgeoisie are naturally diametrically opposed
to ours.

Whenever enmity between the petty bourgeoisie and the proletariat
is not serious enough to warrant direct conflict, we should offer
further concessions [to the petty bourgeoisie]. This we have so far
neglected to do. Hence, at present, even the Left Wing of the Kuomintang does not show good feeling toward us. From the standpoint of
the development of the National Revolution, however, such conflicts
will continue to expand and it is impossible to avoid them. Nevertheless, there are still relatively few bourgeois and petty bourgeois

elements involved in actual conflict [with us]. Conflict is due partly
to the inexperienced action of the bourgeoisie and the petty bourgeoisie and partly to our own mistakes in not giving proper attention to numerous problems and in failing to give concessions to the
petty bourgeoisie.

[31] The most important problem which requires our urgent consideration at the moment is the alliance of foreign imperialism and the
KMT Right Wing with the so-called moderate elements of the KMT,
resulting in internal and external opposition to Soviet Russia, communism, and the labor and peasant movements.

This would be an extremely dangerous thing and is, furthermore,
entirely within the realm of possibility. Under such circumstances,
our Party has decided on the following policies:

1. Urge the masses to render financial and military support to
the National Government. Our aims are: To convince the KMT that
the National Revolution is still in the period of very difficult
struggle and therefore needs mass support, and that ultimate victory is yet to come. We must allay the KMT's fear of the KCT
(fear based on the belief that the KCT is close to the masses and
opposed to the National Government, and that very soon there will
be a communist revolution);

2. Publications of the CC and local committees should concentrate on the following propaganda points:

a) Explain clearly that the National Revolution is still very far
from complete victory. Explain further that the aim of the National
Revolution is not [merely] the transference of political power to
the Kuomintang but thorough reform, and that in the cities and
villages, the influence of imperialism and feudalism still exists.

b) Criticize scornfully the development of bourgeois ideology in
the KMT in order funadmentally to rebuke the bourgeois ideology
of Tai Chi-t'ao and Kai Nan-kuang [Kan Nai-kuang].* Our present
policy toward the bourgeoisie is as follows: In the cities, we
regard [corrupt] officials and compradors as counterrevolutionary
forces; in the villages, we regard landlords, the bad gentry, and
village bullies as counterrevolutionary forces. Labor, the peasantry,
and the revolutionary urban petty bourgeoisie are revolutionary
[32] forces. The bourgeoisie are timid and unstable, wavering between
revolution and counterrevolution. Under no circumstances should
they be considered as belonging to the revolutionary forces. The
bourgeoisie are not independent but subject to powerful class limitations. From the standpoint of their political consciousness and

---

* A mistranslation by the Peking Commission? Kan Nai-kuang was
regarded by the Chinese Communist Party's Central Committee as
a principal leader of the KMT Left Wing which stood opposed to
Tai Chi-t'ao's views. See Part VII, pp. 371-72.

outlook, they do not yet have strong revolutionary determination. For instance, Shanghai is the largest center of the Chinese bourgeoisie but, under militarist pressure, Shanghai newspapers do not publish political articles [?]. Shareholders there are hoping for the dissolution of the Chamber of Commerce so that they may dispose of their property and raise the value of their shares [?].

We should warn the KMT as follows: Although it is not necessary to oppose the bourgeoisie, placing undue trust in their inexperienced views and relying on their help to push forward the Revolution actually places the KMT, wittingly or unwittingly, in the ranks of the bourgeoisie against the real revolutionaries, the masses of workers and peasants. We should create such critical and scornful comments in order to prevent KMT members with Right tendencies from falling for inducements.

c) In our foreign policy, we should concentrate on the anti-British movement. We cannot say that the British policy of international alliance will never succeed. Hence, we should delay extending the anti-imperialist movement to Japan, France, the United States, and other countries, in order to isolate Britain.

These policies are of great importance. If properly executed, they will lead to complete success. They will prevent united attack on us by the foreign powers and eliminate the Kuomintang's fear of the KCT. Our Party organs should thoroughly understand and execute these policies. Only thus can we expect to remedy the critical situation presently developing. The present anti-Red movement can be united within and without the country and become many times

[33] more serious than the incident [the coup d'état] of March Twentieth. While the March Twentieth Incident was an isolated action by Chiang Kai-shek and the Sunyatsenist Society, the present anti-Communist movement involves the Center, the Right Wing, and even a portion of the Left Wing of the Kuomintang.

Document 49 is a Russian report translated into Chinese and published by the Peking Commission under the title, "The Situation of the Split between Chiang and T'ang," in Su-lien yin-mou..., III, "Canton," pp. 65-67. Dated March 5, 1927, the report was apparently written at Hankow. It is unsigned and marked "most secret."

[SOVIET REPORT ON THE SPLIT BETWEEN
CHIANG KAI-SHEK AND T'ANG SHENG-CHIH]

[65] The question of the removal of the National Government has virtually been settled.

Chiang Kai-shek has betrayed his dictatorial conspiracy in opposition to the Kuomintang Left Wing. His attitude was particularly clarified in connection with the appointment [recall] of Wang Ching-wei to the National Government. Chiang at first expressed a great desire for Wang's return but, as soon as Wang had left Paris on his way back to China, Chiang cabled him and hinted that there was no need for him to return. Chiang's cable was delivered to Wang in Berlin; thereupon Wang returned to Paris.

Chiang's conduct eventually became known. Consequently, many wavering elements and a portion of the Kuomintang Right Wing in the National Government have become alienated from him.

In addition to a split among Government and Party members, Chiang has also lost the greater part of his influence in the Army.

The officers of Fukien and Chekiang have declined to render him support and have allied themselves with such other armies as the Second, Third, Fourth, Seventh, Ninth, and Tenth armies.

Following his appointment as Commander-in-Chief [chairman of the provincial government] in Kiangsi, Chu P'ei-te, commander of the Third Army, can no longer support Chiang. The reason is that should the National Government be moved to Nanchang (Chiang's policy), Chu's power in Kiangsi would be entirely lost.

The Fourth and Eleventh armies have been persuaded by T'ang Sheng-chih to turn against Chiang. The commander of the Eleventh Army [Ch'en Ming-shu] formerly commanded the Tenth Division of the Fourth Army, prior to the reorganization of the Tenth Division as the nucleus of the Eleventh Army. Chiang had wanted the Fourth Army to be subordinated instead to Li Tsung-jen, commander of the Seventh Army, as a means to weaken T'ang's [T'ang Sheng-chih's] military power. Due to the opposition of T'ang and the

commander of the Fourth Army [Li Chih-shen], Chiang's plan failed
[66] to materialize. As a consequence, Li Tsung-jen took a wavering
attitude at Kiukiang [in Kiangsi], and planned to ally with a certain
party at the right opportunity. When he came to Hankow, T'ang
Sheng-chih and others succeeded in persuading him to join the
anti-Chiang front and to assume an openly hostile attitude towards
Chiang.

Subsequently, the Ninth and Tenth armies also joined the alliance
against Chiang.

T'ang Sheng-chih won a victory over the Kweichow troops and
cleared out Hunan. He has greatly expanded his military strength.

In short, the best elements of the National Revolutionary Army
are no longer with Chiang Kai-shek. It would be premature to state,
however, that Chiang has been completely defeated and can no longer
figure in the internal struggle.

The people are rather indifferent toward the Revolution and
appear less afraid of the National Government than they did one
month ago. The bourgeois class is uniting and is raising numerous
demands, conditions, and regulations, a part of which have been
approved by the National Government. The revolutionary movement
is now in the stage of economic demands. The All-China Federation
of Labor is taking a cautious attitude and is refraining from making
political demands, in the belief that they are inappropriate at this
time.

The above facts prove that the internal struggle to destroy
Chiang Kai-shek has not been entirely successful, although the
Government has moved to Wuchang.

To supplement previous military plans, the Seventh Army was to
be concentrated in the area around Lotien (northeast Hupeh) on
February 18th, to press the enemy in northern [southern] Anhwei
and, when necessary, give aid to the Hunan Army. The First Division of the Eight Army under Hsia Tou-yin's command should be
dispatched to the area around Nanyang [Hopeh] to aid Fan Hsing-
ming (Fan Chung-hsiu) and to clear up the remnant forces of Wu
P'ei-fu in northwestern Hupeh.

Chiang Kai-shek has changed his plan to attack Shanghai. He has
ordered that Shanghai is not to be attacked following the capture
of Hangchow [in Chekiang] and that the entire forces under Pai
Ch'ung-hsi (the Twenty-sixth Army, the Twenty-first Army, the
Second Army, and the remnant forces of the Twenty-second Division) are to attack Nanking. The attack on Shanghai is to follow the
capture of Nanking.

At the moment, the old forces of Sun Ch'uan-fang, such as the Fifth
and Seventh divisions of Yeh K'ai-hsin and the Sixth Division of
Ch'en Tiao-yuan, are turning south in the direction of Nanking, with
[67] the objective of occupying Nanking before the arrival of Pai's troops.

The following translation of a report on Communist-Kuomintang collaboration in Peking, dated February 10, 1927, is based on the original Chinese document. The author of the report, Po Hai, was Secretary of the Committee on the National Movement of the Chinese Communist Party's Peking Local Committee. The report refers to the KMT as "the People's School," the KCT as "Our School." KMT members are referred to as "Schoolmates of the People's School"; Communists as "Our schoolmates." The original document was published by the Peking Commission in <u>Su-lien yin-mou...</u>, III, "KCT," pp. 157-82.

REPORT ON THE WORK OF THE PEKING LOCAL COMMITTEE IN THE NATIONAL MOVEMENT

157] This is a general report on the Peking Local Committee's work in the national movement for the past few months, not a report on any particular month. Analysis of our current work requires occasional references to facts which are relatively historical in character. Thus, the content of this report becomes more complicated.

<u>Analysis of the Circumstances of Work</u>
    Since the Kuominchün's retreat to Nankow last year [April 15, 1926], the city of Peking has been entirely surrounded by an atmosphere of White terror. Not only has it been impossible to stage open mass demonstrations, but severe setbacks have occurred in the secret work of propaganda and organization. For the past few months, the Peking Local Committee's political work and [work in] the national movement have in fact tended to be one-sided. Kuomintang work has constituted practically the entire work of Our School in the national movement.
    Peking is the asylum of the reactionary political regime. Not only are the reactionary militarists actively destroying the revolutionary forces, but the anti-Red movement of the Kuo-chia chu-i
58] Clique is expanding in the wake of the militarists' anti-Red actions. The people of Peking, sunk in "deep water and hot fire," face imminent personal peril. Only the counterrevolutionary Kuo-chia chu-i Clique could have held the so-called "Support the National Flag" mass meeting at Central Park under the armed protection of the Mukden militarists. Red propaganda is daily suppressed while anti-Red propaganda becomes increasingly violent. This is

due to the anti-Red political environment which is reflected in differentiation of the mass movement.

In the course of the thorough-going anti-Red movement in Peking,
however, a so-called "Red United Front" has materialized. The
major portion of anti-Red propaganda has been transformed into
Red education; Ankuochün Headquarters has virtually become the
ministry of Red education! The masses of Peking with their feudal-
istic ideas are gradually leaning toward the Reds and they hate the
anti-Reds. The intellectuals are divided into two camps, the so-
called Reds and the anti-Reds. The president of Peking Law College openly said to the masses of students: "If we don't go Red,
then should we go White? We do not oppose any political party,
but we welcome the party which represents the interests of the
people." The economics professor of Min-kuo University burned
his books before his students, saying "The economic principles I
studied in the past are unsuited to modern needs, capitalist, and
deceptive. Only Marxist economic principles are true. What a pity
to have wasted more than ten years' efforts."

There are many such objective facts, indicating that the Peking
intelligentsia is leaning to the Left. The organization of Our School
has expanded amidst the dense anti-Red atmosphere from 300 to
more than 1,000. The Kuomintang Municipal Party Headquarters
has expanded from 2,200 to 4,300 persons. However reactionary
the political situation, the revolutionary political parties have made
great progress. The Red United Front has turned from expansion to
gradual stabilization. Such is our concise analysis and summary of
the working environment in Peking.

Working Plans in the National Movement

[159]   1. The movement against the New Right Wing.—The Peking New
Right Wing was born following the May Thirtieth Movement, the
period of the most violent class struggle in China. The doctrine
of the New Right Wing is based on the so-called "Taichitaoism."
Its leaders are those who one year ago were regarded as Peking Kuomintang Leftists. They include Lu Yu-yü, Kuo Ch'un-t'ao, Teng
Fei-huang, Ch'en Tzu-i, Wang Tung-cheng, Wang Chen-chün, and
Liu Chü-ch'üan. When the Old Right Wing held the upper hand, they
had appeared very Leftist and wanted earnestly to cooperate with
Our School against the Right. The policy of Our School then was,
quite naturally, to assist the Left to oppose the Right. Following
the alliance between our schoolmates and the Left, the Right daily
declined until it died. In the last elections of the Municipal Party
Headquarters, the Left scored a complete victory with our assistance. The Old Right then severed connections with Party headquarters. Led by Lin Shen and Chou Lu, it organized the so-called
"Number One, Southern Gardens" Party Headquarters and convened

the famous Western Hills Conference to struggle against the Left Wing.

Drastic differentiation of Chinese society has taken place since the May Thirtieth Movement. Tai Chi-t'ao's theories represent bourgeois interests. Born in Shanghai, they brought about the emergence of the Peking New Right Wing. Members of the New Right Wing are those who before May Thirtieth were the most hard-working Leftists, violently opposed to the Right. The activities of the New Right are not in any way different from those of the Old Right. Though subjectively they still claim to be Leftists, the New Rightists follow the track of the Old Right in their actions. The Old Right opposes Russia, communism, workers and peasants; the New Right also openly rejects the Three Policies of the Russian alliance, the Communist alliance, and [support] of labor and the peasantry bequeathed to us by the late Dr. Sun. It abandons revolutionary work among the masses and at Party Headquarters. Instead, it concentrates on opposing Communists. Its anti-communist propaganda slogans are:

a) The Communist Party monopolizes the Kuomintang.

60]   b) Class struggle is counterrevolutionary—it aids the enemy.

c) CP opposes the Northern Expedition—it is afraid of expanding the Kuomintang's political power.

d) CP alienates relations between Wang [Ching-wei] and Chiang [Kai-shek].

e) CP plots to assassinate Chiang Kai-shek.

The New Right Wing's active anti-Communist propaganda work has of course deceived a certain number of unconscious petty bourgeois elements. The New Right established in Peking the so-called "Great League of Sunyatsenism" based on Taichitaoism. The Great League of Sunyatsenism is the mass organization of the New Right which at its peak had a membership of more than five hundred. However, when the banner of the movement against the New Right Wing was hoisted, the League's Leftist mask was torn off by the masses and its members dispersed like birds and beasts. Our schoolmates led the rising Left elements in striving to expose among the masses the crimes of the New Right. A few months' work suceeded in completely wiping out the masses' confidence in the New Right Wing. Leaders of the League such as Ch'en Tzu-i and others, afraid for their own guilt, dared not face the masses and fled overnight. For a time the Great League was in a state of complete anarchy. Now it is "preparing schemes in the tent." The only New Right leader still around is Wang Chen-chün. Wang is unable, however, to lead the entire New Right Wing which is divided in Peking into three main cliques:

a) The Shantung Clique—leader, Lu Yu-yü.

b) The Hunan Clique—Kuo Ch'un-t'ao, Teng Fei-huang.

c) The Shansi Clique—leader, Wang Chen-chün.

[161]   Of these three, the Shantung Clique under the leadership of Lu
Yu-yü is relatively capable of leading the entire group. Mo T'ung-
jung has joined Our School. He used to be one of the leaders of the
New Right and is able to lead over one hundred Cantonese. Mo now
stands to the Left of the People's School. The masses led by him
are also inclined to the Left, rebelling against the New Right Wing.

For the past few months the New Right Wing has been confronted
with internal and external troubles and is coming to the end of the
road. Its position among the masses is falling rapidly. Our School's
policies and strategies against the New Right Wing constitute the
principle force in exterminating the New Right Wing. We have been
able to utilize the atmosphere of the movement against the New
Right Wing to create the Left United Front. We feel that our former
method of dealing with the Right Wing, under which our comrades
fought hard and singlehandedly against them, is inappropriate. The
current formula of struggle calls for Communists to stand on the
side of the Left masses of the People's School and to unite with the
Left to attack the New Right. Although the struggle is in fact led
by us, the New Right would not dare charge that all who oppose it
are Communists. Lu Yu-yü has done the most in disrupting the
alliance between Our School and the Left. Yet he can merely say to
Hsiao Chung-chen and other Left leaders: "After all, we are
brothers of the same Party; in the last analysis they (meaning CP)
are only outsiders. It is true that our Party needs a left wing, but
it should be an independent left wing of our Party, not a Communist-
directed left wing."

The foregoing is a brief account of our work against the New
Right. Although the Peking New Right Wing may not have entirely
collapsed, its foundation among the masses has been uprooted. It
will be difficult for it to stage a comeback.

2. The Left unification movement.—The Left unification movement
was born in the course of the work against the New Right. It may
also be said that the New Right's life was brought to an end because
of the newly rising Left. Our School's policy is twofold: Unify the
Left and oppose the New Right, simultaneously and without conflict.

[162] In the execution of the anti-Right policy, the Left unified its masses
and published numerous propaganda materials to expose the treacherous intrigues of the New Right. It also defined more firmly its
revolutionary theories and policies. Recently, the atmosphere of
unification of the Peking KMT Left has become very tense and the
Left masses have gradually expanded. To centralize Left forces,
Our School has joined with the Left Wing to establish Peking's
"United Council of the Left," hereafter abbreviated as "United
Left."

The United Left is the highest form of organization of the Left
wing in Peking. Comrade Po Hai is Our School's representative

to the organization. Other Left participating organizations of the
United Left are:

1. Practical Society
2. New Army Society
3. Szechuan Revolutionary Youth Society
4. New Yunnan Society
5. Ch'iung-yai Association
6. Soul of Hainan Society
7. Chung-shan Study Society
8. Reform Society
9. New China Study Society

The United Left has had a history of five months, during which
its work was divided into two stages: the movement against the
Right Wing and seizure of Party power.

During the first period, the United Left completely executed Our
School's policies in fighting the New Right. The Left's foundation
among the masses was gradually expanded and strengthened. The
United Left is the center of Left Wing mass organizations and
directs their activities and work. Basic Left principles include Dr.
Sun's Three Great Policies of alliance with Soviet Russia, alliance
with the Communists, and support of the workers and peasants;
opposition to the Sunyatsenism of the Reform Clique led by Tai
Chi-t'ao; and recognition of Wang Ching-wei as the central leader
of the Left. Propaganda on Leftist principles has had considerable
effect among the masses of the Peking People's School. Since the
publication of the outline of Left principles the differentiation of the
masses into the Right and the Left has become more distinct. To
ascertain whether any particular member of the People's School belongs to the Right or Left, it is only necessary to observe whether his
actions and thoughts violate Dr. Sun's Three Great Policies. Our
[163] Central Committee recently adopted the Three Policies as the
criterion of the Left. Actually, we long ago utilized such theoretical
guidance in working in the Peking People's School (the first period
of the United Left). The work against the New Right Wing, centralization of theories, and the unification movement of the Left constitute
almost entirely the program of the United Left.

We will now discuss the work of the United Left during the second
period (the period of seizing Party power). During the movement
against the New Right Wing, we created among the masses a tense
atmosphere for "handing Party power to the Left." At the same
time the New Right was deeply hated and loathed by the masses.
Hence, it was natural that the New Right Wing was defeated in the
recent elections of the Municipal Party Headquarters. However,
prior to the elections the extent of the New Right Wing's mass
following had not been definitely known. The Leftists therefore had
to redouble their efforts to secure the masses.

This period witnessed the gradual expansion of the organization of Our School and the development of Left organizations. More than twelve hundred of Our School's basic masses were in the People's School. A few months before the elections, we notified our schoolmates that each of them was expected to lead five Leftists of the People's School. Such is the work of the latter period and Our School's preparations and plans.

In short, all the policies of Our School can influence the Left Wing at any time. As the time of re-elections to the Municipal Party Headquarters approached, the list of nominees for the following term was openly brought up. Although there were indications of a fight for power among a small number of Leftists, the result was that all accepted the decision of the United Left. In the elections, an absolute victory was scored by the Left and ourselves due to the unified activities of the United Left.

Analysis of Left Organizations

The failure of the Kuomintang Left to establish a centralized national or local organization is not a question of whether Our School approved of such a step or not. From the standpoint of the Left's class characteristics, Leftists are petty bourgeois revolutionaries. It is difficult if not impossible for the petty bourgeoisie to form a strictly unified organization. Hence, in trying to unify the [164] Left masses, Our School did not adopt a policy of "mixture" but of alliance. This policy seeks to develop Left organizations through alliance, the concentration of forces to fight the objective enemy. However, several Left leaders invented various new schemes while executing our policy. They believed it necessary to centralize all Left organizations in order to achieve success in the revolutionary task. They would have all Left organizations dissolved and then centralized in one organization. We had to employ various facts and theories to dispel their dreams. The Peking masses are highly complicated. It is necessary to have various organizations under different names and with different characteristics to include them all.

Of the Left organizations, the Practical Society enjoys the longest history. When the United Left was first established, we at times used the Practical Society as the center of our work in allying with the Left. We almost always consulted with leaders of the Society, such as Teng Wen-hui, Hsiao Chung-chen, and Li Shu-yung. For instance, the list of nominees for election to the Municipal Party Headquarters was decided upon in consultation with them and the list of nominees to District Party Headquarters was presented to them for consideration before announcement by the United Left. The Practical Society is, relatively speaking, in a position where its mass following is relatively large. However, the current objective situation differs from the past. Our School's attitude towards

Left organizations and individuals should follow changes in the objective situation. A new policy is now necessary.

Left organizations in Peking are showing signs of rapid growth and new Left leaders are constantly emerging out of the actual work. To secure the entire body of the masses, Our School should adopt an unbiased, just attitude and policy toward Left organizations. The following is a chart of Left organizations, listing names, leaders, and the numbers of the masses under their influence.

[165]

Name	Leaders	Leftists	Communist Party	Mass Total	Publication	Remarks
Practical Society	Teng Wen-hui, etc.	300	6	306	Shih-chien	May be regarded as purely Leftist
New Army Society	T'an Tsu-yao	189	75	264	Hsin chün	Entirely led by CP
Szechüan Revolutionary Youth Society	Tu Yen	160	46	206	None	Led by CP
New Yunnan Society	Yang Li-hsien	63	7	70	T'ieh Hua	Led by CP
Reform Society	Liu Yu	140	76	216	None	Led by CP
Soul of Hainan Society	Mo T'ung-jung	116	6	122	None	Led by CP
Ch'iung-yai Association	Cheng Lan-chi	130	?	130	None	[Led by] The Practical Society
Chung-shan Study Society	Yao Yen	40	25	65	Chung-shan sheng-huo	Led by CP
New China Study Society	?	160	45	165[?]	No survey made because many publications have been received from this organization	Long history; not all its members are revolutionary

According to the above chart, the total number of Left masses exceed 1,300. With the addition of more than 1,000 of our schoolmates, there are altogether more than 2,000 persons. The following [166] is an analysis of the various organizations based on the above chart.

1. Practical Society.—The Society has a history of over two years. In the past, its work was simple and its mass following limited. Following the death of Dr. Sun, its members felt that the People's School had lost its center. At the same time, the differentiation of the Party into the Left and Right became daily more apparent. They deplored the counterrevolutionary actions of the Right Wing but did not openly

acknowledge their Left position until the spring of 1926. Since the
Society unfolded its Left banner, the Left masses continued daily
to join it, thereby expanding its organization and work. At the time
when we joined the Left Wing of the Municipal Party Headquarters
(the present New Right Wing) to fight the Old Right Wing, the·
Practical Society had not yet taken a firm Left stand. It even published Tai Chi-t'ao's ideas in its periodical, Shih chien. The Practical Society participated in the united fight against the Old Right
Wing. During the balloting, however, they plotted secretly and voted
contrary to the agreed list of nominees. In the end, they were
sold out by the New Right Wing and failed. Therefore, at one time
we were very cold toward them. In the one year following the
elections in which the Old Right Wing was defeated, the Leftists took
over positions from the Old Right Wing with few exceptions and
have now become the New Right Wing. In October, 1926, several
leaders of the Practical Society and its masses favored the policy
against the New Right Wing and later joined with the CP to sponsor
the great unification of the Peking Left [United Left], to which nine
organizations one after another responded. Subsequently, Left organizations of the Peking People's School expanded rapidly while
the New Right Wing had to retreat before the masses.

Special mention should be made of leaders of the Practical Society
such as Teng Wen-hui, Hsiao Chung-chen, and Li Shu-yung. Known
as the three geniuses of the Practical Society, they command a much
higher position than that of most Leftists of the People's School.
They are fit to be considered as hardworking revolutionaries. They
appear outwardly to hold a respectful attitude towards Our School.
[167] They often say, "Communists [join] two parties; we genuine Leftists should also belong to two parties. After we bring the Chinese
National Revolution to victory, we should immediately engage in the
World Revolution and the proletarian revolution."

We are naturally aware that when in a good mood, the bourgeoisie
can well make all kinds of pretty statements. However, we do not
wish these Left leaders to reject the People's School immediately
and to join Our School instead. Although they often talk of joining
our Party, we have never actually introduced them. Of course those
Left leaders of the People's School who have true class consciousness may join Our School, but it is not necessary or possible for the
three leaders of the Practical Society to do so at this time.

On the one hand, they express willingness to join Our School and,
on the other, they strictly forbid our schoolmates to join the
Practical Society. They even suspect the extreme Leftists of the
Society of being comrades of the CP and CY. Some of them have been
expelled or detained under observation. An injustice was done in
some cases. Although theoretically they favor cooperation with the
Communists, their actions are still anti-Communist. No matter how

we interpret their theories, the facts remain the same. It is not
unusual for such problems to arise in petty bourgeois organizations.
Many of our comrades are resentful of the Society's anti-Communist actions. Some loudly charge that it is inclined toward the
Right, others suggest we break off all cooperation. Not so long ago,
the Left Wing with which we were allied became the New Right Wing
and they believe that the Practical Society may become the New New
Right Wing.

These opinions and actions of our comrades are mistaken. Although the Practical Society will surely become Rightist and reactionary, we must not break with it at the moment because of the
objective situation. It may be said that alliance with the Practical
[168] Society is one of our Party's historical tasks.

Our alliance with the Practical Society has not been interrupted
or broken off because of all these circumstances. Our attitude has
been very polite and tolerant. All misunderstandings are settled
frankly and sincerely at meetings. Up to the present, they have consulted us on major political policies and the work of the Municipal
Party Headquarters. In the recent elections of the Municipal Party
Headquarters four of its members were elected: two as regular
members, one as a reserve member, and another as a supervisory
member. Prior to the elections, the internal situation of the Society
was healthy but, upon the announcement of the election results,
many felt disappointed and its internal troubles multiplied. Our
policy has always been to settle their internal disputes and squabbles
for them so that the union of leftist groups would not be broken.
This is the most concise account and analysis of the past situation
of the Practical Society.

2. <u>New Army Society</u>.—The New Army Society was established in
the spring of 1926 under the sponsorship of Ch'en Ch'i-hsiu and
others. With an original membership of only two score of there-
abouts, it has become an organization exclusively of young students
in a little over a year, its membership having increased to 326.
(The above chart is based on the figures of last month). Within the
period of one month following the Kuomintang elections, over seventy
new members have joined the Society. Our comrades occupy three
fifths and the Leftists two fifths of the seats of the New Army
Society Executive Committee. The Society is a relatively strong
Left organization in Peking and its mass following outnumbers that
of the Practical Society. In terms of strict organization of the lower
masses, it is superior to all other Left organizations. It has set up
basic organizations in every university which meet biweekly to discuss theories and present reports on their activities. Under the
leadership of Our School's cells and our comrades belonging to
the basic organizations, the spirit is good and the work constructive
at these meetings.

The executive organization of the New Army Society has been
[169] very unhealthy. It is in fact completely under our direction. Our
comrades who undertake executive work in the Society often hamper
the work of the Society for the sake of our own Party work, thus
causing loose organization and discipline. The Society's representative [T'an Tsu-yao], recently elected to the Municipal Party Committee, is a comrade of Our School. He has already started reorganizing the setup in preparation for re-elections to facilitate
selection of hard-working Leftists and ourselves for the Executive
Committee so that we may develop our work. Our plan is to make
the New Army Society the central organization of the Left masses
of Peking. At the minimum, it should be of equal standing with the
Practical Society. Poor work in the past had caused the organization to appear excessively Red. Our comrades' activities must
henceforth be "grey" so that we may secure a large mass following
among the petty bourgeoisie. The Society should also absorb enlightened members for executive work, which we must not monopolize.

3. Szechuan Revolutionary Youth Society.—The Society was organized by a group of Szechuan youths at the time of the March
Eighteenth Incident last year. It had only a little over forty members at the start. Owing to its local characteristics, it is difficult
at present for the Society to develop into a mass organization.
Most of its executive positions are occupied by our schoolmates.
Our schoolmates shoulder the responsibility for many activities
both within and without the School. At one time the Society almost
suffered the fate of extinction. In the interest of developing the Society's work, many meetings of Our School's Party fraction in the
Society were held. Last October, a partial reorganization was
affected and the Society's work has since improved. The organization expanded from over forty to over seventy members. In two
months from its partial reorganization last October to registration
for elections in December, great progress was made in its work
and its masses increased from over seventy to over two hundred
persons. As a result of the elections, our schoolmates were elected
to two thirds of the executive committee seats. Our schoolmates
[170] have again taken too great a percentage of seats. However, since
this is an accomplished fact, nothing can be done about it. Fortunately our schoolmates who were elected are not excessively Red.
This organization is entirely under our leadership.

Our schoolmates, Wu Ta-yu, Jan Chao-jung, T'an Tsu-yao, Chu
Chin-chih, and Tu Yen, all have high prestige and position among
the masses. In the re-elections to the Municipal Party Headquarters,
the Szechuan Revolutionary Youth Society's representative who was
elected as reserve executive committee member is also our schoolmate.

The masses of the Youth Society are expanding and its work is becoming complicated. Our School's Party fraction which directs the work of the Society meets weekly to guide the development of work. Basic organizations of the Youth Society in the schools also meet biweekly in rather good spirit.

4. <u>New Yunnan Society</u>.—The New Yunnan Society is a revolutionary organization of a group of Yunnan youths. It has a history of only one year and its organization is not well developed. Membership from the time of its establishment to the present consists merely of a little over seventy persons. For propaganda purposes it publishes <u>T'ieh hua</u> [Iron Flower], edited by our schoolmates. A thousand copies are printed for each issue. The city of Peking is divided into six basic organizations, each of which meets often and in very good spirit. Its membership is not confined to elements of the People's School. At meetings, frequent discussions are held on such topics as "Communism," "Communist Party," "The Three Peoples' Principles," and "Kuomintang." On the theoretical level, our schoolmates have completely secured leadership. Our schoolmate, Yang Li-hsien, has a high standing in the New Yunnan Society.

The Society is national in character, It has organizations in Canton, Shanghai, Hankow, and other important cities. It has close connections with the Fourth National Revolutionary Army, from which it receives economic assistance. We also have a Party fraction within the Society, the secretary of which is our schoolmate [Yang] Li-hsien.

171]   5. <u>The Reform Society</u>.—The Reform Society is a revolutionary organization of Hunan youths which is local in nature. Its mass following increased to over two hundred persons soon after its establishment. Branches of the Society are located at the following universities; National Peking University, Peking Law College, Peking Engineering College, Chiao-t'ung University, Peking Normal College, P'ing University, Chung University, and Ch'ao-yang University. In the past we made the mistake of attempting to make the organization national and set up a central executive committee in Peking. This mistake, however, has since been corrected.

Due to the large number of Hunanese living in Peking, it is not difficult to expand the Society's masses. The Society is also entirely under our direction and many of our schoolmates hold high positions in it. It can be considered the largest mass organization of the Hunanese in Peking. From its establishment to the present, it has accomplished several striking feats which scared the old bureaucrats to death. For instance, in the elections of the Hunan Alumni Association and the activities of the Hunan Natives' Association, the Reform Society has been outstanding. Its victories have almost completely deprived the rotton bureaucrats of their influence and prestige.

Centralization of command and unity of action are the most

prominent features of the Society. Society members are fresh
troops for the mass struggle. We also have a Party fraction in the
Society which meets biweekly. The Society's representative who
was elected as reserve executive committee member of the Municipal Party Headquarters is also our schoolmate. Executive positions
in the Society were formerly divided between our schoolmates and
non-schoolmates. Now, however, it is completely taken over by our
schoolmates. To avoid monopoly and to encourage Leftists to take
part in the work, we are preparing to reorganize the executive organ so that progressive Leftists may participate in its work. The
future development of the Society's work will continue to prosper.

6. Soul of Hainan Society and the Ch'iung-yai Association.—The
Soul of Hainan Society and Ch'iung-yai Association originally
constituted one organization. Differences of opinion among leaders
led to great conflicts and differentiation of its masses, resulting in
division into two organizations of the Ch'iung-yai natives of Kwangtung. One is the Soul of Hainan Society and the other the Ch'iung-yai
Association.

During the first differentiation of the Kuomintang, the Ch'iung-
[172] yai Association stood on the Right, participating in the Western
Hills Conference and affiliating with the Southern Gardens Party
Headquarters. The Soul of Hainan Society stood on the Left. During
the second differentiation of the Kuomintang, however, the so-
called Leftist Soul of Hainan Society stood on the side of the New
Right Wing and the Right-Wing Ch'iung-yai Association turned Leftist against the New Right Wing.

Both organizations have an inglorious history, each attempting to
attack the other as "Rightist" or "New Rightist." However, the
leader of the Soul of Hainan Society, Mo T'ung-jung, has joined
Our School and has introduced many of the Society's progressive
elements to join us also. In fact, more than one hundred members
of the Soul of Hainan Society have now become very good Leftists.
Meanwhile, the Ch'iung-yai Association indicates even more Leftist
leanings. Its leader, Cheng Lan-chi, is called by outsiders a quasi-
Communist. He works very hard. For instance, the Association has
repeatedly issued proclamations on opposing the dispatch of British
troops to China.

These two organizations compete in getting close to Our School,
as if whoever is close to the CP is not counterrevolutionary. By
getting close with the Communist Party, they hope to cope with
the offensives of the counterrevolutionaries. For instance, they
repeatedly asked Comrade Po Hai to deliver political reports and
lectures on communism. Standing between these two organizations,
our outward attitude is of course the same to both, but we are in
reality closer to the Soul of Hainan Society, which has now become
a Party-directed mass organization. The Party plans to eliminate

conflict between them. It would be best for them to thresh out their former differences and unite again.

Our School has a Party fraction within the Soul of Hainan Society. Its representative elected as a committee member of the Municipal Party Headquarters is Comrade Mo T'ung-jung (CP), and the representative of the Association elected to the Municipal committee is Cheng Lan-chi (Leftist).

7. <u>Chung-shan Study Society and New China Study Society.</u>—The Chung-shan Study Society was organized in July, 1926 but is not well developed. In six months its masses do not number over 173] seventy. In fact, those who have real connections with the organization number not over thirty. Among them are many of our schoolmates. Of all Left organizations in Peking, this may be considered the most backward. Also, it has numerous internal troubles. Important persons in its executive organ such as Mi Shih-chen and Lo Szu-jui, have now joined Our School. Yao Yen, the central figure of the Society, is a person of vanity and lust for power. He is the Society's representative elected as a reserve member of the Municipal Party Executive Committee. He was so dissatisfied with the position, however, that he even attempted to form secret connections with the New Right Wing. At the last elections, all the votes of the New Right Wing were cast for Yao Yen. With the New Right Wing's assistance, his name headed the list of reserve members. He has since been promoted to regular membership.

The New China Study Society has had a long history. It was originally not a revolutionary organization but many of our comrades are now among its leaders. Comrades Yü Shu-te and An T'i-ch'eng are members of the Society. Many of the Society's members work in educational institutions. Most of its progressive elements have been introduced by Comrade Shou-ch'ang [Li Ta-chao] to join the People's School. At the same time, quite a number have also joined Our School.

The representative of the New China Study Society elected to the Municipal Party Headquarters is a woman named Liu Yao-hsi. Liu is entirely a bourgeois young lady, absolutely incapable of accomplishing anything. She is understood to have had connections with the New Right Wing. Her present affiliation remains to be investigated.

The foregoing is an analysis of Left organizations in Peking. From this it is clear that, with the exception of the Practical Society, the Ch'iung-yai Association and the New China Study Society, six of the nine Left organizations are entirely under the direction of Our School. The most important work of Our School with reference to Left organizations is to make them mass organizations and revolutionary. Our schoolmates should maintain a gray-colored attitude in order to penetrate petty bourgeois masses and lead them to participate in the revolutionary sturggle.

[174] Recent Elections of the Municipal Party
      Headquarters and Our Policy
    1. The preparatory period of elections.—The recent elections of
the Municipal Party Headquarters was the most important activity
in the national movement in Peking. Our rival was the New Right
Wing. A few months before the elections, we had rallied the Left
masses and, in the course of unifying them, had created a tense
anti-Right atmosphere. The position of the New Right Wing among
the masses wavered, declined, and finally collapsed. Our policy
toward the elections was decided several months before the event.
The one important point was "Handing Party power to the Left
Wing!" a slogan warmly supported by all Leftists of the People's
School. Our School's position among the Left masses was considerably enhanced during the preparatory period. For a time (even now)
the Left masses judged the masses of the People's School as revolutionary or counterrevolutionary according to whether their actions
were anti-Communist or not. With the creation of the tense atmosphere of "Purification of Party Headquarters" and "Down with the
New Right Wing!" during the preparatory period for elections, the
fate of the New Right Wing became as perilous as a candle in the
wind.
    2. Results of elections.—The results of the elections of the Mu-
nicipal Party headquarters witnessed the complete realization of
our slogan, "Handing Party power to the Left Wing!" Our School
and the Leftist groups showed great tolerance during the elections
by accepting the election of one Rightist member although we could
have completely monopolized the elections. Lu Yu-yu, a member
of the New Right Wing, was elected one of the nine members of the
Municipal Party Headquarters Executive Committee. The following
chart presents the results of the elections and the names of members elected to the Executive Committee.

[75]

Regular Members of the Executive Committee, Municipal Party Headquarters	Organization Affiliation	Party Affiliation	Remarks
Wu K'o	CP	CP	Elected as Party representative
Hsieh Pai-yü	CP	CP	same
Teng Wen-hui	Practical Society	Left Wing People's School	
Hsiao Chung-chen	Practical Society	Left Wing People's School	
Mo T'ung-jung	Soul of Hainan Society	CP	
T'an Tsu-yao	New Army Society	CP	
Cheng Lan-chi	[Ch'iung-yai] Association	People's School Left Wing	Connections with Practical Society
Liu Yao-hsi	New China Study Society	Same	Past connections with New Right Wing
Lu Yu-yü	Great League [of Sunyatsenism]	New Right Wing	Has not assumed duty

Of the 51 executive seats in the 17 district Party Headquarters, 37 are occupied by us. If this is the situation at district Party headquarters, it is even more so the situation at subdistrict Party headquarters. Prior to the elections, we had preparations for controlling but not monopolizing low-level organs. And such have been the results! It should be pointed out here that some of the Leftists nominated by us for election were not our schoolmates but joined Our School after the elections. At some district Party headquarters,

[76] the Leftists we nominated were rejected by the Left masses for incompetence. The masses then directly nominated our comrades (though they did not know they were our comrades). The Left Wing sometimes nominated persons on the basis of ability to work. It was also inconvenient to oppose the nominations of the masses. In short, for many reasons we practically monopolize lower-level Party headquarters.

Concerning the elections it must be said that the direction of the responsible comrades of the Local Committee was relatively alert and our tactics relatively effective. There were 2,095 votes cast.

Our schoolmates Wu K'o and Mo T'ung-jung secured the largest
number of votes for the Municipal Party [Headquarters]. They each
got 1,847 votes. This was the first manifestation of the masses of
the Peking Kuomintang. The following table is compiled to give a
clearer picture of the mass strength of all organizations.

Organization	Original Votes	Additional Votes through Maneuvers	Total
Practical Society	250	80	330
Communist Party	1,000	300	1,300
New Army Society	200	40	240
[177] New Yunnan Society	60	20	80
Szechuan Revolutionary Youth Society	150	30	180
Soul of Hainan Society	100	—	100
[Ch'iung-yai] Association	100	—	100
Reform Society	100	—	100
Chung-shan Study Society	30	—	30
New Right Wing	150	30	180

The table sufficiently indicates the large number of votes we
got. Actually, Left organizations are interrelated to a great extent.
One individual may be connected with nine organizations. Thus, if
each of the nine votes for him, his total votes would be equivalent
to those of nine persons although, in reality, there is only one person. From the organizations listed we should find a hard core, a
hard core controlled by our Party. And we may consider all the
masses led by us as our own masses.

In the recent elections we got 70 percent of the total votes; 20
percent went to independent Left organizations such as the Practical
Society; the New Right Wing did not even get 10 percent. Prior to
the voting, we had not realized how few masses the New Right Wing
controlled. We had expected it to poll at least 300 to 400 votes. But
the election results broke its false sign-board to pieces. [As the saying goes,] "Monkeys scatter when the tree falls!"

[178]   During the election fight, our schoolmates unconditionally obeyed
the Party's direction. Although one or two comrades who expressed
a desire for municipal committee work might have had opportunist
tendencies, they dared not openly rebel because they were definitely
a minority. Under the iron discipline they could only admit their
own errors. The situation in Left organizations, excepting a few
organizations under our control, is entirely different. Some Left
elements openly rejected the list of nominees which had been agreed
upon and rebelled against their own organizations at the time of

voting. They had other plans in mind for themselves. (Such problems occurred in the Practical Society.)

3. <u>End of the elections—organization of the new Municipal Committee.</u>—The result of the Municipal Party Headquarters elections was absolute victory for the Left and the Communists. The following table shows the organization of the new Executive Committee of the Municipal Party and the distribution of work of the various departments.

Department	Department Head	Party Affiliation	Remarks
Standing members	Teng Wen-hui T'an Tsu-yao Liu Yao-hsi	Practical Society CP New China Society	Teng- Chairman T'an- Secretary Liu- Treasurer
Organization	Hsieh Pai-yü	CP	――――
Propaganda	Hsiao Chung-chen	Practical Society	――――
Labor	Wu K'o	CP	――――
Peasants	Mo T'ung-jung	CP	――――
Youth	Cheng Lan-chi	[Ch'iung-yai] Association	――――
Merchants	Lu Yu-yü	New Right Wing	Lu has not assumed duties; his substitute is Yao Yen
Women	Chang I-lan	Wavering left	――――

The above table shows the distribution of work among the various departments of the Municipal Party Headquarters. The work of each department is based on positive plans. Our Party fraction in the Municipal Party Headquarters meets once a week with detailed directions for department chiefs. Upon the assumption of duties all department heads immediately announced their political policies and printed department plans for distribution among Party headquarters of all levels. When the masses saw them they declared, "After all, the Party headquarters of the Left is different from the New Right Wing!"

We are deeply aware that the work of the various departments is far too inadequate. Revolutionary Party headquarters of the Left must not be satisfied simply with flattering statements from the masses to the effect that they are "different from the New Right Wing." The new Municipal Party headquarters must do its best to expand its work and positively correct the past mistakes of the New Right Wing. Future work entirely depends on Our School's direction.

<u>The Left's Attitude toward Our School—</u>
<u>The Position of Our School among the Masses</u>

The Peking Local Committee's work in the national movement has passed from the stage in which we prepare to lead the Left to

the stage in which we are actually capable of leading it. Confidence
in [our] Party has been established not only among a few leaders;
we already have an unshakable foundation among the masses. The
attitude of the Left masses toward Our School has been mentioned
in previous reports. We will now cite many facts to illustrate the
Left's general attitude toward Our School.

[179]   1. The New Right Wing's propaganda on the monopoly of the KMT
by the KCT—our Left comrades enumerate facts to prove to the
masses that such rumors are fabricated by the New Right. As a
result, they have come into frequent conflict with the New Right
Wing.

2. The New Right Wing's propaganda on the CP's opposition to
the Northern Expedition—the Left is able to follow our explanation
of Comrade [Ch'en] Tu-hsiu's article, "On the Northern Expedition," [see Part IV, p.230] to counter-attack the New Right, to prove
that it twists the meaning of the article and fabricates rumors.

3. The New Right Wing's anti-Communist propaganda—the Left
is able to attack the New Right Wing for rebelling against Sunyatsenism by citing Dr. Sun's Three Great Policies (Russian alliance,
Communist alliance, and [support of] labor and peastantry).

4. The New Right Wing's propaganda on the KCT's plot to assassinate Chiang Kai-shek—the Left openly points out that the
Right's actions in supporting the imperialists and reactionary
militarists are entirely counterrevolutionary.

In short, the Left accepts our ideas completely in repudiating
among the masses the fancy anti-Communist propaganda of the New
Right Wing. Our School stands completely in the controlling position within the United Council of the Left. It holds the final decision on all questions. The Left's respect for Our School may be
compared with that of a person whose "five members fall prostrate
in obeisance." The outline of the Left's theoretical platform was
proposed by Our School and all political and theoretical reports at
meetings of the United Left are made by comrades of Our School.
Naturally, such a weak Left is not what we had hoped for. This being the case, however, [the only solution] is slow, gradual correction through work of the Left's weaknesses. Whatever controver-
sies arise among Left organizations, the parties concerned would
not be satisfied with any settlement other than that justly brought
about by Our School's representatives. During discussions of all
questions, Our School's representatives must present the final
conclusions in order to satisfy everyone.

[180]   In its work in the national movement, the Peking [Local Commit-
tee] very well accepts the theoretical direction of Our School's
Central Committee on the question of alliance with the Left Wing.
Some of the CC's policies and strategies have already been realized
in Peking. Others are just being carried out. As for the CC's

instructions for Our School's comrades to cope with certain bad
tendencies in the work of the People's School, [we have to point out
that] some of these tendencies have not yet materialized in Peking.
This is because the Peking Local Committee was able to prevent
such bad tendencies from arising in the first place. Since we succeeded in utilizing and completely realizing the Party's direction,
we have been able to avoid any conflict with Left elements of the
People's School which may lead to rupture of relations.

Conclusions

Summarizing the above-mentioned facts and conditions, we may
realize the important mission of Our School in local political work
in Peking. The Peking Leftists have not been able to carry out independently their historical mission. They have to rely on us everywhere. Weak as they are, how can they be expected to fight the
Right and to participate in the actual revolutionary struggle if we
do not help them to develop and grow and to adapt themselves to
the masses and to cultivate their fighting ability?

The KMT's masses in Peking who are truly under the Left's
leadership number at most 600. The Left has even less of a position with the masses in general. The Leftists have a very fantastic
scheme. They think that the Kuomintang Left should merely carry
out the policy [to support] labor and peasantry and that labor and
peasantry should serve as the KMT's class foundation. This is entirely a manifestation of Left infantilism and we have already tried
to correct it. We will now summarize all points as the conclusion
of this report and the objectives of our work.

1. Exert every effort to develop our own Party and to secure the
[181] petty bourgeois masses in the course of the national movement.

2. Develop the Kuomintang methodically. There should be 10,000
members when the next elections of the Municipal Committee take
place. Adapt the Leftists of the People's School to the masses and
lead them to participate in the actual revolutionary struggle.

3. Enable the Left Wing to take over the social mass movement
of the petty bourgeoisie.

4. Continue the anti-Right movement (the anti-Communist movement of the New Right is still continuing).

5. Maintain absolutely the same attitude toward [all organizations of] the Left. Correct the past concept of using the Practical
Society as the center. However, at the Municipal Party Headquarters, which is not a mass organization, we should still unite with
the Practical Society as the center in order to create a three-
party form.

6. Disapprove of the concept that the Left should have a strictly
disciplined and unified organization (because it is impossible).

7. See that Left organizations develop evenly.

8. Continue the United Council of the Left.

9. The Party (the People's School) should be the center of all Left organizations.

10. Unify Left theories and policies but disapprove of the formulation of a special Left political platform.

11. Promote propaganda recognizing Wang Ching-wei as leader of the Left.

12. Cautiously permit the Left to participate in work (under our direction).

13. Strengthen the organizations of the Left's masses and their alliance with Our School.

14. Avoid the principle of "iron discipline" in reforming Party headquarters. Promote the progress of Party members through educational means.

[182]   15. Exert every effort to push Kuomintang work among the masses and correct the past error of not producing any effect among the masses.

CONCLUSIONS

This book has dealt with the major political events during a critical period in modern Chinese history, the years from 1918 to 1927. A knowledge of this period aids in the understanding of China today. The documents presented in translation are authentic, primary sources but because of their random character do not by themselves provide a basis for understanding the events of the period. They have therefore been supplemented by historical exposition.

The book has traced the rise of the modern Nationalist and Communist parties which have dominated the political scene in China for more than thirty years. Their later fratricidal conflict was an aftermath of their union during the early and middle twenties. The ideologies of both parties—their goals of political action—were acquired (or, in the case of the Kuomintang, greatly refined) during this period. So was the system of party organization, of party armies, and of government as the instrument of party. These and a great deal more were learned from Soviet Russia.

Most of the political leaders who have governed China during the past thirty years, and even those who today head the governments in Peking and Taipei, began their careers in the revolutionary movement during the period under review. They are the same actors, grown old.

The history of this period is bewilderingly complex. The vast ocean of the Chinese people with their strongly conservative tradition and urge to stability was nevertheless impelled by extreme tensions to struggle for a different order. Explosive pressure of population, rural poverty, fierce competition for land, and the exploitation of city workers provided a latent revolutionary force. Strong tides of patriotism and resentment against foreign privilege and exploitation waited to be lashed into a fury of anti-imperialism. The rival foreign powers, particularly Britain, Russia, and Japan, competed for a dominant position over great parts of the country. Their competition made more intense the rivalries among the power-hungry militarists and the unstable political cliques all over the country—Chang Tso-lin, Wu P'ei-fu, Feng Yü-hsiang, Sun Ch'uan-fang, and all their satellite politicians and commanders great and small.

Within the revolutionary camp was the triangle of Nationalists, Communists, and Russian advisers, uneasy companions in an adventure in which each had different goals. The Kuomingang was itself a conglomeration of generals and politicians with varying regional interests and local sources of power; these men had their private dreams and ambitions and were constantly scheming and competing as well as allying and cooperating. The Communists, too, had their factions and their bitter disputes over strategy. Likewise among the Russian advisers we catch glimpses of jealousy and rivalry.

The explosive social condition which China had reached by 1920, the dynamic forces which the Communists and the Kuomintang under Russian instruction were able to release, made up the texture of the revolution. But it was enormously complicated by divergent purposes and rivalries among the leaders of the revolutionary camp.

A great conflict within the revolutionary leadership was inevitable from the beginning. The march of events towards the bloody purges of 1927 and the ten years of civil war thereafter is an important theme that forces itself upon this book which records the events as they unfold. The Communist objective in fostering and maintaining the collaboration with the Kuomintang was clear and consistent though hidden from public view—seizure of leadership of the Chinese national revolutionary movement as a transitional step toward the eventual establishment of Communism.

In line with the Comintern's "Theses on the National and Colonial Question," the resolutions adopted by the Third Congress of the Chinese Communist Party instructed members to enter the Kuomintang for joint work in the national revolutionary movement. They were simultaneously to utilize opportunities presented by this membership to expand the Communist Party, organize and absorb the masses, and prepare the Communists' independent forces. In pledging allegiance to Sun Yat-sen's Three Principles of the People, Communists never renounced their ultimate goal of a Communist revolution.

Similarly, the Russians sent to reorganize and strengthen the Kuomintang proceeded on the premise that Soviet control of the Kuomintang would accelerate the development of conditions necessary for the ultimate establishment of a Communist state in China. Perhaps less explicitly, Sun Yat-sen expected to use the Communists for his own ends. Some of the Nationalist leaders—Chiang Kai-shek for example—were suspicious of Russia and hostile to the advisers at the very time they accepted Russian help. They only wanted Russian guns and technical military advice.

The inevitable conflict did not break out in all its violence until the months just after the period covered by this book. Yet it can be foreseen in the emergence of "Taichitaoism," the Western Hills Conference, and the polarization of the Kuomintang into Right and

Left factions over the Communist issue, the conflicts among students in the Whampoa Academy, the March 20th Incident, and the struggles between the Wuhan and the Nanchang centers.

Why the Kuomintang leaders in power tolerated the Communists in their midst as long as they did is rather puzzling when looked at in retrospect. It took some of them only a short time to come to the point of a break; others took much longer. But one by one, at various times and for various combinations of reasons, most of them did come to that position. Ignorance of the Communists' intentions does not provide a good explanation. Suspicions of those intentions based to some extent upon the Communists' own private or public communications were raised officially in the Kuomintang by various leaders in November, 1923, in January, 1924, at the time of the First Kuomintang Congress, and in an impeachment of the Communists on June 18, 1924. Tai Chi-t'ao pointed out the danger in his book published in July, 1925. The members of the Western Hills Conference in November, 1925, denounced the Communists for using the Kuomintang only to expand their own influence and to support Soviet Russia. From then on there was no lack of exposers and denouncers of the Communists' ultimate objectives.

There are several explanations for the postponement of the inevitable conflict. One is lack of real comprehension of Communist intentions among many of the Kuomintang leaders—if lack of comprehension and ignorance may be distinguished. Sun Yat-sen apparently did not really understand their strategy, or minimized the risk to his party if he did. During the earliest phase of the cooperation his influence was a powerful factor in suppressing opposition to his policy of admitting the Communists to the Kuomintang. After his death the prestige of his name was used to uphold the policy. Leaders who disagreed were pushed out of Canton by their colleagues and had to voice their opposition from the sidelines.

Another factor was broad acceptance of the theory of a national revolution in which all revolutionary groups should participate under leadership of the Kuomintang. The general theory had originated with Lenin and been adapted to China by the Comintern. The eyes of many Kuomintang leaders, including Sun, were focused upon unification of the country and the ending of foreign privilege in China: "Anti-militarism" and "anti-imperialism." There was also, apparently, a fascination in being part of a "world revolution." The Communists, too, worked hard for those ends. Why disrupt the revolution by conflict within the revolutionary camp? After the assassination of Liao Chung-k'ai, who was probably the most influential exponent of Sun's policy of cooperation, Wang Ching-wei defined the issue as imperialism versus anti-imperialism. There was no need, he said, to create the issue of Communism. Communist spokesmen were indefatigable, of course, in trying to keep attention focused upon the national revolution and very adept at refuting the charges raised against themselves.

Another explanation for postponement of the conflict lies in the heterogeneous nature of the Kuomintang and the power rivalries within it. The Russian advisers and the Chinese Communists were able to exploit these rivalries. They supported those Kuomintang leaders who approved of the collaboration policy and threw their considerable weight against its opponents. It seems a fair presumption that access to Russian money and arms and support by Communist leaders and their mass organizations were important elements in the Kuomintang power struggle. They helped to maintain in power the leaders who upheld the cooperation policy either from conviction or opportunism. Such dependency prolonged the cooperation.

Another explanation is that the conflict between the two parties was alternately sharpened and then dulled by ambivalence in the strategy of both sides. Each was trying to use the other as long as advantage from the cooperation outweighed risk. Each therefore made compromises and held itself in check.

The Kuomintang had recieved into its ranks some hundreds of ardent workers who, as Communists, were particularly adept at organizing the masses and China's youth and in gaining their support for the revolution. Russian aid, too, seemed to be linked to continued cooperation with the Communists. This aid was extremely important in the Kuomintang's consolidation of its base in Kwangtung and in the long-planned-for Northern Expedition against the rulers of Central and North China.

For their part the Communists, by working within the Kuomintang, could operate with relative freedom in territories under Nationalist jurisdiction. They could propagandize freely, organize the masses, and work among the troops. And since some of their leaders held important posts in high Kuomintang organs, they could influence Kuomintang policy. Yet membership in the Kuomintang imposed severe restraints. Communists dared not push the revolution so fast that it would create a countermovement within the other party strong enough to force them out. They had constantly to compromise, to put the check rein on revolution so as not to imperil their advantageous position. This fundamental inconsistency led to endless dispute over tactics. It finally led nearly to disaster for the Communists.

The Communists were riding a whirlwind from mid-1925 to mid-1927, and some of their leaders knew it. Their Party was entirely inadequate for the role it tried to carry out. When the top leadership decided, upon Comintern advice, to cooperate with the Kuomintang in the national revolution, the combined membership of Party and Youth Corps was between two and three hundred. By the Fourth

Communist Congress in January, 1925, the Party's membership was still under one thousand. Yet by May of that year the Party claimed to have under its leadership over half a million organized workers as well as 400,000 organized peasants in Kwangtung. After the May 30th Incident in 1925, Communist membership increased rapidly—too rapidly for new members to be trained adequately. A resolution of the Central Committee in July, 1926, on the question of organization calculated that a minimum of 355 persons was needed as directing personnel, yet in fact there were only 120. This was just at the start of the Northern Expedition. Rivalry and poor coordination marred the relations of the Communist Party and its Youth Corps. As late as March, 1926, the Party did not even have a peasant movement committee to coordinate work in that field.

Its organizational difficulties were heightened by the fact that the Chinese Communist Party had, from its inception, subscribed to the difficult standards of Marxism-Leninism. Leninist principles of democratic centralism characterized its organization from the start. The norms set up for membership were complete submission of the individual to the Party and "iron discipline." The Party insisted on ideological orthodoxy and sought to suppress all deviations from the Party line, Right or Left. It stressed the superiority of the proletarian point of view for all members. These were difficult standards to achieve in the midst of revolution.

With these organizational problems and weaknesses the Party was trying to carry out a very complicated task. It tried to build and lead a powerful mass movement, particularly to organize industrial labor in Canton, Shanghai, and the Wuhan cities, and to form a peasant movement in Kwangtung and Hunan. It tried to lead the youth, particularly the students, of the entire country. By propaganda and agitation it tried to set in motion a nation-wide anti-imperialist movement which was directed primarily against Great Britain. It tried to steer the policies of the Kuomintang in Canton and at the same time to work in regions under control of hostile militarists—in Peking under the tight control of Chang Tso-lin and among the Red Spears of Chihli, Shantung, and Honan. It tried to convert future officers in training at the Whampoa Academy and to establish Communist cells among officers of the armies associated with the Kuomintang in Kwangtung.

In doing all this the Communists played their dangerous game of joining and cooperating with the Kuomintang with the aim of using it and eventually seizing control of the national revolution. There is a strange contrast between, on the one hand, the self-assured analysis of class forces and the confident assertion of correct strategy that one reads in resolutions of the Central Committee and, on the other hand, the real fears for the safety of their movement which lay behind the inner-Party disputes on strategy.

Since there was intense opposition within the Kuomintang almost from the beginning to Sun's policy of admitting Communists and collaborating with them, and since this opposition grew more and more determined, the Communists under Comintern advice searched for allies within the Kuomintang and tried to strengthen their hand. The basic strategy was to ally with the Left Wing against the Right Wing in order to control the Kuomintang. Moscow appears to have left its agents and the Chinese Communist leaders pretty much to their own devices, however, in implementing this strategy. After Chiang's coup of March Twentieth in 1926, this involved the staggering task of first finding a Left Wing. As the Soviet adviser Nilov so neatly put it, the Left Wing was empty.

Nilov's opinion was shared by members of the Kwangtung Regional Committee of the Chinese Communist Party. They denied that the Left existed and clamoured for direct Communist seizure of leadership of the Kuomintang. Although the Party's Central Committee had to keep the Kwangtung leaders in check, some of its members had doubts about the potentialities of the Left. In October, 1925, the Committee had declared that the Left Wing was "mere talk" and had set up specific criteria to aid Party members in identifying members of the Left.

A resolution of the Central Committee on relations between the Communist Party and the Kuomintang in July, 1926, discussed the persistent anti-Communist offensive within the Kuomintang. It noted that the armed center was in power in Kwangtung and the anti-Red movement of the Right Wing was prevalent throughout the country. Yet it attributed this situation to "the incorrect formula we previously employed in directing the Kuomintang." Its "correct" formula was to expand the Left Wing of the Kuomintang and cooperate with it closely in order to deal with the Center and openly counterattack the reactionary Right [Doc. 27]. In December, 1926, the process of defining the Left reached a climax when, at the Special Conference in Hankow, the Central Committee defined the Left as that portion of the Kuomintang which favored continuation of what they called Sun Yat-sen's "Three Great Policies"—alliance with Soviet Russia, alliance with the Communists, and support of the workers and peasants. Communists were ordered to support and give further concessions to the Left Wing, despite its vacillations and weakness, on the sole condition that the latter uphold Sun's "Three Great Policies." (The available record shows that this term originated not with Sun Yat-sen but with the Communists themselves.)

Aware of the weakness of the Kuomintang Left and the growing strength of reaction and conscious of their organizational weakness,

yet bound by the Comintern strategy of staying within the Kuomintang and trying to guide it, the members of the Communist Central
Committee felt that they had to curb the peasant movement in Hunan
during the Northern Expedition. To combat the great anti-Communist tide which the Committee recognized and to allay the Kuomintang's fear that a Communist revolution would come very soon, the
Committee members decided to urge the masses to support the
National Government. They feared the very dialectical process which
they recognized as fundamental to all change.

Yet the strategy seemed to work—for a time. By March, 1927,
when the Kuomintang ended a meeting of its Central Executive Committee at Wuhan, the united front between the Communists and the
Left Wing of the Kuomintang seemed triumphant. The Left was in
control of the Kuomintang's organization, a powerful alliance of
generals against Chiang Kai-shek seemed in the making, and the
there was in effect a coalition of the two parties in the government
at Hankow.

But dialectical processes were at work. The national reaction to
revolutionary excesses and the reaction of foreign powers to the
Russian challenge had greatly strengthened the anti-Communist
forces within the Kuomintang. The inherent conflict erupted decisively. In April a determined group of Kuomintang leaders,
headed by Chiang Kai-shek, turned upon the Communists and their
radical mass movement. The ranks of the Communists were
decimated in bloody purges, many a Communist leader was executed,
and the organization was left a shattered wreck. By July the whole
policy of cooperating with the Kuomintang to utilize it and control
it had collapsed and the Russian advisers were on their way home-
ward, defeated.

What of the Russians who tried and failed (on this occasion)
to guide the revolution but who left so strong a stamp upon modern
China? Their attempt was overly ambitious. Most of them knew
little about China. They had to depend upon interpreters in order
to speak with their Chinese associates. In retrospect it appears
that they could scarcely understand the social and political forces
which they pretended to harness and direct. It is a risky venture
for one country to attempt to direct the course of political and social
development in another.

The human element in the Soviet adventure in China is perhaps
most strikingly illustrated by the Russians' strenuous effort to
understand and outwit such leaders as Chiang Kai-shek, Feng Yü-
hsiang, and T'ang Sheng-chih. Were they to be considered true
revolutionaries or were they opportunists? Unless this question
were answered satisfactorily, would it not be dangerous to give
them arms? The self-confessed bafflement and exasperation of
Soviet advisers in connection with each of them—as revealed in

documents 23 and 24, 36 and 37, 43 and 44—offer interesting
counterpoint to their conviction that these leaders could be molded
to communist ends provided their characteristics were correctly
estimated.

Soviet confidence was not entirely unwarranted in some fields,
however. The Russian who early in 1926 described the reorganized
Kuomintang as a Soviet creation may have erred in exaggeration but
not in substance. The constitution drafted by Borodin had transformed the Nationalist Party along Leninist lines of democratic
centralism. The Party's platform had also been drafted by Borodin
while its twin slogans of anti-imperialism and anti-militarism
were borrowed from the Chinese Communist Party. Closely allied
with the leaders of the Left Wing who were then in control, the
Russians enjoyed considerable power and prestige.

Under the leadership of Kisanko, the Soviet group in Canton had
deepened its penetration of the Kuomintang's military apparatus in
the winter of 1925-1926. In December, 1925, the chief of the South
China Group could report that the Russians had already secured
good positions in the various departments of the National Revolutionary Army, but that it was impossible to penetrate further and to
obtain complete control [sic!] for two major reasons: shortage of
advisers and lack of interpreters [Doc. 16]. Another report of
February, 1926, states that Rogachev actually acted as chief of
the General Staff and that other instructors were really heads of
all the departments although officially called advisers to the
Chinese chiefs [Doc. 22]. This illusion of having the Kuomintang
under control was shattered by Chiang Kai-shek's coup of March
20, 1926. Thereafter, the failure of the Soviet advisers to gauge
Chiang's real temper and their decision to conciliate him by giving
him greater power and to discourage the formation of an anti-
Chiang alliance proved to be a major strategic error.

Another group of Russian advisers had scant success working
with Feng Yü-hsiang. Despite some early optimism, a Russian
military mission made little headway either in radicalizing or controlling Feng's armies. To what extent was this due to Feng's
personality or to the inability of the Russians to find another adviser with the ability of Borodin? To what extent does the fact
that Feng was a military commander with territorial power in his
own right explain the inability of the Russian mission to exert much
influence over him? They supplied him with arms to the value of
six million rubles in the eleven months between April, 1925, and
March, 1926. Yet during this period, in contrast to what happened
in the south, Feng's power declined relative to that of other northern commanders.

In spite of protestations of loyalty to Sun Yat-sen's Three Principles, Feng did not declare himself for the Kuomintang until after

his attempt to ally with Wu P'ei-fu and other generals had proved
abortive, the Kuominchün had suffered serious reverses, and his
only remaining avenue for supplies was across Mongolia. While
Feng was in Ulan Bator, the capital of Outer Mongolia, on his way
to Moscow, he had long discussions with various Russians, including Borodin and "Henry A. Lin," and with representatives of the
Kuomintang. In Moscow he met many of the Russian leaders and
made a few revolutionary speeches. He also began a study of
Leninism. Only then did he announce his decision to join the Kuomintang.

After his return from Moscow, Feng did stage a military comeback with Russian help. He played an important part in the defeat
of Wu P'ei-fu at the time of the Northern Expedition. But in mid-
1927 he broke with his Russian advisers, just as the Hankow group
of the Kuomintang did also and as Chiang had done a few months
earlier.

Even though the Russians left China defeated, they had made a
powerful impress upon the country. We may wonder why the Russian advisers were as successful as they were. Several of them
appear to have been men of great ability. Borodin, Galen, and Karakhan were men of stature, and this may have been true of some of
the others. The available documents, however, do not produce a
clear picture of the Russians as individuals. Borodin particularly
remains a shadow. The personal reactions between men, between
individual Russian advisers and their Chinese associates, are
historical factors about which we have very little information. Yet
there are enough glimpses to show that the personal factor was
involved both in the success and the defeat of the Russians in
China.

The great asset of the Russians was that they had something
practical to offer to Chinese patriots searching for ways to save
their country. They had a theory of revolution, and technical
skills in the conduct of revolution and war, and they could provide
money and arms. They had their greatest success in the south,
where they began their work with a badly disorganized, power-
hungry, revolutionary group. They were able to help this group to
such an extent that within three years it was master of a considerable part of South China. Such success as they had with Feng Yü-
hsiang seems to have come when he was out of power.

The experience of the Russian advisers in the twenties brings to
mind the much larger number of Soviet technicians and advisers
presently engaged in various activities in the Chinese People's
Republic. Will they be able to avoid the pitfalls which entrapped the
Russians thirty years before? Was the experience which the Russians gained then valuable training for the conduct of relations with
China after 1949? Although the situation encountered by Borodin,

Galen, Kisanko, Stepanov, "Jen Te-chiang," and the others is different from that facing the present-day Soviet advisers, they too have the problem of understanding and dealing with national pride even among hardened Communists.

This is only one facet of the rather startling way in which the events of the twenties seem to have been a dress rehearsal for what has been happening in China under Communism. The cult of learning from Russia finds its precedent in the eagerness of some of the Kuomintang leaders as well as the Communists to absorb revolutionary strategy and tactics from Soviet Russia in the period covered by this book.

The Leninist concept of the exercise of power by a centralized, highly disciplined party found expression in the organization of the revitalized Kuomintang of 1924 just as it underlies the structure of the Chinese People's Republic. The division of the population into two camps, "the people" and "the reactionaries," in Mao Tse-tung's On People's Democratic Dictatorship (July 1, 1949) echoes the reorganized Kuomintang's separation of "anti-imperialist" individuals and groups from those whom they categorized as belonging to the imperialists and militarists. The purposeful organizing and exploiting of nationalist zeal in an anti-imperialist campaign to be used as the motive force of the revolution characterized the Kuomintang's program in the twenties just as it is today a major feature of Communist policy. The deliberate concentration on one power, Great Britain, in the anti-imperialist movement—an integral part of Moscow's global strategy—was a foretaste of the Chinese Communist Party's postwar anti-American campaign, which has culminated (thus far) in the nation-wide movement for "Opposing America and Aiding Korea."

These comparisons between the Kuomintang and its program in the twenties and the Communist Party and its recent program for achieving and consolidating power reemphasize the point that the earlier events are extremely important for understanding recent Chinese history. However, the Kuomintang during the period between its reorganization in January, 1924, and its "purification" in mid-1927 was a rather different organization from what it later became. During its revolutionary period it was strongly under the influence of its Russian advisers, particularly Borodin, and its directing organs were infiltrated with energetic Communists. It is not really surprising, therefore, that there should be these significant resemblances.

The Chinese Communist Party itself has sought, at various stages of its career, to identify its cause with the National Revolution and to claim true succession to Sun Yat-sen. During the period of the United Front in the war of resistance against Japan, the Communists publicized to good effect the allegiance they professed to Sun Yat-sen's Three Principles of the People, to what they called his "Three Great Policies," to the platform of the First Kuomintang Congress, and to Sun Yat-sen's Will. This conscious identification with the nationalist program of the twenties is clearly evident in such key documents as Mao Tse-tung's On New Democracy (January 19, 1940) and On Coalition Government (April 24, 1945).

In 1949, Mao attributed victory to three things: a disciplined party; an army led by that party; and a united front of various revolutionary strata and groups led by the party.

Although the Communists' participation in the National Revolution ended in disaster for them in 1927, they gained invaluable experience in organizing precisely these three things which ultimately led to victory. The Communist Party expanded beyond all expectations of its founders during the heat of the national revolutionary movement. The Kuomintang's experience in organizing a party army with Soviet help and, even more important, the Communists' catastrophe in 1927 due partly to their lack of an army of their own were important lessons for the future.

Of equal importance was the experience gained by the Party in working with and infiltrating other parties and groups and in organizing the masses. Many of the tactics outlined during the twenties for the penetration of the masses were later employed with great effectiveness, particularly during the "Second United Front" of the war against Japan. Some of the key ideas are: attention to low-level work, emphasis on moderation, alertness in utilizing existing conditions, skillful combination of open and secret work, and the need for Communist Party members to get close to the masses in every respect.

In short, the United Front Strategy was a major source of strength in the Communists' rise to power. It was the vehicle for exploiting nationalist sentiment and for fusing nationalist slogans with their own program in accordance with the changing "objective situation."

During the period covered by this book the Kuomintang and the Communists discovered what a powerful force nationalism is in Chinese life. After their split in 1927 both parties strove to capture leadership of this revolutionary force. As this book is written, each party still asserts its claim to be the rightful leader that will guide China to the fulfillment of its nationalist aspirations.

NOTES, GLOSSARIES

BIBLIOGRAPHY

INDEX

NOTES

The Problem of Authenticity

1. The description of the raid is based on the following sources: China Press, April 7 and 8, 1927, Reuters Pacific Service dispatches, Peking, dated April 6, 1927; Shen Pao, April 7, 1927; People's Tribune, April 12, 1927, United Press dispatch, Peking, April 6, 1927; Special Tribune Service dispatch, Peking, April 6, 1927; and Kuo-wen chou-pao, IV, No. 13 (April 10, 1927), 4-5.

2. The number of prisoners has been variously estimated, one source giving as high a figure as 105: 35 Russians and 70 Chinese. See China Weekly Review, (April 16, 1927). Shen Pao, April 8, 1927, gives a total of 97 prisoners: 22 Russians and 75 Chinese. The China Press, April 7, 1927, reports a total of 64 prisoners. According to the official announcement issued by the Ankuochün headquarters on the evening of April 6, 1927, 36 persons who were allegedly Chinese Communists were arrested; see People's Tribune, April 12, 1927, Special Tribune Service dispatch, Peking, April 6, 1927. According to Tass, 15 Russians were taken prisoners; see North China Star, April 14, 1927, Tass dispatch, Peking, April 12, 1927. The discrepancy in the figures may be explained by the fact that a number of Russian women and children and Chinese servants employed at the Soviet offices were released the evening of the raid or shortly thereafter.

3. See, for instance, People's Tribune, April 17, 1927, United Press dispatch, April 13, 1927: "Shadow of War Darkens Peking; Remembers 1914."

4. Oudendyk, Ways and By-Ways in Diplomacy, pp. 348-50. Oudendyk's account is substantiated by contemporary evidence. Interviewed on April 7, 1927, U.S. Minister John Van Antwerp MacMurray confirmed reports that the ministers had granted permission to search the offices of the Chinese Eastern Railway and the Dalbank; see People's Tribune, April 12, 1927, Special Tribune Service dispatch, Peking April 7, 1927. In the British House of Commons, Foreign Secretary Sir Austen Chamberlain made a statement to the same effect on April 11, 1927; see Toynbee, Survey of International Affairs, 1927, p. 343.

5. Shen Pao, April 8, 1927, Reuters Pacific Service dispatch, Peking, April 6, 1927. Oudendyk was reported by Toho News Agency to have said on the evening of April 6, 1927, that the Diplomatic Corps was unable to keep the Chinese police from searching the premises of the Soviet Embassy, as Soviet Russia was not a signa-

tory to the last Boxer Protocol. See China Press, April 9, 1927,
Toho News Agency dispatch, Peking, April 7, 1927.

6. See, for instance, China Press, April 9, 1927, Reuters Pacific
Service dispatch, Peking April 7, 1927.

7. China Press, April 10, 1927, Reuters dispatch, Peking, April
8, 1927; People's Tribune, April 12, 1927, National News Agency
dispatch, Shanghai, April 9, 1927.

8. Kuo-wen chou-pao, IV, No. 13 (April 10, 1927), 5.

9. Chinese Government White Book; see reprint in Chinese Social
and Political Science Review, XI (1927), 153-155.

10. See Part VII, pp. 402-9, on the cooperation between Kuomintang members and Communists in Peking.

11. Hankow Herald, April 22, 1927, Reuters dispatch, April 21,
1927; Chinese Government White Book, pp. 149-151; Soviet Plot in
China, pp. 157-58.

12. People's Tribune, April 13, 1927, Tass dispatch, Moscow,
April 10, 1927; Chinese Government White Book, pp. 144-48;
Soviet Plot in China, pp. 153-57.

13. See Part VII, pp. 397-400.

14. "Letter from the Central Supervisory Committee to the Central
Executive Committee," pp. 53-55.

15. "Important Points concerning the Conference on Party Affairs
Held by Leaders of the Kuomintang," pp. 33-34.

16. Wang Ching-wei, "On Separating the Communists from the
KMT at Wuhan," pp. 600-601.

17. "A Joint Declaration by Leaders of the Kuomintang and the
Chinese Communist Party," pp. 36-37.

18. Shen Pao, April 9, 1927; China Press, April 14, 1927; Chiang
Kai-shek, Chiang Chieh-shih ti ko-ming kung-tso, pp. 240-41.

19. North China Star, April 14, 1927, Reuters dispatch, Moscow,
April 12, 1927.

20. People's Tribune, April 22, 1927. By then there were two
Kuomintang governments. Chiang Kai-shek and his supporters
had formed a government at Nanking in opposition to the Wuhan
Government after taking armed action against the Communists in
Shanghai, Canton, and other areas under their control.

21. I Ch'ing, "The Soviet Embassy Case," pp. 7-9.

22. China Weekly Review, (April 16, 1927); People's Tribune,
April 21, 1927; North China Star, April 29, 1927.

23. People's Tribune, April 12, 1927, Special Tribune Service
dispatch, Peking, April 7, 1927; Chinese Government White Book,
pp. 143-44; Soviet Plot in China, pp. 152-53.

24. People's Tribune, April 12, 1927, Special Tribune Service dispatch, Peking, April 7, 1927. This argument was repeated by a spokesman of the Soviet Embassy on April 12, 1927. See People's Tribune,
April 19, 1927, United Press dispatch, Peking, April 12, 1927.

25. The Times (London), April 9, 1927, dispatch of The Times correspondent from Riga, Latvia, April 8, 1927.

26. See International Press Correspondence, VII (April 14, 1927), 491-92. Relations between Soviet Russia and England were strained and approaching a crisis. On February 23, 1927, the British Foreign Secretary, Sir Austen Chamberlain, handed a note to M. Rosengolz, Soviet representative, charging the USSR with hostility against the British Empire. The note declared that it was futile for the USSR to pretend that attacks on British interests in China were not instigated and directed by the Soviet Union. Note from His Majesty's Government..., pp. 4-5.

27. See note 12 above.

28. "Who is Responsible for the Peking Raid?" p. 547; North China Star, April 14, 1927, Tass dispatch, Moscow, April 11, 1927; China Press, April 13, 1927, Tass dispatch, Moscow, April 11, 1927. Rykov did not indicate the source of the document to which he referred or the reasons for its reliability. The Soviet accusation against White Russians later became more specific. On May 6, 1927, Pravda charged that Russian White-Guardists were experts at making counterfeit anti-Soviet documents, and referred to their close collaboration with the Ankuochün as proof that forged documents could have been smuggled in. See translation in dispatch from Chargé d'Affaires Louis Sussdorf, Jr., Riga, Latvia, to Secretary of State, May 9, 1927; State Department Archives 893.00B/334.

29. See Note 12 above.

30. People's Tribune, April 15, 1927, United Press dispatch, Peking, April 11, 1927.

31. Note of Chinese Foreign Office to the Chinese chargé d'affaires in Moscow. See Note 9 above.

32. The Soviet government took no retaliatory measures against the Peking Government, although the latter had rejected the Soviet's demands. Litvinov's note of April 9, 1927 states that the Soviet government had sufficient technical resources to resort to repressive measures. However, the note went on, the Soviet government was conscious that the imperialists were attempting to provoke the USSR into war and that the Peking Government was merely a tool. Hence, the Soviet government desisted from such repressive measures in the interests of peace. See Note 12 above. Rykov's speech at the All-Russian Congress of Soviets re-emphasized the Soviet intention to pursue a peaceful policy; see Note 28 above. The Soviet attitude was widely interpreted as conciliatory. MacMurray, the United States Minister, suggested that the withdrawal of the Soviet Embassy was not an empty gesture but an acknowledgment of defeat. See "No. 1036. The Minister in China (MacMurray) to the Secretary of State, extracts, Peking, May 10, 1927," in Foreign Relations of the United States (1927), p. 10.

33. China Press, April 7, 1927.

34. The Times (London), April 9, 1927, dispatch from The Times correspondent, Peking, April 8, 1927.

35. Ibid.

36. Telegram from Minister MacMurray, Peking, to Secretary of State, April 27, 1927, in State Department Archives 893.00B/285.

37. Letter from General John Magruder to Professor C. Martin Wilbur, August 8, 1951. The following passages are quoted:

"I witnessed the seizure of the Office of the Soviet Military Attaché, adjacent to the Soviet Embassy compound, from which the documents in question all came....The French and British Military Attachés and myself were the first and for a while the only foreigners permitted to see the documents. The Northern Chinese officials were completely at a loss to know what to do with them or how to exploit them. We three attachés, being in good favor with Chang Tso-lin, were given ready access to the material. After a period of unsystematic fumbling through the papers, we agreed that we should pool our resources....One of my assistant attachés of foreign origin knew the Russian language well and was detailed in charge of the project of selecting the more important documents, photographing some of the originals, and translating them into English. This he did well and methodically, assisted in the translation by some reliable Russians well known to us and who had long been resident in China. These translations into English were published by the Chinese under the direct supervision of my assistant in a series of pamphlets....Assuming that the documents on which you are working are those to which I refer above, I can assure you that the series contained in the original English translation which were chosen and prepared under my personal direction (a) are translations of authentic documents and (b) are authentic and conscientious translations of the documents used....It was thought that the documents we had chosen were the only ones of major significance as bearing upon the situation at that time. From the point of view of historical research today, I am sure that much material of intriguing nature was passed over in those mounds of paper."

38. China Press, April 14, 1927, Reuters dispatch, April 13, 1927.

39. Letter from Ou Tsing [Wu Chin] to Minister MacMurray, April 13, 1927. State Department Archives 701/1927.

40. China Press, April 14, 1927, Reuters dispatch, April 13, 1927; Shen Pao, April 14, 1927.

41. A memorandum in the State Department Archives reports a visit made by United States Senator Hiram Bingham to Chang Tso-lin and Yang Yu-ting, during which Senator Bingham suggested that a "scientist" of established reputation be selected to supervise the examination of evidence found on the premises of the Soviet

Embassy. The enemies of Chang Tso-lin, Bingham pointed out, were sure to attack any evidence as manufactured, and a recognized "scientist" would disarm such criticism both in China and the United States. According to the memorandum, Yang was impressed, asked for a suggestion, then suggested Roy Chapman Andrews. Minister MacMurray was then asked to wire Andrews. (See Memorandum for the Minister, April 25, 1927, signed HB/b [Hiram Bingham?]; State Department Archives 701/1927.) MacMurray subsequently wired the American Consul General in Shanghai to deliver the message to Andrews. (See Telegram, Minister MacMurray to Consul General, Shanghai, April 29, 1927; State Department Archives 701/1927.) Information on ensuing developments was not found.

42. Telegram from Minister MacMurray, Peking, to Secretary of State, April 27, 1927, in State Department Archives 893.00B/295.

43. A group picture taken on that occasion is published in Su-lien yin-mou..., II.

44. The Times (London), April 29, 1927, dispatch from The Times correspondent, Peking, April 28, 1927.

45. Shen Pao, May 1, 1927, Reuters dispatch, April 30, 1927.

46. Memorandum for the Minister, May 3, 1927, signed by John Magruder, State Department Archives 701/1927. Magruder stated that Captain Ratay and the British Military Attaché, Colonel Steward, provided him with this information.

47. Shigeru Honjo, Military Attaché at the Japanese Legation in China, letter of transmittal to Eitaro Hata, Vice-Minister of War, May 26, 1927, in Mitsu dai nikki, 1927, V.

48. The Times (London), April 29, 1927, dispatch from The Times correspondent, Peking, April 28, 1927.

49. Shigeru Honjo, letter of transmittal to Eitaro Hata, May 26, 1927, in Mitsu dai nikki, 1927, V.

50. China Press, April 21, 1927, Reuters dispatch, Peking, April 19, 1927; Shen Pao, April 21, 1927.

51. Oudendyk, for instance, presented his own translation of the document in a reminiscent account of the raid written in 1939. See Oudendyk, Ways and By-Ways in Diplomacy, p. 351.

52. Su-lien yin-mou..., II. We quote the following from Mr. Leo Gruliow's explanatory note, dated October 16, 1951:

"The following is translated from two photographed pages, the left-hand side and bottom of which are either burned off or torn in wavy contours suggestive of burning. On the second page the right-hand side has been sliced off in a straight line or covered over or simply was beyond the camera range, so that the ends of lines, usually only a few letters but in some cases constituting an entire word, do not show. The pages are crumpled and one line in the middle of the page failed utterly to photograph, either because of

highlighting from the crumpling or because it was "washed out" of
the photo. Words of which only a few letters remain and which can
only be guessed are translated in brackets with quotation marks.
Leaders (...) are used for missing words or parts of words. Typing
of this Russian mss. is execrable."

53. Mr Gruliow states, "The typist [of the original Russian
document] started to type 'anti-Chinese,' then overtyped the word
'anti-European.'"

54. Telegram, Minister MacMurray, Peking, to Secretary of
State, April 22, 1927, State Department Archives 893.00B/291.

55. Shen Pao, April 23, 1927; China Press, April 24, 1927,
Reuters Pacific Service dispatch, April 23, 1927; The Times
(London), April 23, 1927, dispatch from The Times correspondent,
Peking, April 22, 1927. Photographs of five original documents, in-
cluding one already released, were received by the U.S. Naval
Attaché in Peking; see telegram, Naval Attaché to Navy Intelligence,
received April 24, 1927, State Department Archives 893.00B/305.
The four documents are (1) instructions to agents for hiring spies
in legations; (2) agreement of Chang Bo-hua for employing spies;
(3) estimate of funds required for military-political work in
China for the first half of year 1925-1926; and (4) minutes of a
meeting of the Military Council of Russian advisers at Canton, July
1, 1925. These documents are available in Chinese Government
White Book and Soviet Plot in China.

56. North China Star, April 29, 1927.

57. The Soviet in China Unmasked: Documents Revealing Bolshevistic Plans and Methods, Seized in the USSR Embassy, Peking,
April 6, 1927.

58. The first of the six pamphlets published by the Peking Metropolitan Police Headquarters under the over-all title of the Soviet Plot
in China and cited herein as the Chinese Government White Book,
appeared on May 17, 1927. The first pamphlet contained five documents. See Hankow Herald, May 17, 1927. By June 30, 1927, four
more pamphlets had been released, bringing the total to 28. The
sixth pamphlet, containing four documents, was not released until
July, 1927. (See dispatch from Minister MacMurray, Peking, to
Secretary of State, June 30, 1927; dispatch from Minister Mac-
Murray, Peking, to Secretary of State, August 1, 1927, State Department Archives 893.00B/384; 893.00B/394.) The Peking and Tientsin
Times issued supplements on May 12, May 24, May 28, and June
16, 1927, containing altogether 27 documents. These were reprinted
by the Tientsin British Committee of Information as a series of
pamphlets, Bolshevik Activities in China (Tientsin, June, 1927).

59. With few exceptions, the same documents were published in the
the press and pamphlets and mentioned in Minister MacMurray's
reports.

60. The Times (London), April 23, 1927, dispatch from The Times correspondent, Peking, April 22, 1927.

61. China Press, April 24, 1927, Reuters dispatch, Peking, April 23, 1927.

62. North China Star, April 26, 1927, dispatch from Randall Gould, Peking, April 26, 1927; People's Tribune, May 14, 1927, dispatch from Randall Gould, United Press staff correspondent.

63. Editorial in The Times (London), May 6, 1927.

64. Su-lien yin-mou..., I.

65. "Foreword," Chinese Government White Book, pp. 153-55; Soviet Plot in China, pp. iii-iv.

66. North China Star, April 26, 1927, Randall Gould dispatch, Peking, April 26, 1927; People's Tribune, May 14, 1927, Randall Gould (UP) dispatch. Randall Gould reiterated his position in 1946, stating that the Soviet representative in Peking exposed the documents as "forgeries of the crudest sort, concocted by White Russians in Chang's entourage and employing the old Russian alphabet." See Randall Gould, China in the Sun, p. 52.

67. People's Tribune, May 5, 1927, dispatch from the Berliner Tageblatt correspondent, Peking, April 29, 1927.

68. "Appeal of the CI against the Monstrous Atrocities in Peking," p. 563. An independent English translation is in a dispatch from Chargé d'Affaires Louis Sussdorf, Jr., Riga, Latvia, to Secretary of State, May 3, 1927, State Department Archives 893.00B/327.

69. The Times (London), May 7, 1927, dispatch from The Times correspondent, Riga, May 6, 1927.

70. China Press, May 7, 1927, Reuters dispatch, Moscow, May 6, 1927.

71. Translation in dispatch from Chargé d'Affaires Louis Sussdorf, Jr., Riga, Latvia, to Secretary of State, May 9, 1927, State Department Archives 893.00B/334.

72. The Times (London), May 7, 1927, dispatch from The Times correspondent, Riga, May 6, 1927. The S.S. "Pamiat Lenina," a Russian merchant steamer en route from Vladivostok to Hankow, was seized at Pukow on February 28, 1927, by Chang Tsung-ch'ang, an ally of Chang Tso-lin. Mrs. Fanny Borodin, a number of Soviet couriers, and the crew were arrested and sent to Tsinan for trial. The Ankuochün asserted on March 17, 1927, that a vast amount of Red propaganda material was found on board the "Pamiat Lenina." See The China Year Book 1928, pp. 789-91.

73. "Events in China," Rokoku narabi-ni Dai-san Intānashyonaru no taigai sakudō ni kansuru shōko tekihatsu jiken.

74. Shigeru Honjo, letters of transmittal to Eitaro Hata, May 26, 1927, June 6, 1927, and June 14, 1927, in Mitsu dai nikki, 1927, V.

75. See, for instance, the telegram from Minister MacMurray,

Peking, to the Secretary of State, April 27, 1927, State Department
Archives 893.00B/295; dispatch, Councilor of Legation Ferdinand
Mayer, Peking, to Secretary of State, May 11, 1927, State Depart-
ment Archives 893.00B/352; dispatch, Consul in Charge, D. C.
Berger, Tientsin Consulate-General, to State Department, May 10,
1927, State Department Archives 893.00B/346; and telegram, Naval
Attaché to Naval Intelligence, received April 24, 1927, State De-
partment Archives, 893.00B/305.

The documents are accepted as authentic in the following accounts
written by foreign diplomatic officers who had seen the documents:
Count Carlo Sforza, "Imperialistic Russia in China," p. 68 (Sforza,
then Italian Ambassador to France, was in Peking immediately after
the raid); Sir Eric Teichman, Affairs of China; p. 65 (Sir Eric
was Chinese Secretary at the British Legation); and Oudendyk,
Ways and By-ways in Diplomacy.

76. Shen Pao, May 1, 1927; The Times (London), April 29, 1927,
dispatch from The Times correspondent, April 28, 1927; "A Note on the
Genuineness of the Documents by a Missionary Who Examined Them,"
Peking, May 3, 1927, in The Soviet in China Unmasked.

77. The Times (London), April 29, 1927, from The Times correspondent dispatch April 28, 1927.

78. The Times (London), April 23, 1927, Times correspondent
dispatch, April 22, 1927.

79. Editorial, The Times (London), May 6, 1927.

80. Enclosed in dispatch from C. E. Gauss, Shanghai Consulate
General to Secretary of State, May 12, 1927, State Department Archives 893.00B/349. The article does not specify which documents
were exhibited.

81. Su-lien yin-mou..., I. A breakdown of the total number of
files follows: (1) Four hundred and sixty-three files of documents in
Russian. The content of each document in each file is listed page
by page. The number of documents in the files varies greatly. A
conservative estimate would be that approximately 3,000 documents in Russian are included in the 463 files; (2) 514 files of original Chinese documents. Judging by the catalogue, which does not list
the content of each document page by page, each file generally contains
one document; (3) 216 files of miscellaneous Chinese and Russian documents. Judging by the catalogue, which does not list the content
of each page of the documents, each file consists of one document.
A wide assortment of documents are included—original documents
of the KMT and KCT, some in Russian translation; Chinese, English, and Japanese newspaper clippings, some in Russian translation; Soviet documents on Chinese groups and organizations;
Soviet news agency dispatches, etc.; and (4) 12 files of documents
in German. The content of each page of each document is listed,
indicating that more than one document is contained in each file.

Most of these documents were presumably stolen from the German Legation in Peking and the German consulates in Shanghai and Hankow.

The catalogue also lists the following as seized from the Soviet Embassy premises: 744 books in German, French, Russian, English, and Japanese; 63 Chinese Communist books; 22 novels; magazines; 295 maps; and 46 account books. Soviet representatives in Peking declared shortly after the raid that most of the seized material was taken from a club library in the Embassy premises; apparently they were referring to this second category. See People's Tribune, May 14, 1927, dispatch from United Press staff correspondent Randall Gould, Peking; North China Star, April 26, 1927.

82. Photographs of 27 Russian documents are printed in the six original pamphlets which make up the Chinese Government White Book. Twenty-three of these, plus two additional photographs, are in the State Department Archives. Photostats are available at the East Asiatic Library, Columbia University. Su-lien yin-mou... is illustrated with 11 photographs.

83. If the seized documents were taken to Japan, it is conceivable that they are in the United States. It is possible also that they are in the USSR if they were not removed from the China mainland to Japan or Taiwan.

84. Su-lien yin-mou... contains 324 Chinese translations of Russian documents and original Chinese documents. A number of additional original documents in Chinese are available in Mitsu dai nikki, 1927, V.

85. Most of the original Chinese documents are published under the heading "Chinese Communist Party," in Su-lien yin-mou..., III, and in Mitsu dai nikki, 1927, V. Twenty-three documents in our collection are translations of original Chinese documents.

86. Most documents in this group are classified under the headings "Canton," "Kuominchün," "Shansi," and "Three Special Areas" in Su-lien yin-mou..., III. Additional documents of this type are available also in Japanese collections. Twenty seven documents in our collection were written in Russian.

87. Documents of this group are published under the headings "Political," "Military," "Secret Agents," "Party Affairs," "Miscellaneous," "Military-Political Conspiracy," in Su-lien yin-mou....

88. The majority of such documents are grouped in the sections "Mongolia," "Chinese Eastern Railway," and "Soviet Trade and Commerce in Manchuria" in Su-lien yin-mou....

89. Ten Kuomintang documents were classified erroneously under the section heading "Chinese Communist Party" in Su-lien yin-mou..., III. They are: "Plans for the Development of Party

Affairs in the Provinces"; "Proposals of the Peking Special Municipal Party Headquarters to the Third Plenum of the Central Executive Committee"; "Telegram of the Peking Executive Headquarters Reporting on the Elections and the Condition of Its
Work"; "Report No. 2 of the Third Executive Committee of the
Peking Special Municipal Party Headquarters"; "Resolutions on
the Labor Movement"; "Report of the 12th District Executive Committee to the Municipal Party Headquarters"; "Interrelationship
between Party Headquarters of All Levels"; "Duties of Party Headquarters of All Levels"; "Urgent Notice of the Secretariat of the
Peking Municipal Party Headquarters"; and "Notices of the Executive Committee of the Peking Special Municipal Party Headquarters."

90. Ch'en Tu-hsiu, "Reactionary tendencies of the KMT New
Right Wing," pp. 1265-67.

91. "Important Documents of the Western Hills Conference
Expelling Communists from the KMT," pp. 14-16.

92. Chang Kuo-t'ao, "An Open Letter to All Members of the
Kuomintang," pp. 1269-70.

93. Central Committees of the Chinese Communist Party and
the Chinese Communist Youth Corps, "Manifesto on the Anti-
Mukden War," pp. 124-26.

94. Central Committees of the Chinese Communist Party and
the Chinese Communist Youth Corps. "Statement to the People of
the Country on the Alliance between Wu P'ei-fu and Mukden against
the Kuominchün," pp. 144-46.

95. Ch'en Tu-hsiu, "The Situation in the South and the Kuomintang," pp. 1459-60.

96. Chung-kuo Kung-ch'an-tang tui-yü shih-chü ti chu-chang.

97. The terms "CY" and "CP" were regularly used in Chinese
Communist literature. See, for instance, articles in Hsiang-tao
chou-pao. The codes "People's School" and "Our School" were
used in "internal" Party documents. See, for instance, "Resolutions
on the Problem of the KMT Left Wing...," pp. 68-77.

98. See the glossary of Chinese names for proper names the
Commission failed to identify.

99. Preface, Su-lien yin-mou..., II.

100. According to a Toho News Agency dispatch from Peking on
April 7, 1927, Li Ta-chao was arrested in Room 28 which was
known as the headquarters of the Communists in Peking, in the
building formerly occupied by the Imperial Russian guards. See
China Press, April 8, 1927.

101. "Instructions from the Kuomintang of China to the Party
Military Academy and the Army," pp. 77-78.

102. Chiang Kai-shek, Chiang Chieh-shih hsien-sheng, XI, 1-8.

103. Chiang Kai-shek, Chiang Chieh-shih hsiao-chang tsai Kuo-
min cheng-fu chün-shih wei-yüan-hui chiang-yen tz'u.

104. Chiang Kai-shek, Chiang Chieh-shih hsien-sheng, XI, 46-49.

105. General Stepanov participated in the First Eastern Expedition against Ch'en Ch'iung-ming in the beginning of 1925 and was appointed adviser with Chiang Kai-shek's army in July, 1925. See "A List of Soviet Officers Who Participated in the Eastern Expedition," May 2, 1925; "Minutes of the Military Conference in Canton on July 1, 1925," Su-lien yin-mou..., III, "Canton," pp. 104, 94.

106. Chiang Kai-shek, Chiang Chieh-shih hsien-sheng, XIV, 82-89.

107. Ao-li-chin served also as vice chief of the Soviet Intelligence Branch in South China. See "A List of Names and Positions of Members of the Soviet Group in South China," Su-lien yin-mou..., III, "Canton," p. 98.

108. Ivanovskii is not on lists of Soviet personnel which were seized in the raid. He is identified in Chiang Kai-shek's diary as a "military member." He was in Canton at the beginning of 1926; he apparently left for Russia at the end of March. See Chiang Kai-shek, Chiang Chieh-shih hsien-sheng, XIV, 82, 87-88. He may have been a member of Kubiak's inspection team. See Part IV, Note 76.

109. V. I. Solovyev is listed as councilor of the Soviet Embassy in Peking in 1926. See The China Year Book, 1926, p. 582.

110. Chiang Kai-shek, Chiang Chieh-shih hsien-sheng, XIII, 73.

111. "Henry A. Lin" is the name assumed by the chief Soviet adviser to Feng Yü-hsiang from September, 1925, to the summer of 1926. He is frequently mentioned in Feng Yü-hsiang's diary and autobiography as "Adviser Lin." Once he is referred to as "Ya-li-shan-ta-lin"; his middle name may have been "Alexander." See Feng Yü-hsiang, Wo ti sheng-huo, III, 54. According to Feng, Lin had been a newspaper reporter in Russia and later joined the army. See Feng Yü-hsiang, Feng Yü-hsiang jih-chi, II, 12.

112. Feng Yü-hsiang, Feng Yü-hsiang jih-chi, II, 126.

113. "Catalogue of Russian Documents of Secondary Importance," Su-lien yin-mou..., I, 5.

114. Preface, Su-lien yin-mou..., II.

115. According to a Soviet personnel list which was apparently drawn up around the end of 1926, "Pavlov" is the assumed name of a Russian who served for a time in the Eighth Army in an unspecified position. See "A List of Real Names, Assumed Names, and Positions in the Army of Members of the Soviet Group in South China," Su-lien yin-mou..., III, "Canton," p. 101.

116. "Theses on the Chinese Question adopted by the Seventh Enlarged ECCI Plenum," and "Resolutions of the Sixth Plenum of the Executive Committee of the Young Communist International," in Su-lien yin-mou..., II, "Political," p. 11, and III, "Party Affairs," p. 7.

117. "Resolutions of the Sixth Plenum of the Executive Committee

of the Young Communist International," Su-lien yin-mou..., III,
"Party Affairs," p. 14.

118. Document 13, "Chiang Kai-shek's letter to Galen, June 26,
1925." The term "t'ung-ling" appears in Chiang's diary (Chiang
Kai-shek, Chiang Chieh-shih hsien-sheng, XI, 3). It appears as
a proper name, "Tung Ling," in Su-lien yin-mou..., III, "Canton,"
p. 17. Presumably the mistake was first made by persons who
translated into Russian Chiang's letter in Chinese. The document
was allegedly found in Russian when seized.

119. "A Brief History of the KCT," Su-lien yin-mou..., III, "KCT,"
p. 3.

120. Document 24, p. 83.

121. Preface, Su-lien yin-mou..., II.

122. Document 1, "A Brief History of the KCT," Su-lien yin
mou..., III, "KCT," p. 45. Checked against an English translation,
A History of Communism in China.

123. Ibid., p. 8. Checked against A History of Communism in
China.

124. Ibid., p. 33.

125. A History of Communism in China, p. 36.

126. See, for instance, Documents 23, 24, 36, 37, 39, and 42.

127. A photograph of the seized Russian copy is printed in the
second pamphlet of the Chinese Government White Book. A photostat made from a photograph in the State Department Archives is
available at the East Asiatic Library, Columbia University. English
translations of this document are in the Chinese Government
White Book, pp. 169-93, and Soviet Plot in China, pp. 2-23. A Chinese translation is in Su-lien yin-mou..., II, "Political," pp. 1-18.
Japanese translations are in Rokoku no tai-shi sekka undō jissō,
Appendix, and Pekin Rōnō Taishikan yori ōshū shitaru himitsu
bunsho, XII. The theses in the original Russian document and in
the English, Chinese, and Japanese translations are numbered one
through 10; the third thesis, however, directly follows the first
one, so there are actually only nine.

128. Puti Mirovoi Revolutsii, II, 435-46; Kommunisticheskii
Internatsional v Dokumentakh, pp. 668-80. Seven theses are given
in the above Russian publications. The third thesis in the copy
allegedly seized in the raid is listed as the second thesis, the fourth
as the third, and so on. The ninth and tenth theses in the allegedly
seized copy are entirely missing. The following English translations
of the "Theses" prepared by Comintern organs have been checked:
International Press Correspondence, Vol. VII, No. 11 (Feb. 3,
1927), pp. 230-34; The Communist, Vol. I, No. 2 (March 19, 1927),
pp. 59-72. Each of these gives eight theses. The Communist version
is introduced as the "final and complete resolution adopted after
an exhaustive discussion at the Chinese Commission held during

the Plenum." The first thesis given in Russian Comintern sources and in the document allegedly seized in the raid is split into two; the second half is entitled "Social Forces of the Chinese Revolution," and is numbered Thesis No. 2. Thus, the numbering of the theses beginning with No. 3 corresponds with the numbering in the allegedly seized copy. The ninth and tenth extra theses of the allegedly seized document are, however, similarly absent in the official Comintern English translations.

129. Compare Point 24 of the first extra thesis, "Armed Forces of the Chinese Revolution," (p. 22) with Point 13 (p. 15); Point 25 (p. 22) with Point 18 (pp. 18-19) and Point 12 (pp. 14-15). The second part of Point 26 (pp. 22-23) is identical with the last paragraph of Point 22 (p. 22), which is itself missing from official Comintern publications. Compare Point 27 (p. 23) with Points 11 and 12 (pp. 13-15). Compare the second extra thesis, "Tasks of the Communist Parties in Imperialist Countries," (p. 23) with Point 3 (p. 5) and Point 18 (p. 19). Page numbers refer to the Soviet Plot in China.

130. Compare Point 23 (Soviet Plot in China, p. 22) with Stalin's speech, "Prospects of the Revolution in China," p. 1582. Also compare it with Point 1 (Soviet Plot in China, p. 3).

131. For instance, according to Robert C. North, M. N. Roy informed him in an interview at Dehra Dun, India, October 15, 1951, that two sets of theses on the Chinese question were prepared. The preliminary theses were drafted by Andrei S. Bubnov, Fedor F. Raskolnikov, and Gregory N. Voitinskii. They were found useless and Stalin asked Bubnov, Bukharin, and Roy to draw up another set. See North, Moscow and Chinese Communists, p. 90. It is doubtful, however, whether Roy's explanation can account for the extra theses, for the implication is that the two sets of theses are entirely different. According to Harold R. Isaacs, the theses were drafted by Bukharin and Stalin. See Isaacs, Tragedy of the Chinese Revolution, p. 117.

132. A dispatch by Randall Gould refers to a statement of Soviet officials in Peking to the effect that translations into English of the allegedly seized Russian documents were being made with great liberty. As proof, Soviet officials cited previously published proceedings of the Comintern which were checked with the English translations released to the Peking press. They found "a difference at several points." See North China Star, April 26, 1927, Randall Gould's dispatch from Peking, April 26, 1927; People's Tribune, May 14, 1927, Randall Gould (UP) dispatch. While Gould did not specify the document in question, it seems likely that the "Theses" was meant, since this was the only Comintern document among the first papers released that had previously been published. As far as we know, the issue of the "extra theses" has never before been raised.

133. Letter from Mr. David J. Dallin to C. Martin Wilbur, March 29, 1954. In another letter of July 19, 1954, Mr. Dallin elaborates on the sentence and term in Point 23 which appear to him inappropriate in a Comintern resolution. He writes:

"Here is the translation of this sentence:

'To this effect it is necessary along [with] energetic political work in the basic corpses of the National Revolutionary armies, to organize and develop by appropriate transfer of political workers for political work [in the midst of] the adhering politically not processed corpses.'

"In parenthesis I have inserted words which, strangely enough are missing in the Russian text: without these words the phrase has as little sense in Russian as it has in English. But even assuming that this omission is an error of the typist, the sentence as a whole is awkward. The author [or the forgers] of this phrase wanted to say that Communist propagandists ('political workers') must be assigned to military units which had recently joined the national revolutionary army; they could not find, however, a better way to express this simple idea than the phrase given above.

"The term which in my view puts in doubt the authenticity of the whole section is the not processed corps. Basically the term 'obrabotannyi' means 'tilled' (or ploughed, or manipulated, or processed). The first time the term was taken over to the political sphere was in 1917, when Russian army units at the German front refused to fight and joined the 'defeatist movement' which, in a way, was identified with Bolshevism. The non-Bolsheviks, especially the rightist press, accused Lenin and his party of sending propagandists into the army to disintegrate it; a regiment which had fallen for the Bolshevik propaganda was in this sense a 'obrabotannyi' (processed) regiment.

"I would not be surprised if the word 'processed army unit' would be found, for instance, in a letter of one private person to another; it is out of the question, however, that the Comintern should have used a term which, in addition, has a touch of slang in it, in a solemn resolution."

134. According to Mr. Leo Gruliow.

135. According to Soviet Plot in China, the "Instructions," enclosing the "Theses," were received by the Soviet Military Attaché on March 28, 1927. See Soviet Plot in China, p. 3. The "Instructions" are not dated, but apparently were drafted after the Hankow Incident of January 3, 1927.

136. Points 2 and 6 of the "Theses." Soviet Plot in China, pp. 4, 8, 9.

137. Point 17 of the "Theses." Ibid., pp. 17-18.

138. Point 12 of the "Theses." Ibid., pp. 14-15.

139. An English translation of the "Instructions to the Soviet

Military Attache" is in <u>Soviet Plot in China</u>, pp. 1-2. A Chinese
translation is in <u>Su-lien yin-mou...</u>, II, "Political," pp. 18-20. The
following are other examples of discrepancies between the alleged
Russian original and the English and Chinese translations. (1) The
English and Chinese translations do not explain that the term
"anti-European" was typed over the term "anti-Chinese" in the
second instruction; (2) While only the word "British" is legible at
the end of the fourth instruction, the English and Chinese translations give the following: "particularly against British." (3) In the
fifth instruction, the English translation reconstructs the words
"the foreigners," against whom the people should be stirred. The
words "repressive measures" are reconstructed in the following
sentence referring to the actions of foreigners. The Chinese translation gives the same words without indicating that they are reconstructed. (4) In the sixth instruction, the phrase "We have categorically ordered Borodin to abstain for the present" precedes "too
strong pressure on capitalist elements" in the English and Chinese
translations. The English translation explains that the phrase
had been erased but that the indentations made by the typewriter
were visible when the sheet was held up to the light. The Chinese
translation does not indicate the phrase was reconstructed. According to Mr. Gruliow, the line in which this phrase occurs is indeci-
pherable in our photostat of the original Russian document. Judging
by several disconnected words which are faintly legible, however,
the above reconstruction is not impossible.

According to the Chinese translation, only half of the allegedly
seized document was salvaged from the fire. Another copy of the
Chinese translation accompanying a facsimile reproduction of the
alleged Russian original in the same volume states that only one
third had been preserved.

140. Letter from David J. Dallin to C. Martin Wilbur, March
29, 1954. Herewith we quote the opinion of Mr Dallin on several
other documents which he suspected. In a letter of November 20,
1952, after examining a collection of 28 translations into English
and 4 original English documents, he wrote:

"I have studied the collection of documents relating to the raid
of the Soviet Embassy compound in Peking in 1927. Offhand my
conclusion is the following: Three documents are certainly forged,
three others are probably false; the greater part of the other
documents are certainly genuine.

"The forged documents are:

"No. 1. 'Instruction to Agents.' It contains Soviet instructions
for hiring spies in other legations. I am certain such instructions
have never been given in writing; besides, they are primitive,
childish and awkward. The document is a poor falsification. [The
document number is that given in the <u>Chinese Government White</u>

Book. In Soviet Plot in China it is numbered 34. Hereafter we give numbers from that collection in parenthesis. The document was allegedly found in English.]

"No. 3. 'Instructions to the Military Attaché.' What is said above about Doc. No. 1 applies here also. [(No. 1) This document has been discussed in our text.]

"No. 29. 'Proletkino.' The Cheka was abolished about three years before the letter had allegedly been written; it is inconceivable that an agency in Moscow should not know the correct name of the Secret Police Department—the GPU. [(No. 44) We venture the comment that the Cheka is mentioned as the subject of a motion picture which may have been produced before the change of name, or which may have been about the earlier period. The document is dated November 23, 1923. The document was allegedly found in English.]

"The three documents which, in my view, are very dubious are:

"No. 2. 'Agreement for employing spies.' [(No. 36) The document was allegedly in English as found.]

"No. 30. No title. At least certain paragraphs are false, f.i., the par. 'In order that these...' The Communist Party of the Soviet Union was called at that time VKP (b). It does not seem probable that a Soviet report should use the obsolete term RKP. [(No. 15) The photograph was illegible. Might these errors be due to the translators?]

"No. 31. 'Regulations Relating to South China.' It is unlikely that the term 'sovietism' should be used in a Soviet document; some other expressions in this document, too, are rather dubious. [(No. 11) Might these errors be due to the translators?]

"While questioning the authenticity of these documents I have no doubts concerning the other papers as far as I have studied them; nor have I any doubts as far as the general political inferences are concerned—about the aims and methods of Soviet intervention in Chinese affairs.

"I have not had the possibility to study thoroughly each of the documents. Such a work would mean weighing every sentence, every word and checking the Russian originals of which the photostats are poor and partly illegible."

Mr. Dallin studied a collection of 25 photographs of Russian documents in March, 1954. In a letter of March 29, 1954, he states:

"1. As to the major part of the documents (marked 'A'), I have no reason to doubt their authenticity. This applies to:

"'Protokol' [Chinese Government White Book, No. 21; Soviet Plot in China, No. 42. 'Report concerning Intelligence Work in Kwangtung'].

"'Obshchaya Svodka' [Chinese Government White Book, No. 24;

(Soviet Plot in China, No. 24). 'General Budget for the "Groups,"
the "Central Apparatus" and the Canton Group.']
"'Uvazhaiemy Tovarishch....' [Soviet Plot in China, No. 34.
'Letter to Moscow Forwarding Documents Stolen from the Japanese
Military Attache's Office.']
"'Ob Oruzhii' [White Book, No 12; Soviet Plot, No. 18. "Statement
of Arms and Ammunition Delivered to the First Kuominchün Army.']
"'Shifrom. Kanton' [White Book, No. 10; Soviet Plot, No. 13.
'Draft of Telegram, Dated July 4th, 1926, to Galen, Canton.']
"'Galinu' [White Book, No. 9; Soviet Plot, No. 12. 'Draft of Tele-
gram, Dated June 15, 1926, to Galen, Canton.']
"'Protokol Zasedaniya V.O.' [White Book, No. 22; Soviet Plot,
No. 43. 'Propaganda among Foreign Troops in Shanghai.']
"'Zapiska' [White Book, No. 14; Soviet Plot, No. 26. 'The Soviet
Military Mission with the First Kuominchün Army.']
"'Dokladnaya Zapiska o Rabote po Priemu Parokhoda "Oleg"'
[White Book, No. 23; Soviet Plot, No. 23. 'Report concerning the
Steamer Oleg.']
"'Opis' [White Book, No. 8; Soviet Plot, No. 8. 'Minutes of Meet-
ings of the Military Council of Soviet Advisers at Canton.']
"'Tov. Berzinu' [English translation not available]."

Mr. Dallin had also examined, though he did not list, the follow-
ing: (The first number is that of the document in the White Book;
the number in parentheses refers to Soviet Plot in China.)
No. 4 (No. 6). "Plan for Employment of Personnel."
No. 5 (No. 25). "Estimate of Funds Required for Military
Political Work in China for the First Half of 1925—1926."
No. 7 (No. 7). "The South China Group of Military-Political
Workers."
No. 11 (No. 14). "Draft of Telegram, Dated August 27th, 1926 to
Borodin, Canton."

"2. There are two documents which, despite certain doubts, I am
inclined to accept as authentic, namely:
"a. The 'Secret Code of the Soviet Embassy for Military Terms.'
This document, which also contains a number of non-military terms,
lists a total of 31 terms; it is amateurish and appears to be incomplete. It might represent the beginning of a genuine attempt to build
up a comprehensive coding system [No. 13 (No. 38)].
"b. 'Instructions to Write Letters in Code.' This document, too,
is short, crude, and amateurish. ('Write in good English,' it says;
'Dear Jhon [with the 'h' before the 'o']). There is no definite proof,
however, against the authenticity of the document [No. 27 (No. 36)].
"3. The document on the 'Organization of Soviet Secret Bureau
in China' is incomplete and bears neither date nor signature. It is

hard to reach a definite conclusion concerning this document. About some passages I am doubtful. The paper gives proofs that the Soviet Embassy serves as a shelter for spies and that the Trade Legations serve similar purposes; that the Soviet Embassy, the GPU, and the Intelligence Service operate on instructions of the Comintern; etc. Despite the fact that such charges were to a great extent correct, the document is too blunt and too frank about matters that are not usually put in writing. However, the document is neither absurd nor impossible. Only a part of it has been turned over to me; if the second part is found, I should be glad to review the whole document [No. 32 (No. 33)].

"4. One document ('Tablitsa') is so illegible that no judgment is possible [No. 17 (No. 21) and No. 18 (No. 22)].

"5. One document ('Posledniye Kantonskie Materialy dlya budushchei svodka') is incomplete; the fragment which is in our possession, however, appears authentic [No. 15 (No. 7)]."

The rest of Mr. Dallin's report concerns the "Instructions to the Military Attaché" and the "Theses on the Chinese Question of the Seventh Enlarged ECCI Plenum," which have been referred to above. Three photographs of the Russian documents were illegible.

In a letter dated May 30, 1954, Mr. Dallin gave his opinion on four photographs of Russian documents published in the Chinese Government White Book which are not included in the collection at the State Department Archives. He states (again, the number given first refers to the White Book, the second number to Soviet Plot in China).

"No. 16 [No. 20]. 'Obligation Signed by Feng Yü-hsiang in 1926 in Moscow.' The upper part of the document is illegible. The rest seems to be authentic.

"No. 19 [No. 19]. 'Statement of Arms and Munitions.' Russian text fairly good. I see no reason to question the authenticity of the document.

"No. 20 [No. 16]. 'Financial Report of the Soviet Military Attaché.' Russian text nearly completely legible. I see no reason to question the authenticity of the document.

"No. 26 [No. 3] is illegible."

Part I: Introduction to "A Brief History of the Chinese Communist Party"

1. The Chinese translation is in Su-lien yin-mou..., III, "KCT," pp. 1-47. The English translation is in A History of Communism in China, pp. 1-54. Our version is keyed to the Chinese but draws upon the substance of both translations. When serious differences arise, we have selected the version to be used on the basis of its relative historical accuracy. While the English translation is on

the whole superior to the Chinese, numerous errors in terms and proper names characterize both. These have been corrected in our translation.

The following lists the proper names of persons which are given incorrectly in the Chinese translation and have been corrected by us. Names given in parenthesis are the incorrect ones used in the Chinese text. They are listed in order of substitution. Shen Hsüan-lu (Shen Chih-lu); Shih Ts'un-t'ung (Shih Ch'eng-t'ung); Yüan Hsiao-hsien (Yüan Hsueh-sun); Huang Ling-shuang (Wang Lin-sheng); Chang Kuo-t'ao (Ch'en Ku-t'a); Teng Chung-hsia (Teng Chu-hsia); Lo Chang-lung (Liu Ch'ang-lung); Liu Jen-ching (Liu Jen-chin); T'an P'ing-shan (T'ang P'ing-san); Ch'en Kung-po (Ch'en Kung-p'o); T'an Chih-t'ang (T'ang Chih-tao); Li Han-chün (Li Han-ch'ing); and Huang Pi-hun (Wang P'ei-huan).

2. Ōtsuka, Shina Kyōsantō shi, I, 8.

3. Independent contemporary sources generally corroborate the account given in the "Brief History." There are, however, discrepancies in relatively minor details. One instance pertains to the First Congress of the Chinese Communist Party in Shanghai. The "Brief History" asserts that it was held in May, 1921, with eleven delegates in attendance (see Doc. 1, p. 15). This conflicts with other sources. However, the composition and date of the First Congress is a controversial subject on which a number of the Congress participants themselves disagree. The following are the accounts of four participants. According to Ch'en T'an-ch'iu and Tung Pi-wu, the Congress was held in July, 1921, with thirteen delegates: Mao Tse-tung, Ho Shu-heng, Tung Pi-wu, Ch'en T'an-ch'iu, Wang Chin-mei, Teng Fn-ming, Liu Jen-ching, Pao Hui-seng, Chou Fu-hai, Chang Kuo-t'ao, Li Han-chün, Li Ta, and Ch'en Kung-po (see Chen Pan-tsu [Ch'en T'an-ch'iu], "Reminiscences of the First Congress of the Communist Party in China," pp. 1361-66; Nym Wales, Red Dust: Autobiographies of Chinese Communists..., p. 39). According to Mao Tse-tung and Chang Kuo-t'ao, twelve delegates attended the Congress. (see Snow, Red Star Over China, p. 157; Chang Kuo-t'ao, "Mao—a New Portrait by an Old Colleague," p. 46). A possible explanation of the conflicting accounts is Tung-Pi-wu's recollection that the Party was founded in Shanghai in May, 1921, by Ch'en Tu-hsiu and Li Ta-chao, but that the First Congress did not take place until July, 1921 (see Nym Wales, Red Dust: Autobiographies of Chinese Communists..., p. 39).

4. The latest incident mentioned in the "Brief History" is the landing of British gunboats at Canton (see Doc. 1, p. 42), which took place on September 3, 1926.

5. Ōtsuka, Shina Kyōsantō shi, I, 9; Shina Kyōsantō undō shi, p. 375.

6. See Part II, pp. 93, 96; Part IV, pp. 225, 227: Part VII, pp. 376-77.

7. See Part IV, p. 225; Part VII, pp. 380, 401-3.

8. The author may have been Gregory Voitinskii, chief Comintern delegate to the Chinese Communist Party at the time the "Brief History" was written. Stationed in Shanghai, Voitinskii faithfully executed the CI's policies and guided the decisions of the CC in the manner prescribed by Moscow. See Part IV, p. 226, and Part VII, pp. 402-3. In the English translation, A History of Communism in China, authorship is credited to one Kisseleff. A person by the name of Nikolai Fedorovich Kiselev was employed as a typist at the Soviet Military Attaché's office in Peking. See Kiselev's case history in Su-lien yin-mou..., II, "Military," pp. 47-48. Kiselev's signature, preceded by the words "True Copy," is attached to many of the seized documents. In one instance, Kiselev signs himself as "secretary in charge of checking documents." See Su-lien yin-mou..., II, "Military," p. 51. Thus, we believe that Kiselev probably signed his name at the end of the "Brief History" as proofreader rather than author. He was among the 15 Russians arrested during the Peking raid. See North China Star, April 14, 1927, p. 9. According to N. Mitarevsky, the "Brief History" was signed in the following manner: "Socialist Republics, Comrade Frunze." See Mitarevsky, World-wide Soviet Plots, p. 113. It is not known whether Mitarevsky is referring to Michael Frunze, who was appointed Minister of War of the USSR in January, 1925. If so, we doubt the correctness of this supposition, because Frunze died on October 31, 1925. The "Brief History" was apparently written after September 3, 1926.

9. For instance, Ōtsuka, Shina Kyōsantō shi; Shina Kyōsantō undō shi.

10. Chin Yü-fu, "A Short History of the Chinese Communist Party Written Twenty-four Years Ago," pp. 22-26.

Part II: The Organizational Policies
of the Chinese Communist Party
1. The Declaration of July 25, 1919, signed by the Deputy Commissar for Foreign Affairs, Leo Karakhan, states: "The Soviet Government has given up all the conquests made by the government of tsars which took away from China Manchuria and other territories... returns to the Chinese people without demanding any kind of compensation, the Chinese Eastern Railway, as well as all the mining concessions, forestry, gold mines, and all the other things which were seized from them...gives up the indemnities payable by China for the insurrection of Boxers in 1900...abolished all the special privileges and all the factories owned by the Russian merchants in the Chinese territory; no Russian official, priest or missionary should be allowed to interfere with Chinese affairs; and if they should commit any crime, they must be judged according to

the local laws in local law courts..." In the Declaration of September 27, 1920, also signed by Karakhan, the Soviet Government proposed seven points in elaboration of the 1919 statement. It also suggested that a special treaty be signed "on the way of working the Chinese Eastern Railway with due regard to the needs of the Russian Socialist Federated Soviet Republic." See "The Declaration of 1919" and "The Declaration of 1920," pp. 867-72. See also Whiting, "The Soviet Offer to China of 1919," pp. 355-64, and his Soviet Policies in China, 1917-1924, pp. 269-75.

2. In a short article written on January 1, 1920, for instance, Ch'en Tu-hsiu declared that there was a causal relationship between conservatism and aggression. The socialist government of Lenin, he said, had proclaimed its desire to help China, whereas the conservative Omsk government had tried to invade Mongolia and Manchuria when it could not even preserve itself. The minds of socialists were filled with principles of humanity, equality, and mutual help. See "Random Thoughts," January 1, 1920, in Tu-hsiu wen-ts'un, II, 78-79.

3. Shina Kyōsantō undō shi, p. 80. This source gives the following list, based on an article by Chou Fu-hai, of nine participants at the conference: Ch'en Tu-hsiu, Chang Tung-sun, Shao Li-tzu, Chou Fu-hai, Ch'en Wang-tao, Li Han-chun, Shen Hsüan-lu, Yang Ming-chai, and Chang T'ai-lei. The "Brief History," which asserts that the conference took place at the beginning of 1920, gives a list of seven participants, four of whom are on Chou Fu-hai's list. See Doc. 1, p. 11.

4. Yasuhara, Sa-rempō to Shina Manshū no Kyōsan undō, p. 454.

5. Chung-kuo hsien-tai ko-ming yün-tung shih, p. 100. Tung Pi-wu recalls that another Comintern delegate, a Russian, also attended the First Congress. See Nym Wales, Red Dust: Autobiographies of Chinese Communists..., p. 39. See Part I, Note 3, on Chinese Communist delegates who attended the Congress.

6. Chen Pan-tsu (Ch'en T'an-ch'iu), "Reminiscences of the First Congress...," pp. 1363-64. Chang Kuo-t'ao confirms that a constitution was adopted at the First Congress (Chang Kuo-t'ao, in an interview with C. Martin Wilbur, Hongkong, November, 1954). The original text is apparently unavailable. The constitution was amended at the Sixth Party Congress in the summer of 1928. For the amended version, see "Constitution of the Chinese Communist Party," pp. 45-60.

7. Nym Wales, Red Dust: Autobiographies of Chinese Communists..., p. 40.

8. Chen Pan-tsu (Ch'en T'an-ch'iu), "Reminiscences of the First Congress...," p. 1364. Li Han-chün's election as a reserve member of the provisional central bureau appears strange, since, according to the "Brief History," he was expelled by the Party; see Doc. 1, p. 17. Other sources do not mention either Li Han-chün

or Liu Jen-ching as having been elected to the bureau. See, for instance, Ōtsuka, Shina Kyōsantō shi, I, 18; Shina Kyōsanto undō shi, p. 81.

9. Ōtsuka, Shina Kyōsantō shi, I, 18; Shina Kyōsantō undō shi, p. 81.

10. According to the "Brief History," Ch'en Tu-hsiu's draft party platform was not adopted at the First Congress, although the delegates approved almost all the principles outlined by him. The party platform was completely passed at the Second KCT Congress in the summer of 1922 (Doc. 1, pp. 16-17, 23).

11. "Manifesto of the Chinese Labor Union Secretariat," pp. 21-22.

12. Chen Pan-tsu (Ch'en T'an-ch'iu), "Reminiscences of the First Congress...," p. 1364; Hu Hua, Chung-kuo hsin min-chu chu-i ko-ming shih, p. 28. Maring visited Sun Yat-sen shortly after the Congress, about August or September, 1921. There is no evidence, however, that he proffered the support of the Chinese Communists to Sun. See Part III, p. 139.

13. Communist International, Theses and Statutes of the Third (Communist) International Adopted by the Second Congress, July 17th-August 7th, 1920, pp. 67-71.

14. For an interesting discussion of the conflicting views of Lenin and M. N. Roy, an Indian Communist, on Communist policy in backward and colonial areas at the Second Congress, see North, Moscow and Chinese Communists, pp. 18-20. Lenin believed it was necessary for the CI and the Communist parties to support bourgeois-democratic movements. Roy stressed the organization of the masses to struggle for their class interests. Both concepts are embodied in the "Theses on the National and Colonial Question."

15. Communist International, The First Congress of the Toilers of the Far East, Held in Moscow January 21st-February 1st, 1922. Closing Session in Petrograd, February 2nd, 1922, p. 214.

16. Ibid., pp. 165-66.

17. Doc. 1, p. 25. The Socialist Youth Corps voted to join the Young Communist International at the First Congress of the Chinese Socialist Youth Corps in May, 1922. See Yasuhara, Sarempō to Shina Manshū no Kyōsan undō, p. 454.

18. Ch'en Tu-hsiu asserts that the "Manifesto of the Second Congress" was based on the resolutions of the First Congress, of the Toilers of the Far East. See Ch'en Tu-hsiu, Kao ch'üan-tang..., p. 2. Chang Kuo-t'ao, who was a delegate at the First Congress of Toilers, recalls that he presented a detailed report on the Congress to the Chinese Communist Party's Central Committee and that the "Manifesto of the Second Congress" and the resolutions adopted at the Congress were drafted on the basis of the spirit and content of the resolutions of the First Congress of Toilers. Chang

Kuo-t'ao, in an interview with C. Martin Wilbur, Hongkong, November, 1954.

19. "Manifesto of the Second Congress of the Chinese Communist Party," pp. 19-23. The Manifesto is dated May, 1922, in our source, which was published in October, 1926, by the Central Committee of the Chinese Communist Party. According to Brandt, Schwartz, and Fairbank, Documentary History of Chinese Communism, pp. 63-65, which gives a partial English translation of the document, the "Manifesto of the Second Congress" is dated in July, 1922, after the "First Manifesto of the Chinese Communist Party." The translation in that source is based on a Japanese version published in Shina ni okeru Kyōsan undō [The Communist movement in China], published in Tokyo in 1933. We believe May, 1922, to be the correct date.

20. Chung-kuo Kung-ch'an-tang tui-yü shih-chu ti chü-chang, pp. 4-5, 11-14.

21. See Part III, p. 140.

22. Ch'en Tu-hsiu, Kao ch'üan-tang..., p. 2.

23. Ibid., pp. 2-3.

24. Maring, in an interview with Harold R. Isaacs, Amsterdam, 1935. See Isaacs, Tragedy of the Chinese Revolution, p. 59.

25. Chang Kuo-t'ao, in an interview with C. Martin Wilbur, Hongkong, November, 1954. While Chang does not think that Maring asserted his authority publicly or in so many words, he does not know whether Maring may have privately asserted the authority of the Comintern to Ch'en Tu-hsiu or whether Ch'en drew the same conclusions from Maring's manner that he, Chang, did. Chang recalls that Maring, who had been secretary of the Commission on Colonial Problems of the Second Comintern Congress, told him many times of his opposition to the position of M. N. Roy, who wanted to oppose Gandhi and the Indian Nationalists. Maring's own views were based upon his experience in Indonesia, where he had organized a party including several revolutionary groups.

26. According to one account, the Kuomintang had 138,000 members at the end of 1922. See A. N. K., "The Part played by the Kuomintang Party in the Chinese Revolution," p. 188. Yang Yu-ch'iung gives the figure of 178,875 members before January, 1924. See Yang Yu-ch'iung, Chung-kuo cheng-tang shih, p. 194.

27. Wang Ching-wei, "On Separating the Communists from the KMT at Wuhan," p. 595. According to T. C. Woo, Li Ta-chao told Sun Yat-sen he could not give up membership in the Chinese Communist Party, not the Comintern. See Woo, The Kuomintang and the Future of the Chinese Revolution, pp. 151-52.

28. Letter to Chiang Kai-shek (Nov. 21, 1922), in Sun Yat-sen, Sun Chung-shan hsien-sheng..., p. 3.

29. Chung-kuo hsien-tai ko-ming yün-tung shih, p. 130.

30. "Resolutions of the Chinese Communist Party on the National Movement and the Kuomintang Problem," pp. 15-16.

31. "Manifesto of the Third Congress of the Chinese Communist Party," p. 228.

32. Chung-kuo hsien-tai ko-ming yün-tung shih, pp. 131-32; Hu Hua, Chung-kuo hsin min-chu chu-i ko-ming shih, pp. 43-44; Ts'ai Ho-shen, "On Ch'en Tu-hsiuism," pp. 43-44.

33. Hu Hua, Chung-kuo hsin min-chu chu-i ko-ming shih, p. 44. Hu Hua's work was published in 1952. Chung-kuo hsien-tai ko-ming yün-tung shih, published in 1940, makes no such claims.

34. Chang Kuo-t'ao, in an interview with C. Martin Wilbur, Hongkong, November, 1954.

35. Hu Hua, Chung-kuo hsin min-chu chu-i ko-ming shih, p. 43.

36. See, for instance, Ts'ai Ho-shen, "On Ch'en Tu-hsiuism," p. 14.

37. "The Petition to Impeach the Communist Party Presented by the Kwangtung Branch of the Kuomintang of China...," p. 6.

38. Ch'en Tu-hsiu, Kao ch'üan-tang...

39. Chang Kuo-t'ao, in an interview with C. Martin Wilbur, Hongkong, November, 1954.

40. "Resolutions of the Second Congress of the Chinese Socialist Youth Corps," pp. 14-15.

41. See Part III, p. 141.

42. Hu Hua, Chung-kuo hsin min-chu chu-i ko-ming shih, p. 42.

43. "The Petition to Impeach the Communist Party presented by the Kwangtung Branch of China...," pp. 5-6.

44. Ch'en Tu-hsiu, Kao ch'üan-tang..., p. 3.

45. See Part III, pp. 151-52.

46. Chang Kuo-t'ao, in an interview with C. Martin Wilbur, Hongkong, November, 1954.

47. Quoted by Liu Lu-yin, "Revolution and Counterrevolution," p. 468. Another source asserts that the policy of forming an alliance with the Left Wing was adopted at a plenum of the CC in July, 1923. See Chung-kuo ko tang-p'ai chih shih-liao yü p'i-p'an, p. 313.

48. "Record of the Questions of CSC Members Hsieh Ch'ih and Chang Chi and the Answers of Borodin," pp. 26-27.

49. Chang Chi, Hsieh Ch'ih, and Teng Tse-ju, "Letter to the Central Executive Committee," pp. 13-14, 20-21.

50. Chang Kuo-t'ao, in an interview with C. Martin Wilbur, Hongkong, November, 1954.

51. Peng Pai (P'eng P'ai), "Memoirs of a Chinese Communist," pp. 117-23. According to P'eng, he had organized 500 peasants in peasant associations by September, 1922. The Haifeng County Peasant Association was established on January 1, 1923, with a membership of 20,000 families, representing 100,000 persons.

52. Central Committee, Chinese Communist Party, Enlarged Plenum, "Letter to the Peasantry," p. 133.

53. Mif, Chin-chi shih-chi..., p. 37.

54. Teng Chung-hsia, Chung-kuo chih-kung yün-tung shih, pp. 158-59.

55. Central Committee, Chinese Communist Party, Enlarged Plenum, "Letter to the Peasantry," p. 133.

56. "Record of the Questions of CSC Members Hsieh Ch'ih and Chang Chi and the Answers of Borodin," p. 28.

57. Quoted by Liu Lu-yin, "Revolution and Counterrevolution," p. 468.

58. "Report of the Young Communist International at the Sixth World Congress of the Communist International," p. 84. The Socialist Youth Corps adopted the name "Chinese Communist Youth Corps," in February, 1925, at the Third Congress of the Corps.

59. Heller, "The Labour Movement in China," pp. 9-11; "National Revolutionary Movement in China and Tactics of the Chinese Communist Party," p. 18; Teng Chung-hsia, Chung-kuo chih-kung yün-tung shih, pp. 189-95.

60. Central Committees of the Chinese Communist Party and the Chinese Communist Youth Corps, "Statement to the People Who Fought for National Independence during May Thirtieth," p. 93.

61. Heller, "The Labour Movement in China," pp. 14-15; "National Revolutionary Movement in China and Tactics of the Chinese Communist Party," pp. 18-21; Teng Chung-hsia, Chung-kuo chih-kung yün-tung shih, pp. 211-27.

62. Ibid.

63. "National Revolutionary Movement in China and Tactics of the Chinese Communist Party," p. 21; Teng Chung-hsia, Chung-kuo chih-kung yün-tung shih, p. 216; "X," "The Revolutionary Movement in the East—Questions at the Coming Enlarged Plenum of the ECCI," p. 103.

64. See Part IV, pp. 206-8.

65. Ch'en Tu-hsiu, Kao ch'üan-tang..., p. 3.

66. Quoted by Liu Lu-yin, "Revolution and Counterrevolution," p. 468.

67. See Part III, p. 149.

68. Prior to May 30, 1925, 90 percent of the members of the Youth Corps were students. By September, 1925, only 49 percent of the members were students. See "Report of the Young Communist International at the Sixth World Congress of the Communist International," p. 84. In November, 1926, students constituted 35 percent of Corps membership; workers, 40 percent; peasants, 5 percent, See "Report on the Communist Movement of Youth in China," A History of Communism in China, p. 54. We have not been able to find reliable comparable figures for the KCT. Mif gives the following breakdown on the Party's membership at the Fifth Congress, April-May, 1927; workers, 53.8 percent; intellectuals, 19.1 percent;

peasants, 18.7 percent; military men, 3.1 percent; middle and small merchants, 0.5 percent. See Mif, Chin-chi shih-chi..., p. 37.

69. Central Committee, Chinese Communist Party, Enlarged Plenum, "Letter to the Peasantry," pp. 137-38.

70. Hu Hua, Chung-kuo hsin min-chu chu-i ko-ming shih, p. 31. Mao Tse-tung was secretary of the Hunan Regional Committee, 1921-1923.

71. Chou Fu-chen, "The Golden Age of the Kwangtung Regional Committee," II, 309-15.

72. The Peasant Department of the Central Committee was established shortly after the July, 1926 Plenum at Shanghai. It was headed by Mao Tse-tung. See Snow, Red Star over China, p. 161. The CC's Military Department was apparently not set up until late 1926 or early 1927. It was headed by Chou En-lai. See Kuei Nien, "Chou En-lai during the Wuhan period," pp. 272-74. Among papers seized at the Soviet Military Attaché's office are documents purporting to be regulations of the CC's Military Department. See "The Military Section (Voyenka) of the Central Committee of the Chinese Communist Party" and "Statutes of the 'Voyenka', " in Soviet Plot in China, pp. 30-34.

73. The Central Committee, at first set up as a provisional organ, was known also as the "Central," "Central Bureau," or the "Central Political Bureau." The politburo was apparently not organized until the Fifth Party Congress held in Wuhan in April and May, 1927. See Ch'ü Ch'iu-pai, Chung-kuo ko-ming yü Kung-ch'an-tang, p. 102.

74. Chang Kuo-t'ao and, later, Ts'ai Ho-shen, were reportedly sent by the CC as special commissioners to the Kwangtung Regional Committee toward the end of 1925 and during the spring of 1926. See Chou Fu-chen, "Golden Age of the Kwangtung Regional Committee," p. 315.

75. Mif, Chin-chi shih-chi..., p. 37.

76. Shina Kyōsantō undō shi, p. 275.

Part III: Consolidation of the Revolutionary
Base in Kwangtung

1. Yang Yu-ch'iung, Chung-kuo cheng-tang shih, pp. 89, 93, 98-99, 104.

2. Wang Ching-wei, "On Separating the Communists from the KMT at Wuhan" p. 593. Wang Ching-wei asserts that the telegram was sent in 1918 or 1919. Li Chien-nung dates it more specifically. He states the wire was sent in 1918, shortly after Sun left Canton for Shanghai. See Li Chien-nung, Tsui-chin san-shih nien..., p. 546.

3. Pravda, March 15, 1925. Quoted by Robert North, Moscow and Chinese Communists, pp. 69-70. According to Katsuji Fuse, Sun met a Soviet representative toward the end of 1920, while Sun was on his way from Shanghai to Canton. Fuse does not identify the

Russian. See Fuse, Su-Wo ti Tung-fang cheng-ts'e, p. 226.

4. Lo Yüan-k'un, Chung-kuo Chin pai-nien shih, II, 20, 22.

5. Chou Lu, Chung-kuo Kuomintang shih-kao, II, 1927.

6. Hu Hua, Chung-kuo hsin min-chu chu-i ko-ming shih, p. 46.
Hu asserts that Sun Yat-sen and Maring met through the introduction of Li Ta-chao.

7. Li Chien-nung, Tsui-chin san-shih-nien..., p. 546. According to
Li, Sun Yat-sen told Liao Chung-k'ai after meeting Maring that
Soviet Russia's New Economic Policy was very similar to his own
Three People's Principles. In 1927, Wang Ching-wei confirms that
Sun met Maring at Kweilin in August or September, 1921. See Wang
Ching-wei, "On Separating the Communists from the KMT at Wuhan,"
p. 593.

8. Chiang Kai-shek, Chiang Chieh-shih hsien-sheng, III, 100.

9. Izvestia, October 9, 1920, quoted by Isaacs, Tragedy of the Chinese Revolution, pp. 61-62.

10. Wang Ching-wei, "On Separating the Communists from the
KMT at Wuhan," p. 594.

11. Fuse, Su-Wo ti Tung-fang cheng-ts'e, p. 310.

12. "China and the Far Eastern Republic," The Nation, CXII
(Feb. 2, 1921), pp. 192-93. The Far Eastern Republic, a pro-Soviet
Siberian state formed in the spring of 1920, served the USSR by establishing contact with countries which did not recognize the Soviet
government. It sent a delegation to the Washington Conference of
1922.

13. Fuse, Su-Wo ti Tung-fang cheng-ts'e, p. 201.

14. Li Chien-nung, Tsui-chin san-shih-nien..., p. 545.

15. Chou Lu, Chung-kuo Kuomintang shih-kao, II, 1027-42; Doc. 1,
p. 26. Chiang Kai-shek, who was with Sun, kept a daily record of the
fifty-six days on the gunboat. See Chiang Kai-shek, "A Record of
President Sun's Calamity in Canton," pp. 1-50.

16. Yang Yu-ch'iung, Chung-kuo cheng tang shih, pp. 149-52;
Chung-kuo hsien-tai ko-ming yün-tung shih, p. 118.

17. Letter to Chiang Kai-shek (Aug. 30, 1922), in Sun Yat-sen,
Sun Chung-shan hsien-sheng..., pp. 5-6.

18. According to Harold R. Isaacs, the Soviet decision to support
Sun Yat-sen was due largely to Maring's influence. In September,
1921, when Maring returned to Moscow, Isaacs asserts, he published
his views in the Communist press calling for support of Sun Yat-
sen. As a consequence, the Comintern reversed the "Irkutsk line"
of attempting to establish links with northern militarists and turned
its attention to Sun. See Isaacs, Tragedy of the Chinese Revolution,
p. 62.

19. Chiang Kai-shek, Chiang Chieh-shih hsien-sheng, IV, 28.

20. Letter to Chiang Kai-shek (Nov. 21, 1922), in Sun Yat-sen,
Sun Chung-shan hsien-sheng..., pp. 2-3.

21. George Sokolsky asserts, for instance, that before turning to Russia, Sun had sent Eugene Chen to confer with British authorities in Hongkong and London for assistance and had sent Morris Cohen to Canada and the United States to recruit World War veterans to help reorganize his army. Both missions failed. Sun had also turned unsuccessfully to Germany for aid. See G. E. Sokolsky, "The Kuomintang," in The China Year Book, 1928, pp. 1320-21.

22. Attendance at the First Congress of the Toilers of the Far East proved to be a disillusioning experience for some of the Kuomintang delegates; see Doc. 1, pp. 21-22. Kuomintang delegates bitterly protested Zinoviev's remark that certain members of the Kuomintang were still flirting with the United States. They also objected to the view expressed by Zinoviev and other Soviet leaders that Japan was the most important factor in the Far East. The chief Kuomintang delegate declared there should be no neglect of the Kuomintang, which had a long record and had the sympathy and support of the masses. He questioned also the Communist position regarding Mongolia. See Communist International, The First Congress of the Toilers of the Far East, Held in Moscow, January 21st-February 1st, 1922. Closing Session in Petrograd, February 2nd, 1922, pp. 181-84.

23. "Joint Manifesto of Sun Yat-sen and A. Joffe," p. 2.

24. Chou Lu, Chung-kuo Kuomintang shih-kao, II, 1072, 1077.

25. Li Chien-nung, Tsui-chin san-shih-nien..., p. 547.

26. Fuse, Su-Wo ti Tung-fang cheng-ts'e, pp. 229-32.

27. See, for instance, Part VII, p. 378.

28. Chiang Kai-shek, Chiang Chieh-shih hsien-sheng, V, 42-73.

29. Tong asserts that Chiang advised Sun Yat-sen against cooperating with the Russians. As was customary, Sun Yat-sen did not return Chiang's report but shelved it. Later, when Sun decided to re-examine the report, of which only one copy was prepared, he found it missing, obviously stolen by the Communists. See Tong, Chiang Kai-shek, pp. 543-44. The text of Chiang's report is not available. A number of unfavorable comments made by Chiang during his visit to Moscow, however, are available in his diary. On October 10, 1923, Chiang expressed fear that Chinese students in Moscow lacked respect for Dr. Sun and were under the control of foreigners. On November 28, 1923, the day before he left Moscow, Chiang came across a set of resolutions on the Kuomintang adopted by the Comintern. Chiang said angrily that the resolutions did not sound like those of a friendly party and that the CI should be ashamed to call itself the center of the World Revolution. See Chiang Kai-shek, Chiang Chieh-shih hsien-sheng, V, 53, 69. Chiang had appeared favorably disposed toward Soviet Russia prior to his sojourn in Moscow. This may be seen, for instance, in a letter

he wrote to Sun Yat-sen, apparently shortly after Canton was re-
captured in October, 1920. In the letter Chiang enthusiastically
praised Soviet Russia's spirit of self-reliance. He declared that the
KMT's previous failures were caused by the excessive importance
which the Party attached to foreign aid. In contrast, Soviet Russia
relied on her own strength to withstand the blockade, armed intervention, and other forms of aggression instituted by the foreign
Powers against her. Chiang warned that foreigners regarded the
KMT as patterned after the socialist system and that therefore
the foreign Powers were bound to obstruct and oppose the Kuomintang although individual foreigners might be friendly. Chiang declared that the Party must consolidate internally and adopt Soviet
Russia's spirit of self-reliance. See Letter to Sun Yat-sen, in
Chiang Kai-shek, Chiang Chung-cheng ch'üan-chi, III, 1-2.

30. Ting Ming-nan, "Soviet Aid to China during the First Revo-
lutionary War, 1925-1927." p. 2. On March 20, 1926, the day of
Chiang's coup d'état, a Russian adviser, Ao-li-chin, "gently rebuked"
Chiang by mentioning Pavlov's death. See Doc. 23, p. 68.

31. Mitarevsky, World-wide Soviet Plots, pp. 130-31.

32. Ibid., p. 132.

33. "Proceedings of the First Congress," p. 3.

34. "The Petition to Impeach the Communist Party Presented
by the Kwangtung Branch of the Kuomintang of China...," p. 2.

35. "Proceedings of the First Congress," pp. 6-9.

36. "Constitution of the Kuomintang of China," pp. 155-76.

37. "Manifesto of the First Congress," pp. 39-40.

38. "Manifesto of the Second Congress of the Chinese Communist
Party," p. 13. The "Brief History" states that the KCT decided to
take up the most pressing problems with the Kuomintang and to build
them up as slogans of the day—"Down with imperialism!" and "Down
with militarism!"—when it began collaborating with that party in
1922. See Doc. 1, pp. 28-30.

39. Chou Lu, Chung-kuo Kuomintang shih-kao, II, 1042-46.

40. Yang Yu-ch'iung, Chung-kuo cheng-tang shih, pp. 149-50.

41. "Manifesto of the First Congress," p. 45.

42. "Manifesto of the First Congress," pp. 41-42.

43. Yang Yu-ch'iung, Chung-kuo cheng-tang shih, p. 149.

44. "Manifesto of the First Congress," p. 42.

45. Ibid., pp. 39-43.

46. Yang Yu-ch'iung, Chung-kuo cheng-tang shih, p. 163.

47. "Manifesto of the First Congress," pp. 45-48.

48. Chiang Kai-shek, Chiang Chieh-shih hsien-sheng, V, 60. Sun's telegram contradicts the assertions of Soviet sources and certain KMT
sources that Borodin was merely a private citizen in the employ
of the Kuomintang. There is, furthermore, the report made by T'an
P'ing-shan at a meeting of the Communist Party's Kwangtung

Regional Committee on November 2, 1923. T'an said that he had been informed by Ch'en Tu-hsiu that Borodin was a representative of the USSR. See Mitarevsky, World-wide Soviet Plots, p. 133.

49. Chiang Kai-shek, Chiang Chieh-shih hsien-sheng, V, 73.

50. Ch'en Tu-hsiu, Kao ch'üan-tung..., p. 3.

51. Chiang Kai-shek, "A Circular Letter to KMT Comrades," p. 2.

52. "The Petition to Impeach the Communist Party presented by the Kwangtung Branch of the Kuomintang of China...," pp. 1-11. While the Kwangtung Branch did not officially question the policy of alliance with Soviet Russia, it stated that it could not say for certain whether Russia's motives in helping the KMT to reorganize were the same as Ch'en Tu-hsiu's.

53. Yang Yu-ch'iung, Chung-kuo cheng-tang shih, p. 169.

54. Wang Ching-wei, "On Separating the Communists from the KMT at Wuhan," p. 504.

55. Quoted by Chang Chi, Hsieh Ch'ih, and Teng Tse-ju, "Letter to the Central Executive Committee," p. 19.

56. "List of the First Central Executive and Supervisory Committees," pp. 188-89.

57. Yang Yu-ch'iung, Chung-kuo cheng-tang shih, p. 163.

58. Chiang Kai-shek, Chiang Chieh-shih hsien-sheng, VI, 2; 53-56.

59. Ibid., p. 59.

60. Ibid., XIV, 7.

61. Ibid., VI, 57-58.

62. Ibid., p. 3.

63. T'ang Leang-li, Foundations of Modern China, p. 167; Ting Ming-nan, "Soviet Aid to China during the First Revolutionary War, 1925-1927," p. 1.

64. T'ang Leang-li, Foundations of Modern China, p. 167; Fuse, Su-Wo ti Tung-fang cheng-ts'e, p. 235.

65. Tong, Chiang Kai-shek, p. 46.

66. Chiang Kai-shek, Chiang Chieh-shih hsien-sheng, VI, 6.

67. Ibid., pp. 20-31. Excerpts translated into English in Tong, Chiang Kai-shek, pp. 544-45.

68. Letter to Sun Yat-sen, in Chiang Kai-shek, Chiang Chung-cheng ch'üan-chi, III, 4-9.

69. Sun Yat-sen, "Party Members Must Strictly Observe Discipline and Work Hard," pp. 13-15.

70. Chang Chi, Hsieh Ch'ih, and Teng Tse-ju, "Letter to the Central Executive Committee," pp. 14-22. No mention was made of the Policy of alliance with Soviet Russia. Wu Chih hui and Li Shih-tseng, the remaining members of the CSC, did not sign the petition.

71. Quoted in "Instructions of the Kuomintang of China on the Admission of Communists into Our Party," pp. 81-82.

72. Ch'ien Tuan-sheng, Sa Shih-ch'iung, and others, Min-kuo

cheng-chih shih, I, 165, 193. According to T'ang Leang-li, the Political Council was composed of nine members and three deputies. See T'ang Leang-li, Foundations of Modern China, p. 169.

73. Yasuhara, Sa-rempō to Shina Manshū no kyōsan undō, pp. 276-80.

74. According to Kisanko's report of January 13, 1926, the Soviet Group at Canton had until then no statutes defining its organization and tasks. See "The South China Group of Military-Political Workers," in Soviet Plot in China, pp. 41-43.

75. Lan Ch'uan, "A Complete Record of the Soviet Embassy Case," Kuo-wen chou-pao, IV, No. 15 (April 24, 1927), p. 1.

76. Chiang Kai-shek, Chiang Chieh-shih hsien-sheng, VIII, 2.

77. P'ing Tzu, "A Record of the Canton Merchant Corps Incident," in Hsien-tai shih-liao, III, 19.

78. Sun Yat-sen, "Manifesto to Foreign Countries on the Merchant Corps Incident," pp. 16-17.

79. Sun Yat-sen, "Telegram to the MacDonald Government Protesting the Ultimatum of the British Consul at Canton," p. 18.

80. "A Declaration Issued by the Kuomintang of China on the Objectives of the Northern Expedition," pp. 15-18.

81. Letter to Chiang Kai-shek (Oct. 7, 1924), in Sun Yat-sen, Sun Chung-shan hsien-sheng..., p. 17.

82. Letter to Chiang Kai-shek (Oct. 9, 1924), in Sun Yat-sen, Sun Chung-shan hsien-sheng..., pp. 7-8.

83. Chiang Kai-shek, Chiang Chieh-shih hsien-sheng, VIII, 8-9. This letter is not in the above collection of Sun Yat-sen's letters to Chiang Kai-shek.

84. Letter to Chiang Kai-shek (Oct. 11, 1924), in Sun Yat-sen, Sun Chung-shan hsien-sheng..., pp. 18-20.

85. Chiang Kai-shek, Chiang Chieh-shih hsien-sheng..., VIII, 9-11.

86. Ibid., pp. 16-17.

87. Ibid., pp. 23-24.

88. Chou Lu, Chung-kuo Kuomintang shih-kao, p. 1095.

89. According to Chiang Kai-shek, Fan Shih-sheng, a divisional commander in the Yunnan Army, conspired with the Canton Merchant Corps. See Chiang Kai-shek, Chiang Chieh-shih hsien-sheng, VIII, 5. The orthodox Communist historian, Hu Hua, accuses Fan of conspiring with the Merchant Corps and Hongkong imperialism. See Hu Hua, Chung-kuo hsin min-chu-chu-i ko-ming shih, p. 52. Certain independent sources also accuse Fan of being bribed. See, for instance, Huang Ku, "On the Merchant Corps Incident," pp. 94-97; P'ing Tzu, "A Record of the Canton Merchant Corps Incident," pp. 7-14. In answer to P'ing Tzu's article, Fan Shih-sheng denies being bribed or disloyal in any way; see Fan Shih-sheng, "After Reading 'A Record of the Merchants Corps Incident,'" pp. 14-20. Chou Lu asserts that Fan Shih-sheng took a neutral stand (Chung-kuo Kuomintang shih-kao, p. 1095).

90. Fan Shih-sheng, "After Reading 'A Record of the Merchant Corps Incident,'" pp. 17-19.

91. Chiang Kai-shek, Chiang Chieh-shih hsien-sheng, VIII, 6-7.

92. Letter to Chiang Kai-shek (Oct. 9, 1924), in Sun Yat-sen, Sun Chung-shan hsien-sheng..., pp. 6-7.

93. Chiang Kai-shek, Chiang Chieh-shih hsien-sheng, VIII, 15.

94. Ibid., XIV, 9.

95. Ibid., 9.

96. See Part VI, pp. 318-20.

97. Quoted in "Manifesto of the Kuomintang of China on the Acceptance of Tsung-li's Will," p. 40. The will is translated into English in Woo, Kuomintang and the Future of the Chinese Revolution, p. 253.

98. Central Executive Committee of the Kuomintang, "Manifesto of the Kuomintang of China Convening the Second Congress," p. 101.

99. "Manifesto of the Kuomintang of China on the Acceptance of Tsung-li's Will," p. 41.

100. "Manifesto of the Kuomintang of China on the Current Situation," p. 60.

101. "Manifesto of the First Congress," p. 45.

102. "Manifesto of the Kuomintang of China on the Acceptance of Tsung-li's Will," p. 60.

103. "Sun Yat-sen's Farewell Messages," p. 286. The Chinese text of Sun's letter is given in several editions of his collected works and also in Hu Hua, Chung-kuo hsin min-chu chu-i ko-ming shih, pp. 55-56.

104. "Sun Yat-sen's Farewell Messages," p. 286.

105. Central Committee, Chinese Communist Party, "Letter to the Central Executive Committee of the Kuomintang," p. 890.

106. "Instructions of the Kuomintang of China on the Admission of Communists into Our Party," pp. 79-83.

107. "Circular Notice from the Kuomintang of China on Party Discipline," p. 75.

108. "Manifesto of the Kuomintang of China on the Acceptance of Tsung-li's Will," p. 41; "Instructions of the Kuomintang of China on the Acceptance of Tsung-li's Will," p. 73.

109. Central Executive Committee of the Kuomintang, "Manifesto of the Kuomintang of China Convening the Second Congress," p. 101. The CEC declared that the decision to move to Canton was made because of the reactionary environment in Peking. By May, 1925, the Kuomintang openly opposed the provisional Peking Government.

110. "An Important Declaration of the Central Executive Committee of the Kuomintang," pp. 43-44. The Kuomintang continued to take precautions against starting hostilities with the British. The Military Council ordered army units not to precipitate conflict with British forces. See Doc. 15, p. 6.

111. Chiang Kai-shek, Chiang Chieh-shih hsien-sheng, XI, 9-34.

112. Central Executive Committee of the Kuomintang, "Resolutions of the Kuomintang on Reorganization of the Army," pp. 61-64.

113. Chiang Kai-shek, Chiang Chieh-shih Hsien-sheng, XIV, 9-10.

114. Central Executive Committee of the Kuomintang, "Manifesto of the Kuomintang of China Convening the Second Congress," pp. 99, 102; Chiang Kai-shek, Chiang Chieh-shih hsien-sheng, XIV, 4-14.

115. "Letter from the Military Council of the National Government to All Officers and Men," pp. 48-50.

116. Chiang Kai-shek, Chiang Chieh-shih hsien-sheng, XI, 68-69.

117. "Instructions from the Kuomintang of China to the Party Military Academy and the Army," pp. 77-78.

118. Ch'ien Tuan-sheng, Sa Shih-ch'iung, and others, Min-kuo cheng-chih shih, pp. 165-67.

119. "Manifesto of the National Government of the Republic of China," pp. 45-47; "Letter to the People from the National Government," pp. 53-57; "Letter to Overseas Chinese from Hu Han-min, Minister of Foreign Affairs of the National Government," pp. 69-71.

120. "Letter to Overseas Chinese from Hu Han-min, Minister of Foreign Affairs of the National Government," pp. 69-71.

121. Chiang Kai-shek, Chiang Chieh-shih hsien-sheng, XI, 66. In an interview with Nym Wales in 1937, Liao Ch'eng-chih, son of Liao Chung-k'ai and now a leading member of the Chinese Communist Party, said: "My father's political position was further to the Left than Sun Yat-sen's. Sun's third book, National Democracy, criticized Marxism in a nonsensical way, but my father never did. He sympathized with the new Communist Party from the beginning and talked of Lenin constantly. Sun Yat-sen never reached the point where he wanted to follow in Lenin's footsteps. Father was loyal to the Kuomintang, but saw clearly that a true democracy must lead to socialism in the end. I think I can say that he had become a real Socialist by the time he died. He was firmly convinced that cooperation with the Communist Party and with Soviet Russia was basic to the realization of the national-bourgeois-democratic revolution." According to Liao Ch'eng-chih, his father held actual power in Canton in the summer of 1925 although Wang Ching-wei was chairman of the National Government. Hu Han-min and others of the Right Wing, he said, were out of power because of Liao Chung-k'ai's power. See Nym Wales, Red Dust: Autobiographies of Chinese Communists, pp. 30-31.

122. Chiang Kai-shek, Chiang Chieh-shih hsien-sheng, XI, 8.

123. Teng Tse-ju, "Letter Impeaching the Political Council," pp. 289-91.

124. "Letter from Wang Ching-wei and Others Rejecting the Letter of Impeachment," pp. 291-92.

125. Chiang Kai-shek, Chiang Chieh-shih hsien-sheng, XI, 65-66.
126. Ibid., 67-68.
127. Ibid., XII, 1, 25.
128. Ibid., XII, 21-23.
129. Ibid., X, 90-91.
130. In a speech on December 25, 1925, Chiang Kai-shek confirmed that the Special Committee overshadowed the Political Council. See Chiang Kai-shek, "A Circular Letter to KMT Comrades," p. 5.
131. Chiang Kai-shek, Chiang Chieh-shih hsien-sheng, XII, 19. Wang Ching-wei took over Liao Chung-k'ai's job as chief Party representative to the Whampoa Academy and the Army.
132. Wang Ching-wei, "Eulogizing Liao Chung-k'ai to Inspire My Comrades," pp. 53-57.
133. Chiang Kai-shek, Chiang Chieh-shih hsien-sheng, XI, 72.
134. Doc. 16, p. 31. Galen had left Canton on leave. See "Plan for Employment of Personnel, etc. Minutes of the Sitting of the Military Council on the 1st of July, 1925," Soviet Plot in China, p. 35.
135. The China Year Book, 1926, p. 582.
136. See Part IV, pp. 208-9.
137. Chiang Kai-shek, Chiang Chieh-shih hsien-sheng, X, 15-16. Ho Ying-ch'in was appointed commander of the First Brigade of the Party Army, which incorporated the Whampoa Training Regiment. However, the unit was placed under the control of Chiang Kai-shek, president of the Academy. Liao Chung-k'ai was appointed Party representative.
138. Te-la-t'e-wen was at the front during the First Eastern Expedition. He was listed as communications adviser at the Military Academy and the General Staff at the beginning of 1926. See "A List of Soviet Officers Who Participated in the Eastern Expedition," May 2, 1925; "A List of Names and Positions of Members of the Soviet Group in South China," Su-lien yin-mou..., III, "Canton," pp. 97, 106.
139. According to a Soviet list presented to Hsü Ch'ung-chih, Russian advisers at the front included Admiral Smirnov, General Rogachev, five other generals, one lieutenant-colonel, five colonels, five captains, and one officer in charge of political training. See "A List of Soviet Officers Who Participated in the Eastern Expedition," May 2, 1925, Su-lien yin-mou..., III, "Canton," pp. 105-6. An article published in a newspaper in Tientsin in 1952 gives a similar list. The advisers served directly as staff officers, according to this source. See Ting Ming-nan, "Soviet Aid to China during the First Revolutionary War, 1925-1927," p. 4.
140. "A List of Names and Positions of Members of the Soviet Group in South China," Su-lien yin-mou..., III, "Canton," p. 98.
141. "Plan for Employment of Personnel, etc. Minutes of the

Sitting of the Military Council on the 1st of July, 1925," Soviet Plot in China, pp. 35-40. At this meeting, no Soviet adviser was appointed below divisional level.

142. Chiang Kai-shek, Chiang Chieh-shih hsien-sheng, XIV, 21.

143. "Joint Meeting of Political Bureau and Military Council," September 22, 1925, Soviet Plot in China, pp. 48-49.

144. "Draft of Telegram, Dated July 4th, 1926, to Galen, Canton," Soviet Plot in China, p. 60.

145. Chiang Kai-shek, Chiang Chieh-shih hsien-sheng, XII, 26.

146. Ibid., p. 73, and XIII, 40.

Part IV: Friction and Reconciliation in the Revolutionary Camp

1. Tai Chi-t'ao was one of the original founders of the Shanghai Communist group. See Doc. 1, p. 11. After the reorganization of the KMT he headed the Propaganda Department. He was transferred to the Shanghai Executive Headquarters, which supervised Party affairs in Kiangsu, Chekiang, Anhwei, and Kiangsi, at the beginning of 1925. Sun Yat-sen proposed the establishment of executive headquarters in Shanghai, Peking, Hankow, and Harbin at the First Plenum of the first CEC in January, 1924. See Ta Te, "A Short History of the Shanghai Executive Headquarters," p. 90.

2. See Part III, pp. 151-52.

3. Tai Chi-t'ao, Kuo-min ko-ming yü Chung-kuo Kuomintang, pp. 50-64, 70-72.

4. Ch'en Tu-hsiu, "Letter to Tai Chi-t'ao," pp. 1196-97.

5. This has become part of the orthodox Communist interpretation of the emergence of Tai Chi-t'ao's theories. According to Tai, he realized after May Thirtieth that Chinese youths lacked political understanding and experience and knew only how to "yell slogans." See Tai Chi-t'ao, Kuo-min ko-ming yü Chung-kuo Kuomintang, pp. 52-53.

6. See Part II, p. 89.

7. Li Ang, Hung-se wu-t'ai, pp. 4-5, 8-9. Li asserts that members of the Kwangtung Regional Committee, particularly Ch'en Yen-nien and Su Chao-cheng, supported Liao Chung-k'ai for the chairmanship instead of Wang Ching-wei. See also Wang Wei-lien, "Election of the First Chairman of the National Government," pp. 2, 5-8; Ho Fu, "Kuomintang Cliques before the Third Plenum," p. 10; Yang Hsin-hua, "Liao Chung-k'ai and Hu Han-min," p. 159. Borodin had reportedly maneuvered against both Hu Han-min and Wang Ching-wei in October, 1924 (see Part III, p. 156). If that was the case, he apparently changed his attitude toward Wang Ching-wei. According to some sources, the Communists were at first hostile to Wang because he did not support, although he did not oppose, Sun Yat-sen's decision to reorganize the KMT. See Wang Wei-lien, "A Record of Wang Ching-wei's Opposition to Com-

munists," p. 8. Liao Ch'eng-chih asserts that Wang Ching-wei
was definitely opposed to KMT reorganization. See Nym Wales,
Red Dust: Autobiographies of Chinese Communists..., p. 30.

8. Liu Lu-yin, "Revolution and Counterrevolution," p. 479; also
see Li Ang, Hung-se wu-t'ai, p. 10.

9. Li Shih, "Organization of the Left Wing before the Kuomintang
Purge," pp. 86-90.

10. See Part III, p. 166.

11. "Important Documents of the Western Hills Conference Expelling Communists from the KMT," pp. 14-16.

12. Ch'en Tu-hsiu, "What are the Right and Left Wings of the
Kuomintang?" pp. 1247-48. Ch'en emphasized that Chinese Communists did not constitute the KMT Left Wing and went to great
lengths to prove this point. He pointed out that not one of the KMT
Left leaders was a Communist. Among the twelve leaders he mentioned was Hu Han-min, a principal target in the anti-Right coup a
few months earlier.

13. Central Executive Committee of the Kuomintang, "Circular
Notice from the Kuomintang of China Explaining Its Revolutionary
Strategy to All Party Members in the Country and Abroad," pp. 95-
97.

14. "Important Documents of the Western Hills Conference Expelling Communists from the KMT," p. 15. Lin Tsu-han had been
elevated to the CEC from the status of a reserve CEC member.

15. Central Executive Committee of the Kuomintang, "Manifesto
of the Kuomintang of China Convening the Second Congress," p.
103.

16. Chiang Kai-shek, "The Meaning of the Soviet Alliance," pp. 9-
10, 13. The passage quoting Sun Yat-sen on Borodin is omitted in
Chiang's diary. See Chiang Kai-shek, Chiang Chieh-shih hsien-
sheng, XIV, 18-22.

17. "A List of Names and Positions of Members of the Soviet
Group in South China," Su-lien yin-mou..., III, "Canton," p. 99;
Lo Yüan-k'un, Chung-kuo chin pai-nien shih, p. 514.

18. "A List of Names and Positions of Members of the Soviet
Group in South China," Su-lien yin-mou..., III, "Canton," p. 98.

19. Russian advisers assigned to divisions were subordinate to
the senior adviser of a given army. The divisional adviser was
assisted by an assistant adviser and an adviser for political affairs.
The chief of the Soviet Group was assisted by a deputy chief and an
assistant for political affairs. The latter maintained contact with
Kuomintang and Chinese Communist organs and political organizations in general and was responsible for political work in the National Revolutionary Army. See "Task and Organization of the South
China Group of Soviet Military-Political Workers," Soviet Plot in
China, pp. 56-58. A hint that Kisanko and Borodin may not have
worked in complete harmony is suggested by Kisanko's request for

the Soviet Military Attaché to send him a copy of the secret code. He explained that only one copy was available at Borodin's place and Borodin's decoding clerk often piled up telegrams without transmitting them. Kisanko remarked that if he could have the secret code for direct communication with the Soviet Military Attaché, it would prove "extremely beneficial." See Doc. 16, p. 62.

20. "Telegram of Greetings from the XIV Party Conference of the R.C.P. to the Kuomintang," p. 4.

21. Tang Shin She, "China and the Kuomintang a Year after Sun Yat-sen's Death," pp. 329-30.

22. "Manifesto of the Second Congress," pp. 62-63.

23. Second Congress of the Kuomintang of China, "Telegram from the Second Congress to the Oppressed Peoples of the World," pp. 148-50.

24. Chang Kuo-t'ao, "Lessons of the Second KMT Congress," p. 1329.

25. Wang Wei-lien, "Election of the CEC at the Second Congress," pp. 94-98. Wang asserts that the Communist Party fraction was directly supervised by the Communist Central Political Bureau. There were eleven officers: T'an P'ing-shan, Chang Kuo-t'ao, Kao Yü-han, Yün Tai-ying, Mao Tse-tung, Lin Tsu-han, Wu Yü-chang, Yang P'ao-an, Han Lin-fu, Hsia Hsi, and Yü Shu-te. Members of the fraction met at least every two days. The officers met daily to discuss problems of the Second Kuomintang Congress, including persons to be supported for election.

26. Nym Wales, Red Dust: Autobiographies of Chinese Communists..., p. 41.

27. "List of the Second Central Executive and Supervisory Committees," p. 190.

28. Chiang Kai-shek, Chiang Chieh-shih hsien-sheng, XIV, 44.

29. Ibid., Others of the nine-man Standing Committee: Wang Ching-wei, T'an Yen-k'ai, Hu Han-min, Ch'en Kung-po, Kan Nai-kuang, T'an P'ing-shan, Lin Tsu-han, and Yang P'ao-an.

30. "Circular Notice from the Kuomintang of China on Party Discipline," p. 75.

31. "Resolutions Impeaching the Western Hills Conference," pp. 75-77.

32. "List of the Second Central Executive and Supervisory Committees," p. 189.

33. See, for instance, Wang Wei-lien, "Election of the CEC at the Second Congress," p. 97.

34. Chiang Kai-shek, "A Circular Letter to KMT Comrades," pp. 1-6.

35. Chiang Kai-shek, Chiang Chieh-shih hsien-sheng, XIII, 17.

36. Ibid., XIV, 43. Chiang had had unfavorable impressions of Soviet Russia as early as late 1923 and early 1924. See Part III, Note 29.

37. Ibid., XIV, 59-60.

38. Ibid., XIV, 61.

39. Ibid., XIV, 64. Chiang's diary does not state to whom this proposal was made.

40. Borodin apparently left for North China to confer with Feng Yü-hsiang shortly after February 3, 1926. On that day, he discussed his trip with Chiang Kai-shek (Ibid., XIV, 58).

41. Chiang Ting-fu (T. F. Tsiang), Chün-cheng ling-hsiu Chiang Chieh-shih, p. 78.

42. Chiang Kai-shek, Chiang Chieh-shih hsien-sheng, XIV, 67-68.

43. Ibid., XIV, 67.

44. Ibid., XIV, 68. The entry for February 19, 1926, states that Chiang was considering making another visit to Soviet Russia because of the unfavorable circumstances at Canton caused by poor relations with his associates and differences of opinion among his subordinates. It adds that when Kisanko learned about Chiang's plans he showed signs of extreme uneasiness (Ibid., XIV, 66-67).

45. Ibid., XIV, 67-68.

46. Li Chi-shen was appointed chief of staff on February 23, 1926 (Ibid., XIV, 67).

47. Ibid., XIV, 72.

48. Ibid., XIV, 78.

49. For instance, on January 26, 1926, during a discussion with Chang Ching-chiang on the situation of the Party and his own personal position, Chiang said he could not help feeling sad that certain Party members should resort to agitation within the Party (Ibid., XIV, 55).

50. Ibid., XIV, 72, 76.

51. Ibid., XIV, 75.

52. Ch'en Kuo-fu, "A Piece of Party History...," p. 60.

53. Yang Yu-ch'iung, Chung-kuo cheng-tang shih, p. 163; Snow, Red Star over China, p. 160; Chou Ts'ui-fen, "Central Party Headquarters during the Canton Period," pp. 40-44; Yü Ming, "Mao Tsetung at the Central Propaganda Department," pp. 341-46.

54. There were far fewer Communist Party representatives in the regiments and companies (Doc. 24, p. 81). According to another source, 80 percent of all Party representatives in the First Army were Communists; the rest were members of the KMT Left. See Huang Hao, "True Picture of the S.S. 'Chung-shan' Incident," p. 105.

55. Sung Hsiao-ch'ing, "A Biographical Sketch of Chou En-lai," p. 145; Chou Ts'ui-fen, "On Lu I," pp. 302-10; Yün T'ien, "Anecdotes about Shao Li-tzu," pp. 78-85; Yang Hsin-hua, "Yün Tai-ying," pp. 294-301.

56. Chiang Kai-shek, Chiang Chieh-shih hsien-sheng, XIV, 81.

57. Ibid., XIV, 83.

58. Ibid., XIV, 83. The official termination of the services of more than ten Russian advisers, including Kisanko and Ao-li-chin,

did not take place until April 14, 1926 (Ibid., XV, 46).

59. Stepanov mentions the departure of a group of Russians on March 24, 1926. (see Doc. 23, p. 69). It appears likely that Kisanko was among them; Rogachev definitely was. See "Letter of C. Chao'es to Comrade Rogacheff," March 24, 1926, in Soviet Plot in China, p. 54. In this letter, the chief of the Operations Department of the General Staff expressed profound shock and grief at Rogachev's sudden departure. Rogachev was subsequently appointed assistant military attaché at the Soviet Embassy, Peking, assuming this post on October 14, 1926. See "A List of Members of the Staff at the Soviet Military Attaché's Office in Peking," January, 1927, in Su-lien yin-mou..., II, "Military," p. 55.

60. Chiang Kai-shek, Chiang Chieh-shih hsien-sheng, XIV, 88.

61. Ibid., XV, 4.

62. Ibid., XIV, 77-78.

63. Quoted by Mif, Chin-chi shih-chi..., p. 26.

64. Ch'en Tu-hsiu, "The Congress of the KMT New Right Wing," pp. 1413-15.

65. Tang Shin She, "The Canton Government and the Revolutionary Movement in China," p. 415.

66. G. Voitinsky (Voitinskii), "The Situation in China and the Plans of the Imperialists," p. 600.

67. Chiang Kai-shek, Chiang Chieh-shih hsien-sheng, XIV, 83-86.

68. Ibid., XIV, 86-87.

69. Ibid., XV, 30. Writing in the fall of 1926, Katsuji Fuse, an astute Japanese journalist, dismissed the incident as the result of a split between the Sunyatsenist Society and the League of Military Youth; see Fuse, Su-Wo ti Tung-fang cheng-ts'e, p. 252.

70. Chiang Kai-shek, Chiang Chieh-shih hsien-sheng, XV, 7-11.

71. Ibid., XV, 7-11.

72. Ibid., XV, 21.

73. In a letter to the students of the Academy dated April 14, 1926. See Chiang Kai-shek, Chiang Chieh-shih hsien-sheng, XV, Ibid., 30.

74. Ibid., XV, 15, 6.

75. Chiang Kai-shek, "Interview with a Reporter of the Min-kuo jih-pao Following the S.S. 'Chung-shan' Incident at Canton," pp. 414-16.

76. Chiang Kai-shek, Chiang Chieh-shih hsien-sheng, XV, 38-47. According to Liu Lu-yin, the March Twentieth Incident was instigated by Kubiak, chief of the Far Eastern Bureau of the Russian Communist Party, as a plot to destroy the KMT. See Liu Lu-yin, "Revolution and Counterrevolution," p. 490. According to Chiang's diary, Kubiak arrived at Canton on March 13, 1926, as a representative of the Soviet Union. He was welcomed by Chiang; see Chiang Kai-shek, Chiang Chieh-shih hsien-sheng, XIV, 78. Kubiak had gone first to Peking. Fuse reports that Kubiak headed an inspection

team composed of important members of the Russian Communist Party. He held important conferences with Borodin and Karakhan in Peking. See Fuse, Su-Wo ti Tung-fang cheng-ts'e, p. 222; Soviet Policy in the Orient, p. 219. Ch'en Tu-hsiu confirms that a Soviet inspection team composed mainly of members of the CC of the Russian Communist Party was in Canton on March 20, 1926. See Ch'en Tu-hsiu, Kao ch'üan-tang..., p. 3.

77. Chiang Kai-shek, Chiang Chieh-shih hsien-sheng, XV, 2-3, 17.

78. Ibid., XV, 15.

79. According to a Japanese source, Chiang Kai-shek had Wu T'ieh-ch'eng arrested and confined at Hu-men for several months. He was released in July, 1926, on the intercession of Madame Sun Yat-sen. See Gendai Shina jimmei kan, p. 716.

80. Confirmed in Chiang's diary, see Chiang Kai-shek, Chiang Chieh-shih hsien-sheng, XIV, 82, 87.

81. Ibid., XIV, 88-89.

82. Ibid., XV, 36, 61.

83. Stepanov mentioned "Mr. Sung" (T. V. Soong?), Li Chi-shen, T'an Yen-k'ai, Chu P'ei-te, and Teng (Yen-ta?). See Doc. 23, p. 68. Except for Teng Yen-ta, these men were among those to whom Chiang conveyed his intention of resigning on March 26, and whose support prompted him to withdraw his resignation that same evening.

84. According to Seifulin's case history, his real name was Albert Yakovlevich Labin (or Rabin). He was born May 28, 1899 and joined the Communist Party in 1916. A graduate of a military academy, Seifulin served in the Russian Red Army and was stationed in the Far Eastern Republic from 1917 to 1921. He was sent to China in 1925. He served as instructor in the First Kuominchün and concurrently as a member of the Soviet Intelligence Branch in Kalgan from April to June, 1925. He served in the Soviet Intelligence Branch in Kaifeng from June to October, 1925, then began working at the Soviet Military's Attaché's office in Peking. He took part in the battle between the First Kuominchün and Li Ching-lin's forces in Tientsin in December, 1925. Seifulin succeeded A. I. Egorov as Soviet Military Attaché for a few months in 1926. See Su-lien yin-mou..., II, "Military," pp. 53-54.

85. "Resolutions on the China Question," pp. 648-49. Hu Han-min was an honored guest at the Plenum.

86. Stalin, "The International Situation," p. 237.

87. Nilov was appointed adviser with Li Chi-shen's Fourth Army in July, 1925. Borodin sent him to Kwangsi with members of the Party and Government, presumably to negotiate on the inclusion of Kwangsi province under Kuomintang jurisdiction. See "Minutes of the Military Conference in Canton on July 1, 1925"; "A List of Soviet Russian Personnel," Su-lien yin-mou..., III, "Canton," pp. 95-100.

88. Huang Hao, "A True picture of the S.S. 'Chung-shan' Incident," p. 102. According to one source, among the strongest proponents of a direct offensive were Ch'en Yen-nien, eldest son of Ch'en Tu-hsiu, who was secretary of the Kwangtung Regional Committee; Chang T'ai-lei, head of the Propaganda Department; and Chou En-lai, head of the Military Committee of the Kwangtung Regional Committee. See Fang Lu, "Liquidation of Ch'en Tu-hsiu," p. 71.

89. Ch'ü Ch'iu-pai, Chung-kuo ko-ming, p. 74.

90. Ch'en Tu-hsiu, Kao ch'üan-tang..., pp. 3-4.

91. See, for instance, Ts'ai Ho-shen, "On Ch'en Tu-hsiuism," p. 22.

92. Quoted by Mif, Chin-chi shih-chi..., p. 25.

93. Yakhontoff, The Chinese Soviets, pp. 123-24. Trotsky had by this time demanded the withdrawal of Communists from the Kuomintang. See Isaacs, Tragedy of the Chinese Revolution, for details on the Stalin-Trotsky dispute on the Chinese Revolution.

94. Chiang Kai-shek, Chiang Chieh-shih hsien-sheng, XV, 55. Borodin arrived at Canton with Hu Han-min, who was back from Moscow.

95. Borodin saw Chiang on the day of his arrival and held conferences with him on succeeding days. Ibid., XV, 53, 54, 58, 62, 66, 73.

96. Borodin saw Chiang on May 12, 13, and 14, the three days before the Plenum convened, and on May 16, the second day of the Plenum. On May 14, Borodin disagreed with Chiang on the question of KMT-KCT relations. He was quieted by Chiang, who admitted that the proposed regulations governing Communist activities were harsh. Chiang asserted that a big party, by allowing a small party to work within it, was actually seeking self-destruction. Since it was Sun Yat-sen's policy to unite all classes, however, Chiang said he did not wish to violate Sun's principles and had thus endured all the necessary pain. On May 16, 1926, Chiang told Borodin that the Revolution must be centralized in order to succeed. Ibid., XV, 62, 66.

97. Nassonov, Fokine, and Albrecht, "The Letter from Shanghai," p. 407.

98. Quoted by Mif, Chin-chi shih-chi..., p. 26. Most sources assert that Borodin and the Kwangtung Communists cooperated closely in Canton. In 1930, Borodin himself stated that there were two wings in the KCT as early as 1923: the Canton Communists and Borodin, standing in opposition to the Shanghai CC led by Ch'en Tu-hsiu. See Yakhontoff, The Chinese Soviets, pp. 125-26.

99. Chiang Kai-shek, Chiang Chieh-shih hsien-sheng, XV, 64-65.

100. "Resolutions of the Plenum of the Central Executive Committee of the Kuomintang," pp. 9-11.

101. Chiang Kai-shek, Chiang Chieh-shih hsien-sheng, XV, 65.

102. Ibid., XV, 67. According to Ch'en Kuo-fu, Chang Ching-chiang left Shanghai for Canton immediately after March Twentieth. He was followed shortly afterward by Ch'en himself, who had been handling enrollment of students for the Central Military and Political Academy at Shanghai. Ch'en Kuo-fu recalled that upon his arrival Chang Ching-chiang told him that the Communists would destroy the Kuomintang if allowed to remain in the Party. Chiang compared Communists to an eared owl, a mother-eating species. See Ch'en Kuo-fu, "A Piece of Party History," p. 62.

103. Chiang Kai-shek, Chiang Chieh-shih hsien-sheng, XV, 77; Chou Ts'ui-fen, "Central Party Headquarters during the Canton Period," p. 44.

104. "Letter from the Chinese Communist Party to the Kuomintang," pp. 1525-26.

105. Chiang Kai-shek, Chiang Chieh-shih hsien-sheng, XV, 73.

106. Chiang's diary confirms that Hu Han-min left Canton for Hongkong on May 9, 1926, on the same boat with Wang Ching-wei; see Ibid., XV, 61. Anti-Communist sources confirm that Borodin played an important part in the series of setbacks suffered by the Right Wing in 1926. According to Liu Lu-yin, for instance, it was Borodin who was responsible for Hu Han-min's departure from Canton (Liu Lu-yin, "Revolution and Counterrevolution," p. 491). Another source asserts that Wu Ch'ao-shu was involved in negotiations with the governor of Hongkong for a $10,000,000 loan to be used against the National Government. Wu was forced out of Canton when Borodin learned of the loan and insisted that the authorities take action against Wu. See Yang Hsin-hua, "Wu Ch'ao-shu and the Hongkong Government," p. 199.

107. Chiang Kai-shek, Chiang Chieh-shih hsien-sheng, XV, 54.

108. Tong, Chiang Kai-shek, p. 59. Writing one year after the event, George Sokolsky asserted that Borodin used the Northern Expedition as a weapon in bargaining with Chiang Kai-shek for his own terms. See Sokolsky, "General Chiang and Wang Ching-wei," p. 92. Among the documents seized in the Peking raid is one purporting to be the record of a meeting of a subsidiary organ of the ECCI in Moscow on August 4, 1926. The commission decided, in view of insufficient information, to put off the question of the "so-called" Northern Expedition until the next sitting. The document then states: "The Commission once more points out the real danger of the assistance extended by Canton to Hunan, which might develop into a great military operation, and objects strongly against the crossing of the borders of Hunan by the Canton Army and is in favor of stopping the further moving of troops out of the province of Kwangtung." The authenticity of the document, however, has yet to be determined. See Soviet Plot in China, pp. 24-29. If authentic, it would indicate that the decision to support the Northern

Expedition was made on the spot, independent of the ECCI in Moscow.

109. T'ang was a divisional commander under Governor Chao Heng-t'i of Hunan. A rift began to develop between T'ang and Chao in the fall of 1925. On February 24, 1925, T'ang occupied Changsha and pursued Chao's forces to Yoyang (Yochow), on the Hunan-Hupeh border. Five days earlier, T'ang had dispatched an emissary to Canton to conduct secret negotiations on an alliance with the National Government. When T'ang was defeated by the forces of Wu P'ei-fu in March, 1926, he again made overtures to Canton for an alliance. By April 24, T'ang had retreated to Hengyang and appealed to the National Government for immediate aid. See Chiang Kai-shek, Chiang Chieh-shih hsien-sheng, XIV, 16, 65, and XV, 48, 76.

110. Ibid., XV, 78.

111. T'ang Leang-li, Foundations of Modern China, p. 174.

112. Chiang Kai-shek, Chiang Chieh-shih hsien-sheng, XV, 79, 91, XVI, 4, 6.

113. Ch'en Tu-hsiu, "On the National Government's Northern Expedition," pp. 1584-85.

114. At the Fifth Congress, Ch'en Tu-hsiu confirmed that the KCT had been reluctant in its support of the Northern Expedition. The Party's attitude was definitely negative, he said. See Mif, Chin-chi shih-chi..., p. 72.

115. The Central Committee referred to the New Right Wing interchangeably as the Center in July, 1926, although in October, 1925, it had declared that there was no such thing as the Center.

116. The orthodox Communist interpretation defines the March 20th coup d'état as the culmination of Taichitaoism. This interpretation was formulated as early as April-May, 1927, in Ch'en Tu-hsiu's political report to the Fifth Congress. See Mif, Chin-chi shih-chi..., p. 26.

117. Ch'en Kuo-fu, "A Piece of Party History...," pp. 64, 65, 68.

Part V: The Chinese Communist Party's
Policies in the Mass Movement

1. The Kuo-chia chu-i Clique was led by Tseng Ch'i, Li Huang, Yü Chia-chü, and Ho Kung-kan, among others. Its nationalistic views were publicized in two major periodicals, Hsing-shih chou-pao [awakened lion weekly] and Ku-chün chou-pao [solitary army weekly], later known as Tu-li ch'ing-nien [independent youth]. Hostility between members of the group and the Chinese Communists dates back to 1921, when Chou En-lai, Chao Shih-yen, Li Li-san, and Ch'en Yen-nien, founders of the Chinese Communist Youth Corps in Paris, engaged in disputes with members of the group. See, for instance, Hatano, "Biography of Chou En-lai," pp. 89-91; T'an I-chung, "A Story about Li Li-san," pp. 151-55.

2. Chung-kuo Kung-ch'an-tang tui-yü shih-chü ti chu-chang, p. 24.

3. Enlarged Plenum of the Central Committee, Chinese Communist Party, "Letter to the Peasantry," p. 128; Central Committees of the Chinese Communist Party and the ₁Chinese Communist Youth Corps, "Letter to the First National Peasant Conference," p. 1438.

Part VI: Kuomintang and Soviet
Relations with Feng Yü-hsiang

1. Feng Yü-hsiang, Feng Yü-hsiang jih-chi, I, 121, 123.

2. Before the Second Mukden-Chihli War, according to Feng, many KMT members, among them Huang Fu, discussed with him plans for overthrowing Wu P'ei-fu. He had frequent contacts with KMT members. H. H. Kung, on Sun Yat-sen's instructions, brought him copies of Sun's writings. Hsü Ch'ien often visited him. The first concrete move to stage a coup occurred on September 10, 1924, when Feng suggested to Sun Yüeh, Commander of the Chihli Army's Fifteenth Mixed Brigade and vice-commander of the Peking garrison, that they cooperate in overthrowing Wu P'ei-fu. Sun Yüeh not only agreed, according to Feng, but suggested that Hu Ching-yi, commander of the First Shensi Army, stationed in Honan, be brought into the alliance. Two weeks later, a definite agreement was reached with Hu Ching-yi through his emissary, Yüeh Wei-chün. This included, Feng asserts, the stipulation that Sun Yat-sen be invited to Peking upon the successful conclusion of the coup. Feng asserts further that he met with Chang Tso-lin's representative at Kupehkow, on the boundary between Chihli and Jehol, and demanded acceptance of his condition that Sun Yat-sen be invited to North China. According to Feng, the very name "Kuominchün" was selected to demonstrate that the coup was a revolution in support of Sun Yat-sen. Since Sun's party was called the Kuomintang, Feng's army was to be known as the Kuominchün. See Feng Yü-hsiang,· Wo ti sheng-huo, III, 1, 2, 5-8, 18, 19.

3. Feng Yü-hsiang, Feng Yü-hsiang jih-chi, I, 136.

4. Chou Lu, Chung-kuo Kuomintang shih-kao, p. 1096.

5. "An Important Declaration of the Generalissimo on the Current Situation," pp. 18-24.

6. Wang Ching-wei, "On Generalissimo Sun's Trip to the North," p. 26.

7. Sun Yat-sen, "The Generalissimo's Circular Telegram on the Reconstruction Conference," pp. 27-29.

8. Central Executive Committee of the Kuomintang, "Circular Telegram Announcing Our Party Will Not Join the Reconstruction Conference," pp. 30-31.

9. Central Committee of the Chinese Communist Party, "Second

Manifesto of the Chinese Communist Party on the Current Situation,"
p. 52.

10. "Fourth Manifesto of the Chinese Communist Party on the
Current Situation," pp. 64-69.

11. Mif, Chin-chi shih-chi..., p. 24. Borodin also allegedly opposed
Sun's decision to go to Peking. Certain KMT sources assert that
Borodin attempted to obstruct Sun's departure from Kwangtung and
even attempted to induce Sun to go to Russia. Hence, his sudden departure for Japan, which served as a detour to Peking. See, for
instance, Liu Lu-yin, "Revolution and Counterrevolution," p. 456.

12. P'eng Shu-chih, "The question of Dr. Sun's attitude," pp. 817-
18.

13. "Manifesto of the Fourth Congress of the Chinese Communist
Party," pp. 833-35.

14. Li T'ai-fen, Kuominchün shih-kao, pp. 314-15.

15. Feng Yü-hsiang, Wo-ti sheng-huo, III, 32-33. According to
Feng's later account, the decision to support Tuan was necessitated
by military expediency. On October 24, 1924, Feng asserts, it was
learned that Wu P'ei-fu had launched a counterattack. Cheng Shih-
ch'i, governor of Shantung, commanded a strategic position, since
he could help Wu's forces attacking the Kuominchün from the south.
Since Cheng was a member of the Anfu Clique, Feng recalls that
Sun Yüeh proposed supporting Tuan Ch'i-jui in order to win over
Cheng, and that this suggestion was unanimously accepted. See Ibid.,
pp. 22-23.

16. Chiang Kai-shek, Chiang Chieh-shih hsien-sheng, XIII, 13,
61, 67-70. Chiang's diary includes detailed annual chronologies of
important events throughout the country. They prove generally accurate when checked against other sources and are particularly valuable in giving exact dating of events.

17. Feng Yü-hsiang, Wo ti sheng-huo, III, 37.

18. Ibid., III, 41-42.

19. Feng Yü-hsiang, Feng Yü-hsiang jih-chi, II, 4.

20. Ibid., II, 37.

21. "Jen Te-chiang" is referred to as "Jen Chiang" in Feng Yü-
hsiang's autobiography. Feng recalls that he had fought in World
War I. When Feng went to Moscow in the summer of 1926, "Jen
Te-chiang" was a general in the Red Army and was in charge of
training the army. See Feng Yü-hsiang, Wo ti sheng-huo, III, 42, 109.

22. "Report on the First Kuominchün," Su-lien yin-mou..., III,
"Kuominchün," p. 30.

23. Chou Lu, Chung-kuo Kuomintang shih-kao, p. 1096.

24. "Lin's report," March 26, 1926, Su-lien yin-mou..., III,
"Kuominchün," p. 44.

25. China Year Book, 1925, p. 922.

26. The following is Li T'ai-fen's version of the first meeting

between Borodin and Feng: Borodin left Canton on March 26, 1925 and stayed at Kalgan for two days. Feng entertained him as a representative of the Canton Government. Borodin informed Feng that the Russians would withdraw aid from the KMT and help him instead if he had better plans for saving the country. Borodin added, however, that if Feng had no such plans, he should join the KMT and work jointly with it for the National Revolution. See Li T'ai-fen, Kuominchün shih-kao, pp. 301-4.

27. According to Feng's autobiography, around the beginning of 1925, Borodin and Karakhan visited him on several occasions and they discussed revolution, religion, and abolition of the unequal treaties, with Eugene Chen acting as interpreter. Feng told them that China was willing to accept as a friend any country which aids her in the struggle for freedom and independence, and finally asked them to introduce advisers to his army. The military experts, about thirty in number, who subsequently arrived were free to leave whenever they so chose, Feng asserts. There were no binding regulations and the advisers had complete freedom of movement. See Feng Yü-hsiang, Wo ti Sheng-huo, p. 42. Feng's diary makes no mention of the negotiations. The only reference to any discussion with Russians is the entry of May 6, 1925, which states that Feng met a certain Russian and held a detailed conversation with him about the manufacture of tanks, the use of the cavalry during the European War, and the work of training in Soviet Russia. See Feng Yü-hsiang, Feng Yü-hsiang jih-chi, II, 60.

28. According to Feng's diary, he stated on many occasions that Russian influence in Outer Mongolia must be restricted. On February 6, 1925, for instance, he said it was necessary to find means to limit Russian rights in Outer Mongolia. On February 17, 1925, he said that Russian troops must withdraw from Outer Mongolia. See Feng Yü-hsiang, Feng Yü-hsiang jih-chi, II, 9, 14.

29. Voronin succeeded A. I. Gecker as Military Attaché. He himself was succeeded by A. I. Egorov.

30. Jen Te-chiang had resigned and returned to Russia. According to Feng, his resignation stemmed from anger over Feng's intervention in a dispute between Jen and a cavalry brigade commander over the distribution of horses, when Feng said that the Russians had no right to interfere in administrative matters. See Feng Yü-hsiang, Wo ti sheng-huo, III, 54.

31. "Telegram on the Dispatch of Students from Feng's Army," Su-lien yin-mou..., III, "Kuominchün," pp. 70-72.

32. This chapter deals primarily with Feng Yü-hsiang's First Kuominchün. For information on the work of Soviet advisers in the Second and Third Kuominchün, see documents in the "Kuominchün" section, Su-lien yin-mou..., III.

33. Feng Yü-hsiang, Wo ti sheng-huo, III, 45.

34. "Lin's Report," March 26, 1926, Su-lien yin-mou..., III, "Kuominchün," pp. 49-50; "The Soviet Military Mission with the First Kuominchün Army," April 19, 1926, Soviet Plot in China, p. 96.

35. Chiang Kai-shek, Chiang Chieh-shih hsien-sheng, XI, 51. Some sources assert that Shao Li-tzu went also as Chiang Kai-shek's personal representative to Feng Yü-hsiang. See, for instance, Yün Tien, "Anecdotes about Shao Li-tzu," p. 83.

36. Gendai Shina jimmei-kan, p. 38.

37. Chiang Kai-shek, Chiang Chieh-shih hsien-sheng, XI, p. 52; "Report on the Activities of Party Members and the Red Spears in Honan," Su-lien yin-mou..., III, "Kuominchün," pp. 40-41.

38. Hsieh Yeh, "Han Lin-fu," pp. 395-406; Han Lin-fu, "Plan for Assisting Armed Civilians in Jehol," Soviet Plot in China, pp. 114-16.

39. "A Honanese," "Early Activities of the Chinese Communist Party in Honan," p. 292.

40. T'an Kung, "Hsiao Ch'u-nü," p. 317.

41. Pai Lin, "The Northern Communist Leader An T'i-ch'eng," p. 294.

42. Lo Yüan-K'un, Chung-kuo chin pai nien shih, II, 43-44.

43. Teng Chung-hsia, Chung-kuo chih-kung yün-tung shih, p. 225; "National Revolutionary Movement in China and Tactics of the Chinese Communist Party," p. 22.

44. I. Heller, "The Labour Movement in China," pp. 12, 15.

45. "National Revolutionary Movement in China and Tactics of the Chinese Communist Party," p. 25.

46. Ibid., p. 23; "The Conference of the Communist Party of China," p. 1166.

47. "National Revolutionary Movement in China and Tactics of the Chinese Communist Party," p. 27.

48. Chiang Kai-shek, Chiang Chieh-shih hsien-sheng, XIII, 70.

49. Ibid., XIII, 71.

50. Ibid., XIII, 73.

51. Central Committees of the Chinese Communist Party and the Chinese Communist Youth Corps, "Manifesto on the Anti-Mukden War," pp. 124-26. The KCT's optimism at this time was confirmed by the CC in July, 1926, when it reported that in October, 1925, it had appeared that the Kuomintang in the South and the Kuominchün in the North might join together to seize political power throughout the country and establish a relatively Red government. See Doc. 26, p. 62.

52. "Manifesto of the Kuomintang of China on the Current Situation," pp. 84-86; Peking Executive Headquarters of the Central Executive Committee of the Kuomintang, "Manifesto of Our Party on the Current Situation," pp. 3-11.

53. Chiang Kai-shek, Chiang Chieh-shih hsien-sheng, XIII, 74.

54. Fuse, Su Wo ti Tung-fang Cheng-ts'e, p. 221.

55. "Manifesto of Our Party on the Current Situation," pp. 11-13.

56. Feng Yü-hsiang, Feng Yu-hsiang jih-chi, II, 135, 136, 138.

57. Central Committees of the Chinese Communist Party and the Chinese Communist Youth Corps, "Statement to the People on the Rebellion of Kuo Sung-ling," pp. 138-40.

58. Central Executive Committee of the Kuomintang, "Manifesto of the Kuomintang of China on the Revolutionary Movement in Peking," p. 98. The Kuomintang's antigovernment struggle coincided with intensification of intra-Party conflicts. With the inauguration of the "New Right Wing" at the Western Hills of Peking in November, 1925, the Peking Kuomintang Left Wing and Communists had to wage war simultaneously against the New Right Wing and the government. Communists accused Chou Lu, a leader of the Right Wing, of forcing Lu Chung-lin to suppress the demonstration of November 28, 1925. See Ch'en Tu-hsiu, "Reactionary Tendencies of the KMT New Right Wing," p. 1267; Chang Kuo-t'ao, "An Open Letter to All Members of the Kuomintang," p. 1270.

59. Entries in Feng's diaries in this period contain frequent references to "Adviser Lin" without explanation of his status or any mention of arrangements with the Russians. Feng's diary also mentions without further explanation the presence of Russian instructors. On September 3, 1925, for instance, Feng ordered battalion commanders to have frequent contacts and discussions with Russian instructors and to learn their good points. On September 11, 1925, he told brigade commanders to utilize the opportunity provided by the Russian instructors to develop the Kuominchün's technical capacity. (See ibid., II, 95, 106). Feng's diary is complete for 1925 except for the period from July 11 to August 31.

60. "Report on the First Kuominchün," Su-lien yin-mou..., III, "Kuominchün," p. 31.

61. Ya-en may have been on Kubiak's inspection team. See Part IV, Note 76.

62. Li T'ai-fen, Kuominchün shih-kao, p. 298.

63. According to his diary, Feng retired because many elements in the First, Second, Third, Fourth and Fifth Kuominchün failed to understand the significance of principles and cared only for money, weapons, and territorial expansion. Furthermore, he recognized his own shortcomings and decided to study abroad in preparation for the task of saving the country. See Feng Yü-hsiang, Feng Yu-hsiang jih-chi, II, 8. In his autobiography, he explains that the retirement resulted from disagreement with the Government's appointment of Sun Yüeh, Third Kuominchün Commander, as military governor of Chihli. Feng wanted Chang Chih-chiang to have the post. See Feng Yü-hsiang, Wo ti sheng-huo, III, 67.

64. On November 15, 1925, for instance, Henry A. Lin asked Feng about his attitude on the current situation. Feng answered that lack of principles was the cause of political disturbances in China. He said the Three People's Principles were his guide. See Feng Yü-hsiang, Feng Yü-hsiang jih-chi, II, 128. The diaries abound with such remarks made to subordinates, visitors, interviewers, and the army.

65. Li T'ai-fen, Kuominchün shih-kao, p. 300.

66. "Lin's report," March 26, 1926, Su-lien yin-mou..., III, "Kuominchün," p. 52.

67. Chiang Kai-shek, Chiang Chieh-shih hsien-sheng, XII, 78. Remnants of Kuo Sung-ling's defeated army were reorganized by Kuo's lieutenant, Wei I-san, into the Fourth Kuominchün. The following are other units of the Kuominchün. The Fifth Kuominchün under the command of Fang Chen-wu was organized on January 18, 1926. Fang had defected from the army of Chang Tsung-ch'ang. The Sixth Kuominchün was organized shortly afterward under the command of Kung Fu-k'uei, who had deserted from the Shansi Army. The Seventh Kuominchün, commanded by Lü Hsiu-ts'ai, was actually organized before the Fourth, Fifth and Sixth Kuominchün. Lü had been a subordinate of the governor of Shantung Cheng Shih-ch'i, whose support of the Kuominchün was allegedly arranged in return for Tuan Ch'i-jui leadership of the provisional government. The Seventh Kuominchün existed for a brief period between November, 1924, and May 15, 1925, when it was defeated by Chang Tsung-ch'ang's army. See Feng Yü-hsiang, Wo ti sheng-huo, III, 141; Li T'ai-fen, Kuominchün shih-kao, p. 287.

68. Chiang Kai-shek, Chiang Chieh-shih hsien-sheng, XX, 108.

69. Ibid., XX, 112. The Second Kuominchün, the largest unit in the Kuominchün combination in the spring of 1925, had undergone a steady reduction in size and strength following the death of Hu Ching-yi. As in Feng's First Kuominchün, the KMT encountered considerable difficulty in its attempt to work within the Second Kuominchün. The commander of the Second Kuominchün, Yüeh Wei-chün also incurred the hostility of the peasants by suppressing all peasant associations in Honan. The Chinese Communists in Honan encouraged this hostility, although officially they supported Yüeh Wei-chün. The opposition to Yüeh on the part of the Honanese peasantry and Red Spears Associations facilitated the defeat of the Second Kuominchün. See "Sinani's Report on a Conversation with Wei-k'o-ch'ia-pu-erh-szu-chi, a Member of the Honan Provincial Committee of the KCT," February 2, 1926, Su-lien yin-mou..., III, "Kuominchün," pp. 40-42; Doc. 29, p. 97.

70. "Report on the Kuominchün," Su-lien yin-mou..., III, "Kuominchün," p. 36.

71. Chiang Kai-shek, Chiang Chieh-shih hsien-sheng, XX, 113.

72. The Diplomatic Corps had first protested the installation of artillery at Taku as a violation of the Boxer Protocol in January, 1926. See Lo Yüan-k'un, Chung-kuo chin pai-nien shih, pp. 49-50.

73. Ibid., pp. 49-50.

74. Chiang Kai-shek, Chiang Chieh-shih hsien-sheng, XX, 113.

75. Feng Yü-hsiang, Feng Yü-hsiang jih-chi, II, 1-2. According to his autobiography, Feng had decided to go to Russia at the time of his resignation in January, 1926. See Feng Yü-hsiang, Wo ti sheng-huo, p. 67.

76. Feng Yü-hsiang, Feng Yü-hsiang jih-chi, II, 5. Feng's autobiography contradicts this. It states that Feng learned of the March Eighteenth Incident from Borodin and others at Ulan Bator.

77. "Lin's report," March 26, 1926, Su-lien yin-mou..., III, "Kuominchün," p. 50-52.

78. Feng Yü-hsiang, Feng Yü-hsiang jih-chi, II, 9. For a record of Feng's discussions and statements during the month at Urga (Ulan Bator), see ibid., II, 2-19.

79. Ibid., II, 9.

80. Feng Yü-hsiang, Wo ti sheng-huo, III, 82. Borodin had apparently left Canton early in February, 1926, to see Feng. Certain sources assert that he was in Peking during the March Eighteenth Incident. When he left for Kalgan under the protection of Lu Chung-lin, he was accompanied by Ku Meng-yü and Hsü Ch'ien, who were under warrant for arrest. Other KMT leaders who accompanied him reportedly included: Chu Chia-hua, Shao Li-tzu, and the Communists T'an P'ing-shan, Yü Shu-te, and An T'i-ch'eng. The group headed for Vladivostok from Urga (Ulan Bator) and from Vladivostok boarded a ship for Canton. See Wang Wei-lien, "Ch'en Ch'i-hsiu's Organization of a New Party," Jung Fu, "Ch'en Yü-jen's Political Career," 37-46.

81. Feng Yü-hsiang, Feng Yü-hsiang jih-chi, II, 9-10.

82. Feng Yü-hsiang, Wo ti sheng-huo, III, 82.

83. Feng Yü-hsiang, Feng Yü-hsiang jih-chi, II, 19.

84. "Feng Yü-hsiang's Wire to Chang Chih-chiang, Li Ming-chung, and Lu Chung-lin," May 3, 1926, Su-lien yin-mou..., III, "Kuominchün," p. 84. According to Feng's diary, he discussed the Kalgan situation with Karpenko at Verkne-Udinsk (Ulan-Ude) on May 3, the day he dispatched the wire. See Feng Yü-hsiang, Feng Yü-hsiang jih-chi, II, 21.

85. "The Soviet Military Mission with the First Kuominchün Army," Soviet Plot in China, p. 96.

86. Tang Shin She, "The Significance of the Coup d'état in Peking," pp. 441-42.

87. G. Voitinsky (Voitinskii), "Situation in China," pp. 62-66.

88. Feng Yü-hsiang, Feng Yü-hsiang jih-chi, II, 24-25. According to his autobiography, Feng reached the decision to enter the Kuo-

mintang under Hsü Ch'ien's influence. See Feng Yü-hsiang, Wo ti sheng-huo, III, 82.

89. Chiang Kai-shek, Chiang chieh-shih hsien-sheng, XX, 38, 114-15.

90. Ibid., p. 114.

91. A Russian adviser reported shortly before the withdrawal to Nankow that Chief of Staff Liu Chi had informed him that the withdrawal would have been ordered sooner had there not been hope of a compromise with Wu P'ei-fu. See "Henkel's Report to Seifulin," Su-lien yin-mou..., III, "KMC," p. 100.

92. Feng Yü-hsiang, Feng Yü-hsiang jih-chi, II, 20.

93. "Report on the First Kuominchün," Su-lien yin-mou..., III, "Kuominchün," p. 32. For itemized lists of supplies, see "Statement of Arms and Ammunition Delivered to the First Kuominchun Army from June 5, 1925, to January 4, 1926," Soviet Plot in China, pp. 72-73; "Statement of Arms and Ammunition delivered to the First Kuominchün Army from April 15, 1925, to July 8, 1926," ibid., pp. 74-75. While in Moscow, Feng Yü-hsiang signed an agreement promising to compensate the government of the USSR for all supplies received. Attached to the agreement were two receipts, certifying the amounts—6,395,642 rubles, and 4,501,999 rubles, respectively —to be repaid. See "Certified Copy of an Agreement Signed by Feng Yü-hsiang, in 1926, While in Moscow," "A Certified Copy of a Receipt for Roubles 6,395,642 Signed by Feng Yü-hsiang, in 1926, While in Moscow," "A Certified Copy of a Receipt for Roubles 4,501,999 Signed by Feng Yü-hsiang, in 1926, While in Moscow," Soviet Plot in China, pp. 76-81.

94. T'an Ong, "A Short History of Sun Yat-sen University in Moscow," pp. 187-220; Ch'ang Jen, "Feng Yü-hsiang's Changes," Hsien-tai shih-liao, III, 67.

95. Feng Yü-hsiang, Feng Yü-hsiang jih-chi, II, 28.

96. Fuse, Su Wo ti Tung-fang cheng-ts'e, pp. 318-19.

97. Feng did not get to meet Stalin, he said, because Stalin was at a Black Sea resort during his stay. See Feng Yü-hsiang, Wo ti sheng-huo, III, 95-101.

98. Feng Yü-hsiang, Feng Yü-hsiang jih-chi, II, 27, 30.

99. Feng Yü-hsiang, Wo ti sheng-huo, III, 93. According to a Soviet personnel list, Usmanov's real name was Sangurskii. See "List of Persons Working in the Northwestern Army," Su-lien yin-mou..., III, "Kuominchün," p. 104.

100. Feng Yü-hsiang, Wo ti sheng-huo, III, 93.

101. Ibid., III, 116.

102. Li T'ai-fen, Kuominchün shih-kao, p. 305. The Kuomintang welcomed Feng into the Party fold. On June 3, 1926, the day before the formal order for the Northern Expedition was issued, Chiang Kai-shek wired to Feng Yü-hsiang asking him to come to

Canton and participate in planning strategy for the Expedition. On July 1, 1926, Chiang Kai-shek, as chairman of the Military Council, announced that the National Revolutionary Army pushing north from Canton should first occupy Hunan and the Wuhan cities in Hupeh and then effect a juncture with Feng Yü-hsiang's Kuominchün. See Chiang Kai-shek, Chiang Chieh-shih hsien-sheng, XX, 78; XVI, 1.

103. Chiang Kai-shek, Chiang Chieh-shih hsien-sheng, XVI, 112, 117.

104. Ibid., XVI, 121.

105. Li T'ai-fen, Kuominchün shih-kao, pp. 314-15; Feng Yü-hsiang, Wo ti sheng-huo, III, 131-32.

Part VII: Kuomintang-Communist Relations during the Northern Expedition

1. Chiang Kai-shek, Chiang Chieh-shih hsien-sheng, XV, 91. The detailed information on units of the Northern Expeditionary Forces in Chiang's diary, generally proves accurate when checked against other sources.

2. Ibid., XVI, 1.

3. Ibid., XV, 32; XVI, 65.

4. Ibid., XVI, 112, 131; XVII, 5.

5. Ibid., XVII, 16, 20; XVIII, 37.

6. Ibid., XVIII, 13.

7. Ibid., XIV, 58; XVI, 1-3.

8. Ibid., XVI, 76, 79. Chiang left Canton on July 26, 1927; ibid., XVI, 59.

9. Ibid., XVI, 106; 124-25.

10. Ibid., XVII, 31, 49, 57. Chiang wired Sun Ch'uan-fang on September 12 and September 17, 1926, asking him to withdraw his troops from Kiangsi. On September 18, 1926, Chiang wired Teng Yen-ta to contact Sun's representatives in Hankow to inform them that Kiangsi could still remain within the combination of the Five Provinces on condition that Sun's army be withdrawn.

11. Ibid., XVII, 60, 72; XVIII, 4.

12. Ibid., XVIII, 51.

13. On October 23, 1926, Chiang wired Chang Ching-chiang, deputy chairman of the CEC, and T'an Yen-k'ai, chairman of the National Government, at Canton, informing them that Sun Ch'uan-fang was reportedly planning to withdraw from Kiangsi and Fukien in order to defend Kiangsu and Chekiang. Chiang suggested that a peaceful agreement might be made with Sun, provided he agreed to turn Chekiang over to the National Government or allowed the province to maintain neutrality. Chiang met with representatives of Sun that same day and again three days later. See ibid., XVIII, 110, 115.

14. Ibid., XVIII, 128, 137-39.

15. Ibid., XVI, 74.

16. Ibid., XVI, 120-21.

17. Kuo Mo-jo, Ko-ming ch'un-ch'iu, p. 294.

18. Chiang Kai-shek, Chiang Chieh-shih hsien-sheng, XVII, 22, 54-55.

19. In his reminiscent account of the Northern Expedition, Kuo Mo-jo recalls that Teruni was a general in the Red Army's cavalry and was wounded several times during the Russian Revolution. He was well versed in political affairs and was a cultivated person; he was particularly fond of poetry. See Kuo Mo-Jo, Ko-ming ch'un-ch'iu, pp. 294, 357.

20. Chiang Kai'shek, Chiang Chieh-shih hsien-sheng, XVIII, 51, 105, 137. Chiang proposed the immediate transfer of the CEC to Wuhan, leaving the Central Party Headquarters and the National Government in Canton, or the transfer of both the Central Party Headquarters and the CEC to Wuhan.

21. See, for instance, P'eng Shu-chih, "On the Transfer of the National Government," pp. 2008-9, on the Communist assertion that the Joint Conference decided on moving to Wuhan. Communists had made no such claims prior to the development of Wuhan-Nanchang conflict on the location of the capital. An article published in the International Press Correspondence in December 1926, for instance, definitely states that the Joint Conference had decided to remain in Canton. See Tang Shin She, "The Removal of the Kuomintang Government to Wuchang," p. 1498.

22. Chiang Ting-fu (T. F. Tsiang), Chün-cheng ling-hsiu Chiang Chieh-shih, p. 99; Tong, Chiang Kai-shek, p. 81.

23. Wan Yah-kang, Rise of Communism in China, p. 10. According to Ch'en Kuo-fu, Communists inspired an unsuccessful attempt to lodge a formal complaint against Chang Ching-chiang at the Joint Conference. See Ch'en Kuo-fu, "A Piece of Party History...," p. 69.

24. The following resolutions were adopted, according to Hu Hua: (1) to raise democracy within the Party; (2) to oppose dictatorship; (3) to develop the peasant and labor movements; and (4) to carry out a 25 percent rent reduction. These resolutions are not confirmed by other sources. See Hu Hua, Chung-kuo hsin min-chu-chu-i ko-ming shih, p. 81.

25. Chiang Kai-shek, Chiang Chieh-shih hsien-sheng, XVIII, 137; XVI, 109. On August 24, 1926, Chiang wired the CEC demanding that the KCT bear responsibility for Ch'en Tu-hsiu's article, "On the National Government's Northern Expedition," which, he said, clearly proved the Communist intention to break the cooperation with the KMT (see XVI, 121). However, Chiang wired Wang Ching-wei directly, asking him to return to his duties and telling him that the future of the Party depended on their cooperation (see XVII, 95-96; XVIII, 5).

26. Ch'ü Ch'iu-pai, Chung-kuo ko-ming..., p. 39. See, for instance, Ch'en Kuo-fu, "A Piece of Party History...," p. 68, and Li Ang, Hung-se wu-t'ai, p. 11, on the assertion that the Movement to Welcome Wang was planned and directed by the Communists. Ch'en Kuo-fu asserts that the Joint Conference was utilized by Communists to carry out the conspiracy of welcoming Wang to overthrow Chiang.

27. Mandalyan, Wei shen-mo Chung-kuo Kung-ch'an-tang ti ling-tao p'o-ch'an, p. 4. Following the break between the Left KMT and the Communists at Wuhan in July, 1927, a group of communists formed the Revolutionary Committee at Nanchang. On August 1, 1927, led by Ho Lung and Yeh T'ing, they staged an uprising, known as the Nanchang Uprising.

28. "Resolutions on the Problem of the KMT Left Wing...," p. 72.

29. Ibid., pp. 72, 76.

30. Ch'ü Ch'iu-pai, Chung-kuo ko-ming yü Kung-ch'an-tang, p. 77.

31. Ibid., p. 42.

32. See Part IV, p. 224.

33. Chiang Kai-shek, Chiang Chieh-shih hsien-sheng, XVIII, 17, 28.

34. Ibid., XVII, 11. On September 12, 1926, Chiang wired Ho Ying-ch'in to declare that peace could be maintained provided the Fukien army were withdrawn (XVI, 31).

35. Ibid., XVIII, 65; XX, 8, 57.

36. Hsia Ch'ao defected to the National Government on October 13, 1926; he was followed by Chou Feng-ch'i. See ibid., XVIII, 45, 51.

37. The autonomous movement in the provinces of Chekiang, Kiangsu, and Anhwei represented an internal anti-Sun Ch'uan-fang movement in support of the National Government.

38. Chiang Kai-shek, Chiang Chieh-shih hsien-sheng, XX, p. 2, 16, 17. Chou Tzu-sheng, "The Northern Expeditionary War of the National Revolutionary Army," p. 32.

39. Chiang Kai-shek, Chiang Chieh-shih hsien-sheng, XIV, 75, 92-93.

40. Ibid., XX, 91.

41. Ibid., XVIII, 8.

42. Ibid., XIX, 112. Referring to troops sent by Chang Tsung-ch'ang to re-enforce Sun's army.

43. Ibid., XX, 6.

44. Chiang Kai-shek, Chiang Chieh-shih hsien-sheng, XX, 81.

45. Ibid., XX, 101.

46. Ibid., XX, 15.

47. Ibid., XX, 18.

48. Chiang and Borodin held a conference two days before the decisions were adopted. Ibid., XX, 15.

49. Ch'en Kuo-fu, "A Piece of Party History...," pp. 67, 70; he explains that in July, 1926, the Communists were not clear about his position. He had never participated in conflicts at Party headquarters and had not been openly affiliated with any clique. Aside from expressing the opinion that there should not be a party within a party, Ch'en had not made any statements opposing the KCT. To avoid friction, Ch'en asserts, he purposely avoided using KMT members who were prominently anti-Communist. Thus, it was not until following the Joint Conference in October, 1926, that the Communists began to attack him.

50. Ibid., pp. 68, 70.

51. Following the defection of Hsia Ch'ao, governor of Chekiang, to the National Government, Hsia sent a regiment to attack Shanghai under an agreement with Niu Yung-chien, KMT representative in Shanghai, calling for an insurrection in Shanghai to support the Chekiang Army. The date was set for October 24, 1926. Hsia's army was defeated, however. According to Communist sources, Niu learned of the defeat but still ordered the uprising to take place; thus only Communists were suppressed. A Russian representative, Ho-mieh-li-fu, reported to Borodin shortly after the insurrection that Niu was not to be trusted. See "Ho-mieh-lieh-fu's report to Borodin on the Work of Agitation in the Army in Shanghai," Su-lien yin-mou..., II, "Military," p. 28.

52. See, for instance, Chiang Kai-shek, Chiang Chieh-shih hsien-sheng, XIX, 30, 67-79.

53. Ibid., XX, 19.

54. Mitarevsky, World-wide Soviet Plots, pp. 118-19.

55. Yang Hsin-hua, "Yün Tai-ying," p. 298. Yün Tai-ying is credited with coining the slogan.

56. Galen had helped Chiang organize the Commander-in-Chief's headquarters in June, 1926. See Chiang Kai-shek, Chiang Chieh-shih hsien-sheng, XV, 80.

57. Ibid., XIX, 21-23.

58. Chen Ta, "Fundamentals of the Chinese Labor Movement," p. 200.

59. Mao Tse-tung, "Report on an Investigation of the Hunan Peasant Movement," pp. 2063-68. Chang Kai-lin, chief of the Department of Finance of the Hunan Provincial Government, reported to the Joint Council on December 27, 1927 that peasant associations frequently executed the gentry and "local bullies." See Mitarevsky, World-wide Soviet Plots, pp. 139-40.

60. Nassonov, Fokine, and Albrecht, "A Letter from Shanghai," p. 398.

61. "Resolutions on the Problem of the KMT Left Wing...," p. 71.

62. Snow, Red Star over China, p. 161. Following his inspection tour, Mao asserts, he recommended the policy of widespread redistribution of land but this was rejected by the CC.

63. Mitarevsky, World-wide Soviet Plots, pp. 135-36.

64. Longva had succeeded Seifulin as Soviet Military Attaché in the fall of 1926. See "List of Staff Members of the Soviet Military Attaché's Office in Peking," Su-lien yin-mou..., II, "Military," p. 87.

65. Mitarevsky, World-wide Soviet Plots, pp. 140-41.

66. "Resolutions on the Problem of the KMT Left Wing...," pp. 69-75.

67. Ch'en Tu-hsiu, "What are the Right and Left Wings of the Kuomintang?" pp. 1247-48.

68. "Resolutions on the Problem of the KMT Left Wing," pp. 75-77.

69. Ts'ai Ho-shen, "On Ch'en Tu-hsiuism," p. 22.

70. Soviet Plot in China, pp. 6, 8-10, 13-14, 16-17; see above, p. 482, note 128.

71. "Sixth Session of the Enlarged Executive Committee of the Young Communist International," pp. 1400-4. The Plenum was convened on November 12.

72. "Resolutions on the Problem of the KMT Left Wing...," p. 72.

73. Chou Ts'ui-fen, "On the Transfer of the Capital to Wuhan," p. 52; Woo, The Kuomintang and the Future of the Chinese Revolution, p. 226. The main body of Party and Government members left Canton on December 7, 1926.

74. Chiang Kai-shek, Chiang Chieh-shih hsien-sheng, XX, 33; Wang Wei-lien, "Teng Yen-ta during the Wuhan Period," p. 270.

75. Tong, Chiang Kai-shek, p. 63.

76. Chiang Kai-shek, Chiang Chieh-shih hsien-sheng, XX, 102.

77. Looting was engaged in by the Ninth and Tenth armies when they captured Ichang and Shasi on December 21 and 22, 1926. The two armies had joined the National Revolutionary Army in August, 1926, and were assigned the task of capturing western Hupeh to coincide with the attack on Wuhan.

P'eng Han-chang, commander of the Ninth Army, and Wang T'ien-p'ei, commander of the Tenth Army, were subordinates of Yüan Tsu-ming, commander of the Kweichow Army and military governor of the Szechuan, Yunnan, and Kweichow Border Area. Negotiations began in the spring of 1926 between the National Government and Yüan, and plans were subsequently made for the amalgamation of Yüan's army with the National Revolutionary Army. When Changsha was captured on July 10, 1926, Yüan Tsu-ming occupied Changteh, Hunan, and launched an offensive in western Hupeh. The campaign in western Hupeh progressed slowly. Ichang was captured on December 21 and Shasi on December 22, 1926. Ho Lung was a divisional commander in P'eng's Ninth Army. See ibid., XV, 73; XVI, 32; XX, 65, 75, 117.

78. Chiang Kai-shek, Chiang Chieh-shih hsien-sheng, XX, 79, 82-83, 104-5.

79. Tung-fang tsa-chih, XXIV, No. 5 (March 10, 1927), 109.

80. Ch'en Ming-shu, "Why We Want to Overthrow the Chinese Communist Party," pp. 365-66.

81. Woo, The Kuomintang and the Future of the Chinese Revolution, pp. 221-23.

82. M. N. Roy, My Experience in China, p. 46.

83. Wu Ch'ih-hui, "Petition to Safeguard the Party and Save the Nation," p. 47.

84. Ch'en Ming-shu, "Why We Want to Overthrow the Chinese Communist Party," p. 265.

85. Chiang Kai-shek, Chiang Chieh-shih hsien-sheng, XX, 105. On December 2, 1926, five days before the scheduled departure for Wuhan of the Party and Government staffs, Chiang wired T'an Yen-k'ai, requesting a stopover at Nanchang for conferences. See ibid., XX, 5.

86. Chiang Kai-shek, "Statement on 'Essential Points of Propaganda on Party Affairs,'" p. 19.

87. Tung-fang tsa-chih, XXIV, No. 5 (March 10, 1927), 100.

88. For an account of Chiang's speeches and the meetings he attended during his trip to Wuhan, see dispatch from Consul General Lockhart, Hankow, to Secretary of State, Jan. 22, 1927. State Department Archives 893.00/8342.

89. See, for instance, Liu Lu-yin, "Revolution and counterrevolution," p. 493.

90. Woo, The Kuomintang and the Future of the Chinese Revolution, p. 225.

91. See Note 21 above.

92. Nassonov, Fokine, and Albrecht, "The Letter from Shanghai," pp. 402, 406-7.

93. The China Year Book, 1928, pp. 739-42.

94. Nassonov, Fokine, and Albrecht, "The Letter from Shanghai," pp. 403, 406.

95. Tung Pi-wu, for instance, asserts that Chiang ordered the execution of many Communists in Kian as soon as he returned to Kiangsi. See Nym Wales, Red Dust: Autobiographies of Chinese Communists..., p. 42.

96. "Documents on the Conference of Party Members of Wuhan, Han-yang, Hsia-k'o," pp. 1-3.

97. Reprinted in Ch'en Tu-hsiu, "Internal Conflicts of the KMT and the Chinese Revolution," pp. 2045-46.

98. Chiang Kai-shek, "Speech at Nanchang General Headquarters," Feb. 21, 1927, pp. 8-9.

99. Chiang Kai-shek, "Statement on 'Essential Points of Propaganda on Party Affairs,'" p. 17.

100. Chiang Kai-shek, "Speech at Nanchang General Headquarters," Feb. 21, 1927, pp. 10-11.

101. Chiang Kai-shek, "Statement on 'Essential Points of Propa-

ganda on Party Affairs,' " p. 17. Wang Ching-wei confirms receiving a number of telegrams from Chiang urging him to return. In February, 1927, said Wang, Chiang again wired, saying that if Wang did not return, Chiang would resign. See Wang Ching-wei, "On Separating the Communists from the KMT at Wuhan," p. 600.

102. Chiang Kai-shek, "Speech at Nanchang General Headquarters," Feb. 21, 1927, p. 9.

103. Chiang Kai-shek, "Letter to Students of the Central Military and Political Academy," March 12, 1927, p. 27.

104. Chiang Kai-shek, "Speech at Nanchang General Headquarters," Feb. 21, 1927, pp. 13-14.

105. Chiang Kai-shek, "Speech at Nanchang General Headquarters," March 7, 1927.

106. Mitarevsky, World-wide Soviet Plots, pp. 137-38.

107. Ch'en Tu-hsiu, "Internal Conflicts of the KMT and the Chinese Revolution," p. 2046. See also Ch'en Tu-hsiu, "Sorrow on the Second Anniversary of Dr. Sun's Death," pp. 2056-57.

108. Chiang Kai-shek, "Speech at Nanchang General Headquarters," March 7, 1927; "Letter to Students of the Central Military and Political Academy," p. 30.

109. Shinsen Dai-jimmei Jiten [new biographical dictionary], 1938, III, p. 173.

110. Gendai Shina jimmei kan, p. 603. On March 12, 1927, Chiang confirmed that Huang Fu had visited him at his headquarters. Chiang said that the visit was made on a personal basis, as he and Huang were old friends. See Chiang Kai-shek, "Letter to Students of the Central Military and Political Academy," p. 28. In May, 1927, following the purge, Huang Fu was appointed mayor of Shanghai.

111. Dispatch from Ambassador MacVeagh, Tokyo, to Secretary of State, January 18, 1927, State Department Archives 794.00/37.

112. Dispatch from Charge d'Affaires Norman Armour, Tokyo, to Secretary of State, May 25, 1927, State Department Archives 893.00/9085. The dispatch mentions the visit of Tai Chi-t'ao to Japan in February, 1927. Tai, said Armour, was generally understood to represent Chiang Kai-shek's faction.

113. Dispatch, Ambassador MacVeagh, Tokyo, to Secretary of State, March 28, 1927, State Department Archives 893.00/4; Dispatch, Ambassador MacVeagh, Tokyo, to Secretary of State, March 20, 1927, State Department Archives, 893.00/91.

114. On March 29, 1927, Minister MacMurray reported to the Secretary of State that he and Japanese Minister Yoshizawa had been called into consultation by British Minister Lampson. Lampson at first suggested offering Eugene Chen, Foreign Minister of the National Government, a chance to show the good faith of the National Government. Yoshizawa, however, urged taking the

matter up with Chiang from whom, he said, more satisfactory action could be expected. The ministers therefore decided to request from their governments permission to present Chiang with an ultimatum demanding punishment of the guilty party, apology, and reparations. (See Dispatch from Minister MacMurray to Secretary of State, March 29, 1927, State Department Archives 893.00/10). On April 1, 1927, MacMurray reported that Yoshizawa had received from the Japanese government agreement to all terms except stipulation of a time limit. The Japanese purpose, said MacMurray, was to induce Chiang to expedite a solution on his own initiative, leaving it to Chiang and other healthy elements to settle the affair. It was most of all important, in the Japanese view, to avoid such steps as might result in facilitating the downfall of Chiang. (See Dispatch, Minister MacMurray to Secretary of State, April 1, 1927, State Department Archives 893.00/16.) In a telegram sent on the same day, MacMurray reported that both Britain and Japan believed it inadvisable to single out Chiang for responsibility, and the ministers had therefore decided to recommend that terms be presented simultaneously to Chiang and Eugene Chen. (See Telegram, Minister MacMurray, Peking, to Secretary of State, April 1, 1927, State Department Archives 893.000/20.) Finally, on April 5, 1927, MacMurray reported that Minister Yoshizawa had received instructions from the Japanese government to request a delay of several days in presenting the terms to Chiang and Eugene Chen in order to give the Japanese consul general in Shanghai time to persuade Chiang Kai-shek to take the initiative in offering to meet the views of the Foreign Powers. (See Telegram, Minister MacMurray to Secretary of State, April 5, 1927, State Department Archives 893.00/37.) The terms were finally presented to Chiang and Chen on April 11, 1927. (See telegram, Consul General C. E. Gauss, Shanghai, to Secretary of State, April 11, 1927, State Department Archives 893.00/57; Telegram, Consul General Lockhart Hankow, to Secretary of State, April 11, 1927, 893.00/60.)

115. Dispatch, Minister MacMurray, Peking, to Secretary of State, April 9, 1927, State Department Archives 893.00/8633.

116. Ch'en Tu-hsiu, "Sorrow on the Second Anniversary of Dr. Sun's Death," p. 2057.

117. Ch'en Ming-shu, "Why We Want to Overthrow the Chinese Communist Party," p. 366.

118. Ho Ying-ch'in, "Speech on the Party Purification Movement," p. 91.

119. Mitarevsky, World-wide Soviet Plots, p. 138.

120. Ch'en Tu-hsiu, "Sorrow on the Second Anniversary of Dr. Sun's Death," pp. 2056-57.

121. Central Executive Committee of the Kuomintang, "Manifesto of the Kuomintang of China Convening the Second Congress,"

pp. 99-100. The five fundamental policies are: (1) Overthrow imperialism; join a united front with Soviet Russia to realize this goal; (2) Unite the forces of the peasantry and labor and lead them to struggle for their own liberation and the liberation of China; (3) Provide the people with arms and proper training. Apply political training to the Army, make it join hands with the people, then make it the people's army; (4) Fill the Party with revolutionary elements so that Party members may lead the masses. Leave no room for counterrevolutionaries, pseudo-revolutionaries, or non-revolutionaries. Admit Communists into the KMT and work together with them for the National Revolution; and (5) Institute strict Party discipline in regulating the activities of Party members so that the Party may realize its principles and policies. Centralize the action of Party members.

122. Mif, Chin-chi shih-chi..., pp. 12-13; see also Nassonov, Fokine, and Albrecht, "The Letter from Shanghai," p. 408.

123. Quoted by Mif, Chin-chi shih-chi..., p. 33.

124. Ch'en Kuo-fu, "A Piece of Party History...," p. 73.

125. According to an anti-Communist source, T'ang Sheng-chih disobeyed Chiang Kai-shek's orders shortly after the capture of Yochow (Yoyang), Hunan (August 22, 1926). He openly criticized Wang Po-lin (vice-commander of the First Army) and Chiang himself. See Pai Shan, "The Wuhan-Nanking Split and T'ang Sheng-chih," p. 34. In mid-March, 1927, Lo Ch'eng, adviser and aid to T'ang Sheng-chih, confidentially informed the American Consul General at Hankow that friction between T'ang and Chiang dated from the Hunan-Hupeh campaign. See dispatch, Consul General F. P. Lockhart, Hankow, to Secretary of State, March 19, 1927, State Department Archives 893.00/9040.

126. Pai Shan, "The Wuhan Nanking Split and T'ang Sheng-chih," pp. 34-36. According to the author, the Alumni Association of Four Military Academies developed great influence in the Fourth, Seventh and Eighth armies. It was also influential in the Second, Third and Sixth armies. Ch'eng Ch'ien, commander of the Sixth Army, allegedly sent a telegram to T'ang Sheng-chih conveying his desire to help develop the organization.

127. Nassonov, Fokine, and Albrecht, "The Letter from Shanghai," p. 418.

128. Quoted by Wu Chih-hui, "Petition to Safeguard the Party and Save the Nation," pp. 43-44. Wu explains that the document was sent to him by someone in Hankow with the request that he take appropriate action against the Communists. The document appears authentic.

129. Sources representing diverse political groups assert that T'ang Sheng-chih and the Communists were allies at Wuhan. See, for instance, Woo, The Kuomintang and the Future of the Chinese

Revolution, p. 149; Tong, Chiang Kai-shek, pp. 80-81; Roy, My Experiences in China, p. 37. T'ang Sheng-chih reportedly made a number of speeches at Wuhan and Changsha declaring that anti-communism would be considered as counterrevolution. See Kuo-wen chou-pao, IV, No. 42 (Oct. 21, 1927), 1. T'ang's speech at the Wuhan Joint Council on December 29, 1926 was noticeably revolutionary in tone (see Doc. 46).

130. Roy, My Experiences in China, p. 37.

131. Chang Fa-k'uei's Twelfth Division of the Fourth Army was reorganized into the Fourth Army, incorporating Yeh T'ing's Third Regiment. Chang was appointed vice-commander of the Fourth Army. Ch'en Ming-shu's Tenth Division of the Fourth Army was reorganized into the Eleventh Army. The Soviet report on Ch'en Ming-shu's sympathies was proved completely erroneous. On March 6, 1927, Ch'en Ming-shu was compelled to leave Wuhan when, according to American Consul General Lockhart, he replied in the negative when asked if he was sympathetic to the Left Wing (see dispatch, American Consul General F. P. Lockhart, Hankow, to Secretary of State, April 14, 1927, State Department Archives 893.00/8953). KMT sources cite the ousting of Ch'en Ming-shu as an important proof of Communist conspiracy. See, for instance, Chiang Kai-shek, "Letter to the Officers and Men of the National Revolutionary Army," p. 84; Liu Lu-yin, "Revolution and Counter-revolution," p. 494.

In connection with Ch'en Ming-shu's political sympathies, it is interesting to note Teruni's report of October 30, 1926, on his own efforts to stir up enmity between Ch'en Ming-shu and T'ang Sheng-chih at a time when the Russians were bent on keeping T'ang Sheng-chih down (see Doc. 44, pp. 4, 15). Apparently, Ch'en Ming-shu's attitude was partly influenced by personal antagonism toward T'ang Sheng-chih and the Communist-T'ang alliance. Independent sources confirm the development of friction between T'ang and Ch'en Ming-shu shortly after the occupation of Wuchang. See, for instance, Kuo-wen chou-pao, IV, No. 42 (Oct. 21, 1927), 1.

132. Li Chih-shen was charged with the defense of Kwangtung and Kwangsi with the major portion of Li Fu-lin's Fifth Army. The disposition of the main forces of the National Government around February, 1927, was as follows: the Fourth and Eighth armies were in Hunan, Hupeh, and southern Honan. The Third Army was in Kiangsi. The First, Second, Sixth and Seventh armies were engaged in the Southeastern campaign. The Seventh Army under Li Tsung-jen formed the nucleus of the Left Bank Army which proceeded along the northern bank of the Yangtze, charged with cutting the Tientsin-Pukow Railway. The Sixth Army under Ch'eng Ch'ien, together with the Second Army commanded by its vice-commander, Lo T'i-p'ing, formed the nucleus of the Right Bank Army. Its mission was to

proceed along the eastern bank of the Yangtze to capture Nanking.
The units of the First Army formed the core of the Eastern Route
Army under Pai Ch'ung-hsi's command which captured Hangchow
on February 17, 1927, and later headed for Shanghai. See Chou
Tzu-sheng, "The Northern Expeditionary War of the National
Revolutionary Army," pp. 35-36.

133. Ch'ü Ch'iu-pai, Chung-kuo ko-ming..., p. 41. Writing in
April, 1928, Ch'ü does not of course mention Ch'en Ming-shu in
the military line-up against Chiang.

134. Mandalyan, Wei shen-mo Chung-kuo Kung-ch'an-tang ti
ling tao p'o-ch'an, p. 9. An anti-Communist source asserts that
with the exception of Ho Yao-tsu's Fortieth Army, the forces at
Nanking, were opposed to Chiang. The Twenty-seventh Army
commanded by Wang P'u and the Thirty-seventh Army commanded
by Ch'en T'iao-yüan, the author asserts, were unreliable as they
had recently defected to the National Government. The Second and
Sixth armies were clearly opposed to Chiang. See Szu Ming, "Ho
Yao-tsu during the Northern Expedition," pp. 185-93. The omission
of the Second and Sixth armies from the anti-Chiang military
combination listed in Document 49, a Soviet report dated March 5,
1927, is interesting in view of the charge that the Nanking Incident
of March 24 was instigated by the radicals to discredit Chiang.

135. Hsüeh Yüeh reportedly made an offer to the Communists to
disobey Chiang's orders to move out of Shanghai and to join with
them to oppose Chiang. The Shanghai Communists, however, declined the offer. See Mif, Chin-chi shih-chi..., p. 17; Mandalyan,
Wei shen-mo Chung-kuo Kung-ch'an-tang ti ling-tai p'o-ch'an,
p. 9; Ch'ü Ch'iu-pai, Chung-kuo ko-ming..., p. 47.

136. The American Consul General at Shanghai reported on
March 27, 1927 (the day after Chiang entered Shanghai) that Chiang
could maintain the situation in Shanghai only by the use of military
force against the radicals, but that it was doubtful whether he had
sufficient or loyal forces for this purpose. See telegram, American
Consul General C. E. Gauss, Shanghai, to Secretary of State,
March 27, 1927, State Department Archives 899.00/8506. On April,
4, 1927, Gauss again reported that it was doubtful whether Chiang
commanded the loyalty of the troops. See telegram, American Consul General C. E. Gauss, Shanghai, to Secretary of State, April 4,
1927, 893.00/8547.

137. Pai Shan, "The Wuhan-Nanking Split and T'ang Sheng-chih,"
pp. 35-36.

138. Roy, My Experiences in China, pp. 46, 50.

139. Nassonov, Fokine, and Albrecht, "The Letter from Shanghai,"
p. 409.

140. Chiang Kai-shek, Chiang Chieh-shih hsien-sheng, XX, 120,
26, 88. The Kuominchün had in the meantime sustained a series of

defeats in northern and northwestern China. Under joint attack by Wu P'ei-fu, Chang Tsung-ch'ang, and Chang Tso-lin, the Kuomin-chün lost Kalgan, Chahar, on August 17, 1926. Paotow, Suiyuan, was evacuated on December 25, 1926.

141. Feng Yü-hsiang, Wo ti sheng-huo, p. 208; Feng Yü-hsiang, Wo so jen-shih ti Chiang Chieh-shih, pp. 2-3.

142. Mitarevsky, World-wide Soviet Plots, pp. 117, 124-25. One of the CC's reports states that Feng Yü-hsiang praised the Soviet Union and the Chinese Communist Party. Feng reportedly declared he had rushed back to China to work for the Revolution because he was inspired by the enthusiasm of the Russian comrades for liberating oppressed nations. The CC further reported that Feng said there was no difference between the Chinese Communist Party and the Kuomintang and that the two parties would eventually amalgamate.

143. Mif, Chin-chi shih-chi..., pp. 32-34. Mif asserts that Ch'en Tu-hsiu cited the example of the Taiping Rebellion of the mid-19th century to support the "Northwest Theory." Ch'en allegedly pointed out that the defeat of the powerful peasant movement (which established its capital at Nanking) was achieved largely through imperialist intervention. Thus, it was desirable to establish a base in the Northwest, away from imperialist influence in the Southeast. See also Ts'ai Ho-shen, "On Ch'en Tu-hsiuism," p. 23. The Taiping Rebellion was also cited by the Communists in early 1927 in opposing Nanking as the national capital. See P'eng Shu-chih, "On the Transfer of the National Government," p. 2008.

144. Telegram, American Consul General Douglas Jenkins, Canton, to Secretary of State, March 24, 1927, State Department Archives 893.00/8427.

145. "The Recent National Political Situation and Tendencies in the Revolutionary Movement," pp. 64-65.

146. "Letter from the Central Political Bureau to the Comrades of the Regional Committees of Hunan, Hupeh, and Kiangsi," pp. 67-68.

147. Mitarevsky, World-wide Soviet Plots, p. 138.

148. Hu Hua, Chung-kuo hsin min-chu-chu-i ko-ming shih, p. 82.

149. Liu Lu-yin, "Revolution and Counterrevolution," p. 493. According to Ch'en Kuo-fu, T'an Yen-k'ai decided on his own to go to Wuhan and Chiang instructed Ch'en Kuo-fu to accompany him. They arrived at Wuhan on March 7, 1927. See Ch'en Kuo-fu, "A Piece of Party History...," p. 72. Chiang Kai-shek and Chang Ching-chiang remained at Nanchang.

150. The discussion of the Third CEC Plenum is based on election lists, minutes of meetings, statutes, and resolutions of the Plenum published in Min-kuo jih-pao, the official organ of the KMT, March 8 -March 18, 1927, translated into English in Dispatch No.

478, American Consul General F. P. Lockhart, Hankow, to Secretary of State, April 6, 1927, State Department Archives 893.00/8910.

151. According to Ch'en Kuo-fu, reorganization of the Communist-controlled Kwangtung Provincial Party Headquarters was one of the first tasks he set himself in the summer of 1926. Reorganization of the Kiangsi Provincial Party Headquarters, previously dominated by the Communist, Fang Chih-ming, was accomplished in February, 1927. See Ch'en Kuo-fu, "A Piece of Party History...," pp. 65-71.

152. Borojin Fujin hobaku kokin jiken. Takao said he believed the dismissal of Borodin was related to intraparty conflicts in the KMT, and that it was a very significant development. Since Borodin's departure from Hankow would be desirable for Japan, Takao stated, he was requesting an opinion on this matter. Takao's own view was that Japanese intercession on behalf of Mrs. Borodin would not invite suspicion from either the Right or Left KMT. He thought it might be a good idea to dispatch a man, one Major Okamura, to contact Chang Tsung-ch'ang and Sun Ch'uan-fang and suggest unofficially that they release Mrs. Borodin.

153. Dispatch, American Consul General F. P. Lockhart, Hankow, to Secretary of State, March 18, 1927, State Department Archives 893.00/9040. Lo Ch'eng told Lockhart that he believed that Borodin could not be prevailed upon to leave Hankow, He added, however, that all the Russians would be divested of authority when the KMT won complete control of the country and no longer needed Russian aid. While there was no definite plan for such action, Lo said he believed military strength could accomplish it.

154. Telegram, Minister MacMurray, Peking, to Secretary of State, March 24, 1927, enclosing dispatch from the American Consul General, Canton, dated March 19, 1927; State Department Archives 893.00/8427.

155. See "The Problem of Authenticity," pp. 10-11.

156. See, for instance, Woo, The Kuomintang and the Future of the Chinese Revolution, p. 230; Mandalyan, Wei shen-mo Chung-kuo Kung-ch'an-tang ti ling-tao p'o-ch'an, p. 7; Mif, Chin-chi shih-chi..., p. 10.

157. Wu Ch'ih-hui, "Petition to Safeguard the Party and Save the Nation," pp. 43-44; Chiang Kai-shek, "Letter to Officers and Men of the National Revolutionary Army," pp. 83-84; Chiang Kai-shek, "Proclamation on the Closing of the General Political Department of the Army," pp. 23-24. Chiang accused Teng Yen-ta, Chairman of the General Political Department, of filling the department with men who wished to destroy the National Revolution. Teruni cooperated closely with Teng Yen-ta (see Doc. 44, pp. 4, 5, 21). Although Communist Party representatives withdrew from the First Army in April, 1926, Communists regained access to political

work in the National Revolutionary Army when the Northern Expedition was launched. The Communists Li Fu-ch'un and Lin Tsu-han headed the Political Department of the Second and Sixth armies respectively. See Chung-kuo hsien-tai ko-ming yün-tung shih, p. 169. At the Special Conference in December, 1926, the CC decided to organize Communist cells among commanders of the National Revolutionary Army. However, it decided against organizing cells among the soldiers. See Nassonov, Fokine, and Albrecht, "The Letter from Shanghai," p. 421.

158. See, for instance, Ts'ai Ho-shen, "On Ch'en Tu-hsiuism," p. 23.

159. Mif, Chin-chi shih-chi..., pp. 10, 13, 15-16. The Second Shanghai Insurrection took place on February 22, 1927. It was preceded by a general strike called by the General Labor Union on February 18, 1927, when the National Revolutionary Army occupied Kashing, 60 kilometers from Shanghai. The Second Insurrection was suppressed. On March 21, 1927, as the National Revolutionary Army reached Lunghwa, the General Labor Union again ordered a general strike, which was immediately followed by the Third Insurrection; by the afternoon of March 22, 1927, the insurrection was successful and the First Army entered Shanghai. Beginning around April 12, workers and Communists were suppressed.

160. Ch'ü Ch'iu-pai, Chung-kuo ko-ming..., p. 81.

161. Mif, Chin-chi shih-chi..., pp. 12-13.

162. Ch'en Tu-hsiu, Kao ch'üan-tang..., pp. 4-5.

163. Nassonov, Fokine, and Albrecht, "The Letter from Shanghai," pp. 406, 410, 421, 426. The authors of the letter declared that it was absolutely necessary to recall Voitinskii, but that Ch'en Tu-hsiu could remain as one of the Party leaders. The following are excerpts concerning Voitinskii: "In tactical questions in the past he cannot be separated from the Central Committee; on the contrary, every time that the Party hesitated and began to seek new paths, he forced it back into the old swamp of petty combinations, tricks of political jugglery, which have nothing in common with revolutionary tactics. Completely lacking in principle, he adapted himself to the party and frequently excelled the other leaders in his zeal.... He sent Moscow bastardized information, held back material, and concealed the real situation in the Party from the ECCI. Without principles, as well as without political courage, he viewed everything as a functionary and did not stop at pushing the CC into absurd decisions.... Such a representative of the ECCI can only ruin the work" (pp. 430-32).

164. Stalin, "The International Situation," p. 236. Stalin defended his policies against the Opposition, led by Trotsky, which had demanded the organization of workers', peasants', and soldiers'

Soviets and the complete independence of the Chinese Communist Party from the Kuomintang.

165. Quoted by Isaacs, Tragedy of the Chinese Revolution, p. 162. Isaacs asserts that Stalin made this remark at a meeting of 3,000 Party functionaries in Moscow. On the authenticity of the speech, see Isaacs, pp. 351-52.

166. See Part IV, pp. 209, 232-33; Part VII, pp. 381, 396-97.

167. Ch'ü Ch'iu-pai, Chung-kuo ko-ming, pp. 54-56.

168. "Membership List of the Peking Local Committee's National Movement Committee," Su-lien yin-mou..., III, "KCT," p. 185.

169. "Report of the Peking Executive Headquarters on the Elections and Conditions of Work," February 5, 1927, Su-lien yin-mou..., III, "KCT," p. 126.

170. "Membership List of the Communist Party Fraction in the New Army Society," Su-lien yin-mou..., III, "KCT," p. 185.

171. Ibid., pp. 185-86.

172. "Membership List of the Communist Party Fraction in the Soul of Hainan Society," Su-lien yin-mou..., III, "KCT," p. 186.

173. "Membership List of the Communist Party Fraction at the Municipal Party Headquarters," Su-lien yin-mou..., III, "KCT," pp. 189-90.

174. See Part IV, pp. 209-12; Part VI, pp. 329-30.

175. "The Waichiao Pu to the Soviet Chargé d'Affaires, April 6th, 1927," Chinese Government White Book, p. 141.

176. "An Urgent Circular Notice to All District Party Headquarters from the Peking Municipal Party Headquarters," November 8, [1926], Su-lien yin-mou..., III, "KCT," pp. 219-20.

177. See People's Tribune, May 17, 1927, for a list of prisoners and their sentences announced by Chang Tso-lin on April 28, 1927. See Document 50, p. 175, for a list of members of the executive committee of the Peking Municipal Party Headquarters.

178. "The Waichiao Pu to the Soviet Chargé d'Affaires, April 6th, 1927," Chinese Government White Book, p. 141.

179. People's Tribune, May 17, 1927.

180. Yao Yen was arrested shortly before April 6, 1927. See People's Tribune, May 8, 1927. The confessions of Yao and other prisoners confirmed that Li Ta-chao and others were sheltered in the Soviet Embassy. See "The Waichiao Pu the Soviet Chargé d'Affaires, April 6th, 1927," Chinese Government White Book, p. 141.

181. "The Waichiao Pu to the Soviet Chargé d'Affaires, April 6th, 1927," "Cablegram from the Waichiao Pu to Chinese Chargé d'Affaires at Moscow, April 16, 1927," Chinese Government White Book, pp. 141, 149.

182. Quoted by Mif, Chin-chi shih-chi..., p. 26.

183. China Press, April 8, 1927, Toho News Agency dispatch, Peking, April 7, 1927.

GLOSSARY A

SPECIAL TERMS AND NAMES OF ORGANIZATIONS
AND PARTY ORGANS

[policy of] Admission of Communists	Jung-kung [cheng-ts'e]	容共〔政策〕
Agrarian united front	Hsiang-ts'un lien-ho chan-hsien	鄉村聯合戰綫
All-China Federation of Labor	Chung-hua ch'üan-kuo tsung-kung-hui	中華全國總工會
Anfu Clique	An-fu hsi	安福系
Anhwei Clique	An-hui hsi	安徽系
Army of National Pacification	Ankuochün	安國軍
Autonomous movement	Tzu-chih yün-tung	自治運動
Basic organization	Chi-t'uan	基團
Black Spears Association	Hei-ch'iang hui	黑槍會
Cadres [KMT and KCT]	Kan-pu	幹部
Cell or Party cell [KCT]	Chih-pu	支部
Center	Chung-p'ai	中派
Central [Committee] [KCT]	Chung-yang	中央
Central Bureau [KCT]	Chung-yang chü	中央局
Central Committee or CC [KCT]	Chung-yang wei-yüan-hui	中央委員

Central Executive Committee, or CEC [KMT]	Chung-yang chih-hsing wei-yüan-hui	中央執行委員會
Central Military and Political Academy	Chung-yang chün-shih cheng-chih hsüeh-hsiao	中央軍事政治學校
Central Party Headquarters [KMT]	Chung-yang tang-pu	中央黨部
Central Political Bureau [KCT]	Chung-yang cheng-chih chü	中央政治局
Central Supervisory Committee or CSC [KMT]	Chung-yang chien-ch'a wei-yüan-hui	中央監察委員會
Chairman	Chu-hsi	主席
Chihli Clique	Chih-li hsi	直隸系
Chinese Communist Party, KCT "CP," "Our School"	Chung-kuo Kung-ch'an-tang, "wo-men ti hsüeh-hsiao"	中國共産黨,"我們的學校"
Chinese Communist Youth Corps, CY	Chung-kuo Kung-ch'an-chu-i ch'ing-nien t'uan	中國共産主義青年團
Chinese Labor Union Secretariat	Chung-kuo lao-tung tsu-ho shu-chi-pu	中國勞動組合書記部
Chinese Socialist Youth Corps, SY	Chung-kuo she-hui-chu-i ch'ing-nien-t'uan	中國社會主義青年團
Ch'iung-yai Association	Ch'iung-yai hsieh-chin-hui	瓊崖協進會
Chung-shan Study Society	Chung-shan hsüeh-she	中山學社
Closed-door [principle]	Kuan-men [chu-i]	關門主義
Comintern, see Communist International		
Commander-in-Chief's Headquarters	Tsung ssu-ling-pu	總司令部

Committee on the Labor Movement [KCT]	Chih-kung yün-tung wei-yüan-hui	職工運動委員會
Committee on the Military Movement [KCT]	Chün-shih yün-tung wei-yüan-hui	軍事運動委員會
Committee on the National Movement	Kuo-min yün-tung wei-yüan-hui	國民運動委員會
Committee on the Peasant Movement [KCT]	Nung-min yün-tung wei-yüan-hui	農民運動委員會
Committee on the Relief Movement	Chi-nan yün-tung wei-yüan-hui	濟難運動委員會
Communist International, or Third International, or Comintern, or CI	Kung-ch'an Kuo-chi or Ti-san Kuo-chi	共產國際 or 第三國際
Communist Party member, or "our schoolmate"	Kung-ch'an-tang yüan, "wo-men ti t'ung-hsüeh"	共產黨員 "我們的同學"
Conference of active elements [KCT]	Huo-tung fen-tzu ta-hui	活動分子大會
Conference of responsible comrades [KCT]	Fu-tse kung-tso t'ung-chih ta-hui	負責工作同志大會
Congress [National Congress]	Ch'üan-kuo tai-piao ta-hui	全國代表大會
District Party Headquarters [KMT]	Ch'ü-tang-pu	區黨部
Eastern Expedition(s)	Tung-cheng	東征
Educational propagandists [KCT]	Chiao-yü hsüan-ch'uan-yüan	教育宣傳員
Enlarged plenum	K'uo-ta ch'üan-t'i hui-i	擴大全體會議
Executive Headquarters [KMT]	Chih-hsing-pu	執行部
Exorbitant taxes and irregular levies	K'o-chüan tsa-shui	苛捐雜稅

Foreign Language School	Wai-kuo yü-yen hsüeh-hsiao	外國語言學校
General Labor Union	Tsung kung hui	總工會
General Political Department [KMT]	Tsung cheng-chih pu	總政治部
Generalissimo	Ta-yüan-shuai	大元帥
Great League of Sunyatsenism	Chung-shan chu-i ta-t'ung-meng	中山主義大同盟
Hsien	County	縣
Hsien (or County) Party headquarters [KMT]	Hsien tang-pu	縣黨部
Hunan Alumni Association	Hsiang hsiao-hui	湘校會
Hunan Regional Committee [KCT]	Hsiang ch'ü wei-yüan-hui or Hsiang-ch'ü	湘區委員會 or 湘區
Joint Committee	Lien-ho wei-yüan-hui	聯合委員會
Joint Conference	Lien-hsi hui-i	聯席會議
Joint Council	Lien-hsi hui-i	聯席會議
Kiangsi Provincial Party Headquarters [KMT]	Chiang-hsi Sheng tang-pu	江西省黨部
Kiangsu-Chekiang Regional Committee [KCT]	Chiang-Che Ch'ü wei-yüan-hui or Chiang-Che ch'ü-wei	江浙區委員會 or 江浙區委
Kuo-chia chu-i clique	Kuo-chia chu-i p'ai	國家主義派
Kuo-min ko-ming chün	National Revolutionary Army	國民革命軍
Kuominchün	People's Army(ies) or National Army(ies)	國民軍
Kuomintang, or KMT, or "People's School"	Kuo-min-tang, "Min-hsiao"	國民黨,"民校"
Kuomintang member, see Nationalist		

Kwangsi Clique	Kuang-hsi hsi	廣西系
Kwangtung Branch of the Kuomintang of China	Chung-kuo Kuomintang Kuang-tung chih-pu	中國國民黨廣東支部
Kwangtung Provincial Party Headquarters [KMT]	Kuang-tung Sheng tang-pu	廣東省黨部
Kwangtung Regional Committee [KCT]	Kuang-tung ch'ü wei-yüan-hui or Kuang-tung ch'ü-wei or Kuang-tung ch'ü	廣東區委員會 or 廣東區委 or 廣東區
Labor Department [KMT]	Kung-jen pu	工人部
League of Military Youth	Ch'ing-nien chün-jen lien-ho hui	青年軍人聯合會
Left Wing	Tso p'ai	左派
"Li Jui-hsiang," see Northern Regional Committee		
Local bullies and bad gentry	T'u-hao lieh-shen	土豪劣紳
Local committee [KCT]	Ti-fang wei-yüan-hui or ti-wei	地方委員會 or 地委
March Eighteenth Incident	San-i-pa shih-pien or San-i-pa ta-t'u-sha	三一八事變 or 三一八大屠殺
March Twentieth Incident	San-yüeh erh-shih jih shih-pien or Chung-shan chien an	三月廿日事變 or 中山艦案
Marxist Study Group [KCT]	Ma-k'o-ssu-chu-i yen-chiu-hui	馬克斯主義研究會
Merchant Corps, or "Paper Tigers," or "Tiger Party"	Shang-t'uan, "chih-hu" "Lao-hu tang"	商團,"紙虎","老虎黨"
Military Council	Chün-shih wei-yüan-hui	軍事委員會
Military Personnel Department [KMT]	Chün-jen pu	軍人部

Min-t'uan	People's Corps	民團
Mukden Clique	Feng-t'ien hsi	奉天系
Municipal Party head- quarters [KMT]	Shih-tang-pu	市黨部
National Army(ies)	Kuominchün	國民軍
National assembly	Kuo-min hui-i	國民會議
National Government	Kuo-min cheng-fu	國民政府
National Government Council	Kuo-min cheng-fu wei-yüan-hui	國民政府委員會
National Labor Congress	Ch'üan-kuo lao-tung ta-hui	全國勞動大會
National Peasant Conference	Ch'üan-kuo nung-min ta-hui	全國農民大會
National Revolution- ary Army	Kuo-min ko-ming chün	國民革命軍
Nationalist, or Kuo- mintang member, or "schoolmate of the People's School"	Kuo-min-tang tang- yüan, "min-hsiao t'ung-hsüeh"	國民黨黨員"民 校同學"
New Army Society	Hsin-chün she	新軍社
New China Study Society	Hsin Chung hsüeh-hui	新中學會
New Right Wing	Hsin yu-p'ai	新右派
New Student Society	Hsin hsüeh-sheng she	新學生社
New Yunnan Society	Hsin T'ien she	新滇社
Northern Expedition or Northern Punitive Expedition	Pei-fa	北伐
Northern Regional Committee, "Li Jui- hsiang" [KCT]	Pei-fang ch'ü wei- yüan-hui or Pei-fang ch'ü wei or Pei-fang ch'ü	北方區委員會 or 北方區委 or 北 方區"李瑞祥"
Old Right Wing	Chiu yu-p'ai	舊右派

Organization Department [KMT and KCT]	Tsu-chih pu	組織部
"Our School," see Chinese Communist Party		
"Our schoolmate," see Communist Party member		
Overseas Department [KMT]	Hai-wai pu	海外部
"Pai Wei," see Peking Local Committee		
Paoting Clique	Pao-ting hsi	保定系
"Paper Tigers," see Merchant Corps		
Parliament (Peking Parliament)	Kuo-min hui-i	國民會議
Party Army	Tang-chün	黨軍
Party fraction [KMT and KCT]	Tang-t'uan	黨團
Party headquarters	Tang-pu	黨部
Party Purification Movement	Ch'ing-tang yün-tung	清黨運動
Party representative	Tang-tai-piao	黨代表
Peasant Department [KMT]	Nung-min pu	農民部
Peasant Movement Training Institute [KMT]	Nung-ming yün-tung hsün-lien so	農民運動訓練所
Peking Executive Headquarters [KMT]	Pei-ching chih-hsing-pu	北京執行部
Peking Kuomintang Comrades' Club	Pei-ching Kuo-min-tang t'ung-chih chü-le-pu	北京國民黨同志俱樂部
Peking Local Committee, or "Pai Wei" [KCT]	Pei-ching Ti-fang wei-yüan-hui	北京地方委員會 "柏蔚"

Peking Municipal Party Headquarters [KMT]	Pei-ching shih-tang-pu	北京市黨部
People's Army(ies)	Kuo-min chün	國民軍
People's Corps	Min-t'uan	民團
"People's School," see Kuomintang		
Plenum	Ch'üan-t'i hui-i	全體會議
Political Bureau [KCT]	Cheng-chih chü	政治局
Political commissar [KMT]	Cheng-chih wei-yüan	政治委員
Political Council [KMT]	Cheng-chih hui-i or Cheng-chih wei-yüan-hui	政治會議 or 政治委員會
Political Department [KMT]	Cheng-chih pu	政治部
Political Training Class [KMT]	Cheng-chih hsün-lien pan	政治訓練班
Political Training Department [under Military Council]	Cheng-chih hsün-lien pu	政治訓練部
Political Training Institute [under KMT CEC]	Cheng-chih hsün-lien so	政治訓練所
Practical Society	Shih-chien she	實踐社
Preparatory Committee	Ch'ou-pei wei-yüan-hui	籌備委員會
Presidium	Chu-hsi-t'uan	主席團
Principles of Sun Yat-sen, see Sunwenism		
Principles of Tai Chi-t'ao, see Taichitaoism		
Progressive Society	Ch'ien-chin she	前進社
Propaganda Department [KMT and KCT]	Hsüan-ch'uan pu	宣傳部

Propaganda mobili-zation	Hsüan-ch'uan tung-yüan	宣傳動員
Provincial Party Headquarters [KMT]	Sheng tang-pu	省黨部
Provisional Central Executive Commit-tee [KMT]	Lin-shih Chung-yang chih-hsing wei-yüan-hui	臨時中央執行會
Publications Depart-ment [KCT]	Ch'u-pan pu	出版部
Reactionary Right Wing	Fan-tung yu-p'ai	反動右派
Reconstruction Con-ference	Shan-hou hui-i	善後會議
Red Beards	Hung-hu-tzu	紅鬍子
Red Spears Associ-ation	Hung-ch'iang-hui	紅槍會
Reform Society	Ko-hsin she	革新社
Regional Committee [KCT]	Ch'ü wei-yüan-hui or Ch'ü-wei	區委員會 or 區委
Relief Association	Chi-nan hui	濟難會
Reorganization	Kai-tsu	改組
Revolutionary Com-mittee [KMT]	Ko-ming wei-yüan-hui	革命委員會
Right Wing	Yu p'ai	右派
"Schoolmate of The People's School," see Nationalist		
Secretariat	Shu-chi-ch'u	書記處
Section formed by grouping neighboring cells [KCT]	Pu	部
Sectional Committee [KCT]	Pu wei-yüan-hui or pu-wei	部委員會 or 部委
Self-defense army	Tzu-wei chün	自衛軍

Self-study Group	Tzu-hsiu yen-chiu-hui	自修研究會
Shanghai Executive Headquarters, [KMT]	Shang-hai chih-hsing-pu	上海執行部
Shanghai Hsin-hai Comrades Club	Shang-hai Hsin-hai T'ung-chih chü-le-pu	上海辛亥同志俱樂部
Small unit of large Party cell [KCT]	Hsiao-tsu	小組
Soul of Hainan Society	Ch'iung-tao hun she	瓊島魂社
Special Commissioner [KCT]	T'e-p'ai-yüan	特派員
Special Committee [KMT]	T'e-pieh wei-yüan-hui	特別委員會
Special Plenum	T'e-pieh ch'uan-t'i hui-i	特別全體會議
Standing Committee [KMT]	Ch'ang-wu wei-yüan-hui	長務委員會
Strike Committee	Pa-kung wei-yüan-hui	罷工委員會
Sub-district Party Headquarters [KMT]	Ch'ü-fen-pu	區分部
Sunwenism, or Sunyat-senism, or Principles of Sun Yat-sen	Sun Wen chu-i	孫文主義
Sunyatsenism, see Sunwenism		
Sunyatsenist Society	Sun Wen chu-i hsüeh-hui	孫文主義學會
Szechuan Revolution-ary Youth Society	Ssu-ch'uan ko-ming ch'ing-nien she	四川革命青年社
Taichitaoism, or Prin-ciples of Tai Chi-t'ao	Tai Chi-t'ao chu-i	戴季陶主義
Ten-person group	Shih-jen t'uan	十人團
Third International, see Communist International		

Three Great Policies (alliance with Soviet Russia, alliance with Communists, and [support of] workers and peasants)	San-ta cheng-ts'e (Lien-Wo, Lien-Kung, Kung-Nung)	三大政策（聯俄，聯共，工農）
Three People's Principles	San-min chu-i	三民主義
"Tiger Party," see Merchant Corps		
Tsung-li [Dr. Sun Yat-sen]	Director-General	總理
United Council of the Left	Tso-p'ai lien-hsi hui-i or Tso-lien	左派聯席會議
Western Hills Faction [or clique, or group]	Hsi-shan p'ai	西山派
Whampoa Academy	Huang-p'u Chün-hsiao	黃埔軍校
Woman's Department [KMT]	Fu-nü pu	婦女部
Women's Department [KCT]	Fu-nü pu	婦女部
Women's Movement Training Institute [KMT]	Fu-nü yün-tung hsün-lien so	婦女運動訓練所
Workers Club	Kung-jen chü-le-pu	工人俱樂部
Workers pickets	Kung-jen chiu-ch'a-tui	工人糾察隊
Young Communist International	Shao-nien Kung-ch'an Kuo-chi or Shao-Kung Kuo-chi	少年共產國際 or 少共國際
Youth Department [KMT]	Ch'ing-nien pu	青年部

GLOSSARY B

NAMES OF CHINESE PERSONS MENTIONED
IN THE DOCUMENTS AND ESSAYS

This glossary includes the most common forms of names, together
with aliases, variants, and incorrect renderings.

Names		Aliases, Variant Names, and Wrong Characters Used by Peking Commission
An T'i-ch'eng	安體誠	
Chang Chi	張 繼	
Chang Chih-chiang	張之江	
Chang Ching-chiang	張靜江	(Chang Jen-chieh 張人傑)
Chang Ch'iu-pai	張秋白	
Chang Ch'ün	張 羣	
Chang Fa-k'uei	張發奎	
Chang Heng-fang	張恆芳	
Chang I-lan	張艷蘭	
Chang Kuo-ch'en	張國忱	
Chang Kuo-t'ao	張國燾	(Chang T'e-li 張特立 . Incorrectly written as Ch'en Ku-t'a 陳古塔)
Chang Min-ta	張民達	(Incorrectly written as Chang Ming-ta 張明達)
Chang Shih-chao	張士釗	
Chang T'ai-lei	張太雷	

Names		Aliases, Variant Names, and Wrong Characters Used by Peking Commission
Chang T'ai-yen	張太炎	
Chang Tso-lin	張作霖	
Chang Tsung-ch'ang	張宗昌	
Chang Tung-sun	張東蓀	
Chang Tzu-p'ing	張資平	
Chao Heng-t'i	趙恆惕	
Chao Shih-yen	趙世炎	(Alias Shih Yang 施洋)
Chen, Eugene [Ch'en Yu-jen]	陳友仁	
Ch'en Ch'i-hsiu	陳啟修	
Ch'en Ch'i-mei	陳其美	
Ch'en Ch'iung-ming	陳炯明	
Ch'en Hsing-yu	陳興亞	
Ch'en K'o-yü	陳可鈺	(Incorrectly written as Ch'en K'o-chüeh 陳可珏)
Ch'en Kung-po	陳公博	(Incorrectly written as Ch'en Kung-p'o 陳拱坡)
Ch'en Kuo-fu	陳果夫	
Ch'en Lien-po	陳廉伯	
Ch'en Ming-shu	陳銘樞	
Ch'en T'an-ch'iu	陳潭秋	
Ch'en T'iao-yüan	陳調元	
Ch'en Tu-hsiu	陳獨秀	(Ch'en Shih-an 陳實庵)
Ch'en Tzu-i	陳資一	
Ch'en Wang-tao	陳望道	

Names			Aliases, Variant Names, and Wrong Characters Used by Peking Commission
Ch'en Yen-nien	陳	延 年	
Cheng Lan-chi	鄭	蘭 積	
Cheng Shih-ch'i	鄭	士 琦	
Ch'eng Ch'ien	程	潛	
Chia Te-yao	賈	德 耀	
Chiang Ching-kuo	蔣	經 國	
Chiang Kai-shek [Chiang Chieh-shih]	蔣	介 石	(Chiang Chung-cheng 蔣中正)
Chin Yü-fu	金	毓 黼	
Chin Yün-e	靳	雲 鶚	
Chin Yün-p'eng	靳	雲 鵬	
Chou Ao-shan	周	鰲 山	(Incorrectly written as Chou Hao-shan 周浩山)
Chou En-lai	周	恩 來	(Alias Shao Shan 少山 . Incorrectly written as Chou Wen-lai 周文賴)
Chou Feng-ch'i	鄒	鳳 岐	
Chou Fu-hai	周	佛 海	
Chou Lu	鄒	魯	(Chou Hai-pin 鄒海濱)
Chu Chia-hua	朱	家 驊	
Chu Chin-chih	朱	近 之	
Chu P'ei-te	朱	培 德	
Ch'ü Ch'iu-pai	瞿	秋 白	
Chün (Pseudonym?)	駿		
Fan Hsing-min	樊	醒 民	(Fan Chung-hsiu 樊鍾秀)

Names				Aliases, Variant Names, and Wrong Characters Used by Peking Commission
Fan Shih-sheng	范	石	生	
Fang Chen-wu	方	振	武	
Fang Pen-jen	方	本	仁	
Feng Chü-p'o	馮	菊	坡	
Feng Shao-min	馮	紹	閔	
Feng T'ien-chu	馮	天	柱	(Incorrectly written as Fei Kuo-cho 費國卓)
Feng Tzu-yü	馮	自	由	
Feng Yü-hsiang	馮	玉	祥	(Feng Huan-chang 馮煥章)
Fu Ping-ch'ang	傅	秉	常	
Han Lin-fu	韓	麟	符	
Ho Chien	何		鍵	(Incorrectly written as Ho Chia 何嘉)
Ho Hsiang-ning (Mrs. Liao Chung-k'ai)	何	香	凝	
Ho Kung-kan	何	公	敢	
Ho Lung	賀		龍	
Ho Shu-heng	何	叔	衡	
Ho Yao-tsu	賀	耀	祖	
Ho Ying-ch'in	何	應	欽	
Hsia Ch'ao	夏		超	
Hsia Hsi	夏		曦	
Hsia Tou-yin	夏	斗	寅	
Hsiao Ch'u-nü	蕭	楚	女	
Hsiao Chung-chen	蕭	忠	貞	

Names			Aliases, Variant Names, and Wrong Characters Used by Peking Commission
Hsieh Ch'ih	謝	持	
Hsieh Pai-yü	謝伯	俞	
Hsiung K'o-wu	熊克	武	
Hsiung Pin	熊	斌	
Hsü Ch'ien	徐	謙	(Hsü Chi-lung 徐季龍 George Hsu)
Hsü Ch'ung-chih	許崇	智	(Hsü Ju-wei 許汝為)
Hsü Shih-ying	許世	英	
Hsüeh Yüeh	薛	岳	
Hu Ching-yi	胡景	翼	
Hu Han-min	胡漢	民	(Hu Chan-t'ang 胡展堂)
Hu Hua	胡	華	
Hu I-sheng	胡毅	生	
Hu Shih	胡	適	
Hu Tsung-to	胡宗	鐸	
Huang Fu	黃	郛	(Huang Ying-pai 黃膺白)
Huang Ling-shuang	黃凌	霜	(Incorrectly written as Wang Lin-sheng 王林陞)
Huang Pi-hun	黃璧	魂	(Incorrectly written as Wang P'ei-huan 王丕環)
I P'ei-chi	易培	基	
Jan Chao-jung	冉昭	融	
Kan Nai-kuang	甘乃	光	(Incorrectly written as Kai Nan-kuang 蓋南光)

Names		Aliases, Variant Names, and Wrong Characters Used by Peking Commission
Kao Chün-yü	高君宇	
Kao Yü-han	高語罕	
Koo, Wellington [Koo Wei-chün]	顧維鈞	
Ku Meng-yü	顧孟餘	
Ku Ying-fen	古應芬	
Kung, H. H. [K'ung Hsiang-hsi]	孔祥熙	
Kung Fu-k'uei	弓富魁	
Kung Hao	龔 浩	(Incorrectly written as Kuan Hao 關浩)
Kuo Ching-wei	郭經緯	
Kuo Ch'un-t'ao	郭春濤	
Kuo Mo-jo	郭沫若	
Kuo Sung-ling	郭松齡	
Lai Shih-huang	賴世璜	
Lei Chu-huan	雷鑄寰	(Incorrectly written as Lei Chen-huang 雷震黃)
Li Chi-shen	李濟琛	
Li Chih-lung	李之龍	(Incorrectly written as Li Ch'eng-lung 李成龍)
Li Ching-lin	李景林	
Li Ch'un-fan	李春蕃	
Li Fu-ch'un	李富春	
Li Fu-lin	李福林	(Incorrectly written as Liao Fu-lin 廖福林)

Names		Aliases, Variant Names, and Wrong Characters Used by Peking Commission
Li Han-chün	李漢俊	(Incorrectly written as Li Han-ch'ing 李翰卿)
Li Huang	李璜	
Li Li-san	李立三	(Li Lung-chih 李隆郅 , alias Pai Shan 柏山)
Li Ling-yung	李陵溶	
Li Ming-chung	李鳴鐘	
Li Pao-chang	李寶章	
Li P'in-hsien	李品仙	
Li Po-hai	李渤海	
Li Shih-tseng	李石曾	
Li Shu-yung	李壽雍	
Li Ta	李達	
Li Ta-chao	李大釗	(Li Shou-ch'ang 李守常)
Li T'ai-fen	李泰芬	
Li Tsung-jen	李宗仁	
Li Yüan-hung	黎元洪	
Liang Hung-k'ai	梁鴻楷	
Liang Shih-i	梁士詒	
Liao Ch'eng-chih	廖承志	(Alias Ho Liu-hua 何柳華)
Liao Chung-k'ai	廖仲愷	
Liao Hsing-ch'ao	廖行超	(Incorrectly written as Liao Chung-chou 廖仲舟)
Lin Shen	林森	

Names		Aliases, Variant Names, and Wrong Characters Used by Peking Commission
Lin Shih-mien	林直勉	
Lin Tsu-han	林祖涵	(Lin Pai-ch'ü 林伯渠)
Lin Chen-huan	劉震寰	
Liu Chi	劉驥	
Liu Chia-Hsing	劉嘉興	
Liu Chü-ch'üan	劉巨全	
Liu Fen	劉芬	
Liu Jen-ching	劉仁靜	(Incorrectly written as Liu Jen-chin 劉仁津)
Liu Jung	劉榮	
Liu Tso-lung	劉佐龍	
Liu Wen-tao	劉文島	(Incorrectly written as Li Wan-tao 李萬道; Liu Wan-tao 劉萬道)
Liu Yao-hsi	劉耀西	
Liu Yü	劉愈	
Liu Yü-fen	劉郁芬	
Liu Yüeh-chih	劉嶽峙	(Incorrectly written as Liu Liang-chen 劉樑珍)
Lo Chang-lung	羅章龍	(Incorrectly written as Liu Ch'ang-lung 劉長龍)
Lo Ch'eng	羅誠	
Lo Ch'i-yüan	羅綺園	
Lo I-nung	羅亦農	
Lo Szu-jui	羅思睿	

Names		Aliases, Variant Names, and Wrong Characters Used by Peking Commission
Lu Chin-shan	盧金山	
Lu Chung-lin	鹿鐘麟	
Lu I	魯易	
Lu Ti-p'ing	魯滌平	
Lu Yu-yü	路友于	
Lü Hsiu-ts'ai	呂秀才	
Ma Su	馬素	
Mao Tse-tung	毛澤東	(Mao Jun-chih 毛潤之)
Mi Shih-chen	米市珍	
Mo Jung-hsin	莫榮新	
Mo T'ung-jung	莫同榮	
Nieh Jung-chen	聶榮臻	
Niu Yung-chien	鈕永建	
Ou-yang Chü	歐陽駒	(Incorrectly written as Ou-yang Ch'i 歐陽歧)
Pai Ch'ung-hsi	白崇禧	
Pai Wen-wei	柏文蔚	
P'an Yu-ch'iang	潘佑強	
Pao Hui-seng	包惠僧	
P'eng Han-chang	彭漢章	
P'eng P'ai	彭湃	
P'eng Shu-chih	彭述之	
P'eng Tse-hsiang	彭澤湘	

Names

		Aliases, Variant Names, and Wrong Characters Used by Peking Commission
P'eng Yang-kuang	彭養光	(Incorrectly written as P'eng Yang-ch'ung 彭養充)
Shao Li-tzu	邵力子	
Shao Yüan-ch'ung	邵元冲	
Shen Hsüan-lu	沈玄盧	(Shen Ting-i 沈定一 . Incorrectly written as Shen Chih-lu 沈之 錄)
Shih Ts'un-t'ung	施存統	(Incorrectly written as Shih Ch'eng-t'ung 史 成同)
Soong, T. V. [Sung Tzu-wen]	宋子文	
Su Chao-cheng	蘇兆徵	
Sun Ch'uan-fang	孫傳芳	
Sun Fo [Sun K'o]	孫 科	(Sun Che-sheng 孫哲 生)
Sun Yat-sen [Sun I-hsien]	孫逸仙	(Sun Wen 孫文 Sun Chung-shan 孫 中山)
Sun Yüeh	孫 岳	
Sung Che-yüan	宋哲元	
Sung Ch'ing-ling (Madame Sun Yat-sen)	宋慶齡	
Tai Chi-t'ao	戴季陶	(Tai Ch'üan-hsien 戴 傅賢)
T'an Chih-t'ang	譚植棠	(Incorrectly written as T'ang Chih-tao 唐直 道)
T'an P'ing-shan	譚平山	(Incorrectly written as T'ang P'ing-san 唐 聘三)
T'an Tsu-yao	譚祖堯	

Names		Aliases, Variant Names, and Wrong Characters Used by Peking Commission
T'an Yen-k'ai	譚延闓	
T'ang Chi-yao	唐繼堯	
T'ang Shao-i	唐紹儀	
T'ang Sheng-chih	唐生智	(T'ang Meng-hsiao 唐孟瀟)
T'ang Yüeh-liang	唐悅良	
Teng Chung-hsia	鄧中夏	(Incorrectly written as Teng Chu-hsia 鄧竹霞)
Teng En-ming	鄧恩銘	
Teng Fei-huang	鄧飛黃	
Teng Pen-yin	鄧本殷	(Incorrectly written as Teng P'ei-ying 鄧培英)
Teng Shou-ch'üan	鄧壽荃	(Incorrectly written as T'an Shou-sui 譚壽歲; T'ang Shou-sui 唐壽歲)
Teng Tse-ju	鄧澤如	
Teng Wen-hui	鄧文輝	
Teng Yen-ta	鄧演達	(Teng Tse-sheng 鄧澤生)
Teng Ying-ch'ao (Mrs. Chou En-lai)	鄧穎超	
T'ien Wei-ch'in	田維勤	
Ting Wei-fen	丁惟汾	
Tong, Hollington K. [Tung Hsien-kuang]	董顯光	
Ts'ai Ho-shen	蔡和森	
Ts'ao Hao-shen	曹浩森	

Names		Aliases, Variant Names, and Wrong Characters Used by Peking Commission
Ts'ao K'un	曹 錕	
Tseng Ch'i	曾 琦	
Tu Yen	杜 炎	
Tuan Ch'i-jui	段 琪 瑞	
Tung Pi-wu	董 必 武	
Wang, C. T. [Wang Cheng-t'ing]	王 正 廷	
Wang Chen-chün	王 振 鈞	
Wang Chin-mei	王 盡 美	
Wang Ching-wei	汪 精 衛	(Wang Chao-ming 汪兆銘)
Wang Chün	王 鈞	
Wang Ch'ung-hui	王 寵 惠	
Wang Hu	王 瑚	
Wang Jo-fei	王 若 飛	
Wang Li-chai	王 勵 齋	
Wang Mou-kung	王 懋 功	
Wang Po-ling	王 柏 齡	(Wang Mei-yu 王梅友)
Wang P'u	王 普	
Wang T'ien-p'ei	王 天 倍	
Wang Tung-chen	王 冬 珍	
Wei I-san	魏 益 三	
Wei Pang-p'ing	魏 邦 平	
Wu Ch'ao-shu	伍 朝 樞	
Wu Chih-hui	吳 稚 暉	(Wu Chin-heng 吳敬恆)

Names			Aliases, Variant Names, and Wrong Characters Used by Peking Commission
Wu Chin	吳	晉	
Wu Chün-sheng	吳	俊陞	
Wu Chung-hsin	吳	忠信	(Incorrectly written as Wu Chi-hsin 吳濟新; Wu Chi-hsing 吳濟興)
Wu K'o	吳	可	
Wu P'ei-fu	吳	佩孚	
Wu Ta-yu	吳	大猷	
Wu T'ieh-ch'eng	吳	鐵城	(Incorrectly written as Wu T'i-hsin 吳體新)
Wu T'ing-shen	吳	廷琛	
Wu Yü-chang	吳	玉章	
Yang Hsi-min	楊	希閔	(Incorrectly written as Yang Shih-min 楊師閔)
Yang Li-hsien	楊	立賢	
Yang Ming-chai	楊	明齋	
Yang P'ao-an	楊	鲍安	
Yang Shen	楊	森	
Yang Yin-chih	楊	引之	
Yang Yü-t'ing	楊	宇霆	
Yao Yen	姚	彥	
Yeh Chi	葉	琪	(Incorrectly written as Yeh Ch'i 葉齊)
Yeh Ch'u-cheng	葉	楚傖	
Yeh K'ai-hsin	葉	開鑫	
Yeh T'ing	葉	挺	

Names		Aliases, Variant Names, and Wrong Characters Used by Peking Commission
Yen Hsi-shan	閻錫山	
Yi Yang-ts'ai	易養材	
Yü Ch'ia-ch'ing	虞洽卿	
Yü Chia-chü	余家菊	
Yü Fang-chou	于方舟	
Yü Shu-te	于樹德	
Yü Yu-jen	于右任	
Yüan Hsiao-hsien	阮嘯仙	(Incorrectly written as Yüan Hsüeh-sun 袁學孫)
Yüan Shih-k'ai	袁世凱	
Yüan Tsu-ming	袁祖銘	
Yüeh Wei-chün	岳維峻	
Yün Tai-ying	惲代英	

NAMES OF RELATIVELY OBSCURE RUSSIANS MENTIONED
IN THE DOCUMENTS AND ESSAYS

English Equivalent or Transliteration of Name Appearing in the Documents	Romanization of Chinese Rendering	Chinese Rendering	Transliteration of Japanese Rendering
Abumori			Abumori
Ao-li-chin	Ao-li-chin	鄂利金	
Chi-lieh-fu, Colonel (rendering of real name)	Chi-lieh-fu	基列夫	
Egorov, A. I. (real name)	Yeh-ko-lo-fu	葉葛羅夫	
Fu-lin-t'e	Fu-lin-t'e	弗林特	
Gecker, A. I. (real name)	Ko-k'o-erh	格克爾	
Hei-hsing	Hei-shing	黑興	
Henkel	Han-k'o-erh	漢克爾	
Ho-mieh-lieh-fu	Ho-mieh-lieh-fu	賀乜列夫	
Ivanovskii	I-wan-no-fu-szu-chi	伊萬諾夫斯基	
"Jen Te-chiang"	Jen Te-chiang	任德江	
Karachev	Ch'ia-la-ch'ih-fu	卡拉赤夫	Karachefu
Karpenko	K'o-erh-p'ien-k'uo	喀爾偏闊	
Kisanko	Ch'i-sang-k'o	琪桑喀	

English Equivalent or Transliteration of Name Appearing in the Documents	Romanization of Chinese Rendering	Chinese Rendering	Transliteration of Japanese Rendering
Kiselev, Nikolai Fedorovich (real name)	Chi-hsieh-lieh-fu Ni-k'o-lai-i Fei-to-lo-wei-ch'ih	基謝列夫尼柯拉依費多羅維赤	
K'o-erh-te	K'o-erh-te	柯爾得	
Ko-lei	Ko-lei	菖雷	
Kuibyshev (real name)			Kuibuishefu
"Henry A. Lin"	Heng-li Lin	亨利林	
Longva	Lung-ko-wa-erh-fu	龍格窪爾夫	
Nikitin (real name; assumed name, Hsi-lin)	Ni-chi-ch'in Hsi-lin	尼濟欽西林	
Nikitin (assumed name; real name rendered as Kuo-lieh-fu)	Ni-chi-chin Kuo-lieh-fu	尼及金果列夫	Nikiichin
Nilov	Ni-lo-fu	尼羅夫	
Orishevskii (real name; assumed name, Ao-ni-i-ch'i)	Ao-li-nieh-fu-szu-chi; Ao-ni-i-ch'i	奧利聶甫斯及奧尼依奇	Orishefusukii
Pavlov, General	P'a-fu-lo-fu	帕夫羅夫	
Pavlov	P'a-fu-lo-fu	帕夫羅夫	
Pei-tzu-szu-ch'a-szu-t'e-no-fu, General	Pei-tzu-szu-ch'a-szu-t'e-no-fu	貝茲斯察斯特諾夫	
Remi	Lieh-mu	列穆	
Rogachev, Victor P., General	Lo-ka-chi'ao-fu	羅嘎喬夫	
Seifulin (assumed name; real name, Albert Yakovlevich Labin or Rabin)	Hsieh-fu-lin; A-li-pi-erh-t'e Ya-k'uo-wei-ch'ih La-pin	謝福林阿立亞特瑞弃拉列爾闓賓	

English Equivalent or Transliteration of Name Appearing in the Documents	Romanization of Chinese Rendering	Chinese Rendering	Transliteration of Japanese Rendering
Sinani	Hsi-na-ni	希那尼	Shinani
Smirnov, Admiral	Szu-mi-erh-no-fu	斯密爾諾夫	
Solovyev, V. I. (real name)	So-lo-wei-yeh-fu	索洛維也夫	
Stepanov, General	Szu-ch'i-p'an-no-fu	斯切潘諾夫	
T'a-hsin	T'a-hsin	塔新	
Te-la-t'e-wen, Colonel	Te-la-t'e-wen	德拉特文	
Teruni	T'ieh-lo-ni	鐵羅尼	Teruni
Usmanov (assumed name; real name, Sangurskii)	Wu-szu-ma-no-fu Shan-ku-erh-ssu-chi	烏斯馬諾夫 山古爾斯 基	
Voronin	Wei-lo-ning	倭羅寧	
Ya-en	Ya-en	牙恩	

BIBLIOGRAPHY

Unless otherwise noted, all publications listed below are to be found in either Butler Library or the East Asiatic Library of Columbia University.

The titles of articles and essays originally published in Chinese have been listed in translation; titles of books, however, are listed in the romanized form, followed by a translation.

Titles of publications which are mentioned but not cited are preceded by an asterisk.

PRINCIPAL COLLECTIONS AND TRANSLATIONS OF
DOCUMENTS SEIZED FROM
THE SOVIET MILITARY ATTACHÉ'S OFFICE,
PEKING, APRIL 6, 1927

Chinese Collection

Su-lien yin-mou wen-cheng hui-pien [collection of documentary evidence of the Soviet Russian conspiracy]. Ed. and trans. Peking Metropolitan Police Headquarters, Inspection Bureau, Commission for Translation and Compilation. Peking, Metropolitan Police Headquarters, 1928.

蘇聯陰謀文證彙編

A collection of 324 Chinese translations of Russian documents and original Chinese documents, printed in two nearly identical sets. One consists of four volumes, bound Western style and with Western-style pagination. The other consists of ten volumes, bound Chinese style and with Chinese-style pagination. Page numbers in our translations are keyed to the four-volume set; when using the ten-volume set, divide the page numbers by two. The collection includes photographs of articles and stacks of papers seized in the raid and facsimile reproductions of eleven Russian documents. The set bound in Chinese style is supplemented by an eleventh volume, a group of English translations published under the title Soviet Plot in China (see under that heading below).

English Collections

Bolshevik Activities in China: Some Documents Seized in the Soviet
  Military Attaché's Office at Peking on April 6, 1927. 4 vols.
  Tientsin, Tientsin British Committee of Information, June, 1927.
  Twenty-seven documents with prefaces signed by "H. G. W. W."
  [H. G. W. Woodhead?]. They were originally issued as supple-
  ments to the Peking and Tientsin Times, May 12, May 24, May 28,
  and June 17, 1927. State Department Archives.
Chinese Government White Book.
  Six pamphlets containing 32 of the documents issued by the Peking
  Metropolitan Police Headquarters under the title Soviet Plot in
  China (see also that heading below). The first pamphlet was published on May 17, the sixth in July, 1927. The series includes
  photographs of 27 Russian documents. The pamphlets were known
  as the "Chinese Government White Book" when first published and
  are cited under that title in this work to avoid confusion with Soviet
  Plot in China (see below). The 32 documents are reprinted without
  facsimiles of Russian texts in Chinese Social and Political Science
  Review, XI (1927), 141-272. Citations in the notes are of this re-
  print. The six original pamphlets are available at the Library of
  Congress.
A History of Communism in China. n.p., 1927. 67 pp.
  Translations of five documents reprinted from the Peking and
  Tientsin Times. State Department Archives.
Mitarevsky, N. World-wide Soviet Plots, as Disclosed by Hitherto
  Unpublished Documents Seized at the USSR Embassy in Peking.
  Tientsin, Tientsin Press, Ltd., n.d. 203 pp.
  The author was associated with the Commission for Translation
  and Compilation appointed by the Peking Metropolitan Police
  Headquarters. The work bears no date of publication, but internal
  evidence indicates that it was completed in the latter part of 1927.
  Mitarevsky gives extracts from or mentions some 135 documents,
  more than half of which are unavailable in other collections. However, the book betrays serious ignorance of Chinese political
  conditions and particularly of the Kuomintang and the Chinese
  Communist Party.
The Soviet in China Unmasked: Documents Revealing Bolshevistic
  Plans and Methods. Seized in the USSR Embassy, Peking, April 6,
  1927. Shanghai, North China Daily News and Herald, Ltd., 1927.
  48 pp.
  Fourteen documents with facsimiles of Russian texts reprinted
  from the North China Daily News of May 11, 1927. State Department Archives; New York Public Library.
Soviet Plot in China. Peking, Metropolitan Police Headquarters,
  1928. 162 pp. Published as the eleventh volume of Su-lien yin-mou
  wen-cheng hui-pien. 45 documents are given, including slightly

revised versions of the 32 documents printed in the Chinese
Government White Book.

Japanese Collections

Mitsu dai nikki [confidential great daily records]. 1927, V. Japanese
Ministry of War.

密大日記

The "confidential great daily records" contain chronologically
filed copies of correspondence and reports received by the Japanese Ministry of War. The following translations and copies of
documents seized in the Peking Raid are filed in the records of
1927: parts 8, 10-13, and 14-23, dated from June 29 to August 4,
1927, of Pekin Ro-Taishikan ōshū himitsu bunsho (see below);
copies of 15 original Chinese documents and Japanese translations
of three Russian documents, which were sent with letters of transmittal by Major General Shigeru Honjo, Japanese Military Attaché
in Peking, to Eitarō Hata, Vice-Minister of War, on May 26,
June 6, and June 14, 1927; and copies of five original Chinese
documents grouped under the heading "Correspondence of the
Organization Department, Northern Regional Committee." Thirteen of the original Chinese documents are not available in Su-lien
yin-mou wen-cheng hui-pien. Mitsu dai nikki, 1927, V, is stored
in the National Archives under the title: RG 242, World War
Collection of Seized Enemy Records. Japan. NA 14678.

Ōshū bunsho naiyō kankei [the contents of the seized documents].
2 or 4 vols. See Zai Pekin So Taishikan sōsaku jiken.

押收文書内容關係

Pekin Ro-Taishikan ōshū himitsu bunsho [secret documents seized
at the Russian Embassy in Peking]. Ed. Masayoshi Miyazaki.
Dairen, South Manchurian Railway, Intelligence Section, 1927.
Classified "secret."

北京露大使館押收秘密文書.　　宮崎正義

This collection of mimeographed Japanese translations is arranged
in 23 parts. Parts 1-6 and 8-13, dated from June 8 to 27, 1927,
and containing 32 documents, are available at the Library of Congress. Other parts are filed in Mitsu dai nikki, 1927, V (see above).
Sixty-nine documents in all are available. More than half of these
have been translated into Chinese or English in other collections.

Pekin Rōnō Taishikan yori ōshū shitaru himitsu bunsho [secret
documents seized at the Russian Embassy in Peking]. Comp.
Army General Staff. Tokyo, 1927. Classified "secret."

北京勞農大使館より押收したる秘密文書

At least 13 volumes containing 148 documents were compiled.
Volumes 3, 4, and 11-13, containing 57 documents, are available
at the Library of Congress. Most of them are also available in
Chinese, English, and other Japanese translations.

Rokoku no tai-Shi sekka undō no jissō [the truth about Russian activities to sovietize China]. Ed. Gorō Koguchi. 3d ed. Peking, Association for the Investigation of Chinese Conditions, September 5, 1927. 101 pp.
露國 の 對支赤化運動 の 實相   小口五郎
This series consists of 33 documents, all of which are available in Chinese, English, or other Japanese translations. Library of Congress.

Roshiya Taishikan ōshū shorui no naiyō [contents of documents seized at the Russian Embassy]. n.p., Russian News Agency, n.d.
ロシア大使館押收書類 の 内容
The present whereabouts of this series is not known.

Zai Pekin So Taishikan sōsaku jiken [the incident of the search of the Soviet Embassy in Peking]. 1 or 4 vols.
在北京蘇大使館搜索事件
This collection and also Ōshū bunsho naiyō kankei, both now missing, are known to have been compiled by the Japanese Foreign Office. They formed parts of a larger collection, Shina Seifu no sorempō Kyōsan shugi senden bōshi kankei jiken zakken (see under that heading in the following section of the bibliography), and bore the classification numbers C/R 3/1/1 and C/R 3/1.

ARTICLES, DOCUMENTS, ESSAYS,

NEWSPAPERS, AND BOOKS

A. N. K. "The Part Played by the Kuomintang Party in the Chinese Revolution," International Press Correspondence, VI, No. 13 (February 18, 1926), 187-88.

"Appeal of the CI against the Monstrous Atrocities in Peking," International Press Correspondence, VII, No. 28 (May 7, 1927), 562-63.

Borojin Fujin hobaku kōkin jiken [Documents relating to the arrest and confinement of Mrs. Borodin]. March, 1928 through July, 1929. Tokyo, Japanese Foreign Office. 76 pp.
ボロヂン夫人捕縛拘禁事件
On microfilm at Columbia.

Brandt, Conrad, Benjamin Schwartz, and John K. Fairbank. A Documentary History of Chinese Communism. Cambridge, Harvard University Press, 1952. 552 pp.

Central Committee, Chinese Communist Party. "Letter to the Central Executive Committee of the Kuomintang," March 15, 1925, Hsiang-tao chou-pao, No. 107 (March 21, 1925), p. 890.

____ "Letter to the First National Peasant Conference," April 20, 1926, Hsiang-tao chou-pao, No. 151 (May 1, 1926), p. 1438.

Also in Chung-kuo Kung-ch'an-tang wu-nien lai chih cheng-chih chu-chang, pp. 204-5.

―――"Second Manifesto of the Chinese Communist Party on the Current Situation," July, 1923, in Chung-kuo Kung-ch'an-tang wu-nien lai chih cheng-chih chu-chang, pp. 48-53.

Central Committee, Chinese Communist Party, Enlarged Plenum. "Letter to the Peasantry," Oct. 10, 1925, in Chung-kuo Kung-ch'an-tang wu-nien lai chih cheng-chih chu-chang, pp. 127-37.

Central Committees of the Chinese Communist Party and the Chinese Communist Youth Corps. "Manifesto on the Anti-Mukden War," Oct. 20, 1925, in Chung-kuo Kung-ch'an-tang wu-nien lai chih cheng-chih chu-chang, pp. 124-26.

―――"Statement to the People of the Country on the Alliance between Wu P'ei-fu and Mukden against the Kuominchün," Feb. 7, 1926, in Chung-kuo Kung-ch'an-tang wu nien lai chih cheng-chih chu-chang, pp. 144-46.

―――"Statement to the People on the Rebellion of Kuo Sung-ling," Dec. 1, 1925, in Chung-kuo Kung-ch'an-tang wu-nien lai chih cheng-chih chu-chang, pp. 138-40.

―――"Statement to the People Who Fought for National Independence during May Thirtieth," July 10, 1925, in Chung-kuo Kung-ch'an-tang wu-nien lai chih cheng-chih chu-chang, pp. 93-100.

Central Executive Committee of the Kuomintang. "Circular Notice from the Kuomintang of China Explaining Its Revolutionary Strategy to All Party Members in the Country and Abroad," Dec. 4, 1925, in Chung-kuo Kuomintang chung-yao hsüan-yen hsün-ling chi, pp. 95-97.

―――"Circular Telegram Announcing Our Party Will Not Join the Reconstruction Conference," Feb. 2, 1925, in Chung-kuo Kuomintang chung-yao hsüan-yen hsün-ling chi, pp. 30-31.

―――"Manifesto of the Kuomintang of China Convening the Second Congress," Dec. 12, 1925, in Chung-kuo Kuomintang chung-yao hsüan-yen hsün-ling chi, pp. 99-103. Also in Chung-kuo Kuomintang tsui-chin tui-yü shih-chü chih chu-chang, pp. 15-19.

―――"Manifesto of the Kuomintang of China on the Revolutionary Movement in Peking," Dec. 8, 1925, in Chung-kuo Kuomintang chung-yao hsüan-yen hsün-ling chi, p. 98.

―――"Resolutions of the Kuomintang on Reorganization of the Army" [Third CEC Plenum], in Chung-kuo Kuomintang chung-yao hsüan-yen hsün-ling chi, pp. 61-64.

Chang Chi, Hsieh Ch'ih, and Teng Tse-ju. "Letter to the Central Executive Committee," June 18, 1924, in Tan-ho Kung-ch'an-tang liang ta yao-an, pp. 13-23.

Chang Kuo-t'ao. "Lessons of the Second Kuomintang Congress," Hsiang-tao chou-pao, No. 145 (Feb. 20, 1926), pp. 1329-30.

_____"Mao—A New Portrait by an Old Colleague," The New York Times Magazine (Aug. 2, 1953), pp. 5, 46-47.

_____"An Open Letter to All Members of the Kuomintang," Hsiang-tao chou-pao, No. 139 (Dec. 24, 1925), 1269-70.

Ch'ang-jen. "Feng Yü-hsiang's Changes," in Hsien-tai shih-liao, III, 56-78.

Chen Pan-tsu [Ch'en T'an-ch'iu]. "Reminiscences of the First Congress of the Communist Party of China," Communist International, American Edition, XIII (October, 1936), 1361-66.

Chen Ta. "Fundamentals of the Chinese Labor Movement," The Annals of the American Academy of Political and Social Sciences, Vol. 152 (November, 1930), 196-205.

Ch'en Kuo-fu. "A Piece of Party History in the Years 1926-1927," in Pen-tang yü fei-tang po-tou shih-shih, pp. 61-74.
A reprint of an article published in the newspaper Chung-yang jih-pao (Taiwan, Nov. 15, 1950), written in commemoration of Chang Ching-chiang's death. Ch'en Kuo-fu hails Chang as the guiding spirit behind the KMT's "Purification" program. Useful for details.

Ch'en Ming-shu. "Why We Want to Overthrow the Chinese Communist Party," in Ko-ming yü fan-ko-ming, pp. 360-70.

Ch'en Tu-hsiu. "The Congress of the KMT New Right Wing," Hsiang-tao chou-pao, No. 150 (April 23, 1926), pp. 1413-15.

_____"Internal Conflicts of the KMT and the Chinese Revolution," Hsiang-tao chou-pao, No. 190 (March 6, 1927), pp. 2045-46.

_____Kao ch'üan-tang t'ung-chih shu [a letter to all comrades of the Party], Dec. 10, 1929. 17 pp.
陳獨秀　告全黨同志書
Hoover Institute and Library on War, Revolution, and Peace; on microfilm at Columbia. Translated into English in The Militant, III, No. 33 (Nov. 15, 1930), 5; III, No. 34 (Dec. 1, 1930), 4; IV, No. 1 (Jan. 1, 1931), 5; IV, No. 2 (Jan. 15, 1931), 8; IV, No. 3 (Feb. 1, 1931), 6. At the New York Public Library.
Ch'en Tu-hsiu announces his final split with the Chinese Communist Party. He denies the charges of the Comintern and the KCT leadership that he was primarily responsible for Communist failure in 1927, and asserts that he had faithfully carried out Comintern policies while leader of the KCT. Ch'en's assertions need to be checked.

_____"Letter to Tai Chi-t'ao," August 30, 1925, Hsiang-tao chou-pao, No. 130 (Sept. 18, 1925), pp. 1196-97.

_____"On the National Government's Northern Expedition," Hsiang-tao chou-pao, No. 161 (July 7, 1926), pp. 1650-51.

_____"Reactionary Tendencies of the KMT New Right Wing," Hsiang-tao chou-pao, No. 139 (Dec. 24, 1925), pp. 1265-67.

_____ "The Situation in the South and the Kuomintang," Hsiang-tao chou-pao, No. 153 (May 15, 1926), pp. 1459-60.

_____ "Sorrow on the Second Anniversary of Dr. Sun's Death," Hsiang-tao chou-pao, No. 191 (March 12, 1927), pp. 2056-57.

_____ Tu-hsiu wen-ts'un [collected works of Ch'en Tu-hsiu]. 3 vols. Shanghai, Ya-tung Bookstore, 1923.

陳獨秀　獨秀文存

_____ "What are the Right and Left Wings of the Kuomintang?" Hsiang-tao chou-pao, No. 137 (Dec. 3, 1925), pp. 1247-48.

Ch'en Tu-hsiu p'ing-lun [discussions on Ch'en Tu-hsiu]. Ed. Ch'en Tung-hsiao. Peking, Tung-ya Bookstore, 1933. 256 pp.

陳獨秀評論　　陳東曉

A collection of newspaper and periodical articles on Ch'en Tu-hsiu written at the time of his arrest and trial in 1932-33. All shades of opinion are represented. Chinese-Japanese Library, Harvard University.

*Chi-nan hua-pao [relief pictorial review]. Organ of the relief association.

濟難畫報

Chiang Kai-shek. Chiang Chieh-shih hsiao-chang tsai Kuo-min-cheng-fu Chün-shih wei-yüan-hui chiang-yen tz'u [speech of Academy President Chiang Kai-shek to the Military Council of the National Government]. n.p., Political Department of the First National Revolutionary Army, n.d. 16 pp.

蔣介石　蔣介石校長在國民政府軍事委員會演講詞

Library of Congress; on microfilm at Columbia. Extracts in Chiang Kai-shek, Chiang-Chieh-shih hsien-sheng, XI, 46-49. The speech is dated July 26, 1925, in this source.

_____ Chiang Chieh-shih hsien-sheng—Min-kuo shih-wu-nien i-ch'ien chih Chiang Chieh-shih hsien-sheng [Mr. Chiang Kai-shek—Mr. Chiang Kai-shek before 1926]. Ed. Mao Szu-ch'eng. 20 vols. n.p., n.d.

蔣介石先生—民國十五年以前之蔣介石先生　　毛思誠

This collection contains the diaries of Chiang Kai-shek through December, 1926, with emphasis on the period 1924 to 1926, which takes up 15 of the 20 volumes. The collection bears no date of publication, but was presumably published near the end of 1936. (The editor's postscript is dated October, 1936.) It provides a rich store of documentary material—summaries of Chiang's conversations, his speeches, reports, letters, and telegrams, as well as important documents of the Kuomintang and the National Government. Detailed annual chronologies add further to the collection's usefulness. When checked against contemporary texts, the documentary data is usually accurate, although there are omissions, apparently intentional.

_____Chiang Chieh-shih ti ko-ming kung-tso [Chiang Kai-shek's revolutionary work]. Ed. Wen Chih. 2 vols. Shanghai, T'ai-p'ing-yang Bookstore, June, 1927.
蔣介石　蔣介石的革命工作　　文砥
A collection of Chiang Kai-shek's speeches, letters, telegrams, essays, and reports. The documents are undated, but most appear to fall between 1925 and the spring of 1927. They are preceded by a brief biographical sketch.

_____Chiang Chieh-shih tsui-chin chih yen-lun [Recent speeches of Chiang Kai-shek]. Peking, Min She, September, 1926. 126 pp.
蔣介石　蔣介石最近之言論
A collection of Chiang's speeches delivered in 1925 and the first half of 1926. Published in September, 1926, many months before the split of April, 1927, the collection is extremely valuable.

_____Chiang Chung-cheng ch'üan-chi [collected writings of Chiang Kai-shek]. Ed. Hsin-hsüeh Publishing Co. 3 vols. n.p., Chin-ch'eng Bookstore, n.d.
蔣介石　蔣中正全集
This collection of Chiang's articles, speeches, and letters was apparently published in 1936, judging by the preface. The second half of the third volume contains important private letters dated in the early 1920s which are not available in other collections. Cornell University Library.

_____"A Circular Letter to KMT. Comrades," Dec. 25, 1925, in Chiang Kai-shek, Chiang Chieh-shih tsui-chin chih yen-lun, pp. 1-6.
Also in Chiang Chieh-shih hsien-sheng, XIII, 42-50.

_____"Interview with a Reporter of the Min-kuo jih-pao Following the S.S. 'Chung-shan' Incident at Canton," in Chiang Kai-shek, Chiang Chieh-shih ti ko-ming kung-tso, II, 414-16.

_____"Letter to Officers and Men of the National Revolutionary Army," in Ch'ing-tang yün-tung, pp. 79-84.

_____"Letter to Students of the Central Military and Political Academy," March 12, 1927, in Ch'ing-tang yün-tung, pp. 26-32.

_____"The Meaning of the Soviet Alliance," Dec. 11, 1925, in Chiang Kai-shek, Chiang Chieh-shih tsui-chin chih yen-lun, pp. 7-14.

_____"Proclamation on the Closing of the General Political Department of the Army," April, 1927, Kuo-wen chou-pao, IV, No. 16 (May 1, 1927), 23-24.

_____"A Record of President Sun's Calamity in Canton," in Chiang Kai-shek, Chiang Chieh-shih ti ko-ming kung-tso, I, 1-50.

_____"Speech at Nanchang General Headquarters," Feb. 21, 1927, in Ch'ing-tang yün-tung, pp. 7-16.
Also in Chiang Kai-shek, Chiang Chieh-shih ti-ko-ming kung-tso, II, 384-96.

———"Speech at Nanchang General Headquarters," March 7, 1927, in Ch'ing-tang yün-tung, pp. 19-26.
Also in Chiang Kai-shek, Chiang Chieh-shih ti ko-ming kung-tso, II, 400-409.

———"Statement on 'Essential Points of Propaganda on Party Affairs,'" Feb. 27, 1927, in Ch'ing-tang yün-tung, pp. 15-19.
Also in Chiang Kai-shek, Chiang Chieh-shih ti ko-ming kung-tso, II, 384-96.

Chiang Ting-fu (T. F. Tsiang). Chün-cheng ling-hsiu Chiang Chieh-shih [military and political leader: Chiang Kai-shek]. Shanghai, Ch'ang-feng Bookstore, 207 pp.
蔣鼎黼　軍政領袖蔣介石
A condensed translation into Chinese of the first edition of Hollington K. Tong's Chiang Kai-shek.

*Ch'ien-feng [vanguard]. Organ of the Chinese Communist Party.
前鋒

Ch'ien Tuan-sheng, Sa Shih-ch'iung, and others. Min-kuo cheng-chih shih [a history of political institutions under the republic] 2 vols. Shanghai, Commercial Press Ltd., 1946.
錢端升　薩師炯　民國政制史

Chin Yu-fu. "A Short History of the Chinese Communist Party Written Twenty-four Years Ago," in the newspaper Chin-pu jih-pao (Tientsin, 1951). Translated in American Consulate General, Hongkong, Survey of China Mainland, No. 163 (Aug. 28, 1951), pp. 22-26.

China Press. Shanghai.
Files in the New York Public Library.

The China Year Book. Shanghai, The North China Daily News and Herald, Ltd., 1923-1928.

Ch'ing-tang yün-tung [the party purification movement]. Ed. Association for the Party Purification Movement. n.p., Association for the Party Purification Movement, June, 1927. 302 pp.
清黨運動
This extremely important collection of documents on the Party Purification Movement is divided into six sections. The first is a collection of Chiang Kai-shek's speeches. The second is a group of documents on conferences of KMT leaders. The third contains documents of the Central Supervisory Committee of the Kuomintang. The fourth and fifth sections contain declarations announcing the Purification Movement and the establishment of the Nanking Government. The last section groups together essays by KMT leaders who were sponsors of the Purification Movement. Most of the documents are dated between March and May, 1927.

Chou Fu-chen. "The Golden Age of the Kwangtung Regional Committee," in Hsien-tai shih-liao, II, 309-15.

Chou Lu. Chung-kuo Kuomintang shih-kao [draft history of the Kuomintang]. 2 vols. Shanghai, Min-chih Bookstore, October, 1929.

鄒魯　中國國民黨史
A comprehensive documentary history of the Kuomintang up to
early spring, 1925 written by a leading member of the KMT Right
Wing.

Chou Mu-chai. Hsin Chung-kuo fa-chan shih [a history of the development of the New China]. Shanghai, Kuang-ming Bookstore,
November, 1939. 168 pp.
周木齋　新中國發展史
An orthodox Communist history dealing with the period from
1911 to 1937.

Chou Ts'ui-fen. "Central Party Headquarters During the Canton
Period," in Hsien-tai shih-liao, II, 40-48.
"On Lu I," in Hsien-tai shih-liao, IV, 302-10.
"On the Transfer of the Capital to Wuhan," in Hsien-tai shih-
liao, II, 48-52.

Chou Tzu-sheng. "The Northern Expeditionary War of the National
Revolutionary Army," Tung-fang tsa-chih, XXV, No. 15 (Aug. 10,
1928, 21-32; XXV, No. 16 (Aug. 25, 1928), 25-39.

Ch'ü Ch'iu-pai. Chung-kuo ko-ming yü Kung-ch'an-tang [the Chinese
Revolution and the Chinese Communist Party]. n.p., June 1, 1928.
298 pp.
瞿秋白　中國革命與共產黨
This is a report to the Sixth Congress of the Chinese Communist
Party, July-September, 1928. The author had replaced Ch'en Tu-
hsiu as Secretary-General of the KCT at the Emergency Conference of August 7, 1927. His report surveys the Party's history
and "the Kuomintang problem". Ch'ü's thesis, in accordance with
the orthodox Communist interpretation, is that Ch'en Tu-hsiu's
opportunist leadership sabotaged the correct policies of the Comintern. Ch'ü gives interesting details, however, which are not
found in orthodox Communist histories. The article has only
casual documentation. Library of Congress; on microfilm at
Columbia.

*Chung-kuo ch'ing-nien [Chinese youth]. Organ of the Chinese Com-
munist Youth Corps.
中國青年

*Chung-kuo fu-nü [Chinese women]. Organ of the Federation of
Women.
中國婦女

Chung-kuo hsien-tai ko-ming yün-tung shih [a history of modern
revolutionary movements in China]. Ed. Committee for Research
on Chinese Modern History. 3d ed. n.p., China Publishing Co.,
1940. 236 pp.
中國現代革命運動史
Orthodox Communist interpretation. In parts identical with Hua
Kang's work. Little documentation.

Chung-kuo ko tang-p'ai chih shih-liao yü p'i-p'an [a brief history
  and criticism of political parties in China]. Peiping, Hsüan-wei-
  t'ien Publishing Co., 1947. 318 pp.
  中國各黨派之史略與批判
Chung-kuo Kung-ch'an-tang tui-yü shih-chü ti chu-chang [manifesto
  of the Chinese Communist Party on the current situation]. June
  15, 1922. n.p., Central Committee of the Chinese Communist
  Party, June 17, 1922. 14 pp.
  中國共產黨對於時局的主張
  Library of Congress. Also in Chung-kuo Kung-ch'an-tang wu-nien
  lai chih cheng-chih chu-chang, pp. 24-39. Translated from a Russian version in Brandt, Schwartz, and Fairbank, pp. 54-63.
Chung-kuo Kung-ch'an-tang tui-yü shih-chü ti chu-chang [manifesto
  of the Chinese Communist Party on the current situation]. n.p.,
  Enlarged Plenum of the Central Committee of the Chinese Communist Party, July 12, 1926. 27 pp.
  中國共產黨對於時局的主張
  Known as the "Fifth Manifesto of the Chinese Communist Party."
  Library of Congress. Also in Chung-kuo Kung-ch'an-tang wu-nien
  lai chih cheng-chih chu-chang, pp. 159-77.
Chung-kuo Kung-ch'an-tang wu-nien lai chih cheng-chih chu-chang
  [political policies of the Chinese Communist Party in the last
  five years]. 2d ed. n.p., Central Committee of the Chinese Communist Party, October 10, 1926. 214 pp.
  中國共產黨五年來之政治主張
  A collection of 38 documents of the Chinese Communist Party,
  dated from May, 1922, to October, 1926. Most are signed by the
  Central Committee of the Party alone or together with the CC of
  the CY. Published nearly a year before the emergence of the
  orthodox Communist interpretation, the collection has great
  historical value. Library of Congress.
*Chung-kuo kung-jen [Chinese workers]. Organ of the All-China
  Federation of Labor.
  中國工人
Chung-kuo Kuomintang chung-yao hsüan-yen hsün-ling chi [Impor-
  tant declarations and instructions of the Kuomintang of China].
  n.p., Political Department of the Military Academy of the Kuomintang of China, December 1925. 121 pp.
  中國國民黨重要宣言訓令集
  A superb collection of 35 Kuomintang documents dated from
  January, 1924, to January, 1926. "Internal" documents, such as
  instructions and circular notices to Party members, are included
  as well as published Party manifestos. Library of Congress.
Chung-kuo Kuomintang ti-i-erh-san tz'u ch'üan-kuo tai-piao ta-hui
  hui-k'an [collection of documents on the first, second, and third
  congresses of the Kuomintang of China]. n.p., Propaganda

Department of the Central Executive Committee of the Kuomintang of China, October, 1931. 193 pp.
中國國民黨第一二三次全國代表大會彙刊.
A collection of manifestos and selected documents of the first
three KMT congresses, with brief summaries of the agendas of
the congresses. The texts dealing with the First and Second Congresses prove accurate when checked against a collection of documents of the First Congress published in April, 1924, and another
collection of documents of the First and Second Congresses published in 1926. These two earlier collections, Chung-kuo Kuomintang ti-i tz'u ch'üan kuo tai-piao ta-hui hui-i-k'an and Chung-kuo
Kuomintang ti-i-erh tz'u ch'üan kuo tai-piao ta-hui hui-i-k'an,
are available at the Library of Congress.
Chung-kuo Kuomintang tsui-chin tui-yü shih-chü chih chu-chang
    [most recent declarations of the Kuomintang of China on the cur-
    rent situation]. n.p., Peking Executive Headquarters of the Cen-
    tral Executive Committee of the Kuomintang, December, 1925.
    22 pp.
    中國國民黨最近對於時局之主張.
    A collection of six documents, issued toward the end of 1925.
*Chung-shan sheng-huo [life of Sun Yat-sen]. Organ of the Chung-
    shan Study Society, Peking.
    中山生活.
"Circular Notice from the Kuomintang of China on Party Discipline,"
    Circular Notice No. 147, July, 1925, in Chung-kuo Kuomintang
    chung-yao hsüan-yen hsün-ling chi, pp. 75-76.
The Communist. Organ of the Communist Party of Great Britain.
    Issues for 1927.
The Communist International. Organ of the ECCI. English edition,
    1925-1927.
Communist International. The First Congress of the Toilers of the
    Far East, Held in Moscow January 21st - February 1st, 1922.
    Closing Session in Petrograd, February 2nd, 1922. Petrograd,
    Communist International, 1922. 248 pp.
    ____ Theses and Statutes of the Third (Communist) International—
    Adopted by the Second Congress, July 17th - August 7th, 1920.
    Moscow, Publishing Office of the Communist International, 1920.
    85 pp.
"The Conference of the Communist Party of China," International
    Press Correspondence, V, No. 77 (Oct. 29, 1925), 1166.
"Constitution of the Chinese Communist Party," Mantetsu Shina
    gesshi, VII, No. 5 (May, 1930), 45-60.
"Constitution of the Kuomintang of China," Chung-kuo Kuomintang
    ti-i-erh-san-tz'u ch'üan-kuo tai-piao ta-hui hui-i-k'an, pp. 155-76.
    Translated into English in Arthur N. Holcombe, The Chinese
    Revolution (Cambridge, Harvard University Press, 1931, pp. 356-70.

"A Declaration Issued by the Kuomintang of China on the Objectives of the Northern Expedition," Sept. 18, 1924, in Ta-yüan-shüai kuan-yü Pei-fa chih ming-ling chih hsüan-yen, pp. 15-18. Also in Chung-kuo Kuomintang chung-yao hsüan-yen hsün-ling chi, pp. 19-21.

"The Declaration of 1919" and "The Declaration of 1920," in The China Year Book, 1924, pp. 867-72.

Department of State. Foreign Relations of the United States (1927). 2 vols. Washington, D. C., U. S. Government Printing Office, 1942.

Documents Illustrating the Hostile Activities of the Soviet Government and Third International against Great Britain. Russia No. 2 (1927). Cmd. 2874. London, His Majesty's Stationery Office, 1927. 31 pp.

"Documents on the Conference of Party Members of Wuhan, Hanyang and Hsia-k'o," Feb. 24, 1927, Kuo-wen chou-pao, IV, No. 16 (May 1, 1926), 1-3.

Fan Shih-sheng. "After Reading 'A Record of the Merchant Corps Incident,'" in Hsien-tai shih-liao, III, 14-20.

Fang Lu. "Liquidation of Ch'en Tu-hsiu," in Ch'en Tu-hsiu p'ing-lun, pp. 60-80.

Feng Yü-hsiang. Feng Yü-hsiang jih-chi [Feng Yu-hsiang's diaries]. 2 vols. 2d ed. Peking, Association for Editing the Historical Materials of the Republic, December, 1932.

馮玉祥　馮玉祥日記

Feng's diaries cover the period from November, 1920, through 1927. The first edition appeared in July, 1930. Preceded by a brief chronology, they give detailed information about Feng's activities and include selected documents. There are considerable gaps in the record. The reader is informed that the records for certain periods had been lost. It is admitted in the preface, however, that much data of importance had been left out because of political considerations. Harvard library.

―――Wo so jen-shih ti Chiang Chieh-shih [the Chiang Kai-shek I know]. Shanghai, Wen-hua Publishing Co., March, 1949. 232 pp.

我所認識的蔣介石

―――Wo ti sheng-huo [my life]. 3 vols. 2d ed. Chungking, San-min Bookstore, August, 1944.

我的生活

The third volume of Feng's autobiography covers the period from shortly before his coup d'état of October 23, 1924, to the Cheng-chou Conference of June 12, 1927. Written many years after the events, it contains attempts at self-justification and rationalization.

"Fourth Manifesto of the Chinese Communist Party on the Current Situation," November, 1924, in Chung-kuo Kung-ch'an-tang wu-nien lai chih cheng-chih chu-chang, pp. 64-69.

This is also translated into English from a Japanese version in
Brandt, Schwartz, and Fairbank, pp. 74-77.

Fuse, Katsuji. Su-Wo ti Tung-fang cheng-ts'e [Soviet Russia's
policies in the East]. Trans. Pan Su. 5th ed. Shanghai, T'ai-
p'ing-yang Bookstore, February, 1929. 396 pp.

布施勝治　蘇俄的東方政策　　　　半粟.

The author was a correspondent for the Osaka Mainichi and the
Tokyo Nichi Nichi. He drew upon extensive personal experience
in preparing this book, which was completed at the end of September, 1926. For an English translation see Katsuji Fuse Soviet
Policy in the Orient. East Peking, Enjinsha, 1927. 409 pp.

Gendai Shina jimmei kan [who's who in China today]. Ed. Intelligence
Bureau of the Foreign Office. Tokyo, Research and Editorial
Department of the East Asia Society, October, 1928. 957 pp.

現代支那人名鑑

A useful biographical dictionary.

Gould, Randall. China in the Sun. Garden City, N.Y., Doubleday
and Co., 1946. 403 pp.

Hankow Herald. Hankow. Files in the New York Public Library.

Hatano, Ken'ichi. "A Biography of Chou En-lai," Kaizo, XIX (July,
1937), 89-91.

Heller, I. "The Labour Movement in China," Communist International, No. 17, pp. 3-17. [English edition, n.d., probably? Oct.
or Nov., 1925]

Ho Fu. "Kuomintang Cliques before the Third Plenum," in Hsien-
tai shih-liao, II, 1-33.

Ho Ying-ch'in. "Speech on the Party Purification Movement,"
May 2, 1927, in Kuomintang Ch'ing-tang yün-tung lun-wen chi,
pp. 86-95.

"A Honanese." "Early Activities of the Chinese Communist Party
in Honan," in Hsien-tai shih-liao, II, 286-98.

Hsiang-tao chou-pao [guide weekly].

嚮導週報

Organ of the Chinese Communist Party. Files in the Library of
Congress; also on microfilm at Columbia. September, 1922-1927.

Hsieh Yeh. "Han Lin-fu," in Hsien-tai shih-liao, IV, 395-406.

Hsien-tai p'ing-lun (The Contemporary Review). Shanghai, 1927.

現代評論

Hsien-tai shih-liao [materials of modern history]. Ed. Hai-t'ien
Publishing Co. 4 vols. Shanghai, Hai-t'ien Publishing Co., Vols.
I, II, III, 1934; Vol. IV, 1935.

現代史料

A collection of articles and essays on Chinese political parties
and leaders of the 1920s and early 1930s, approximately half of
them dealing with the period of KMT-KCT cooperation in the
1920s. Most articles are undated, but were apparently written

in the early 1930s. Many appear to have been previously published. Authorship is usually obscure since only pseudonyms are supplied in most cases. Some articles are brief anecdotes; others attempt historical analysis but without documentation. There is great variation in quality. The authors generally convey a sense of intimate involvement in the events discussed. While they provide a wealth of detailed information, they frequently reveal bias on personal or political grounds, sometimes both. The entire collection is pervaded by an anti-Communist point of view. Many authors write as if they were ex-Communists, but they do not appear to reveal any bias for any other group or party. This is a valuable collection provided the contents of each article are carefully checked. Hoover Institute and Library on War, Revolution, and Peace.

*Hsin ch'ing-nien (La Jeunesse). Shanghai, Ch'ün-i Shu-she.

新青年

*Hsin Chün [new army]. Organ of the New Army Society, Peking.

新軍

*Hsing-shih chou-pao [awakened lion monthly]. Shanghai, Hsing-shih Weekly Association.

醒獅週報

Hsü Shan-fu. "History of Splits within the KCT," in Hsien-tai shih-liao, I, 221-51.

Hu Hua. Chung-kuo hsin min-chu-chu-i ko-ming shih [a history of the new democratic Chinese revolution]. 2d ed. Canton, New China Bookstore, 1951. 251 pp.

胡華 中國新民主主義革命史

A recent orthodox Communist history covering the period from the May Fourth Movement to the end of the Sino-Japanese War in 1945.

Hua Kang. Chung-kuo min-tsu chieh-fang yün-tung shih [a history of the Chinese national liberation movement]. 2 vols. Shanghai, Vol. I, n.p., Chi-ming Publishing Co., 1940; Vol. II, Shanghai, Tu-shu Publishing Co., 1940.

華崗 中國民族解放運動史

An orthodox Communist history of Chinese revolutionary movements from the first Anglo-Chinese War (Opium War) to 1927.

Huang Hao. "A True Picture of the S.S. 'Chung-shan Incident,'" in Hsien-tai shih-liao, II, 98-103.

Huang Ku. "On the Merchant Corps Incident," in Hsien-tai shih-liao, II, 94-97.

*Huo-yu [the employee]. Publication of the Shanghai Communist Group, 1920-1921.

影友

I Ch'ing. "The Soviet Embassy Case," Hsien-tai p'ing-lun, V, No. 123 (April 16, 1927), 7-9.

"An Important Declaration of the Central Executive Committee of the Kuomintang," June 23, 1925, in Sha-ch'i t'u-sha chung Tang-li chün-hsiao shou-nan che, pp. 43-44.

"An Important Declaration of the Generalissimo on the Current Situation," Nov. 10, 1924, in Ta-yüan-shuai kuan-yü Pei-fa chih ming-ling chih hsüan-yen, pp. 18-23.

"Important Documents of the Western Hills Conference Expelling Communists from the KMT," November, 1925, Kuo-wen chou-pao, IV, No. 14 (April 17, 1927), 14-16.

"Important Points Converning the Conference on Party Affairs Held by Leaders of the Kuomintang," April 7, 1927, in Ch'ing-tang yün-tung, pp. 33-34.

"Instructions from the Kuomintang of China to the Party Military Academy and the Army," Instructions No. 12, July, 1925, in Chung-kuo Kuomintang chung-yao hsüan-yen hsün-ling chi, pp. 77-78.

"Instructions of the Kuomintang of China on the Acceptance of Tsung-li's Will," Instructions No. 13, July, 1925, in Chung-kuo Kuomintang chung-yao hsüan-yen hsün-ling chi, pp. 72-74.

"Instructions of the Kuomintang of China on the Admission of Communists into Our Party," Instructions No. 10, July, 1925, in Chung-kuo Kuomintang chung-yao hsüan-yen hsün-ling chi, pp. 79-83.

International Press Correspondence. Organ of the ECCI. English Edition.

Isaacs, Harold R. The Tragedy of the Chinese Revolution. Rev. ed., Stanford University Press, 1951, 382 pp.

*Jen-min chou-k'an [people's weekly]. Organ of the Kwangtung Regional Committee of the Chinese Communist Party.
人民週刊

"A Joint Declaration by Leaders of the Kuomintang and the Chinese Communist Party," April 4, 1927, in Ch'ing-tang yün-tang, pp. 36-37.

"Joint Manifesto of Sun Yat-sen and A. Joffe," Jan. 26, 1923, Kuo-wen chou-pao, IV, No. 14 (April 17, 1927), 2.
Translated in Brandt, Schwartz, and Fairbank, pp. 70-71.

Jung Fu. "Ch'en Yu-jen's Political Career," in Hsien-tai shih-liao, IV, 37-46.

*Ko-ming ch'ang-shih [common knowledge on revolution]. A projected publication of the Propaganda Department of the Central Committee of the Chinese Communist Party.
革命常識

Ko-ming yü fan-ko-ming [revolution and counterrevolution]. Ed. Lang Hsin-shih. Shanghai, Min-chih Publishing Co., October, 1928. 612 pp.
革命與反革命   郎醒石

An important collection of 21 essays by leaders of the Nanking Government. Undated, the essays apparently were written in the latter half of 1927 and in 1928. While the primary purpose of the collection was to battle communism on the ideological level, many of the essays also attack Wang Ching-wei. Two speeches delivered by Wang in November, 1927, are included in the appendix.

Kommunisticheskii Internatsional V Dokumentakh [Communist International in documents]. Ed. Bela Kun. Moscow, Party Press, 1933. 1007 pp.

*Ku-chün chou-pao [solitary army weekly]. Shanghai, Ku-chün Magazine Association.

孤軍週報

*Kuang-ming pan-yüeh-k'an [brightness semi-monthly]. Organ of the relief association.

光明半月刊

Kuei Nien. "Chou En-lai During the Wuhan Period," in Hsien-tai shih-liao, IV, 272-80.

Kung-ch'an-tang (The Communist).

共產黨

A periodical published by the Shanghai Communist group in the fall of 1920. The following issues are available at the Library of Congress: No. 3 (April 7, 1921), 41 pp.; No. 5 (June 7, 1921), 48 pp.; and No. 6 (July 7, 1921), 60 pp. The contents consist largely of translations from Russian and English of theoretical and general articles, documents of the Communist International and the communist parties of various countries, and news of conditions within Soviet Russia and the communist movement abroad.

*Kung Nung or Lao Nung [workers and peasants]. Publication of the Central Committee of the Chinese Communist Party. (Planned)

工農　　勞農

*Kuo-min jih-pao [national daily]. Organ of the Kuomintang.

國民日報

Kuomintang Ch'ing-tang yün-tung lun-wen chi [collection of essays on the Kuomintang party purification movement]. Ed. "J. E." Shanghai, New China Society, June, 1927. 184 pp.

國民黨清黨運動論文集

Twenty-two essays by KMT leaders; dated around spring, 1927.

Kuo Mo-jo. Ko-ming ch'uh-ch'iu [revolutionary spring and autumn]. Shanghai, Hai-yen Bookstore, May, 1947. 437 pp.

郭沫若　革命春秋

This is the second volume of Kuo's autobiography, Mo-jo tzu-ch'üan. Written in 1932 and 1933, it contains recollections of his experiences during the Northern Expedition from August 24 to early in November, 1926, when he was chairman of the Propaganda Section of the General Political Department of the National

Revolutionary Army. Translated into English in Kuo Mo-jo, "A
Poet with the Northern Expedition," trans. Josiah W. Bennet, Far
Eastern Quarterly, III (1943-1944), 5-36, 144-71, 237-59, 362-80.
Kuo-wen chou-pao (Kuowen Weekly Illustrated). Tientsin, Kuowen
Weekly Association.
國民週報
An independent periodical offering weekly analyses of domestic
and international news and important contemporary documents.
Particularly valuable is a collection of documents on Kuomin-
tang-Communist relations, 1922-1927, in Volume IV, Nos. 14, 15,
and 16.
*Lao-tung-che [the laborer]. Publication of the Shanghai Communist
Group, 1920-1921.
勞動者
*Lao-tung sheng [the laborer's voice]. Publication of the Canton
Communist Group, 1920-1921.
勞動聲
*Lao-tung yin [the laborer's sound]. Publication of the Peking
Communist Group, 1920-1921.
勞動音
"Letter from the Central Political Bureau to the Comrades of the
Regional Committees of Hunan, Hupeh, and Kiangsi," quoted by
Wu Chih-hui in "Another Discussion with Wang Ching-wei on
the Basis of Definite Evidence," pp. 67-68.
"Letter from the Central Supervisory Committee to the Central
Executive Committee," April, 1927, in Ch'ing-tang yün-tung,
pp. 53-55.
"Letter from the Chinese Communist Party to the Kuomintang,"
June 4, 1926, Hsiang-tao chou-pao, No. 157 (June 9, 1926),
1525-26.
"Letter from the Military Concil of the National Government to
All Officers and Men," July 6, 1925, in Chung-kuo Kuomintang
chung-yao hsüan-yen hsün-ling chi, pp. 48-50.
"Letter from Wang Ching-wei and Others Rejecting the Letter of
Impeachment," July 1, 1925, in Teng Tsu-ju, Chung-kuo Kuomin-
tang erh-shih nien shih-chi, pp. 291-92.
"Letter to Overseas Chinese from Hu Han-min, Minister of Foreign
Affairs of the National Government," July, 1925, in Chung-kuo
Kuomintang chung-yao hsüan-yen hsün-ling chi, pp. 69-71.
"Letter to the People from the National Government," in Chung-kuo
Kuomintang chung-yao hsüan-yen hsün-ling chi, pp. 53-57.
Li Ang. Hung-se wu-t'ai [the red stage]. Chengtu, Sheng-li Publish-
ing Co., May, 1942. 198 pp.
李昂　紅色舞臺
The author asserts that he worked as a translator on Borodin's
staff during the mid-1920s. His first chapter, which is on this

period, resembles Wang Wei-lien's article, "Election of the First Chairman of the National Government." Both need careful checking.

Li Chien-nung. Tsui-chin san-shih nien Chung-kuo cheng-chih shih [political history of China for the past thirty years]. Shanghai, T'ai-p'ing-yang Bookstore, 1930. 652 pp.

李創農　最近三十年中國政治史

An objective, partially documented history spanning the years from 1894 to the conclusion of the Northern Expedition.

Li Shih. "Organization of the Left Wing before the Kuomintang Purge," in Hsien-tai shih-liao, I, 86-90.

Li T'ai-fen. Kuominchün shih-kao [draft history of the Kuominchün]. n.p., October, 1930. 511 pp.

李泰棻　國民軍史稿

Official history of the Kuominchün up to August, 1928. Library of Congress.

Lieh-ning ch'ing-nien. Organ of the Chinese Communist Youth Corps.

列寧青年

Files in the Library of Congress. Oct. 1928-1929.

"List of the First Central Executive and Supervisory Committees," in Chung-kuo Kuomintang ti-i-erh-san tz'u ch'üan-kuo tai-piao ta-hui hui-i-k'an, pp. 188-89.

"List of the Second Central Executive and Supervisory Committees," in Chung-kuo Kuomintang ti-i-erh-san-tz'u ch'üan-kuo tai-piao ta-hui hui-i-k'an, pp. 189-91.

Liu Lu-yin. "Revolution and Counterrevolution," Ko-ming yü fan-ko-ming, pp. 427-75.

An important KMT Right Wing interpretation of KMT-Communist relations. The author, who opposes Wang Ching-wei as well as the Communists, quotes liberally from Chinese Communist sources, some of which are important and apparently genuine.

Lo Yüan-k'un. Chung-kuo chin pai-nien shih [a history of China for the last hundred years]. 2 vols. Shanghai, Commercial Press Ltd., 1933.

羅元鯤　中國近百年史

Mandalyan. Wei shen-mo Chung-kuo Kung-ch'an-tang ti ling-tao p'o-ch'an [why did the leadership of the Chinese Communist Party fail?]. Trans. Yin Szu-mei. Moscow, Sun Yat-sen University, 1927. 13 pp.

曼特林　為什麼中國共產黨的領破產　　尹思美

The author, a representative of the Russian Communist Party in China, presents one of the earliest attempts to charge the KCT leadership with opportunism. The booklet was apparently written immediately after the Nanchang Uprising of August 1, 1927, and before the Emergency Conference, held on August 7, 1927, judging by the incomplete copy of a Chinese translation at the Library of Congress.

"Manifesto of the Chinese Labor Union Secretariat," Kung-ch'an-tang, No. 6 (July 7, 1921), 21-22.

"Manifesto of the First Congress," in Chung-kuo Kuomintang ti-i-er-san-tz'u ch'üan-kuo tai-piao tai-hui hui-i-k'an, pp. 33-48. Translated in T. C. Woo, The Kuomintang..., pp. 258-69.

"Manifesto of the Fourth Congress of the Chinese Communist Party," Jan. 22, 1925, Hsiang-tao chou-pao, No. 100 (Jan. 28, 1925), pp. 933-35. Also in Chung-kuo Kung-ch'an-tang wu-nien lai chih cheng-chih chu-chang, pp. 71-77.

"Manifesto of the Kuomintang of China on the Acceptance of Tsung-li's Will," May 20, 1925, in Chung-kuo Kuomintang chung-yao hsüan-yen hsün-ling chi, pp. 37-41.

"Manifesto of the Kuomintang of China on the Current Situation" [Third CEC Plenum], in Chung-kuo Kuomintang chung-yao hsüan-yen hsün-ling chi, pp. 58-60.

"Manifesto of the Kuomintang of China on the Current Situation," Oct. 24, 1925, in Chung-kuo Kuomintang chung-yao hsüan-yen hsün-ling chi, pp. 84-86. Also in Chung-kuo Kuomintang tsui-chin tui-yü shih-chü chih chu-chang, pp. 1-3.

"Manifesto of the National Government of the Republic of China," July 1, 1925, in Chung-kuo Kuomintang chung-yao hsüan-yen hsün-ling chi, pp. 45-47.

"Manifesto of Our Party on the Current Situation," Nov. 28, 1925, in Chung-kuo Kuomintang tsui-chin tui-yü shih-chü chih chu-chang, pp. 11-13.

"Manifesto of the Second Congress," in Chung-kuo Kuomintang ti-i-erh-san-tz'u ch'üan-kuo tai-piao ta-hui hui-i-k'an, pp. 49-72.

"Manifesto of the Second Congress of the Chinese Communist Party," May, 1922, in Chung-kuo Kung-ch'an-tang wu-nien lai chih cheng-chih chu-chang, pp. 1-23. Partially translated into English from a Japanese version in Brandt, Schwartz, and Fairbank, pp. 63-65.

"Manifesto of the Third Congress of the Chinese Communist Party," Hsiang-tao chou-pao, No. 30 (June 20, 1923), p. 228. Also in Chung-kuo Kung-ch'an-tang wu-nien lai chih cheng-chih chu-chang, pp. 45-47. Translated into English in Brandt, Schwartz, and Fairbank, pp. 71-74.

Mao Tse-tung. "Report on an Investigation of the Hunan Peasant Movement," Hsiang-tao chou-pao, No. 191 (March 12, 1927, pp. 2063-68. Translated into English in Brandt, Schwartz, and Fairbank, pp. 80-89.

*Mei-chou p'ing-lun [weekly review]. Peking.

每週評論

Mif, Pavel. Chin-chi shih-ch'i chung ti Chung-kuo Kung-ch'an-tang [the Chinese Communist Party in critical days]. Trans. into Chinese from Russian. Moscow, Sun Yat-sen University, 1928. 79 pp.

緊急 時期中的中國共產黨

This was originally published in Bolshevik, Nos. 23 and 24 (1927) and No. 5 (1928). The preface, dated June, 1928, states that its purpose is to expose all manifestations of opportunism betrayed by the KCT leadership. Mif, sent to China by the Comintern in early 1927, concentrates on the period from July, 1926, to July, 1927.

*Min-kuo jih-pao (Republican Daily News). Organ of the Kuomintang.

民國日報

Nassonov, N., N. Fokine, and A. Albrecht. "The Letter from Shanghai," March 17, 1927, trans. from the French in Leon Trotsky, Problems of the Chinese Revolution, pp. 397-432.
Three Comintern delegates criticize the policies of the KCT Central Committee and of Voitinskii, chief CI delegate, particularly during the Northern Expedition.

"National Revolutionary Movement in China and Tactics of the Chinese Communist Party," The Communist International, No. 17, pp. 18-29. [English edition, n. d., probably? Oct. or Nov., 1925]

North, Robert C. Moscow and Chinese Communists. Stanford University Press, 1953. 306 pp.

North China Star. Tientsin.
Files in the New York Public Library.

Note from His Majesty's Government to the Government of the Union of Soviet Socialist Republics Respecting the Relations Existing between the Two Governments and Note in Reply. Russia No. 1 (1927). Cmd. 2822. London, His Majesty's Stationery Office, 1927. 31 pp.

*Nu-li chou-pao (The Endeavor). Peking.

努力週報

Ōtsuka, Reizō. Shina Kyōsantō shi [a history of the Chinese Communist Party]. 2 vols. Tokyo, Seikatsu Sha, July, 1940.

大塚令三 支那共產黨史

Oudendyk, William J. Ways and By-Ways in Diplomacy. London, Peter Davies, 1939. 386 pp.

Pai Lin. "The Northern Communist Leader An T'i-ch'eng," in Hsien-tai shih-liao, IV, 288-94.

Pai Shan. "The Wuhan-Nanking Split and T'ang Sheng-chih," in Hsien-tai shih-liao, I, 32-36.

*Pei-ching cheng-chih sheng-huo [political life in Peking]. Publication of the Chinese Communist Party.

北京政治生活

Peking Executive Headquarters of the Central Executive Committee of the Kuomintang. "Manifesto of Our Party on the Current Situation," Oct. 26, 1925, in Chung-kuo Kuomintang tsui-chin tui-yü shih-chü chih chu-chang, pp. 3-11.

Pen-tang yü fei-tang po-tou shih-shih [historical records on our party's struggle against the bandit party]. n.p., Publications Supply Association of the [KMT] Central Reform Committee, March, 1951. 74 pp.
本黨與匪黨搏鬪史實

Peng Pai [P'eng P'ai]. "Memoirs of a Chinese Communist," The Living Age, Vol. 344 (April, 1933), 117-29.

P'eng Shu-chih. "On the Transfer of the National Government," Feb. 13, 1927, Hsiang-tao chou-pao, No. 188 (Feb. 16, 1927), pp. 2008-9.
P'eng was a close follower of Ch'en Tu-hsiu during the latter's leadership of the Communist Party. He later followed Ch'en into the Trotskyite fold and was arrested with Ch'en on October 15, 1932. P'eng is one of the chief targets of attack in orthodox Communist histories. The views he expressed during the period of KMT-KCT collaboration are significant because of his identification with Ch'en.

_____"The Question of Dr. Sun's Attitude," Hsiang-tao chou-pao, No. 98 (Jan. 7, 1925), pp. 817-18.

People's Tribune. Organ of the National Government in Hankow. Files in the New York Public Library. March-August, 1927.

"Petition to Impeach the Communist Party Presented by the Kwangtung Branch of the Kuomintang of China and Tsung-li's Criticisms and Explanations," Nov. 29, 1923, in Tan-ho Kung-ch'an-tang liang ta yao an, pp. 1-11.
Sun Yat-sen's comments are translated into English in Brandt, Schwartz, and Fairbank, pp. 72-73.

P'ing Tzu. "A Record of the Canton Merchant Corps Incident," in Hsien-tai shih-liao, III, 7-14.

"Proceedings of the First Congress," in Chung-kuo Kuomintang ti-i-erh-san-tz'u ch'üan-kuo tai-piao ta-hui hui-i-k'an, pp. 3-18.

Puti Mirovoi Revolutsii [road of world revolution]. 2 vols. Moscow, Executive Committee of the Communist International, 1927.

"The Recent National Political Situation and Tendencies in the Revolutionary Movement," Secret Regional Correspondence No. 14, quoted in Wu Chih-hui, "Another Discussion with Wang Ching-wei on the Basis of Definite Evidence," pp. 64-66.
An important document on Chinese Communist policy, probably issued by the Kiangsu-Chekiang Regional Committee of the Chinese Communist Party around early March, 1927. It appears to be authentic.

"Record of the Questions of CSC Members Hsieh Ch'ih and Chang Chi and the Answers of Borodin," June 25, 1924, in Tan-ho Kung-ch'an-tang liang ta yao an, pp. 25-30.

"Report of the Young Communist International at the Sixth World Congress of the Communist International," Lieh-ning ch'ing-nien, I, No. 10 (February 15, 1929), pp. 69-94.

Files in the Library of Congress.

"Resolutions Impeaching the Western Hills Conference," translated into Japanese in Shunzō Satō, Shina no kokunai tōsō..., pp. 75-77.

"Resolutions of the Chinese Communist Party on the National Movement and the KMT Problem," quoted in Chang Chi, Hsieh Ch'ih, and Teng Tse-ju, "Letter to the Central Executive Committee," p. 15-16.

Excerpts from the resolutions adopted at the Third Congress of the KCT in the summer of 1923.

"Resolutions of the Plenum of the Central Executive Committee of the Kuomintang," Kuo-wen chou-pao, IV, No. 15 (April 4, 1927), pp. 9-11.

"Resolutions of the Second Congress of the Chinese Socialist Youth Corps," published by the Central Committee of the Chinese Socialist Youth Corps, August 25, 1923, quoted in Chang Chi, Hsieh Ch'ih, and Teng Tse-ju, "Letter to the Central Executive Committee," pp. 14-15.

The resolutions are quoted in the petition to impeach the Communist Party presented on June 18, 1924. The quotes appear to be authentic.

"Resolutions on the China Question," International Press Correspondence, VI, No. 40 (May 13, 1926), 648-49.

"Resolutions on the Problem of the KMT Left Wing Adopted at the Recent Special Conference of the Central Committee," Secret Regional Correspondence No. 7, in Wu Chih-hui, "Another Discussion with Wang Ching-wei on the Basis of Definite Evidence," pp. 69-77.

Presumably issued by the Kiangsu-Chekiang Regional Committee of the Chinese Communist Party, these are resolutions adopted at the conference of the Central Committee in Hankow in December, 1926. The document seems to be authentic, and is extremely important.

Rokoku narabi ni Dai-san Intānashyonaru no taigai sakudō ni kansuru shōko tekihatsu jiken [documents relating to the exposure of proof of the conspiracy of the USSR and the Third International]. Japanese Foreign Office, European and American Section, March, 1928. Special Studies No. 112. 70 pp.

露國 竝 第三インターナショナルノ對外策動二關スル
證據摘發事件

On microfilm at Columbia.

Roy, M. N. My Experience in China. 2d ed. Calcutta, Renaissance Publishers, January, 1945, 70 pp.

First published in January, 1938, this is based on the author's

Sokolsky, George. "General Chiang and Wang Ching-wei," North China Herald, April 9, 1927.

Stalin, J. "The International Situation," in Lun Chung-kuo ko-ming [on the Chinese revolution], ed. Sino-Soviet Friendship Association. Mukden, New China Bookstore, 1950; pp. 220-61.
Chinese translation of a speech delivered on August 1, 1927, at the Joint Plenum of the Central Committee and Central Control Commission of the Communist Party of the Soviet Union.

―――"Prospects of the Revolution in China," Nov. 30, 1926, International Press Correspondence, VI, No. 90 (Dec. 23, 1926), 1581-84.

Sun Yat-sen. "The Generalissimo's Circular Telegram on the Reconstruction Conference," in Chung-kuo Kuomintang chung-yao hsüan-yen hsün-ling chi, pp. 27-29.

―――"Manifesto to Foreign Countries on the Merchant Corps Incident," Sept. 1, 1924, in Chung-kuo Kuomintang chung-yao hsüan-yen hsün-ling chi, pp. 16-17.

―――"Party Members Must Strictly Observe Discipline and Work Hard," Circular Notice No. 24, March 16, 1924, in Chung-kuo Kuomintang chung-yao hsüan-yen hsün-ling chi, pp. 13-15.

―――Sun Chung-shan hsien-sheng shou-cha mo-chi [original copies of Mr. Sun Yat-sen's handwritten letters]. n.p., n.d. 33 pp.
孫中山　孫中山先生手扎墨蹟
Facsimile reproduction of 33 letters to Chiang Kai-shek written in 1924, except for three dated in 1922. The collection was probably published in 1926, judging by T'an Yen-k'ai's postscript, which is dated April, 1926. Some of the letters are published in other collections of Sun Yat-sen's writings, in Chiang Kai-shek's diaries, and in Kuo-wen chou-pao, IV, No. 14 (April 17, 1927), 1-5.

―――"Telegram to the MacDonald Government Protesting the Ultimatum of the British Consul at Canton," Sept 10, 1924, in Chung-kuo Kuomintang chung-yao hsüan-yen hsün-ling chi, p. 18.

"Sun Yat-sen's Farewell Messages," Moscow, March 14, 1925, International Press Correspondence, V, No. 20 (March 19, 1925), 286.

Sung Hsiao-ch'ing. "A Biographical Sketch of Chou En-lai," in Hsien-tai shih-liao, I, 144-47.

Szu Ming. "Ho Yao-tsu during the Northern Expedition," in Hsien-tai shih-liao, II, 185-93.

Ta Te. "A Short History of the Shanghai Executive Headquarters," in Hsien-tai shih-liao, I, 90-94.

Ta-yüan-shuai kuan-yü Pei-fa chih ming-ling chih hsüan-yen [manifestos and instructions of the Generalissimo on the Northern Expedition]. n.p., Propaganda Department of the Central Executive Committee, n.d. 23 pp.
大元帥關於北伐之命令之宣言

Seven documents issued by Sun Yat-sen and the Kuomintang between September and November, 1924. Library of Congress.

Tai Chi-t'ao. Kuo-min ko-ming yü Chung-kuo Kuomintang [the National Revolution and the Kuomintang of China]. Shanghai, "Chi-t'ao's Office," July, 1925. 103 pp.

戴季陶　國民革命與中國國民黨

An extremely important source on Communist-Kuomintang relations. The ideas expressed here were labelled "Taichitaoism," and defined by the Communists as the ideological foundation of the KMT New Right Wing.

Tan-ho Kung-ch'an-tang liang ta yao-an [two important cases of impeachment of the Communist Party]. n.p., Kuomintang Central Supervisory Committee, September, 1927. 30 pp.

彈劾共產黨兩大要案

Tan Ong. "A Short History of Sun Yat-senist University at Moscow," in Hsien-tai shih-liao, IV, 187-220.

T'an I-chung. "A Story about Li Li-san," in Hsien-tai shih-liao, I, 151-55.

T'an Kung. "Hsiao Ch'u-nü," in Hsien-tai shih-liao, IV, 310-19.

Tang Shin She. "The Canton Government and the Revolutionary Movement in China," International Press Correspondence, VI, No. 27 (April 8, 1926), 415.

——"China and the Kuomintang a Year after Sun Yat-sen's Death," International Press Correspondence, VI, No. 21 (March 18, 1926), 329-30.

——"The Removal of the Kuomintang Government to Wuchang," International Press Correspondence, VI, No. 87 (Dec. 16, 1926), 1497-98.

——"The Significance of the Coup d'état in Peking," International Press Correspondence, VI, No. 29 (April 15, 1926), 441-42.

*Tang-wu ch'ang-shih [common knowledge of party tasks]. Publication of the Propaganda Department of the Central Committee of the Chinese Communist Party. (Planned).

黨務常識

*Tang-yüan hsü-chih [what party members should know]. Publication of the Chinese Communist Party, 1925.

黨員須知

T'ang Leang-li. The Foundations of Modern China. London, Noel Douglas, 1928. 290 pp.

——The Inner History of the Chinese Revolution. London, George Routledge and Sons, Ltd., 1930. 362 pp.

Presents the point of view of the Left Wing led by Wang Ching-wei. Undocumented.

Teichman, Sir Eric. Affairs of China: A Survey of the Recent History and Present Circumstances of the Republic of China. London, Methuen Publishers, 1938. 312 pp.

"Telegram of Greetings from the XIV Party Conference of the R.C.P. to the Kuomintang," International Press Correspondence, VI, No. 1 (Jan. 7, 1926), 4.

Teng Chung-hsia. Chung-kuo chih-kung yün-tung chien shih [a brief history of the Chinese labor movement]. n.p., Chieh-fang She, July, 1949. 272 pp.

鄧中夏　中國職工運動簡史

A posthumous edition of a book originally published in Moscow in 1930. The author was an important Communist leader.

Teng Tse-ju. Chung-kuo Kuomintang erh-shih nien shih-chi [historical records of the Kuomintang of the past twenty years]. Shanghai, Cheng-chung Bookstore, June, 1948. 502 pp.

鄧澤如　中國國民黨二十年史蹟

——"Letter Impeaching the Political Council," June 30, 1925, in Teng Tse-ju, Chung-kuo Kuomintang erh-shih nien shih-chi, pp. 289-91.

*T'ieh-hua [iron flower]. Organ of the New Yunnan Society, Peking.

鐵花

Ting Ming-nan. "Soviet Aid to China during the First Revolutionary War, 1925-1927," in the newspaper Chin-pu jih-pao Tientsin, June 28, 1952. English translation in. American Consulate General, Current Background, No. 194 (July 24, 1952), pp. 1-6. This recent article in a leading Chinese Communist newspaper is not documented. It is interesting, however, that much of the information is indentical with the data found in documents seized in the Peking raid.

Tong, Hollington K. Chiang Kai-shek. Rev. ed. Taipei, China Publishing Co., 1953, 562 pp.

A completely revised edition of a work first published in 1938. It offers interesting interpretations of Chiang's attitude and activities in the mid-1920s. The author was given access to Chiang's personal documents. The book is not documented, however.

Toynbee, Arnold J. Survey of International Affairs, 1927. London, Oxford University Press, 1929. 613 pp.

Trotsky, Leon. Problems of the Chinese Revolution. New York, Pioneer Publishers, 1932. 432 pp.

Ts'ai Ho-shen. "On Ch'en Tu-hsiuism," in Ch'en Tu-hsiu p'ing-lun, 5-26.

This article originally appeared in Pu-erh-sai-wei-k'o [Bolshevik], IV, No. 5 (Sept. 10, 1931), 82-114. Orthodox Communist interpretation.

*Tu-li ch'ing-nien [independent youth]. Shanghai, Tu-li ch'ing-nien magazine association.

獨立青年

Tung-fang Tsa-chih (The Eastern Miscellany). Shanghai, the Com-
    mercial Press Ltd., 1924-1927.
    東方雜誌

Voitinsky, G. [G. Voitinskii]. "Situation in China," April 21, 1926,
    Communist International, No. 21, 49-69. [English edition, n.d.]
    ____"The Situation in China and the Plans of the Imperialists,"
    International Press Correspondence, VI, No. 39 (May 6, 1926),
    599-601.

Wales, Nym (Mrs. Edgar Snow). Red Dust: Autobiographies of
    Chinese Communists, as Told to Nym Wales. Stanford University
    Press, 1952. 238 pp.

Wan Yah-kang. The Rise of Communism in China. Trans. D.S.F.
    Chen; ed. C.S. Kwei. Hongkong, Chung-shu Publishing Co., 1952.
    77 pp.

Wang Ching-wei. "Eulogizing Comrade Liao Chung-k'ai to Inspire
    My Comrades," Aug. 22, 1925, in Wang Ching-wei hsien-sheng
    chiang-yen chi, pp. 53-57.
    ____"On Generalissimo Sun's Trip to the North," May 1, 1925, in
    Wang Ching-wei hsien-sheng chiang-yen chi, pp. 24-27.
    ____"On Separating the Communists from the KMT at Wuhan,"
    Nov. 5, 1927, in Ko-ming yü fan-ko-ming, pp. 590-611.
    Four months after the split between the Left KMT and the Com-
    munists, Wang Ching-wei explains the events from April 1, 1927,
    when he arrived at Shanghai from abroad, up to mid-July, 1927.
    He also reviews the entire history of collaboration with the Com-
    munists. Important for Wang's point of view.
    ____Wang Ching-wei hsien-sheng chiang-yen chi [collected speeches
    of Mr. Wang Ching-wei]. Ed. Ai-chih She. 2d ed., Shanghai, Ai-
    chih She, December, 1926. 130 pp.
    汪精衛   汪精衛先生講演集
    A valuable collection of 16 speeches first published in March,
    1926, just before Wang Ching-wei's retirement. Some are not
    dated. All were apparently delivered in 1925 and in January,
    1926.

Wang Wei-lien. "Ch'en Ch'i-hsiu's Organization of a New Party,"
    in Hsien-tai shih-liao, I, 281-85.
    "Election of the CEC at the Second Congress," in Hsien-tai
    shih-liao, I, 94-98.
    ____"Election of the First Chairman of the National Government,"
    Hsien-tai shih-liao, I, 2-5.
    ____"Mao Tse-tung," in Hsien-tai shih-liao, I, 133-37.
    ____"A Record of Wang Ching-wei's Opposition to Communists,"
    in Hsien-tai shih-liao, I, 8-11.
    ____"Teng Yen-ta during the Wuhan Period," in Hsien-tai shih-liao,
    I, 267-71.

Whiting, Allen S. "The Soviet Offer to China of 1919," Far Eastern Quarterly, X, No. 4 (August, 1951), 355-64.

——Soviet Policies in China, 1917-1924. New York, Columbia University Press, 1954. 350 pp.

"Who Is Responsible for the Peking Raid?" International Press Correspondence, VII, No. 27 (April 28, 1927), 545-47.

Woo, T. C. The Kuomintang and the Future of the Chinese Revolution. London, George Allen and Unwin Ltd., 1928. 278 pp.
Point of view of the Left Kuomintang led by Sung Ch'ing-ling and Eugene Chen. Undocumented.

Wu Chih hui. "Another Discussion with Wang Ching-wei on the Basis of Definite Evidence," in Ko-ming yü fan-ko-ming, pp. 62-80. Also in Kuomintang Ch'ing-tang yün-tung lun-wen chi, pp. 114-54, and Ch'ing-tang yün-tung, pp. 269-83. Writing shortly after the split in April, 1927, Wu Chih-hui cited several Communist documents to prove that the KCT was engaged in a conspiracy against the KMT.

——"Petition to Safeguard the Party and Save the Nation," in Ch'ing-tang yün-tung, pp. 41-47.
Also in Kuomintang ch'ing-tang yün-tung lun-wen chi, pp. 165-74. A basic document of the Party Purification Movement. Presented on April 2, 1927, by the author, a member of the KMT CSC, the petition states the charges against the Communists and the reasons for party purification.

"X." "The Revolutionary Movement in the East—Questions at the Coming Enlarged Plenum of the ECCI," Communist International, Nos. 18 and 19, 97-115. [English edition, n.d., probably? Nov. or Dec., 1925]

Yakhontoff, Victor A. The Chinese Soviets. New York, Coward-McCann, Inc., 1934. 296 pp.

Yang Hsin-hua, "Liao Chung-k'ai and Hu Han-min," in Hsien-tai shih-liao, II, 158-63.

——"Wu Ch'ao-shu and the Hongkong Government," in Hsien-tai shih-liao, II, 196-220.

——"Yün Tai-ying," in Hsien-tai shih-liao, IV, 294-301.

Yang Yu-ch'iung. Chung-kuo cheng-tang shih [a history of Chinese political parties]. Shanghai, Commercial Press, Ltd., 1936. 370 pp.
楊 幼 炯　中國政黨史

Yasuhara, Yoshihiro. Sa-rempō to Shina Manshū no kyōsan undō [the Soviet Union and the Chinese and Manchurian Communist movements]. Tokyo, Shinkō Association, September, 1934. 613 pp.
安原祺博　ザ聯邦と支那満洲の共産運動

Yü Ming. "Mao Tse-tung at the Central Propaganda Department," in Hsien-tai shih-liao, IV, 341-46.

Yün T'ien. "Anecdotes about Shao Li-tzu," in Hsien-tai shih-liao, III, 78-85.

Zai Shi Ro-jin no jyōkyō chōsa [an investigation of the situation of
  Russians in China]. Japanese Foreign Office, European and
  American Section. December, 1928. Special Studies No. 114.
  365 pp.
  在支露人ノ状況調査
  On microfilm at Columbia.

INDEX

Glossaries A, B, and C give original Chinese forms of organizations, terms, and persons.

Agrarian problems: at Second and Third KCT congresses, 59, 68; difficulties of KCT in field of, 78; equalization of land tenure in Manifesto of First KMT Congress, 147-48; Communist policies with regard to, 376-77, 379; see also Peasant movement

Air Force: organization of, 185, 196-97; Russian influence in, 212

All-China Federation of Labor, 290-91, 436

Alumni Association of Four Military Academies, 393, 530

An T'i-ch'eng, 324

Anarchists, 49-50, 51

Andrews, Roy Chapman, 475

Anfu Clique: opposition to, 46, 63; pro-Japanese attitude of, 46-47; Feng Yü-hsiang's attacks against, 320

Anhwei, situation in, 419, 524

Ankuochün, 8, 14, 373, 404

Anti-Mukden Wars, 25, 318, 324-26, 427, 429

Ao-li-chin: visits to Chiang Kai-shek, 28, 249; as chief adviser of Political Council, 189-90, 190n; posts held, 481; termination of services, 508-9

Armaments: Soviet shipments to national Revolutionary Army, 18, 154, 169, to Kuominchün armies, 18, 322, 333, 339, 521, to Feng Yü-hsiang, 18, 333, 339, 521; supplies of Kuominchün armies, 349-50; Feng Yü-hsiang's agreement to compensate USSR for, 521

Armour, Norman, 390

Army, see Kuominchün; Military schools; National Revolutionary Army

Army of National Pacification (Ankuochün), 8, 14, 373, 404

Artillery school (Kuominchün), 344, 346, 355

Assembly, freedom of, 148

Authenticity, problem of, 8-37; Soviet attitude on, 6, 11-12, 13, 19, 36; external evidence, 8-22; arguments against authenticity; 18-20, 21-22; arguments for authenticity, 20-21; original Chinese documents, 22, 23-27; Russian documents, 22, 27-37; internal evidence, 22-36; Magruder on, 474; Dallin on, 485-88

Aviation, see Air Force

Aviation Bureau, 197, 212, 245

Belgium, stolen documents and, 15

Berliner Tageblatt, on authenticity problem, 18, 19

Bingham, Hiram, 474-75

Black Spears Associations, 304

Blucher, Vassili, see Galen

Borah, Senator William E., 431

Borodin, Mrs. Fanny: arrest of, 400, 477; Japanese intercession on behalf of, 534

Borodin, Michael: dismissal of, 11, 24, 534; report on KMT Revolutionary Committee by, 29, 171-73; on KCT and CY members joining KMT, 90; role in KMT's alliance with USSR, 144; influence of, in KMT, 144, 148, 464, 505; role in organizing Whampoa Academy, 150;

Borodin, Michael (Continued)
   Sun Yat-sen and, 153, 515; influence
   on KMT Revolutionary Committee,
   156; Chiang Kai-shek, conferences
   with and policies toward, 156, 227–
   28, 384, 395, 511; influence on KMT
   Left Wing, 166, 208; attitude toward
   Northern Expedition, 228, 230;
   Feng Yü-hsiang, negotiations with
   and attitude toward, 322, 330–31,
   336–37, 338–39, 396, 516, 520; position in China, 499–500
Bourgeoisie: development of, in China,
   43; national revolutionary movement
   and, 73, 273–74, 274–75, 276; KCT
   objectives and, 76, 82–83, 274–75,
   276, 432–33; May Thirtieth Movement and, 91; in curriculum of KCT
   Party schools, 130; KMT and, 246
Boxer Protocol, Taku ultimatum to
   Peking government by signatories
   of, 329
"Brief History of the Chinese Communist Party, A" (Doc. 1), 41–78;
   internal evidence and authenticity of,
   25–26; distortions in, 31; introduction to, 38–40; KCT alliance with
   KMT and, 84; English version of,
   488–89; authorship problem, 490
British-American Tobacco Company,
   55
Bubnov, Andrei S., 483
Buddhism, T'ang Sheng-chih and, 411
Bukharin, Nikolai Ivanovich, 483

Canton: Chiang Kai-shek's March
   Twentieth coup d'état, 218–21, 248–
   53, 264; Communist Group, organization of, 50–52; Ch'en Ch'iung-ming's
   coup against Sun Yat-sen, 60–61, 83,
   140; strikes in, 64, 72, 160; landing
   of British gunboats at, 74, 489; headquarters of Kwantung Regional Committee, 96; Sun Yat-sen's opposition
   government in, 138; Soviet position
   in, 153, 166–67; Chiang Kai-shek's
   military victory at, 162; as Left
   Wing stronghold, 165; attack and
   blockade of, 187–88; Soviet reports
   from, 245–47, 255, 266–70; labor
   movement in, 294; CY work in, 424;
   work of Soviet group under leadership of, 464

Canton government, see National
   Government
Capitalism: attacks on, in "Brief
   History of KCT," 41–42; in
   Party schools curriculum, 130,
   131, 133
Cavalry school (Kuominchün), 345,
   346–47, 355, 356
Cells, see Party cells
Central Bank, losses of, 267
Central Military and Political
   Academy, 168, 203–4, 218
Chambers of commerce, merchant
   movement and, 306–7
Chang Chi, 89–90, 151, 210, 214
Chang Chih-chiang: military gov-
   ernor of Chahar, 320; Feng
   Yü-hsiang's power delegated to,
   328; on the reform of learning,
   363
Chang Ching-chiang: election as
   chairman of KMT's CEC, 229;
   as Chiang Kai-shek's deputy
   during Northern Expedition, 230;
   attempts to tighten KMT setup,
   233
Chang I-lan, 453
Chang Kuo-ch'en, 13
Chang Kuo-t'ao: open letter in
   relation to Document 21 by, 24;
   as member of Peking Chinese
   Communist Group, 50; posts
   held by, 54, 80, 149, 496; opposition to KCT's alliance with KMT,
   84; on KCT organizational policies, 86; anti-Chiang policy and,
   393; on First KCT Congress,
   491; delegate at First Congress
   of the Toilers of the Far East,
   492; on Maring, 493
Chang T'ai-yen, 234
Chang Tso-lin: raid on premises
   of Soviet Embassy in Peking and,
   10, 12, 391; Soviet policy toward,
   12, 16, 20, 324–25; national liberation movement and, 46; control
   of Peking government by Wu
   P'ei-fu and, 139–40; defeat of,
   140; KMT policy toward, 318,
   324, 373–74; alliance with Chang
   Tsung-ch'ang and Wu P'ei-fu,
   328; Feng Yü-hsiang's opposition to, 338; Ankuochün organiza-

tion and, 373; Chiang Kai-shek's alleged negotiations with, 373-74, 389, 391; repressive measures against Communist activities in Peking by, 404; executions following raid on Soviet Embassy, 408; tactics to oppose Northern Expeditionary Forces, 427; authenticity of documents question and, 474-75

Chang Tsung-ch'ang, 373, 400, 427

Chang Tzu-p'ing clique, 411

Changsha, 64, 368

Chao Heng-t'i, 513

Chekiang, situation in, 373, 420, 522, 524

Chen, Eugene: note to Chicherin on raid on Soviet Embassy in Peking, 11; posts held by, 156, 268, 381; role of, at Wuhan, 370, 381, 399; intercession on behalf of Mrs. Borodin, 400; attitude toward Chiang Kai-shek, 401; see also Ch'en-O'Malley notes

Ch'en Ch'i-hsiu, 445

Ch'en Ch'iung-ming: Kwantung's capture by, 50; coup d'état against Sun Yat-sen by, 60-61, 83, 140; reconquest of Canton by, 139; Merchant Corps' alliance with, 154; attack on Canton, and extermination of army of, 187-88

Ch'en Hsin-ya, 8

Ch'en Kung-po, 50, 53

Ch'en Kuo-fu: posts held by, 229; attempts to tighten KMT setup, 233; Communist attacks against, 374, 375; failure at election of Third CEC Plenum, 398; political attitudes and outsting of, 512, 525, 531; reorganization of provincial party headquarters, 534

Ch'en Lien-po, 154

Ch'en Ming-shu, 411, 435, 531; role of, in Northern Expedition, 367; Teruni's efforts to strengthen power of, 370; on conflicts between Chiang Kai-shek and Wuhan KMT leaders, 382-83; accusations against Communists by, 391; as garrison commander of Wuchang, 414; Russian advisers and, 418

Ch'en-O'Malley notes, 384

Ch'en T'an-ch'iu, 80

Ch'en Tu-hsiu: article by, compared

to Document 20, 23-24; glorification of, in "Brief History," 39; role of, in beginnings of KCT, 47-48, 50-51, 79, 87; draft of party platform and, 52, 53, 54, 492; posts held by, 54, 80; on KCT-KMT relationship, 83-84, 86, 402; admission of Communists to KMT and, 92, 149, 227; reaction to Tai Chi-t'ao's theories, 207; policy toward KMT and Chiang Kai-shek, 220-21, 226-27, 393; Northern Expedition, opposition to, 231; accusations against, 379, 392, 393; on Lenin's government, 491

Ch'en Tzu-i, 438, 439

Ch'en Wang-tao, 48

Ch'en Yen-nien, 96, 511

Ch'en Yu-jen, see Chen, Eugene

Cheng Lan-chi, 449, 451, 453

Cheng Shih-ch'i, 515

Ch'eng Ch'ien, 192

Chi-lieh-fu, 262

Chiang Ch'iu-pai, 58

Chiang Kai-shek: March Twentieth coup d'état, 5-6, 75, 218-21, 248-53, 264, 509-10; Stepanov on, 5-6, 219-21, 251-52, 255; position in KMT, 10, 165-66, 230, 232, 266, 267, 374-75, 398; attitude toward raid on Soviet Embassy, 11; letter to Galen, 27, 176-80; speech to Military Council, 28, 181-82; on Sun Yat-sen-Maring meeting, 139; trip to USSR and study of Soviet system, 143-44, 498-99; on Whampoa Academy, 150-51; Chinese Communists, attitude toward, 150-51, 221, 267, 388, 463; attack on Merchant Corps, 155; as member of Revolutionary Committee, 156; Borodin, relations and negotiations with, 156, 227-28, 384, 395, 511; United Kingdom, attitude toward, 161, 176; on army reorganization, 161-62; as commander of First Army, 163, 191; antiforeign attacks, 163-64; Galen's letter to, 174-75; Soviet advisers, attitude toward, 212, 215-17, 222-23, 254-55, 257, 388, 458; policy

Chiang Kai-shek (Continued)
  and attitudes toward Soviet Russia,
  214, 375, 388; Soviet conciliatory
  policy toward, 219-21, 255, 267-68,
  403, 463-64; plans for Northern
  Expedition and role played in, 220,
  230, 368-69, 521-22; KCT's policy
  toward, 220-21, 255, 374-75, 384-
  85, 389, 391-93; on KMT-KCT relations, 221-22, 228-29, 511; attitudes and policies on assumption of
  power after March Twentieth coup
  d'état, 221-24; Soviet advisers on,
  248-53, 264-65; relations between
  Wu Ch'ao-shu and, 261-62; Communists in KMT and, 267, 374-75,
  388; negotiations with Sun Ch'uan-
  fang, 367-68; T'ang Sheng-chih, relations with, 369-70, 393-94, 435-
  36, 530; question of transfer to
  Wuhan and, 370-71, 383-84, 387,
  523; Chang Tso-lin, negotiations
  with, 373-74, 389-90; conflicts
  with Joint Council at Wuhan, 382;
  Wang Ching-wei, attitude toward,
  387, 429, 435; Japan, relations
  with, 388-91; Mukden Clique,
  alleged negotiations with, 389, 391;
  Sino-Anglo-American consultations
  and policies toward, 390, 528-29;
  anti-Chiang military and political
  alliances, 393-96, 435-36, 532;
  split between T'ang Sheng-chih and,
  436-37; strategic errors of Soviet
  advisers in dealings with, 464;
  threatened resignation of, 510;
  Feng Yü-hsiang, relations with,
  521-22
Chiang T'ai-lei, 143
Chicherin, Chen's note to, 11
Chin-pu jih-pao (Tientsin paper), 40
Chin Yu-fu, 40
Chin Yun-e, 427
Chin Yun-p'eng, 427
China: effects of World War I in,
  43; anti-Japanese movement in, 47,
  63; participation in First Congress
  of Toilers of the Far East, 57, 82;
  unequal treaties, pledges to abolish, 67, 146, 157, 160, 161
Chinese Communist Party (KCT):
  original Chinese documents, and,
  23-27; Anti-Mukden War and, 25,
  325; Russian translations of KCT
  documents, 27-28; question of
  authenticity of KCT documents,
  37; "Brief History of KCT," 38-40,
  41-78; membership, 41, 64, 71, 74,
  80, 84, 87, 90, 94-95, 102, 109,
  276, 310, 438, 460-61, 495-96;
  labor unions and labor movement,
  policies and work with regard to,
  46, 54, 55-57, 64-65, 80, 87, 282,
  284, 285-86, 288-95, 375; establishment of, 47-48, 49, 50, 79-81;
  Ch'en Tu-hsiu's role in, 47-48, 50;
  Shanghai Communist Group, 48-
  49; Peking Communist Group, 49-
  50, 491; Canton Communist Group,
  50-52; publications, 54, 125;
  Chinese participation in First
  Congress of the Toilers of the
  Far East, 57-58; Comintern, decision to join, 59; denunciation of
  imperialism and militarism in
  policy of, 59, 62-63, 146, 459; national assembly, plans for, 71, 319-
  20; Hongkong strike and, 72-73, 74;
  role and strategy of, in Chinese
  Revolution, 73, 76-78, 85, 86, 91,
  100, 457-58; weaknesses of and
  mistakes of, 74-75, 87, 251, 258,
  276-77, 461; personnel shortages,
  74-75, 310; organizational structure and policies of, 76, 79, 85-119,
  461; Northern Expedition and, 76-
  77, 230-31; work in the army of,
  78, 79, 258, 316-17, 506-7, 535;
  Comintern guidance, 79, 403; policy toward Sun Yat-sen, 80-81;
  closed-door policy, 81, 86; effect
  of May Thirtieth Movement, 90-
  95; emphasis on independent
  character of, 92, 93-95, 207, 279-
  80; policy of alliance with Left
  Wing of KMT against the Right,
  92-93, 208-9, 225, 231-33, 235,
  244, 247, 259-60, 275, 372, 375,
  377-79, 392, 396-97, 404, 438, 440,
  454, 462; cell organization, 95-96,
  104-9; relations with Youth Corps,
  97, 117-19, 121, 423; propaganda
  policies and training, 97-99, 122-
  24, 235, 240; Chiang Kai-shek on,
  150-51, 388; reaction to Tai Chi-
  t'ao's theories, 208; Chiang Kai-

shek, policy toward, 220–21, 255, 374–75, 384–85, 389, 391–93; relief movement, policy regarding, 282, 313–15; student movement, policies regarding, 282–83, 311–12; policies in mass movement, 282–317; Christian Church, policy toward, 286, 299–300; Peasant movement, policy in, 301–2, 375–77; Merchant Movement, policies toward, 306–7; Tuan Ch'i-jui's attitude toward, 327, 329; Kuominchün, relations with, 363–64; Wang Ching-wei's recall and, 371, 374–75; Three People's Principles, 378, 458; neglect of land revolution and, 378–79; policy in Wuhan-Nanchang controversy, 384; foreign policy, 388, 434; "Northwest Theory" and, 396; policies and position in Peking, 403–9, 437–56; Red United Front in Peking and, 438, 440–41; strategy of infiltration in Left organizations in Peking, 442–49; Peking Municipal Party Headquarters elections and, 450–53; Central Political Bureau, officers of, 507; Ch'en Kuo-fu's attitude toward, 525; see also Kuomintang-Communist relations

——Central Committee: resolutions at Enlarged Plenum (Oct., 1925), 6, 92, 100–103, 122–24; resolutions at Second Enlarged Plenum (July, 1926), 24–25, 39, 110–16, 125–29, 227, 296–317; First Manifesto of KCT, 25, 83; diverging currents on policy toward KMT, 227, 231; political reports, 271–77, 427–30, 431–34; Red Spears movement, resolutions on, 283, 303–5; women's movement, resolutions on, 308–10; military movement, resolutions on, 316–17; position in Hankow Incident, 384–85; Wuhan Communists and, 393; organization of, 496

——Congresses: First Party Congress, 52–55, 80, 486, 491; Second Party Congress, 58–60, 82–83, 492–93; Third Party Congress, 66–69, 85–87, 458; Fourth Party Congress, 71–72; Sixth Party Congress, 401–3

Chinese Communist Party (postwar), comparison between postwar Communist Party and KMT, 466–67

Chinese Communist Youth Corps: Anti-Mukden War and, 25; members of, at Foreign Language School, 49; in Kwantung, 52; membership, 71, 74, 84, 90, 96–97, 118, 460–61, 495; resolutions on joining KMT, 88; KMT accusations against members of, 90; relations between KCT and, 97, 107, 117–19, 121, 423; importance of work development of, 103; resolutions on the, 120–21; role in labor movement, 292; struggle with KCT to strengthen KMT Left Wing, 381; resolutions on, at Sixth Plenum of the Young Communist International, 422–24

Chinese Eastern Railway, 8, 9

Chinese Government White Book, 18, 476, 479, 482

Chinese People's Republic, work of present Soviet advisers in, 465–66

Chinese Socialist Youth Corps, 79–80

Ch'iung-yai Association, 443, 448–49, 451, 452

Chou Ao-shan, 410

Chou En-lai, 218, 496

Chou En-lai, Mrs. (Teng Ying-ch'ao), 217

Chou Fu-hai, 80

Chou Lu, 155, 187, 210, 214, 241, 438

Christian Church, KCT policy toward, 286, 299–300

Chu P'ei-te: commander of Third Army, 163; member of Military Council, 183; opposition to Chiang Kai-shek, 224, 249; position of, 435

Ch'ü Ch'iu-pai: policies of, 86, 226; election to Reserve CEC of KMT, 149; recall of Wang Ching-wei and, 371; anti-Chiang campaign and, 393, 395; report to Sixth KCT Congress, 401–2

"Chung-shan" (S.S.), 196, 218, 248

Chung-shan Study Society, 443, 449, 542

CI, see Communist International

Class struggle: in curriculum of KCT Party schools, 130, 131; need for, in National Revolution, 240; Chiang Kai-shek's attitude toward, 432; KCT policy and, 432

Comintern, see Communist International

Commissar system: function and prerogatives of, 27; KMT's first use of, in Whampoa Academy, 150; in National Revolutionary Army, 163, 168, 191, 200-202, 218, 222, 254, 259; Chiang Kai-shek's attitude toward, 222, 254; KCT mistakes in, 259

Commission for Translation and Compilation of Soviet Documents, 13

Communist International: instructions to Soviet Military Attaché, 15, 34-36; formal denial of authenticity of documents, 19; resolutions of Seventh Enlarged Plenum of Executive Committee, 19-20, 33-34, 483; in "Theses on the Chinese Question," 32-34; KCT vote to join, at Second Congress, 59, 82-83; policy in China and toward KMT and KCT, 79, 85, 159, 225, 403; policy in "Theses on the National and Colonial Question," 81; penetration of National Government, key policy of, 379; on Chinese Revolution, 380; instructions to Chinese Communists on policy toward KMT, 403; Sun Yat-sen, attitude toward, 497; opposition to Northern Expedition, 512

Communist Party (China), see Chinese Communist Party

Communist Party (Soviet Union), help to China by, 42

Communist University for the Toilers of the East, 98

Communist Youth Corps, see Chinese Communist Youth Corps

Comprador class, 273-74, 306-7

Contract labor, abolition of, 68-69

CY, see Chinese Communist Youth Corps

Dalin (delegate of YCI), 83, 140-41

Dallin, David J., on authenticity problems, 33-34, 36, 484, 485-88

Debuchi, 390

Diplomatic Corps at Peking, Soviet denunciations against, 12-13

Documents: exhibit of, 14; supression of some, 15; criticism of handling of, 17-18; present location of originals, 22; original Chinese, 23-27; Russian, 27-37; number of files, 478-79; see also Authenticity, problem of

East Asiatic Library (Columbia University), 104

Eastern Expeditions, 157, 162, 170, 212, 504

Education and training: KCT propaganda and indoctrination, 68, 97-99, 124; cell functions in connection with, 95, 104, 105, 107-8, 112, 113; school reports to Propaganda Department, 128; outline of curriculum of KCT Party schools, 130-34; concrete guide to the work of training, 135-37

Eighth Army, Pavlov's report on, 410-12

Engineering school (Kuominchün), 345-46, 355

Espionage, 17, 18, 32

Factories, Party cells and fractions in, 95, 112, 113, 114, 289

Fan Hsing-ming, 419

Fan Shih-sheng, 156, 501

Fang Chen-wu, 519

Fang Pen-jen, 256, 258

February Seventh Incident, 65, 70, 87

Federation of Railway Unions, 293

Feng Chu-p'o, 217

Feng T'ien-chu, 410

Feng Tzu-yu, 149, 160, 232, 234

Feng Yü-hsiang, 318-66; shipment of Soviet supplies to, 18, 333, 339, 521; Soviet advisers to and problems related with, 29, 322, 327-28,

334, 336–40, 341–43, 347–49, 358, 464–65, 516, 518; coup d'état (Oct. 23, 1924), 70–71, 318–19; seizure of Peking by, 157; commander in chief of Kuominchün, 318; KMT, relations with, 319, 323, 327, 332, 342, 343; Tuan Ch'i-jui, relations with, 320, 321, 515; Soviet relations with, 321–23, 324, 327–28, 331–32, 334–40, 352, 441–43, 463–64; Soviet appraisal of character of, 322, 331–32, 338–39; attacks on Mukden Clique, 324; support of Peking Government by, 326–27; retirement of, 328, 518; March Eighteenth Incident at Peking and, 330; journey to Moscow, 330, 331, 333–34; political attitude toward Soviet Union and Chinese Communists, 330, 331, 342, 365–66, 395–96, 533; entry into KMT, 333, 334–35; appointment as party representative in Northwest, 334; Jen Te-chiang's letter to Frunze on alliance with, 336–40; Chang Tso-lin, position toward, 338; letter to Karakhan on, 341–43; Japan, relations with, 352–53; anti-Chiang alliances and, 395–96; Sun Yat-sen, attitude toward, 514; Borodin's meetings with, 516, 520; Chiang Kai-shek, relations with, 521–22

Fifth Army (National Revolutionary Army), 163, 169, 189, 192

First Army (National Revolutionary Army): Chiang commander of, 163; commissar system in, 168, 218, 508; organization of, 177, 191; in Second Eastern Expedition, 188; Whampoa Academy and, 194–95; withdrawal of party representatives from, 221, 254

First Kuominchün Army: strength of, and training in, 322, 323; KMT work in, 323, 343; defeat of, in Second Tientsin War, 329; Russian criticism of, 331; Soviet reports on, 344–54, 365–66; work of Soviet advisers with, 350–51, 356–58; in Ya-en's report, 355–56; KCT, relations with, 363–64; Feng Yü-hsiang's restrictions on political

work in, 365; see also Kuominchün

Foreign Language School (Shanghai), 49, 56

Fourth Army (National Revolutionary Army): reorganization of, 163, 177, 192, 531; in Second Eastern Expedition, 188; in Wuchang battle, 413–14

Fractions, see Party fractions

France, 13, 431

Frunze, Michael, Jen Te-chiang's letter to, 336–40

Fukien, 373, 419

Fukien Army, see Fifth Army

Fuse, Katsuji, 140, 143, 496

Galen (Vassili Blucher): Chiang Kai-shek's letter to, 27, 176–80; role of, in organizing Whampoa Academy, 150; army reorganization and, 167; letter to Chiang Kai-shek, 174–75; opposition to Chiang Kai-shek's strategy in southeastern campaign, 382, 383; Chiang Kai-shek's march on Shanghai and, 395

Gauss, C. E., 532

Gecker, A. I., 322, 336

General Labor Union, see Shanghai General Labor Union

General Staff of Kuominchün, 347, 348

General Staff of the Military Council, 167, 184, 190, 212, 245

German documents, 478–79

Gould, Randall, on authenticity problem, 17, 18, 477, 483

Great Britain, see United Kingdom

Great League of Sunyatsenism, 439

Gruliow, Leo, 15, 475–76

Hainan Island, attacks against, 186, 189

Han Lin-fu, 149, 323

Hankow: antiforeign incidents, 17; strikes, 64, 72; labor movement, 294; occupation of British Concession, 384; capture by Revolutionary Army, 418; transfer of National Government to, 429

"Henry A. Lin," 29, 326, 330, 344–54 passim, 481

Ho Chien, 411

Ho Lung, 419
Ho Ying-ch'in, 373, 504
Honan: Communist nuclei established, 51; labor movement, 56; Red Spears Associations, 296, 303-5
Hongkong: strike in, and Communist guidance, 72-73, 74; blockade of, 185; KMT situation, 187, 268; labor movement, 294
Hongkong-Shanghai Banking Corporation, 154
Honjo, Shigeru, 15, 20, 100
Hsia Ch'ao, 373, 525
Hsiang-tao (publ.), 125
Hsiao Ch'u-nu, 324
Hsiao Chung-chen, 408, 442, 444, 451, 453
Hsieh Ch'ih, 89-90, 151, 210, 214, 241
Hsieh Pai-yu, 406, 451, 453
Hsien Peasant Associations, 248, 297
Hsin ch'ing-nien (publ.), 125
Hsin-Hai Comrades Club (Shanghai), 234
Hsü Ch'ien: Feng Yü-hsiang and, 331; role of, at Wuhan, 381, 397, 399; on Communist participation in KMT work, 386
Hsü Ch'ung-chih, 156, 165, 183, 188, 208
Hsü Shih-ying, 326
Hsüeh Yüeh, 532
Hu Ching-yi, 185, 318, 321, 514
Hu Han-min: on KMT-KCT cooperation, 61, 62; instructor in Whampoa Academy, 150; question of inclusion on Revolutionary Committee, 156, 171n; fall from power, 164, 165; as KMT representative to Soviet Russia, 165; member of Military Council, 183; exile of, 188, 230, 512; Communist opposition to, 208, 505; position in KMT's Right Wing, 266-67
Hu Hua, 139
Hu Shih, 61, 63
Huang Fu, 389
Huang Ling-shuang, 49-50
Huang Pi-hun, 57-58
Hunan: Communist nuclei established, 51; labor movement, 57, 296; military operations, 230, 269-70, 368, 427-28; situation in, 256, 265, 428; KCT policy, 272; provincial government established by KMT, 368; progress of peasant movement, 376; rift between Chao Heng-t'i and T'ang Sheng-chih, 513
Hunan Army, see Second Army (national Revolutionary Army)
Hunan Clique in Peking, 439
Hunan Regional Committee, 96
Hupeh: Communist nuclei established, 51; political and military situation in, 369, 370, 382, 425-26, 428, 429; policies of KCT and CY regional committees, 394; organization of provincial government in, 420; Yüan Tsu-ming's campaign in, 526

Imperialism: anti-imperialist program outlined in "Theses," 35; attacks on, in "Brief History," 41; KCT's struggle against, 59, 62-63, 146, 459; big bourgeoisie and, 76; in curriculum of KCT Party schools, 131-32, 133; KMT policy against, 146, 459; Sun Yat-sen and, 155, 158; Chiang's attacks against, 163, 181-82; attempts to form military anti-Red united front, 272; policy toward China, 273; Christian Church as vanguard of, 299-300; Merchant Movement and, 306-7; Feng Yü-hsiang's attitude toward, 342; tactics followed, 432; alliance between KMT Right Wing and foreign imperialism, 433
Infantry school (Kuominchün), 344-45, 346, 366
"Instructions to Agents," 485
"Instructions to Soviet Military Attaché": English translation of document, 15-16; question of authenticity of, 19, 21, 34-36, 37; Dallin on, 36, 486; discrepancies between Russian original and English and Chinese translations, 484-85
"Instructions to Write Letters in Code," 487
Intelligence school (Kuominchün), 346, 355

Intelligentsia, 73, 103

Italy, documents stolen from Italian Legation among Soviet documents, 14

Ivanovskii, 28, 481

Japan: documents stolen from Japanese Legation among Soviet documents, 14; authenticity of documents question and, 20; influence and policies in China, 43, 273, 324, 389, 457; Chinese opposition to, 46, 47, 63; strikes against Japanese-owned factories, 91, 160; efforts to form anti-Red united front, 272; Feng Yü-hsiang's relations with, 352-53; KCT attitude against, 388; Chiang Kai-shek and, 389, 390, 528-29; intercession on behalf of Mrs. Borodin, 400, 534; negotiations with T'ang Sheng-chih, 417; support to Mukden Army by, 429; surtax problem and, 431

Jen Te-chiang: Soviet negotiations with Feng Yü-hsiang and, 321-22; need for Russian advisers stressed by, 327; letter to Frunze on alliance with Feng Yü-hsiang, 336-40; as possible writer of letter to Karakhan on Feng Yü-hsiang, 341-43; Feng Yü-hsiang on, 515; resignation of, 516

Joffe, Adolph, 140, 141-42, 143

Judiciary reforms, in political platform of Third KCT Congress, 68

Kalgan Group, Ya-en's report on, 355-59

Kan Nai-kuang, 229, 233, 371

Karachev, 377

Karakhan, Leo: negotiations at Peking, 144; views on policies toward Feng Yü-hsiang, 337; criticism on directions to Soviet advisers, 339-40; letter to, on Feng Yü-hsiang, 341-43; at Soviet Embassy meeting in Peking, 344-54; Declaration of July 15, 1919, 490-91

Karpenko, 331

KCT, see Chinese Communist Party

Kiangsi: situation in, 256, 419, 428; military operations in, 368, 369, 372-73, 414-15; autonomous movement, 524; reorganization of Provincial Party Headquarters, 534

Kisanko: on Liao Chung-k'ai's assassination, 166; on party commissars in the army, 168; report on military developments in Kwantung, 186-99; influence on KMT military apparatus, 212-13; Chiang Kai-shek's attacks on, 215-16; March Twentieth coup d'état and, 249; work of Soviet group in Canton under leadership of, 464; termination of services of, 508

Kiselev, Nikolai Fedorovich, 490

KMT, see Kuomintang

Ko-ming ch'ang-shih (book), 127

Kollontai, Alexandra, 57

Koo, Wellington, 9

Ku Meng-yü, 229, 399

Kubiak, 509-10

Kuibyshev, V., 268n

Kung-ch'an-tang, see Chinese Communist Party

Kung Fu-k'uei, 519

Kuo-chia chu-i Clique, 437, 513

Kuo Ching-wei, 195

Kuo Ch'un-t'ao, 438, 439

Kuo Sung-ling, 271, 328, 352

Kuominchün: establishment of, and revolutionary movement, 71; conflict between Wu P'ei-fu and Chang Tso-lin and, 256; KMT, relations with, 271, 324, 330, 331, 517, 519; static condition of, and militarist political regimes, 272-73; KCT propaganda in, 317, 323-24; organization of, 318, 519; Soviet advisers' influence and work in, 322-23, 327, 331, 347-49, 350-51; military reverses, 328-29, 532-33; question of responsibility in March Eighteenth Incident, 329; Communist criticism of armies, 332; Soviet shipments of military supplies to, 332, 333, 339, 521; Mukden Army and, 333, 427; possible alliance with National Revolutionary Army and KMT, 334, 517; military schools discussed at meeting at Peking Soviet Embassy, 344-47; General Staff, 347, 348; armaments and army strength, 349-50; organiza-

Kuominchün (Continued)
  tion of civilian volunteer militia in
  Peking and, 360-61; naming of,
  and Feng Yü-hsiang's coup, 514;
  see also Feng Yü-hsiang; First
  Kuominchün Army
Kuomintang: purges and expulsion
  of Communists from, 3, 10, 11,
  463; intraparty struggle between
  Right and Left wings, 10, 233, 235,
  239, 243-44, 267-68, 275, 278,
  280, 404; Party Purification Movement, 10, 401; denunciation of raid
  on Soviet Embassy, 11; in "Instructions to Soviet Military Attaché,"
  15-16; shipment of Soviet supplies
  to, 18, 154, 169; questions regarding KMT documents, 27-28, 37;
  Revolutionary Committee, Borodin's report on, 29, 156, 171-73;
  imperialism, militarism, and,
  35, 77, 146; participation in Congresses of the Toilers of the Far
  East, 57, 58, 498; admission of
  Communists into 84, 86-87, 88-
  89, 92-93, 141, 148-49, 151-53,
  159, 206-7, 462; functions in labor
  movement, 87; division into Right,
  Center, and Left groups, 89, 236,
  246; organization of KCT Party
  fractions within, 89-90; Soviet
  influence on and relations with,
  141, 142-43, 144, 145, 149, 153,
  159, 213, 216-17, 460; organization and functions, 141, 144-48,
  149, 205, 505; Whampoa Academy,
  organization of, 150-51; Central
  Supervisory Committee's petition
  to impeach Communists, 151-52;
  Merchant Corps threat to authority
  of, 154; effect of Sun Yat-sen's
  death on policies of, 157-60; United
  Kingdom, policy toward, 160-62,
  502; Special Committee, activities
  of, 165; Tai Chi-t'ao's theories
  and, 206-7; Western Hills Conference, 209-12, 214; Communist
  seats in organs of, and influence
  exerted, 217-18, 242-43, 370-71;
  380, 400, 403, 404-6, 460; restrictions of Communist activities in,
  228-29, 267-68, 511; general policies of various groups, 237 (table);

  growing friction between Chiang
  Kai-shek and Communists, 267,
  374-75, 388; Kuominchün, relations
  with, 271, 324, 330, 331, 517, 519;
  power rivalries within, 275, 460,
  518; strategy and alliances during
  Northern Expedition, 318, 368;
  Chang Tso-lin, negotiations with,
  318, 373-74; Feng Yü-hsiang and,
  319, 321, 323, 327, 331-35, 342,
  343; support of Anti-Mukden forces,
  325; Tuan Ch'i-jui and, 327; outline
  on organization of a volunteer militia in Peking, 360-62; Wuhan-
  Nanchang controversy, 370-71, 381-
  88, 523; opposition to Chiang Kai-
  shek within, 372, 384; Movement to
  Restore Party Power, 398; Peking
  Municipal Party Headquarters
  elections and membership, 404-6,
  438, 442, 445, 450-53; support of
  Soviet Peking Embassy to work of,
  408; Youth Department and CY,
  424; growing opposition toward
  USSR and Chinese Communists,
  432; role of, in Chinese Revolution,
  457-58; comparison between present Communist Party in China and,
  466-67; membership, 493; opposition to provisional Peking Government, 502
—Congresses, policies of: First
  Congress, 88, 141, 145-48; Second
  Congress, 213-15, 529-30
—Central Executive Committee, 10,
  144-45, 148-49; elections and Communist seats, 149, 214, 217; army
  reorganization plans at Third Plenum, 161-62; manifesto of Fourth
  Plenum, 210; Standing Committee,
  members of, 217, 400, 507; Chiang
  Kai-shek's proposals at Second
  Plenum, 222, 228-29; policy of
  strengthening, and abolition of
  chairmanship, 386, 398; resolutions
  at Third Plenum in Wuhan, 398-99;
  transfer to Canton, 502
—Political Council: organization
  and functions, 152-53, 162, 163,
  183, 205, 242, 398; relationship between Military Council and, 162-
  63, 183; Teng Tse-ju's attacks on,
  164

Liang Shih-i, 391

Liao Ch'eng-chih, 503

Liao Chung-k'ai: KMT-KCT cooperation, approval of, 61; plans drafted by Joffe with, 143; posts held, 148, 150, 156, 162, 163, 164, 171, 183; action against Merchant Corps, 156; assassination of, 165, 166; Communist opposition to, 208; political position of, 503; as candidate for first chairman of National Government, 505

Likin, abolition of, 68

Lin, Henry A.: Feng Yü-hsiang and, 29, 326, 330; report at meeting at Soviet Embassy in Peking, 344-54 passim; identification of, 481

Lin Shen, 210, 214, 241, 438

Lin Shih-mien, 165

Lin Tsu-han, posts held by, 148, 149, 214, 217, 381

Litvinov, M. M.: on raid of Soviet Embassy, 10, 12, 473; authenticity of documents question and, 19, 20

Liu Chen-huan, 162, 166, 187

Liu Chi, 327, 347, 348

Liu Chia-hsin, 410

Liu Fen, 217

Liu Jen-ching, 50

Liu Jung, 410

Liu Tso-lung, 414, 418-19

Liu Wen-tao, 410

Liu Yao-hsi, 449, 451, 453

Liu Yüeh-chih, 410

Lo Chang-lung, 50

Lo Ch'eng, 400

Lo I-nung, 402

"Lo Keng-ti," 117

Local committees (KCT); functions of, in party organization, 101, 108-9, 113, 114; special commissioners to inspect work of, 112; reports to Propaganda Department, 127-28; work in labor movement, 292

Lockhart, 400-401

Lu Chung-lin, 320, 324

Lu I, 218

Lu Yu-yü: execution of, 408; as a leader of New Right Wing of KMT, 438, 439, 440; election to Municipal Party Headquarters Executive Committee, 450, 451, 453

Lü Hsiu-ts'ai, 519

Machine-gun school (Kuominchün), 345, 355, 356

MacMurray, John Van Antwerp, 13, 17, 391, 471, 528-29

Mac Veagh, 390

Magruder, John, 14, 474

Mandalyan, 371

Mao Tse-tung: formulations at Third KCT Congress, 86; posts held by, 149, 217, 496; land policy of, 376-77, 525

March Eighteenth Incident (Peking, 1926), 329-30, 363-64

March Twentieth coup d'état: Stepanov's report on, 5-6, 218-19, 248-53; Communist reaction to, 75, 218-21; Russian advisers' opinions on, 264; charges of instigation by Kubiak of, 509-10

Maring: KCT's establishment and, 80; on KMT-KCT alliance, 83-84, 87; Sun Yat-sen and, 139, 497; Chang Kuo-t'ao on, 493

Matsumura, Feng Yü-hsiang's relations with, 351-52

May Fourth Movement, birth of KCT and, 47

May Thirtieth Incident (1952) and Movement following, 73, 90-92, 160

Mechanics' Union, 49, 260-61

Mei-chou p'ing-lun (Communist weekly), 48

Merchant Corps: threat to KMT authority by, 154; suppression of, 155-56, 246; KMT Revolutionary Committee against, 172, 173; KCT policies and, 283-84, 306-7; Fan Shih-sheng's collaboration with, 501

Mif, Pavel, 393, 401

Militarism: attacks on, in "Brief History of KCT," 41; KCT's anti-militarist policy, 59, 62-63, 146, 287; attitude of militarists toward KMT, 77, 431-32; suppression of labor movement attempted by, 91; Communist propaganda in militarist armies, 116; Chiang Kai-shek's attacks against, 181-82; politicial power of militarist regimes, 271, 272; anti-Red movement of militarists, 273; Merchant Movement

Militarism (Continued)
and, 306-7; Red Spears Associations and militarist regimes, 303-5
Military Council (National Revolutionary Army), 183-85; interrelationship between Political Council and, 162-63, 183, 205; Chiang Kai-shek's speech to, 181-82; interrelationship between General Staff and, 184, 190, 245; in Kisanko's report on military developments in Kwangtung, 189-90; functions and membership, 193, 398
Military Court, 191
Military Movement, KCT resolution on, 316-17
Military schools: Whampoa Academy, 150-51, 157, 168, 174, 178-79, 194-95, 263, 267; Central Military and Political Academy, 168, 203-4, 218; of National Revolutionary Army, 194-96; of Kuominchün, 344-47, 355-56, 366
Military supplies, see Armaments
Min-t'uan (People's Corps), 286, 298-99
Miners' movement, 293
Mo Jung-hsin, 50
Mo T'ung-jung: joining of Communist Party by, 405, 440; posts held by, 448, 449, 451, 452, 453
Mongolia, 68, 342, 516
Mukden Clique: Mukden Chihli conflict, 70; suppression of labor movement and, 91; KCT policy and, 271-72; Feng Yü-hsiang's attacks on, 324; Chiang Kai-shek's alleged negotiations with, 389, 391; military operations and alliances, 427, 429
Mukden Wars, 25, 70, 318, 324-26, 429

Nanchang: military operations in, 368; Wuhan-Nanchang conflict, 381-88, 397, 523; revolutionary committee formed by Communists, 524
Nanking Incident, 16-17, 390, 528-29
National assembly, question of convocation of, 71, 319-20
National Government: British pro-
vocation of, 74; inauguration of, 163; KCT's Left Wing influence on, 164; Hongkong situation and, 187; political and military situation of, 187-88, 250, 428-29; regulations on organs of, 205; ECCI praise of, 225; weaknesses of, in Soviet report from Canton, 246; reforms by, 269; external relations, 269-70; Wuhan-Nanchang controversy, 370-71, 383-84, 523; question of Communist penetration and participation in, 380, 399-400; attitude toward Wuhan problem, 420; meeting of Provisional Joint Council of KMT's Central Executive Committee and, 425-26; Yen Hsi-shan's attitude toward, 428; conflict among leaders of, 429; people's attitude toward, 436; candidates for election to first chairmanship, 505
National Labor Conference (1926), 290
National Labor Congress (1925), 72
National Revolutionary Army: military supplies situation and Soviet shipments, 18, 154, 169, 192-93; enlistment in, in political platform of Third KCT Congress, 68; KCT work and propaganda in, 78, 259, 317; Chiang Kai-shek and, 161-62, 177-80, 181-82; 222, 254; organization of, 161-63, 167, 177-80, 187, 191-94, 253; main armies of, 162; commissar system in, 163, 168, 191, 200-202, 218, 222, 254, 259; General Staff, 167, 184, 190, 212, 245; Soviet advisers' work and organization in, 167, 197-99, 212-13, 245, 257, 259, 504, 506-7; Soviet penetration and influence in, 167, 212-13, 216-17, 218, 253, 257, 464, 534-35; financial problems, 169, 177, 179-80, 187; communications problems in, 174-75, 193; Kisanko's report on military developments in Kwantung, 186-99; distribution of armies in Second Eastern Expedition, 188-89; political training and departments, 190-91, 197-98, 200-202, 203-4; arsenal, 193-94; army schools, 194-96; plans on establishment of

Central Political Academy, 203-4; weaknesses of, in Soviet report, 246; strength of, 250, 381-82; recall of Communists from, 260; enmity between Chiang Kai-shek and Li Chi-shen, 269; alliance with Kuominchün by, 334; opposition to Chiang Kai-shek within, 394, 435-36, 532; Soviet report on Eighth Army, 410-12; T'ang Sheng-chih on, 411, 425-26; CY work in, 423; alliances against Mukden Army, 429; amalgamation of Yüan Tsu-ming's army with, 526; influence of Alumni Association of Four Military Academies, 530; see also Military Council; Northern Expedition; Whampoa Academy

National Revolutionary Movement: Soviet strategy and policy in, 32-33, 79, 250-51, 457, 463-67, 490-91; in "Brief History of KCT," 46-47; development of, 72-74; KCT-KMT collaboration and, 81; peasant movement role in, 296; Feng Yü-hsiang and, 323-24; report on work of Peking Local Committee of KCT, 437-56

Nationalism, Principle of, 146

Nationalization, in political platform of Third KCT Congress, 67

Navy: Chiang Kai-shek's plans for, 178; budget for, 179; organization of, 185, 196; Communist influence in Navy Bureau, 212, 218; subordination to Military Council, 245; Chiang Kai-shek's influence in, 262

New Army Society, 445-46; Communist work in, 405, 407; activities in Peking universities, 406; organization, 443, 452

New China Study Society, 443, 449, 451

New Yunnan Society, 443, 452

Nieh Jung-chen', 218

Nikitin, 337, 415n

Nilov, 232-33, 426, 510

Niu Yung-chien, 374, 525

North, Robert C., 483

North China: trade-union movement in, 56; KCT policy in, 71, 101, 272; Feng Yü-hsiang's change of sides, 157; KCT attitude toward KMT in,

238-43; Stepanov's report on conditions in, 256; see also Peking; Peking government; Peking Local Committee (KCT)

North China Daily News (newspaper), 17, 21

North China Star (newspaper), 17

Northern Expedition, 367-459; KCT attitude toward, 76-77, 230-31; Chang Tso-lin's defeat in First, 140; Sun Yat-sen launches Second, 154-55; Military Council on, 184; Chiang Kai-shek's plans for, 216, 220, 230, 521-22; Borodin's attitude toward, 228, 230; distribution of armies for, 256; financial problems, 256-57; objectives of, 261; strategy and military operations, 367-69, 373, 391, 414-16, 419, 427, 436, 531-32; discord among generals, 413-21 passim; military operations against Mukden Army, 427; early Soviet opposition to, 512

Northern Regional Committee (KCT), 23, 96, 101, 117, 118

"Northwest Theory," 533

Organization Department of KMT, 217, 229

"Organization of Soviet Secret Bureau in China," 487-88

Orishevskii, 417n

Orthography, and authenticity question, 18, 19, 20, 21, 34

Otsuka, Reizo, 38

Ou-yang Chü, 223, 254

Oudendyk, William J., 9

Outer Mongolia, 342, 516

Pai Ch'ung-hsi, 418, 436

Pai Wen-wei, 323

Paikes, A. K., 140

"Pamiat Lenina" (S.S.), seizure of, 477

Paoting Clique, 393-94, 411, 418

Party cells (KCT): organization and functions, 95, 104-8; educational propaganda, 97, 99, 102, 123, 128; criticism of work of, 112-14; 276; role in labor movement, 289, 292; role in relief movement, 313; in militarist armies, 317

Party fractions (KCT): activities in KMT, 89; organization and functions, 89, 102, 114–15; in labor movement, 289, 292; work in Peking, 405, 407

Pavlov: Soviet adviser with KMT, 144; on T'ang Sheng-chih's power, 368–69; report on the Eighth Army, 410–12; in Soviet personnel list, 481

Peasant associations: Communist Party fractions in, 89, 114; organization of, 94, 297–98; in Hunan, 376; membership of Haifeng County Peasant Association, 494

Peasant Department (KMT), 217

Peasant movement: legislation at Second KCT congress, 59; KCT support of, 68, 76, 82–83, 94, 103; Party cells and, 113; propaganda among peasants, 122, 128–29; equalization of land tenure, 147–48; as force in national revolution and KCT policy toward, 273, 274, 275; criticism of, 277; resolutions of KCT's Central Committee on, 296–302; relations between KMT and, 300–301; Red Spears movement, 303–5; women's movement and, 309; Communist position in, 375–76

Pei-tzu-szu-ch'a-szu-t'e-no-fu, 262n

Peking: anti-Japanese riots, 47; Communist Group in, 49–50; trade-union movement, 56; strikes, 72; influence of KMT's Right Wing in, 238–39; student movement, 311; conquest by Feng Yü-hsiang, 318; November Twenty-eighth demonstration, 326–27, 353; plans for volunteer militia, 328, 360–62; March Eighteenth Incident (1926), 329–30, 363–64; Kuominchün withdrawal from, 333, 347–48; Communist and KMT Left Wing strength, 403–9; KMT Municipal Party Headquarters elections and Communist victories, 404–6; United Council of the Left (Red United Front), formation of, 405, 438, 440–42, 454; anti-Red movement, 437–38; in report of KCT Local Committee, 437–56; Left organizations, analysis of, 442–49; see also Peking Government; Raid on Soviet Embassy in Peking

Peking Executive Headquarters of KMT, 241, 404–6

Peking Government: position on raid on Soviet Embassy, 9–10, 13, 408, 409, 473; papers stolen from Foreign Office among seized documents, 15; Soviet relations with, 140, 153, 473; November Twenty-eighth demonstration against, 326–27; Taku Ultimatum by Boxer Protocol signatories, 329; executions of Communists by, 408

Peking-Hankow railway: labor union of workers on the, 44; strikes, 45–46, 65, 87; strategic importance of, 428

Peking KMT Comrades Club, 234

Peking Local Committee (KCT): original Chinese documents and, 23; reaction to Western Hills Conference, 210; attitude toward KMT, 238–43; report on work of, 437–56; policies of, 454–55

P'eng Han-chang, 526

P'eng P'ai, 90, 494

P'eng Shu-chih, 226, 320, 393, 402

P'eng Tse-hsiang, 324

P'eng Yang-kuang, 234

People's Army, see Kuominchün

People's Corps (Min-t'uan), 286, 298–99

People's Livelihood, Principle of, 147–48, 149

Personnel: requirements of, 115; concrete guide to the work of training, 135–37; interpreters shortages, 197; problems among Soviet advisers, 261, 358–59; in organization of labor movement, 295; lists of Soviet advisers, 481

"Po Hai," 404, 440

Political Council (KMT): organization and functions, 152–53, 398; interrelationship between Military Council and, 162–63, 183, 205; Right Wing proposal to dissove, 242

Political Training Department (KMT), 190–91

Practical Society, 407, 442, 443-45, 451, 452, 455

Pravda (Soviet newspaper), 12, 19-20

Press, freedom of, 148

Printers' union (Shanghai), 49

Progressive Society, 209

"Prolektino," 486

Proletariat: development of, following industrial expansion, 43; KCT work and policies toward, 73, 100, 103, 122-23, 128-29, 273-75, 285, 432; role of, in Chinese Revolution, 82-83, 273, 274, 275, 380; CY influence on, 423; conflict with bourgeoisie and Communist policies, 432-33

Propaganda: antiforeign, in China, 16, 19; on meaning of labor unions, 46; slow progress at beginnings of KCT, 55, 56; KCT policies and resolutions on, 97-99, 122-24, 125-29, 235; Party cells, functions in connection with, 104, 105, 107-8; publications, translation and distribution of, 124; concrete guide to the work of training, 135-37; KCT plans in North China, 240; lack of, in criticism of KCT work, 276-77; in peasant movement, 284-85, 298; in National Revolutionary Army, 317; Communist, in Kuominchün, 317, 323-24, 350-51; against Chiang Kai-shek, 389; among tasks of Soviet advisers, 430; by KCT, to counteract anti-Communist tide in KMT, 433-34; anti-Red, in Peking, 437-38, 439

Propaganda Department, 125-29, 217

Publications: publishing office established by KCT, 54; translations and distribution of, 124; problems concerning, 125-26; 127; increase in women's, 309

Raid on Soviet Embassy in Peking, 8-9; Diplomatic Corps responsibility on, 9, 10; position of Peking Government, USSR, and KMT on, 9-13; circumstances of raid favoring authenticity arguments, 21; executions following, 408; prison-ers taken, 471, 536; Magruder on, 477

Railways, labor movement in, 44, 292-93; strikes, 45-46, 64-65, 87

Raskolnikov, Fedor F., 483

Ratay, John P., 14

Red Spears movement, 283, 296, 303-5

Reform Society, 443, 447-48

Regional committees (KCT): functions of, in Party organization, 96, 101, 113, 114; reports to Propaganda Department, 127-28; work in labor movement, 292

Relief movement, 313-15

Religion, freedom of, 148

Resolutions on the Question of Cooperation between Our Party Members and the First Kuominchün (Doc. 41), 363-64

Revolutionary Committee (KMT), Borodin's report on, 29, 156, 171-73

Rogachev, Victor P.: as chief of General Staff, 167, 184, 464; Chiang Kai-shek's attacks on, 215; participation in Eastern Expedition, 504; termination of services, 509

Roy, M. N., 382, 483, 492

Russian advisers, see Soviet advisers

Russian documents: question of authenticity of, 27-32, 32-36; translations into English, 483

Russian Revolution, 79, 134

Rykov, Alexis I., 12

Saburi, Sadao, 389, 390-91

Schools, see Education and training; Military schools

Seamen's Union, 293

Second Army (Kuominchün), 321-22, 323, 328-29, 519

Second Army (National Revolutionary Army): T'an Yen-k'ai commander of, 163; reorganization of, 163, 177, 191; in Second Eastern Expedition, 189; schools of, 195

"Secret Code of the Soviet Embassy for Military Terms," 487

Sectional committees (KCT), 101, 113, 114

Seifulin, 228, 266–70, 510

Sforza, Count Carlo, 478

Shameen Massacre, 160–61

Shanghai: prominence of, in "Brief History," 39; labor movement in 48, 55, 276, 277, 290, 293–94; as center of KCT organization, 48–49, 50; Foreign Language School, 49, 56; strikes, 55, 64, 72, 91; May Thirtieth Incident, 73, 160; student movement, 311; insurrections in, 374, 525, 535; Communist policy, 402; autonomous movement, 428, 429; Chiang Kai-shek's position, 532; conquest by First Army, 535

Shanghai General Labor Union, 91, 160, 293, 535

Shanghai Hsin-hai Comrades Club, 234

Shansi, 354

Shansi Clique (Peking), 439

Shantung, 296, 303–5

Shantung Clique, 439, 440

Shao Li-tzu, 323

Shao Yüan-ch'ung, 210, 214

Shen Hsuan-lu, 48, 210, 214

Shensi, 296

Shidehara (Japanese Foreign Minister), 390

Shih Ts'un-t'ung, 48

Sinani, 417n

Sino-Japanese relations, 43, 273, 324, 389, 457

Smirnov, 504

Sneevliet, see Maring

Socialism, development of, in curriculum of KCT Party schools, 133

Socialist Youth Corps, 492, 495

Solovyev, in meetings with Chiang Kai-shek, 28, 220, 249, 250

Soong, T. V., 249, 370, 399

Soul of Hainan Society, 405, 406, 443, 448–49, 451, 452

South China, Soviet penetration in, 465

Soviet advisers: Chiang Kai-shek's coup d'état and, 5–6, 218–21, 248–53; to Feng Yü-hsiang, problems connected with, 29, 322, 327–28, 334, 336–40, 341–43, 347–49, 350, 358–59, 464–65, 516, 518; at Whampoa Academy, 150; work and organization of, in National Revo-

tionary Army, 167, 197–99, 212–13, 245, 257, 259, 504, 506–7; Chiang Kai-shek's attitude toward, 215–17, 222–23, 375, 388; conciliatory policy of, toward Chiang Kai-shek, 219, 224–225, 267–68, 395, 464; criticism and mistakes of, 219, 250–51, 464; report from Canton, 245–47; personnel problems, 261, 358–59; instructions by Foreign Commissariat and criticism of Kharakan's directions, 339–40; record of meeting at Soviet Embassy in Peking, 344–54; Ya-en's report on Kalgan Group, 355–59; report on political attitude of Feng Yü-hsiang and First Kuomin-chün officers, 365–66; T'ang Sheng-chih and, 416–18; tasks discussed at meeting of Provisional Joint Council and National Government Council, 429–30; report on split between Chiang Kai-shek and T'ang Sheng-chih, 435–36; role and strategy, 457–58, 465; KMT, role in, 458; present work of, in Chinese People's Republic, 465–66; personnel lists, 481; termination of services, 508–9

Soviet Embassy in Peking: coordination system through, 154; record of meeting at, 344–54; support to KCT work, 408; see also Raid on Soviet Embassy in Peking

Soviet Union, see Union of Soviet Socialist Republics

Spain, documents stolen from Spanish Legation among Soviet papers, 14

Speech, freedom of, 148

Stalin, Joseph V., 159, 403, 535–36

Stepanov: account of March Twentieth coup d'état by Chiang Kai-shek, 5–6, 28, 218–19, 248–53; conciliatory policy toward Chiang Kai-shek, 219–20; report of meeting of Soviet Group at Canton, 254–65; posts held by, 481

Strikes: railways, 45–46, 65, 87; in British-American Tobacco Company, 55; in Canton, 64, 72, 160; strike waves, 64–66, 91; Hongkong strike against Great Britain, 72–73, 74

Student movement: KCT direction of, and policy toward, 73, 76, 91, 274, 275, 282–83, 311–12; importance of CY work in, 103; Party fractions in, 114; CY and KCT in relation to, 121; destructive activities of Sunyatsenist Society, 260; as force in national revolution, 273, 274; women's movement and, 309; New Army Society and, 445–46; Reform Society and, 447–48

Student Society, 209

Su Chao-cheng, 399

Su-lien yin-mou wen-cheng hui-pien (publication), 26, 27, 29–30

Sun Ch'uan-fang: alliance with Fang Pen-jen, 258; Canton Government, relations with, 269; role of, in Anti-Mukden War, 271, 325; Feng Yü-hsiang and, 352; negotiations between Chiang Kai-shek and, 368–69; organization of Ankuochün, 373; military situation of, 415, 436, 522; T'ang Sheng-chih's relations with, 415–16, 417

Sun Fo, 370, 381, 399

Sun Yat-sen: invitation by Ch'en Ch'iung-ming to Kwangtung, 50; Huang Pi-hun's attempt to assassinate, 58; Ch'en Ch'iung-ming's coup d'état against, 60–61, 83, 140; KMT-KCT cooperation and, 61–62, 83–84; KCT policy toward, at First Party Congress, 80–81; on Communist admission into KMT, 88, 141, 148–49, 160; establishment and reorganization of government in Canton, 138, 143; relations with USSR, 138–40, 141–42, 144, 150–51, 158–59, 497, 498; Maring's meetings with, 139, 497; Chiang Kai-shek's relations with, 141–42, 150–51; Bordin's influence over, 144, 153; First KMT Congress, 145, 148; creation of Political Council of KMT, 152–53; accusations against United Kingdom of supporting Merchant Corps, 154; Second Northern Expedition and, 154–55; Revolutionary Committee and, 156–57, 171; 'Tsung-li's Will,' 157, 158, 184; effect of death of, on Kuomintang policies, 157–60; Feng Yü-hsiang and, 318, 514; Tuan Ch'i-jui, negotiations with, 319, 320, 321; Three Policies, question of formulation of, 392; policy toward Communists, 458, 459; efforts to obtain assistance from Great Britain, Canada, and the United States, 498; trip to Peking by, 514, 515

Sun Yat-sen, Madame (Sung Ch'ing-ling), 370, 381

Sun Yat-sen University for Chinese Toilers, 98

Sun Yüeh, 318, 320, 514, 518

Sun Che-yüan, 345

Sung Ch'ing-ling (Madame Sun Yat-sen), 370, 381

Sunyatsenist Society, 200, 260, 263

Surtax problem, 431

Szechuan, labor movement in, 296

Szechuan Revolutionary Youth Society, 443, 446–47, 452

T'a-hsin, 337

Tai Chi-t'ao: position of, in KMT Right Wing, 48–49; growing influence of, 92; emergence of theories of, 206–7; Western Hills Conference and, 210–214; political posts held by, 214, 505; leader of New Right Wing, 232; activities in North China, 238; attacks on KMT, 241–42; visit to Japan, 528

Taichitaoism: growing influence of, and KCT reaction, 92; Communist appraisal of and attitude toward, 238–39, 240, 241; revival of, in Peking, 438, 439

Takao, 400, 534

T'an Chih-t'ang, 50

T'an P'ing-shan: as member of Communist Group in Canton, 50; as head of Organization Department of KMT, 93, 149, 217; member of CEC of KMT, 149, 214; Revolutionary Committee, 156, 171; Minister of Agriculture in National Government, 399; election to KMT Standing Committee, 400; on Borodin's position in China, 499–500

T'an Tsu-yao, 405, 446, 451, 453

T'an Yen-k'ai: posts held by, 183, 224; Chiang Kai-shek attitude

T'an Yen-k'ai (Continued)
toward, 224, 249; power of, in
Hunan, 265; as leader among
Wuhan Communists, 399; trip to
Wuhan, 533
Tang Shin She, 332
Tang-wu ch'ang-shih (book), 126
T'ang Shao-i, 234
T'ang Sheng-chih: attitude toward
National Government, 256, 513;
situation of army of, 269-70, 436;
Pavlov's appraisal of, 368-69;
power and character of, 368-69,
411, 436; opposition to Chiang Kai-
shek, 369-70, 393-94, 416, 435-36,
530; position of, in Wuhan, 382,
394, 413-14, 420; cliques in civil
organization of, 410; Sun Ch'uan-
fang's relations with, 415-16;
Russian advisers and, 416-18; re-
port on military movements and
conditions in Western Hupeh, 425-
26; Soviet policy toward, 435-36,
463-64; rift between Chao Heng-t'i
and, in Hunan, 513; attitude toward
Communism, 530-31; antagonism
between Ch'en Ming-shu and, 531
T'ang Yueh-liang, 363
Tariffs, 273, 431
Taxation problems, 68, 296, 431
Te-la-t'e-wen, 167, 174, 504
Teng Chung-hsia, 50
Teng Fei-huang, 438, 439
Teng Shou-ch'üan, 410, 411
Teng Tse-ju, 89-90, 151, 164
Teng Wen-hui, 408, 442, 444, 451,
453
Teng Yen-ta, 381, 382, 420, 534
Teng Ying-ch'ao (Mrs. Chou En-lai),
217
Teruni: on relations between Chiang
Kai-shek, T'ang Sheng-chih, and
the Russians, 369-70; on strategy
in southeastern campaign, 383;
report on situation at Wuhan, 413-
21; Kuo Mo-jo on, 523
"Theses on the Chinese Question,"
32-34, 35, 37, 482, 483
"Theses on the National and Colonial
Question," 81, 86
Third Army (Kuominchün), 322, 323
Third Army (National Revolutionary
Army): Chu P'ei-te commander of,

163; organization of, 177, 191-92;
in Second Eastern Expedition, 189;
schools of, 195-96
Three Great Policies: Communist
charges of violation of, 392; as
basis of United Left in Peking,
441
Three People's Principles: in
Manifesto of KMT's First Congress, 145-46; as basis of KMT
policy, 160; Communists and, 206,
548; KMT Left Wing support of,
211
Tibet, self-determination of, at
Third KCT Congress, 68
T'ien Wei-ch'in, 333
Tientsin: labor movement in, 56,
294; strikes, 64, 72; Russian ad-
visers in battle for, 327
Tigers, see Merchant Corps
Times of London, 14, 17-18
Toilers of the Far East: Chinese
participation in First Congress of,
57-58, 142, 498; policy defined,
81-82
Tong, Hollington K., 143
Trade unions, see Labor unions
Translations of documents, 14, 17,
29-32
Transliteration of Chinese proper
names, in Russian, 29-30
Trotzky, Leon, on policies in China,
535-36
Ts'ai Ho-shen, 84, 379, 496
Ts'ao K'un, 319
Tsingtao, 72, 294
"Tsung-li's Will" (Sun Yat-sen),
157, 158, 184
Tuan Ch'i-jui: question of convok-
ing national assembly and, 71;
policies of, complicating relations
between KMT and Feng Yü-hsiang,
319; Sun Yat-sen's negotiations
with, 319, 320; KCT criticism of,
320; Feng Yü-hsiang's relations
with, 320, 321, 515; November
Twenty-eighth demonstration and,
326-27; March Eighteenth Incident
and, 329; tyranny of, 364

Union of Soviet Socialist Republics:
on authenticity of documents, 6,
11-12, 13, 19, 36; position on raid

on premises of Soviet Embassy in Peking, 10, 12, 473; instructions to Military Attaché in Peking, 15; supplies shipped to National Revolutionary Army, 18, 154, 169; supplies shipped to Feng Yü-hsiang, 18, 333, 339, 521; accusations against White Russians, 19, 473; report from China and question of authenticity of, 28-29, 37; strategy and policy in Chinese Revolution, 32-33, 79, 250-51, 457, 463-67, 490-91; documents on Soviet organization in China, 32-37; endorsement of KCT-KMT collaboration, 84; Chinese Communists training in, 98-99; Sun Yat-sen, relations with, 138-40, 141-42, 144, 150-51, 158-59, 497, 498; Wu P'ei-fu, negotiations with, 139-40; KMT, policies toward and relations with, 141, 142-43, 144, 145, 149, 153, 158, 159, 166, 213, 216-17, 460; Chiang Kai-shek's report on, 143-44, 498-99; influence in Whampoa Academy, 150-51; position in Canton, 166-67; Tai Chi-t'ao on Sino-Soviet relations, 207; position toward Chiang Kai-shek, 219-20, 227-28, 255, 267-68, 370, 403, 463-64; China's policy of alliance with, 241; Feng Yü-hsiang, relations with, 321-23, 324, 327-28, 331-32, 336-40, 341-43, 521; Foreign Commissariat instructions to Soviet advisers in China, 339-40; position toward T'ang Sheng-chih, 370; temporary defeat of advisers in China, 465; activities in present Chinese People's Republic, 465-67; relations between United Kingdom and, 473

United Kingdom: denunciation by USSR in connection with raid on Soviet Embassy, 12, 20; documents stolen from Legation of, 14; aid to Communist Party in, 42; training of Chinese factory workers, 43; Hongkong strike against, 72-73; National Government, policies toward, 74, 165, 429; strikes against British-owned factories in China, 91; accusations against, of supporting Merchant Corps, 154; Shameen Incident, 160-61; KMT policies toward, 160-62, 502; Chiang's attacks on, 161, 163, 176; efforts to form united anti-Red front, 272; imperialist policies in China, 273, 457; Hankow incident, 384; KCT policy with regard to, 388, 434; surtax conflict and, 431; relations between USSR and, 473; attitude toward Chiang Kai-shek after Nanking Incident, 528-29

United Press, 18-20

United States: role of, in translation of documents, 13; attitude on authenticity of documents, 20; attacks on, in "Brief History of KCT," 42; policies in China, 43, 273; Feng Yü-hsiang's friendly attitude toward, 342; post-World War II campaign against, 466

Universities, Communist penetration in Peking through Left Wing organizations, 406

Versailles Peace Conference, 43

Voitinskii, Gregory: mission in China, 79; on independent character of KCT, 89, 92; on Communist leadership in labor movement, 90; meeting with Sun Yat-sen, 138-39; conciliatory policy toward Chiang Kai-shek, 226; attacks on Feng Yü-hsiang, 332; on Communist policy in Shanghai, 402; drafting of "theses" and, 483; possible author of "A Brief History of the KCT," 490; accusations against work of, 535

Wang Chen-chün, 438, 439

Wang Ching-wei: attitude toward Communists, 10-11, 149, 459; KMT-KCT cooperation and, 61; as instructor in Whampoa Academy, 150; posts held by, 156, 162, 164, 171-72, 183, 208, 398-99, 505; power vested in, 165; Communist support of, 208, 371, 374-75; expulsion from KMT by Western Hills Group, 212, 214; attitude toward Soviet advisers, 217; Chiang

Wang Ching-wei (Continued)
  Kai-shek, relations with, 223–24,
  255, 268–69, 386, 429, 435; disap-
  pearance and retirement of, 224,
  250, 254; as leader of KMT's Left
  Wing, 233; recall of, and Communist policies, 371, 402–3
Wang Hu, 354
Wang Jo-fei, 323–24
Wang Po-lin, 263, 368
Wang T'ien-p'ei, 526
Washington Naval Conference, 57
Wei I-san, 519
Western Hills Conference, 209–12,
  459
Whampoa Academy: organization of,
  150–51, 194–95; cadets' role in
  suppression of Merchant Corps,
  157; political orientation and influ-
  ences in, 168, 263; army communi-
  cations problems and, 174;
  Chiang's plans for expansion of,
  178–79; anti-Communist action by,
  267
Whampoa Alumni Association, 393
White Book, by Chinese Government,
  18, 476, 479, 482
White Russians, 19, 473
Women's movement: Huang Pi-hun
  and, 57–58; legislation at Second
  KCT congress, 59; at Third KCT
  Congress, 67; Party cells and, 113;
  resolutions of KCT's Central Committee on, 308–10
Workers' Clubs, 99, 123, 124
World War I, effect of, in China, 43
Wu Ch'ao-shu: member of Military
  Council, 162, 184; negotiations in
  Hongkong for loan and expulsion
  from Canton, 230, 512; relations
  between Chiang Kai-shek and,
  261–62
Wu Chih-hui, 210
Wu Chin, 9
Wu Chung-hsin, 192
Wu K'o, 451, 452, 453
Wu P'ei-fu: railway workers and,
  44, 45; Feng Yü-hsiang and, 71,
  514; Soviet negotiations with, 139–
  40; second Northern Expedition and,
  155, 184, 318; efforts to form anti-
  Red united front and, 272; support
  of Sun Ch'uan-fang, 325; negotia-

tiations with Kuominchün, 333;
  end of power in Hupeh, 368
Wu T'ieh-ch'eng, 223, 262, 268, 510
Wu Yü-chang, 214, 371, 381, 400
Wuchang, battle for, 367, 368, 369,
  413–15
Wuhan Communists: Third CEC
  Plenum and, 10, 397; question of
  transfer of capital to Wuhan, 370–
  71, 381–88, 523; situation of, 393,
  420; alliance between T'ang
  Sheng-chih and, 394; Communist
  alliance with, 396; chief leaders,
  399; Teruni's report to Borodin
  on situation of, 413–21; break
  between KMT Left Wing and,
  524
Wuhan Government: Joint Council,
  formation and work, 381, 397–98;
  anti-Chiang Kai-shek policies of,
  393, 401–2; minutes of meeting
  of Provisional Joint Council of
  KMT's Central Executive Committee and National Government
  Council, 425–26
Wuhan-Nanchang controversy, 370–
  71, 381–88, 523

Ya-en: on Soviet relations with
  Feng Yü-hsiang, 327–28; report
  on the Soviet Kalgan Group,
  355–59
Yakhontoff, Victor A., 227
Yang Hsi-min, 162, 166, 186
Yang Li-hsien, 447
Yang Ming-chai, 79
Yang P'ao-an, 214
Yang Shen, 269, 419
Yang Yü-t'ing, 474
Yao Yen: arrest, confessions, and
  execution, 408, 536; leader of
  Chung-shan Study Society, 449
Yeh Ch'u-cheng, 210, 229
Yen Hsi-shan, 428, 429
Yi Yang-ts'ai clique, 411
Yoshizawa, 528–29
Young Communist International,
  380, 422–24
Youth Corps, see Chinese Commu-
  nist Youth Corps
Youth movement, 446–47
Yü Fang-chou, 149
Yü Shu-te, 149, 214, 323

Yüan Hsiao-hsien, 48
Yüan Tsu-ming, 269, 526
Yüeh Wei-chün, 320, 321, 519
Yün Tai-ying, 214

Yunnan, 186, 258
Yunnan Society, 447
Yurin, Ignatius, 140
Zinoviev, 498